NEUROPSYCHOLOGY OF EVERYDAY FUNCTIONING

THE SCIENCE AND PRACTICE OF NEUROPSYCHOLOGY

A Guilford Series

Robert A. Bornstein, *Series Editor*

Neuropsychology of Everyday Functioning

Edited by

THOMAS D. MARCOTTE
IGOR GRANT

Series Editor's Note by Robert A. Bornstein

THE GUILFORD PRESS
New York   London

© 2010 The Guilford Press
A Division of Guilford Publications, Inc.
72 Spring Street, New York, NY 10012
www.guilford.com

Printed in the United States of America

This book is printed on acid-free paper.

Last digit is print number: 9 8 7 6 5 4 3 2

Library of Congress Cataloging-in-Publication Data

Neuropsychology of everyday functioning / edited by Thomas D. Marcotte, Igor Grant.
     p. cm.–(The science and practice of neuropsychology)
   Includes bibliographical references and index.
   ISBN 978-1-60623-459-4 (hbk.)
   1. Neuropsychology.   2. Cognitive psychology.   3. Cognitive
neuroscience.   I. Marcotte, Thomas D. II. Grant, Igor, 1942–
   QP360.N4948 2010
   612.8′2—dc22

                                                    2009016121

To Wendy, Kyle, and Kathryn,
who prove that despite its day-to-day challenges,
the real world is a wondrous place to be

And to my parents, Bob and Carol,
who always encouraged and supported me

—T. D. M.

To JoAnn Nallinger Grant, my partner in life

—I. G.

About the Editors

Thomas D. Marcotte, PhD, is Associate Professor in the Department of Psychiatry at the University of California, San Diego (UCSD), and Center Manager of the HIV Neurobehavioral Research Center at UCSD. His research focuses on the development of methods for assessing and predicting the impact of cognitive impairments on the ability to carry out everyday activities, in particular, driving an automobile. Dr. Marcotte also has a program of research investigating HIV-related neurocognitive dysfunction, particularly in the international context. He has published numerous articles and book chapters on these topics and served on the editorial boards of the *Journal of the International Neuropsychological Society* and *Neuropsychology.*

Igor Grant, MD, is Distinguished Professor of Psychiatry and Director of the HIV Neurobehavioral Research Center at the University of California, San Diego. He has contributed extensively to the literature on neuropsychiatry, particularly the effects of alcohol abuse, drug abuse, HIV, and other disease states on neurocognitive functioning and underlying brain disease. Dr. Grant's work has also touched on the effects of life stress on health, in particular, physiological changes and coping among chronically stressed caregivers of patients with Alzheimer's disease. He is Founding Editor of the *Journal of the International Neuropsychological Society* and *AIDS and Behavior.*

Contributors

Amarilis Acevedo, PhD, ABPP/CN, Department of Psychiatry and Behavioral Sciences, Miller School of Medicine, University of Miami, Coral Gables, Florida

Peter A. Arnett, PhD, Department of Psychology, Pennsylvania State University, University Park, Pennsylvania

J. Hampton Atkinson, MD, Department of Psychiatry, University of California, San Diego, La Jolla, California

Karlene Ball, PhD, Center for Research on Applied Gerontology, University of Alabama at Birmingham, Birmingham, Alabama

Terry R. Barclay, PhD, Department of Psychiatry and Biobehavioral Sciences, University of California, Los Angeles, Los Angeles, California

Carolyn M. Baum, PhD, OTR/L, FAOTA, Program in Occupation Therapy/Neurology, Washington University School of Medicine, St. Louis, Missouri

Patricia Boyle, PhD, Rush Alzheimer's Disease Center, Chicago, Illinois

Mariana Cherner, PhD, Department of Psychiatry, University of California, San Diego, La Jolla, California

Cara B. Fausset, MS, School of Psychology, Georgia Institute of Psychology, Atlanta, Georgia

Igor Grant, MD, Department of Psychiatry and HIV Neurobehavioral Research Center, University of California, San Diego, La Jolla, California

Michael F. Green, PhD, Department of Psychiatry and Biobehavioral Sciences, University of California, Los Angeles, and VA Greater Los Angeles Healthcare System Los Angeles, California

Robert K. Heaton, PhD, ABPP/CN, Department of Psychiatry, University of California, San Diego, La Jolla, California

Charles H. Hinkin, PhD, ABPP, Department of Psychiatry and Biobehavioral Sciences, University of California, Los Angeles, and VA Greater Los Angeles Healthcare System, Los Angeles, California

Rujvi Kamat, BS, Joint Doctoral Program in Clinical Psychology, San Diego State University, San Diego, California

Robert M. Kaplan, PhD, Department of Health Services, University of California, Los Angeles, Los Angeles, California

Noomi Katz, PhD, OTR, Research Institute for the Health and Medical Professions, Ono Academic College and School of Occupational Therapy, Hebrew University, Jerusalem, Israel

Ida L. Kellison, MS, Department of Clinical and Health Psychology, University of Florida, Gainesville, Florida

Kristina Kowalski, MSc, Department of Psychology, University of Victoria, Victoria, British Columbia, Canada

Rema A. Lillie, MSc, Department of Psychology, University of Victoria, Victoria, British Columbia, Canada

David Loewenstein, PhD, Department of Psychiatry and Behavioral Sciences, Miller School of Medicine, University of Miami, Coral Gables, Florida

Mark R. Lovell, PhD, Center for Sports Medicine, University of Pittsburgh Medical Center, Pittsburgh, Pennsylvania

Paul Malloy, PhD, Department of Psychiatry and Human Behavior, Warren Alpert Medical School of Brown University, Providence, Rhode Island

Susan E. Maloney, MA, Department of Psychology, Division of Behavioral Neuroscience, University of Missouri–St. Louis, St. Louis, Missouri

Thomas D. Marcotte, PhD, Department of Psychiatry and HIV Neurobehavioral Research Center, University of California, San Diego, La Jolla, California

Catherine A. Mateer, PhD, RPsych, Department of Psychology, University of Victoria, Victoria, British Columbia, Canada

Brent T. Mausbach, PhD, Department of Psychiatry, University of California, San Diego, La Jolla, California

Andrew K. Mayer, MS, School of Psychology, Georgia Institute of Technology, Atlanta, Georgia

Nicole C. R. McLaughlin, PhD, Department of Psychiatry and Human Behavior, Butler Hospital, Warren Alpert Medical School of Brown University, Providence, Rhode Island

David J. Moore, PhD, Department of Psychiatry, University of California, San Diego, La Jolla, California

Suzanne Moseley, BS, Veterans Medical Research Foundation, La Jolla, California

Jamie E. Pardini, PhD, Center for Sports Medicine, University of Pittsburgh Medical Center, Pittsburgh, Pennsylvania

Brigitte N. Patry, PhD, RPsych, Department of Psychology, Queen Elizabeth II Health Sciences Center, Halifax, Nova Scotia, Canada

Thomas L. Patterson, PhD, Department of Psychiatry, University of California, San Diego, La Jolla, California

Robert H. Paul, PhD, ABPP/ABCN, Department of Psychology, Division of Behavioral Neuroscience, University of Missouri–St. Louis, St. Louis, Missouri

Matthew Rizzo, MD, Department of Neurology, Carver College of Medicine, University of Iowa, Iowa City, Iowa

Wendy A. Rogers, PhD, School of Psychology, Georgia Institute of Technology, Atlanta, Georgia

Lesley A. Ross, PhD, Center for Research on Applied Gerontology, Department of Psychology, University of Alabama at Birmingham, Birmingham, Alabama

Joseph R. Sadek, PhD, Department of Psychiatry, University of New Mexico, and Behavioral Health Care Line, New Mexico VA Health Care System, Albuquerque, New Mexico

J. Cobb Scott, PhD, HIV Neurobehavioral Research Center, University of California, San Diego, La Jolla, California, and Department of Psychiatry, Yale University, New Haven, Connecticut

Claire Sira, PhD, RPsych, Outpatient Neurorehabilitation Program, Victoria General Hospital, Victoria, British Columbia, Canada

Megan M. Smith, PhD, Department of Psychiatry, University of Iowa, Iowa City, Iowa

Holly Tuokko, PhD, RPsych, Department of Psychology and Centre on Aging, University of Victoria, Victoria, British Columbia, Canada

Wilfred G. van Gorp, PhD, Department of Psychiatry, Columbia Presbyterian Medical Center, New York, New York

Sarah Viamonte, MA, Minneapolis VA Medical Center, Minneapolis, Minnesota

Matthew J. Wright, PhD, Department of Psychiatry and Biobehavioral Sciences, University of California, Los Angeles, Los Angeles, California

Series Editor's Note

The field of neuropsychology has continued to evolve over the past six decades. The initial focus of the field on questions related to detection of cognitive dysfunction in various disorders, and the use of neurobehavioral investigations to better understand brain–behavior relationships, has now been amplified by an increased focus on taking neuropsychology out of the laboratory and into the real world. This emphasis on understanding the generalizability of laboratory phenomena to everyday functioning will be a critical next step as the field embraces the concepts of evidence-based science and practice. Until recently clinicians' judgments about the real-world implications of their evaluations were predicated on presumptions about which cognitive abilities were central to the performance of activities of daily living. The increasing engagement of occupational therapists, neuropsychologists, speech and language pathologists, rehabilitation psychologists, and other disciplines in the direct examination of the link between the laboratory and daily life is an important step forward.

In this volume, editors Thomas D. Marcotte and Igor Grant have assembled leaders from diverse perspectives that reflect the complexity of the issues that impact our understanding of the relationship of laboratory findings and daily function. For example, in Chapter 2, Wendy A. Rogers, Andrew K. Mayer, and Cara B. Fausset introduce the field of ergonomics and human factors, which has obvious implications for the study of everyday implications, but is a field to which most neuropsychologists have had little exposure. Similarly, Carolyn M. Baum and Noomi Katz, in Chapter 3, present the perspective of the discipline of occupational therapy, which has a robust tradition of helping patients adapt to their environments and vice versa. As Baum and Katz point out, and as many neuropsychologists know, occupational therapists have a distinct approach to cognitive assessment that is explicitly oriented to functional abilities. Section B of Part I of the volume focuses on approaches to the measurement of specific functional domains such as medication management and driving, as well as the relationship of neuropsychological status with vocational performance and instrumental activities of daily living. Part III addresses questions of everyday function in the setting of several common neurological and psychiatric disorders and normal aging, and also discusses the impact of cognitive impairment on quality of life.

This volume is the fifth in the Guilford series The Science and Practice of Neuropsychology. The goal of this series is to integrate the scientific foundations and clinical applications of knowledge of brain–behavior relationships. In the modern era, which emphasizes translational research, the contributors to this volume exemplify the application of evidence from the research and clinical laboratory to the real world.

ROBERT A. BORNSTEIN, PhD

Preface

Life is a neuropsychological test.
—ROBERT K. HEATON

Navigating through daily life is a complex and dynamic process. We must constantly filter an overabundance of new information, prioritize minute-to-minute actions, attend to time-sensitive problems while deliberating on others, engage in risky activities (e.g., driving), track appointments and deadlines, interact with others, and change strategies as needed. The human brain, fortunately, is efficient and adaptive, and despite these challenges it is rare to experience significant failure on most common everyday tasks. But brain damage can profoundly affect these abilities, and even individuals with mild neurocognitive impairments can struggle in completing their day-to-day activities. Although our ability to predict performance in the "wild" from assessments in the controlled laboratory or clinic has grown over the decades, it nonetheless remains inadequate.

The aims of this book are twofold: (1) to explore the rationale, theory, and practical aspects of assessing everyday functioning, and (2) to review the impact of key neurological and psychiatric conditions on the ability to complete real-world tasks. Our hope is to provide a volume that stimulates critical thinking regarding current methods and to foster future research.

This book is divided into two major parts.

Part I addresses general approaches to evaluating the relationship between cognition and everyday functioning. Numerous professions focus on this issue, yet there is often limited dialogue between the groups. Methodologies are sometimes comparable and, at other times, divergent. One goal of this book is to expose the reader to these various methods. We therefore begin the volume in Section A with overviews of the neuropsychological, human factors, and occupational therapy approaches to examining real-world functioning. These chapters include contributions from distinguished researchers who have also served as presidents of one of the organizations serving their profession (Robert K. Heaton, International Neuropsychological Society; Wendy A. Rogers, Human Factors and Ergonomics Society; Carolyn M. Baum, American Occupational Therapy Association).

Section B consists of chapters addressing the theoretical bases and practical issues involved in assessing specific components of everyday functioning. For this volume, we selected four aspects of real-world functioning that are challenging but common: instrumental activities of daily living (IADLs), vocational functioning, medication management, and automobile driving. Given the increasing diversity of many societies, as well as the growing emphasis on international research, we also include a chapter focusing on cross-cultural issues in the assessment of functional abilities.

Part II reviews the impact of specific neurological and psychiatric conditions on real-world performance. We begin by examining how neurocognitive impairments affect overall quality of life, and follow with a discussion of normal aging and everyday functioning. The remainder of Part II addresses conditions commonly seen in the clinic: dementia/mild cognitive impairment, vascular dementia, traumatic brain injury, sports injuries and concussion, multiple sclerosis, HIV-associated neurocognitive disorders, depression, and schizophrenia. Each chapter includes background on the condition of interest and a discussion of its effects on IADLs, vocational performance, medication management, and driving.

In the final chapter, based on the material presented throughout the book, we provide our opinions regarding directions for future work on the prediction of everyday functioning from laboratory measures.

There are a number of individuals we would like to thank. In seeking contributors to this book, it was readily apparent that although many investigators may publish a study or two on everyday functioning, only a limited number of researchers are dedicated to addressing the theoretical and methodological issues associated with the prediction of real-world performance. We were fortunate to find such individuals for this book and are grateful to the authors who contributed to this volume.

Our knowledge and interest in the importance of using neuropsychological measures to predict real-world functioning grows in part from our collaborations with Robert Heaton, PhD. Bob is a long-time colleague (IG) and mentor/colleague (TDM). His decades-long emphasis on the real-world impact of brain dysfunction has kept this issue at the forefront throughout our association.

Last, we'd like to thank Robert F. Bornstein, PhD, editor of The Science and Practice of Neuropsychology series, who originally proposed this volume; Margaret Ryan, whose expert editing made this a much better product; and especially Rochelle Serwator, our editor at The Guilford Press, who so patiently nurtured this book into existence.

Contents

PART II. EVERYDAY IMPACT OF NORMAL AGING AND NEUROPSYCHIATRIC DISORDERS

PART I

ASSESSMENT CONCEPTS AND METHODS

SECTION A

Approaches to Assessing the Relationship
between Cognition and Everyday Functioning

CHAPTER 1

Neuropsychology and the Prediction of Everyday Functioning

Thomas D. Marcotte, J. Cobb Scott, Rujvi Kamat, and Robert K. Heaton

M odern neuropsychology rose to prominence as a discipline during the middle of the 20th century, based on the ability of neuropsychologists, armed with a toolkit of cognitive, motor, and sensory tests, to help localize brain lesions and contribute to the diagnosis of neurological and neuropsychiatric conditions. Over the past few decades, the need to use cognitive tests for lesion localization has waned, as new imaging techniques have enabled clinicians to locate brain abnormalities with increasing sensitivity and accuracy. However, brain imaging is not a panacea, as commonly used techniques frequently are not helpful in diagnosing some neurological conditions (e.g., mild traumatic brain injury or early dementing processes), and imaging can lack some specificity, in that brain lesions can be seen in a large proportion of otherwise "normal" adults, especially as they age (de Leeuw et al., 2001). Neuropsychological assessment is still critical, however, if one wants to know the nature and severity of any behavioral manifestations that may result from brain abnormalities. Indeed, increasingly a primary reason for referrals for neuropsychological testing is to answer questions regarding the effects that brain alterations are likely to have on everyday functioning, such as the ability to be successful at work, live independently (Rabin, Barr, & Burton, 2005), handle finances, or drive an automobile. In addition to being a common clinical question (Chelune & Moehle, 1986; Heaton & Pendleton, 1981), it is particularly a focus in forensic referrals, where decisions on financial compensation may depend on estimates of a client's functional levels, and in referrals that seek to identify treatment targets for rehabilitation efforts.

The neuropsychological approach to assessment, in the psychological tradition, usually integrates results on tests that have been well standardized and carefully characterized in terms of reliability and validity. Such measures can be useful for tracking the effects of disease progression, as well as any beneficial effects of rehabilitation programs or treatment of the underlying brain abnormality. In addition, by delineating an individual's cognitive deficits, as well as strengths, neuropsychologists aim to understand how these might impact functioning in day-to-day life.

However, since the foundations of neuropsychology include lesion localization and clinical diagnosis (e.g., assessment of cognitive decline), the neuropsychologist typically uses measures originally designed to address these issues rather than the prediction of how an individual might function in everyday life, given a particular injury or decline (Chaytor & Schmitter-Edgecombe, 2003). For example, measures such as the Stroop Color–Word Interference Test and Tower of London were not originally designed to be used as clinical measures (Burgess et al., 2006). These instruments later found their way into the clinical realm and have been used to help predict difficulties with everyday functioning primarily based on the assumption that they assess functions/constructs that are important to carrying out real-world activities. As an example, with regard to the Stroop, one might hypothesize that the ability to inhibit an automatic, overlearned response would, at times, be beneficial to the safe driving of an automobile, such as being able to withhold a reflex to press the brakes if a traffic light turns red when the driver is halfway through the intersection.

The approach of predicting everyday functioning using neuropsychological measures designed for other purposes has been questioned, because it is not always clear how performance on basic abilities translates to behavior within the varying environments found in the real world (Goldstein, 1996). Indeed, despite many advances in neuroscience we still know surprisingly little about how the brain enables us to interact with the environment and organize everyday activities, even ostensibly simple actions such as cooking (Burgess et al., 2006). In response, investigators have developed new measures that have a strong neuropsychological bent but focus on cognitive constructs specifically hypothesized to relate to real-world performance—measures designed to assess more directly the abilities needed to carry out everyday tasks.

In this chapter we review key issues in the assessment of everyday functioning, including factors that complicate the relationship between performance on laboratory tests and real-world performance. In addition, we briefly summarize the literature on the use of different types of neuropsychological measures to predict real-world performance. We limit our discussion regarding specific neuropsychological predictors and outcomes, as this aspect is covered in the chapters throughout this book.

Ecological Validity

Originally coined by Brunswik (1955), the term "ecological validity" refers to whether the findings obtained within a controlled experiment or environment can be generalized to what we see in the real world, where the organism exhibits "free behavior in the open environment" (Franzen, 2000). With respect to neuropsychology, Sbordone (1996) defined ecological validity as the "functional and predictive relationship between the patient's performance on a set of neuropsychological tests and the patient's behavior in a variety of real world settings" (p. 15). (Although the term "real world" has been criticized as being nonspecific [Rogers, 2008] and suggesting that behavior in the lab does not count as "real-world" behavior [Goldstein, 1996], we find it useful to indicate the environment outside the confines of the laboratory/clinic.)

Veridicality and *verisimilitude* are two general approaches to ecological validity, as described by Franzen and Wilhelm (1996). Veridicality is "the extent to which test results reflect or can predict phenomena in the open environment" (p. 93). This usually involves using neuropsychological measures or combinations of measures to predict real-world performance (e.g., employment status). Most neuropsychological measures would fall into this category, because they do not directly measure everyday behaviors but do assess some basic requirements of such behaviors and therefore may predict functioning outside of the laboratory.

Verisimilitude refers to the "the topographical similarity of the data collection method to a task in the free environment" (Franzen, 2000, p. 47). In other words, the test resembles a task people perform in everyday life, and the test is developed considering the theoretical relationship between the demands of the test procedures and the behavior that is being predicted. The tests more closely approximate everyday tasks, so the inferential leap from test performance to real-world performance can be made easily (Spooner & Pachana, 2006). In reality, of course, perfect verisimilitude is impossible, since one cannot completely replicate the environment in which the behavior of interest will ultimately take place (Goldstein, 1996). Furthermore, it would appear impossible to capture in a standardized task all important differences that people experience in the specific requirements of their everyday roles of shopper, parent, financial manager, and so on. In addition, a test based on verisimilitude is not necessarily ecologically valid (Chaytor & Schmitter-Edgecombe, 2003), and several have yet to be validated with respect to their true, real-world counterparts (Rabin, Burton, & Barr, 2007).

Verisimilitude is an increasingly popular approach, however, and a growing number of instruments that more closely resemble real-world tasks have become widely available. Examples of more commonly used tests include the Rivermead Behavioral Memory Test (Wilson, Cockburn, & Baddeley, 1985), Behavioral Assessment of the Dysexecutive Syndrome (Wilson, Alderman, Burgess, Emslie, & Evans, 1996), and the Test of Everyday Attention (Robertson, Ward, Ridgeway, & Nimmo-Smith, 1996).

Examples Relating Neuropsychological Performance and Everyday Functioning

A recurring question in the field is whether tests originally developed for detection and localization of brain pathology can predict real-world functioning (Heaton & Pendleton, 1981). Because of the importance of this question, a considerable amount of research has used traditional neuropsychological tests to predict outcomes such as academic performance, financial management, medication management, and automobile driving. Despite the fact that investigators have used a large variety of neuropsychological tests, ranging from a select number of measures to comprehensive batteries, and varying operational definitions of functional outcomes, it is clear that basic cognitive functioning (measured via neuropsychological tests) *is* related to one's ability to carry out such real-world tasks. The strength of this relationship can best be characterized as "moderate." Below we provide a few brief examples of this type of research; additional examples are provided in chapters throughout this volume.

Academic Achievement

Intelligence tests were originally designed to predict academic achievement, and then secondarily were found to be sensitive to brain pathology. Numerous studies have examined the relationship between neurocognitive functioning and either concurrent or future academic success (most often defined as the number of years of schooling completed, or grades in school). There is generally a strong relationship between intelligence quotient (IQ) and academic success, with a correlation in the vicinity of .50 (Matarazzo, 1972; Sternberg, Grigorenko, & Bundy, 2001). IQ at age 7 has been found to be predictive of adult educational attainment (McCall, 1977), suggesting that, in general, cognitively more able people tend to succeed more and go further in school. Performance on IQ tests does not explain all of the variance seen in academic achievement, and many other factors may be important, such as home and school environment, parental expectations, self-efficacy, and individual motivational levels, as well as abilities not assessed by IQ tests (e.g., learning efficiency and various "executive functions"). Matarazzo (1972) has argued that a minimum IQ threshold may be necessary to reach certain academic levels (e.g., high school diploma, graduate school), and that these additional factors may influence success beyond those levels. The interplay between IQ and education is complex, and the issue continues to be investigated with a variety of methods (Deary, Strand, Smith, & Fernandes, 2006; Rohde & Thompson, 2006). Regardless, since academic functioning in neurological patients can be impacted by neuropsychological deficits beyond pre- and postmorbid changes in IQ, a comprehensive neuropsychological test battery is recommended if one wants to determine the full impact of neurological conditions (Heaton & Pendleton, 1981).

Instrumental Activities of Daily Functioning

Activities of daily living (ADLs) have generally been divided into two types: *basic* ADLs, comprised of activities such as grooming, dressing, feeding, toileting, and bathing, and *instrumental* ADLs (IADLs), which involve more complex tasks such as money management, shopping, medication management, and handling transportation needs. Basic ADLs are often significantly impacted by physical impairments, but clinicians should remain cognizant that physical impairments may affect IADL success as well.

Neuropsychologists are most commonly asked to predict IADL functioning since the capacity to execute basic ADLs is more clinically apparent. Neuropsychological performance has been associated with IADL abilities in numerous groups, including individuals diagnosed with Alzheimer's disease (Cahn-Weiner, Ready, & Malloy, 2003), vascular dementia (Boyle, Paul, Moser, & Cohen, 2004), postacute brain injury (Farmer & Eakman, 1995), HIV infection (Heaton, Marcotte, et al., 2004), and schizophrenia (Jeste et al., 2003), as well as in community-dwelling older adults (Bell-McGinty, Podell, Franzen, Baird, & Williams, 2002; Royall, Palmer, Chiodo,

& Polk, 2005). However, the relationship between neuropsychological performance and IADLs varies according to the task and patient group. As examples, in an HIV-infected group, deficits in learning, abstraction/executive functioning, and attention/working memory were significant predictors of IADL failures and objectively assessed functional impairments (Heaton, Marcotte, et al., 2004), whereas action fluency was most predictive of IADL dependence using a different test battery and cohort (Woods et al., 2006). In a study of patients with Alzheimer's disease, the executive component of working memory was related to money management (Earnst et al., 2001), although disproportionate impairments of episodic memory are generally seen as most disabling in Alzheimer's disease.

Vocational Functioning/Employment

In patients of working age, perhaps the most common question posed to neuropsychologists is whether the patient will be able to return to work, and if so, what types of work will he or she be able to perform? Vocational outcomes have been defined via dichotomous, or multitiered, endpoints (e.g., fully employed/partially employed/unemployed), or at a more granular level, as hours worked or a qualitative assessment of whether there has been a decline in efficiency.

Neuropsychological impairment status has been a modest predictor of vocational functioning in clinical groups, and is perhaps better at predicting failure than success (Guilmette & Kastner, 1996). In a review of vocational functioning and IQ in cognitively normal individuals (i.e., assessing the premorbid or developmental aspect of neuropsychological functioning), Heaton and Pendleton (1981) concluded that IQ was related to job level, in that IQ scores were generally lower in unemployed individuals and higher in employed persons with more challenging positions. Using a meta-analytic approach across various patient groups, Kalechstein, Newton, and van Gorp (2003) found that intellectual functioning, executive system functioning, verbal learning and memory, and episodic learning and memory were the strongest predictors of employed versus unemployed status.

As expected, the relationship between neuropsychological predictors and vocational status varies by neuromedical condition. For example, memory and attention predicted employment in traumatic brain injury (TBI) (Brooks, McKinlay, Symington, Beattie, & Campsie, 1987), whereas verbal learning predicted return to work in an HIV cohort (van Gorp et al., 2007), and executive functioning, working memory, and speed of information processing related to vocational functioning in patients with schizophrenia (McGurk & Mueser, 2006). Return-to-work analyses can be complicated by non-neuropsychological issues, such as the presence of litigation, the patient's disability income, and motivation to return to work, as well as factors such as premorbid functioning, age, and the availability and quality of rehabilitation resources. Even with such complications, neuropsychological tests are still valuable predictive tools in examining vocational outcomes. For example, in a comprehensive study of TBI and vocational functioning, Machamer, Temkin, Fraser, Doctor, and Dikmen (2005) found that neuropsychological tests were useful in predicting postinjury work status, even after controlling for a variety of preinjury factors and injury severity. However, given the potential impact of these other factors, Guilmette and Kastner (1996) recommended that all assessments used to predict vocational functioning include evaluations of psychosocial/psychological functioning in order to improve predictive power.

Automobile Driving

Driving is perhaps the most complex, and dangerous, everyday activity for many adults. Safe driving requires numerous abilities, including intact attention, perception, tracking, choice reactions, sequential movements, spatial judgment, and planning. Attempts to predict on-road driving behavior through the use of traditional neuropsychological tests have met with mixed success. Some studies have found neuropsychological performance to be associated with on-road abilities (Fitten et al., 1995; Hunt, Morris, Edwards, & Wilson, 1993; Odenheimer et al., 1994) and driving simulator performance (Marcotte et al., 1999; Rebok, Bylsma, Keyl, Brandt, & Folstein, 1995; Rizzo, Reinach, McGehee, & Dawson, 1997; Szlyk, Myers, Zhang, Wetzel, & Shapiro, 2002), whereas others have found poor relationships between driving abilities and cognitive assessments (Bieliauskas, Roper, Trobe, Green, & Lacy, 1998; Fox, Bowden, Bashford, & Smith, 1997). As with most studies addressing everyday functioning, attempts to summarize the field of driving research are complicated by the variety of populations sampled and methods used across studies. Researchers have used divergent test batteries and different gold standards regarding "driving impairment" (Molnar, Patel, Marshall, Man-Son-Hing, & Wilson, 2006; Reger et al., 2004; Withaar, Brouwer, & van Zomeren, 2000). For example, driving impairments have been determined via on-road drives, performance on driving simulators, and reviews of real-world crash or moving violation history.

Using attention as one example of a cognitive ability associated with driving performance, lapses in attention have been cited in epidemiological studies as a key factor in accidents, perhaps occurring in 15–40% of all accidents (e.g., Stutts, Reinfurt, & Rodgman, 2001). In one project, the "100-Car Naturalistic Driving Study," over the course of a year the investigators unobtrusively recorded data from 241 nonpatient drivers (a total of 2 million miles). There were 83 crashes and 761 near-crashes (i.e., requiring a rapid, severe evasive maneuver to avoid a crash). Driver inattention was cited as the cause in 78% of the crashes and 65% of the near-crashes that occurred during the study (Klauer, Dingus, Neale, Sudweeks, & Ramsey, 2006). This study was done with healthy control participants. In patient groups, performance on measures of attentional processes such as divided attention have shown a strong relationship to driving performance (Brouwer, 2002; Lengenfelder, Schultheis, Al-Shihabi, Mourant, & DeLuca, 2002; Uc et al., 2006b). The Useful Field of View (UFOV) test (Ball, Beard, Roenker, Miller, & Griggs, 1988; Sims, Owsley, Allman, Ball, & Smoot, 1998), a computerized measure that assesses both divided and selective attention by measuring the amount of time it takes an individual to accurately acquire both central and peripheral visual information without head or eye movements, may be a particularly sensitive indicator of driving impairment. UFOV declines with normal aging and is significantly reduced in many patient populations, including persons with TBI (Fisk, Novack, Mennemeier, & Roenker, 2002), multiple sclerosis (Schultheis, Garay, & DeLuca, 2001), stroke (Fisk, Owsley, & Mennemeier, 2002; Mazer et al., 2003), HIV (Marcotte et al., 2006), and mild Alzheimer's disease (Duchek, Hunt, Ball, Buckles, & Morris, 1998). Reduced UFOV performance has been correlated with higher rates of past (Ball, Owsley, Sloane, Roenker, & Bruni, 1993) and future automobile crashes (Owsley et al., 1998) and associated with poor performance during on-road driving evaluations (Duchek et al., 1998; Myers, Ball, Kalina, Roth, & Goode, 2000).

Attention, of course, is but one example of the cognitive domains that may need to be intact to drive safely. Depending on the patient group and outcomes, other cognitive domains implicated in driving performance include visuospatial functioning (Amick, D'Abreu, Moro-de-Casillas, Chou, & Ott, 2007; Galski, Bruno, & Ehle, 1992; Grace et al., 2005; Hunt et al., 1993; Lundberg, Hakamies-Blomqvist, Almkvist, & Johansson, 1998; Reger et al., 2004; Schanke & Sundet, 2000), executive functioning (Daigneault, Joly, & Frigon, 2002; Marcotte et al., 2004; van Zomeren, Brouwer, & Minderhoud, 1987; Whelihan, DiCarlo, & Paul, 2005), and processing speed (Stolwyk, Charlton, Triggs, Iansek, & Bradshaw, 2006; Uc et al., 2006b; Worringham, Wood, Kerr, & Silburn, 2006). However, there is currently no consensus regarding which neuropsychological measures best identify high-risk drivers. There is a general agreement, though, that cognitively impaired individuals as a group perform significantly worse than controls on driving measures, and the risk of a crash increases with higher levels of cognitive impairment (Withaar et al., 2000). Many factors beyond neuropsychological ability can affect driving performance, including motivation, personality, driving experience, use of medications and other substances with CNS effects, and road conditions. See Marcotte and Scott (2009) for a more detailed discussion of neuropsychology and the prediction of driving ability.

As yet, there is no clear answer as to which neuropsychological tests are most predictive of the many components of real-world functioning, even, as noted above, when narrowing the question down to specific real-world tasks and neurological disorders. Whereas a number of studies has shown "modest" results in using specific neuropsychological tests to predict driving ability, for example, it is worth noting that in most cases these studies do not yield cutpoints that can guide the clinician in determining fitness to drive for an individual person.

We can have the most confidence in the very general statement that global cognitive impairment is associated with worse performance on everyday functioning measures. Neuropsychologically, overall impairment levels can often be best estimated using summary scores such as the Average Impairment Rating from the Halstead–Reitan Battery, or a Global Deficit Score calculated from a reasonably comprehensive battery (Carey et al., 2004; Heaton, Miller, Taylor, & Grant, 2004). At the domain-specific level, a broad review of the literature suggests that executive measures may be the strongest and most consistent predictors of everyday functioning, in concurrence with the notion that complex measures better correlate with the complex aspects of real-world functioning (Chaytor & Schmitter-Edgecombe, 2003; Goldstein, 1996; McCue, Rogers, & Goldstein, 1990). Thus, it has been argued that future research should specifically focus on executive functioning as a predictor of real-world performance (Cahn-Weiner et al., 2003; Guilmette & Kastner, 1996). In addition, recent studies have implicated learning/memory in predicting real-world behavioral functioning (Heaton, Marcotte, et al., 2004; van Gorp et al., 2007). But these conclusions are by no means universally true, and the utility of specific measures, and even specific cognitive domains, still remains to be determined.

Defining "Everyday Functioning" Outcomes

One of the challenges in relating neuropsychological performance to real-world functioning is the lack of agreed-upon best methods for determining impairments in everyday abilities. Should we simply ask patients how they are doing in their daily lives? Should we require documentation of their daily performance, something that is often difficult to come by, if not entirely nonexistent? How about asking a third party who may only witness the patient performing tasks under specific circumstances? Or is it best to try to objectively measure the patient's ability to carry out an everyday task, even though this test would be conducted in a controlled environment and perhaps have limited real-world applicability?

As noted by Goldstein (1996), "tests or predictors and outcome measures or criteria are both surrogates for actual abilities and behaviors" (p. 84). There is a tendency in the literature to accept various outcome measures as being closely related to real-world functioning, but we must pay as much attention to the outcome, how it is measured, and its relationship to actual real-world tasks/functioning as to the predictors themselves. For example, is slowing on a task in which the individual is required to press a brake pedal when a stimulus on a computer screen changes color evidence of a reduction in "driving ability"?

The use of outcome measures is addressed in various chapters in this volume; here we touch upon them briefly since they are critical in understanding the relationship, or lack thereof, between performance on neuropsychological measures and "real-world" outcomes.

Self-Report

Directly asking patients/participants how they are functioning in the world is the most relied-upon method for assessing real-world outcomes; in many cases it is the most practical and may give a reasonably accurate representation of real-world performance. This method is also advantageous because it provides important information regarding patients' perception of their status, even if it lacks external validity in some cases. One example of a self-report instrument is the Patient's Assessment of Own Functioning Inventory (Chelune, Heaton, & Lehman, 1986), in which participants detail complaints regarding the frequency of everyday difficulties with memory, language, communication, use of hands, and higher-level cognitive and intellectual functions.

However, self-report measures often have a less clear relationship to formal testing than reports from informants or clinical ratings, particularly in neurological populations (Chaytor & Schmitter-Edgecombe, 2003). Numerous studies have demonstrated that self-report is susceptible to biases based on the individual's mood and cognitive status. For example, depressed individuals tend to manifest negative self-judgments across multiple domains and may underestimate their true abilities (see Moore et al., Chapter 17, in this volume, for a detailed discussion of depression and everyday functioning). In fact, Heaton, Chelune, and Lehman (1978) found that cognitive complaints were more closely related to results on the Minnesota Multiphasic Personality Inventory (MMPI) than to neuropsychological test results. On the other hand, individuals with impairments in metacognition and self-awareness may be prone to underreporting their real-world deficits (Cahn-Weiner et al., 2003; Patterson, Goldman, McKibbin, Hughs, & Jeste, 2001). Other factors such as litigation and the possibility of secondary gain may also influence self-report.

Significant Others (Collateral/Proxy)

Another common approach to assessing real-world outcomes is to ask for input from an informant, such as a spouse or caregiver. Such persons may be in a position to give the most accurate reports of how the patient handles everyday activities, but there are limitations to this approach. The informant may be biased, not know the patient well, or see the person only in situations in which his or her functioning is maximized (or minimized). Caregivers may be particularly influenced by certain obvious deficits; for example, ratings of memory functioning may be more influenced by word-finding difficulties than by actual memory impairments (Cahn-Weiner et al., 2003). There are indications that many informants tend to overestimate patients' abilities (Loewenstein et al., 2001). And, of course, the patient and caregiver may disagree regarding each other's assessments, perhaps making it difficult to determine which view is more accurate.

Ratings by Clinicians

Clinician ratings are often used as an outcome measure. Examples include the Global Assessment of Functioning (GAF) and the Clinical Dementia Rating Scale. A key disadvantage to this approach is that clinicians have only what they see before them in the clinic—a snapshot of the person's functional level. Moreover, clinicians are also subject to biases and often place significant emphasis on input from the patient and/ or caregiver (studies suggest that caregiver input carries the most influence). Some studies have found that the clinician's judgment more closely matches performance on neuropsychological tests than the caregiver's reports, possibly because the neuropsychological and clinical evaluations occur in the same structured environment. Although the approaches may lead to common conclusions, they still may not reflect real-world performance as closely as reports of an observer in the everyday living environment.

Manifest Functioning

Another approach is to seek external documentation of real-world deficits, such as examining employment history, official driving records, or medical records (e.g., for medication adherence measurements). This approach better reflects how people function in their everyday lives and perhaps provides insights regarding whether, due to noncognitive factors, individuals perform better (e.g., using compensatory strategies) or worse (e.g., due to environmental limitations) than one would expect, based on their functional capacities as assessed in the laboratory. This approach, however, also can be prone to error. For example, employability can be influenced by factors other than capacity (mood disorders, environmental factors, reluctance to give up disability income support, etc.). And in the case of driving ability, crashes are rare, often only reported to authorities in more severe cases and may be related to many external factors (e.g., other drivers, road conditions). Crash history can also be influenced by risk exposure (i.e., driving mileage, urban vs. rural driving, traffic conditions) and may thus not provide an accurate reflection of a person's true driving ability.

Actual everyday functioning can be assessed at the "molar" level (e.g., is the individual employed vs. unemployed?) (Goldstein, 1996) or at a more granular level (e.g., is the individual as effective at his or her job as in the past?). It appears that composite global cognitive test measures often best predict molar outcomes, perhaps because both types of variables encompass a broad range of abilities (Franzen & Wilhelm, 1996).

Direct Observation in the Real World

Arguably, the most valid determination of "real-world" outcomes would be direct observation of the person in the real world. Ideally, this observation would occur unobtrusively, without the person's awareness, since the act of being observed can change behavior. This approach is very difficult to implement, however, and likely to be costly and time-consuming, although new technologies make it feasible to observe certain behaviors with increased subtlety and across extended periods of time. For example, in the 100-Car Naturalistic Driving Study of automobile driving (Klauer et al., 2006), healthy individuals agreed to have their own automobiles outfitted with equipment that recorded not only data (e.g., steering and braking), but also video of the driver and the view out the windows. Investigators could then witness each person's behavior right before a crash or near-crash. Of course, such methods can potentially engender ethical concerns (e.g., what if the investigator witnesses illegal behavior of someone who has not consented to be observed?) as well as analysis challenges (e.g., how does the investigator conduct data reduction on 42,300 hours of multimodal data?), among other issues. But such advances do represent exciting new options for observing how patients with neurological conditions truly behave in the open environment.

Factors Complicating the Relationship between Neuropsychological Performance and Everyday Functioning

As one considers everyday functioning, a distinction needs to be made between an individual's capacity to do a task and the actual execution of that capacity. Goldstein (1996) refers to this distinction as the difference between *ability*—a skill or talent within the individual, which is assessable via neuropsychological testing—and *function*—the exercise of that ability in an environmental context. A person develops an *impairment* in ability (e.g., attention), which may then lead to *functional deficits* or *disability* (e.g., in driving an automobile). Clinic-based tests typically focus on capacity/ability, whereas in predicting real-world behavior, in addition to understanding what the person is capable of doing, we are also concerned with what the person actually *does*. In order to understand the limitations in using laboratory measures to predict real-world functioning, it is also important to remain cognizant that the person being evaluated must function within a changing environment and under varying contexts (Tupper & Cicerone, 1990), which can make success in the activity more or less likely. Unlike the laboratory testing situation, everyday functioning is not standardized across people and time. Below we briefly review some of the factors that might complicate the relationship between test performance and real-world functioning.

Testing Environment

Neuropsychological assessment typically emphasizes the elicitation of "optimal performance" from an individual in order to determine the person's underlying capacity (Lezak, Howieson, & Loring, 2004). By design, external factors (e.g., noise, distracting stimuli), task complexity (e.g., multitasking), and task length (many tests are relatively brief) are kept to a minimum. Even the newer ecologically oriented instruments (Rabin et al., 2007), which may encompass a variety of tasks, are often designed to be carried out within a clinic setting where distractions are minimized. In contrast, in the real world tasks are typically undertaken in environments where there are distractions, no direction, and limited encouragement.

Specificity of the Neuropsychological Test

Neuropsychological tests are often cited as measures of specific cognitive constructs. Yet identification of these constructs can vary from author to author, adding to the difficulty in consistently identifying cognitive domains that are critical to real-world functioning. For example, the Trail Making Test Part B (Army Individual Test Battery, 1944; Reitan & Davidson, 1974) is often considered one of the measures most sensitive to brain dysfunction. In the literature it has been referred to as a measure of "complex visual scanning," "speed of executive functioning," "cognitive flexibility," "visual–perceptual processing speed," and "set switching ability" (Gunstad et al., 2008; Kennedy, Clement, & Curtiss, 2003; Lezak et al., 2004; Schwab et al., 2008; Wobrock et al., 2007). Factor analyses have led investigators to consider it among measures of focused attention and perceptuomotor speed (Kelly, 2000; Mirsky, Anthony, Duncan, Ahearn, & Kellam, 1991), executive functioning (Heaton et al., 1995), or rapid alternation between mental sets (Tchanturia et al., 2004). The truth, of course, is that it has aspects of all of these constructs and receives a label of "X" due to the specific factor analysis that was conducted, the other measures included in the analyses, the subject group, or the author's own interpretation of the measure.

Multiple Cognitive Determinants of Real-World Functioning

As noted earlier in this chapter, most everyday tasks involve multiple cognitive processes, even tasks that may appear simple, such as making toast (Hart, Giovannetti, Montgomery, & Schwartz, 1998) or coffee (Giovannetti, Schwartz, & Buxbaum, 2007). Thus, determining the relationship between the cognitive ability and performance of a real-world task depends not only on how important the specific ability is to the task, but also the person's degree of impairment in that ability. Some activities may have a threshold whereby significant impairment in a single domain, even if it is not considered critical to the task, can impact the ability to carry out the task. For example, attention and basic arithmetic skills may be key to managing a checkbook, but severe visuospatial impairments may outweigh the relevance of the intact domains.

Limited Sampling of Behavior

Neuropsychological testing provides only a brief snapshot of behavior (Chaytor & Schmitter-Edgecombe, 2003), whereas real-world tasks can take place over a long time period. A client may be able to rally resources for a brief testing period but have difficulty when that time is extended, perhaps due problems with stamina and fatigue (Chaytor & Schmitter-Edgecombe, 2003) or limited attentional capacity. A real-life example can be seen in studies of the effects of high altitude/oxygen depletion on cognition. Barcroft and colleagues (1923), as quoted in Gerard and colleagues (2000), reported on the difference in test performance and real-world performance during their time on the Peruvian mountain Cerro de Pasco (altitude of 4,330 meters): "When we were undergoing a test, our concentration could by an effort be maintained over the length of time taken for the test, but under ordinary circumstance it would lapse. It is, perhaps, characteristic that, whilst each individual mental test was done as rapidly at Cerro as at the sea-level, the performance of the series took nearly twice as long for its accomplishment. Time was wasted there in trivialities and 'bungling,' which would not take place at sea-level" (pp. 59–60). Such may also be the case when individuals with neurological disorders attempt to carry out a brief laboratory test versus a day's worth of activities.

Environmental Factors and Resources

The ability to carry out everyday functions can be significantly impacted by the environment. For example, being able to safely drive an automobile may differ depending on whether a person is alone in the car, using a cell phone, or transporting a group of middle schoolers. Environmental factors differ between individuals and for the individual from moment to moment: During the course of a commute an individual may drive on both a rural roadway and a congested city street, and weather-related driving conditions may change. A person's work environment may also determine if cognitive declines impact vocational functioning: Mild declines may be very evident in a highly demanding work environment, and less so when the responsibilities are not as challenging (Chaytor & Schmitter-Edgecombe, 2003). Environmental factors can be beneficial as well as detrimental. The availability of resources and support systems, such as electronic reminders or individuals who can guide the person through specific tasks and provide moral/emotional support, may help a person to be more successful in the real world than suggested by a laboratory assessment of his or her functional capacity. Unfortunately, as important as it is to assess environmental demands for each person, few studies incorporate such evaluations in a standardized manner.

Psychiatric and Substance Use Disorders

Many psychiatric conditions, such as schizophrenia (Green, Kern, & Heaton, 2004), bipolar disorder (Martinez-Aran et al., 2007), and major depression (Covinsky, Fortinsky, Palmer, Kresevic, & Landefeld, 1997; Rytsala et al., 2005), can affect a person's ability to initiate and complete ADLs and impact the reliability of self-reported functioning (Heaton, Marcotte, et al., 2004). Although medications for these conditions often improve functioning, they can potentially have negative effects as well (e.g., on automobile driving). Acute, and in some cases chronic, substance use can also affect key everyday activities such as employment, financial management, and driving ability (Hser, Huang, Chou, & Anglin, 2007; Johansson, Alho, Kiiskinen, & Poikolainen, 2007; Logan, 1996; Najavits & Lester, 2008; Semple, Patterson, & Grant, 2003), although the literature using objective measures of functional capacity in these groups is limited.

Experience/Functional Reserve

It is generally accepted that certain individuals, typically those with higher IQs, educational level, or occupational attainment, may be able to suffer greater brain insults before such damage manifests itself clinically (Satz, 1993; Stern, 2003). It has been hypothesized that individuals may have a "cognitive reserve" based on innate levels or, alternatively, reserve is expanded by exposure to schooling and other stimulating activities. For most individuals, repeated exposure increases the "automaticity" with which tasks can be completed, enhances their expertise, and perhaps increases reserve. One example of an everyday activity modifying brain structure can be found in a study of London taxi drivers. In this project, the more time the participant spent as a driver, the larger the hippocampal volumes (Maguire et al., 2000), suggesting the possibility of increased reserve. One might hypothesize that the more experienced individuals could suffer more brain abnormality prior to reaching a point where they no longer work at a minimally competent level.

Individualized Approaches to Problem Solving

Even neurologically normal individuals approach the same task differently (Chaytor & Schmitter-Edgecombe, 2003). For example, some people may spend a great deal of time ineffectively "organizing" their to-do lists, whereas others may focus on completing the tasks that are in front of them. Others may routinely and effectively use shopping lists or map out a driving route ahead of time. These idiosyncratic approaches to everyday life complicate the prediction of real-world performance; in some cases, a well-developed "list-making" approach may help individuals should they suffer a decline in functional capacity in the future.

Motivation

Clients may be motivated to do their best during testing but perhaps have less motivation in the real world, or vice versa. For example, they may be able to avoid undesirable tasks at home if they feign an inability to do the tasks. In the example of forensic cases, clients may see benefits in not performing their best during an evaluation in order to get increased compensation. Even in nonlitigation cases, clients may simply lack the motivation to try their best across a battery of neuropsychological or everyday functioning tests. These motivational issues argue for the use of skilled examiners, conversant with such problems, even when computerized measures are being administered. A number of instruments assesses "effort," symptom validity, and malingering in the clinic/lab (Green, Allen, & Astner, 1996; Hiscock & Hiscock, 1989; Morgan & Sweet, 2008; Rey, 1964; Tombaugh, 1997).

Physical Impairments

As noted earlier, physical impairments can affect both ADLs and IADLs and should be considered in many neuropsychological or functional evaluations. The impact of physical impairments is evident in many neurological conditions (e.g., stroke, traumatic brain injury, multiple sclerosis) and across many real-world tasks (e.g., driving and vocational functioning).

Education and Literacy

Although it is clear that educational levels and neuropsychological test performance travel together on many tests, and IQ is closely linked to educational and ultimately job attainment, little attention has been paid to the direct relationship between education and the ability to carry out everyday tasks. At lower levels of education, in particular, literacy (numeracy, reading and writing) may be an issue. Many resource-limited countries have high illiteracy rates. Inadequate numeracy ("the ability to understand and use numbers in daily life") may adversely impact health outcomes and everyday functioning in tasks such as reading food labels, interpreting bus schedules, and refilling prescriptions (Rothman, Montori, Cherrington, & Pignone, 2008). However, education and literacy are not completely synonymous, as individuals learn many life skills (e.g., how to count money) without formal education.

Compensatory Strategies

Because clinic/laboratory assessments are typically highly structured and assess only a limited number of abilities, these evaluations may at times underestimate an individual's capacity to perform in the open environment by not providing opportunities to implement compensatory strategies (Franzen & Wilhelm, 1996). Individuals may have learned strategies such as monitoring tasks using a to-do list or setting an alarm as a medication reminder. Thus they may function adequately in their daily life but do poorly in the clinic/laboratory when asked to learn a list of items or do a task at a certain time. On the other hand, they may make a concerted effort to strategize during a testing session, but not do so in everyday life. For example, a person might use semantic clustering to remember items on a memory test, but not use such a strategy when trying to remember a shopping list (Chaytor & Schmitter-Edgecombe, 2003). In addition to providing information regarding an individual's deficits, neuropsychological testing can provide valuable information regarding a person's cognitive strengths, which may also suggest ways that he or she could potentially compensate for deficits. This is one reason why neuropsychologists should always consider assessing multiple domains, and not just those in which they hypothesize likely impairment (Heaton & Marcotte, 2000).

Given the many factors that might affect everyday functioning, it is not surprising that, as with most behavioral research, measures of cognitive status alone remain only "moderately" related to real-world performance. Improving assessment in the areas mentioned above might enhance laboratory predictions of behavior in the open environment.

Selection of Neuropsychological Test Variables

Is a common, underlying set of cognitive abilities necessary in order to adequately perform all everyday activities? Alternatively, is it the case that some key abilities (e.g., attention) are necessary, but perhaps not sufficient, to carry out many tasks, and specific activities require specific skill sets? Can we predict human behavior by examining performance on cognitive constructs individually and in isolation, or do we need to know how they work in concert? Although these questions remain unanswered, there appears to be general agreement among practicing neuropsychologists regarding the key abilities that should be assessed when predicting everyday functioning. These include attention, executive functions, intelligence, language, motor skills, verbal and nonverbal (visual) memory, construction, and visuospatial skills. Nevertheless, there remains significant variability with respect to which tests are used to assess these domains (Rabin et al., 2007). When predicting everyday functioning, most neuropsychologists use traditional tests and then may augment their battery with one or more ecologically oriented measures (see below).

Neuropsychological tests can yield a number of performance variables: raw scores, scaled scores, and demographically adjusted scores. In order to determine whether there has been a decline in functioning, the examiner needs to know the patient's premorbid functional level. However, neuropsychological testing is rarely available for the period prior to an insult (e.g., head injury). A variety of methods has been developed to estimate prior functioning, including measures based on educational and occupational attainment, as well as performance on tests that are relatively insensitive to acquired brain abnormalities (e.g., Barona & Chastain, 1986; Gladsjo, Heaton, Palmer, Taylor, & Jeste, 1999). Neuropsychological performance tends to travel with characteristics such as age, education, gender, and ethnicity (Heaton, Taylor, & Manly, 2004), and the use of norms that adjust for these factors are particularly helpful in estimating differences between observed and expected levels of performance.

Although the method of using demographically adjusted normative standards works well for determining whether individuals are impaired relative to expected levels, it may be that the use of adjusted scores is not the best method for predicting performance of activities that most of the population can accomplish routinely. For example, although we might expect a person with a PhD in engineering to perform better on cognitive tests than an individual with a high school education, we would not necessarily expect that person to be a better driver or more adept at managing his or her medications.

When addressing the relationship between cognition and everyday functioning, we are not so much concerned with whether someone has declined from a previous level of neurocognitive performance, but rather whether his or her functioning is adequate for everyday functioning requirements *now*. One approach to predicting competence in everyday skills would be to simply consider raw scores, such as time to complete the Trail Making Test Part B, or the learning rate on the California Verbal

Learning Test. However, raw scores are difficult to compare across tests and to interpret in relation to expected functioning of the general population. For example, one measure may be timed, in which a fewer number of seconds indicates good performance, whereas higher scores on another measure (e.g., a list-learning test) are indicative of good performance. These differences also make it difficult to combine such variables into summary scores. For these reasons we have recommended the use of scaled scores in predicting everyday functioning (Heaton & Marcotte, 2000). Scaled scores are uncorrected (e.g., for age) scores that are generated from a population of normal controls (ideally representing a broad range of demographic characteristics, similar to the society of interest; e.g., based on a national census), and transformed so that they are normally distributed (often with a mean of 10 and a *SD* of 3). Since each test variable is put onto this common metric, one can then compare performance across measures and generate summary scores, such as estimates of overall or domain-specific functioning (Heaton, Miller, et al., 2004).

There remains a fair amount of variability in whether investigators use raw, scaled, or *T*-scores. A recent study directly compared the use of adjusted and unadjusted scores (Silverberg & Millis, 2009) in a group of patients with TBI. Real-world outcomes were based on patient and caregiver reports. The authors used the normative data provided by Heaton, Miller, and colleagues (2004) to generate "absolute scores"—unadjusted scores that were placed upon the *T*-scale metric, where the overall mean of the normative group is 50, with a standard deviation of 10, in order to facilitate comparisons of the two methods. They then created two overall test battery mean scores (for absolute and adjusted scores) in order to predict outcomes on their questionnaires. The authors found that (1) absolute and adjusted scores were often divergent, usually based, as would be expected, on the degree to which the patient differed from the normative group average on demographic factors (age, education, gender, ethnicity); and (2) whereas both measures predicted everyday functioning, the results tended to favor the use of absolute scores. It should be noted, however, that the superiority of absolute scores for predicting everyday functioning may depend on whether the tasks are those that all or most adults would be expected to perform successfully. If the everyday tasks are exceptionally demanding and normally performed only by people with high levels of education (e.g., physicians, attorneys, scientists, university professors), use of education-corrected scores may be better predictive of success or failure.

Additional studies comparing these methods may yield useful insights as to the best way to use neuropsychological test results to predict real-world behavior. For example, such studies might identify absolute levels of functioning in various domains that are needed to accomplish specific tasks, such as medication management. The findings might vary by neurological group, but over time investigators could build a common base of knowledge that would inform clinicians and future studies.

Instruments Focusing on Ecological Validity

There has been an increasing interest in developing test instruments and batteries that emphasize ecological validity. These instruments more closely resemble the activities individuals would be expected to undertake in everyday life, with the hope of better predicting real-world functioning. Many of these "performance-based" measures are designed to assess functional capacity—that is, the person's ability to perform tasks under optimal circumstances. The focus is not on differentiating normal and patient groups, per se, but on "identifying people who have difficulty performing real-world tasks, regardless of the etiology of the problem" (Chaytor & Schmitter-Edgecombe, 2003, p. 182). Thus, in theory, these tests should be applicable to many different patient groups and, in some cases, people within normal populations. Such tests are often well accepted by patients/participants, given their strong face validity.

These measures typically have multiple subtests; examples of the types of tasks utilized include remembering names associated with faces, recalling a hidden object and its location, recalling an appointment when a timer sounds (Rivermead Behavioral Memory Test; Wilson et al., 1985); searching maps, looking through telephone directories, and listening to broadcasts of lottery numbers (Test of Everyday Attention; Robertson et al., 1996); clock reading, preparing a letter for mailing, eating skills (Direct Assessment of Functional Status [DAFS]; Loewenstein et al., 1989); role-playing household chores (cooking, shopping), route-planning for public transportation, and planning recreational activities (UCSD Performance-Based Skills Assessment [UPSA]; Patterson et al., 2001); managing medications, cooking, and performing financial management and vocationally oriented tasks (Heaton, Marcotte, et al., 2004).

In a survey of almost 750 members of the major neuropsychological societies (International Neuropsychological Society, National Academy of Neuropsychology, American Psychological Society Division 40 [Neuropsychology]), Rabin and colleagues (2007) found no clear consensus regarding which ecologically oriented measures were most useful for predicting everyday functioning. The most common standardized measure was used by less than 10% of the respondents. In decreasing order, the following methods for assessing the domains of memory, attention, executive functioning, and determination of ability to return to work were the most frequently mentioned:

- *Memory*: Rivermead Behavioral Memory Test (Wilson et al., 1985), Autobiographical Memory Interview (Kopelman, Wilson, & Baddeley, 1990), Contextual Memory Test (Toglia, 1993), Brief Test of Attention (Schretlen, 2005), prospective memory tests.
- *Attention*: Test of Everyday Attention (Robertson et al., 1996), Behavioral Inattention Test (Wilson, Cockburn, & Halligan, 1987), observe patient's compensatory strategies, clinical interview with functional questions, review work record and past job responsibilities.
- *Executive functioning*: Tinkertoy Test (Lezak, 1982), Behavioral Assessment of Dysexecutive Syndrome (Wilson et al., 1996), Behavior Rating Inventory of Executive Function (Gioia, Isquith, Guy, & Kenworthy, 2000), Six Elements Test (Shallice & Burgess, 1991), Dysexecutive Questionnaire (Wilson et al., 1996).
- *Return to work*: Driving evaluation, functional assessment, structured work trial, clinical assessment of current job demands, expectations, requirements; interview with coworkers/supervisors.

As can be seen, there were many cases in which neuropsychologists emphasized clinical acumen and nonstandardized evaluations rather than published tests. Of those who used the ecologically oriented instruments (35% of the sample), 65% used only one measure, and 95% used three or fewer measures, even though 70% of all respondents reported encountering at least one rehabilitation-related assessment referral question. As the authors note, this research "highlights the disparity between the proportion of neuropsychologists who conduct assessments that focus on ecological issues and the proportion who use the instruments designed for ecological purposes" (p. 736).

If these instruments hold promise, why have neuropsychologists hesitated to incorporate such measures into their standard test batteries? Spooner and Pachana (2006) propose the following possibilities: (1) the assumption that traditional tests are ecologically valid, despite limited evidence that this is the case; (2) the tendency to stay with those instruments on which one received graduate training, or to remain committed to a particular theory of assessment approach; (3) the view that verisimilitude is synonymous with face validity, suggesting a less rigorous or "unscientific" evaluation of the ecological validity of the measure, even though many of these instruments have undergone such evaluations; (4) the belief that tests based on verisimilitude overlap with the occupational therapy approach and thus encroach on another discipline; (5) the belief that traditional tests measure specific constructs, even though "the application of labels to cognitive domains is not necessarily reflective of unambiguous empirical findings" (p. 334).

Although many such instruments hold promise, mimicking everyday tasks in the clinic/lab does not necessarily mean that the findings will directly relate to how patients/participants function in the real world, where they must deal with competing tasks, prioritizing, paying attention in the context of distractions, and so on. As such, some investigators have tried to assess the sequencing and multitasking aspects of daily life.

Burgess and colleagues (2006) advocate a "function-led approach" to creating clinical tasks—models that proceed from a directly observable everyday behavior backward to examine how a sequence of actions leads to behavior, and how that behavior might become disrupted. Ecological validity may be improved because of more specific delineation of cognitive processes, even in seemingly simple behaviors (e.g., making toast and coffee) (Schwartz, 2006).

As an example, although various executive functions have been proposed to be cognitive skills that are integral to the successful execution of everyday activities, "executive functions" can refer to a range of cognitive processes (e.g., planning, conceptualization, set shifting, attention, monitoring), any of which, if impaired, could lead to problems with everyday functioning. Isolating these processes is difficult because neuropsychological tests used to assess executive functioning (e.g., Trail Making Test Part B, Wisconsin Card Sorting Test, category test, Stroop tests, Tower of London test, fluency tests) generally assess more than one of these processes. Thus, taking a "function-led" approach, researchers have examined everyday behaviors that are problematic for patients with executive dysfunction by developing tasks informed by cognitive models of these behaviors. Many patients with dementia and frontal lobe disorders display problems with organization and execution of "everyday action"

(Schwartz & Buxbaum, 1997), such as errors in carrying out a sequence of actions (e.g., preparing a lunch). One hypothesis is that the actual generation and sequencing of actions might be deficient in such a scenario. This hypothesis has been explored through tasks of script generation, in which individuals are asked to generate and properly sequence all the steps needed to complete an action (e.g., doing the laundry). Script generation deficits have been found in individuals with frontal lobe lesions (Sirigu et al., 1995), Parkinson's disease (Godbout & Doyon, 2000), attention-deficit/hyperactivity disorder (Braun et al., 2004), and schizophrenia (Chan, Chiu, Lam, Pang, & Chow, 1999), and these deficits have been related to problems in everyday functioning (Chevignard et al., 2000). Assessing the generation and organization of such action sequences may be important in certain patient groups.

On the other hand, the actual execution of an action sequence may result in errors in carrying out the task due to errors of omission (e.g., leaving out a critical step), commission (e.g., adding unnecessary steps), or substitution (e.g., using an object not relevant to the task). This possibility has been investigated with standardized laboratory tests that mimic everyday, multistep tasks, such as the Naturalistic Action Test (Schwartz, Buxbaum, Ferraro, Veramonti, & Segal, 2003), in which patients are asked to make toast, pack a lunchbox, and so on. On this and similar tasks, individuals with closed head injuries (Schwartz et al., 1998), stroke (Schwartz et al., 1999), schizophrenia (Kessler, Giovannetti, & MacMullen, 2007), and progressive dementia (Giovannetti, Libon, Buxbaum, & Schwartz, 2002) have a high number of errors relative to normal comparison participants. In addition, different patterns of performance on such tasks might distinguish clinical groups (Giovannetti, Schmidt, Gallo, Sestito, & Libon, 2006; Kessler et al., 2007), emphasizing the possible clinical utility of such an approach.

Another possibility is that the coordination of various action sequences (i.e., switching between sequences) creates deficits in everyday action. This roughly corresponds with the construct of "multitasking," in which an individual is required not only to plan and organize based on temporal and conditional associations between actions, but also to maintain this conditional and temporal information in working memory, along with other information such as the immediate environmental stimuli, goals, and subgoals. Given that this process was disrupted in a number of their patients with neurological conditions who displayed adequate performance on traditional executive function tests, Shallice and Burgess developed the Six Elements Test (1991) and Multiple Errands Test (Shallice, 1991) to provide patients with similar task demands as everyday life situations and thereby assess multitasking abilities. In each of these tests, individuals are asked to complete a number of simple tasks without breaking a series of prescribed rules. Subsets of patients with frontal lobe lesions (Burgess, 2000), depression (Channon & Green, 1999), schizophrenia (Evans, Chua, McKenna, & Wilson, 1997), Parkinson's disease (Kamei et al., 2008), or multiple sclerosis (Roca et al., 2008) have shown profound deficits on such tests, with concomitant problems in real-world functioning.

Importantly, despite their open-ended and naturalistic nature, such measures have generally displayed adequate psychometric properties (Knight, Alderman, & Burgess, 2002; Schwartz et al., 2002) and have shown moderately high correlations with independent outcomes assessing everyday functioning (Burgess, Alderman, Evans, Emslie, & Wilson, 1998). As such, they may offer ecologically relevant additions to a battery of assessment instruments when such everyday problems are suspected.

Prospective memory, or the ability to execute a future intention (i.e., "remembering to remember") in the absence of explicit cues, is another area garnering interest among investigators interested in predicting real-world performance. Examples include remembering to take a medication after a meal or mail a letter on the way home from work. Prospective memory is conceptually dissociable from retrospective memory, which refers to remembering information from the past in response to overt prompts. Initial studies attest to the ecological relevance of prospective memory, suggesting that it may even be a stronger contributor to the independent performance of IADLs than retrospective memory (Park & Kidder, 1996). Prospective memory is theorized to be dependent on the integrity of frontostriatal circuits (Simons, Scholvinck, Gilbert, Frith, & Burgess, 2006) and has been shown to be reduced in a number of conditions that affect these systems, including aging (Einstein, Holland, McDaniel, & Guynn, 1992; Maylor, Smith, Della Sala, & Logie, 2002), HIV infection (Carey, Woods, Rippeth, Heaton, & Grant, 2006), Parkinson's disease (Katai, Maruyama, Hashimoto, & Ikeda, 2003), and schizophrenia (Kondel, 2002; Woods, Twamley, Dawson, Narvaez, & Jeste, 2007). Furthermore, prospective memory has been predictive of everyday functioning in individuals with schizophrenia (Twamley et al., 2008) and HIV infection (Martin et al., 2007; Woods, Carey, et al., 2007; Woods et al., 2008). Prospective memory may therefore be a unique and ecologically important aspect of cognitive functioning that, although ubiquitous in daily life, is not captured by traditional assessment techniques.

In some cases, individuals display a number of errors on such assessment instruments while performing adequately on more traditional measures of similar constructs. However, many of the instruments that have been developed using a function-led approach are still being used predominantly in clinical research and await further validation and normative standards before being widely used in clinical care.

Challenges in Developing Ecologically Oriented Measures

Ideally, it would be useful to employ ecologically oriented measures that encompass a broad range of skill levels (easy to challenging) and are able to detect subtle declines (in the case of early-stage neurological disorders) or improvements (in the case of pharmaceutical treatments). However, it is very difficult to develop measures that reflect everyday functioning—tasks that most people successfully perform in their daily lives—and are still challenging enough to provide a distribution of functioning across "normal" individuals (i.e., so that not everyone either receives a perfect score or fails the test). As the difficulty of a task increases, it becomes a challenge to keep the measure from being "test-like" (Goldstein, 1996) or game-like. For example, how much complexity can be added to a money management task before the testee would need to be a certified public accountant to succeed on the test, or at what point does adding difficulty to a driving simulation (e.g., accident avoidance scenarios) produce the look and feel of an arcade videogame, thus losing the real-world aspects of the measures? The Rivermead Behavioral Memory Test is an example of a measure that was "extended" when the earlier version was found to be insufficiently challenging to delineate functioning within normal individuals (de Wall, Wilson, & Baddeley, 1994). From our own experience, our battery of functional measures (cooking, shopping, financial management, medication management, vocational abilities) underwent a number of modifications before achieving a reasonable balance between task difficulty and real-world applicability (Heaton, Marcotte, et al., 2004). In addition, given that most healthy individuals perform near ceiling on many everyday measures, it is also often challenging to establish test–retest reliability via traditional correlational methods.

Using Both Traditional and Ecologically Oriented Instruments to Predict Everyday Functioning

Measures specifically designed to assess abilities related to an everyday task, but not directly mirroring the task of interest, may provide incremental improvement on the prediction of everyday functioning achieved using traditional neuropsychological measures. For example, in a study of automobile driving with HIV infection, poor neuropsychological functioning was associated with recent on-road crashes (Marcotte et al., 2006). However, by further stratifying participants according to performance on the UFOV test (Ball et al., 1993; Ball & Roenker, 1998), a computerized measure of visual divided attention, we were able to identify those participants who had the highest number of crashes. It is thus possible that individuals with impaired visual attention and concomitant executive deficits are less likely to be aware of their attentional deficits and thus fail to take steps to compensate for their impairments (e.g., driving more slowly).

In addition, measures that more closely reflect real-world tasks may also add incremental information useful in predicting real-world performance. For example, in a different study of driving abilities of HIV-positive individuals (Marcotte et al., 2004), we examined performance on a structured, on-road driving assessment. Participants completed a detailed neuropsychological test battery and interactive PC-based driving simulations assessing routine driving and accident avoidance skills, as well as navigational abilities (i.e., using a map, participants were asked to drive to a location within a virtual city and then return to their starting location). Global neuropsychological performance was a significant predictor of passing or failing the on-road drive. However, performance on the simulations explained additional variance beyond traditional testing in predicting on-road performance, suggesting that the simulations may provide information on real-world behaviors that are not captured by the neuropsychological measures, such as the ability to anticipate high-risk situations or respond to complex demands when under time pressure.

What Is the Best Lab-/Clinic-Based Approach to Predicting Real-World Behavior?

As noted earlier, the existing literature suggests a "moderate" relationship between traditional neuropsychological measures and real-world functioning, and no single test, or battery of tests, is predictive of all aspects of everyday functioning across all groups. However, the neuropsychological approach brings many advantages, in that many tests have good psychometric properties, established reliability and validity, and norms; in addition, there is abundant evidence that performance on traditional neuropsychological tests relates to aspects of everyday functioning. Few studies have done direct comparisons between approaches emphasizing veridicality versus verisimilitude, and comparisons between studies are complicated by the use of different test instruments, different outcome measures, and different samples. However, in a review of studies using one, or both, approaches, Chaytor and Schmitter-Edgecombe (2003) found some evidence favoring the verisimilitude approach in predicting everyday performance, at least with respect to memory and executive functioning. But the matter is still unresolved.

At this juncture, it appears that the best approach remains one in which, in most circumstances, the neuropsychologist uses demographically adjusted scores to determine whether there has likely been a decline from previous cognitive levels. If the decline appears to be of sufficient magnitude to affect everyday functioning, the examination of nonadjusted scaled or absolute scores can be used to predict most real-world activities (Silverberg & Millis, 2009). Greater precision of this prediction is likely to be possible if future studies help clarify basic levels needed to perform specific tasks. In some cases of particularly highly demanding positions (e.g., physician, pilot), it is advisable to continue to focus on expected levels of cognitive functioning, using demographic corrections, since an average level of scaled scores may not adequately encompass the cognitive expertise needed for the most challenging real-world tasks. Based on a broad review of the literature, a focus on executive functioning (Guilmette & Kastner, 1996) and perhaps learning and memory (Chaytor & Schmitter-Edgecombe, 2003; Heaton, Marcotte, et al., 2004) may provide the greatest yield regarding the prediction of real-world functioning. Additional cognitive domains specific to the real-world tasks in question could also be assessed. As noted earlier, since one is also interested in cognitive strengths (e.g., for potential compensatory mechanisms), we recommend the administration of a comprehensive battery whenever the prediction of real-world functioning is the goal.

It should also be clear that there are benefits to the multimodal assessment of an individual's ability to carry out everyday tasks successfully. Such assessments would include information gleaned from some of the well-developed, ecologically oriented measures discussed throughout this chapter, as well as perceptions regarding how well the individual is functioning in his or her daily life (based on self-reports and knowledgeable informants). Traditional neuropsychological tests and performance-based everyday functioning measures inform us of the individual's capacity, but the clinician also needs to be familiar with other factors (e.g., environmental, emotional, psychosocial) that might cause differences between capacity and implementation.

Future Directions

Traditional neuropsychological measures continue to prove useful, as just noted. However, although there will always be a need for measures that assess specific cognitive constructs (e.g., for diagnosis), the field is still faced with the question of how to develop new tests or more effectively use the old ones to better predict functioning in the real world. We are seeing a merging of traditional approaches and ones based on verisimilitude, and it appears that such methods can be used in a complementary way to predict real-world functioning and also be standardized with good psychometric properties.

Yet some have argued for an even more significant paradigm shift in how we go about identifying and measuring the cognitive abilities involved in carrying out everyday tasks. For example, as noted earlier, Burgess and colleagues (2006) make a case for going from "function to construct," rather than adapting tests developed from experimental investigations. Using this function-led approach in developing their Multiple Errands Test, they progressed from designing a measure of "real-world" behavior that they believed captured the behavioral disorganization seen in patients with neurological conditions, to a series of studies ultimately examining the neural underpinnings of subfunctions, ending with an hypothesized construct of an attentional "gateway" (Burgess et al., 2006).

In a similar vein, Kingstone, Smilek, and Eastwood (2008) contend that the usual approach of emphasizing invariance and control in cognitive research, using constrained laboratory paradigms, is "incompatible with the ecological goal." Stating that general systems theory "has demonstrated that tight experimental control can be effective at revealing the basic characteristics of simple linear systems but it is ineffective at revealing the characteristics of complex, non-linear systems, which must surely include the human cognitive system," these authors emphasize observing and describing behavior as it occurs in the real world, rather than expecting models developed in the lab to pertain to the open environment (p. 320). They also encourage the elicitation of input from participants themselves, in order to garner their subjective and introspective experience and better understand individual approaches to a task. This approach, termed "cognitive ethology," is described as more compatible with basic research and discovery. It may not have immediate application with respect to predicting real-world performance from an office setting, but it may yield new insights that inform the development of implementable, and standardized, measures.

Consistent prediction of real-world behavior is also complicated by the fact that, for the ecologically oriented instruments that have been developed, most have yet to gain widespread use, either by different research groups or across different neurological populations. Many tools are "home grown" and applied within a single laboratory or across only a few patient groups, thus limiting their utility to the field at large. Until these approaches are more widely implemented, it is likely that the field will progress slowly. Since such movement is unlikely to occur when initiated by only a handful of investigators sharing a common interest, and funding for such development is scarce, it is recommended that neuropsychological organizations or government entities invested in understanding outcomes (e.g., the National Institutes of Health) foster such collaborations, perhaps assembling expert panels to weigh in on the design of new instruments, as well as methods of implementing them across multiple sites. This recommendation is certainly not meant to inhibit the critical role played by the individual investigator creatively developing novel measures. But to truly advance the field to a point where such instruments can become the standard of care, there needs to be widespread acceptance and application of these measures.

Another area warranting both increased individual initiative and a fostering of collaboration is the application of ecologically oriented measures as outcomes in clinical trials. Over the past decade greater importance has been placed on the question of whether behavioral or pharmaceutical interventions significantly improve real-world functioning and quality of life. Further development of neuropsychological norms for change—an approach that will help clinicians determine whether improvements or declines are "unusual"—will only enhance the utility of the neuropsychological approach (Heaton & Marcotte, 2000). However, these neuropsychological measures do not necessarily meet the spirit of the requirement to assess functional outcomes (e.g., is significant improvement in Trails B time important if it fails to translate into a functional change in daily life?). For this reason, there have been calls for better measurement of outcomes relating to everyday functioning. For example, the U.S. Food and Drug Administration (FDA) requires that clinical trials for the treatment of Alzheimer's disease (Laughren, 2001) and schizophrenia (Buchanan et al., 2005) include co-primary measures that assess a clinically meaningful/relevant functional outcome. There thus may be greater movement toward measures that include a verisimilitude approach to predicting real-world behavior, if indeed such measures are better predictors.

As noted here, and throughout this book, one needs to pay as much attention to the measurement of outcomes as to predictors. This lack of attention to outcomes is still a limitation for many studies examining real-world functioning, since the "real-world" outcome is itself poorly defined. In the field of automobile driving, for example, the relationship between cognitive performance and "driving" may differ if driving performance is assessed via reaction time to a video, a fully interactive desktop simulator, a full-motion car cab, a closed-course challenge drive, an open-road assessment, or a tally of real-world crashes. New technologies hold promise for unobtrusively observing some important behaviors in the open, real-world environment. As described earlier, in the "100-Car Naturalistic Driving Study" the investigators outfitted the research participants' own cars with equipment to measure, and video, individuals' behavior on the real road over the course of a year (Klauer et al., 2006). Other techniques have been used to monitor natural movement of impaired individuals in their homes (Hayes et al., 2008). Although such approaches can raise ethical issues and present data informatics challenges, they offer an exciting preview of a coming capacity to observe how normal, and impaired, individuals behave in their day-to-day life.

The ability of neuropsychological testing to predict everyday functioning has been clearly established. However, performance on these clinic-based measures does not capture all of the variance associated with behavior in the open environment. Advances in theoretical conceptualizations, test development, technology, and multimodal methods of assessing predictors and outcomes portend a promising future for our ability to understand the relationship between brain function and behavior in the real world.

Acknowledgment

We wish to thank Rachel Meyer for her assistance in the preparation of this chapter.

References

Amick, M. M., D'Abreu, A., Moro-de-Casillas, M. L., Chou, K. L., & Ott, B. R. (2007). Excessive daytime sleepiness and on-road driving performance in patients with Parkinson's disease. *J Neurol Sci, 252*(1), 13–15.

Army Individual Test Battery. (1944). *Manual of directions and scoring.* Washington, DC: War Department, Adjutant General's Office.

Ball, K., Owsley, C., Sloane, M. E., Roenker, D. L., & Bruni, J. R. (1993). Visual attention problems as a predictor of vehicle crashes in older drivers. *Invest Ophth Vis Sci, 34*(11), 3110–3123.

Ball, K., & Roenker, D. (1998). *Useful field of view.* San Antonio, TX: Psychological Corporation.

Ball, K. K., Beard, B. L., Roenker, D. L., Miller, R. L., & Griggs, D. S. (1988). Age and visual search: Expanding the useful field of view. *J Opt Soc Am A, 5*(12), 2210–2219.

Barcroft, J., Binger, C. A., Bock, A. V., Doggart, J. H., Forbes, H. S., Harrop, G., et al. (1923). Observations upon the effect of high altitude on the physiological processes of the human body, carried out in the Peruvian Andes, chiefly at Cerro de Pasco. *Philos T Roy Soc B, 211*, 351–480.

Barona, A., & Chastain, R. L. (1986). An improved estimate of premorbid IQ for blacks and whites on the WAIS-R. *Int J Clin Neuropsy, 8*, 169–173.

Bell-McGinty, S., Podell, K., Franzen, M., Baird, A. D., & Williams, M. J. (2002). Standard measures of executive function in predicting instrumental activities of daily living in older adults. *Int J Geriatr Psych, 17*(9), 828–834.

Bieliauskas, L. A., Roper, B. R., Trobe, J., Green, P., & Lacy, M. (1998). Cognitive measures, driving safety, and Alzheimer's disease. *Clin Neuropsycholog, 12*(2), 206–212.

Boyle, P. A., Paul, R. H., Moser, D. J., & Cohen, R. A. (2004). Executive impairments predict functional declines in vascular dementia. *Clin Neuropsychol, 18*(1), 75–82.

Braun, C. M., Godbout, L., Desbiens, C., Daigneault, S., Lussier, F., & Hamel-Hebert, I. (2004). Mental genesis of scripts in adolescents with attention deficit/hyperactivity disorder. *Child Neuropsychol, 10*(4), 280–296.

Brooks, N., McKinlay, W., Symington, C., Beattie, A., & Campsie, L. (1987). Return to work within the first seven years of severe head injury. *Brain Inj, 1*(1), 5–19.

Brouwer, W. H. (2002). Attention and driving: A cognitive neuropsychological approach. In M. Leclercq & P. Zimmermann (Eds.), *Applied neuropsychology of attention* (pp. 230–254). New York: Psychology Press.

Brunswik, E. (1955). Symposium of the probability approach in psychology: Representative design and probabilistic theory in a functional psychology. *Psychol Rev, 62*, 193–217.

Buchanan, R. W., Davis, M., Goff, D., Green, M. F., Keefe, R. S., Leon, A. C., et al. (2005). A summary of the FDA-NIMH-MATRICS workshop on clinical trial design for neurocognitive drugs for schizophrenia. *Schizophr Bull, 31*(1), 5–19.

Burgess, P. W. (2000). Strategy application disorder: The role of the frontal lobes in human multitasking. *Psychol Res, 63*(3–4), 279–288.

Burgess, P. W., Alderman, N., Evans, J., Emslie, H., & Wilson, B. A. (1998). The ecological validity of tests of executive function. *J Int Neuropsychol Soc, 4*(6), 547–558.

Burgess, P. W., Alderman, N., Forbes, C., Costello, A., Coates, L. M., Dawson, D. R., et al. (2006). The case for the development and use of "ecologically valid" measures of executive function in experimental and clinical neuropsychology. *J Int Neuropsychol Soc, 12*(2), 194–209.

Cahn-Weiner, D. A., Ready, R. E., & Malloy, P. F. (2003). Neuropsychological predictors of everyday memory and everyday functioning in patients with mild Alzheimer's disease. *J Geriatr Psych Neur, 16*(2), 84–89.

Carey, C. L., Woods, S. P., Gonzalez, R., Conover, E., Marcotte, T. D., Grant, I., et al. (2004). Predictive validity of global deficit scores in detecting neuropsychological impairment in HIV infection. *J Clin Exp Neuropsychol*, 26(3), 307–319.

Carey, C. L., Woods, S. P., Rippeth, J. D., Heaton, R. K., & Grant, I. (2006). Prospective memory in HIV-1 infection. *J Clin Exp Neuropsychol*, 28(4), 536–548.

Chan, A. S., Chiu, H., Lam, L., Pang, A., & Chow, L. Y. (1999). A breakdown of event schemas in patients with schizophrenia: An examination of their script for dining at restaurants. *Psychiatry Res*, 87(2–3), 169–181.

Channon, S., & Green, P. S. (1999). Executive function in depression: The role of performance strategies in aiding depressed and non-depressed participants. *J Neurol Neurosurg Psychiatry*, 66(2), 162–171.

Chaytor, N., & Schmitter-Edgecombe, M. (2003). The ecological validity of neuropsychological tests: A review of the literature on everyday cognitive skills. *Neuropsychol Rev*, 13(4), 181–197.

Chelune, G. J., Heaton, R. K., & Lehman, R. A. W. (1986). Neuropsychological and personality correlates of patients' complaints of disability. In G. Goldstein & R. E. Tarter (Eds.), *Advances in clinical neuropsychology* (Vol. 3, pp. 95–126). New York: Plenum Press.

Chelune, G. J., & Moehle, K. (1986). Neuropsychological assessment and everyday functioning. In D. Wedding, J. Horton, A. Webster, & J. Webster (Eds.), *The neuropsychology handbook: Behavioral and clinical perspectives* (pp. 489–525). New York: Springer.

Chevignard, M., Pillon, B., Pradat-Diehl, P., Taillefer, C., Rousseau, S., Le Bras, C., et al. (2000). An ecological approach to planning dysfunction: Script execution. *Cortex*, 36(5), 649–669.

Covinsky, K. E., Fortinsky, R. H., Palmer, R. M., Kresevic, D. M., & Landefeld, C. S. (1997). Relation between symptoms of depression and health status outcomes in acutely ill hospitalized older persons. *Ann Intern Med*, 126(6), 417–425.

Daigneault, G., Joly, P., & Frigon, J. Y. (2002). Executive functions in the evaluation of accident risk of older drivers. *J Clin Exp Neuropsyc*, 24(2), 221–238.

Deary, I. J., Strand, S., Smith, P., & Fernandes, C. (2006). Intelligence and educational achievement. *Intelligence*, 35(1), 13–21.

de Leeuw, F. E., de Groot, J. C., Achten, E., Oudkerk, M., Ramos, L. M., Heijboer, R., et al. (2001). Prevalence of cerebral white matter lesions in elderly people: A population based magnetic resonance imaging study. The Rotterdam Scan Study. *J Neurol Neurosur Ps*, 70(1), 9–14.

de Wall, C., Wilson, B. A., & Baddeley, A. D. (1994). The Extended Rivermead Behavioural Memory Test: A measure of everyday memory performance in normal adults. *Memory*, 2(2), 149–166.

Duchek, J. M., Hunt, L., Ball, K., Buckles, V., & Morris, J. C. (1998). Attention and driving performance in Alzheimer's disease. *J Gerontol*, 53(2), P130–P141.

Earnst, K. S., Wadley, V. G., Aldridge, T. M., Steenwyk, A. B., Hammond, A. E., Harrell, L. E., et al. (2001). Loss of financial capacity in Alzheimer's disease: The role of working memory. *Aging Neuropsychol C*, 8, 109–119.

Einstein, G. O., Holland, L. J., McDaniel, M. A., & Guynn, M. J. (1992). Age-related deficits in prospective memory: The influence of task complexity. *Psychol Aging*, 7(3), 471–478.

Evans, J. J., Chua, S. E., McKenna, P. J., & Wilson, B. A. (1997). Assessment of the dysexecutive syndrome in schizophrenia. *Psychol Med*, 27(3), 635–646.

Farmer, J. E., & Eakman, A. M. (1995). The relationship between neuropsychological functioning and instrumental activities of daily living following acquired brain injury. *Appl Neuropsychol, 2*(3–4), 107–115.

Fisk, G. D., Novack, T., Mennemeier, M., & Roenker, D. (2002). Useful field of view after traumatic brain injury. *J Head Trauma Rehab, 17*(1), 16–25.

Fisk, G. D., Owsley, C., & Mennemeier, M. (2002). Vision, attention, and self-reported driving behaviors in community-dwelling stroke survivors. *Arch Phys Med Rehab, 83*(4), 469–477.

Fitten, L. J., Perryman, K. M., Wilkinson, C. J., Little, R. J., Burns, M. M., Pachana, N., et al. (1995). Alzheimer and vascular dementias and driving: A prospective road and laboratory study. *JAMA, 273*(17), 1360–1365.

Fox, G. K., Bowden, S. C., Bashford, G. M., & Smith, D. S. (1997). Alzheimer's disease and driving: Prediction and assessment of driving performance. *J Am Geriatr Soc, 45*, 949–953.

Franzen, M. D. (2000). *Reliability and validity in neuropsychological assessment.* New York: Springer.

Franzen, M. D., & Wilhelm, K. L. (1996). Conceptual foundations of ecological validity in neuropsychological assessment. In R. J. Sbordone & C. J. Long (Eds.), *Ecological validity of neuropsychological testing* (pp. 91–112). Delray Beach, FL: GR Press/St. Lucie Press.

Galski, T., Bruno, R. L., & Ehle, H. T. (1992). Driving after cerebral hemorrhage: A model with implications for evaluation. *A J Occup Ther, 46*, 324–332.

Gerard, A. B., McElroy, M. K., Taylor, M. J., Grant, I., Powell, F. L., Holverda, S., et al. (2000). Six percent oxygen enrichment of room air at simulated 5,000 m altitude improves neuropsychological function. *High Alt Med Biol, 1*(1), 51–61.

Gioia, G. A., Isquith, P. K., Guy, S. C., & Kenworthy, L. (2000). *Behavior Rating Inventory of Executive Function.* Odessa, FL: Psychological Assessment Resources.

Giovannetti, T., Libon, D. J., Buxbaum, L. J., & Schwartz, M. F. (2002). Naturalistic action impairments in dementia. *Neuropsychologia, 40*(8), 1220–1232.

Giovannetti, T., Schmidt, K. S., Gallo, J. L., Sestito, N., & Libon, D. J. (2006). Everyday action in dementia: Evidence for differential deficits in Alzheimer's disease versus subcortical vascular dementia. *J Int Neuropsychol Soc, 12*(1), 45–53.

Giovannetti, T., Schwartz, M. F., & Buxbaum, L. J. (2007). The Coffee Challenge: A new method for the study of everyday action errors. *J Clin Exp Neuropsychol, 29*(7), 690–705.

Gladsjo, J. A., Heaton, R. K., Palmer, B. W., Taylor, M. J., & Jeste, D. V. (1999). Use of oral reading to estimate premorbid intellectual and neuropsychological functioning. *J Int Neuropsychol Soc, 5*(3), 247–254.

Godbout, L., & Doyon, J. (2000). Defective representation of knowledge in Parkinson's disease: Evidence from a script-production task. *Brain Cogn, 44*(3), 490–510.

Goldstein, G. (1996). Functional considerations in neuropsychology. In R. J. Sbordone & C. J. Long (Eds.), *Ecological validity of neuropsychological testing* (pp. 75–89). Delray Beach, FL: GR Press/St. Lucie Press.

Grace, J., Amick, M. M., D'Abreu, A., Festa, E. K., Heindel, W. C., & Ott, B. R. (2005). Neuropsychological deficits associated with driving performance in Parkinson's and Alzheimer's disease. *J Int Neuropsychol Soc, 11*(6), 766–775.

Green, M. F., Kern, R. S., & Heaton, R. K. (2004). Longitudinal studies of cognition and functional outcome in schizophrenia: Implications for MATRICS. *Schizophr Res, 72*(1), 41–51.

Green, P., Allen, L. M., & Astner, K. (1996). *The Word Memory Test: A user's guide to the oral and computer-administered forms.* Durham, NC: CogniSyst.

Guilmette, T. J., & Kastner, M. P. (1996). The prediction of vocational functioning from neuropsychological data. In R. J. Sbordone & C. J. Long (Eds.), *Ecological validity of neuropsychological testing* (pp. 387–409). Delray Beach, FL: GR Press/St. Lucie Press.

Gunstad, J., Spitznagel, M. B., Keary, T. A., Glickman, E., Alexander, T., Karrer, J., et al. (2008). Serum leptin levels are associated with cognitive function in older adults. *Brain Res, 1230*, 233–236.

Hart, T., Giovannetti, T., Montgomery, M. W., & Schwartz, M. F. (1998). Awareness of errors in naturalistic action after traumatic brain injury. *J Head Trauma Rehabil, 13*(5), 16–28.

Hayes, T. L., Abendroth, F., Adami, A., Pavel, M., Zitzelberger, T. A., & Kaye, J. A. (2008). Unobtrusive assessment of activity patterns associated with mild cognitive impairment. *Alzheimers and Dement, 4*(6), 395–405.

Heaton, R. K., Chelune, G., & Lehman, R. (1978). Using neuropsychological and personality tests to assess likelihood of patient employment. *J Nerv Ment Dis, 166*, 408–416.

Heaton, R. K., Grant, I., Butters, N., White, D. A., Kirson, D., Atkinson, J. H., et al. (1995). The HNRC 500: Neuropsychology of HIV infection at different disease stages. *J Int Neuropsych Soc, 1*, 231–251.

Heaton, R. K., & Marcotte, T. D. (2000). Clinical neuropsychological tests and assessment techniques. In F. Boller, J. Grafman, & G. Rizzolatti (Eds.), *Handbook of neuropsychology* (pp. 27–52). Amsterdam: Elsevier.

Heaton, R. K., Marcotte, T. D., Mindt, M. R., Sadek, J., Moore, D. J., Bentley, H., et al. (2004). The impact of HIV-associated neuropsychological impairment on everyday functioning. *J Int Neuropsychol Soc, 10*(3), 317–331.

Heaton, R. K., Miller, S. W., Taylor, M. J., & Grant, I. (2004). *Revised comprehensive norms for an expanded Halstead–Reitan Battery: Demographically adjusted neuropsychological norms for African American and Caucasian adults.* Lutz, FL: Psychological Assessment Resources.

Heaton, R. K., & Pendleton, M. G. (1981). Use of neuropsychological tests to predict adult patients' everyday functioning. *J Consul Clin Psych, 49*(6), 807–821.

Heaton, R. K., Taylor, M., & Manly, J. (2004). Demographic effects and use of demographically corrected norms with the WAIS-III and WMS-III. In D. Tulsky, D. Saklofske & R. K. Haton (Eds.), *Clinical interpretation of the WAIS-III and WMS-III* (pp. 181–209). San Diego, CA: Academic Press.

Hiscock, M., & Hiscock, C. K. (1989). Refining the forced-choice method for the detection of malingering. *J Clin Exp Neuropsyc, 11*, 967–974.

Hser, Y., Huang, D., Chou, C., & Anglin, M. D. (2007). Trajectories of heroin addiction: Growth mixture modeling results based on a 33-year follow-up study. *Evaluation Rev, 31*(6), 548–563.

Hunt, L., Morris, J. C., Edwards, D., & Wilson, B. S. (1993). Driving performance in persons with mild senile dementia of the Alzheimer type. *J Am Geriatr Soc, 41*, 747–753.

Jeste, S. D., Patterson, T. L., Palmer, B. W., Dolder, C. R., Goldman, S., & Jeste, D. V. (2003). Cognitive predictors of medication adherence among middle-aged and older outpatients with schizophrenia. *Schizophr Res, 63*(1–2), 49–58.

Johansson, E., Alho, H., Kiiskinen, U., & Poikolainen, K. (2007). The association of alcohol dependency with employment probability: Evidence from the population survey "Health 2000 in Finland." *Health Econ, 16*(7), 739–754.

Kalechstein, A. D., Newton, T. F., & van Gorp, W. G. (2003). Neurocognitive functioning is associated with employment status: A quantitative review. *J Clin Exp Neuropsychol, 25*(8), 1186–1191.

Kamei, S., Hara, M., Serizawa, K., Murakami, M., Mizutani, T., Ishiburo, M., et al. (2008).

Executive dysfunction using behavioral assessment of the dysexecutive syndrome in Parkinson's disease. *Mov Disord*, 23(4), 566–573.

Katai, S., Maruyama, T., Hashimoto, T., & Ikeda, S. (2003). Event based and time based prospective memory in Parkinson's disease. *J Neurol Neurosurg Psychiatry*, 74(6), 704–709.

Kelly, T. P. (2000). The clinical neuropsychology of attention in school-aged children. *Child Neuropsychol*, 6(1), 24–36.

Kennedy, J. E., Clement, P. F., & Curtiss, G. (2003). WAIS-III processing speed index scores after TBI: The influence of working memory, psychomotor speed and perceptual processing. *Clin Neuropsychol*, 17(3), 303–307.

Kessler, R. K., Giovannetti, T., & MacMullen, L. R. (2007). Everyday action in schizophrenia: Performance patterns and underlying cognitive mechanisms. *Neuropsychology*, 21(4), 439–447.

Kingstone, A., Smilek, D., & Eastwood, J. D. (2008). Cognitive ethology: A new approach for studying human cognition. *Br J Psychol*, 99(Pt. 3), 317–340.

Klauer, S. G., Dingus, T. A., Neale, V. L., Sudweeks, J. D., & Ramsey, D. J. (2006). *The impact of driver inattention on near-crash/crash risk: An analysis using the 100-Car Naturalistic Driving Study data*. Washington, DC: National Highway Traffic Safety Administration.

Knight, C., Alderman, N., & Burgess, P. W. (2002). Development of a simplified version of the multiple errands test for use in hospital settings. *Neuropsychol Rehabil*, 12, 231–255.

Kondel, T. K. (2002). Prospective memory and executive function in schizophrenia. *Brain Cognition*, 48, 405–410.

Kopelman, M., Wilson, B. A., & Baddeley, A. D. (1990). *The autobiographical memory interview*. Bury St. Edmunds, UK: Thames Valley Test.

Laughren, T. (2001). A regulatory perspective on psychiatric syndromes in Alzheimer disease. *Am J Geriatr Psychiatry*, 9(4), 340–345.

Lengenfelder, J., Schultheis, M. T., Al-Shihabi, T., Mourant, R., & DeLuca, J. (2002). Divided attention and driving: A pilot study using virtual reality technology. *J Head Trauma Rehabil*, 17(1), 26–37.

Lezak, M. D. (1982). The problem of assessing executive functions. *Int J Psychol*, 17, 281–297.

Lezak, M. D., Howieson, D. B., & Loring, D. W. (2004). *Neuropsychological assessment* (4th ed.). New York: Oxford University Press.

Loewenstein, D. A., Amigo, E., Duara, R., Guterman, A., Hurwitz, D., Berkowitz, N., et al. (1989). A new scale for the assessment of functional status in Alzheimer's disease and related disorders. *J Gerontol*, 44(4), 114–121.

Loewenstein, D. A., Arguelles, S., Bravo, M., Freeman, R. Q., Arguelles, T., Acevedo, A., et al. (2001). Caregivers' judgments of the functional abilities of the Alzheimer's disease patient: A comparison of proxy reports and objective measures. *J Gerontol B Psychol Sci Soc Sci*, 56(2), P78–84.

Logan, B. K. (1996). Methamphetamine and driving impairment. *J Forensic Sci*, 41(3), 457–464.

Lundberg, C., Hakamies-Blomqvist, L., Almkvist, O., & Johansson, K. (1998). Impairments of some cognitive functions are common in crash-involved older drivers. *Accident Anal Prev*, 30(3), 371–377.

Machamer, J., Temkin, N., Fraser, R., Doctor, J. N., & Dikmen, S. (2005). Stability of employment after traumatic brain injury. *J Int Neuropsychol Soc*, 11(7), 807–816.

Maguire, E. A., Gadian, D. G., Johnsrude, I. S., Good, C. D., Ashburner, J., Frackowiak, R.

S., et al. (2000). Navigation-related structural change in the hippocampi of taxi drivers. *Proc Natl Acad Sci USA, 97*(8), 4398–4403.

Marcotte, T. D., Heaton, R. K., Wolfson, T., Taylor, M. J., Alhassoon, O., Arfaa, K., et al. (1999). The impact of HIV-related neuropsychological dysfunction on driving behavior. *J Int Neuropsych Soc, 5*(7), 579–592.

Marcotte, T. D., Lazzaretto, D., Scott, J. C., Roberts, E., Woods, S. P., Letendre, S., et al. (2006). Visual attention deficits are associated with driving accidents in cognitively-impaired HIV-infected individuals. *J Clin Exp Neuropsyc, 28*(1), 13–28.

Marcotte, T. D., & Scott, J. C. (2009). Neuropsychological performance and the assessment of driving behavior. In I. Grant & K. M. Adams (Eds.), *Neuropsychological assessment of neuropsychiatric disorders* (3rd ed., pp. 652–687). New York: Oxford University Press.

Marcotte, T. D., Wolfson, T., Rosenthal, T. J., Heaton, R. K., Gonzalez, R., Ellis, R. J., et al. (2004). A multimodal assessment of driving performance in HIV infection. *Neurology, 63*(8), 1417–1422.

Martin, E. M., Nixon, H., Pitrak, D. L., Weddington, W., Rains, N. A., Nunnally, G., et al. (2007). Characteristics of prospective memory deficits in HIV-seropositive substance-dependent individuals: Preliminary observations. *J Clin Exp Neuropsychol, 29*(5), 496–504.

Martinez-Aran, A., Vieta, E., Torrent, C., Sanchez-Moreno, J., Goikolea, J. M., Salamero, M., et al. (2007). Functional outcome in bipolar disorder: The role of clinical and cognitive factors. *Bipolar Disord, 9*(1–2), 103–113.

Matarazzo, J. D. (1972). *Wechsler's measurement and appraisal of adult intelligence* (5th ed.). Oxford, UK: Williams & Wilkins.

Maylor, E. A., Smith, G., Della Sala, S., & Logie, R. H. (2002). Prospective and retrospective memory in normal aging and dementia: An experimental study. *Mem Cognit, 30*(6), 871–884.

Mazer, B. L., Sofer, S., Korner-Bitensky, N., Gelinas, I., Hanley, J., & Wood-Dauphinee, S. (2003). Effectiveness of a visual attention retraining program on the driving performance of clients with stroke. *Arch Phys Med Rehab, 84*(4), 541–550.

McCall, R. B. (1977). Childhood IQ's as predictors of adult educational and occupational status. *Science, 197*(4302), 482–483.

McCue, M., Rogers, J. C., & Goldstein, G. (1990). Relationships between neuropsychological and functional assessment in elderly neuropsychiatric patients. *Rehabil Psychol, 35*, 91–99.

McGurk, S. R., & Mueser, K. T. (2006). Cognitive and clinical predictors of work outcomes in clients with schizophrenia receiving supported employment services: 4-year follow-up. *Adm Policy Ment Hlth, 33*(5), 598–606.

Mirsky, A. F., Anthony, B. J., Duncan, C. C., Ahearn, M. B., & Kellam, S. G. (1991). Analysis of the elements of attention: A neuropsychological approach. *Neuropsychol Rev, 2*(2), 109–145.

Molnar, F. J., Patel, A., Marshall, S. C., Man-Son-Hing, M., & Wilson, K. G. (2006). Clinical utility of office-based cognitive predictors of fitness to drive in persons with dementia: A systematic review. *J Am Geriatr Soc, 54*(12), 1809–1824.

Morgan, J. E., & Sweet, J. J. (Eds.). (2008). *Neuropsychology of malingering casebook*. New York: Psychology Press.

Myers, R. S., Ball, K. K., Kalina, T. D., Roth, D. L., & Goode, K. T. (2000). Relation of Useful Field of View and other screening tests to on-road driving performance. *Percept Motor Skill, 91*(1), 279–290.

Najavits, L. M., & Lester, K. M. (2008). Gender differences in cocaine dependence. *Drug Alcohol Depen, 97*(1–2), 190–194.

Odenheimer, G. L., Beaudet, M., Jette, A. M., Albert, M. S., Grande, L., & Minaker, K. L. (1994). Performance-based driving evaluation of the elderly driver: Safety, reliability, and validity. *J Gerontol*, *49*(4), M153–M159.

Owsley, C., Ball, K., McGwin, G., Jr., Sloane, M. E., Roenker, D. L., White, M., et al. (1998). Visual processing impairment and risk of motor vehicle crash among older adults. *J Amer Med Assoc*, *279*(14), 1083–1088.

Park, D. C., & Kidder, D. P. (1996). Prospective memory and medication adherence. In M. Brandimonte, G. O. Einstein, & M. A. McDaniel (Eds.), *Prospective memory: Theory and applications* (pp. 369–390). Mahwah, NJ: Erlbaum.

Patterson, T. L., Goldman, S., McKibbin, C. L., Hughs, T., & Jeste, D. V. (2001). UCSD Performance-Based Skills Assessment: Development of a new measure of everyday functioning for severely mentally ill adults. *Schizophr Bull*, *27*(2), 235–245.

Rabin, L. A., Barr, W. B., & Burton, L. A. (2005). Assessment practices of clinical neuropsychologists in the United States and Canada: A survey of INS, NAN, and APA Division 40 members. *Arch Clin Neuropsychol*, *20*(1), 33–65.

Rabin, L. A., Burton, L. A., & Barr, W. B. (2007). Utilization rates of ecologically oriented instruments among clinical neuropsychologists. *Clin Neuropsychol*, *21*(5), 727–743.

Rebok, G. W., Bylsma, F. W., Keyl, P. M., Brandt, J., & Folstein, S. E. (1995). Automobile driving in Huntington's disease. *Movement Disord*, *10*(6), 778–787.

Reger, M. A., Welsh, R. K., Watson, G. S., Cholerton, B., Baker, L. D., & Craft, S. (2004). The relationship between neuropsychological functioning and driving ability in dementia: A meta-analysis. *Neuropsychology*, *18*(1), 85–93.

Reitan, R. M., & Davidson, L. A. (Eds.). (1974). *Clinical neuropsychology: Current status and applications*. Washington, DC: Winston.

Rey, A. (1964). *L'examen clinique en psychologie* (2nd ed.). Paris: Presses Universitaires de France.

Rizzo, M., Reinach, S., McGehee, D., & Dawson, J. (1997). Simulated car crashes and crash predictors in drivers with Alzheimer disease. *Arch Neurol*, *54*(5), 545–551.

Robertson, I. H., Ward, T., Ridgeway, V., & Nimmo-Smith, I. (1996). The structure of normal human attention: The Test of Everyday Attention. *J Int Neuropsychol Soc*, *2*(6), 525–534.

Roca, M., Torralva, T., Meli, F., Fiol, M., Calcagno, M., Carpintiero, S., et al. (2008). Cognitive deficits in multiple sclerosis correlate with changes in fronto-subcortical tracts. *Mult Scler*, *14*(3), 364–369.

Rogers, W. A. (2008). Editorial. *J Exp Psychol-Appl*, *14*(1), 1–4.

Rohde, T. E., & Thompson, L. A. (2006). Predicting academic achievement with cognitive ability. *Intelligence*, *35*(1), 83–92.

Rothman, R. L., Montori, V. M., Cherrington, A., & Pignone, M. P. (2008). Perspective: The role of numeracy in health care. *J Health Commun*, *13*(6), 583–595.

Royall, D. R., Palmer, R., Chiodo, L. K., & Polk, M. J. (2005). Normal rates of cognitive change in successful aging: The freedom house study. *J Int Neuropsychol Soc*, *11*(7), 899–909.

Rytsala, H. J., Melartin, T. K., Leskela, U. S., Sokero, T. P., Lestela-Mielonen, P. S., & Isometsa, E. T. (2005). Functional and work disability in major depressive disorder. *J Nerv Ment Dis*, *193*(3), 189–195.

Satz, P. (1993). Brain reserve capacity on symptom onset after brain injury: A formulation and review of evidence for threshold theory. *Neuropsychology*, *7*, 273–295.

Sbordone, R. J. (1996). Ecological validity: Some critical issues for the neuropsychologist. In R. J. Sbordone & C. J. Long (Eds.), *Ecological validity of neuropsychological testing* (pp. 55–41). Delray Beach, FL: GR Press/St. Lucie Press.

Schanke, A. K., & Sundet, K. (2000). Comprehensive driving assessment: Neuropsychological testing and on-road evaluation of brain injured patients. *Scand J Psychol, 41*(2), 113–121.

Schretlen, D. (2005). *Brief Test of Attention.* Lutz, FL: Psychological Assessment Resources.

Schultheis, M. T., Garay, E., & DeLuca, J. (2001). The influence of cognitive impairment on driving performance in multiple sclerosis. *Neurology, 56*(8), 1089–1094.

Schwab, S. G., Plummer, C., Albus, M., Borrmann-Hassenbach, M., Lerer, B., Trixler, M., et al. (2008). DNA sequence variants in the metabotropic glutamate receptor 3 and risk to schizophrenia: An association study. *Psychiatr Genet, 18*(1), 25–30.

Schwartz, M. F. (2006). The cognitive neuropsychology of everyday action and planning. *Cogn Neuropsychol, 23*, 202–221.

Schwartz, M. F., & Buxbaum, L. J. (1997). Naturalistic action. In L. G. Rothi & K. M. Heilman (Eds.), *Apraxia: The neuropsychology of action.* Hove, UK: Psychology Press.

Schwartz, M. F., Buxbaum, L. J., Ferraro, M., Veramonti, T., & Segal, M. (2003). *The Naturalistic Action Test.* Bury St. Edmunds, UK: Thames Valley Test Corporation.

Schwartz, M. F., Buxbaum, L. J., Montgomery, M. W., Fitzpatrick-DeSalme, E., Hart, T., Ferraro, M., et al. (1999). Naturalistic action production following right hemisphere stroke. *Neuropsychologia, 37*(1), 51–66.

Schwartz, M. F., Montgomery, M. W., Buxbaum, L. J., Lee, S. S., Carew, T. G., Coslett, H. B., et al. (1998). Naturalistic action impairment in closed head injury. *Neuropsychology, 12*(1), 13–28.

Schwartz, M. F., Segal, M. E., Veramonti, T., Ferraro, M., & Buxbaum, L. J. (2002). The Naturalistic Action Test: A standardized assessment for everyday-action impairment. *Neuropsychol, Rehabil, 12*, 311–339.

Semple, S. J., Patterson, T. L., & Grant, I. (2003). Binge use of methamphetamine among HIV-positive men who have sex with men: Pilot data and HIV prevention implications. *AIDS Educ Prev, 15*(2), 133–147.

Shallice, T. (1991). Higher-order cognitive impairments and frontal lobe lesions in man. In H. S. Levin, H. M. Eisenberg, & A. L. Benson (Eds.), *Frontal lobe function and injury* (pp. 125–138). Oxford, UK: Oxford University Press.

Shallice, T., & Burgess, P. W. (1991). Deficits in strategy application following frontal lobe damage in man. *Brain, 114*(Pt. 2), 727–741.

Silverberg, N. D., & Millis, S. R. (2009). Impairment versus deficiency in neuropsychological assessment: Implications for ecological validity. *J Int Neuropsychol Soc, 15*(1), 94–102.

Simons, J. S., Scholvinck, M. L., Gilbert, S. J., Frith, C. D., & Burgess, P. W. (2006). Differential components of prospective memory?: Evidence from fMRI. *Neuropsychologia, 44*(8), 1388–1397.

Sims, R. V., Owsley, C., Allman, R. M., Ball, K., & Smoot, T. M. (1998). A preliminary assessment of the medical and functional factors associated with vehicle crashes by older adults. *J Am Geriatr Soc, 46*(5), 556–561.

Sirigu, A., Zalla, T., Pillon, B., Grafman, J., Agid, Y., & Dubois, B. (1995). Selective impairments in managerial knowledge following pre-frontal cortex damage. *Cortex, 31*(2), 301–316.

Spooner, D. M., & Pachana, N. A. (2006). Ecological validity in neuropsychological assessment: A case for greater consideration in research with neurologically intact populations. *Arch Clin Neuropsychol, 21*(4), 327–337.

Stern, Y. (2003). The concept of cognitive reserve: A catalyst for research. *J Clin Exp Neuropsychol, 25*(5), 589–593.

Sternberg, R. J., Grigorenko, E. L., & Bundy, D. A. (2001). The predictive value of IQ. *Merrill–Palmer Quart, 47*(1), 1–41.

Stolwyk, R. J., Charlton, J. L., Triggs, T. J., Iansek, R., & Bradshaw, J. L. (2006). Neuropsychological function and driving ability in people with Parkinson's disease. *J Clin Exp Neuropsychol, 28*(6), 898–913.

Stutts, J. C., Reinfurt, D. W., & Rodgman, E. A. (2001). The role of driver distraction in crashes: An analysis of 1995–1999 Crashworthiness Data System data. *Annu Proc Assoc Adv Automot Med, 45,* 287–301.

Szlyk, J. P., Myers, L., Zhang, Y., Wetzel, L., & Shapiro, R. (2002). Development and assessment of a neuropsychological battery to aid in predicting driving performance. *J Rehabil Res Dev, 39*(4), 483–496.

Tchanturia, K., Anderluh, M. B., Morris, R. G., Rabe-Hesketh, S., Collier, D. A., Sanchez, P., et al. (2004). Cognitive flexibility in anorexia nervosa and bulimia nervosa. *J Int Neuropsychol Soc, 10*(4), 513–520.

Toglia, J. P. (1993). *Contextual Memory Test.* San Antonio, TX: Pearson.

Tombaugh, T. (1997). *TOMM: Test of Memory Malingering manual.* Toronto: Multi-Health Systems.

Tupper, D. E., & Cicerone, K. D. (1990). Introduction to the neuropsychology of everyday life. In D. E. Tupper & K. D. Cierone (Eds.), *The neuropsychology of everyday life* (pp. 3–17). Boston: Kluwer.

Twamley, E. W., Woods, S. P., Zurhellen, C. H., Vertinski, M., Narvaez, J. M., Mausbach, B. T., et al. (2008). Neuropsychological substrates and everyday functioning implications of prospective memory impairment in schizophrenia. *Schizophr Res, 106*(1), 42–49.

Uc, E. Y., Rizzo, M., Anderson, S. W., Sparks, J. D., Rodnitzky, R. L., & Dawson, J. D. (2006a). Driving with distraction in Parkinson disease. *Neurology, 67*(10), 1774–1780.

Uc, E. Y., Rizzo, M., Anderson, S. W., Sparks, J., Rodnitzky, R. L., & Dawson, J. D. (2006b). Impaired visual search in drivers with Parkinson's disease. *Ann Neurol, 60*(4), 407–413.

van Gorp, W. G., Rabkin, J. G., Ferrando, S. J., Mintz, J., Ryan, E., Borkowski, T., et al. (2007). Neuropsychiatric predictors of return to work in HIV/AIDS. *J Int Neuropsychol Soc, 13*(1), 80–89.

van Zomeren, A. H., Brouwer, W. H., & Minderhoud, J. M. (1987). Acquired brain damage and driving: A review. *Arch Phys Med Rehabil, 68*(10), 697–705.

Whelihan, W. M., DiCarlo, M. A., & Paul, R. H. (2005). The relationship of neuropsychological functioning to driving competence in older persons with early cognitive decline. *Arch Clin Neuropsychol, 20*(2), 217–228.

Wilson, B. A., Alderman, N., Burgess, P. W., Emslie, H., & Evans, J. J. (1996). *Behavioral Assessment of the Dysexecutive Syndrome (BADS).* Bury St. Edmunds, UK: Thames Valley Test Company.

Wilson, B. A., Cockburn, J., & Baddeley, A. D. (1985). *The Rivermead Behavioural Memory Test.* Reading, UK: Thames Valley Test.

Wilson, B. A., Cockburn, J. M., & Halligan, P. (1987). *The Behavioral Inattention Test.* Bury St. Edmunds, UK: Thames Valley Test.

Withaar, F. K., Brouwer, W. H., & van Zomeren, A. H. (2000). Fitness to drive in older drivers with cognitive impairment. *J Int Neuropsych Soc, 6*(4), 480–490.

Wobrock, T., Sittinger, H., Behrendt, B., D'Amelio, R., Falkai, P., & Caspari, D. (2007). Comorbid substance abuse and neurocognitive function in recent-onset schizophrenia. *Eur Arch Psychiatry Clin Neurosci, 257*(4), 203–210.

Woods, S. P., Carey, C. L., Moran, L. M., Dawson, M. S., Letendre, S. L., & Grant, I. (2007). Frequency and predictors of self-reported prospective memory complaints in individuals infected with HIV. *Arch Clin Neuropsychol, 22*(2), 187–195.

Woods, S. P., Iudicello, J. E., Moran, L. M., Carey, C. L., Dawson, M. S., & Grant, I. (2008).

HIV-associated prospective memory impairment increases risk of dependence in every-day functioning. *Neuropsychology, 22*(1), 110–117.

Woods, S. P., Morgan, E. E., Dawson, M., Scott, J. C., Grant, I., & the HNRC Group. (2006). Action (verb) fluency predicts dependence in instrumental activities of daily living in persons infected with HIV-1. *J Clin Exp Neuropsychol, 28*(6), 1030–1042.

Woods, S. P., Twamley, E. W., Dawson, M. S., Narvaez, J. M., & Jeste, D. V. (2007). Deficits in cue detection and intention retrieval underlie prospective memory impairment in schizophrenia. *Schizophr Res, 90*(1–3), 344–350.

Worringham, C. J., Wood, J. M., Kerr, G. K., & Silburn, P. A. (2006). Predictors of driving assessment outcome in Parkinson's disease. *Mov Disord, 21*(2), 230–235.

CHAPTER 2

Understanding the Relevance of Human Factors/ Ergonomics to Neuropsychology Practice and the Assessment of Everyday Functioning

Wendy A. Rogers, Andrew K. Mayer, and Cara B. Fausset

Understanding human–system interactions is the broad goal of the field of human factors/ergonomics (HF/E). The characteristics of the human that are relevant to such interactions include physical as well as cognitive capabilities. The "system" can range from something as simple as a can opener to something as complex as the cockpit of a jet airplane or the control room of a nuclear power plant. This chapter focuses on the cognitive capabilities of humans that influence their interactions with systems encountered in the context of everyday activities, such as computers, medical devices, medications, and transportation systems.

HF/E practitioners investigate the capabilities and limitations of people and the demands placed upon them when performing activities from the most basic everyday tasks to the most complex vocational tasks. Our goal here is to illustrate the relevance of the knowledge base and the tools of the HF/E field to issues faced by neuropsychologists and their patients. For example, neuropsychologists and occupational therapists could use HF/E tools and techniques to understand more completely the cognitive and perceptual functioning of a patient with traumatic brain injury; this knowledge could then guide interventions to facilitate everyday functioning for that individual. These tools can also be used to develop strategies that help individuals with general memory deficits to perform demanding tasks such as managing a medication regimen. One of the major benefits of the HF/E tools and techniques discussed herein is their potential applicability to a wide range of people and systems.

The chapter is organized as follows. We first provide an overview of the HF/E field. Next, we describe the tools and techniques used in HF/E to understand human–system interactions, identify problems, and develop solutions (i.e., asking the right questions and answering them). We then provide illustrative examples of these tools and techniques as they have been applied in various domains. The domains we selected mirror the activities of everyday functioning that are addressed in the other chapters of this volume. We conclude with a brief discussion of some future directions in HF/E, including neuroergonomics and adaptive automation.

Defining the Discipline of Human Factors/Ergonomics

HF/E is a "unique and independent discipline that focuses on the nature of human–artifact interactions, viewed from the unified perspective of the science, engineering, design, technology, and management of human-compatible systems, including a variety of natural and artificial products, processes, and living environments" (Karwowski, 2006, p. 4). In the United States a distinction is often made between "human factors," referring to perceptual and cognitive characteristics of people and the systems with which they are interacting, and "physical ergonomics," referring to anthropometry and biomechanics. In other nations the broad term "ergonomics" is used to refer to the whole discipline. In this chapter we use the abbreviation HF/E.

HF/E practitioners are generally interested in three goals: to enhance system performance, increase safety, and increase user satisfaction (Wickens, Lee, Liu, & Becker, 2004). These goals are generally achieved by analyzing and understanding the cognitive and physical capabilities and limitations of the user as well as the physical and information systems with which he or she interacts through the use of appropriate analytic tools. Adding HF/E tools to neuropsychologists' and occupational therapists' toolkits provides them with the means to better understand neurological populations and the systems with which they interact.

The breadth of the field is illustrated by the range of technical specialties within it. The Human Factors and Ergonomics Society (HFES) was founded in 1957 and currently has approximately 5,000 members. HFES has technical groups to support the exchange of knowledge within specialty areas; these technical groups are listed in Table 2.1. This list demonstrates the range of HF/E applications (e.g., aging, communication, health care, the Internet, transportation) as well as the varied research methodologies used in the field (e.g., cognitive engineering, human performance modeling, test and evaluation).

TABLE 2.1. Technical Groups of the Human Factors and Ergonomics Society

Aerospace systems	Industrial ergonomics
Aging	Internet
Cognitive Engineering and Decision Making	Macroergonomics
Communications	Perception and Performance
Computer Systems	Product Design
Education	Safety
Environmental Design	Surface Transportation
Forensics Professional	System Development
Human Performance Modeling	Test and Evaluation
Health Care Systems	Training
Individual Differences in Performance	Virtual Environments

Note. Data from *www.hfes.org.*

Asking the Right Questions—and Answering Them

HF/E is a diverse discipline that ranges from transportation to health care and from nuclear power plants to the football field. How can the tools and techniques used by HF/E practitioners span such a seemingly broad chasm of domains? Simple: by asking the right questions in the right situations.

The purpose of asking the right questions is to identify user–system problems, to pinpoint the source(s) of the problems, and to understand and identify potential solutions. Although there is no formula to guide the question-asking process, there are commonly asked questions that may serve as a starting point (see Table 2.2). Given the HF/E focus on the person, the system, and the interaction between them, the relevant questions encompass these variables. The basic tenet of HF/E is to "know thy user." The corollaries are to understand the system and the context of use.

The first step is to understand the person. What are the capabilities and limitations in terms of the physical, perceptual, and cognitive characteristics of the people who are interacting with the system? This question can be answered through observation, interviews, and surveys, as well as through an understanding of the typical capabilities and limitations for the user group (e.g., children, older adults, those with visual impairments). The person analysis must be specific. For example, we would not assess engineers to ascertain the problems individuals with cognitive impairments would have navigating through an environment or interacting with a system; we would assess individuals with such impairments. This point may seem obvious, but unfortunately decisions are often based on the beliefs of designers, rather than on specific user capabilities and limitations.

The system characteristics must also be analyzed. What are the physical, perceptual, and cognitive demands imposed by the system itself? Does it require fine motor control, processing of multiple sources of information, or the comprehension of complex instructions? Is monitoring of automated components required? System analysis can be accomplished through task analysis and process diagrams (described later). Understanding the characteristics of the system is essential to link users' capabilities and limitations to the system's demands and requirements.

The third set of questions relates to understanding more about the interaction between the person and the system. What is the context of use (e.g., time pressure)? What type of instruction and feedback is provided during the interaction? Is the situation static or dynamically changing? Consider an analysis of a person using an in-vehicle navigation system. It is important to know if the user is an experienced driver, has familiarity with the system, can process both visual and auditory information, has constraints on attention or working memory, and so on. Details of the system must also be understood, such as the type of input device that is used to interact with the system, the amount of information that is displayed, and the format in which it is displayed, among other factors. It is also relevant to understand the context of the interaction; for example, if the system will be used while the person is driving, the display can be viewed only for limited amounts of time (while taking eyes off the road), input can be made with only one hand, and decisions may have to be made quickly. The person, the system, and the interaction must all be analyzed to understand where, why, and how errors might occur and to develop solutions that will minimize errors and lead to a safe, effective, and efficient person–system interaction.

TABLE 2.2. General List of Questions Relating to the User, the System, and the User–System Interaction

Questions relating to the user

General characteristics

- Who are the users?
- Is the design for a single user or for multiple users?
- What are the cultural differences between users?
- What is the average age of the intended user population?

Physical characteristics

- What is the average body size of the user population?
- Do users have mobility problems that restrict normal body movements?
- What are the strength characteristics of the users?

Perceptual characteristics

- What are the visual capabilities of the users?
- What are the auditory capabilities of the users?
- Do important perceptual differences exist between users?

Cognitive characteristics

- What are the users' memory capabilities and limitations?
- What are the users' attentional capabilities and limitations?
- What decisions does the user have to make?
- What learning is required of the user?

Questions relating to the system

Environmental characteristics

- What are the lighting conditions of the environment?
- How much clutter is in the environment?
- How much noise is in the environment and what are its sources?
- Is the system operating indoors or outdoors?
- What is the temperature of the system environment?

System characteristics

- What is the purpose of the system?
- What tasks are involved?
- Is the system automated?
- What are the system inputs and outputs?
- What sort of feedback is provided by the system?
- What instructions have been provided?
- What is the context of use?

Questions relating to the user–system interaction

- What are the cognitive (memory, attention, information-processing) demands on the user?
- What are the perceptual (visual and auditory) demands on the user?
- What are the users' experiences in relation to the system?
- What are the task demands?
- Are multiple users interacting?
- How much workload is placed on the user?

HF/E Tools and Techniques

To meet the goals of HF/E, various techniques are used to identify problem areas within a user–system unit, describe the problems and their sources, and suggest solutions to remedy those issues. In the following sections we highlight a few techniques that are widely used throughout the field and across various domains.

Surveys and Questionnaires

Surveys and questionnaires are often used in descriptive studies to gather data from the user's perspective (see, e.g., Leonard, Jacko, Yi, & Sainfort, 2006; Stanton, Salmon, Walker, Baber, & Jenkins, 2005; Vu & Proctor, 2006). An advantage of surveys and questionnaires is that the data can be qualitative or quantitative, by asking either open-ended questions or ranking responses on a numerical scale. These methods also offer flexibility in assessing a wide range of variables, and data can be obtained from a large group of users in a relatively short period of time. However, it may be difficult to obtain a representative sample of respondents for a survey, and the development of materials and analysis of qualitative data can be time-consuming and laborious. Moreover, both the developers' and the users' biases may affect the validity of the results.

Interviews and Focus Groups

Interviews and focus groups can also be used to collect descriptive data from users (Stanton, Salmon, et al., 2005; Vu & Proctor, 2006). Interviews are conducted in a one-on-one environment, whereas focus groups are conducted with a moderator leading a small group, ideally with around five individuals of similar backgrounds.

Interviews are appealing in that the interviewer can direct the questioning to elicit responses, especially about cognitive components of an activity. In the small-group environment of the focus group, ideas can emerge that may not have been realized by an individual. Although the data collected from interviews and focus groups are rich in detail and thus very informative, the analysis of such qualitative data can be challenging and time-consuming.

Task Analysis and Process Diagrams

No matter how simple a task may seem, there are often several unseen steps that a casual observer might never consider. To fully understand human–system interactions, it is imperative that all user activities, physical or cognitive, required in a user–system process are identified. A valuable tool for developing such a detailed understanding is a *task analysis*, which can be used "to identify and characterize the fundamental characteristics of a specific activity or set of activities" (Hollnagel, 2006, p. 373).

Task analysis is a broad term that includes many techniques for collecting, organizing, and analyzing information about user–system activities (for details, see Kirwan & Ainsworth, 1992). Generally an activity is selected, the goals of that activity are defined, and then there is a delineation of each step that must be performed to attain the final goal of the activity. Sample task analysis techniques include (1) *hierarchical task analysis*, wherein each task is divided into a hierarchy of subtasks with goals, operations, and plans defined; (2) *link analysis*, in which the relationships between a user and parts of the system are identified; (3) *operational sequence analysis*, for which the sequence of movements and information acceptance or dissemination are detailed, and (4) *timeline analysis*, wherein the time for each task element is recorded.

Although a task analysis is often necessary to develop an understanding of human–system interactions, the analysis may also require resources, such as time and video or audio equipment (Stanton, Salmon, et al., 2005). Given the detail required for an accurate task representation, it is often useful to have multiple raters analyze a task, because each analyst may create different representations of the same activity. Moreover, even within-rater reliability is not a guarantee, as an analyst may create a different representation of the same activity on different occasions.

Aspects of the task analysis can be compiled into pictorial representations called "process flow diagrams." Standardized symbols that depict the required actions, decisions, movements, information flow, time, and effort of an activity can convey the process in an easy-to-understand format (Kirwan & Ainsworth, 1992). Figure 2.1 provides an example of a flow diagram for the relatively simple task of making coffee. The benefit of this approach is that it provides a detailed overview of the task, with every step indicated in the order in which it should be performed. Moreover a flow diagram can illustrate the actual complexity (i.e., number of steps involved) of tasks and indicate why such tasks may be overwhelming for individuals with diminished cognitive capacity.

Perhaps the most important advantage of process diagrams is that an entire user–system activity can be visualized easily without pages of text that describe each step; however, the more complex the task is, the more visually overwhelming the diagram becomes. These diagrams, which are easy to learn to create and use, can depict a range of tasks. However, they represent only one aspect of a task analysis in that they do not indicate where errors are likely to occur and the potential error sources.

Workload Analysis

The task analysis and process diagrams provide general overviews of task requirements. However, the same task may impose different demands across individuals and contexts of use. Workload analysis is a means of measuring workload at the individual level. Workload can be broadly defined as "the amount of work that a machine, employee, or group of employees can be or is expected to perform" (Random House, 1998, p. 2189).

Workload can be measured using physiological indices such as heart rate, measures of brain activity, or pupil dilation (Tsang & Vidulich, 2006). However, such measures may be costly or interfere with the tasks being performed. Another approach to workload analysis is to measure subjective workload. Two commonly used methods have been tested extensively for both validity and reliability: the National Aeronautics and Space Administration—Task Load Index (NASA-TLX) and the Subjective Workload Assessment Technique (SWAT).

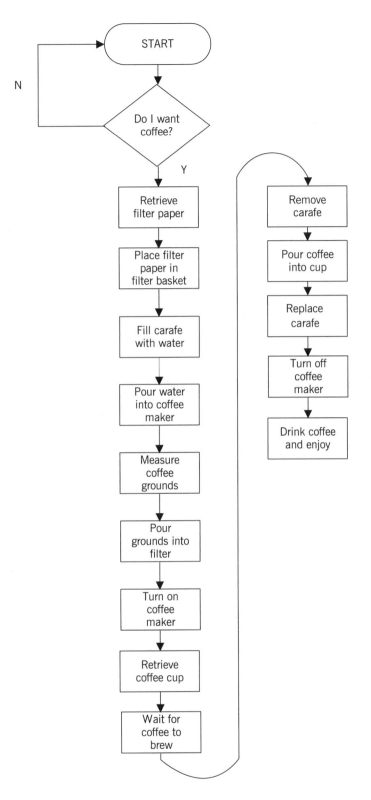

FIGURE 2.1. Process diagram for making coffee.

The NASA-TLX assesses six categories and uses the ratings to derive an overall workload score (Hart & Staveland, 1988). Users quantitatively rate six factors: mental demand, physical demand, temporal demand, performance, effort, and frustration. Advantages of the NASA-TLX are that it is quick and easy to use, and the general categories allow this technique to be applied across various domains. Disadvantages of the NASA-TLX are that the data from the six categories are complex to analyze and apply only to individual workload assessments (Stanton, Salmon, et al., 2005). Table 2.3 provides sample application of the NASA-TLX and the type of output that it provides. Note that the individual dimensions can be analyzed independently to identify the specific sources of workload for an individual.

The SWAT is also a multidimensional scale like the NASA-TLX but considers different categories (Reid & Nygren, 1988). The dimensions measured are time load, mental effort load, and psychological stress load. The advantages of SWAT are similar to the NASA-TLX in that it is quick and easy to use and generalizable across domains; however, some studies have suggested that it is less sensitive than the NASA-TLX (Stanton, Salmon, et al., 2005).

Usability Assessment Tools

Thus far we have described tools that are useful for understanding the user and the system. There are also techniques wherein the focus is specifically on the interaction of the user with the system. For example, usability testing can reveal critical features of the user–system interaction.

One method of usability testing is user trials, wherein users perform tasks with a product or device to evaluate features of the product and issues that may arise during use (Stanton, Salmon, et al., 2005). The flexibility and simplicity of user trials are

TABLE 2.3. Using the NASA-TLX to Assess Subjective Workload for Two Hypothetical Diabetes Management Systems

Step 1:	Have patient interact with first device or system of interest
Step 2:	Have patient complete NASA-TLX
Step 3:	Have patient interact with second device or system of interest
Step 4:	Have patient complete NASA-TLX

Scale	System 1: Diabetes management system using directive instructions		System 2: Diabetes management system using cooperative instructions	
	Value	Weight	Value	Weight
Mental Demand	25	0.13	80	0.27
Physical Demand	20	0	35	0
Temporal Demand	50	0.33	80	0.13
Performance	30	0.20	65	0.13
Effort	25	0.13	80	0.33
Frustration	20	0.20	75	0.13
Total workload	33.33		77.33	

Note. The overall subjective workload is clearly lower for System 1; consequently that support system might be selected for this particular patient. However, even for System 1 the reported temporal demand is high, and the system might thus be redesigned to reduce that aspect of demand.

an appealing advantage, but the time-consuming nature of this technique must also be considered. Often, user trials involve a lengthy analysis because large amounts of data are collected; however, these data are extremely informative for identifying issues and assessing how the system will be used.

Another approach is a "walkthrough" analysis "whereby experienced system operators perform a walkthrough or demonstration of a task or set of tasks using the system under analysis" (Stanton, Salmon, et al., 2005, p. 479). The actual system is not required in a walkthrough analysis, because the operator can simply describe the steps of the tasks performed. This technique allows assessment without interrupting real-time system operations. Although this method is very useful, its reliability is not well established because there is no prescribed technique for conducting a walk-through analysis. Consequently it is useful to have more than one person perform the walkthrough and then to compare the results.

Knowledge Engineering

Another approach to understanding the human–system interaction, called "knowl-edge engineering," can be used to identify the users, their goals, their tasks, the system, and the interaction of these components. Knowledge engineering involves developing a complete understanding of the system and its goals and then using focus groups and other knowledge acquisition techniques to elicit users' knowledge (Bowles, Sanchez, Rogers, & Fisk, 2004). Knowledge engineering may reveal how operators actually use systems (perhaps in contrast to their intended use), how skilled operators differ from novices, gaps in operator knowledge about system functions, and information requirements for successful system use.

Developing Solutions

Asking the right questions is the first step in an HF/E analysis: Who are the users, what will they be doing and in what context, what kinds of difficulties are they likely to encounter, and so on. The next step is to develop solutions. We discuss three gen-eral classes of solutions: training, environmental support, and system redesign.

Training

Training the individual is one way to alleviate problems identified or to prevent prob-lems from occurring. Training can be broadly defined as "the systematic acquisition of knowledge, skills, and attitudes that together lead to improved performance in a particular environment" (Salas, Wilson, Priest, & Guthrie, 2006, p. 473). Training can be particularly worthwhile when people are learning to use complex systems.

However, there is no single training method that can be applied to all tasks. Training can include the use of instructional materials, feedback, simplification of the task, or other methods. For example, part-task training involves dividing a com-plex task into component tasks (Kirlik, Fisk, Walker, & Rothrock, 1998) and can be accomplished in different ways (e.g., by segmenting the task or by simplifying it). The judgment regarding the optimal approach will depend on the specific task demands. It is therefore important to conduct a training needs analysis before beginning any training program (Salas et al., 2006). Training needs can be identified using HF/E techniques (e.g., task analysis, knowledge engineering). Once training needs have been identified, the appropriate training technique can be implemented.

Another critical component of training is the provision of feedback to guide performance and learning (Salas et al., 2006). The feedback must be timely and task relevant as well as allow the trainee to learn to adjust and improve behavior for future interactions.

There is a large literature on training (for a review, see Alvarez, Salas, & Garofano, 2004) that can provide guidance for the development of training programs. One general principle to remember is that the training must be tailored to the task goals, the context of use, and the capabilities and limitations of the user (Rogers, Campbell, & Pak, 2001).

Environmental Support

Another method of solving human–system interaction problems is to provide an environmental support to aid the user in handling the cognitive aspects of a task (see Morrow & Rogers, 2008). An environmental support could be a map or outline of material on a webpage, for example, a stimulus that promotes recall of a particular characteristic, or a technological aid such as a personal data assistant (PDA). Environmental supports have proved particularly beneficial to people with limited cognitive abilities in the areas of memory and attention (Nichols, Rogers, & Fisk, 2006); these types of supports can be used to remind and guide individuals in the accomplishment of tasks, thereby improving their function in everyday situations.

One way to provide environmental support—through automation—involves the reallocation of functions previously performed by a human to a computer or electronic device (Sheridan & Parasuraman, 2006). Automation of tasks can free up memory resources by reducing the number of items the user must remember (e.g., an automated appointment reminder on a PDA). By alerting users of when to focus attention (e.g., an alarm in the car indicating that the oil is low) instead of requiring them to sustain attention, automation can free up attentional resources. However, although automation has the potential to support aspects of everyday life, it is not a panacea. Issues such as how people's trust in, and reliance upon, the automated device interact with system reliability, error type, and error consequence are not yet well understood (Sanchez, Fisk, & Rogers, 2006).

Redesign

Human–system interactions can also be optimized through design. For example, Rogers, Mykityshyn, Campbell, and Fisk (2001) used a task analysis to analyze a blood glucose monitor whose manufacturer claimed it was "as easy as 1, 2, 3." However, rather than requiring 3 easy steps, there were 52 substeps to perform! Based on this analysis, Rogers and colleagues were able to provide redesign suggestions along five dimensions: (1) modify the test strips (e.g., make them longer), (2) modify the meter (e.g., reduce amount of programming required), (3) modify the features (e.g., reduce processing time), (4) modify the blood sampling procedure (e.g., reduce required amount of blood), and (5) modify major systems (e.g., eliminate need for calibration). Opportunities for system redesign abound (see Norman, 1988, for examples).

Summary of HF/E Tools

HF/E provides guidance for understanding human–system interactions by asking the right questions, assessing user–system interactions, identifying problems, and providing solutions. The first step is to ask the right questions about the user and the system. What are the perceptual and/or cognitive demands on a user? What are the characteristics of the system being used? The next step is to choose an approach to answer the question. From task analyses to focus groups to usability testing, many methods can be used. However, one must carefully consider both the advantages and disadvantages of each approach. The final step is to provide a solution: Training, environmental support, and redesign are all potential solution options.

We have provided only a brief introduction to the discipline of HF/E. We recommend the following texts for more details:

- *Engineering Psychology and Human Performance* (Wickens & Hollands, 2000)
- *"Extra-ordinary" Ergonomics: How to Accommodate Small and Big Persons, the Disabled and Elderly, Expectant Mothers, and Children* (Kroemer, 2006)
- *Handbook of Human Factors and Ergonomics Methods* (Stanton, Hedge, Brookhuis, Salas, & Hendrick, 2005)
- *Handbook of Human Factors and Ergonomics* (2nd and 3rd editions; Salvendy, 1997, 2006)
- *Human Factors Methods: A Practical Guide for Engineering and Design* (Stanton, Salmon, et al., 2005)

Illustrative Examples

The following sections illustrate the application of the HF/E methods described above. The goal of these examples is to demonstrate how HF/E has been applied to diverse domains, including everyday activities, work, health promotion, and navigation. Cultural differences are also discussed as a "person characteristic" that must be considered at all stages of analysis.

Everyday Activities

Everyday activities can be broadly defined in terms of three categories: (1) Activities of Daily Living (ADLs), such as bathing, toileting, and eating, that a person must perform to live successfully by oneself (Clark, Czaja, & Weber, 1990); (2) Instrumental Activities of Daily Living (IADLs), such as housework, managing medication, and preparing nutritional meals (Lawton, 1990); and (3) Enhanced Activities of Daily Living (EADLs), which are activities that individuals perform in adapting to changing environments (e.g., using an ATM or e-mailing) and learning new skills to cope with these challenges (Rogers, Meyer, Walker, & Fisk, 1998).

Declining cognitive and physical functioning can hamper performance of these activities, and much of the research in this domain has focused on aging. Researchers have assessed how people's abilities change with age and how these changes impact independent functioning in the home. Despite the focus on aging in this area, the research approach is relevant to all ages.

HF/E Questions Relevant to ADLs, IADLs, and EADLs

What kinds of difficulties in ADLs are encountered by a person with arthritic hands? How does this person open a jar of spaghetti sauce, insert a key into a lock, or type on a keyboard? What if a person has limited leg mobility? How would that person climb stairs, make the bed, sweep the floor, or take a shower? The physical demands of daily living activities should not be overlooked; see Clark and colleagues (1990) for a direct assessment of the physical demands required to perform various ADLs.

Also relevant here is developing an understanding of the cognitive component of everyday activities. For example, a specific question relevant to EADLs might be, "What is the relationship between World Wide Web strategy use and search success for experienced younger and older users?" (Stronge, Rogers, & Fisk, 2006). Researchers have also studied the frustrations and difficulties older adults experience in the context of performing ADLs, IADLs, and EADLs (Rogers et al., 1998). Other HF/E questions relevant to these activities may include the attentional demands of cooking a meal. There may be multiple ingredients to track, events that must be sequenced properly, as well as timing of various components and monitoring to prevent burning. HF/E analysis can provide insight into these issues.

HF/E Techniques

Using task analysis techniques, the physical demands associated with ADLs were detailed by videotaping older adults performing certain tasks (Clark et al., 1990). Via this method, tasks such as making the bed were divided into elemental physical units such as bending, reaching, grasping, and pulling. Although this study focused on the physical actions required of ADL tasks and the capabilities and limitations of older adults, this method can be used to assess cognitive components of ADL tasks for users of any age or ability. For instance, the cognitive demands of preparing a meal can be identified by using task analysis. This method can illustrate how an individual remembers which ingredients have been added or how he or she monitors meal preparation progress.

To understand the task components of strategies in searching the Web, participants were monitored as they executed specific queries (Stronge et al., 2006). Process diagrams were created from these observations to visualize the various Web search strategies used, and knowledge engineering was used to assess the declarative knowledge of Web users. These methods provided detailed descriptions of each step in a complex process. This study illustrated different strategies and processes that can be used to successfully search the Web.

Focus groups were conducted to collect descriptive data about the frustrations older adults encounter in ADLs, IADLs, and EADLs (Rogers et al., 1998). The questions centered on the constraints of interacting with devices and performing everyday tasks. The benefit of this method is that the group dynamic can move the conversations into a data-rich domain that the interviewer may not have considered. These HF/E methods yield valuable data relevant to solving user problems in the domain of everyday activities.

Solutions or Potential Solutions

Environmental supports, assistive technologies, and support services were identified by Clark and colleagues (1990) as solutions to remedy the physical problems experienced by older adults when performing ADLs. The data collected from the focus groups indicated that nearly 40% of the problems encountered in ADLs, IADLs, and EADLs by older adults were a result of physical limitations, whereas 30% were attributable to cognitive limitations (Rogers et al., 1998). Automated aids such as the Cook's Collage, which gives the user feedback about which ingredients have been added to a recipe, may assist those with memory deficits in the realm of everyday activities (Sanchez, Calcaterra, & Tran, 2005). Training was identified by Rogers and colleagues (1998) and Stronge and colleagues (2006) as a solution to aid older adults in EADLs. Other suggested solutions included redesign of the Internet search engines studied by Stronge and colleagues.

Work and the Workplace

The workplace can be anywhere. For taxi drivers it is the car, for accountants it is an office, for golf course maintenance teams it may be riding a mower. No matter the occupation, there are several aspects of work that must be considered and assessed to foster optimal work performance. With the diversity of work and workplaces, it is important to understand the physical and cognitive aspects of a job to make it safer and its performance more efficient.

HF/E Questions Related to Work and the Workplace

Physically fitting the workspace to the human operator is important to prevent injury and to increase work efficiency (Spath, Braun, & Hagenmeyer, 2006). Some HF/E questions related to physical considerations involve the diversity of size of the users. For example, in any office environment it is critical to ask how users differ in size and shape. Also, what are the physical capabilities and limitations of the users? Do any of the users have injuries or deficits that restrict movements? Other issues relate to the layout of the workspace—for example, the placement of items required for the job, such that they are physically accessible to users. Investigation of the layout leads to questions concerning the most important items and which items are most frequently used.

In addition to physical considerations, the cognitive aspects of a job must be addressed. For example, consider the cognitive aspects of using a riding mower at a golf course. Relevant cognitive questions might concern the types of decisions that the operator must make while operating the mower. What cues does the operator have available on which to base those decisions? What are the memory demands of the task (e.g., things that have already been done and things that still need to be done)? To what does the operator need to pay attention? How much workload is placed on the operator while completing the task?

HF/E Techniques

Knowledge engineering techniques have been applied to the analysis of commercial mowing at a golf course (Sanchez, Bowles, Rogers, & Fisk, 2006). Product manuals, subject matter experts, focus groups, and process flow diagrams were used to understand the task of mowing a golf course. The focus group data gave insight into what operators do when faced with a specific problem (i.e., slipping in wet grass), the decision sequence that takes place to solve the problem (i.e., reduce pressure on gas, lift blades, etc.), and the reasons behind the decisions. Knowledge engineering also provided insight into areas where the operators' understanding of the system was inaccurate. This was accomplished by comparing the actions of the operators to the information available in the instruction materials. The comparison revealed that operators were unaware of the benefits of a key mower feature (i.e., the traction control knob) that was described by the subject matter expert as essential for successful operation.

How a user operates a piece of machinery (e.g., a golf course mower) or makes a decision within a system is influenced by the amount of workload placed on the user. The amount of workload will differ depending on the tasks that must be completed or monitored at a given time, the complexity of the tasks, or the amount of time available to complete tasks (Gonzalez, 2005). Different individuals have different workload capacities, of course, and people with limited cognitive abilities are likely to be more affected by workload. The subjective workload associated with the task can be measured for each individual using one of the methods discussed previously (i.e., NASA-TLX, SWAT). For example, during dynamic decision-making tasks, decisions that are made in real time and that are affected by the environment in which they are being made are negatively impacted under high workload and when individuals have limited cognitive abilities (Gonzalez). Thus, when designing tasks and jobs for individuals, it is important to examine, understand, and, if appropriate, adjust the workload placed on the user.

Solutions or Potential Solutions

The knowledge engineering study conducted by Sanchez and colleagues (2006) provided insights into the potential for solution in the three categories described above (training, environmental support, and redesign). Training could help operators learn to use the mower to its maximum efficiency, for example, by teaching operators how to use the traction control system. Environmental support might be provided through automating the traction control such that it automatically engages when the mower slips. Future redesigns of the mower could make the traction control feature more salient either by emphasizing it in the instructions or by placing the control in a visible location. Other solutions might reduce or manage workload: training to improve the skill of the user so that the task becomes easier, environmental support to aid memory or other taxed cognitive resources, or redesign of the system to reallocate functions from the person to the machine.

Health Promotion

Health improvement is an important everyday activity that can benefit from HF/E analysis. For example, medication noncompliance has been shown to be a serious problem both for the individuals as well as for the entire health care system. According to the American Heart Association (2006), "The number one problem in treating illness today is patients' failure to take prescriptions medications correctly." In fact, it is estimated that more than half of all Americans suffering from chronic illnesses do not adhere to their health care provider's medication guidance. Using HF/E techniques, researchers have identified problem areas and suggested solutions to improve adherence.

Medication adherence is only one area in the health domain that HF/E researchers have examined. Other areas include medical device use and nutrition label effectiveness. Much research in this domain has focused on an aging population, likely because older adults take more medications and have more health issues than younger adults. Also, as the average expected lifespan increases, people are more likely to have chronic diseases that they must manage. However, this research is relevant to all ages and all conditions because the same HF/E techniques can be used to identify issues, suggest solutions, and direct future research.

HF/E Questions Related to Health Promotion

Managing one's health is easy when one is very healthy. However, how does health management change when one is not very healthy? For instance, what are the demands of managing multiple medications when a person's health declines? How difficult are prescription instructions to follow? How effective are cognitive aids, such as pill organizers and organizational charts, in facilitating adherence to a medication regimen (Park, Morrell, Frieske, & Kincaid, 1992)? What is the best way to train individuals to use a sequential, multiple-step device, such as a glucometer (Mykityshyn, Fisk, & Rogers, 2002)? How simple are "simple" medical devices (Rogers, Mykityshyn, et al., 2001)? How should a nutrition label be designed to ensure optimal reader comprehension (Marino & Mahan, 2005)?

HF/E Techniques

Rogers, Mykityshyn, and colleagues (2001) used a task analysis to assess the physical and cognitive steps required in using a medical device. This analysis clearly demonstrated that the device (a glucometer) has multiple steps that must be performed in a specific sequence to attain the end goal of proper use. These steps can tax the working memory of the users and likely increase stress. To assess the mental workload of using a medical device, participants in the Mykityshyn and colleagues (2002) study completed the NASA-TLX after each step. This provided the researchers with a subjective measure of the mental workload placed on the users.

Solutions or Potential Solutions

Training, support, and redesign are all potential solutions to health promotion issues faced by individuals. Video training led to more successful medical device use than a text manual in the Mykityshyn and colleagues (2002) study. The video training likely provided more environmental support by minimizing working memory load and visualization demands placed on the user compared to reading a manual. By supporting comprehension, working memory, long-term memory, and prospective memory, Park and colleagues (1992) found that combining a pill organizer and an organizational chart resulted in the highest medication adherence. By following HF/E information display principles, Marino and Mahan (2005) showed that current nutrition labels are inadequate in the demands that they place on readers. They found that information integration of current labels imposed working memory demands upon readers; participants made more correct nutrition judgments when the label design was displayed pictorially. System redesign was suggested by Rogers, Mykityshyn, and colleagues (2001) when the usability testing revealed that the "user-unfriendly" device design could not be remedied by training alone.

Getting Around: Issues of Driving and Navigation

Most people think about "getting around" as simply a matter of jumping in a car and driving to a destination. However, transportation issues are also found in navigating through an environment on foot or using public transportation. In this section, we discuss not only driving and the cognitive factors involved in it, but also wayfinding and navigation.

HF/E Questions Related to Driving and Navigation

Navigating through the environment or finding one's way can be reasonably easy if a person is in a familiar environment and perceptual or cognitive resources are not being overly taxed. However, when a person is in an unfamiliar place, with the added complexities of driving, navigating the environment can become very demanding. For individuals with cognitive impairments, these problems may be exacerbated (Sohlberg, Todis, Fickas, Hung, & Lemoncello, 2005). Relevant questions then relate to understanding the capabilities and limitations of individuals with respect to the task of navigating an environment or driving a vehicle. System analysis is also critical: Which characteristics of the environment and the vehicle are placing demands on the user, and what exactly are those demands? The questions should address all aspects of navigating an environment or driving a car, from determining a route to reading street signs and from visually searching an environment for hazards to deciding to proceed through an intersection.

HF/E Techniques

Task analysis indicates that three domains of ability or human functioning relate to successfully getting around: sensoriperceptual (vision and audition), cognitive (attention, memory, spatial processing), and movement control (Watson, 2001). Being able to see or hear is crucial to successful navigation. Vision deficiency can be problematic when navigating. The ability to read street signs and directions and the ability to adjust to differing light conditions (e.g., those that occur when going from outside to inside) are important to finding one's way. Visual attention—that is, the visual information that can be attended to during a brief period of time—has a significant effect on the ability to drive and avoid accidents (Goode et al., 1998). Visual attention can be measured using the Useful Field of View (UFOV) test, which indicates the size of the area to which individuals can visually attend. The size of the UFOV has been shown to predict crash involvement and to assess risk of crashing in older adults who generally have smaller UFOVs (Goode et al.).

Given the nature of driving today, with the demand of performing multiple tasks at a given time, the driver's capacity to divide attention is also important. Drivers may simultaneously talk on a cell phone, adjust the radio, listen to music, or talk to a passenger (not to mention put on makeup or eat lunch). Individuals with fewer attentional resources have more difficulty performing multiple tasks successfully and may put themselves and others at risk by attempting to do so (Caird, Edwards, Creaser, & Horney, 2005). Research shows that when attention is divided while driving, people react more slowly, show greater speed variation, follow at a greater distance, and are involved in more rear-end collisions (Strayer & Drews, 2004). In addition, when attentional resources are being taxed by, for example, searching for objects in the environment, such as street signs and other vehicles, drivers are slower and less accurate (McPhee, Scialfa, Dennis, Ho, & Caird, 2004). Dividing attention can leave less reaction time for evasive action (McPhee et al., 2004) and negatively impact decisions while navigating complex environments such as intersections (Caird et al., 2005). When attention is taxed, individuals based driving decision on fewer cues in the environment.

To assess these effects for individuals from specific populations, surveys, interviews, and focus groups with populations of interest can be used. These methods are an excellent way of ascertaining the source and subsequent outcomes of many functional limitations associated with navigation and wayfinding. For example, Sohlberg and colleagues (2005) used these techniques to assess the challenges faced by cognitively impaired individuals. These individuals expressed concerns about getting lost and the challenges associated with problem solving while en route; their concerns resulted in fewer medical and business visits and reduced social interaction. The interviews and focus groups enabled the researchers to delve more deeply into the individuals' problems and their reported strategies to overcome them. These data indicated potential areas for solutions to these problems.

Solutions or Potential Solutions

Human beings are very good at adapting to situations and overcoming obstacles—up to a point. Although some people may experience problems navigating an environment, many develop "survival" strategies. Sohlberg and colleagues (2005) found that people often use explicit written directions received in advance to reduce memory demands. Landmarks were found to be unhelpful because, when memory is a problem, cognitively impaired individuals do not remember having passed landmarks. The authors also found that it is important for cognitively impaired individuals to have backup plans if the primary strategy fails (e.g., if the directions are lost). Such plans include asking people for directions or carrying a cell phone to receive directions from family or friends. These survival strategies can inform our solutions to navigational problems.

Training has proved effective for improving problems associated with UFOV and risk awareness in drivers. For example, the size of UFOV was expanded when participants were trained on speed of processing, a fundamental ability influencing UFOV (Roenker, Cissell, Ball, Wadley, & Edwards, 2003). Risky driving behavior was decreased by training inexperienced drivers to reduce their exposure to dangerous situations (Fisher et al., 2002). Furthermore, training individuals to focus attention on appropriate locations in complex driving situations may enable them to compensate for taxed attentional resources.

Cultural Considerations: Globalizing HF/E

With the increased cultural interactions in the present global economy, considering users with cognitive, perceptual, and motor differences outside of Western society is essential for the acceptance and integration of systems and technology worldwide. Important cultural distinctions—cognitive, perceptual, and physical—may be relevant to proposed HF/E solutions.

Anthropometric data used by human factors specialists are based primarily on measurements derived from Western populations. However, there are significant physical differences between cultures. For example, on average, Japanese people are shorter than people from Western countries (Lippa & Klein, 2005). A mismatch between the physical size of users and the physical size of where or what they are operating can lead to reduced efficiency in the workplace and increased safety risks.

Cultural differences can also be seen in differences of perception. Culture—defined by Webster's (2006) as the belief system and values of the society in which one is raised—can have a significant influence on how one perceives the world. A study of Nepalese people showed that they exhibited significantly higher pain thresholds compared to Western people (Clark & Clark, 1980), which were not attributed to neurosensory variations but to differences related to pain-reporting criteria, brought on by a different cultural value system. It is therefore important to be cognizant of cultural differences in the context of human–system interaction. These differences might impact measures of subjective workload, for example.

Research also indicates that there are cultural differences in the way we think. For example, a comparison of Asian and American cultures revealed distinct differences in the way each uses intuition versus formal reasoning to overcome conflict (Norenzayan, Smith, Kim, & Nisbett, 2002). Americans were more likely to use formal reasoning compared to Chinese and Koreans, who relied more heavily on intuitive strategies for solving conflict. Nisbett, Peng, Choi, and Norenzayan (2001) found that Westerners were more analytical compared to East Asians, who tended to be more holistic in their systems of thought. These fundamental cultural differences can influence cognition and motivation.

In a study comparing American and Asian cognitive styles, Rau, Choong, and Salvendy (2004) found that American cognitive style tends to classify stimuli based on inferences about those stimuli or their functions. In contrast, some Asian cultures tend to classify stimuli based on their interrelationships. The Asian way of thinking tends to be more relational compared to American way, which tends to be more analytical. The result is that Asian cultures rely on experience and do not separate the person from objective facts, whereas Americans do separate subjective experience from objective reality. An implication of cultural differences in cognition is that the mental models on which designs are based may not work for people from other cultures and, in fact, may be detrimental to their efficiency and safety when interacting with the product/system.

Cultural differences can play a big role when applying HF/E tools and techniques. For example, Chavan (2005) pointed out that the Indian culture generally accepts the current state of a situation and then looks for ways around it. This mental set can pose a problem when conducting usability studies in that people from the Indian culture do not like giving negative opinions. In addition, people from collectivist cultures (e.g., most Asian cultures) may have trouble providing an individual opinion and will likely give an opinion that he or she thinks the collective would hold. Therefore, when applying HF/E tools it is important to consider cultural differences and how they affect the collection and interpretation of data.

Summary of Illustrative Examples

As the above examples illustrate, HF/E techniques have been used in a wide range of domains. From task analysis to focus groups and from driving a car to managing medications, HF/E techniques have been used to identify problem areas; describe the user, the system, and their interaction; and suggest solutions. The advantage of these tools is that they can be applied to any domain or any system that involves a human user. HF/E techniques consider the user's capabilities and limitations and the context in which the user is interacting with the system.

Looking to the Future

The discipline of HF/E has much to offer the practice of neuropsychology. In fact, there is an emerging area called "neuroergonomics" that represents the intersection between HF/E and neuropsychology (see Parasuraman, 2003). Neuroergonomic analysis involves understanding the neural bases of perception and cognition as they relate to human–system interactions. Parasuraman provided examples of how this approach may involve assessments of cognitive workload, attention, and oculomotor control. Such measures may prove useful to detect when workload is overloading for individual patients, for example, while they are performing a particular task. Neurological measures would be particularly useful if the person were unable to provide an accurate report of subjective workload.

The concept of adaptive automation also has potential for supporting patients' needs. In adaptive automation, functions are assigned (allocated) either to the system or to the person, based on different parameters such as workload, stress, or ability. For example, in a low stress or low workload situation it may be desirable to have the human perform a task (e.g., wayfinding) so that he or she can maintain and possibly improve functional abilities. However, in high-stress or high workload situations it might be critical to have an automated system provide the needed information. This type of adaptive system could support patient's learning during the rehabilitation process yet recognize situations of overload and provide technological support as needed.

Adaptive automation is reliant on valid and timely assessments of workload that might be attained through neuroergonomic assessments—measuring brain function during task performance. Such measures can be continuous and nonintrusive. According to Parasuraman (2003), "Measures of brain function can indicate not only *when* an operator is overloaded, drowsy, or fatigued, but also *which* brain networks and circuits may be affected. In short, neuroergonomic measures offer new avenues for adaptive interventions aimed at enhancing system performance" (p. 12).

The broad discipline of HF/E has well-developed methods to enable understanding of human–system interactions in a variety of contexts. These methods provide ways of asking questions that lead to the development of solutions through training, provision of environmental support, or system redesign. Such solutions can be implemented for groups of people or for single patients—in either case these solutions have the potential to improve the safety, efficiency, and effectiveness of human–system interactions.

Acknowledgments

We were supported in part by Grant No. P01 AG17211 from the National Institutes of Health (National Institute on Aging) under the auspices of the Center for Research and Education on Aging and Technology Enhancement (CREATE). Order of the second and third authors is random—they contributed equally.

References

Alvarez, K., Salas, E., & Garofano, C. M. (2004). An integrated model of training evaluation and effectiveness. *Hum Resource Devel Rev, 3*, 385–416.

American Heart Association. (2006). *Statistics you need to know.* Dallas, TX: Author. Retrieved September 7, 2006, from *www.americanheart.org/presenter.jhtml?identifier=107*.

Bowles, C. T., Sanchez, J., Rogers, W. A., & Fisk, A. D. (2004). Knowledge engineering: Applying the process. In *Proceedings of the Human Factors and Ergonomics Society 48th annual meeting* (pp. 2411–2415). Santa Monica, CA: Human Factors and Ergonomics Society.

Caird, J. K., Edwards, C. J., Creaser, J. I., & Horrey, W. J. (2005). Older driver failures of attention at intersections: Using change blindness methods to assess turn decision accuracy. *Hum Factors, 47*, 235–249.

Chavan, A. L. (2005). Another culture, another method. *Proceedings of the 11th international conference on human–computer interaction: Vol. 10. Internationalization, online communities and social computing: Design and evaluation.* Mahwah, NJ: Erlbaum.

Clark, M. C., Czaja, S. J., & Weber, R. A. (1990). Older adults and daily living task profiles. *Hum Factors, 32*, 537–549.

Clark, W. C., & Clark, S. B. (1980). Pain responses in Nepalese porters. *Science, 209*, 410–412.

Fisher, D. L., Laurie, N. E., Glaser, R., Connerney, K., Pollatsek, A., Duffy, S. A., et al.

(2002). Use of a fixed-base driving simulator to evaluate the effects of experience and PC-based risk awareness training on drivers' decisions. *Hum Factors, 44,* 287–302.

Gonzalez, C. (2005). Task workload and cognitive abilities in dynamic decision making. *Hum Factors, 47,* 92–101.

Goode, K. T., Ball, K. K., Sloane, M., Roenker, D. L., Roth, D. L., Myers, R. S., et al. (1998). Useful field of view and other neurocognitive indicators of crash risk in older adults. *J Clin Psychol Med S, 5,* 425–439.

Hart, S. G., & Staveland, L. E. (1988). Development of NASA-TLX (task load index): Results of empirical and theoretical research. In P. A. Hancock & N. Meshkati (Eds.), *Human mental workload* (pp. 139–183). New York: Elsevier.

Hollnagel, E. (2006). Task analysis: Why, what, and how. In G. Salvendy (Ed.), *Handbook of human factors and ergonomics* (3rd ed., pp. 373–383). Hoboken, NJ: Wiley.

Karwowski, W. (2006). The discipline of ergonomics and human factors. In G. Salvendy (Ed.), *Handbook of human factors and ergonomics* (3rd ed., pp. 3–31). Hoboken, NJ: Wiley.

Kirlik, A., Fisk, A. D., Walker, N., & Rothrock, L. (1998). Feedback augmentation and part-task practice in training dynamic decision-making skills. In J. A. Cannon-Bowers & E. Salas (Eds.), *Making decisions under stress: Implications for individual and team training* (pp. 91–113). Washington, DC: American Psychological Association.

Kirwan, B., & Ainsworth, L. K. (1992). *A guide to task analysis.* London: Taylor & Francis.

Kroemer, K. H. E. (2006). *"Extra-ordinary" ergonomics: How to accommodate small and big persons, the disabled, and elderly, expectant mothers, and children.* Boca Raton, FL: CRC Press and HFES.

Lawton, M. P. (1990). Aging and performance of home tasks. *Hum Factors, 32,* 527–536.

Leonard, V. K., Jacko, J. A., Yi, J. S., & Sainfort, F. (2006). Human factors and ergonomic methods. In G. Salvendy (Ed.), *Handbook of human factors and ergonomics* (3rd ed., pp. 292–321). Hoboken, NJ: Wiley.

Lippa, K., & Klein, H. A. (2005). Making "human factors" truly human: Cultural considerations in human factors research and practice. *Proceedings of the Human Factors and Ergonomics Society, 49,* 941–945.

Marino, C. J., & Mahan, R. P. (2005). Configural displays can improve nutrition-related decisions: An application of the proximity compatibility principle. *Hum Factors, 47,* 121–130.

McPhee, L. C., Scialfa, C. T., Dennis, W. M., Ho, G., & Caird, J. K. (2004). Age differences in visual search for traffic signs during a simulated conversation. *Hum Factors, 46,* 674–685.

Merriam-Webster Online. (2006). *Culture.* Retrieved August 14, 2006, from *www.m-w.com/dictionary/culture.*

Morrow, D. J., & Rogers, W. A. (2008). Environmental support: An integrative framework. *Hum Factors, 50,* 589–613.

Mykityshyn, A. L., Fisk, A. D., & Rogers, W. A. (2002). Learning to use a home medical device: Mediating age-related differences with training. *Hum Factors, 44,* 354–364.

Nichols, T. A., Rogers, W. A., & Fisk, A. D. (2006). Design for aging. In G. Salvendy (Ed.), *Handbook of human factors and ergonomics* (3rd ed., pp. 1418–1445). Hoboken, NJ: Wiley.

Nisbett, R. E., Peng, K., Choi, I., & Norenzayan, A. (2001). Culture and systems of thought: Holistic vs. analytic cognition. *Psychological Review, 108,* 291–310.

Norenzayan, A., Smith, E. E., Kim, B. J., & Nisbett, R. E. (2002). Cultural preferences for formal versus intuitive reasoning. *Cognitive Science, 26,* 653–684.

Norman, D. (1988). *The psychology of everyday things*. New York: Basic Books.

Parasuraman, R. (2003). Neuroergonomics: Research and practice. *Theor Issues Ergon, 4*, 5–20.

Park, D. C., Morrell, R. W., Frieske, D., & Kincaid, D. (1992). Medication adherence behaviors in older adults: Effects of external cognitive supports. *Psychol Aging, 7*, 252–256.

Random House Webster's unabridged dictionary (2nd ed.). New York: Author.

Rau, P. P., Choong, Y., & Salvendy, G. (2004). A cross cultural study on knowledge representation and structure in human computer interfaces. *Int J Ind Ergonom, 34*, 117–129.

Reid, G. B., & Nygren, T. E. (1988). The subjective workload assessment technique: A scaling procedure for measuring mental workload. In P.A. Hancock & N. Meshkati (Eds.), *Human mental workload* (pp. 185–218). New York: Elsevier.

Roenker, D. L., Cissell, G. M., Ball, K. K., Wadley, V. G., & Edwards, J. D. (2003). Speed-of-processing and driving simulator training result in improved driving performance. *Hum Factors, 45*, 218–233.

Rogers, W. A., Campbell, R. H., & Pak, R. (2001). A systems approach for training older adults to use technology. In N. Charness, D. C. Park, & B. A. Sabel (Eds.), *Communication, technology, and aging: Opportunities and challenges for the future* (pp. 187–208). New York: Springer.

Rogers, W. A., Meyer, B., Walker, N., & Fisk, A. D. (1998). Functional limitations to daily living tasks in the aged: A focus group analysis. *Hum Factors, 40*, 111–125.

Rogers, W. A., Mykityshyn, A. L., Campbell, R. H., & Fisk, A. D. (2001) Analysis of a "simple" medical device. *Ergon Des, 9*, 6–14.

Salas, E., Wilson, K. W., Priest, H. A., & Guthrie, J. W. (2006). Design, delivery, and evaluation of training systems. In G. Salvendy (Ed.), *Handbook of human factors and ergonomics* (3rd ed., pp. 472–512). Hoboken, NJ: Wiley.

Salvendy, G. (1997). *Handbook of human factors and ergonomics* (2nd ed.). New York: Wiley.

Salvendy, G. (2006). *Handbook of human factors and ergonomics* (3rd ed.). Hoboken, NJ: Wiley.

Sanchez, J., Bowles, C. T., Rogers, W. A., & Fisk, A. D. (2006). Human factors goes to the golf course: Knowledge engineering of commercial mowing. *Ergon Des, 14*, 17–23.

Sanchez, J., Calcaterra, G., & Tran, Q. Q. (2005). Automation in the home: The development of an appropriate system representation and its effects on reliance. In *Proceedings of the Human Factors and Ergonomics Society 49th annual meeting* (pp. 1859–1862). Santa Monica, CA: Human Factors and Ergonomics Society.

Sanchez, J., Fisk, A. D., & Rogers, W. A. (2006). What determines appropriate trust of and reliance on an automated collaborative system?: Effects of error type and domain knowledge. In *Proceedings of the 9th international conference on control, automation, robotics, and vision* (pp. 98–103). New York: IEEE.

Sheridan, T. B., & Parasuraman, R. (2006). Human automation interaction. In R. S. Nickerson (Ed.), *Reviews of human factors and ergonomics* (pp. 89–129). Santa Monica, CA: Human Factors and Ergonomics Society.

Sohlberg, M. M., Todis, B., Fickas, S., Hung, P., & Lemoncello, R. (2005). A profile of community navigation in adults with chronic cognitive impairments. *Brain Injury, 19*, 1249–1259.

Spath, D., Braun, M., & Hagenmeyer, L. (2006). Human factors and ergonomics in manufacturing and process control. In G. Salvendy (Ed.), *Handbook of human factors and ergonomics* (3rd ed., pp. 1597–1625). Hoboken, NJ: Wiley.

Stanton, N. A., Hedge, A., Brookhuis, K., Salas, E., & Hendrick, H. (2005). *Handbook of human factors and ergonomics methods*. Boca Raton, FL: CRC Press.

Stanton, N. A., Salmon, P. M., Walker, G. H., Baber, C., & Jenkins, D. P. (2005). *Human factors methods: A practical guide for engineering and design*. Burlington, VT: Ashgate.

Strayer, D. L., & Drews, F. A. (2004). Profiles in driver distraction: Effects of cell phone conversations on younger and older drivers. *Hum Factors, 46*, 640–649.

Stronge, A. J., Rogers, W. A., & Fisk, A. D. (2006). Web-based information search and retrieval: Effects of strategy use and age on search success. *Hum Factors, 48*, 443–446.

Tsang, P. S., & Vidulich, M. A. (2006). Mental workload and situation awareness. In G. Salvendy (Ed.), *Handbook of human factors and ergonomics* (3rd ed., pp. 243–268). Hoboken, NJ: Wiley.

Vu, K. L., & Proctor, R. W. (2006). Web site design and evaluation. In G. Salvendy (Ed.), *Handbook of human factors and ergonomics* (3rd ed., pp. 1317–1343). Hoboken, NJ: Wiley.

Watson, T. L. (2001). There's got to be a better way (finding system). *Ergon Des, 9*, 20–26.

Wickens, C. D., & Hollands, J. G. (2000). *Engineering psychology and human performance* (3rd ed.). Upper Saddle River, NJ: Prentice-Hall.

Wickens, C. D., Lee, J., Liu, Y., & Becker, S. G. (2004). *An introduction to human factors engineering* (2nd ed.). Upper Saddle River, NJ: Pearson Education.

CHAPTER 3

Occupational Therapy Approach to Assessing the Relationship between Cognition and Function

Carolyn M. Baum and Noomi Katz

Occupational therapy is concerned with enabling the individual to do the activities, tasks, and roles that are self-identified as necessary for daily life. This approach, known as the person, environment, and occupation (PEO) approach, requires scientists to discover and then clinicians to address in practice the relationship among person factors (psychological, cognitive, sensory, motor, physiological), occupations (what the individual needs and wants to do to maintain self and engage in work, family, and community activities), and environment social support (social capital, the physical environment, and culture).

The Occupational Therapy Approach

There are several contemporary PEO models in the occupational therapy literature: the person–environment–occupational performance model (Christiansen & Baum, 1991, 1997, 2005); the model of human ecology (Dunn, Brown & McGuigan, 1994; Dunn, Brown, & Youngstorm, 2003); the model of human occupation (Kielhofner, 2002, 2008); the person–environment–occupation model, (Law et al., 1996); the Canadian model of occupational performance (Townsend et al., 1997); and occupational performance—Australia (Chapparo & Ranka, 1997). Each of these models includes the three central elements—person, occupation, and environment—and each acknowledges the importance of the stages of development as they influence motivation, skills, and roles. Moreover, they share views of the individual that emphasize the complex relationship of biological, psychological, and social phenomena and the importance of a satisfactory match between the person, the task, and the situational characteristics. This interaction is known as "occupational performance," the term occupational therapists use to describe the function of an individual interacting with the environment while doing the activities that are important for him or her to do.

The PEO concepts were articulated by scholars in occupational therapy through-out the 20th century (Fidler & Fidler, 1973; Meyer, 1922; Mosey, 1974; Reilly, 1962) and form the basis for views of occupational therapy practice that address the occu-pational performance issues of individuals. The PEO models are based on research and knowledge from the behavioral and social sciences (such as psychology, anthro-pology, and sociology), the neurosciences, as well as from work in newer areas such as rehabilitation science, disability studies, and occupation science. Each provides a unique perspective and emphasizes the concepts differentially but based on the same foundation.

Occupational therapy intervention is viewed as a process of using a broad range of purposeful client-centered strategies that engage the individual to develop or use his or her resources to enable successful performance. The satisfactory performance of occupations is seen as a consequence of individual goals in relation to environmental characteristics that either limit or support an individual's participation. Intervention strategies may or may not involve an individual's direct engagement in occupation. In some cases, it is possible to modify environments to make them accessible and man-ageable. The client's active involvement may consist of working with the therapist and the family to identify goals and strategies that will remove barriers and enable participation in tasks and roles. Occupational therapists almost never do things *to* people; they more frequently do things *with* people.

Many people with chronic health conditions and disabilities have cognitive prob-lems that limit their performance in daily life activities. Moving through daily life requires the individual to formulate goals, plan how to achieve them, and carry out plans (Lezak, Howieson, & Loring, 2004). Occupational therapists work with chil-dren and adults who have difficulties formulating and maintaining the focus on their goals. Goal-directed activities include caring for self and others; maintenance of the home; work, fitness, leisure, and sport activities; as well as community, social, and spiritual activities. These types of activities give meaning to people's lives. Imple-menting goal-directed activities requires individuals to use higher-level cognitive pro-cesses to self-correct, make decisions, use judgment, and make wise choices as they navigate through life's challenges and difficulties (Goel, Grafman, Tajik, Gana, & Danto, 1997; Lezak, 1982; Lezak et al., 2004). Impairment or loss of these abilities compromises individuals' ability to participate fully in society.

Emphasis on both occupational performance activities and participation in the community requires the practitioner to employ a client-centered strategy (Baum & Law, 1997; Fisher, 1998; Mathiowetz & Haugen, 1995). The practitioner must first determine with the client what he or she perceives to be the issues that are limiting his or her participation and causing difficulty in carrying out tasks related to produc-tivity and work, personal care, home maintenance, sleep, recreation, and/or leisure. This approach is defined as a top-down one because it starts with the individual's performance to identify any physiological, psychological, cognitive, neurobehavioral, and/or spiritual factors that may be interfering with, or supporting, the individual's performance; as well, it identifies the environmental factors that may serve as enablers or barriers to performance.

It is important to determine an individual's capacity for real-world everyday per-formance (Alderman, Burgess, Knight, & Henman, 2003; Allen & Blue, 1998; Allen, Earhart, & Blue, 1992; Fisher, 1998; Giles, 2005; Gioia & Isquith, 2004; Keil &

Kaszniak, 2002; Levy & Burns, 2005; Shallice & Burgess, 1991). Real-world performance requires multitasking that occurs in environments that may or may not be supportive. Testing of real-world performance requires behavioral observations in the context in which the individual will be required to do the tasks (Burgess et al., 2006). The information obtained by occupational therapists from such assessments enables them to work with individuals and their families to maximize function in those with cognitive loss.

Occupational therapists assess cognition to determine individuals' capacities to live alone safely and comfortably, to work, or to do any task that is important and meaningful for them. They also address the impact that executive function has on performance. By assessing cognitive capacities in the performance of daily tasks, it is possible to determine their strengths, limitations, and challenges as they learn skills and environmental strategies that support them in their daily lives. It is possible to observe key executive constructs in the performance of daily life tasks even in those with mild cognitive deficits (Bar-Haim Erez, Rothschild, Katz, Tuchner, & Hartman-Maeir, in press; Baum & Edwards, 1993; Burgess et al., 2006; Edwards, Hahn, Baum, & Dromerick, 2006). These tasks include initiation, the process that precedes the performance of a task; organization, the physical arrangement of the environment, tools, and materials to facilitate efficient and effective performance (Katz & Hartman-Maeir, 2005; Lezak et al., 2004); judgment (Goel et al., 1997; Lezak, 1982); and completion (Baum et al., 2008; Goel et al., 1997). Occupational therapists measure cognition and function not just to know what a person can do, but to know what to do to foster that individual's engagement in daily life—because occupation is a basic human need, a determinant of health, and a source of meaning (Katz, 2005; Townsend, 1997).

Occupational Therapy Cognitive Theoretical Models

The last decade has seen the development of occupational therapy treatment models for persons with cognitive loss (Katz, 2005). Two major approaches are discussed here. The first, strategy learning and awareness, reviews the work of Toglia (a dynamic interactional approach to cognitive rehabilitation) and Polatajko (cognitive orientation to daily occupational performance [CO-OP]). The second approach, adaptive and functional skill training, reviews the work of Giles (a neurofunctional approach) and Levy and Burns (the cognitive disabilities model for rehabilitation in dementia) based on the work of Allen (1985; Allen et al., 1992).

A Strategy Learning and Awareness Approach

Theoretical Foundations for a Dynamic Interactional Model of Cognition

Traditional cognitive rehabilitation approaches have been guided by the assumption that cognition can be divided into subskills (Trexler, 1987). Toglia (1993, 2005) proposes an alternative to syndrome-specific approaches and encourages clinicians to discover the underlying conditions and processing strategies that influence performance. Treatment focuses on helping the person become aware of how deficits require the modification of activity demands and the environment and developing strategies that accomplish these modifications. The approach is based on the cognitive and educational psychology literature as well as on neuropsychology, cognitive rehabilitation, and neuroscience theories that address how people process, learn, and generalize information (Toglia, 1991, 2005; Toglia & Kirk, 2000).

Lidz (1987) defines cognition as the capacity to acquire and use information to learn and generalize. Individuals must take in, organize, assimilate, and integrate new information with previous experiences; adaptation involves using information that has been previously acquired to plan and structure behavior for goal attainment under changing conditions. Using this definition, cognition is not divided into subskills such as attention, memory, organization, or reasoning. Instead the approach requires understanding the person's ability to use strategies, monitor performance, and learn. Such an approach is necessary because cognition is neither static nor stable; interaction with the external world requires such flux (Feuerstein & Falik, 2004; Lidz, 1987; Lidz & Elliot, 2000). This model conceptualizes cognition as an ongoing product of the dynamic interaction among the person, the activity, and the environment and as modifiable under certain conditions. Because there is a fixed or structural limit in the capacity to process information, there are differences in the way that capacity can be used. The same activity can require different amounts of processing capacity depending on how it is performed; thus it must be used efficiently. The efficient allocation of limited processing resources is central to learning and all forms of cognition (Flavell, Miller, & Miller, 1993). The multicontext approach is directed at teaching the person to use strategies and to self-monitor performance, while simultaneously adapting the activity and environmental demands to be at a level slightly above the "just right challenge" (Toglia, 2005). This treatment approach focuses on the person's use of strategies and level of awareness in graded transfer levels from near to far transfer. The approach requires the occupational therapist to present opportunities for the individual to experience different environments, different levels of demands in the activity, and to bring to consciousness a new level of awareness. The measurement methods developed for this model include a dynamic graded cueing approach to assess the current abilities of the individual, the potential performance with mediation, as well as steps to identify the level of awareness for the performance requirements within the assessments (see Table 3.4, on page 74).

Theoretical Foundations for CO-OP

CO-OP is a client-centered, performance-based, problem-solving approach that enables skill acquisition, generalization, and transfer of learning through a process of strategy use and guided discovery (Polatajko & Mandich, 2004, 2005). The foundational theories are drawn from behavioral and cognitive psychology, movement science, and occupational therapy. Behavioral theories focus on the relationship between stimulus, response, and consequence, and learning is viewed as a permanent change in the form, duration, or frequency of a behavior. Reinforcement is seen as an integral component of learning. CO-OP uses reinforcement, modeling, shaping, prompting, fading, and chaining techniques to support skill acquisition (Polatajko & Mandich, 2004) and also builds on a cognitive view of learning as an active mental process of acquiring, remembering, and using knowledge. The mental organization of knowledge (problem solving, reasoning, and thinking) plays an important role in the acquisition and performance of skills (Schunk, 2000).

The problem-solving strategy used in CO-OP—"Goal–Plan–Do–Check"—was adopted from Meichenbaum (1977, 1994) as a framework for guiding the discovery of self-generated domain-specific strategies that support skill acquisition. After an individual chooses a goal he or she wants to accomplish or a skill to learn, the clinician guides the client in the use of the Goal–Plan–Do–Check strategy, first to determine where task performance is breaking down, and then to identify the strategies that can be used to overcome the breakdown and perform the task. For example, a 42-year-old man with a right hemiplegia wanted to be able to play cards with his friends again. By attempting to shuffle, he was guided to discover what was not working for him. He figured out that the way he wanted to shuffle required both hands to be equally active, which could not work, so he tried other approaches to shuffling. Using this method, he created an approach that both worked for him *and* was acceptable to him. In his new method he used his weaker hand only to assist in shuffling the cards. Though this is a single task, with it he learned how to set the goal, develop the plan, implement the strategy, and evaluate the strategy (in this case it helped him to accomplish his goal).

CO-OP fosters the learning of skills that support occupational performance. The actual performance of tasks requires motor skills, and this component requires us to consider theories of motor learning. Motor learning is an internal processes that leads to a change in the learner's capacity for skilled motor performance (Rose, 1997). The process of learning a new skill is not observable but can be inferred by observing the individual's motor performance. The learning of a motor skill also requires the individual to interact with the environment in which the task is performed. Dynamic systems theory emphasizes the relationship between the person and the environment (Thelen, Kelso, & Fogel, 1987; Turvey, 1990); behavior is seen as arising from a hierarchical, dynamic interaction of the sensory, motor, perceptual, and anatomical systems (Thelen, 1995). The Fitts and Posner (1967) three-stage model of motor learning provides theoretical support for CO-OP. The *cognitive stage* guides the individual as he or she seeks to understand the task and how to perform it; in the *associative stage* the individual focuses attention and performs with greater speed and precision; and in the *autonomous stage* the skill is performed consistently and in a coordinated pattern. CO-OP is based on a learning paradigm that acknowledges that new skills emerge from an interaction with the environment; the occupational therapist, in turn, creates the learning environment to support optimal learning. In this approach cognition acts as the mediator between the individual's ability and the performance that is the goal of the individual; as such a certain level of cognitive abilities is required to develop the new skills. Such an approach creates a learning paradigm that helps the individual develop skills that can then be used to accomplish multiple tasks that support their daily occupations.

Functional Skill Training

Theoretical Foundations for the Neurofunctional Retraining Approach

The aim of the functional skill training approach is to enhance abilities and participation by providing training in each activity the person with severe cognitive impairment needs to perform and modifying the activity demands and contexts. This approach helps the individual develop habits and routines by retraining him or her in the use of real-world skills with the goal of developing behavioral automaticity and a greater reliance on the environment, including cueing (Giles, 2005). Clients are trained in behavioral routines when there is little expectation of a generalized application of strategies to novel circumstances encountered in the real world. For example, a person might be trained to accomplish a specific morning routine by repeating the sequence of activities over many days until it becomes automatic. Or a person could be trained to walk to the same restaurant on the same route with specific points indicating where to turn, how to look before crossing a street, how to obey street lights, and so on. Once arriving at the restaurant, where there would be familiarity with the staff, the person would be trained in how to use the menu and order a dish. The aim is to help the individual learn how to maintain a schedule that becomes routine, with the same activities done in the same sequence each day.

Neurofunctional retraining considers the person's learning capacity in the design and implementation of programs. Memory, attention, and frontal lobe impairments create problems for individuals that make it difficult for them to achieve independence. Though specific cognitive capacities are not the target of direct interventions, the capacities must be considered in the design of functional skill training. Memory obviously is central to performance because the individual must remember to actually execute the skilled behaviors. By knowing which memory systems are affected, it is possible to improve performance. For example, nondeclarative (procedural) memory supports performance in that it is central to habituation and learning can occur without the client's awareness (Giles, 2005). Attention is necessary to sustain performance of appropriate tasks and to orient the individual to surroundings and safety. Cognitive control is central to the acquisition of new learning (Schneider, Dumais, & Shiffrin, 1984) and to both focus attention and divide it when multitasking is required (Stuss et al., 1989). If individuals have a divided attentional deficit, they may have insufficient attention to do more than one thing at a time; even walking and listening to someone speak to them may cause them to lose their balance (Giles, 2005). Because task performance is influenced by competing demands on attention (Kewman, Yanus, & Kirsch, 1988), a client's ability to sustain and divide attention under varying conditions must be understood.

Impairments in conscious decision-making capacities of the executive function may contribute to increased environmental dependence (Lengfelder & Gollwitzer, 2001). To support daily life it is important to help the person integrate awareness into the interventions.

Deficits in the individual's memory, attention, and executive function create constraints that must be overcome as the occupational therapist addresses the occupational performance needs of the person with brain injury. The neurofunctional approach considers these constraints in the development of treatment programs that train individuals to perform routines and make use of environmental affordances that support their daily life functioning. The behavioral treatment approach used in this model is also in line with an errorless learning training method, wherein errors are prevented as much as possible (Wilson, Baddeley, Evans, & Shiel, 1994; Ylvisaker, Hanks, Johnson-Green, 2003), compared to a trial-and-error learning model wherein errors are corrected. The model uses a range of assessment techniques for initial screening of neurofunction, specifically in the areas of metacognition, attention, memory, and executive functions (see instruments in Tables 3.3 and 3.4, on page 74), however, the primary mode of evaluation is observation in real-life functioning according to the needs of the client.

Theoretical Foundations for the Cognitive Disabilities Model of Rehabilitation in Dementia

Occupational therapists work with individuals and their families who are dealing with the consequences of dementia. The cognitive disabilities model uses an information-processing approach to uncover the patterns of impaired and preserved cognitive functions that impact occupational performance of the individual, in turn impacting the family (Levy & Burns, 2005). The cognitive psychology and occupational therapy frameworks provide the knowledge to inform clinical interventions. Individuals with dementia have limitations in sensoriperceptual memory, thus limiting their longer-term storage of information. Initially the decline in sensoriperceptual memory was thought to be of limited practical significance (Craik & Jennings, 1992; Mendez, Mendez, Martin, Smyth, & Whitehouse, 1990); however, studies have found that an impairment in visual sensory abilities interferes with the perception and storage of visual cues that contribute to visuospatial abilities (Tetewsky & Duffy, 1999). Because the sensoriperceptual memory store represents visual and auditory memory, it is affected by the visual and auditory deficits experienced by older adults, making it necessary to determine if a visual or hearing problem requires accommodation in order to deliver the needed visual or auditory cues.

Working memory is important for the maintenance and manipulation of information. The central role of working memory is to reduce the individual's reliance on automatic actions and to allow for the mental representation of alternatives (Goldberg, 2001). Working memory is critical to numerous functions: conscious attention, concentration, the overriding of automatic reactions when needed, moving from concrete to abstract concepts, understanding language, setting goals, planning, problem solving, decision making, and carrying out meaningful activities. Most everyday tasks, including those involved in leisure/fitness and social activities, are very dependent on working memory. As working memory becomes progressively limited, well-established long-term memories may be activated from internally generated thought processes or those cued by stimuli in the environment. These long-term memories, which can be language-based, visuospatial, visuoperceptual, and/or procedural, deteriorate in a reversed ontogenetic order (Levy, 1974, 1986; Reisberg, Franssen, Souren, Auer, & Kenowsky, 1998; Reisberg, Kenowsky, Franssen, Auer, & Souren, 1999; Reisberg et al., 2002). Old memories may be recalled but more recent memories may remain inaccessible (Haist, Gore, & Mao, 2001; Lopez, 2000). These principles of retrogenesis (Reisberg et al., 1998, 1999, 2002) echo theoretical work developed in the original cognitive disabilities model literature (Allen, 1985; Allen et al., 1992; Levy, 1974, 1986; Levy & Burns, 2005).

The hippocampus, a primary site for new memories, is the first site of deterioration in Alzheimer's disease. Because there is an inability to store new memories, the individual experiences each event as a new one, causing family members great difficulty; he or she cannot report any recent experience, including whether they have gone to the bathroom or what they have just eaten. The progression of the disease to areas responsible for spatial orientation, recognition of objects, and body information causes even more limitations in the performance of daily life activities. The areas that seem to be somewhat spared are the cerebellum and basal ganglia, which are the sites of procedural and other implicit-type memories. Interventions are required to help individuals maintain routines—those tasks and activities they have consistently performed over long periods of time (Averbuch & Katz, 2005; Baum & Edwards, 1993; Baum, Edwards, & Morrow-Howell, 1993; Camp, Foss, O'Hanlon, & Stevens, 1996). Indeed, there is growing evidence that even severely impaired people with Alzheimer's disease can learn and retain procedural tasks for at least 1 month (Camp et al., 1996; Dick et al., 1996). When procedural memories are cued (activated) under constant practice conditions, procedural skills can be retrieved by reactivating the relevant synapses in the brain. The act of retrieval appears to have a mnemonic effect. This learning is task and situation specific, and generalization is limited (Levy & Burns, 2005); however, it does offer a strategy to capitalize on for training.

Recall deficits occur earlier in the disease than recognition deficits because recall is a demanding working memory task. Memories remain inactive until a cue acts as a reminder and causes them to be activated and retrieved. The cognitive disabilities model employs environmental cues to compensate for the decline in working and explicit memory. It capitalizes on procedural (implicit) and cued recognition capacities (episodic and semantic), using what remains to retrieve information; such a strategy enables individuals to optimize their occupational performance using the capacities that remain (Levy & Burns, 2005). It also provides strategies for the family to use to maximize their loved one's potential to successfully interact with others.

The cognitive disabilities model was originally developed by Allen for patients suffering from long-term psychiatric disabilities, then further extended to use with the dementia population and their caregivers. It provides a hierarchy of six cognitive functional levels to analyze and understand the client's level of performance. Its measurement approach emphasizes the assessment of cognitive functional abilities in daily task performance (see Tables 3.2, on page 71, and 3.3, on page 74) and a corresponding activity analysis. Levy and Burns (2005) use the same hierarchy to explain the information processing and occupational behavior that occur at each level.

The evolving exploration of brain and behavior has provided knowledge for occupational therapists to apply in working with clients who have developmental, acquired, or chronic debilitating cognitive conditions. The next step in our efforts to support and expand cognitive rehabilitation is to link brain function, behavior, and performance/participation in daily life to more accurately evaluate the effectiveness of intervention strategies. Individuals' real-world performance can then inform our knowledge of the function and structure of the brain.

Evaluation Process for Individuals with Suspected Cognitive Disabilities

The purpose of occupational therapy intervention for individuals with suspected cognitive disabilities is to minimize their limitations and enhance their participation in everyday activities (Toglia, 2003). The knowledge base underlying occupational therapy cognitive models comes from recent cognitive/neuroscience developments of rehabilitation theories and techniques that target the underlying mechanisms of the deficits; and psychosociobiological and holistic approaches that examine the relations between occupational performance and participation in the community and define intervention outcomes.

The practitioner must begin intervention by collecting information. One system for this process, the Cognitive Functional Evaluation (CFE; Hartman-Maeir, Katz, & Baum, 2009), provides the following: (1) a description of cognitive strengths and weaknesses (lower- and higher-level cognitive functions) and their impact/implications on occupational performance; (2) a recommendation concerning the type and amount of assistance required for safe and meaningful occupational performance; and (3) clinical reasoning to guide the practitioner in selecting the treatment method (e.g., considering the severity of deficits, learning ability, degree of awareness, variation in skills, environmental conditions, occupational goals) that will be employed and in providing the family with the knowledge and skills to support successful interactions with their loved one.

Stages in the Development of a CFE

The development of a CFE proceeds through the following stages:

1. Interview and background information, including an occupational history.
2. Cognitive screening and baseline status tests.
3. Measures of cognition in task performance.
4. In-depth testing of specific cognitive domains: laboratory-like tests.
5. In-depth assessment of performance in functional activities.
6. Evaluation of environmental/contextual factors.

Interview and Background Information

In persons with suspected cognitive deficits, it cannot be assumed that they have a realistic view of their condition; therefore the first step is to determine their level of awareness. There are different methods to evaluate awareness, including the use of interviews with questionnaires, comparison between the answers of the individual and a proxy (e.g., relative, other caregiver, therapist), comparison to test performance, and prediction before and evaluation after task performance (Katz & Hartman-Maeir, 2005; Katz, Hartman-Maeir, Ring, & Soroker, 2000; Prigatano, 1986; Toglia, 1993, 2005). We recommend the *Self-Awareness of Deficits Interview* (SADI; Fleming, Strong, & Ashton, 1996) at this first stage. Following evaluation of the person's self-awareness, information about occupational history and activities performed in daily functioning is obtained to determine his or her interests and experience with activities that can be used to build daily routines. This information is obtained with an *Occupational Questionnaire* (Smith, Kielhofner, & Watts, 1986) that lists activities during a typical 24-hour day, and the *Activity Card Sort* (ACS) for adults (Baum, 1995; Baum & Edwards, 2001, 2008; Katz, Karpin, Lak, Fuman, & Harman-Maeir, 2003; Sachs & Josman, 2003) or the *Pediatric Activity Card Sort* for children (Mandich, Polatajko, Miller, & Baum, 2004). To complete the initial interview the *Canadian Occupational Performance Measure* (COPM; Law et al., 1998) is administered to gain understanding of the client's occupational goals and the tasks of his or her choice (see Table 3.1).

TABLE 3.1. Components of the Initial Interview

- Self-Awareness of Deficits Interview (SADI; Fleming et al., 1996)
- Brief occupational history; Occupational Questionnaire, 24 hours of a typical day (Smith et al., 1986), *www.moho.uic.edu*; Model of Human Occupation clearinghouse-related resources
- Activity Card Sort (ACS; Baum 1995; Baum & Edwards, 2001, 2008)
- Canadian Occupational Performance Measure (COPM; Law et al., 1998)

Cognitive Screening and Baseline Status Tests

In order to acquire a basic knowledge of the cognitive abilities and deficits of the client, the occupational therapist administers the appropriate tests depending on the client's age, diagnosis, stage of illness, setting, and so on. The instruments listed in Table 3.2 are standardized, and their psychometric properties were established with various populations.

The *Mini-Mental State Examination* (MMSE; Folstein & Folstein, 1975) and the *Short Blessed Test* (Katzman et al., 1983) are used extensively as screening tools for dementia, and *clock drawing* tests are used in a variety of ways to assess visual–spatial deficits, spatial organization, memory, and executive functions (Freedman et al., 1994; Royall, Cordes, & Polk, 1998).

The *Allen Cognitive Level Screen–5* (ACLS-5) and the *Large ACLS-5* (LACLS-5) are short screening tests using a leather lacing task with three different stitches graded in difficulty from one step at a time to two steps and error corrections. A cognitive function score between 3 and 6 is provided, as is a more refined score ranging from 3.0 to 5.8. Extensive research to support the reliability and validity has been done with this instrument (Allen et al., 1992, 2007).

The *Cognistat* (Mueller, Kierman, & Langston, 2007) was developed by neurologists for bedside testing and also has a profile format that includes attention, language (naming, comprehension), calculations, and reasoning (similarities and judgment). It is used extensively by occupational therapists. Studies in a variety of client populations in which brain dysfunction is suspected show that the Cognistat is sensitive in detecting cognitive impairments, differentiating between groups, as

TABLE 3.2. Cognitive Screening and Baseline Status Tests

- Mini-Mental State Evaluation (MMSE; Folstein & Folstein, 1975)
- Short Blessed test (Katzman et al., 1983)
- Clock Drawing Test (Freedman et al., 1994; Royall et al., 1998)
- Allen Cognitive Levels–5 (ACLS-5; Allen et al., 2007; *www.allen-cognitive-network.org*)
- Cognistat (Mueller et al., 2007; *www.cognistat.com*)
- Loewenstein Occupational Therapy Cognitive Assessment (LOTCA; Izkovich et al., 2000; *www.maddak.org*)
  Loewenstein Occupational Therapy Cognitive Assessment—Geriatric (LOTCA-G; Elazar et al., 1996; *www.maddak.org*)
- Dynamic Occupational Therapy Cognitive Assessment for Children (DOTCA-Ch; Katz, Parush, et al., 2005; *www.maddak.org*)

well as measuring changes over time (Katz, Elazar, & Itzkovich, 1996; Katz, Hartman-Maeir, Weiss, & Armon, 1997; Lezak et al., 2004; Logue, Tupler, D'amico, & Schmitt, 1993; Osmon, Smet, Winegarden, & Gandhavadi, 1992). It was also found that the instrument is among the 20 most frequently used to evaluate cognitive baseline (Rabin, Barr, & Burton, 2005).

The *Loewenstein Occupational Therapy Cognitive Assessment* (LOTCA), *LOTCA Geriatric Version* (LOTCA-G), and the *Dynamic Occupational Therapy Cognitive Assessment for Children* (DOTCA-Ch) are standardized instruments that have been studied in various populations (Elazar, Itzkovich, & Katz, 1996; Itzkovich, Averbuch, Elazar, & Katz, 2000; Katz, Parush, & Traub Bar-Ilan, 2005). They were developed by occupational therapists to assess cognitive skills that underlie everyday functioning in the areas of orientation, visual and spatial perception, praxis, visuomotor construction, thinking operations and memory; all together, 25 subtests in 5 areas. Both adult and elderly versions were studied extensively, and reliability as well as validity were determined in various populations (healthy adults and elderly patients following stroke and traumatic brain injuries [TBI]) and countries (Averbuch & Katz, 2005; Bar-Haim Erez & Katz, 2003; Cermak et al., 1995; Katz, Itzkovich, Averbuch, & Elazar, 1989; Katz, Kizony, & Parush, 2002). The DOTCA for children has data on typical children ages 6–12 years as well as data differentiating significantly between typical children and children with learning disabilities and TBI (Katz, Goldstand, Traub Bar-Ilan, & Parush, 2007; Ziviani et al., 2004). The aim of these assessments is to identify the cognitive skills necessary for occupational performance. As such, the specific deficit areas clarify clients' difficulties in task performance and point to particular strategies that can be incorporated into treatment planning.

At this stage of the process the occupational therapist should have a good idea about the clients' level of self-awareness, their previous and current occupational performance and participation, as well as their cognitive strengths and limitations. Although screening tools may have reduced sensitivity to subtle impairments, when paired with performance-based assessment, they do give a clinical indication of problems that require attention if the person is having difficulty performing tasks.

Measures of Cognition in Task Performance

Six instruments are included as examples in this category. Two standardized tests stem from the cognitive disabilities model (Allen et al., 1992): the *Cognitive Performance Test* (CPT) and the *Routine Task Inventory—Extended* (RTI-E). They include a battery of activities of daily living (ADLs) and instrumental activities of daily living (IADLs) (the CPT), including six tasks of medication use, shopping, preparing toast, using the phone, choosing appropriate dressing for an outing, and travel (Bar-Yosef, Weinblatt, & Katz, 1999; Burns, 2006; Levy & Burns, 2005). As well as a rating scale based on observations of everyday functioning that include 30 tasks in 4 areas—ADLs, IADLs, communication, and work readiness, the RTI-E includes descriptions of 6 levels for each task, and the rater chooses the level that best describes the current performance (Allen, 1989; Katz, 2006). The RTI-E can be conducted by the caregiver, the therapist, or the individuals themselves if they are able. The CPT and RTI-E follow the hierarchy of cognitive levels developed by Allen. The reliability and validity of these two tests have been extensively researched in psychiatric and dementia populations (Allen et al., 1992; Allen & Blue, 1998; Katz, 2006; Levy & Burns, 2005).

The *Kitchen Task Assessment* (KTA; Baum & Edwards, 1993) is a standardized performance-based assessment of cognition and executive function. The investigator records the level of support needed to perform a simple cooking task (making pudding). Support levels include verbal cueing, need for physical assistance, or an indication that the person is not capable of performing the task. The individual is scored on his or her ability to initiate the task, execute the task (including organization, sequencing, judgment, and safety), and complete the task. The KTA serves three purposes: to determine which executive functions are causing performance problems (initiation, organization, sequencing, judgment, and/or completion); to determine an individual's capacity for independent functioning; and to determine the level of assistance needed to complete the task (Baum & Edwards, 1993). Caregivers can then adjust the level of support they provide accordingly.

The *Kettle Test* (Hartman-Maeir, Armon, & Katz, 2005) is a brief performance-based test that involves a task of assembling an electric tea kettle and preparing two different hot beverages. Following completion of the task, the therapist engages the client in a debriefing that focuses on the client's evaluation of the performance. Task selection is designed to require basic cognitive abilities such as attention, perception, praxis, and memory, as well as requiring higher-order executive functions by providing unusual, novel, and complex conditions (the kettle is empty and disconnected; target ingredients are situated within distracters). Initial results with an older adult group ($N = 41$) showed significant (moderate to high) correlations with ADL and IADL measures as well as with tests of cognition. More recently Hartman-Maeir, Harel, and Katz (in press) found high interrater reliability between two sets of raters of 20 clients in stroke rehabilitation. Stroke survivors ($N = 36$) at discharge from rehabilitation were found to require significantly more assistance on the Kettle Test than matched controls, and their scores on the Kettle Test were moderately but significantly correlated with conventional cognitive and functional outcome measures.

The *Observed Tasks of Daily Living—Revised* (OTDL-R) is a performance-based test that requires problem solving in IADL tasks (Diehl et al., 2005). It includes nine tasks in three areas: medication use, telephone use and financial management. The test discriminates between groups with cognitive impairments and those that are healthy. Categorization and deductive reasoning measures predict performance on the OTDL-R (Goverover & Hinojosa, 2002; Goverover & Josman, 2004).

The *Assessment of Motor and Process Scale* (AMPS; Fisher, 2006a, 2006b) is based on the model of human occupation (Kielhofner, 2002) and was developed to assess the subsystem supporting an individual's performance. In the context of this chapter the Process scale of the instrument is of interest as it measures integrated cognitive functions. The instrument includes a list of about 50 ADLs, mostly IADL tasks, from which the client and therapist choose two to three tasks that are familiar to the person and then the therapist observes as the person performs them. Such items may be making a sandwich, washing dishes, or paying a bill. The scoring yields both a motor and a process score and also identifies four levels of independence. The instrument was developed using a Rasch model (an item-response model that transfers the total score to a linear score to create a value that can be used in analysis more readily than the raw total score, which has floor and ceiling effects) and applied to

TABLE 3.3. Measures of Cognition in Task Performance

- Routine Task Inventory (RTI-E; Allen, 1989; *www.allen-cognitive-network.org*; Katz, 2006)
- Cognitive Performance Test (CPT; Burns, 2002, 2006)
- Kitchen Task Assessment (KTA; Baum & Edwards, 1993)
- Kettle Test (Hartman-Maeir et al., 2005, in press)
- Revised Observed Tasks of Daily Living (OTDL-R; Diehl et al., 2005)
- Assessment of Motor and Process Scale (AMPS; Fisher, 2006a, 2006b)

large and diverse populations (Fisher, 1993, 2006a, 2006b; Fisher, Liu, Velozo, & Pan, 1992; Kizony & Katz, 2002).

In general, after the third stage of the evaluation process it is determined if more in-depth cognitive testing is necessary. When severe deficits are detected in the screening/baseline process, the cognitive testing can be stopped, unless specific deficits such as unilateral spatial neglect, attention, memory, or executive functions require further testing to guide interventions (see Table 3.3).

In-Depth Testing of Specific Cognitive Domains

Under laboratory-like tests occupational therapists use those tests that were developed with the idea of simulating behavioral components of performance. The test batteries listed in Table 3.4—the *Behavioral Inattention Test* (BIT), *Test of Everyday Attention* (TEA), *Rivermead Behavioural Memory Test* (RBMT), and the *Behavioural Assessment of Dysexecutive Syndrome* (BADS)—all target specific domains in a variety of ways to assess the extent of the difficulties a client has in spatial neglect, attention, memory, and/or executive functions. Data from these tests enable therapists to form a more in-depth understanding of the problem a client has in performing daily routine tasks as well as complicated and novel occupations that may require multitasking abilities (Robertson, Ward, Ridgeway, & Nimmo-Smith, 1994; Wilson, Alderman, Burgess, Emslie, & Evans, 1996; Wilson, Cockburn, & Baddeley, 1985; Wilson, Evans, Emslie, Alderman, & Burgess, 1998). All four instruments are standardized and have been studied extensively with various populations.

Attention and visuospatial neglect can also be tested by a new computerized program, the *Visual Spatial Search Task* (VISSTA; Bar-Haim Erez, Kizony, Shahar, &

TABLE 3.4. Cognitive Tests for Specific Domains

- Behavioral Inattention Test (BIT; Wilson et al., 1987)
- Visual Spatial Search Task (VISSTA; Bar-Haim Erez et al., 2006)
- Test of Everyday Attention (TEA; Robertson et al., 1994)
- Rivermead Behavioural Memory Test (RBMT; Wilson et al., 1986)
- Behavioral Assessment of the Dysexecutive Syndrome (BADS; Wilson et al., 1996)
- Contextual Memory Test (Toglia, 1993)
  Toglia Categorization Test (Toglia, 1994)
  Both tests: Awareness of performance assessed pre- and posttesting.

Katz, 2006), which was developed to enable precise measure of success rate and reaction time in a random and graded search task. The VISSTA shows significant construct validity in differentiating between groups of stroke patients and controls and good test–retest reliability with standards for different age groups (Bar-Haim Erez, Katz, Ring, & Soroker, 2009). The program has different modules and is intended for training as well as assessment.

Two additional instruments listed in this category are the *Contextual Memory Test* (CMT) and the *Toglia Categorization Assessment* (TCA) with Deductive Reasoning (DR); they were developed by Toglia in line with the dynamic model described above. The unique feature of these two tests is the dynamic component, whereby a graded cueing system provides a current level of ability in memory or categorization, as well as a level of ability when mediation is provided, namely, the potential ability. The discrepancy between the two scores, termed by Vygotsky (1978) the "zone of proximal development," is the basis for much of the dynamic testing approach (Feuerstein, 1979; Grigorenko, & Sternberg, 1998; Sternberg & Grigorenko, 2002). In addition, these tests include an online evaluation of emergent awareness that enables the therapist to see whether clients' level of awareness changed while they performed a task (Toglia & Kirk, 2000). Both tests were developed for clients with TBIs but were further studied in clients with schizophrenia as well as children with TBI and attention-deficit/hyperactivity disorder (ADHD) (Goverover & Hinojosa, 2004; Josman, 2005; Josman, Berney, & Jarus, 2000a, 2000b).

If further cognitive testing is required, particularly for mild cases, or when functional problems are reported but no deficits were found on initial measures, referral for extensive neuropsychological assessment is recommended and further exploration of the impact of the deficit on daily life must be determined. The tests described below may be useful in these cases.

Specific Cognitive Measures of Daily Functions

At this point the specific cognitive area of deficit in daily functions has to be observed and measured in daily functions. The *ADL Checklist for Neglect* (Hartman-Maeir & Katz, 1995) and the *Catherina Bergego Scale* (Azouvi et al., 2003) both measure deficits in activities such as grooming, dressing, and eating, as well as reading, writing, and mobility. Namely, does the client neglect the left or right side of his or her personal or extrapersonal space without the knowledge that it occurs? This phenomenon is one of the most detrimental to rehabilitation of clients following stroke (Heilman, Watson, & Valenstein, 2003; Katz, Hartman-Maeir, Ring, & Soroker, 1999).

Executive functions have been tested traditionally with neuropsychological measures such as the Wisconsin Card Sorting Test (WCST), Tower of London Test, and so on. However, it is now acknowledged by many researchers that to fully identify executive function deficits, tests in complicated, novel situations that require multitasking in daily activities should be conducted (Burgess et al., 2006; Katz & Hartman-Maeir, 2005; Stuss & Alexander, 2000) (see Table 3.5 on the next page). The *Executive Function Performance Test* (EFPT) was developed based on the KTA previously described (Baum, Morrison, Hahn, & Edwards, 2007; Baum et al., 2008) to record executive functions in the performance of a task. The EFPT includes four standardized IADL tasks (cooking, telephone use, medication management, and money management).

TABLE 3.5. Cognitive Measures in Daily Functions for Specific Domains

- Unilateral Neglect in ADL (Hartman-Maeir & Katz, 1995) or Catherina Bergero Scale (Azouvi et al., 2003)
- Executive Function Performance Test (EFPT; Baum et al., 2007)
- Multiple Errands Test (MET) hospital and simplified versions (Alderman et al., 2003; Knight et al., 2002)
- Pro-Ex Profile of Executive Control System (Braswell et al., 1993)
- Prigatano Competency Rating Scale (PCRS; Prigatano, 1986)
- Assessment of Awareness of Disabilities (AAD; Kottorp & Tham, 2005; Tham et al., 1999)

The therapist provides graded cues and determines a score for components of initiation, planning, execution of the task with error detection and correction, safety and judgment, and task completion. The EFPT has been validated in studies with older adults, with individuals with stroke, and with clients with schizophrenia (Baum et al., 2008; Katz, Felzen, Tadmor, & Hartman-Maeir, 2007).

The *Multiple Errands Test* (MET) by Shallice and Burgess (1991) was further adapted and studied with clients with TBI (Alderman et al., 2003; Knight, Alderman, & Burgess, 2002) and those following stroke (Dawson et al., 2005; Rand, Weiss, & Katz, in press) and provides a more complicated multiple subgoal task performed in a shopping district. As Burgess and colleagues (2006) emphasize, the only accurate way to determine executive function abilities is to study them in natural environments with as much similarity as possible to the daily requirements of standards of performance in social community settings.

In addition to the above performance measures the *Pro-Ex* (Braswell et al., 1993) is a 7-point rating scale that the therapist scores in the areas of initiation, planning, goal management, and awareness based on observations, interview with caregiver, or functional testing in daily occupational performance.

Finally, evaluation of self-awareness in daily activities is needed to understand how much clients can and may be willing to cooperate in their rehabilitation process, based on their level of awareness/unawareness. The *Prigatano Competency Rating Scale* (PCRS) questionnaire (Prigatano, 1986) is comprised of 30 daily activities or social encounters that the client and a proxy (e.g., relative, therapist) complete. The discrepancy between the two scores indicates overestimation (client rates self higher than the proxy) and suggests that the client is unaware of his or her daily performance and social behavior. The instrument was studied extensively and found to be reliable and valid (Hoofien & Sharoni, 2006; Katz, Fleming, Keren, Lightbody, & Hartman-Maeir, 2002; Prigatano, 1999, 2005; Prigatano, Borgaro, Baker, & Wethe, 2005).

The *Assessment of Awareness of Disabilities* (AAD; Kottorp & Tham, 2005; Tham, Bersnpang, & Fisher, 1999; Tham, Ginsburg, Fisher, & Tenger, 2001) is a guided interview with seven questions that measures the discrepancy between the client's observed ADL ability on the AMPS and his or her perceived ability. Preliminary Rasch analysis suggests acceptable validity and affirms that the instrument measures one construct of awareness of disability. The AAD has demonstrated acceptable reliability (between raters and over time), internal consistency, and sensitivity to change (Tham et al., 1999, 2001).

Evaluation of Environmental/Contextual Factors

Occupational therapists understand that an individual's abilities can be optimized by environments that support their ability to use their skills. Thus they closely consider the immediate natural environment of the person, especially the physical and human environment, focusing on resources and potential barriers to clients' successful performance. For example, what are their living conditions? Are they safe? Do they live alone? Who can be "recruited" for assistance (family, friends, etc.).

Many practitioners visit the client's home to determine the safety of the physical environment. The environment must be assessed for people with cognitive loss to determine if they have the capacity to live alone safely. Three assessments that focus on home safety are discussed here: the *Home Occupational Environmental Assessment* (HOEA; Baum & Edwards, 1998), the *Safety Assessment of Function and the Environment for Rehabilitation* (SAFER tool; Chui et al., 2006), and the *Home Environmental Assessment Protocol* (HEAP; Gitlin et al., 2002, in Asher, 2007) (see Table 3.6).

The HOEA is a checklist designed to identify how the home environment supports occupational performance and the safety of the person being assessed. It is particularly useful for clients with visual and cognitive impairments. It is completed by a therapist while in the client's home and requires approximately 20 minutes. The HOEA checklist covers issues such as accessibility within the home, sanitation, food storage, safety issues, and lighting at the point of common tasks. The scoring indicates the independence of the person.

The SAFER tool was designed to help therapists assess the client's ability to safely carry out functional activities at home. It can be used with adults who have cognitive impairments, mental health problems, physical disabilities, and/or complex needs. It includes 97 items in 14 areas of concern, including mobility, kitchen use, fire hazards, wandering, and communication. Level of safety risk is rated on a 4-point scale, with higher scores indicating severer environmental problems. Internal consistency reliability and initial support for validity are reported (Asher, 2007). Most clinicians report that the SAFER tool is valuable because it provides a comprehensive assessment of safe functioning at home and useful ideas for environmental interventions.

The HEAP is comprised of a caregiver interview and direct observation designed to assess the home environment of individuals with dementia and provide recommendations for home modifications. It includes 192 items in 8 areas of the house, such as bedroom, kitchen, and bathroom, which are scored for presence/absence of safety hazards, adaptations, visual cues, and comfort. High interrater agreement was found, and preliminary studies support content and convergent validity (Gitlin et al., 2002).

TABLE 3.6. Environmental Assessments

- Home Occupational Environmental Assessment (HOEA; Baum & Edwards, 1998)
- Safety Assessment of Function and the Environment for Rehabilitation (SAFER; Chui et al., 2006).
- Home Environmental Assessment Protocol (HEAP; Asher, 2007; Gitlin et al., 2002)

Summary

An important skill in the training of occupational therapists is the capacity to do activity/occupational analysis. A task is evaluated for its cognitive, motor, sensory, psychological, and physiological demands. Occupational therapists are knowledgeable in the analysis of routine activities, taking into account the typical way the activity is performed, with special attention to cultural differences in the performance of tasks (Pierce, 2001). Utensil use is just one example, with some cultures eating with their hands, others with the fork in the right and knife in the left hand. There are many differences in how self-care, work, and community activities are valued and placed into routines. In all cases the occupational therapist lets the client define the goals that will be the basis of treatment.

Few systems of analysis have been developed in occupational therapy that focus on the cognitive demands of desired/target occupations. The most established one is the activity analysis within the cognitive disabilities model developed by Allen (1985), which corresponds to the hierarchy of cognitive levels (Allen et al., 1992). Levy and Burns (2005) extended the analysis using the dimensions of attentional processes, working memory processes, and occupational behavioral responses at each of the six cognitive levels, with rehabilitation potential predicted from this analysis. In the multicontext treatment approach (Toglia, 2003, 2005), a system of subgoaling, according to areas of concern, is developed that outlines strengths within skill areas, subskills, and strategies that need to be strengthened, first using simulated tasks agreed upon with the client. Thus activities are chosen with the client and awareness strategies, techniques, and processing strategies are learned to accomplish desired performance of the activities (Toglia, 2005).

Occupational therapists use the person's capacities and the affordances offered by the environment to foster his or her occupational performance. These professionals work with people in hospitals, rehabilitation hospitals, in the home, and in the work environment to help people gain the skills that will support their recovery and learn strategies to manage any residual cognitive impairments. The Cognitive Functional Evaluation (CFE) provides a description of cognitive strengths and weaknesses and their implications for occupational performance. It further provides recommendations concerning the type and amount of assistance currently required for safe and meaningful occupational performance, and it provides the basis for clinical reasoning in selecting a cognitive model for intervention and a treatment approach. The factors that enter into the decision-making process follow the three perspectives of a PEO model:

- *Person*: severity of cognitive deficits and variance of cognitive profile (areas of strengths and deficits), learning potential (declarative and procedural memory capacities), awareness of deficits and disabilities, psychological factors, disease/injury variables (time postonset, severity, progressive, etc.)
- *Environment*: safety of the environment; human, physical, economical, and/or cultural resources or barriers to rehabilitation
- *Occupation*: previous and current activities that can be used in the intervention to sustain and support independence, health, sense of self and identity, social interaction, and meaningful activities.

Recent Intervention Studies by Occupational Therapists

Intervention studies are essential to provide evidence-based practice and constitute a future direction for the field of occupational therapy. Recent controlled group intervention studies have been conducted to investigate the effectiveness of a range of intervention methods, with different populations and at different stages of disabilities, that focus on cognitive domains and aim to increase participation in daily life. Several studies are summarized to highlight the strategies that are being employed.

Bar-Haim Erez (2006) studied the effectiveness of phasic alerting (PA) treatment (Robertson, Mattingley, Rorden, & Driver, 1998) combined with visuospatial search training (using the VISSTA program; Bar-Haim Erez et al., 2009) for patients with right-hemisphere strokes and unilateral spatial neglect (USN) at the postacute stage. Eighteen patients were randomly assigned to three groups (experimental—PA + spatial training; only spatial training; no spatial training). All patients were tested with an extensive assessment battery (including paper-and-pencil and functional tests) at three points in time (pre-, posttreatment at 2–3 weeks following 10 sessions, and follow-up after 5 additional weeks). Results show a significant advantage of the experimental group receiving PA treatment with spatial search task. On average the experimental group showed a recovery trend of significant improvement immediately posttreatment that was maintained at the follow-up stage. The other two groups improved to a lesser degree, and this improvement was detected mostly at the follow-up stage after an additional 5 weeks, not immediately after the treatment stage. The relative improvement of the experimental group was apparent in USN measures as well as in functional measures such as the ADL checklist (Azouvi et al., 2003), room description (Frassinneti, Angeli, Meneghello, Avanzi, & Ladavas, 2002) and general daily functions (Functional Independence Measure [FIM]; Granger, 1993). The findings suggest that the use of alerting methods combined with visuospatial training in the acute stage poststroke is beneficial and has effects on USN itself as well as functional implications.

Katz, Ring, and colleagues (2005) aimed to determine whether nonimmersive interactive virtual environments are an effective medium for training individuals who suffer from USN as a result of a right-hemisphere stroke, and to compare it to a standard computer visual scanning training method within a rehabilitation program. Participants included 19 patients with right-hemisphere stroke randomly assigned to two groups: 11 in an experimental group were given computer desktop-based virtual reality (VR) street-crossing training, and 8 in a control group were given computer-based visual scanning tasks, both for a total of 12 sessions, 9 hours total, over 4 weeks. Measures included USN assessments, paper-and-pencil tests, and an ADL checklist; a test on the VR street program; and actual street crossing videotaped. Testing was performed pre- and postintervention. Results showed that, on the USN measures, the VR group achieved results that equaled those achieved by the control group treated with conventional visual scanning tasks. However, the VR group improved more on the VR test and did better on some measures of the real street crossing. Despite some inequality in the group assignment, the findings support the effectiveness of the VR street program in the treatment of stroke patients with USN, and suggest further development of VR programs with ecological significance (Weiss, Kizony, Fientuch, & Katz, 2006).

Rand, Abu-Rukun, Weiss, and Katz (2009) studied the validity of an intervention using VR of a supermarket (VMall) as an assessment tool for executive functions, followed by the study of its effectiveness with postacute stroke survivors for improving their shopping in a real mall. An additional question of the study related to whether the intervention would improve executive functioning (Rand et al., 2009). Seven stroke survivors living at home 5–27 months postevent participated in the study. A series of single-subject studies using an A-B-A design was conducted. Intervention included 10 sessions over 3 weeks, and testing took place at four points in time (baseline, pre- and postintervention, and 2-week follow-up). Patients were assessed with executive function measures, including the Zoo Map from the BADS (Wilson, Alderman, Burgess, Emslie, & Evans, 1996) and the MET (Knight et al., 2002) as well as a virtual version of the MET, the VMET. The VMET was performed in a virtual large supermarket VMall programmed as an application within GestureTek's Gesture Xtreme (GX) video-capture VR system (Rand, Katz, Shahar, Kizony, & Weiss, 2005; Weiss, Rand, Katz, & Kizony, 2004). Participants see their performance on the screen, thus receiving immediate feedback while manipulating the environment with the upper extremity. The performance of the shopping task provides multiple opportunities to make decisions, plan strategies, and multitask. Results show that the number of mistakes made while performing the MET in both the real shopping mall and the VMall decreased following the intervention. Percent improvement on all MET measures was substantial (26–50%). All patients returned to shopping in a real supermarket on their own or with caregivers and expressed high satisfaction and enjoyment from the intervention. Findings suggest that executive functions as well as IADL performance can be improved using VR intervention (Rand et al., in press).

In another study that focused on executive function deficits, Keren (2006) studied the effectiveness of the goal management treatment (GMT) method (Levine et al., 2000) developed as an occupational goal intervention (OGI) with a population of clients with schizophrenia. The OGI uses a five-stage process (*stop, define, list, learn, check*) in a variety of graded individualized occupational tasks (Keren & Katz, 2005). Eighteen subjects—six in each of three groups—comprising two experimental groups (OGI and frontal-executive program [FEP]; Delahunty & Morice, 1996) and a control group participated. Evaluations included measures of executive functions (BADS, EFPT), cognition in task performance (RTI-E), and participation (Activity Card Sort [ACS], Return to Normal Living [RNL]). Clients were assessed at three points, pre- (T0), posttreatment (T1; treatment lasted 6 weeks and included 18 one-hour sessions), and at 6-month follow-up (T2). Results show that participants in the study groups (OGI and FEP) improved significantly in executive function measures at T1 in comparison to the control group. A significant improvement was found in the OGI group on most measures of activity and participation outcomes at T1, whereas less significant improvements were found in the other groups. The majority of the participants' achievements were maintained when tested at T2. The results support the effectiveness of the OGI for patients with schizophrenia in improving both executive functioning and daily activities and participation. However, further studies are needed to validate the findings.

Finally, Hartman-Maeir, Eliad, and colleagues (2007) studied the effectiveness of a community intervention program for functional status, leisure activity, and satisfaction of adult first-stroke survivors, and compared these outcomes with those of stroke survivors not attending any program (Hartman-Maeir, Soroker, Ring, Avni, & Katz, 2007). Participants were living at home at least 1 year post onset. Twenty-seven were participants in a community rehabilitation program and 56 were nonparticipants. Outcome measures included the Stroke Impact Scale (SIS; Duncan et al., 1999), FIM, IADL, activity card sort, and the Life-Satisfaction–9 questionnaire (Li-Sat-9; Fugl-Meyer, Branholm, & Fugl-Meyer, 1991). Results revealed severe stroke impact and low functioning in ADLs/IADLs in the participant group, but the level of participation in leisure activities improved significantly after attending the program. The comparison with the nonparticipant group revealed that participants were significantly more disabled in ADLs/IADLs than nonparticipants (this outcome was expected because some of the participants were in a chronic state and still needed rehabilitation). Despite their disability status, the satisfaction rates of participants were significantly higher than nonparticipants from "life as a whole" and from their leisure situation. Findings suggest that stroke survivors participating in a community-based rehabilitation program did not show an advantage in terms of disability levels over nonparticipants. However, their activity level increased, presumably due to the program, and their satisfaction scores were higher than those of nonparticipants.

In summary, the issues faced by individuals with neurological dysfunctions demand interdisciplinary work to link brain function with behavior, performance, and everyday life. The science is evolving to inform interventions. The next step is to continue to determine the effectiveness of interventions and to disseminate the strategies to clinicians who work with people with neurological dysfunctions and to families who are central to supporting the recovery and adaptation process.

References

Alderman, N., Burgess, P. W., Knight, C., & Henman, C. (2003). Ecological validity of a simplified version of the multiple errands shopping test. *J Int Neuropsych Soc, 9,* 31–44.

Allen, C. K. (1985). *Occupational therapy for psychiatric diseases: Measurement and management of cognitive disabilities.* Boston: Little, Brown.

Allen, C. K. (1989). Treatment plans in cognitive rehabilitation. *Occup Ther Pract, 1,* 1–8.

Allen, C. K., Austin, S., Davis, S., Earhart, C., MaCearth, D., & Riska-Williams, L. (2007). *Allen Cognitive Level Screen (ACLS-5) and LACLS-5.* Camarillo, CA: ACLS and LACS Committee.

Allen, C. K., & Blue, T. (1998). Cognitive disabilities model. In N. Katz (Ed.), *Cognition and occupation in rehabilitation: Models for intervention in occupational therapy* (pp. 225–280). Bethesda, MD: American Occupational Therapy Association.

Allen, C. K., Earhart, C. A. & Blue, T. (1992). *Occupational therapy treatment goals for the physically and cognitively disabled.* Rockville, MD: American Occupational Therapy Association.

Asher, I. E. (2007). *Occupational therapy assessment tools* (3rd ed.). Bethesda, MD: American Occupational Therapy Association.

Averbuch, S., & Katz, N. (2005). A retraining model for clients following brain injuries. In N. Katz (Ed.), *Cognition and occupation across the life span: Models for intervention in occupational therapy* (pp. 113–138). Bethesda, MD: American Occupational Therapy Association.

Azouvi, P., Olivier, S., Montety, G., Samuel, C., Louise-Dreyfus, A., & Luigi, T. (2003). Behavioral assessment of unilateral neglect: Study of the psychometric properties of the Catherine Bergego Scale. *Arch Phys Med Rehab, 84*, 51–57.

Bar-Haim Erez, A. (2006). *Effect of phasic alerting treatment on the recovery of patients post right stroke with unilateral spatial neglect: Using functional imaging and standardized neurobehavioral and functional tests.* Unpublished doctoral dissertation, Hebrew University, Jerusalem, Israel.

Bar-Haim Erez, A., & Katz, N. (2003). Cognitive profiles of individuals with dementia and healthy elderly: The Loewenstein Occupational Therapy Cognitive Assessment (LOTCA-G). *Phys Occup Ther Geriatr, 22*, 29–42.

Bar-Haim Erez, A., Katz, N., Ring, H., & Soroker, N. (2009). Assessment of spatial neglect using computerized feature and conjunction visual search tasks. *Neuropsychol Rehabil, 9*, 11–19.

Bar-Haim Erez, A., Kizony, R., Shahar, M., & Katz, N. (2006, September). *Visual Spatial Search Task (VISSTA): A computerized assessment and training program.* Paper presented at the International Conference on Disability, Virtual Reality, and Associated Technologies (ICDVRAT), Esjberg, Denmark.

Bar-Haim Erez, A., Rothschild, E., Katz, N., Tuchner, M., & Hartman-Maeir, A. (in press). Executive functioning, awareness and participation in daily life after mild traumatic brain injury: A preliminary study. *Am J Occup Ther.*

Bar-Yosef, C., Weinblatt, N., & Katz, N. (1999). Reliability and validity of the Cognitive Performance Test (CPT) in Israel. *Phys Occup Ther Geriatr, 17*, 65–79.

Baum, C. M. (1995). The contribution of occupation to function in persons with Alzheimer's disease. *J Occup Sci: Australia, 2*, 59–67.

Baum, C. M., Connor, L. T., Morrison, M. T., Hahn, M., Dromerick, A. W., & Edwards, D. F. (2008). The reliability, validity, and clinical utility of the Executive Function Performance Test: A measure of executive function in a sample of persons with stroke. *Am J Occup Ther, 62*, 446–455.

Baum, C. M., & Edwards, D. F. (1993). Cognitive performance in senile dementia of the Alzheimer's type: The Kitchen Task Assessment. *Am J Occup Ther, 47*, 431–438.

Baum, C. M., & Edwards, D. F. (1998). *Home Occupational Environmental Assessment: An environmental checklist for treatment planning.* Unpublished manuscript, Washington University School of Medicine, St. Louis, MO.

Baum, C. M., & Edwards, D. F. (2008). *Activity Card Sort (ACS)* (2nd ed.). Bethesda, MD: American Occupational Therapy Association.

Baum, C. M., Edwards, D. F., & Morrow-Howell, N. (1993). Identification and measurement of productive behaviors in senile dementia of the Alzheimer type. *Gerontologist, 33*, 403–408.

Baum, C. M., & Law, M. (1997). Occupational therapy practice: Focusing on occupational performance. *Am J Occup Ther, 51*, 277–288.

Baum, C. M., Morrison, T., Hahn, M., & Edwards, D. (2007). *Executive Function Performance Test: Test protocol booklet.* Unpublished program in Occupational Therapy Washington University School of Medicine, St. Louis, MO.

Braswell, D., Hartry, A., Hoornbeek, S., Johansen, A., Johnson, L., Schultz, J., et al. (1993). *Profile of executive control system: Instruction manual and assessment.* Wake Forest, NC: Lash and Associates Publishing/Training.

Burgess, P. W., Alderman, N., Forbes, C., Costello, A., Coates, L. M.-A., Dawson, D. R., et al. (2006). The case for the development and use of "ecologically valid" measures of executive function in experimental and clinical neuropsychology. *J Int Neuropsychol Soc, 12*, 194–209.

Burns, T. (2002). *Cognitive Performance Test (CPT)*. Minneapolis, MN: Geriatric Research, Education and Clinical Center, Minneapolis Veterans Affairs Medical Center.

Burns, T. (2006). *Cognitive Performance Test (CPT)*. Pequannock, NJ: Maddak.

Camp, C., Foss, J., O'Hanlon, A., & Stevens, A. (1996). Memory interventions for persons with dementia. *Appl Cog Psychol, 10*, 193–210.

Cermak, S. A., Katz, N., McGuire, E., Greenbaum, S., Peralta, C., & Maser-Flanagan, V. M. (1995). Performance of American and Israeli individuals with CVA on the Loewenstein Occupational Therapy Cognitive Assessment (LOTCA). *Am J Occup Ther, 49*, 500–506.

Chapparo, C., & Ranka, J. (1997). *Occupational performance model* (Australia) (Monograph 1). Sydney: Total Print Control. Available at *www.occupationalperformance.com*.

Christiansen, C., & Baum, C. M. (Eds.). (1991). *Occupational therapy: Overcoming human performance deficits*. Thorofare, NJ: Slack.

Christiansen, C., & Baum, C. M. (Eds.). (1997). *Occupational therapy: Enabling function and well-being* (2nd ed.). Thorofare, NJ: Slack.

Christiansen C., & Baum, C. M. (Eds.). (2005). *Occupational therapy: Performance, participation and well-being*. Thorofare, NJ: Slack.

Chui, T., Oliver, R., Ascott, P., Choo, L. C., Davis, T., Gaya, A., et al. (2006). *Safety Assessment of Function and the Environment for Rehabilitation (SAFER) version 3*. Toronto, ON: COTA Health. Available online at *www.cotahealth.ca*.

Craik, F. I., & Jennings, J. (1992). Human memory. In F. Criak & T. Salthous (Eds.), *Handbook of memory disorders*. New York: Wiley.

Dawson, D. R., Anderson, N. D., Burgess, P. W., Levine, B., Rewilak, D., Cooper, E. K., et al. (2005, February). *The ecological validity of the Multiple Errands Test—Hospital Version: Preliminary findings*. Poster presented at the meeting of the International Neuropsychological Society, St Louis, MO.

Delahunty, A., & Morice, R. (1996). Rehabilitation of frontal/executive impairments schizophrenia. *Aust NZ J Psychiat, 30*, 760–767.

Dick, M., Shankle, R., Bet, R., Dick-Muehlke, C., Cotman, C., & Kean, M. (1996). Acquisition and long-term retention of a gross motor skill in Alzheimer's disease patients under constant and varied practice conditions. *J Gerontol, 51B*, P103–P111.

Diehl, M., Marsiska, M., Horgas, A. L., Rosenberg, A., Saczynski, J. S., & Willis, S. L. (2005). The Revised Observed Tasks of Daily Living: A performance based assessment of everyday problem solving in older adults. *J Appl Gerontol, 24*, 211–230.

Duncan, P. W., Lai, S. M., Wallace, D., Embretson, S., Johnson, D., & Studenski, S. (1999). *Stroke Impact Scale version 3.0*. Kansas City, MO: University of Kansas Medical Center.

Dunn, W., Brown, C., & McGuigan, A. (1994). The ecology of human performance: A framework for considering the effect of context. *Am J Occup Ther, 48*, 595–607.

Dunn, W., Brown, C., & Youngstorm, M. J. (2003). Ecological model of occupation. In P. Kramer, J. Hinojosa, & C. B. Royeen (Eds.), *Perspectives in human occupation* (pp. 222–263). Philadelphia: Lippincott Williams & Wilkins.

Edwards, D. F., Hahn, M., Baum, C., & Dromerick, A. W. (2006). The impact of mild stroke on meaningful activity and life satisfaction. *J Stroke Cerebrovasc Dis, 15*, 151–157.

Elazar, B., Itzkovich, M., & Katz, N. (1996). Geriatric version: *Loewenstein Occupational Therapy Cognitive Assessment (LOTCA-G) battery*. Pequannock, NJ: Maddak.

Feuerstein, R. (1979). *The dynamic assessment of retarded performers: The Learning Potential Device, theory, instruments and techniques*. Baltimore: University Park Press.

Feuerstein, R., & Falik, L. H. (2004). *Cognitive modifiability: A needed perspective on learn-*

ing for the 21st century. Retrieved April 2004 from *www.icelp.org/asp/Dynamic_Cognitive_Assessment.shtm.*

Fidler, G. S., & Fidler, J. W. (1973). Doing and becoming: Purposeful action and self-actualization. *Am J Occup Ther, 32,* 305–310.

Fisher, A. G. (1993). The assessment of IADL motor skills: An application of many faceted Rasch analysis. *Am J Occup Ther, 47,* 319–329.

Fisher, A. G. (1998). Uniting practice and theory in an occupational framework. *Am J Occup Ther, 52,* 509–521.

Fisher, A. G. (2006a). *Assessment of motor and process skills: Vol. 1. Development, standardization, and administration manual* (6th ed.). Fort Collins, CO: Three Star Press.

Fisher, A. G. (2006b). *Assessment of motor and process skills: Vol. 2. User manual* (6th ed.). Fort Collins, CO: Three Star Press.

Fisher, A. G., Liu, Y., Velozo, C., & Pan, A. (1992). Cross cultural assessment of process skills. *Am J Occup Ther, 47,* 878–884.

Fitts, P. M., & Posner, M. I. (1967). *Learning and skilled performance in human performance.* Belmont, CA: Brook-Cole.

Flavell, J. H., Miller, P. H., & Miller, S. A. (1993). *Cognitive development* (3rd ed.). Englewood Cliffs, NJ: Prentice-Hall.

Fleming, J. M., Strong, J., & Ashton, R. (1996). Self-awareness of deficits in adults with traumatic brain injury: How best to measure? *Brain Injury, 10,* 1–15.

Folstein, M. F., & Folstein, S. E. (1975). Mini-Mental State: A practical method for grading the cognitive state of patients for clinician. *J Psychiat Res, 12,* 189–198.

Frassinneti, F., Angeli, V., Meneghello, F., Avanzi, S., & Ladavas, E. (2002). Long-lasting amelioration of visuospatial neglect by prism adaptation. *Brain, 125,* 608–623.

Freedman, M., Leach, L., Kaplan, E., Winocur, G., Shulman, K., & Delis, D. C. (1994). *Clock drawing: A neuropsychological analysis.* New York: Oxford University Press.

Fugl-Meyer, A. R., Branholm, I. B., & Fugl-Meyer, K. S. (1991). Happiness and domain-specific life satisfaction in adult northern Swedes. *Clin Rehabi, 5,* 25–33.

Giles, G. M. (2005). A neurofunctional approach to rehabilitation following severe brain injury. In N. Katz (Ed.), *Cognition and occupation across the life span: Models for intervention in occupational therapy* (pp. 139–166). Bethesda, MD: American Occupational Therapy Association.

Gioia, G. A., & Isquith, P. K. (2004). Ecological assessment of executive function in traumatic brain injury. *Develop Neuropsychol, 25,* 135–158.

Gitlin, L. N., Schinfeld, S., Winter, L., Corcoran, M., Boyce, A. A., & Hauck, W. W. (2002). Evaluating home environments of persons with dementia: Inter rater reliability and validity of the Home Environmental Assessment Protocol (HEAP). *Disabil Rehabil, 24,* 59–91.

Goel, V., Grafman, J., Tajik, J., Gana, S., & Danto, D. (1997). A study of the performance of patients with frontal lobe lesions in a financial planning task. *Brain, 120,* 1805–1822.

Goldberg, E. (2001). *The executive brain: Frontal lobes and the civilized mind.* New York: Oxford University Press.

Goverover, Y., & Hinojosa, J. (2002). Categorization and deductive reasoning: Predictors of instrumental activities of daily living performance in adults with brain injury. *Am J Occup Ther, 56,* 509–516.

Goverover, Y., & Hinojosa, J. (2004). Interrater reliability and discriminant validity of the deductive reasoning test. *Am J Occup Ther, 58,* 104–108.

Goverover, Y., & Josman, N. (2004). Everyday problem solving among four groups of individuals with cognitive impairments: Examination of the discriminant validity of the Observed Tasks of Daily Living—Revised. *Occup Ther J Res, 24,* 103–112.

Granger, C. V. (1993). *Guide for the uniform data set for medical rehabilitation (adult FIM), version 4.0.* Buffalo: State University of New York.

Grigorenko, E. L., & Sternberg, R. J. (1998). Dynamic testing. *Psychol Bull, 124,* 75–111.

Haist, F., Gore, J., & Mao, H. (2001). Consolidation of human memory over decades revealed by functional magnetic resonance imaging. *Nat Neurosci, 4,* 1139–1145.

Hartman-Maeir, A., Armon, N., & Katz, N. (2005). *The Kettle test: A cognitive functional screening test.* Unpublished protocol, Helene University, Jerusalem, Israel.

Hartman-Maeir, A., Eliad, Y., Kizony, R., Nahaloni, I., Kelberman, H., & Katz, N. (2007). Evaluation of a long-term community based rehabilitation program for adult stroke survivors. *J Neurol Rehab, 22,* 295–301.

Hartman-Maeir, A., Harel, H., & Katz, N. (in press). The Kettle Test—a brief measure of cognitive functional performance: Reliability and validity in stroke rehabilitation. *Am J Occup Ther.*

Hartman-Maeir, A., & Katz, N. (1995). Validity of the Behavioral Inattention Test (BIT): Relationships with task performance. *Am J Occup Ther, 49,* 507–511.

Hartman-Maeir, A., Katz, N., & Baum, C. (2009). Cognitive Functional Evaluation (CFE) for individuals with suspected cognitive disabilities. *Occup Ther Health Care, 23,* 1–23.

Hartman-Maeir, A., Soroker, N., Ring, H., Avni, N., & Katz, N. (2007). Activities, participation and satisfaction one-year post stroke. *Disabil and Rehabil, 29,* 559–566.

Heilman, K. M., Watson, R. T., & Valenstein, E. (2003). Neglect and related disorders. In K. M. Heilman & E. Valenstein (Eds.), *Clinical neuropsychology* (4th ed., pp. 296–346). Oxford, UK: Oxford University Press.

Hoofien, D., & Sharoni, L. (2006). Measuring unawareness of deficits among patients with traumatic brain injury: Reliability and validity of the Patient Competency Rating Scale—Hebrew Version. *Israeli J Psychiatry and Related Sci, 43,* 296–305.

Itzkovich, M., Averbuch, S., Elazar, B., & Katz, N. (2000). *Loewenstein Occupational Therapy Cognitive Assessment (LOTCA) battery* (2nd ed.). Pequannock, NJ: Maddak.

Josman, N. (2005). The dynamic interactional model in schizophrenia. In N. Katz (Ed.), *Cognition and occupation across the life span: Models for intervention in occupational therapy* (pp. 169–185). Bethesda, MD: American Occupational Therapy Association.

Josman, N., Berney, T., & Jarus, T. (2000a). Evaluating categorization skills in children following severe brain injury. *Occup Ther J Res, 20,* 241–255.

Josman, N., Berney, T., & Jarus, T. (2000b). Performance of children with and without traumatic brain injury on the contextual memory test (CMT). *Phys Occup Ther Pedi, 19,* 39–51.

Katz, N. (2005). *Cognition and occupation across the life span: Models for intervention in occupational therapy.* Bethesda, MD: American Occupational Therapy Association.

Katz, N. (2006). *Routine Task Inventory—RTI-E manual, prepared and elaborated on the basis of Allen, C.K.* Available online at *www.allen-cognitive-network.org.*

Katz, N., Elazar, B., & Itzkovich, M. (1996). Validity of the Neurobehavioral Cognitive Status Examination (Cognistat) in assessing patients post CVA and healthy elderly in Israel. *Israel J Occup Ther, 5,* E185–E198.

Katz, N., Felzen, B., Tadmor, I., & Hartman-Maeir, A. (2007). Validity of the Executive Function Performance Test (EFPT) in persons with schizophrenia: An occupational performance test. *Occup Ther J Res, 27,* 1–8.

Katz, N., Fleming, J., Keren, N., Lightbody, S., & Hartman-Maeir, A. (2002). Unawareness and/or denial of disability: Implications for occupational therapy intervention. *Canadian J Occup Ther, 69,* 281–292.

Katz, N., Goldstand, S., Traub Bar-Ilan, R., & Parush, S. (2007). The Dynamic Occupational Therapy Cognitive Assessment for Children (DOTCA-Ch): A new instrument for assessing learning potential. *American Journal of Occupational Therapy, 61,* 41–52.

Katz, N., & Hartman-Maeir, A. (2005). Higher-level cognitive functions: Awareness and executive functions enabling engagement in occupation. In N. Katz (Ed.), *Cognition and occupation across the life span: Models for intervention in occupational therapy* (pp. 3–25). Bethesda, MD: American Occupational Therapy Association.

Katz, N., Hartman-Maeir, A., Ring, H., & Soroker, N. (1999). Functional disability and rehabilitation outcome in right-hemispheric-damaged patients with and without unilateral spatial neglect. *Arch Phys Med Rehab, 80,* 379–384.

Katz, N., Hartman-Maeir, A., Ring, H., & Soroker, N. (2000). Relationship of cognitive performance and daily function of clients following right hemisphere stroke: Predictive and ecological validity of the LOTCA battery. *Occup Ther J Res, 20,* 3–17.

Katz, N., Hartman-Maeir, A., Weiss, P., & Armon, N. (1997). Comparison of cognitive status profiles of healthy elderly persons with dementia and neurosurgical patients using the neurobehavioral cognitive status examination. *NeuroRehabilitation, 9,* 179–186.

Katz, N., Itzkovich, M., Averbuch, S., & Elazar, B. (1989). The Loewenstein Occupational Therapy Cognitive Assessment (LOTCA) battery for brain-injured patients: Reliability and validity. *Am J Occup Ther, 43,* 184–192.

Katz, N., Karpin, H., Lak, A., Furman, T., & Hartman-Maeir, A. (2003). Participation in occupational performance: Reliability and validity of the Activity Card Sort. *Occup Ther J Res, 23,* 1–9.

Katz, N., Kizony, R., & Parush, S. (2002). Cross-cultural comparison and developmental change of Ethiopian, Bedouin, and mainstream Israeli children's cognitive performance. *Occup Ther J Res, 22,* 1–10.

Katz, N., Parush, S., & Traub Bar-Ilan, R. (2005). *The Dynamic Occupational Therapy Cognitive Assessment for Children (DOTCA-Ch) manual.* Pequannock, NJ: Maddak.

Katz, N., Ring, H., Naveh, Y., Kizony, R., Feintuch, U., & Weiss, P. L. (2005). Interactive virtual environment training for safe street crossing of right hemisphere stroke patients with unilateral spatial neglect. *Disabil Rehabil, 29,* 177–181.

Katzman, R., Brown, T., Fuld, P., Peck, A., Schechter, R., Schimmel, H., et al. (1983). Validation of a short orientation–memory–concentration test of cognitive impairment. *Am J Psychiat, 140,* 734–39.

Keil, K., & Kaszniak, A. W. (2002). Examining executive function in individuals with brain injury: A review. *Aphasiology, 16,* 305–335.

Keren, N. (2006). *Evidence from an occupational goal intervention program for executive dysfunction in schizophrenia on occupational performance.* Unpublished doctoral dissertation, Hebrew University, Jerusalem, Israel.

Keren, N., & Katz, N. (2005, April). *Effectiveness of an occupational goal intervention for executive dysfunction in schizophrenia and occupational outcomes: A RCT study in progress.* Paper presented at the annual meeting of the American Occupational Therapy Association, Long Beach, CA.

Kewman, D. G., Yanus, B., & Kirsch, N. (1988). Assessment of distractibility in auditory comprehension after traumatic brain injury. *Brain Injury, 2,* 131–137.

Kielhofner, G. (Ed.). (2002). *A model of human occupation: Theory and application* (3rd ed.). Baltimore: Williams & Wilkins.

Kielhofner, G. (2008). *A model of human occupation: Theory and application* (4th ed.). Baltimore: Lippincott Williams & Wilkins.

Kizony, R., Josman, N., Katz, N., Rand, D., & Weiss, P. L. (2008). Virtual reality and rehabilitation of executive functions: annotated bibliography. *Israeli J Occup Ther, 17,* E47–E61.

Kizony, R., & Katz, N. (2002). Relationships between cognitive abilities and the process scale and skills of the Assessment of Motor and Process Skills (AMPS) in patients with stroke. *Occup Ther J Res, 22,* 82–92.

Knight, C., Alderman, N., & Burgess, P. W. (2002). Development of a simplified version of the Multiple Errands Test for use in hospital settings. *Neuropsychol Rehabil, 12*, 231–255.

Kottorp, A., & Tham, K. (2005). *Assessment of awareness of disability (Test Manual).* Stockholm, Sweden: Karolinska Institute, Division of Occupational Therapy.

Law, M., Baptiste, S., Carswell, A., McColl, M. A., Polatajko, H., & Pollock, N. (1998). *The Canadian Occupational Performance Measure* (3rd ed.). Toronto: Canadian Association of Occupational Therapists.

Law, M., Cooper, B., Strong, S., Stewart, D., Rigby, P., & Letts, L. (1996). The person-environment–occupation model: A transactive approach to occupational performance. *Canadian J Occup Ther, 63*, 9–23.

Lengfelder, A., & Gollwitzer, P. M. (2001). Implementation intentions and efficient action initiation. *J Pers Soc Psychol, 81*(5), 946–960.

Levy, L. L. (1974). Movement therapy for psychiatric patients. *Am J Occup Ther, 28*, 354–357.

Levy, L. L. (1986). A practical guide to the care of the Alzheimer's disease victim: The cognitive disability perspective. *Topics Ger Rehabil, 1*, 16–26.

Levy, L. L., & Burns, T. (2005). Cognitive disabilities reconsidered: Rehabilitation of older adults with dementia. In N. Katz (Ed.), *Cognition and occupation across the life span: Models for intervention in occupational therapy* (pp. 347–388). Bethesda, MD: American Occupational Therapy Association.

Lezak, M. D. (1982). *Neuropsychological assessment* (2nd ed.). New York: Oxford University Press.

Lezak, M. D., Howieson, D. B., & Loring, D. W. (2004). *Neuropsychological assessment.* New York: Oxford University Press.

Lidz, C. S. (1987). Cognitive deficiencies revisited. In C. S. Lidz (Ed.), *Dynamic assessment: Evaluating learning potential* (pp. 444–478). New York: Guilford Press.

Lidz, C. S., & Elliot, J. G. (2000). *Advances in cognition and educational practice: Vol. 6. Dynamic assessment.* Amsterdam: Elsevier Science.

Logue, P. E., Tupler, L. A., D'amico, C., & Schmitt, F. A. (1993). The Neurobehavioral Cognitive Status Examination: Psychometric properties in use with psychiatric inpatients. *J Clin Psychol, 49*, 80–89.

Lopez, J. (2000). Shaky memories in indelible ink. *Nat Rev Neurosci, 1*, 6–7.

Mandich, A., Polatajko, H., Miller, L., & Baum, C. M. (2004). *The Paediatric Activity Card Sort (PACS).* Ottawa: Canadian Occupational Therapy Association.

Mathiowetz, V., & Haugen, J. B. (1995). Evaluation of motor behavior: Traditional and contemporary views. In C. A. Trombly (Ed.), *Occupational therapy for physical dysfunction* (pp. 157–185). Baltimore: Williams & Wilkins.

Meichenbaum, D. (1977). *Cognitive behavioral modification: An integrative approach.* New York: Plenum Press.

Meichenbaum, D. (1994). *A clinical handbook/practical therapist manual for assessing and treating adults with posttraumatic stress disorder.* Waterloo, ON: Institute Press.

Mendez, M. F., Mendez, M. A., Martin, R., Smyth, K. A., & Whitehouse, P. J. (1990). Complex visual disturbances in Alzheimer's disease. *Neurology, 40*, 439–443.

Meyer, A. (1922). The philosophy of occupation therapy. *Arch Occup Ther, 1*, 1–10.

Mosey, A. C. (1974). An alternative: The biopsychosocial model. *Am J Occup Ther, 28*, 137–140.

Mueller, J., Kierman, R., & Langston, J. W. (2007). *Cognistat manual.* Fairfax, CA: Northern California Behavioral Group. Available at *www.cognistat.com.*

Northern California Neurobehavioral Group. (2007). *Cognistat: The Neurobehavioral Cognitive Status Examination manual* (2nd ed.). Fairfax, CA: Author.

Osmon, D. C., Smet, I. C., Winegarden, B., & Gandhavadi, B. (1992). Neurobehavioral Cognitive Status Examination: Its use with unilateral stroke patients in a rehabilitation setting. *Arch Phys Med, 73,* 414–418.

Pierce, D. (2001). Untangling occupation and activity. *Am J Occup Ther, 55,* 138–146.

Polatajko, H. J., & Mandich, A. (2004). *Enabling occupation in children: The cognitive orientation to daily occupational performance (CO-OP) approach.* Ottawa, ON: Canadian Association Occupational Therapists Publications ACE.

Polatajko, H. J., & Mandich, A. (2005). Cognitive orientation to daily occupational performance with children with developmental coordination disorders. In N. Katz (Ed.), *Cognition and occupation across the life span: Models for intervention in occupational therapy* (pp. 237–259). Bethesda, MD: American Occupational Therapy Association.

Prigatano, G. P. (1986). *Neuropsychological rehabilitation after brain injury.* Baltimore: Johns Hopkins University Press.

Prigatano, G. P. (1999). Disorders of self-awareness after brain injury. In G. P. Prigatano (Ed.), *Principles of neuropsychological rehabilitation* (pp. 265–293). New York: Oxford University Press.

Prigatano, G. P. (2005). Disturbance of self-awareness and rehabilitation of patients with traumatic brain injury: A 20-year perspective. *J Head Trauma Rehab, 20,* 19–29.

Prigatano, G. P., Borgaro, S., Baker, J., & Wethe, J. (2005). Awareness and distress after traumatic brain injury: A relative perspective. *J Head Trauma Rehab, 20,* 359–67.

Rabin, L. A., Barr, W. B., & Burton, L. A. (2005). Assessment practices of clinical neuropsychologists in the United States and Canada: A survey of INS, NAN, and APA Division 40 members. *Archives of Clinical Neuropsychology, 20,* 33–65.

Rand, D., Abu-Rukun, S., Weiss, P. T., & Katz, N. (2009). Validation of the virtual MET as an assessment tool for executive functions. *Neuropsychol Rehabil, 19,* 583–602.

Rand, D., Katz, N., Shahar, M., Kizony, R., & Weiss, P. L. (2005). The virtual mall: A functional virtual environment for stroke rehabilitation. *Ann Rev Cyberther Telemedicine, 3,* 193–198.

Rand, D., Katz, N., & Weiss, T.P. (2007). Evaluation of virtual shopping in the VMall: Comparison of post-stroke participants to healthy control groups. *Disabil Rehabil, 29,* 1–10.

Rand, D., Weiss, P. T., & Katz, N. (in press). Training multitasking in a virtual supermarket: A novel intervention following stroke. *Am J Occup Ther.*

Reilly, M. (1962). Occupational therapy can be one of the great ideas of 20th century medicine. *Am J Occup Ther, 16,* 300–308.

Reisberg, B., Franssen, E., Souren, L., Auer, S., Akram, I., & Kenowsky, S. (2002). Evidence and mechanisms of retrogenesis in Alzheimer's and other dementias: Management and treatment import. *Am J Alzheimer's Other Dementias, 17,* 160–174.

Reisberg, B., Franssen, E., Souren, L., Auer, S., & Kenowsky, S. (1998). Progression of Alzheimer's disease: Variability and consistency: Ontogenic models, their applicability and relevance. *J Neural Transm, 54,* 9–20.

Reisberg, B., Kenowsky, S., Franssen, E., Auer, S., & Souren, L. (1999). Toward a science of Alzheimer's disease management: A model based upon current knowledge of retrogenesis. *Int Psychogeriatr, 11,* 7–23.

Robertson, I. H., Mattingley, J. B., Rorden, C., & Driver, J. (1998). Phasic alerting of neglect patients overcomes their spatial deficit in visual awareness. *Nature, 395,* 169–172.

Robertson, I. H., Ward, T., Ridgeway, V., & Nimmo-Smith, I. (1994). *The Test of Everyday Attention manual.* Bury St. Edmund, UK: Thames Valley Test.

Rose, D. J. (1997). *A multilevel approach to the study of motor control and learning.* Newton, MA: Allyn & Bacon.

Royall, D. R., Cordes, J. A., & Polk, M. (1998). CLOX: An executive clock drawing task. *J Neurol Neurosurg Ps, 64,* 588–594.

Sachs, D., & Josman, N. (2003). The Activity Card Sort: A factor analysis. *Occup Ther J Res*, *23*, 165–174.

Schneider, W., Dumais, S. T., & Shiffrin, R. M. (1984). Automatic and control processing and attention. In R. Parasuraman & D. R. Davis (Eds.), *Varieties of attention* (pp. 1–27). London: Academic Press.

Schunk, D. (2000). *Learning theories: An educational perspective* (3rd ed.). Upper Saddle River, NJ: Prentice-Hall.

Shallice, T., & Burgess, P. W. (1991). Deficits in strategy application following frontal lobe damage in man. *Brain*, *114*, 727–741.

Smith, N., Kielhofner, G., & Watts, J. (1986). The relationship between volition, activity pattern and life satisfaction in the elderly. *Am J Occup Ther*, *40*, 278–283.

Sternberg, R. J., & Grigorenko, E. L. (2002). *Dynamic testing: The nature and measurement of learning potential*. Cambridge, UK: Cambridge University Press.

Stuss, D. T., Stethem, L., Huggenholtz, H., Picton, T., Pivik, J., & Richards, M. T. (1989). Reaction time after head injury: Fatigue, divided attention, and consistency of performance. *J Neurol Neurosur Ps*, *52*, 742–748.

Tetewsky, S., & Duffy, C. (1999). Visual loss and getting lost in Alzheimer's disease. *Neurology*, *52*, 958–965.

Tham, K., Bersnpang, B., & Fisher, A. (1999). The development of the awareness of disabilities. *Scand J Occup Ther*, *6*, 184–190.

Tham, K., Ginsburg, E., Fisher, A. G., & Tenger, R. (2001). Training to improve awareness of disabilities in clients with unilateral neglect. *Am J Occup Ther*, *55*, 46–54.

Thelen, E. (1995). Motor development: A new synthesis. *Am Psychol*, *50*, 79–95.

Thelen, E., Kelso, J. A. S., & Fogel, A. (1987). Self-organizing systems and infant motor development. *Dev Rev*, *7*, 739–765.

Toglia, J. P. (2005). A dynamic interactional approach to cognitive rehabilitation. In N. Katz (Ed.), *Cognition and occupation across the life span: Models for intervention in occupational therapy* (pp. 29–72). Bethesda, MD: American Occupational Therapy Association.

Toglia, J. P. (1991). Generalization of treatment: A multicontextual approach to cognitive perceptual impairment in the brain-injured adult. *Am J Occup Ther*, *45*, 505–516.

Toglia, J. P. (1993). *Contextual Memory Test*. San Antonio, TX: Psychological Corporation.

Toglia, J. P. (1994). *Dynamic assessment of categorization: The Toglia Category Assessment manual*. Pequannock, NJ: Maddak.

Toglia, J. P. (2003). The multicontext approach. In E. B. Crepeau, E. S. Cohn, & B. A. B. Schell (Eds.), *Willard and Spackman's occupational therapy* (10th ed., pp. 264–267). Philadelphia: Lippincott Williams & Wilkins.

Toglia, J. P., & Kirk, U. (2000). Understanding awareness deficits following brain injury. *NeuroRehabilitation*, *15*, 57–70.

Townsend, E. S. (1997). Occupation: Potential for personal and social transformation. *J Occup Sci: Australia*, *4*, 18–26.

Townsend, E. S., Stanton, M., Law, H. J., Polatajko, S., Baptiste, T., Thompson-Franson, C., et al. (1997). *Enabling occupation: An occupational therapy perspective*. Toronto: Canadian Association of Occupational Therapy.

Trexler, L. (1987). Neuropsychological rehabilitation in the United States. In M. Meier, A. Benton, & L. Diller (Eds.), *Neuropsychological rehabilitation* (pp. 437–460). New York: Guilford Press.

Tulving, E. (1985). How many memory systems are there? *Am Psychol*, *40*, 385–398.

Turvey, M. T. (1990). Coordination. *Am Psychol*, *45*, 938–953

Vygotsky, L. S. (1978). *Mind in society: The development of higher psychological processes*. Cambridge, MA: Harvard University Press.

Weiss, P. L., Kizony, R., Fientuch, U., & Katz, N. (2006).Virtual reality in neurorehabilitation. In M. E. Selzer (Ed.), *Textbook of neural repair and rehabilitation* (Vol. II, pp. 182–197). Cambridge, UK: Cambridge University Press.

Weiss, P. L., Rand, D., Katz, N., & Kizony, R. (2004). Video capture virtual reality as a flexible and effective rehabilitation tool. *J NeuroEngineering Rehab*, *1*, 12.

Wilson, B. A., Alderman, N., Burgess, P. W., Emslie, H., & Evans, J. J. (1996). *Behavioural assessment of dysexecutive syndrome*. Bury St. Edmunds, UK: Thames Valley Test.

Wilson, B. A., Baddeley, A., Evans, J. J., & Shiel, A. (1994). Errorless learning in the rehabilitation of memory impaired people. *Neuropsychol Rehabil*, *4*, 307–326.

Wilson, B. A., Cockburn, J., & Baddeley, A. (1985). *The Rivermead Behavioural Memory Test*. Reading, UK: Thames Valley Test.

Wilson, B. A., Cockburn, J., & Halligan, P. W. (1987). *Behavioural Inattention Test manual*. Fareham, UK: Thames Valley Test.

Wilson, B. A., Evans, J. J., Emslie, H., Alderman, N., & Burgess, P. (1998). The development of an ecologically valid test for assessing patients with a dysexecutive syndrome. *Neuropsychol Rehabil*, *8*, 213–228.

Ziviani, J., Rodger, S., Pacheco, P., Rootsey, N., Smith, A., & Katz, N. (2004). The Dynamic Occupational Therapy Cognitive Assessment for Children (DOTCA-Ch): Pilot study of inter-rater and test retest reliability. *New Zealand J Occup Ther*, *51*, 17–24.

SECTION B

Assessment of Specific Functional Abilities
and Assessment Considerations

CHAPTER 4

The Relationship between Instrumental Activities of Daily Living and Neuropsychological Performance

David Loewenstein and Amarilis Acevedo

In order for individuals to live independently, they must have the ability to take care of themselves and to function autonomously in their environment. Difficulties with independent function as a result of cerebral impairment have profound effects on both the physical and psychological well-being of the patient and his or her family. Functional impairment also has significant financial consequences for individuals as well as for society as a whole. The ability to accurately assess both higher- and lower-order functional abilities is critical to the remediation and management of persons with brain-related impairments.

Functional abilities are typically divided into two groups: basic activities of daily living (BADLs) and instrumental activities of daily living (IADLs). BADLs are those tasks that are related to basic self-care, such as feeding, dressing, self-transfer, toileting, and grooming (see Kane & Kane, 1981; Katz, Ford, Moskowitz, Jackson, & Jaffe, 1963). On the other hand, IADLs refer to activities of daily living that, as the name implies, are instrumental in allowing the individual to effectively interact with the environment to obtain needed goods and services. IADLs have higher cognitive complexity than BADLs, which are more rudimentary in nature. IADLs are required for independent living at home and within the community and allow the individual to cope with the demands of everyday life. IADLs include, but are not limited to, shopping, taking medications, cooking and performing other household chores, managing money and personal finances, and using means of communication (e.g., telephone, mail) and transportation (e.g., driving, taking the bus or subway) (Kane & Kane, 1981; Lawton & Brody, 1969; Tuokko, 1993). IADLs are generally distinguished from specific vocational or work-related skills that are necessary for gainful employment. Although IADLs typically refer to activities in the home environment, IADL impairment in areas such as utilizing transportation or using different means of communication may adversely impact upon work attendance and/or performance.

93

The interest in the assessment of the ability to perform activities of daily living has its origins in rehabilitation medicine and occupational therapy (Bennet, 2001; Loewenstein & Mogosky, 1999). The primary goal of the functional assessment of activities of daily living is to identify the patient's strengths and weaknesses so that these are incorporated in treatment planning and in rehabilitation and management efforts. Depending on the expertise of the health professional and the clinical setting, he or she may be asked to render an opinion regarding the degree to which an individual is able to independently and safely carry out BADLs or IADLs. For example, physicians who specialize in physical medicine and rehabilitation, and occupational and physical therapists who work in rehabilitation institutions with individuals with severe head injury or advanced neurological diseases or dementias, are frequently asked to determine the degree to which BADLs may be compromised in a given individual. In contrast, neuropsychologists working in private practice, in outpatient settings with mildly impaired brain injury, or other nonrehabilitation settings are more likely to be asked to render an opinion about an individual's cognitive status and its impact on his or her ability to drive, manage finances, self-administer medications, and carry out other IADLs. The opinions of these professionals could lead to changes in the home environment to protect the individual's safety, and could have a profound impact on the individual's autonomy, including decisions about guardianship and living arrangements.

In addition to patient care, the assessment of an individual's ability to carry out IADLs is an essential part of diagnostic procedures that require the identification of functional deficits thought to be present in various psychiatric and neurodegenerative disorders. As an example, the *Diagnostic and Statistical Manual of Mental Disorders* (DSM-IV; American Psychiatric Association, 1994) requires that deterioration in social and/or occupational functioning be present for a diagnosis of most major psychiatric conditions or dementia. In fact, one of the primary differences between an individual who meets criteria for dementia, according to the National Institute for Neurological and Communicative Diseases and Stroke—Alzheimer's Disease and Related Disorders Association (NINCDS-ADRDA; McKhann et al., 1984) and an individual with mild cognitive impairment (MCI) is that the former requires the presence of functional impairment whereas the latter requires relatively intact functional status in the presence of cognitive deficits.

The discussion that follows examines the ability to perform IADLs from a cognitive standpoint. In our view there are three key elements that need to be considered when assessing the impact of cognitive status on the ability of individuals to perform IADLs: the elements of causation, change, and specificity. The *element of causation* refers to the fact that the loss of the ability to perform an IADL needs to be cognitive in nature and not secondary to physical limitations. As an example, a right-handed patient may be unable to write checks because of the loss of control of the right arm after a left-hemisphere stroke. If the patient is conceptually able to describe all the steps that would be needed to complete the task correctly, including what information needs to be included in the check and where it should be placed, then there has been no cognitive-functional loss in his or her ability to write a check. This point underscores the importance of conducting a thorough medical evaluation to rule out physical factors (e.g., poststroke paresis, loss of vision secondary to diabetes retinopathy) as the main reason for impairments in the performance of an IADL. In cases where physical and cognitive factors coexist in a given individual, it is usually difficult to disentangle the relative contribution of each factor in the resulting functional deficit. For example, a young adult who lost motor control of his arm as a result of a traumatic brain injury and an older adult who has limited vision may both have memory problems superimposed upon their physical limitations. Clearly, the interdisciplinary collaboration of physicians, neuropsychologists, occupational therapists, and physical therapists is needed for the comprehensive evaluation and treatment planning of such cases.

The *element of change* refers to the need to compare an individual's current ability to perform an IADL with his or her ability and to carry out the task in the past. For example, if a patient was never able to balance a checkbook or had never engaged in balancing a checkbook and is still unable to do the task, then there has been no functional loss in that ability. In other words, the inability of a person to perform a functional task that he or she has never performed or mastered may not constitute actual functional decline. In our work with older adults from heterogeneous backgrounds, we find that many of our patients have never performed banking transactions electronically or by using automated menu-driven telephone systems. Thus, the fact that they may not be able to perform this task at present does not constitute change and should not be conceptualized as evidence of cognitive-functional decline. The requirement that functional deterioration be present to meet DSM-IV criteria for dementia assumes that the clinician has adequate understanding of a person's premorbid functioning and that deterioration in function parallels decline in cognitive abilities rather than merely reflecting lack of familiarity with a task. In addition, health professionals must be aware that there are instances in which a person who never learned to drive, prepare meals, or manage finances may be suddenly jeopardized by the loss of a significant other who once performed those activities. In these cases, these skills were never learned but may remain important targets for assessment and intervention.

The *element of specificity* can be divided into three types that frequently coincide: task-, person-, and environment-specificity. Different IADLs have different cognitive characteristics and demands. Thus, an individual may be unable to perform a specific IADL but may still be able to perform other IADLs without difficulty. For example, individuals who have amnesic MCI (see Petersen et al., 1999) are more likely to have difficulty with IADLs that have strong episodic memory demands (e.g., remembering to take medications) than with those with more procedural motor demands (e.g., dialing a telephone number). Some tasks have multiple cognitive determinants, any one of which can adversely affect functional performance. For example, paying bills is an important component of the ability to manage finances. However, a component analysis of this task reveals that an individual might not be able to pay a bill after a brain injury because of the inability to understand the bill or because he or she has forgotten that the bill arrived. Provided that the person has intact prospective memory (i.e., the ability to remember to perform an intended action), which would allow him or her to remember the intended action of paying the bill, the person may still be unable to pay the bill because of confusion as to how to write a check or prepare a letter for mailing. There are also instances in which the individual manages to pay a bill but because of difficulties in balancing his or her checkbook, the checking account may have insufficient funds. All of these possible causes for not paying the bill may potentially lead to deleterious consequences (i.e., losing the electricity in one's home, discontinuation of telephone services). Thus, it is not only important to understand functional deficits in terms of task-specific performance but also by gaining an appreciation for specific elements that underlie a particular functional deficit.

Task-specific factors interact with person-specific variables such as cognitive and functional reserve. Given a similar pattern and degree of cerebral dysfunction, an individual who may have worked as an accountant may evidence better performance on functional tasks related to finances relative to someone who recently had to learn this skill because of the death of a spouse. Other person-specific variables may include the individual's ethnocultural/linguistic background, premorbid strengths and weaknesses, compensatory abilities and motivation, amount of practice with certain IADLs, and degree to which a task has been overlearned. In fact, many caregivers of patients with dementia become aware of the patient's functional changes when they observe the difficulties faced by their loved ones when trying to perform IADLs in new circumstances or unfamiliar environments (e.g., preparing a meal in an unfamiliar kitchen). Preparation of a meal requires an interaction between task- and subject-specific characteristics; difficulties encountered in an unfamiliar kitchen reflect environment-specific characteristics. Persons with brain injury or cognitive impairment typically fare better when performing routinized tasks in familiar environments and in the presence of overlearned situational cues.

Assessment of IADLs

To assess an individual's ability to perform IADLs, clinicians typically utilize information from one or more of the following sources: (1) self-report by the individual, (2) information provided by the individual's informant(s) (e.g., relatives, close friends, proxy), or (3) direct observation of the individual's ability to perform tasks that are similar to the functional task in question. Each of these methods of assessment has inherent strengths and weaknesses (see Loewenstein & Mogosky, 1999).

Self-Report and Informant Report

Information about the patient is usually provided by the patient him- or herself and/or by informants. Both the self-report by the individual and the report by the informant(s) are usually elicited in a clinical interview, which may be supplemented by information obtained from questionnaires and/or rating scales.

Although most clinicians seem to agree about the importance of asking the patient about his or her functional status, there are conflicting reports in the literature regarding the extent to which self-reports of functional status should be considered valid. Myers, Holliday, Harvey, and Hutchinson (1993) reported a high correspondence between the self-report of older adults regarding their functional abilities and their actual performance in the home. In contrast, other investigators have shown that, relative to younger adults, old and very old individuals may be less accurate in their judgment of their own functional capacities (Hoeymans, Wouters, Feskens, van den Bos, & Kromhout, 1997; Sinoff & Ore, 1997). Other studies have questioned the relative weight that should be given to the report of patients themselves versus their informants. Various investigations have shown that patients with dementia often overestimate their functional abilities, whereas caregivers may either overestimate or underestimate these abilities (Argüelles, Loewenstein, Eisdorfer, & Argüelles, 2001; Loewenstein et al., 2001; Mangone et al., 1993; Weinberger et al., 1992). While neurologically impaired patients commonly underestimate their deficits because of agnosia, it is also possible that those with significantly depressed mood may complain more about their inability to carry out daily functional activities. Furthermore, depressed caregivers may be particularly susceptible to overreporting functional impairment.

There are a plethora of self-report measures and of informant-based rating scales for assessing patients' ability to perform BADLs and IADLs (Lindeboom, Vermeulen, Holman, & De Haan, 2003). The reader is referred to Loewenstein and Mogosky (1999) for a description of the strengths and weaknesses of many available measures. Perhaps the most widely used method of ascertaining a patient's ability to perform IADLs is via informant report by a relative or close friend who has had the opportunity to observe the patient in his or her real-world environment. One of the first measures created using this approach was the Instrumental Activities of Daily Living Scale (IADLs) by Lawton and Brody (1969). This measure taps abilities to engage in activities such as shopping, managing finances, taking medications, preparing food, doing laundry, and using the telephone. Other commonly used IADL scales administered to the patient and/or the informant include the Bayer Activities of Daily Living Scale (BADLS; Erzigkeit et al., 2001), the Disability Assessment for Dementia (DAD; Gelinas, Gauthier, McIntyre, & Gauthier, 1999), the Older Adults Resource Center Scale (OARS; Fillenbaum & Smyer, 1981), and the Functional Activities Questionnaire (FAQ; Pfeffer, Kurosaki, Harrah, Chance, & Filos, 1982).

One of the advantages of utilizing self-report scales is the ease of administration and scoring and the fact that they can be filled out by the patient and/or informant while in the waiting room. A major disadvantage of self-report measures when evaluating neurologically impaired patients such as those with Alzheimer's disease or specific right-hemisphere cerebral infarctions is that they may exhibit varying degrees of anosognosia. Given that these patients may be unaware of their deficits and changes in their functional abilities, self-report measures may overestimate their actual functional status. Another disadvantage of self-report methods is that even individuals who are aware of their deficits may choose not to report changes in their functional status for fear of social stigma and/or losing their independence (e.g., especially driving privileges).

An advantage of informant-based scales is that the informant usually rates the patient based on real-world functional performance of IADLs. Thus, informant-based scales tend to be less susceptible to those fluctuations in the patient's cognitive status and motivation that may affect the performance and behavior in the clinician's office. In addition, given that the informant is likely to interact with the patient over long periods of time and in many situations, his or her report may serve as an overall estimate of the individual's functional status across settings and time. Specifically, information provided by a knowledgeable informant is helpful to the clinician who is attempting to establish the degree to which an individual has evidenced functional deterioration relative to his or her premorbid level of function. On the other hand, an informant may feel uncomfortable reporting changes in the patient's functional ability out of a sense of loyalty or for fear that the family member might lose critical privileges, including driving. The level of stress and depression, marital dynamics, and individual personality styles that involve minimization and denial as well as over-exaggeration may further serve to affect the accuracy of the self-report of the spouse and other family members.

Performance-Based Approach

The performance-based approach usually requires the patient to perform the particular activity under the observation of the examiner, who utilizes behaviorally based measures to assess different aspects of functional capacity. Performance-based assessments have the advantage of providing an objective behavioral evaluation of functional skills that are required for daily living, such as using the telephone, meal preparation, medication management, writing a check, balancing a checkbook, and making change for a purchase. Such direct assessment is particularly useful in the evaluation of patients who may not have an informant, in cases where there is doubt about the validity of information provided by a sole informant, and in cases where there are discrepant opinions among multiple informants. Direct observation of the individual as he or she carries out the functional tasks can be conducted in the clinic and/or the patient's home.

Various research groups have developed standardized testing protocols so that the assessment of an individual's functional capacity can be objectively assessed and quantified. Such tests have typically been developed for older adults and those with cognitive impairment and include some of the measurements described in further detail below.

Performance Test of Activities of Daily Living

The Performance Test of Activities of Daily Living (PADL; Kuriansky, Gurland, & Fleiss, 1976) categorizes patients into one of three levels of functional independence (independent, moderately dependent, or dependent) through the administration of 16 tasks related to basic and independent activities of daily living (IADLs). Most tasks include the manipulation of props, which can be assembled into a portable kit and administered in remote settings. The PADL includes the assessment of grooming, hygiene, eating, dressing, communication, time orientation (e.g., telling time on a clock), and safety awareness (e.g., turning a light switch on and off). The PADL was designed so that tasks could be easily understood and carried out by the patient. Task instructions are simple and direct, and facilitate translation of the instrument for use in other languages. The props help convey, nonverbally, what is expected. A trained paraprofessional can administer the PADL in about 20 minutes.

Direct Assessment of Functional Status Scale

The Direct Assessment of Functional Status (DAFS; Loewenstein et al., 1989) scale was originally developed to assess functioning in Alzheimer's disease and related disorders, but researchers have also found it useful with other patient populations, such as those with schizophrenia (Evans et al., 2003; Patterson et al., 1998) and Huntington's disease (Hamilton, 2000). The test measures functional ability across multiple tasks in both BADL and IADL domains, including time orientation, communication, transportation, financial skills, shopping, grooming, and eating. Two unique features of the DAFS include a memory task in the shopping subscale (recall and recognition of a grocery list) and the optional transportation subscale, which assesses an individual's ability to understand and respond to road signs. Examining functional capacity on the transportation subscale is important for patients who are still driving but for whom driving competence may be a concern. The DAFS has also been translated for use in non-English-speaking populations and takes 30–35 minutes to administer.

Structured Assessment of Independent Living Scales

The Structured Assessment of Independent Living scales (SAILS; Mahurin, De Bettignes, & Pirozzolo, 1991) divides 50 ADL tasks into 10 subscales, including fine motor, gross motor, dressing, eating, expressive language, receptive language, time orientation, money-related skills, instrumental activities, and social interaction (e.g., appropriate responses to social greetings). In addition to the total score, reflective of overall functioning, the SAILS generates a motor score and a cognitive score. Administration and scoring of the SAILS is guided by detailed, behaviorally anchored descriptions and can be used in both clinical and research settings. Overall, the tasks take approximately 60 minutes to complete.

Assessment of Motor and Process Skills

Designed as a tool for occupational therapists, the Assessment of Motor and Process Skills (AMPS; Fisher, Leu, Velozo, & Pan, 1992) measures the quality of performance by the effort, efficiency, safety, and level of independence involved in both ADL motor and process skills. Motor skills include actions in which the client moves him- or herself or an object, whereas process skills are actions involving a logical sequence of steps, appropriate tool/material selection, and adaptation to problems as they occur. The AMPS inventory contains 83 standardized ADL tasks, varying in degree of difficulty, and a brief interview is used to help the client choose two tasks that are particularly relevant and familiar. For performance comparisons, the AMPS computer package adjusts scores for task/item difficulty and rater severity. Training to administer and score the AMPS includes a 5-day workshop plus follow-up reliability and tester calibration requirements; however, the test has been standardized cross-culturally and internationally (e.g., the United States, England, Sweden, Japan) on over 100,000 individuals for use in research and clinical practice. Administration typically takes about 45 minutes, but the time required varies by tasks chosen and individual level of functioning.

Cognitive Performance Test

The Cognitive Performance Test (CPT; Burns, Mortimer, & Mechak, 1994) is comprised of six common daily tasks, including dressing, shopping, toast making, telephone use, washing, and traveling. The assessment focuses on the degree to which an individual's functional abilities and deficits affect performance on these tasks; simple task completion is not the main variable of interest. Performance is classified into one of six ordinal levels of functional disability that range from profoundly disabled to normal functioning (these levels are based on Allan's [1982] cognitive disability theory). During testing, as deficits or competencies appear, the tester changes the task demands according to a standardized procedure, thus tailoring the test for each individual throughout the administration. The degree and type of help required for task completion are then reflected in the rating. For example, an individual whose task performance is organized, efficient, and without error would be rated as a level 6 (normal), whereas a participant who shows a trial-and-error approach and often needs additional specific directions to complete the task is functioning at level 4 (moderate functional decline). Completion of the battery takes approximately 45 minutes.

Kitchen Task Assessment

The Kitchen Task Assessment (KTA; Baum & Edwards, 1993) focuses solely on the ADL task of cooking, and analyzes performance in terms of the cognitive processes involved and the subsequent level of cognitive support needed to complete the task. During the KTA, which can be administered in the clinic or the home, the individual is asked to make cooked pudding. The tester evaluates the performance across multiple components, and scoring is based on whether each component was completed independently, with verbal assistance, with physical assistance, or not completed at all. From task observation and the scored results, the tester or clinician can recommend appropriate strategies that caregivers can use to help the impaired individual complete other ADLs. The KTA takes less than 30 minutes to administer and is appropriate for use in both clinical and research settings.

Test of Everyday Functional Ability

The Test of Everyday Functional Ability (TEFA; Weiner, Gehrmann, Hynan, Saine, & Cullum, 2006), which was originally called the Texas Functional Living Scale, was designed as a brief measure of functional competence. This 21-item test includes subscales related to dressing, time, money, instrumental activities (e.g., addressing an envelope, using a telephone), and memory (e.g., remembering to take medications). The TEFA can be administered in about 15 minutes by a bachelor's-level tester.

Functional assessments have also been developed for use in other populations. The UCSD Performance-Based Skills Assessment (UPSA; Patterson, Goldman, McKibbin, Hughs, & Jeste, 2001) was designed for persons with schizophrenia or schizoaffective disorder and was developed to tap skills in areas such as communication, finance, household chores, transportation, and recreational activities. The ability to manage medications in individuals with schizophrenia can also be assessed employing instruments such as the Medication Management Ability assessment (MMA; Patterson et al., 2002). Heaton and colleagues (2004) have described the use of performance-based tasks that tap financial skills, medication management, shopping, and cooking as well as specific vocationally related skills in individuals with HIV infection.

Despite the abovementioned strengths, the performance-based approach has its limitations. Performance on tests of functional capacity may not always capture patient-specific or environment-specific variables that affect real-life performance and that, although present in the testing situation, may not be present in the patient's everyday environment. Some of these variables involve the ability to self-initiate and complete a task, the overall motivation of the patient, and the presence of environmental variables that cue the patient that the task needs to be performed. Moreover, the same task that can be completed in the laboratory under optimal conditions may not be as successfully performed in an environment with multiple cognitive and task demands or with less structure. An illustration of this principle is often seen in acquired brain injury. In a quiet office, a secretary recovering from a brain injury may have the cognitive, motivational, and functional capacity to use the telephone, take a message, and type. However, if placed in a busy office in which attention has to be divided among various distractors (e.g., patients presenting at a reception area, the ringing of the telephone, a letter that is being typed), the individual's functional performance may be severely compromised.

Clinician-Based Evaluations

It has been increasingly recognized that good clinical judgment may depend on data garnered from a wide variety of sources. For example, physicians, occupational therapists, and physical therapists in outpatient rehabilitation settings may rely on their direct observations of performance-based behaviors, staff ratings of the patient's functional ability, and judgments of family members who have a chance to evaluate the patient in his or her real-world environment. In some instances, a wealth of functional information may be derived from home visits conducted by a nurse, occupational therapist, physical therapist, or a social worker. An advantage of this interdisciplinary approach is that the effects of physical limitations, cognitive limitations, and motivational factors can be weighed when arriving at a diagnostic determination and a comprehensive treatment plan.

The Role of Neuropsychological Assessment in the Assessment of Ability to Perform IADLs

From its earliest days, clinical neuropsychology aspired to understand the impact of brain lesions and diseases on cognitive functioning. Early work with individuals who suffered penetrating brain injury, blunt head trauma, or strokes culminated in a rich understanding of the relationship between the damaged brain structures and the multiple facets of memory and of other cognitive processes (e.g., attention, executive function). Our knowledge of the cognitive sequelae of brain injury continues to be enriched by advances in psychometrics, neuroimaging, and cognitive neuroscience.

A long-held assumption in the field of neuropsychology is that cognitive processes involved in memory, language, visuospatial skills, attention, and executive function underlie most IADLs. A logical conclusion of such an assumption is that the measurement of cognitive status should allow the clinician to infer the functional status of the patient (see Loewenstein & Mogosky, 1999). Certainly, it is likely that those with substantial cognitive impairment will have difficulties on many higher-order functional tasks, particularly those that involve multistep cognitive operations or divided attention. It is difficult to imagine an individual with profound generalized neuropsychological impairment managing his or her finances, driving an automobile, or returning to the many functional demands of everyday life. In actual clinical practice, however, persons frequently have only mild or moderate cognitive impairments in specific domains, with some areas evidencing only minimal or no cognitive deficits. Varying strengths and weaknesses and differences in cognitive reserve among individuals (see Scarmeas & Stern, 2004; Whalley, Deary, Appleton, & Starr, 2004) may act as mediating factors between actual brain injury or disease and the individual's ability to function. In our work, we have encountered persons with brain injuries who have significant cognitive impairment but who nevertheless continue to show relatively preserved functional abilities. This suggests that, in addition to cognitive reserve, individuals may also vary in their *functional reserve*. As previously discussed, the ability to perform IADLs is likely related to a combination of person-, task-, and environmental-specific factors. This complexity may explain in part why knowledge of neuropsychological function alone may not provide sufficient information in many cases to make judgments about the person's ability to perform IADLs in real-world settings.

In general, the literature across different patient groups suggests that there is an association between neuropsychological test performance and the ability to perform IADLs. Neuropsychological function, most notably executive ability, has been shown to relate to functional competence in diverse groups such as community-dwelling older adults (Bell-McGinty, Podell, Franzen, Baird, & Williams 2002; Cahn-Weiner, Boyle, & Malloy, 2002; Cahn-Weiner, Malloy, Boyle, Marran, & Salloway, 2000; Rapp et al., 2005; Royall, Palmer, Chiodo, & Polk, 2005) and in patient populations diagnosed with Alzheimer's disease (Boyle, Paul, Moser, & Cohen, 2004; Cahn-Weiner, Ready, & Malloy, 2003), cerebrovascular disease (Jefferson, Paul, Ozonoff, & Cohen, 2006), postacute head injury (Farmer & Eakman, 1995; Goverover, 2004), heart transplantation (Putzke, Williams, Daniel, Bourge, & Boll, 2000), schizophrenia (Jeste, Patterson, et al., 2003), and HIV infection (Albert et al., 2003; Heaton et al., 2004).

Early cognitive deficits have been related to an increased risk of functional decline among older adults (McGuire, Ford, & Ajani, 2006) and to increased mortality (McGuire et al., 2006; Schupf et al., 2005). Early functional deficits have also been related to cognitive decline in longitudinal studies of older adults (Plehn, Marcopulos, & McLain, 2004). In addition, there are specific patterns of neuropsychological deficits that may be related to functional performance. Earnst and colleagues (2001) found that performance on neuropsychological tests tapping the executive component of working memory was strongly associated with performance on a test of functional capacity that assessed basic money skills and ability to manage bank statements and a checkbook. In a study of 69 older patients who presented for clinical assessment, Baird, Podell, Lovell, and McGinty (2001) found that in addition to the Dementia Rating Scale, seven out of nine neuropsychological measures entered into regression equations predicting scores on a scale that assesses the ability to carry out IADLs. In a recent investigation, Hoskin, Jackson, and Crowe (2005) found that neuropsychological performance was related to the capacity of persons with acquired brain injury to manage their personal finances. These investigators compared participants who were handling money independently with those who had been appointed an administrator by the court to help them manage their finances. Results indicated that measures of working memory, impulse control, and cognitive flexibility correctly classified 83.7% of individuals in the correct functional group. Interestingly, measures of memory had no discriminatory power. Woods and colleagues (2006) found that the ability to retrieve words that refer to action (i.e., verbs) was more strongly associated with IADL dependence among HIV-infected individuals, relative to the ability to retrieve words that start with a specific letter or that belong to a particular category, resulting in an overall hit rate of 76%.

In addition, performance on neuropsychological measures such as memory, attention, and conceptual abilities has been related to medication adherence and management (Hinkin et al., 2002; Jeste, Dunn, et al., 2003; Putzke et al., 2000). Cognitive performance has also been associated with performance on driving simulators and on-road driving evaluations (Grace et al., 2005; Lundqvist et al., 1997; Marcotte et al., 2004; Reger et al., 2004; Rizzo, McGehee, Dawson, & Anderson, 2001). A particularly effective predictor of driving performance has been the Useful Field of View (UFOV), a test tapping visual attention (see Clay et al., 2005).

A primary goal of neuropsychological assessment is to determine patterns of cognitive strengths and weaknesses as they relate to important real-world outcomes (Sbordone, 1996). In their review of the literature, Franzen and Wilhelm (1996) and Spooner and Pachana (2006) differentiate between veridicality and verisimilitude in describing the ecological validity of neuropsychological tests. "Veridicality" refers to the extent to which performance on neuropsychological tests relates to measured performance on real-world tasks, whereas "verisimilitude" refers to the degree that the task demands of a test reflect the actual demands imposed on the person by the real-world environment. Clearly, most studies in the field are concerned with veridicality. Increasingly, there has been recognition that neuropsychological measures administered in controlled conditions that facilitate optimal performance may not tap the real-world demands of higher-order functional tasks that often must be completed in the presence of many environmental demands. In our laboratory we have worked on paradigms designed to increase verisimilitude. For example, in our studies of MCI in older adults, we have been developing and refining paradigms that tap time- and event-related prospective memory as well as face–name associations and memory for common, everyday objects. Thus, we have focused on paradigms that more closely tap some of the real-world difficulties reported by subjects with MCI. Although traditional tests of auditory list learning, memory for story passages, and memory for designs are often useful as cognitive tests, their applicability to real-life demands (e.g., remembering to take medications at a specific time, putting a name together with a face) may be more limited. We first developed the DAFS (see above) to assess the real-world abilities of persons with mild dementia. More recently, and in conjunction with Dr. Sara Czaja and her human factors team at the University of Miami, we have developed assessment and outcome measures such as the ability to navigate telephone menu systems and to use an automated teller machine (ATM) (Loewenstein & Acevedo, 2006).

Limitations of Neuropsychological Studies Based on Correlation Analyses

At face value, the above-mentioned studies indicate that there is a significant association between neuropsychological test performance and the ability to carry out IADLs. However, one must be cautious about applying group findings to individual cases and about making causal inferences on data that assess statistical associations. Although most studies demonstrate statistically significant relationships between neuropsychological measures and functional performance, the degree of variability in neuropsychological performance and functional performance frequently does not exceed the unexplained variance associated with the dependent variable (see Loewenstein & Mogosky, 1999; Silver, 2000). Specifically, even if the association between the variables of interest exceeds a healthy correlation of .7, more than 50% of the performance variability on functional measures remains unexplained.

In our judgment, more informative methods to determine the utility of neuropsychological measures in predicting actual functional performance include techniques such as logistic regression, discriminant function analysis, and receiver operating characteristic (ROC) curve analysis. These approaches yield estimates of sensitivity and specificity, providing information to the clinician about how many persons with functional impairment are accurately identified as impaired and how many persons without functional impairment are accurately identified as unimpaired by neuropsychological tests. The next step would be to calculate positive and negative predictive values based on the base rates of impairment in specific settings. Unfortunately, there is a paucity of such studies in the literature.

Many clinicians would feel comfortable concluding that an individual with a normal neuropsychological profile is likely to be able to drive and to manage his or her medications or finances. On the other hand, it is difficult to imagine that a clinician would feel comfortable recommending these activities for an individual scoring below the 1st percentile on a broad array of commonly employed neuropsychological measures of memory, language, attention, executive function, and visuospatial skills. The patients who fall in the mild-to-intermediate impairment ranges in neuropsychological test performance are the ones who often constitute a challenge when trying to make judgments about their degree of functional impairment.

While there is little debate that specific cognitive abilities underlie functional capacity, it should be recognized that neuropsychological measures are not unidimensional but rather tap multiple cognitive functions. More importantly, given that functional performance in real life is often dependent on the complex interaction of person-, task-, and environmental-specific variables, it is not surprising that there is far from a one-to-one correspondence between neuropsychological test results and IADLs. Indeed, in our work on cognitive remediation techniques for those with early Alzheimer's disease, we pay special attention to task specificity. We have found that the use of spaced retrieval (see Camp & Stevens, 1990) and procedural motor memory practice can lead to improvements in performance on functionally relevant tasks in individuals with mild Alzheimer's disease. The concept of spaced retrieval is based on paradigms that require the individual to make associations between two targets (e.g., face–name association) and to gradually lengthen the interval between the presentation of the target and recall of the association by the patient. If the individual fails at a longer interval, the interventionist returns to the last previous shorter interval in which there was success. Procedural learning involves more implicit motor memory subserved by basal ganglia systems and is not as dependent on explicit memory, which is very dependent on the integrity of hippocampal and entorhinal cortex structures. In contrast, we have found that simply training different component cognitive processes (e.g., attention, concentration) thought to underlie task performance has no effect on outcome (Loewenstein & Acevedo, 2006; Loewenstein, Acevedo, Czaja, & Duara, 2004).

Minimizing Errors of Clinical Judgment

In general, functional assessment is most complete when information is obtained from multiple sources. It is important to gather as much information as possible from collateral informants regarding the patient's current and past ability to perform specific IADLs. In addition, an examination of the patient's performance on neuropsychological measures may be helpful when making treatment recommendations and when deciding if referrals or additional assessments (preferably in home) are necessary. For example, an individual, his or her spouse, and their children may insist that the patient is able to drive independently, manage finances, and buy needed goods. However, on direct functional assessment, the patient is unable to count currency, make change for a purchase, write a check, or balance a checkbook. Neuropsychological testing may also evidence severe impairments in memory, attention, visuospatial skills, concept formation, speed of processing, and in the ability to shift cognitive sets. Despite the reports of the patient and family members, it is likely that the patient is at risk. In many states across the country, the results of such an evaluation would prompt a report to the state of concerns about the patient's driving ability and a recommendation that an on-road driving test be conducted. The issue is not merely whether the person has the procedural knowledge and motor skills to operate a vehicle but whether he or she has the cognitive capacity to recognize changing environmental conditions, such as watching out for children in a school zone or taking an alternate route if a road is blocked. Additionally, it might be necessary for a nurse or a social worker to perform a home visit to ensure that the person is actually capable of managing his or her finances and medications in the everyday environment. The nature of the neurological status of the patient as well as the possible need of serial assessments should also be taken into consideration. For example, an individual with a head injury may have a functional disability that dissipates over time and that will show improvement in subsequent evaluations. Conversely, a person with early Alzheimer's disease may not demonstrate functional impairments at a given time but may evidence these deficits on follow-up assessments.

Future Directions

It has been argued that the development of neuropsychological tasks that tap the demands of everyday life (i.e., verisimilitude) should be an important goal for future test development in neuropsychology (Chaytor & Schmitter-Edgecombe, 2003; Spooner & Pachana, 2006). Spooner and Pachana (2006) mention the possible applicability of tests such as the original Rivermead Behavioral Memory Test (RBMT; Wilson, Cockburn, & Baddeley, 1985) and an extended version of the test (RMBT-E; de Wall, Wilson, & Baddeley, 1994; Wilson, Clare, Baddeley, Watson, & Tate, 1999) in the identification of everyday memory impairments, especially those related to prospective memory deficits. Indeed, they endorse the further development of neuropsychological tests that can be administered to neurologically intact as well as medically or neurologically impaired patients.

There is a great need for the development of more sensitive and ecologically valid neuropsychological measures that would allow us to further understand the effects of medications and medical conditions on cognitive test performance, especially among older adults. Emerging technologies using computer microprocessors may enable the development of more sophisticated performance-based measures to assess attention, cognitive processing speed, and working memory, and to examine the relationship of these cognitive processes to functional test performance. In this regard, human factors engineers have made significant contributions to the field by studying how to optimize human–machine interfaces that are used in everyday appliances and systems such as cell phones, telephone menu navigation systems, and even the automobiles that we drive (Czaja & Sharit, 2003).

It is increasingly evident that new empirically based approaches are needed to more fully capture the demands of real-world activities of daily living. In addition, there is increasing emphasis on assessing the practical everyday implications of theoretical research that studies constructs such as memory and executive function. Neuropsychologists, occupational therapists, and other allied health professionals have been at the forefront in developing performance-based instruments for older adults. There is also an increasing appreciation of the value of developing new paradigms that integrate information from related fields of cognitive psychology, human factors, and behavioral medicine. In fact, the challenge to neuropsychology is to appreciate the richness of alternative approaches developed by allied disciplines and to find ways of incorporating these approaches in our continuing pursuit of scientific knowledge.

Researchers and clinicians recognize that those neuropsychological tests that may be useful for diagnosis may not necessarily be the same measures that are most useful for monitoring cognitive and functional change over time. Similarly, the neuropsychological tests that may be useful for diagnostic purposes may not be the optimal measures to predict real-world functional performance. Real-life situations are usually based on open systems where environmental circumstances are fluid and may be unpredictable. In contrast, strict standardization procedures require the administration of cognitive measures in a controlled testing environment that minimizes distractions and maximizes test performance. A continuing challenge to the field is to develop standardized instruments that adequately capture the multiple demands that are placed simultaneously on the individual's cognitive resources.

The limitations of available cognitive tests in the prediction of functional performance in the real world are sometimes not appreciated by neuropsychologists who may be asked to render an opinion about the patient's functional status. The professional opinion rendered by a neuropsychologist may be used by physicians, rehabilitation treatment teams, the schools, and the courts to make decisions that may dramatically affect the patient's quality of life, autonomy, and independence. For example, a cognitively normal, older, non-native, English-speaking immigrant with 6 years of education, whose sole work experience has been repetitive manual labor, may score at the impaired level on neuropsychological tests frequently used by neuropsychologists, such as the Rey–Osterrieth Figure Test, the Boston Naming Test, the Trail Making Test, and subtests of the Wechsler Adult Intelligence Scale (e.g., Similarities, Block Design). If the neuropsychologist conceptualizes the test results as a true reflection of the patient's cognitive status without consideration of the limitations of many mainstream neuropsychological tests when used with individuals of different ethnocultural/linguistic backgrounds, he or she may erroneously conclude that the patient's "cognitive impairment" is likely to result in inability to carry out IADLs. In fact, several cross-cultural studies examining the functional status of older adults have had to rely on IADLs that differ from those traditionally assessed in scales used in the United States (see Fillenbaum et al., 1999; Senanarong et al., 2003). In other words, IADLs vary across cultures and those that may be essential in certain cultural groups may be irrelevant in others.

On the other hand, the neuropsychologist may be evaluating a patient who scores within normal limits on memory for stories on the Wechsler Memory Scales and who exhibits normal expressive and receptive language function on the Boston Diagnostic Aphasia Examination. Unfortunately, normal performance on these measures does not guarantee that the patient will be able to manage and process the welter of discourse material that individuals must manage in their everyday environment. Similarly, normal performance on a list-learning task does not necessarily imply that the person will remember to buy needed grocery items, to pay the electricity bill, or to appropriately respond to environmental cues that signal that the bill should be paid or that it was already paid. The expertise of neuropsychologists in test development and construction places neuropsychology in a unique position to develop tests with verisimilitude. In addition, it allows our field to advance our knowledge of factors, including ethnocultural/linguistic factors, that mediate the relationship between cognition and real-life functioning.

Conclusions

It is increasingly recognized that measures that presumably tap specific cognitive processes rarely tap a unitary cognitive construct and that, rather, performance on widely employed instruments frequently tap various cognitive domains. The notion that cognition, as reflected by neuropsychological tests, is the sole requisite for independent real-world function is, at best, misguided. It is important that we further our knowledge of person-, task-, and environment-specific variables that may affect real-world functioning. Pioneering work by Wilson and colleagues (Wilson, 1993; Wilson et al., 1999) and the cogent arguments presented by Spooner and Pachana (2006) underscore the importance of examining the practical aspects of memory (e.g., prospective memory) that are rarely assessed in traditional neuropsychological measures, thus limiting their ecological validity. This laudable goal would be facilitated by an integration of information stemming from allied disciplines such as rehabilitation medicine, occupational therapy, human factors engineering, and behavioral neurology. Already, psychologists in rehabilitation settings are developing sophisticated treatment approaches that go beyond a specific cognitive domain and that directly train the acquisition and maintenance of functional skills (see Loewenstein & Acevedo, 2006).

To enhance clinical utility, future studies should assess the impact of varied neurological conditions on specific IADLs. In addition, empirical studies should utilize techniques such as ROC curves, logistic regression, and discriminant function analysis to examine outcomes of interest (e.g., sensitivity, specificity, positive and negative predictive values) in different clinical populations and in groups of varied ethnocultural/linguistic backgrounds. The identification of factors other than neuropsychological test performance that can augment the prediction of ability to carry out IADLs in real life would further advance our knowledge in this important field.

The complexity that neuropsychologists face in understanding the multifactoral nature of functional performance on different IADLs can appear daunting. The alternative, however, is to refuse to accept the limitations associated with existing practices and the consequences of making inaccurate judgments that can adversely affect the lives of our patients and the fulfillment of our professional obligations.

Acknowledgment

We would like to thank Rachel Meyer for her assistance in reviewing and summarizing the available measures of functional capacity.

References

Albert, S. M., Flater, S. R., Clouse, R., Todak, G., Stern, Y., & Marder, K. (2003). NEAD Study Group, medication management skill in HIV: I. Evidence for adaptation of medication management strategies in people with cognitive impairment. II. Evidence for a pervasive lay model of medication efficacy. *AIDS Behav*, 7, 329–338.

Allan, C. K. (1982). Independence through activity: The practice of occupational therapy. *Am J Occup Ther*, 36(11), 731–739.

American Psychiatric Association. (1994). *Diagnostic and statistical manual of mental disorders* (4th ed.). Washington, DC: Author.

Argüelles, S., Loewenstein, D. A., Eisdorfer, C., & Argüelles, T. (2001). Caregivers' judgments of the functional abilities of the Alzheimer's disease patient: Impact of caregivers' depression and perceived burden. *J Geriatr Psych Neurol*, 14, 91–98.

Baird, A., Podell, K., Lovell, M., & McGinty, S. B. (2001). Complex real-world functioning and neuropsychological test performance in older adults. *The Clin Neuropsychol*, 15, 369–379.

Baum, C., & Edwards, D. F. (1993). Cognitive performance in senile dementia of the Alzheimer's type: The Kitchen Task Assessment. *The Am J Occup Ther*, 47, 431–436.

Bell-McGinty, S., Podell, K., Franzen, M., Baird, A. D., & Williams, M. J. (2002). Standard measures of executive function in predicting instrumental activities of daily living in older adults. *Int J Geriatr Psych*, 17, 828–834.

Bennet, T. L. (2001). Neuropsychological evaluation in rehabilitation planning and evaluation of functional skills. *Arch Clin Neuropsych*, 16, 237–253.

Boyle, P. A., Paul, R. H., Moser, D. J., & Cohen, R. A. (2004). Executive impairments predict functional declines in vascular dementia. *Clin Neuropsychol*, 18, 75–82.

Burns, T., Mortimer, J., & Mechak, P. (1994). Cognitive performance test: A new approach to functional assessment in Alzheimer's disease. *J Geriatr Psych Neur*, 7, 46–54.

Cahn-Weiner, D. A., Boyle, P. A., & Malloy, P. F. (2002). Tests of executive function predict instrumental activities of daily living in community-dwelling older individuals. *Appl Neuropsychol*, 9, 187–191.

Cahn-Weiner, D. A., Malloy, P. F., Boyle, P. A., Marran, M., & Salloway, S. (2000). Prediction of functional status from neuropsychological tests in community-dwelling elderly individuals. *Clin Neuropsychol*, 14, 187–195.

Cahn-Weiner, D. A., Ready, R. E., & Malloy, P. F. (2003). Neuropsychological predictors of everyday memory and everyday functioning in patients with mild Alzheimer's disease. *J Geriatr Psych Neur*, 16, 84–89.

Camp, C. J., & Stevens, A. B. (1990). Spaced-retrieval: A memory intervention for dementia of the Alzheimer's type (DAT). *Clin Gerontol*, 10, 58–60.

Chaytor, N., & Schmitter-Edgecombe, M. (2003). The ecological validity of neuropsychological tests: A review of the literature on everyday cognitive skills. *Neuropsychol Rev*, 13, 181–197.

Clay, O. J., Wadley, V. G., Edwards, J. D., Roth, D. L., Roenker, D. L., & Ball, K. K. (2005). Cumulative meta-analysis of the relationship between useful field of view and driving performance in older adults: Current and future implications. *Optometry Vision Sci*, 82, 724–731.

Czaja, S. J., & Sharit, J. (2003). Practically relevant research: Capturing real world tasks, environments, and outcomes. *The Gerontologist*, 43, 9–18.

de Wall, C., Wilson, B. A., & Baddeley, A. D. (1994). The Extended Rivermead Behavioral Memory Test: A measure of everyday memory performance in normal adults. *Memory*, 2, 149–166.

Earnst, K. S., Wadley, V. G., Aldridge, T. M., Steenwyk, A. B., Hammond, A. E., Harrell, L. E., et al. (2001). Loss of financial capacity in Alzheimer's disease: The role of working memory. *Aging Neuropsychol C*, 8, 109–119.

Erzigkeit, H., Lehfeld, H., Pena-Casanova, J., Bieber, F., Yekrangi-Hartmann, C., Rupp, M., et al. (2001). The Bayer-Activities of Daily Living Scale (B-ADL): Results from a validation study in three European countries. *Dement Geriatr Cogn*, 12, 348–358.

Evans, J. D., Heaton, R. K., Paulsen, J. S., Palmer, B. W., Patterson, T., & Jeste, D. V. (2003). The relationship of neuropsychological abilities to specific domains of functional capacity in older schizophrenia patients. *Biol Psychiat*, 53, 422–430.

Farmer, J. E., & Eakman, A. M. (1995). The relationship between neuropsychological functioning and instrumental activities of daily living following acquired brain injury. *Appl Neuropsychol*, 2, 107–115.

Fillenbaum, G. G., & Smyer, M. A. (1981). The development, validity, and reliability of the OARS multidimensional functional assessment questionnaire. *J Gerontol*, 36, 428–434.

Fisher, A. G., Leu, Y., Velozo, C. A., & Pan, A. W. (1992). Cross cultural assessment of process skills. *Am J Occup Ther*, 46, 876–885.

Franzen, M. D., & Wilhelm, K. L. (1996). Conceptual foundations of ecological validity in neuropsychological assessment. In R. J. Sbordone & C. J. Long (Eds.), *Ecological validity of neuropsychological testing* (pp. 91–112). Boca Raton, FL: St. Lucie Press.

Gelinas, I., Gauthier, L., McIntyre, M., & Gauthier, S. (1999). Development of a functional measure for persons with Alzheimer's disease: The disability assessment for dementia. *Am J Occup Ther*, 53, 471–481.

Goverover, Y. (2004). Categorization, deductive reasoning, and self-awareness: Association with everyday competence in persons with acute brain injury. *J Clin Exp Neuropsyc*, 26, 737–749.

Grace, J., Amick, M. M., D'Abreu, A., Festa, E. K., Heindel, W. C., & Ott, B. R. (2005). Neuropsychological deficits associated with driving performance in Parkinson's and Alzheimer's disease. *J Int Neuropsych Soc*, 11, 766–775.

Hamilton, J. M. (2000). Cognitive, motor, and behavioral correlates of functional decline in Huntington's disease. *Dissertation Abstracts International: Section B: The Sciences and Engineering*, 61(5-B), 2761–2941.

Heaton, R. K., Marcotte, T. D., Mindt, M. R., Sadek, J., Moore, D. J., Bentley, H., et al. (2004). The impact of HIV-associated neuropsychological impairment on everyday functioning. *J Int Neuropsych Soc, 10*, 317–331.

Hinkin, C. H., Castellon, S. A., Durvasula, R. S., Hardy, D. J., Lam, M. N., Mason, K. I., et al. (2002). Medication adherence among HIV+ adults. *Neurology, 59*, 1944–1950.

Hoeymans, N., Wouters, E. R., Feskens, E. J., van den Bos, G. A., & Kromhout, D. (1997). Reproducibility of performance-based and self-reported measures of functional status. *J Gerontol Biol Sci Med Sci, 52*, 363–368.

Hoskin, K. M., Jackson, M., & Crowe, S. F. (2005). Can neuropsychological assessment predict capacity to manage personal finances? A comparison between brain impaired individuals with and without administrators. *Psychiatry, Psychol Law, 12*, 56–67.

Jefferson, A. L., Paul, R. H., Ozonoff, A., & Cohen, R. A. (2006). Evaluating elements of executive functioning as predictors of instrumental activities of daily living (IADLs). *Arch Clin Neuropsych, 21*, 311–320.

Jeste, D. V., Dunn, L. B., Palmer, B. W., Saks, E., Halpain, M., Cook, A., et al. (2003). A collaborative model for research on decisional capacity and informed consent in older patients with schizophrenia: Bioethics unit of a geriatric psychiatry intervention research center. *Psychopharmacology, 171*, 68–74.

Jeste, S. D., Patterson, T. L., Palmer, B. W., Dolder, C. R., Goldman, S., & Jeste, D. V. (2003). Cognitive predictors of medication adherence among middle-aged and older outpatients with schizophrenia. *Schizophr Res, 63*, 49–58.

Kane, R. A., & Kane, R. A. (1981). *Assessing the elderly: A practical guide to measurement.* Lexington, MA: Lexington Books.

Katz, S., Ford, A. B., Moskowitz, R. W., Jackson, B. A., & Jaffe, M. W. (1963). Studies of illness in the aged. The index of ADL: A standardized measure of biological and psychosocial function. *JAMA, 185*, 914–919.

Kuriansky, J. B., Gurland, B. J., & Fleiss, J. L. (1976). The assessment of self-care capacity in geriatric psychiatric patients by objective and subjective methods. *J Clin Psychol, 32*, 95–102.

Lawton, M., & Brody, E. (1969). Assessment of older people: Self maintaining and instrumental activities of daily living. *Gerontologist, 9*, 179–186.

Lindeboom, R., Vermeulen, M., Holman, R., & De Haan, R. J. (2003). Activities of daily living instruments: Optimizing scales for neurologic assessments. *Neurology, 60*, 738–742.

Loewenstein, D., & Acevedo, A. (2006). Training of cognitive and functionally relevant skills in mild Alzheimer's disease: An integrated approach. In D. K. Attix & K. A. Welsh-Bohmer (Eds.), *Geriatric neuropsychology: Assessment and intervention* (pp. 261–274). New York: Guilford Press.

Loewenstein, D. A., Acevedo, A., Czaja, S. J., & Duara, R. (2004). Cognitive rehabilitation of mildly impaired Alzheimer's disease patients on cholinesterase inhibitors. *Am J Geriat Psychiat, 12*, 395–402.

Loewenstein, D. A., Amigo, E., Duara, R., Guterman, A., Hurwitz, D., Berkowitz, N., et al. (1989). A new scale for the assessment of functional status in Alzheimer's disease and related disorders. *J Gerontol, 44*, 114–121.

Loewenstein, D. A., Argüelles, S., Bravo, M., Freeman, R. Q., Argüelles, T., Acevedo, A., et al. (2001). Caregivers' judgments of the functional abilities of the Alzheimer's disease patient: A comparison of proxy reports and objective measures. *J Gerontol B-Psychol, 56*, 78–84.

Loewenstein, D. A., & Mogosky, B. (1999). Functional assessment in the older adult patient. In P. Lichtenberg (Ed.), *Handbook of assessment in clinical gerontology* (pp. 529–554). New York: Wiley.

Lundqvist, A., Alinder, J., Alm, H., Gerdle, B., Levander, S., & Ronnberg, J. (1997). Neuropsychological aspects of driving after brain lesion: Simulator study and on-road driving. *Appl Neuropsychol*, *4*, 220–230.

Mahurin, R. K., De Bettignes, B. H., & Pirozzolo, F. J. (1991). Structured assessment of independent living skills: Preliminary report of a performance measure of functional abilities in dementia. *J Gerontol*, *46*, 58–66.

Mangone, C. A., Sanguinetti, R. M., Bauman, P. D., Gonzalez, R. C., Pereyra, S., Bozzola, F. G., et al. (1993). Influence of feelings of burden on the caregiver's perception of the patient's functional status. *Dementia*, *4*, 287–293.

Marcotte, T., Wolfson, T., Rosenthal, T. J., Heaton, R. K., Gonzalez, R., Ellis, R. J., et al. (2004). A multimodal assessment of driving in HIV infection. *Neurology*, *63*(8), 1417–1422.

McGuire, L. C., Ford, E. S., & Ajani, U. A. (2006). Cognitive functioning as a predictor of functional disability in later life. *Am J Geriat Psychiat*, *14*, 36–42.

McKhann, G., Drachman, D., Folstein, M., Katzman, R., Price, D., & Stadlan, E. M. (1984). Clinical diagnosis of Alzheimer's disease: Report of the NINCDS-ADRDA Work Group under the auspices of Department of Health and Human Services Task Force on Alzheimer's disease. *Neurology*, *34*, 939–944.

Myers, A. M., Holliday, P. J., Harvey, K. A., & Hutchinson, K. S. (1993). Functional performance measures: Are they superior to self-assessments? *J Gerontol*, *48*, 196–206.

Patterson, T. L., Goldman, S., McKibbin, C. L., Hughs, T., & Jeste, D. V. (2001). UCSD Performance-Based Skills Assessment: Development of a new measure of everyday functioning for severely mentally ill adults. *Schizophrenia Bull*, *27*, 235–245.

Patterson, T. L., Klapow, J. C., Eastham, J. H., Heaton, R. K., Evans, J. D., Koch, W. L., et al. (1998). Correlates of functional status in older patients with schizophrenia. *Psychiat Res*, *80*, 41–52.

Patterson, T. L., Lacro, J., McKibbin, C. L., Moscona, S., Hughs, T., & Jeste, D.V. (2002). Medication management ability assessment: Results from a performance-based measure in older outpatients with schizophrenia. *J Clin Psychopharm*, *22*, 11–19.

Petersen, R. C., Smith, G. E., Waring, S. C., Ivnik, R. J., Tangalos, E. G., & Kokmen, E. (1999). Mild cognitive impairment. *Arch Neurol-Chicago*, *56*, 303–308.

Pfeffer, R. I., Kurosaki, T. T., Harrah, C. H., Chance, J. M., & Filos, S. (1982). Measurement of functional activities in older adults in the community. *J Gerontol*, *37*, 323–329.

Plehn, K., Marcopulos, B. A., & McLain, C. A. (2004). The relationship between neuropsychological test performance, social functioning, and instrumental activities of daily living in a sample of rural older adults. *Clin Neuropsychol*, *1*, 101–113.

Putzke, J. D., Williams, M. A., Daniel, F. J., Bourge, R. C., & Boll, T. J. (2000). Activities of daily living among heart transplant candidates: Neuropsychological and cardiac function predictors. *J Heart Lung Transpl*, *19*, 995–1006.

Rapp, M. A., Schnaider Beeri, M., Schmeidler, J., Sano, M., Silverman, J. M., & Haraoutunian, V. (2005). Relationship of neuropsychological performance to functional status in nursing home residents and community-dwelling older adults. *Am J Geriat Psychiat*, *13*, 450–459.

Reger, M. A., Welsh, R. K., Watson, G. S., Cholerton, B., Baker, L. D., & Craft, S. (2004). The relationship between neuropsychological functions and driving ability in dementia: A meta-analysis. *Neuropsychology*, *18*(1), 85–93.

Rizzo, M., McGehee, D. V., Dawson, J. D., & Anderson, S. N. (2001). Simulated crashes in intersections in drivers with Alzheimer's disease. *Alz Dis Assoc Dis*, *15*(1), 10–20.

Royall, D. R., Palmer, R., Chiodo, L. K., & Polk, M. J. (2005). Normal rates of cognitive change in successful aging: The Freedom House study. *J Int Neuropsych Soc*, *11*, 899–909.

Sbordone, R. J. (1996). Ecological validity: Some critical issues for the neuropsychologists. In R. J. Sbordone & C. J. Long (Eds.), *Ecological validity of neuropsychological testing* (pp. 15–41). Boca Raton, FL: St. Lucie Press.

Scarmeas, N., & Stern, Y. (2004). Cognitive reserve: Implications for diagnosis and prevention of Alzheimer's disease. *Curr Neurol Neurosci Rep, 4,* 374–380.

Schupf, N., Tang, M-X, Albert, S. M., Costa, R., Andrews, H., Lee, J. H., et al. (2005). Decline in cognitive and functional skills increases mortality risk in nondemented elderly. *Neurology, 65,* 1218–1226.

Silver, C. H. (2000). Ecological validity of neuropsychological assessment in childhood traumatic brain injury. *J Head Trauma Rehab, 15,* 973–988.

Sinoff, G., & Ore, L. (1997). The Barthel Activities of Daily Living Index: Self-reporting versus actual performance in the old-old. *J Am Geriatr Soc, 45,* 832–836.

Spooner, D. M., & Pachana, N. A. (2006). Ecological validity in neuropsychological assessment: A case for greater consideration and research with neurologically intact populations. *Arch Clin Neuropsych, 21,* 327–337.

Tuokko, H. (1993). Psychosocial evaluation and management of the Alzheimer's patient. In R. W. Parks, R. Zec, & R. S. Wilson (Eds.), *Neuropsychology of Alzheimer's disease and other dementias* (pp. 565–588). New York: Oxford University Press.

Weinberger, M., Samsa, G. P., Schmader, K., Greenberg, S. M., Carr, D. B., & Wildmand, D. S. (1992). Comparing proxy and patient's perceptions of patient's functional status: Results from an outpatient geriatric clinic. *J Am Geriatr Soc, 40,* 585–588.

Weiner, M. F., Gehrmann, H. R., Hynan, L. S., Saine, K. C., & Cullum, C. M. (2006). Comparison of the test of everyday functional abilities with a direct measure of daily function. *Dement Geriatr Cogn, 22,* 83–86.

Whalley, L. J., Deary, I. J., Appleton, C. L., & Starr, J. M. (2004). Cognitive reserve and the neurobiology of cognitive aging. *Ageing Res Rev, 3,* 369–382.

Wilson, B. A. (1993). Ecological validity of neuropsychological assessment: Do neuropsychological indexes predict performance in everyday activities? *Appl Prev Psychol, 2,* 209–215.

Wilson, B. A., Clare, L., Baddeley, A. D., Watson, P., & Tate, R. (1999). *The Rivermead Behavioral Memory Test—Extended Version.* Bury St. Edmunds, UK: Thames Valley Test.

Wilson, B. A., Cockburn, J., & Baddeley, A. D. (1985). *The Rivermead Behavioral Memory Test—Extended Version.* Bury St. Edmunds, UK: Thames Valley Test.

Woods, S. P., Morgan, E. E., Dawson, M., Scott, J. C., Grant, I., & the HIV Neurobehavioral Research Center (HNRC) Group. (2006). Action (verb) fluency predicts dependence in instrumental activities of daily living in persons infected with HIV. *J Clin Exp Neuropsyc, 28,* 1030–1042.

CHAPTER 5

The Prediction of Vocational Functioning from Neuropsychological Performance

Joseph R. Sadek and Wilfred G. van Gorp

Despite the fact that a range of neuroimaging procedures has greatly reduced the need for neuropsychological tests to determine presence and lesion location, neuropsychological tests continue to have an important place in the clinical assessment of brain dysfunction and cognitive capabilities, relative weaknesses and frank deficits. Relating findings on neuropsychological tests to "real-world functioning" represents one of the most valued uses, today, of neuropsychological assessment. However, the current array of neuropsychological tests was not designed to predict real-world abilities in any but the broadest manner (such as an IQ score predicting general ability to function, overall). Unfortunately, neuropsychological tests do not correlate perfectly with functional outcomes, including vocational outcomes in persons with acquired brain disease. One way to characterize the problem (Franzen & Wilhelm, 1996) is that neuropsychological tests have limited "veridicality," which is the ability to accurately predict real-world outcomes such as future employment or job performance, and that they lack "verisimilitude," which is the similarity to real-world tasks (including work skills). Although we do not have, as yet, an array of neuropsychological tests that are known to directly predict specific aspects of real-world functioning, the tests we use today still have a very important role in assessing outcomes. Neuropsychological tests remain the most direct way to assess cognitive and emotional abilities that are important for vocational and academic performance. However, the challenge remains to develop and validate a new generation of neuropsychological tests that relate to both brain function as well as predict some aspects of specific real-world abilities. This chapter discusses these important issues.

Conditions that affect a person's cognitive functioning can have a profound impact on his or her ability to work. Although acquired or traumatic brain injury (TBI) is the most widely studied condition, with annual estimated costs in lost productivity and medical care around $60 billion (Finkelstein, Corso, & Miller, 2006), other conditions that result in cognitive impairment (e.g., stroke, brain tumors, multiple sclerosis, HIV/AIDS) have also been shown to result in lost productivity relating to work and other outcomes. Some psychiatric disorders (e.g., posttraumatic stress disorder, bipolar disorder, major depression, and schizophrenia, among others) are also associated with cognitive impairment and resulting loss of work productivity. In most of these disorders, there is little research on the relative contribution of affective symptoms versus cognitive impairment to loss of work productivity. In schizophrenia we know that neuropsychological impairment is an independent predictor of unemployment (Heaton et al., 1994; McGurk & Mueser, 2004, 2006; Twamley et al., 2006). Most treatment approaches aim to maximize a person's functional independence, including return to work, and there is a clear need for research on cognitive factors that predict return to work in any condition associated with neuropsychological impairment.

It is, of course, unrealistic to expect that every important behavior relevant to performance in any job for each person undergoing a neuropsychological assessment can be assessed by one or more neuropsychological tests. Reviews of the cognitive aptitudes required for occupations are listed in the *Dictionary of Occupational Titles* (DOT—Lees-Haley, 1990; U.S. Department of Labor, 1991). In the updated DOT, called the Occupational Information Network (O*NET; U.S. Department of Labor, 2006), there are 21 possible "cognitive abilities" listed, an additional 10 "psychomotor abilities" and 12 "sensory abilities" that are considered "worker characteristics"— enduring characteristics that may influence both performance and the capacity to acquire knowledge and skills required for effective work performance (see Table 5.1 for O*NET worker abilities). Many of the abilities are ones that neuropsychologists have also traditionally measured (e.g., auditory attention and finger dexterity). It is important to note that the abilities considered important for various job titles were determined by expert panels and not by empirical validation using actual tests.

A brief electronic review of the Mental Measurements Yearbook (MMY; Buros Institute of Mental Measurement, 2005) using the keyword *vocation* indicates that at least 100 performance-based assessment tools have been published. These assessments may maximize verisimilitude, but it is unlikely that, even if valid, an individual professional could learn to administer and interpret performance on every job-specific performance assessment tool. Therefore, a different approach is required.

One perspective on neuropsychological tests in relation to real-world functioning is that the tests measure meta-abilities that are generally applicable to performance of a broad range of vocations (a global "g" [or general] factor, if you will, of "real-world ability") rather than predicting discrete or specific vocations. A closer inspection of the various descriptions of the vocation-specific measures listed in the MMY reveals that each can be classified into one of two groups. One group contains measures that assess a job-specific skill, such as specific clerical or mechanical skills. The other group contains measures that assess a broader cognitive ability that can be applied in many vocations, such as verbal, computational, or visuospatial abilities. Of the 100 vocation-specific tests we identified, almost half (53) assess some aspect of cognition such as vocabulary, problem solving, or verbal comprehension.

Although there are no studies that directly compare the predictive validity of neuropsychological versus vocation-specific assessments, it seems reasonable to expect that neuropsychological tests perform as well as many of these cognitively themed vocational tests in assessing vocational performance, since they both measure

TABLE 5.1. Abilities—Enduring Attributes of the Individual That Influence Performance

Cognitive abilities	Psychomotor abilities	Sensory abilities
Verbal abilities Oral comprehension Written comprehension Oral expression Written expression *Idea generation and reasoning abilities* Fluency of ideas Originality Problem sensitivity Deductive reasoning Inductive reasoning Information ordering Category flexibility *Quantitative abilities* Mathematical reasoning Number facility *Memory* Memorization *Perceptual abilities* Speed of closure Flexibility of closure Perceptual speed *Spatial abilities* Spatial orientation Visualization *Attentiveness* Selective attention Time sharing	*Fine manipulative abilities* Arm–hand steadiness Manual dexterity Finger dexterity *Control movement abilities* Control precision Peripheral vision Multilimb coordination Response orientation Rate control *Reaction time and speed abilities* Reaction time Wrist–finger speed Speed of limb movement Physical abilities *Physical strength abilities* Static strength Explosive strength Dynamic strength Trunk strength *Endurance* Stamina *Flexibility, balance, and coordination* Extent flexibility Dynamic flexibility Gross body coordination Gross body equilibrium	*Visual abilities* Near vision Far vision Visual color discrimination Night vision Depth perception Glare sensitivity *Auditory and speech abilities* Hearing sensitivity Auditory attention Sound localization Speech recognition Speech clarity

Note. From U.S. Department of Labor, National O*NET Consortium. O*NET OnLine (interactive web application). Available at *online.onetcenter.org*.

the similar construct of cognitive abilities. If this expectation proves true, neuropsychological tests may be a useful alternative to the administration of job-specific tests, especially in circumstances in which the issue of brain dysfunction exists. The neuropsychological test can, therefore, assess both the effect of central nervous system dysfunction as well as at least some aspects of real-world capability.

This chapter reviews recent data on the ability of neuropsychological tests to predict both the ability to resume working and the quality of work performance after an acquired brain dysfunction. Here we emphasize the ability of neuropsychological tests to predict vocational performance in the context of specific illnesses or conditions. If, for example, future job performance were best predicted in a TBI population by the presence and duration of posttraumatic amnesia, and neuropsychological tests added little or no predictive power beyond this factor, there would be limited utility and rationale for then administering neuropsychological tests if we were most interested in job performance. Of course, when the details of the TBI are unknown, some sort of testing may be the only basis for predicting future vocational performance. As we review here, studies that control for disease severity demonstrate that neuropsychological tests do have predictive validity above and beyond disease characteristics. And because neuropsychological studies of vocational outcomes have not been performed in every disease population, it is necessary to extrapolate findings from the few populations that have been studied (e.g., TBI, HIV/AIDS) to populations that have not been studied as extensively (e.g., multiple sclerosis, neurotoxic substance exposure). In this chapter we present a model of the relationship between neuropsychological tests, brain dysfunction, and vocational outcomes, and we review studies of the ability of neuropsychological tests to predict employment outcomes. We also review recent literature on specific neuropsychological abilities, such as executive function and memory, to predict vocational outcomes, and we briefly review performance-based assessment of work skills. We conclude with recommendations for future directions for the development and validation of a new generation of neuropsychological tests to relate to vocational outcomes.

Other disciplines, such as occupational therapy and human factors research, have objectives related to vocational functioning, but from a slightly different perspective. In general, occupational therapy focuses on treatment of disabled populations to maximize functional outcomes, including vocational functioning (Greig, Nicholls, Bryson, & Bell, 2004; Tsang, 2003). As described below in the theoretical models section, occupational therapy is more broadly focused on all factors that impact employment outcome, in addition to cognition, whereas neuropsychology is focused solely on cognition. Human factors is an interdisciplinary field devoted to the advancement and implementation of knowledge about human characteristics as they relate to the design of systems and devices. There is emphasis in this field on both theoretical model development (Gonzalez, 2005; Gonzalez, Thomas, & Vanyukov, 2005) and on changing systems and devices to adapt to human characteristics (Wilson, 2006). We let the other chapters in this volume address issues from their respective positions, but it is likely that the same problems regarding the best way to measure outcome are faced by all who are involved in this line of research.

Measurement of Vocational Outcome

Vocational outcomes can be measured in a variety of ways. Most studies employ outcome as a dichotomous variable: a patient either resumes employment (or other productive societal role) or does not. Recently, however, there has been an emerging emphasis on assessing the *quality* of employment as one measure of outcome as well. Other studies have measured the *stability* of employment outcomes. For example, employment status may be measured at two different time points. In Nybo, Sainio, and Muller's (2004) study, patients with TBI sustained injury as children between 1959 and 1969, were assessed again in 1985, and for the most recent assessment were seen again in 2001. The authors still used a dichotomous variable in that everyone was classified as either employed or unemployed, but they were able to compare employment outcomes approximately 40 years postinjury to those measured approximately 24 years postinjury. Twenty of the 27 participants had no change in employment status compared to the prior evaluation, and of the remaining seven cases, four transitioned from full-time or subsidized work to not working, whereas three transitioned to full-time work.

Employment can be measured in terms of quality. One group (Klonoff, Lamb, & Henderson, 2001) assessed outcomes of their rehabilitation program by characterizing their participants' 11-year outcomes as productive or nonproductive, with "productive" defined as full-time or part-time work or school, volunteering, or homemaking; "nonproductive" was defined as retired or not working. They also characterized their sample as either full-time paid work or not. Some studies characterize outcomes as return to work either at premorbid levels or at a "modified" (i.e., reduced) level (e.g., Ruffolo, Friedland, Dawson, Colantonio, & Lindsay, 1999). An interesting and unique approach to vocational outcomes controls for unemployment rates within the region where patients live (Doctor et al., 2005). These authors devised a predicted employment rate based on current employment statistics and compared a brain-injury unemployment rate versus a predicted rate that took into account demographic factors. As might be expected, they found that the unemployment rate for the brain-injured group far exceeded that predicted by each participant's demographic profile.

One of the most detailed assessments of vocational stability was conducted by Machamer and colleagues (Machamer, Temkin, Fraser, Doctor, & Dikmen, 2005), who assessed job stability 3–5 years post-TBI and defined job stability in several ways, including number of months worked full time, number of full-time jobs, and duration of uninterrupted full-time work. This study represents one of the most sophisticated assessments of job stability in the neuropsychological literature and is an example of the kinds of advances that should be made in studies that assess vocational outcome. From a rehabilitation perspective, Machamer and colleagues' (2005) approach allows for the measurement of key elements of job performance that are related to self-sufficiency, the maximization of which is the goal of rehabilitation. The only missing variable is whether the person can sustain financial independence, but this is understandably difficult to measure. Measurement of vocational outcomes should always control for non-neuropsychological confounding factors that might affect motivation to return to work, especially the existence of litigation to obtain compensation for the injury or the presence of disability benefits that might reduce motivation to return to work. Later in the chapter we review performance-based measures of employment functioning. Such direct measurement of job performance yields the most valid measures of employment outcomes and should become a focus of vocational outcome studies in the future.

Theoretical Underpinnings Regarding the Relationship between Cognitive Performance and Vocational Functioning

The major models of functional outcome (including vocational outcome) in relation to brain dysfunction come from the TBI literature (Kendall & Terry, 1996; Ownsworth & McKenna, 2004). These models are comprehensive and rightly include all factors that impact outcome, of which cognitive abilities are just one. Other noncognitive contributors include premorbid factors such as preillness intellectual abilities, demographic factors, substance use history, premorbid employment history, available resources (e.g., socioeconomic status of the patient, social support), situational factors (e.g., status of the job market, the ability of a job to accommodate certain disabilities), and injury factors (e.g., physical impairment). Figure 5.1 depicts the model proposed by Kendall and Terry (1996). These authors devised this model because they believed that most studies and clinical decisions assumed that in TBI, neurological factors (e.g., characteristics of the injury, cognitive impairment) explained psychological adjustment and well-being. These authors reviewed the literature on non-neurological factors that influenced adjustment post-TBI and found that many factors (e.g., preinjury factors) can contribute to outcomes. Though they do not define "psychosocial outcomes" or any of the other constructs in their model, the model nevertheless has had significant influence on researchers and rehabilitation specialists because it formalized the role of non-neurological factors in determining outcome.

Ownsworth and McKenna (2004) proposed a model that focused on rehabilitation after brain injury, in which they highlight intrapersonal factors such as self-awareness and other metacognitive and emotional factors (Figure 5.2) as they relate to successful rehabilitation (Ownsworth & McKenna, 2004). This model was developed based on a systematic review of the empirical literature. They characterized the

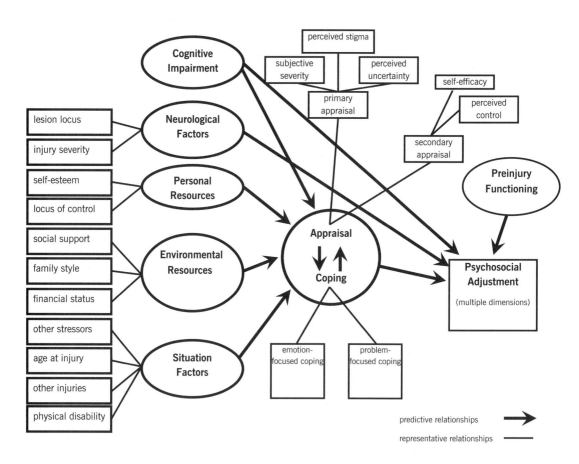

FIGURE 5.1. Model of functional outcomes proposed by Kendall and Terry (1996). Reprinted with permission from Taylor & Francis, Ltd.

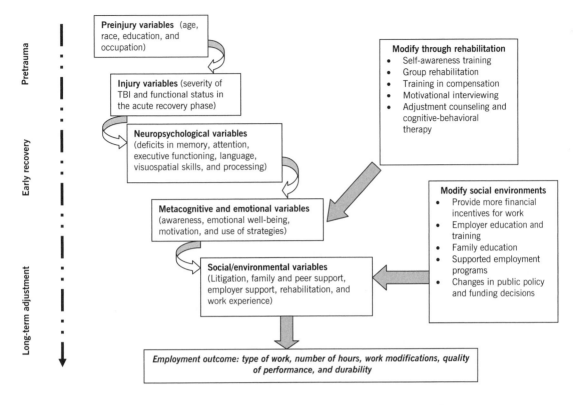

FIGURE 5.2. Model of employment outcomes proposed by Ownsworth and McKenna (2004). Reprinted with permission from Taylor & Francis, Ltd.

quality of studies included in their review and identified well-defined injury and pre-injury factors to assess the level of support the data suggest for each factor's influence on outcomes. This model was designed specifically to assess vocational outcomes, in contrast to Kendall and Terry's (1996) psychosocial outcomes model. Intrapersonal factors are among the targets of their rehabilitation approach, such as developing insight and compensation strategies. Other targets for rehabilitation are categorized as environmental factors, such as employer education and training, family education, and supported employment.

Although the topic of rehabilitation is beyond the scope of this chapter, the distinction must be made between impairment and disability (Wilson, 2000). The World Health Organization (WHO; 2001) has adopted the International Classification of Functioning, Disability, and Health (ICF). The ICF represents a movement away from the concept of disability and a disease-oriented concept of activities. For the purposes of our discussion, we retain the idea of disability since this chapter has a disease-oriented focus. It can be said that "impairment" is the deficit caused by physical or mental structures, whereas "disability" and "functioning" are the behavioral outcomes caused by impairment (Wilson, 2000). The concept of disability focuses on the behavioral deficits that can be observed, whereas functioning is a more neutral term that characterizes both intact and impaired abilities. The models proposed by

Kendall and Ownsworth also focus on impairment and disability (Kendall & Terry, 1996; Ownsworth & McKenna, 2004). In this chapter we focus on the relationship between impairment and work disability. The model we utilize is a simplified version of previous models in which brain dysfunction results in cognitive, emotional, and behavioral impairment, which in turn results in specific disabilities and poor vocational functioning.

Although the models developed by Kendall and Ownsworth were designed around TBI, we believe that the models are just as applicable to other etiologies of cognitive impairment. The existing models are neutral with regard to what course the disability will take, except that they assume that rehabilitation can change the outcome. This issue is important because the prediction of impairment is, of course, complex and multifactorial, taking into account such factors as premorbid characteristics, current resources, and emotional, behavioral, and environmental factors. As Sherer and colleagues (2002) concluded from their review, the timing of the neuropsychological evaluation relative to the onset of the disease can have an impact on the predictive utility of the neuropsychological test data. In the discussion below of Sherer's review, we note that methodological concerns in this line of research limit any interpretation of the conceptual implications of early versus late neuropsychological assessment in TBI.

Wilson and Watson (1996) proposed a model consisting solely of cognitive abilities based on Backman and Dixon's (1992) theory of the development of compensatory behavior. Both models center on an acquired discrepancy between a person's skills and environmental demands on those skills. In relation to brain disease, there is a decrease in skill caused by the disease or condition while the environmental demands remain either the same or increase. In this model "mechanisms" (e.g., treatments) are applied to create a match between environmental demands and skills. There is a distinction between normal compensation in an unimpaired person versus the extraordinary compensation that is used for the individual with brain damage. Such compensatory behaviors are considered extraordinary because the unimpaired person would not normally use them, such as the use of visual cues to focus attention in the patient with hemispatial neglect. The final component of the model is the consequence of the adaptive behavior, with the successful consequence being that which results either in the matching of the disabled skill level to the environmental demands and/or adequate performance of the desired behavior.

We now turn our attention to a review of the research on neuropsychological impairment and its relationship to vocational functioning.

Sequential Model

Because this chapter focuses on the role of cognitive performance in vocational functioning, we assume a model similar to that depicted in Figure 5.3, in which brain dysfunction causes cognitive impairment, and the cognitive impairment then causes impaired vocational functioning. We focus on studies of brain conditions that reduce a person's previously intact vocational performance. The key assumptions of our model is that intact cognitive abilities are required for adequate work performance, and that brain disease directly causes cognitive impairment, which then directly causes vocational impairment.

FIGURE 5.3. Hypothetical model with directional causal relationships among constructs.

In general, there are three trajectories of cognitive performance associated with acquired brain disease: (1) abrupt onset with gradual recovery to premorbid level, (2) abrupt onset with recovery to static impairment, and (3) gradual onset with progressive worsening over time. The first two courses are commonly seen after TBI, stroke, brain tumor, encephalitis/meningitis, and delirium, whereas the third course is typically seen in progressive dementia conditions or other degenerative neurological diseases. Most developmental disorders such as mental retardation, pervasive developmental disorders, learning disabilities, and attention-deficit/hyperactivity disorder typify a static course with no change in abilities.

Controlling for Confounding Factors

In order to draw sound conclusions about the predictive power of neuropsychological abilities, Sherer and colleagues (2002) provide a detailed method for rating studies on generalizability, reliability, and methodology in assessing employment outcome. They based their rating system on a more general rating system proposed by the Committee on Empirically Supported Practices of Division 40 (Division of Neuropsychology) of the American Psychological Association (Heaton, Barth, Crosson, Larrabee, & Reynolds, 2002). The committee's recommendation contained five categories of study types, including studies that are strongly supportive, supportive, tentatively supportive, insufficiently or inconclusively, or studies that contraindicate a practice from being useful. Sherer and colleagues expanded this criteria set into two sets of criteria. One set focused on generalizability and reliability of the actual study, and the other set focused on the adequacy of the methodology. We highlight here the importance of controlling confounding factors in studies of vocational outcomes, especially predysfunction employment status such as poor preillness vocational attainment. In addition, other factors to consider are premorbid intellectual and neuropsychological abilities, psychiatric disorders, substance use disorders, and the age at which the disease or injury occurred.

A special note should be made of the issue of age at disease onset. Some studies have noted that older age predicts worse employment outcomes. The issues surrounding age are complex and are not reviewed in detail here (see Hedge, Borman, & Lammlein, 2006, for a comprehensive review). They include the potential for older age to amplify the cognitive impact of brain disease, psychosocial issues such as age discrimination in the workplace, and the additional impact of an employer's unwillingness to hire a person who suffered a neurological insult. It has also been reported in a long-term follow-up of persons who sustained a TBI that age at the time of injury uniquely predicted independent functioning 5–20 years after leaving a rehabilitation program (i.e., working, going to school full time, or living alone) (Wilson, 1992). Some studies have also hypothesized that persons who suffer brain disease at an advanced age may be less motivated to return to work, since they have fewer years of productive work remaining. Researchers have observed in a state-run vocational rehabilitation program that patients with brain injury who were older than the age of 44 had no worse employment outcomes than those who were injured at younger ages (Skeel, Bounds, Johnstone, Lloyd, & Harms, 2003). When it is considered as a continuous variable rather than a categorical one (Wood & Rutterford, 2006), age may not independently predict employment outcomes more that 10 years after TBI. Because of the divergence in findings regarding age of disease onset, more studies are needed to fully understand the impact of age on vocational outcomes in TBI and other brain diseases.

Review of Neuropsychological Studies and Vocational Outcomes

In the following section we review studies in which neuropsychological tests were used to predict vocational outcome. Most studies use inclusion and exclusion criteria to control for many premorbid factors, such as premorbid IQ, learning disabilities, substance use, and so on, but most do not control for age at disease onset. One area that is rarely considered is that of possible environmental factors affecting employment outcome, especially market factors and presence and quality of rehabilitation.

Prior Reviews of Neuropsychology and Vocational Functioning

There are several reviews of the literature on neuropsychological predictors of vocational functioning (Guilmette & Kastner, 1996; Heaton & Pendleton, 1981; Kalechstein, Newton, & van Gorp, 2003; Sbordone & Guilmette, 1999; Sherer et al., 2002). Here we summarize the previous reviews and evaluate new studies since those reviews were published.

In one of the first manuscripts to focus on neuropsychological tests and vocational outcome, Heaton and Pendleton (1981) reviewed neuropsychological predictors of everyday functioning, including vocational functioning. In their review they included studies of both normal and impaired populations and described several studies that established the well-accepted association between vocational functioning and IQ. The general finding from all of the studies of IQ is that unemployed people have lower IQ scores than employed people, and that occupations considered to be of a higher or more challenging level were associated with higher IQ scores (Heaton & Pendleton, 1981). A very important finding in studies in which a correlation is reported between IQ and some index of vocational performance is that IQ is known to correlate approximately .5, accounting for only 25% of the variance in vocational performance. Heaton and Pendleton also described the few studies (at that time) of neuropsychological test performance predicting vocational functioning. They observed that in studies in which the Halstead–Reitan Battery was used, the average impairment rating was an independent and more powerful predictor of vocational performance or employment status than IQ test scores. They also observed, as reported by Heaton, Chelune, and Lehman (1978), that Minnesota Multiphasic Personality Inventory (MMPI) clinical scales are an additional independent predictor of employment status in a cross-sectional design (Heaton et al., 1978). When this group later attempted to replicate the MMPI findings using a prospective design (Newnan, Heaton, & Lehman, 1978), they found that MMPI results were less predictive of future employment than in their cross-sectional study. Thus the predictive power of neuropsychological tests was demonstrated more than 25 years ago, but neither IQ nor neuropsychological test scores explain even a majority of the variance in employment status or vocational performance.

Guilmette and Kastner (1996) reviewed the literature on neuropsychological tests and prediction of vocational functioning and provided 13 conclusions. Among their conclusions: The greater the degree of impairment, the less employable a person was; neuropsychological tests were better at predicting failure than success; neuropsychological tests should be supplemented with psychosocial/psychological tests to improve predictive validity; and future research would benefit from consistent neuropsychological batteries across studies and validation of brief batteries tailored to specific occupational groups. An important observation of these authors is that because of the limitations of existing studies, the field of neuropsychology is lacking consensus on the predictive power of neuropsychological tests on occupational outcome. They conclude that neuropsychological assessment can predict vocational performance only modestly until further research provides grounds for stronger predictions (Guilmette & Kastner, 1996).

As described above, Sherer and colleagues (2002) conducted a rigorous literature review that assessed studies of the predictive power of neuropsychological tests in TBI by using guidelines established by Division 40 of the American Psychological Association for empirical support of neuropsychological practice (Heaton et al., 2002). This review is notable because the quality of the studies was considered in their recommendations. This review of 23 studies revealed that the best prediction of reemployment after TBI occurs when neuropsychological testing is performed soon after posttraumatic amnesia resolves. In addition, they noted that regardless of when neuropsychological testing is performed relative to the injury, the continued presence (i.e., at the time of testing) of neuropsychological impairment is significantly associated with unemployment or decline in quality of employment relative to preinjury status. The authors concluded that the use of neuropsychological testing is strongly supported in the prediction of employment outcome in TBI, especially when neuropsychological testing is performed close in time to the TBI. As noted above, the review emphasized that the time at which neuropsychological assessment is performed is important.

Studies in which neuropsychological testing was performed closer in time to the measurement of employment status (i.e., late in recovery process or concurrent with measurement of employment status) did not provide clear evidence that neuropsychological testing is useful in predicting employment status. Although the latter studies contained methodological issues (e.g., small sample size, excessive number of statistical analyses, inadequate sample description) that possibly clouded interpretability of neuropsychological predictiveness, the authors raise the very important issue of the timing of neuropsychological assessment, with the weight of evidence suggesting that in TBI, the earlier neuropsychological testing is conducted the more value it may have in predicting vocational outcome. However, as noted by Sherer (2002, p. 176), "There is no conceptual basis for believing that neuropsychological findings obtained closer in time to assessment of employment outcome should be less predictive of this outcome than neuropsychological findings obtained at an earlier time." Indeed, the authors noted that the studies of late neuropsychological assessment may be of poorer methodology and thus may not have detected a relationship that is actually there.

Other authors (e.g., Kalechstein et al., 2003) have used a quantitative, analytical approach to reviewing the literature on the ability of neuropsychological tests to discriminate employed versus unemployed status. Although their meta-analysis relied on a small number of studies, all seven studies demonstrated at least small effect sizes when employed versus unemployed patients were compared on neuropsychological test scores. The innovative approach of this meta-analysis is that the authors subdivided the neuropsychological tests from each of the studies into one of eight cognitive domains. Tests in every domain were able to discriminate employed from unemployed persons. The effect sizes were greatest (medium) for the domains of intellectual functioning, executive systems functioning, verbal learning and memory, and nonverbal learning and memory. The smallest effect size was observed for tests of language. The authors reviewed the numerous limitations of this kind of analysis, including the inability to account for job complexity, demographic factors, and so on. Nevertheless, the important contribution of this study is the finding that abilities in some neuropsychological areas may be better at discriminating employment status than others.

Recent Studies of Neuropsychology and Vocational Functioning

Ever since Heaton and colleagues (1978) reported discriminant function analyses that neuropsychological test scores, in combination with MMPI scales, could classify employment status in greater than 80% of their mixed clinical sample, there has been an abundance of research on the association between neuropsychological test scores and employment, as can be seen from the reviews described above. In this section we review several studies that were not included in the published reviews to provide an updated summary of the state of the literature.

One research group (Machamer et al., 2005) went beyond the simple prediction of return to work by observing the stability of employment after TBI in a sample of 165 consecutively admitted patients. As noted above, they measured employment stability as number of months worked full time, number of full-time jobs held, and maintenance of employment once returned to full-time work. Their sample was largely a mild-to-moderate TBI group, with more than half of their subjects having a Glasgow Coma Scale (GCS) of 13–15 (mild) and being able to follow commands within 24 hours. Neuropsychological testing was conducted 1 month postinjury, and the post injury follow-up period was between 3 and 5 years for the assessment of employment stability. When they categorized patients by percent of time worked during the follow-up period (0%, 1–50%, 51–89%, and ≥90%), they found that less time worked was associated with lower GCS scores, longer time postinjury before commands were followed, worse neuropsychological performance, and preinjury job instability. They used stepwise multiple regression to predict percent of time worked half-time or more and maintenance of employment. The models included the following predictors: age, education, gender, preexisting conditions, preinjury yearly earnings, preinjury work stability, TBI severity evaluated by time to follow commands, other system injury severity, and neuropsychological outcome at 1-month postinjury.

The model that explained the most variance ($r^2 = .428$) in predicting percent of time worked during the follow-up period included the digit symbol test, preinjury earnings, and preinjury arrest record. Maintenance of employment was best predicted (logistical regression) by Performance IQ score, arrest record, and preinjury earnings. This study is important because it goes beyond the simple outcome measure of employed versus unemployed and provides evidence that postinjury work stability is uniquely associated with neuropsychological test performance even when many preinjury factors and injury severity are taken into account. The use of stepwise regression has its problems, including the fact that the final model does not say how well neuropsychological test scores predict work outcomes when injury characteristics are controlled.

Doctor and colleagues (2005) presented a novel analysis of TBI employment outcome by comparing 1-year relative risk ratios for a TBI sample and a control sample on failure to return to work. This approach is significant because the rate of return to work is compared to that of the general population to answer the question of whether unemployment is greater than that for the population in general. As might be expected, having a TBI presented more than a fourfold increase in unemployment risk compared to the general population, and lower test scores 1-month postinjury were significantly associated with greater risk for unemployment. Unfortunately, multivariate analyses were not conducted to determine if neuropsychological impairment was uniquely predictive of unemployment risk, although this question has been addressed by other studies.

Careful selection of participants contributes to the ability of a study to draw conclusions about predictors of employment outcomes. Cattelani, Tanzi, Lombardi, and Mazzucchi (2002) studied a group of patients with TBI involving the severest injuries, as indicated by a GCS score of 3–8 on admission (severe), coma of at least 3 days, and posttraumatic amnesia (PTA) of at least 7 days. The group was also well selected to rule out premorbid confounding factors to future employment: All were employed or in school and none had a history of substance abuse or dependence, mental retardation, psychiatric disorder, or were undergoing treatment for any "situational or psychosocial problems." They divided their 35 eligible participants into demographically matched groups of 19 reemployed (resumed preinjury employment or academic status) and 16 non-reemployed groups. The authors observed that TBI characteristics, including combined PTA and coma duration, distinguished the two groups (28 days for reemployed vs. 108 days for non-reemployed). They observed that worse early activities of daily living (ADL) problems (Barthel Index) predicted worse resumption of preemployment vocational status. Although they also found that lower Wechsler Adult intelligence Scale—Revised (WAIS-R) scores and lower examiner ratings of neuropsychological abilities predicted worse outcome, they did not perform any analyses to determine if cognitive performance predicted outcome independently of TBI severity.

Specific Neuropsychological Abilities That Predict Vocational Outcome

One problem across the spectrum of studies of neuropsychological and vocational outcome is the variability in the test batteries administered (Guilmette & Kastner,

1996). While norming different batteries for different populations or purposes (Ryan, Morrow, Bromet, & Parkinson, 1987) is one solution, another solution is to routinely include a summary score across the entire battery (like a mean t-score, deficit score, or domain summary scores) that can be used to predict outcome. Research with HIV-infected adults (Carey et al., 2004) provides evidence that sufficient sensitivity and specificity can be achieved by neuropsychological batteries that contain different tests but that, when average impairment across tests is used, the different batteries can yield similar classification rates of impairment. This research suggests that the use of summary scores may generalize across batteries and might be an approach to overcome some methodological variability across studies. Average impairment in this study was measured using the deficit score approach, as outlined in a widely used normative manual (Heaton, Miller, Taylor, & Grant, 2007), in which demographically corrected T-scores are assigned a degree of deficit on a scale of 0 (no deficit) to 5 (severe deficit) in 5-point decrements in the T-score. A "global deficit score" is calculated as the average deficit score across all measures and serves as an index of overall impairment. In another example, Newnan and colleagues (1978) found that a cutoff score of 1.61 on the Russell Average Impairment Rating classified 78% of their subjects as employed or unemployed, with a positive predictive value of 81% and a negative predictive value of 70%. Indeed, the research does not support the predictive validity of individual tests for outcomes and diagnoses, but there is substantial evidence that IQ scores and summary scores can predict outcomes.

On the other hand, different batteries (including psychosocial measures) may need to be developed for different purposes. There are two considerations here: first, that a neurological problem may have unique neuropsychological ability deficits, and that these disease-specific deficits may explain vocational problems. For example, in TBI, memory and attention were significant predictors of employment outcome (Brooks, McKinlay, Symington, Beattie, & Campsie, 1987), whereas in mental retardation motor and vocabulary predicted better functional independence (Blackwell, Dial, Chan, & McCollum, 1985). In multiple sclerosis unemployment is best predicted by verbal memory and numerical reasoning (Paced Auditory Serial Addition Test; Benedict et al., 2006), whereas in HIV, verbal learning (California Verbal Learning Test, total trials 1–5) was the strongest predictor of return to work (van Gorp et al., 2007). Second, psychosocial and behavioral factors such as those measured by the MMPI-2, Beck Depression Inventory (BDI), or the various frontal system questionnaires (Malloy & Grace, 2005) can add to or even replace predictive validity of neuropsychological performance (Heaton et al., 1978). Again, disease-specific factors may dictate the tools that provide the best predictive validity. Further research is required before the impact of emotional versus cognitive factors—particularly in clinical situations where psychological distress is more salient than cognitive impairment—is fully understood in each clinical condition (Heaton et al., 2004).

One of the most thoroughly studied psychiatric populations with regard to neuropsychological predictors of return to work is schizophrenia. As a significant public health problem, it is natural that schizophrenia, whose symptoms can be treated pharmacologically, is a target for rehabilitation. Some studies (e.g., McGurk & Mueser, 2003) have reported that intact executive functioning and verbal learning predict more wages earned and more hours worked over a 2-year follow-up period. In addition, this group reported that worse cognitive abilities predicted greater utilization of supported employment services, suggesting that cognitive impairment results in more rehabilitation resource consumption. This same group followed their sample through 4 years of supported employment (McGurk & Mueser, 2006). Cognitive and symptom measurements taken 2 years after beginning a work rehabilitation program were correlated with total hours of competitive work 3–4 years after beginning the program and total wages earned during that period. The authors observed that both of these markers of employment (total hours and wages) were correlated with symptoms (autistic preoccupation from the Positive and Negative Symptom Scale [PANSS]) and cognitive performance. The specific cognitive abilities that predicted more hours and higher wages included executive functioning (Wisconsin Card Sorting Test [WCST] percent perseveration, Trail Making Test Part B), working memory (letter–number sequencing, digit span backward, digit span forward), and speed of information processing (Trail Making Test A, digit symbol substitution). Unfortunately, the authors did not perform a multivariate analysis to determine whether neuropsychological test performance independently predicted work performance when psychiatric symptoms were taken into account. And, similar to their 2-year follow-up study, their 4-year follow-up data also showed that worse performance on neuropsychological tests predicted greater utilization of supported employment services, including contact hours with counselors.

Studies of cognitive predictors of employment that also use a work performance measure are rare. One study of employment outcome involved a sample of 112 patients with schizophrenia who enrolled in work rehabilitation programs (Evans et al., 2004). This study utilized an inventory that involves ratings by a research assistant directly observing the patient's work performance and by interview with the patient's immediate supervisor (Work Behavior Inventory; Bryson, Bell, & Lysaker, 1997). This study also measured employment status using the Work Placement Scale (Meyer, Bond, Tunis, & McCoy, 2002) consisting of a 5-point gradient ranging from integrated employment to unemployed, with higher scores representing more independent employment activity. Although the study is complicated by a heterogeneous sample (patients from different vocational rehabilitation programs) and incomplete data (work performance measures were available only for a subsample from one vocational program), the pattern of neuropsychological predictors of work placement and work performance was consistent: baseline verbal learning and memory were related to 4-month vocational outcomes regardless of the outcome measure. Interestingly, executive functioning (WCST and Trail Making Test Part B) was not associated with outcome. Many people posit that executive functioning deficits in schizophrenia are central to the disability associated with the disease (Iachini, Sergi, Ruggiero, & Gnisci, 2005; Nuechterlein et al., 2004; Sergi, Kern, Mintz, & Green, 2005; Velligan, Bow-Thomas, Mahurin, Miller, & Halgunseth, 2000). This research raises the possibilities that executive functioning is not a core deficit or that the executive functioning ability is a complex construct that is better explained by core components such as learning. It has also been reported that better immediate memory predicted full- or part-time employment status in a sample of patients with bipolar disorder, although executive functioning was not thoroughly assessed in this sample (Dickerson et al., 2004).

Predicting Vocational Outcomes Independent of Disease Variables

From the studies reviewed above, it is clear that neuropsychological tests do predict employment status following brain disease or injury. In general, most studies have not attempted to demonstrate whether neuropsychological abilities uniquely predict vocational functioning above and beyond easily obtained indices of disease status. The central question that should be asked is whether neuropsychological tests are necessary to serve as predictors once disease variables are known.

Verbal learning (California Verbal Learning Test [CVLT] total trials 1–5) independently predicted return to work 2 years after initial assessment in a sample of 118 prospectively studied HIV-infected persons who were seeking to return to work, even when disease severity (AIDS status, viral burden, immunosuppression) and education level were taken into account (van Gorp et al., 2007). In a TBI sample Novack and colleagues analyzed 1-year outcome data using path analysis, which is a form of structural equation modeling that, because of its multivariate nature, is well suited to answering the question of whether neuropsychological performance predicts outcome when other factors, such as premorbid status and disease characteristics, are taken into account (Novack, Bush, Meythaler, & Canupp, 2001). In this model premorbid status, injury severity, and 6-month cognitive, emotional, and functional status were used to predict 12-month outcome. The 12-month outcome factor included the Community Integration Questionnaire, Disability Rating Scale, and "productivity level" (employment or high school/college enrollment). One advantage of path analysis is that measured variables, such as individual neuropsychological test scores or specific questionnaire scores, can be grouped together into conceptual categories called "endogenous variables." Then direct and indirect relationships among the endogenous variables can be estimated using path analysis to determine which constructs are or are not significant direct predictors of the outcome. These researchers found that the only significant direct predictors of outcome were cognitive status (consisting of nine cognitive and five observation-based neurobehavioral rating scores from the Neurobehavioral Rating Scale) and premorbid factors (consisting of age, education, employment status, and alcohol, drug, and social histories). Importantly, injury severity and premorbid factors were significantly predictive of cognitive status and thus only indirectly associated with TBI outcome (including employment). This study is an excellent example of the utility of neuropsychological assessment to predict future vocational functioning even when disease characteristics are considered. These findings were replicated with a separate sample by the same group (Bush et al., 2003).

Performance-Based Assessment of Vocational Functioning

As described at the beginning of this chapter, there are many performance-based assessments for career planning, applicant screening, and job placement purposes used primarily by persons involved in vocational and career planning outside a clinical context. There are few performance-based assessments of vocational functioning specifically designed for rehabilitation of clinical populations; the Behavioral Assessment of Vocational Skills (Butler, Anderson, Furst, & Namerow, 1989) is one such test, and it consists of a standardized measurement of a person's ability to assemble a wheelbarrow using printed instructions. Trained examiners rated patients on their ability to follow directions, maintain their attention, tolerate frustration, and on several other variables in the face of preplanned interruptions and criticisms by the examiner. The test was designed to mimic actual demands faced in a typical manual labor work environment, including a predefined goal and the presence of common distracting events. In their sample of 20 participants with brain injury, this test predicted ratings of employment performance during a 3-month trial work placement, independent of neuropsychological test scores. We await additional validation data on the instrument, as few other studies that have used this measure to date.

Commercially developed vocational assessment instruments have been studied in neuropsychologically impaired persons with HIV infection (Heaton et al., 1994). The instrument (the COMPASS; Valpar International Corporation, Tucson, AZ) purports to assesses work skills, although in reality it is weighted toward general cognitive and motor skills (e.g., reasoning, arithmetic, language comprehension, immediate memory) that are then scored along dimensions deemed important work-related skills and abilities by the 1991 DOT (described above). The addition of manual tasks that require fine motor control (wiring task) as well as sequencing and upper limb dexterity (machine tending and alignment and driving tasks) broadens the scope to behaviors not assessed with traditional neuropsychological tests. Because the study was cross-sectional, the findings are limited to a snapshot in time that supports the validity of neuropsychological impairment as a significant predictor of lower scores on the COMPASS. In this study there was no direct assessment of whether COMPASS scores were worse in the unemployed participants.

In a later manuscript that included the COMPASS in a larger battery of everyday functioning tests, Heaton and colleagues (2004) observed that failing scores on the COMPASS (relative to a neuropsychologically normal group with HIV infection) were associated with lower scores in the neuropsychological domains of Abstraction/Mental Flexibility (Category Test, Trail Making Test Part B) and Working Memory (WAIS-III Digit Span and Arithmetic, and Paced Auditory Serial Addition Test). In addition to the ability of the COMPASS to serve as a performance-based assessment of vocational skills, its integration with the DOT allows comparison of a person's current level of vocational abilities measured by the COMPASS with an estimate of abilities the person had at his or her highest occupational achievement. An estimate of decline can be obtained, in addition to an estimate of the number of jobs a person might be able to perform both at his or her highest functioning and at the measured functioning. As the first study demonstrated, it is possible to quantify the loss of job opportunities as a result of measured decline in functional abilities (Heaton et al., 1994). These studies suggest that performance-based assessment can be associated with cognitive abilities. However, further research is required to determine whether the COMPASS predicts unemployment (which seems likely), and if the COMPASS or any other performance-based vocational measure can predict work performance in an employed clinical sample. There are no studies that address which type of assessment—neuropsychological testing or performance-based vocational testing—has better predictive validity of employment status or long-term employment outcomes.

One group compared neuropsychological test performance to ratings and recommendations of a trained vocational expert when the patient performed simulated work tasks (Leblanc, Hayden, & Paulman, 2000). These authors determined that general cognitive abilities (WAIS-R, combinations of various neuropsychological tests) best predicted expert employment performance ratings. Consistent with the notion that individual tests are not useful predictors, no single neuropsychological test or ability correlated significantly with the vocational evaluator's recommendation that a person could or could not return to competitive employment. However, specific neuropsychological tests were associated with specific ratings of performance on simulated work activities. For example, Wechsler Memory Scale Logical Memory II (delayed recall) was associated with examiner ratings of patient memory during work tasks, and a number of tests in their executive functioning factor (Rey Complex Figure, Booklet Category Test, WAIS-R Object Assembly and Block Design) were associated with examiner ratings of visual and verbal problem solving. While the data appear to provide some evidence for domain-specific ecological validity of the neuropsychological tests, the vocational expert was not blind to the neuropsychological test findings, and indeed based the choice of vocational tasks in part on the neuropsychological profile. This aspect of the methodology suggests that the examiner's ratings (the outcome variables of the study) could have been biased by the neuropsychological test scores (the predictor variables). The study did not assess whether neuropsychological or performance-based ratings predicted actual work outcomes in this TBI sample. Future studies should address the relative value of vocational rehabilitation approaches to measuring work outcomes.

In summary, there is little research on performance-based vocational assessment in clinical populations. Because "vocational functioning" encompasses such a broad domain that includes physical as well as cognitive abilities, and because it is impossible to design a single test or series of tests to measure the myriad of complex work skills required in today's occupations, it is not surprising that research in this area is scant. However, some studies in the human factors arena (e.g., Gonzalez, 2005; see also Rogers et al., Chapter 2, this volume) hold promise for development of computerized assessment tools that can simulate specific job demands and obtain objective data with normative reference. More importantly, such approaches can help define new conceptual cognitive domains (e.g., dynamic decision making; Edwards, 1962) that might have better predictive validity for vocational performance than traditional neuropsychological domains.

Focus of Future Research to Improve Predictive Validity

As we have noted (Sherer et al., 2002), group studies consistently find that neuropsychological test results are statistically associated with employment status and vocational outcomes. However, the predictive validity of specific neuropsychological tests is often lacking in these studies. It would be very useful, for example, for future research to utilize statistical approaches such as discriminant function, odds ratios, positive and negative predictive values, or other classification approaches to determine how accurate neuropsychological performance is when disease-specific variables (e.g., PTA and loss of consciousness in TBI, AIDS status in HIV, or lesion location and volume in stroke), demographic and premorbid variables, and neuropsychological performance (e.g., mean T-score or deficit score) in statistical models predicting the outcome of interest, such as return to premorbid employment status or likelihood of any postdisease employment. A major criticism of most of the cited studies is that they are conducted on groups of participants, with the primary conclusion that neuropsychological tests are predictive of vocational functioning *on average*, with little data that can be applied to the individual about his or her current or future prospects for employment. The exception to this rule is found in the cases of severely impaired individuals, where gainful employment is highly unlikely. The most useful studies will address how patients who are not completely disabled and who have some preserved abilities can be helped in vocational rehabilitation.

A second focus of future research should examine remediation of cognitive deficits and assessment of the effectiveness of the remediation. An example of such research is offered by Jensen and colleagues, who treated reading and writing impairments in a sample of individuals with learning disabilities and demonstrated positive outcomes on employment measures (Jensen, Lindgren, Andersson, Ingvar, & Levander, 2000). The often stated claim that neuropsychological profiles can provide a "map" of cognitive strengths and weaknesses that can then guide rehabilitation is a claim that is largely unsubstantiated, even if ultimately proven to be true. Although several studies have found associations between baseline cognitive abilities and vocational outcomes some time later (Evans et al., 2004; McGurk & Mueser, 2006; van Gorp et al., 2007), no studies to our knowledge have assessed whether individualized treatment plans based on neuropsychological profiles improve employment outcomes.

A third focus of future research is the development of task-independent standardized rating scales that would formally rate work behaviors that are directly observed. The first step in this direction has been developed by LeBlanc and colleagues (2000) and is called a "situational vocational evaluation" (SEval). In its current form, as described above, a certified vocational evaluator has the subject perform simulated work activities, and then rates his or her performance on 16 indices in one of three general categories (visual processing, memory, executive functioning). The main problems requiring further research with this approach include developing standardized rating criteria that would result in sufficient interrater reliability and ensuring that all relative domains were assessed. If such a generalized rating system could be developed, then the clinician would have a standard instrument (much like the Functional Independence Measure [FIM] that is widely used in physical and occupational therapy outcome studies) that could be applied regardless of the specific vocation.

A fourth focus of future research should exploit technological advances such as virtual environments or virtual reality. The human factors literature, including such studies as Gonzales (2005) and Gonzalez and colleagues (2005) and that exemplified in a special issue of the *International Journal of Human–Computer Studies* on "Interaction with Virtual Environments" (Volume 64, Issue 3), provides some promising directions, but as noted by Wilson (2006, p. 157), "human factors empirical work has been extraordinarily difficult to plan and carry out, given the very large number of variables involved."

We agree with many of the conclusions made by Sbordone, including these: (1) Individual predictions of vocational abilities need to be weighted by the facts that no neuropsychological test score can accurately predict vocational performance, and that neuropsychological testing as a predictor of vocational ability should be interpreted with caution since the procedure is not an actual measure of vocational performance and since the testing situation is rarely similar to the actual employment environment; and (2) many factors other than neuropsychological test scores need to be considered when predicting vocational abilities, such as preinjury work performance and job stability, past or current substance abuse, psychological disorders and stressors, and any medical, neurological, or developmental disorders (Sbordone, 2001). The more these issues can be addressed with an empirical approach, the less guesswork will be required and the less uncertainty will result from current treatment of individuals with acquired brain disorders.

Acknowledgments

We would like to thank Patrick Cordova and Christine Karver for their help in preparing this chapter.

References

Backman, L., & Dixon, R. A. (1992). Psychological compensation: A theoretical framework. *Psychol Bull*, *112*, 259–283.

Benedict, R. H. B., Cookfair, D., Gavett, R., Gunther, M., Munschauer, F., Garg, N., et al. (2006). Validity of the minimal assessment of cognitive function in multiple sclerosis (MACFIMS). *J Int Neuropsych Soc*, *12*, 549–558.

Blackwell, S. C., Dial, J. G., Chan, F., & McCollum, P. S. (1985). Discriminating functional levels of independent living: A neuropsychological evaluation of mentally retarded adults. *Rehabil Couns Bull*, *29*, 42–52.

Brooks, N., McKinlay, W., Symington, C., Beattie, A., & Campsie, L. (1987). Return to work within the first seven years of severe head injury. *Brain Inj*, *1*, 5–19.

Bryson, G., Bell, M., & Lysaker, P. (1997). Affect recognition in schizophrenia: A function of global impairment or a specific cognitive deficit. *Psychiat Res*, *71*, 105–113.

Buros Institute of Mental Measurements. (2005). The sixteenth *mental measurements yearbook*. Lincoln, NE: Author. Available at *www.unl.edu/buros*.

Bush, B. A., Novack, T. A., Malec, J. F., Stringer, A. Y., Millis, S. R., & Madan, A. (2003). Validation of a model for evaluating outcome after traumatic brain injury. *Arch Phys Med Rehabil*, *84*, 1803–1807.

Butler, R. W., Anderson, L., Furst, C. J., & Namerow, N. S. (1989). Behavioural assessment in neuropsychological rehabilitation: A method for measuring vocational-related skills. *Clin Neuropsychol*, *3*, 235–243.

Carey, C. L., Woods, S. P., Gonzalez, R., Conover, E., Marcotte, T. D., Grant, I., et al. (2004). Predictive validity of global deficit scores in detecting neuropsychological impairment in HIV infection. *J Clin Exp Neuropsyc*, *26*, 307–319.

Cattelani, R., Tanzi, F., Lombardi, F., & Mazzucchi, A. (2002). Competitive re-employment after severe traumatic brain injury: Clinical, cognitive and behavioural predictive variables. *Brain Inj*, *16*, 51–64.

Dickerson, F., Boronow, J. J., Stallings, C., Origoni, A. E., Cole, S. K., & Yolken, R. H. (2004). Cognitive functioning in schizophrenia and bipolar disorder: Comparison of performance on the Repeatable Battery for the Assessment of Neuropsychological Status. *Psychiat Res*, *129*, 45–53.

Doctor, J. N., Castro, J., Temkin, N. R., Fraser, R. T., Machamer, J. E., & Dikmen, S. S. (2005). Workers' risk of unemployment after traumatic brain injury: A normed comparison. *J Int Neuropsychol Soc*, *11*, 747–752.

Edwards, W. D. (1962). Dynamic decision theory and probabilistic information processing. *Hum Factors*, 4, 59–73.

Evans, J. D., Bond, G. R., Meyer, P. S., Kim, H. W., Lysaker, P. H., Gibson, P. J., et al. (2004). Cognitive and clinical predictors of success in vocational rehabilitation in schizophrenia. *Schizophr Res*, 70, 331–342.

Finkelstein, E. A., Corso, P. S., & Miller, T. R. (2006). *The incidence and economic burden of injuries in the United States.* New York: Oxford University Press.

Franzen, M. D., & Wilhelm, K. L. (1996). Conceptual foundations of ecological validity in neuropsychological assessment. In R. J. Sbordone & C. J. Long (Eds.), *Ecological validity of neuropsychological testing* (pp. 91–112). Delray Beach, FL: GR Press/St. Lucie Press.

Gonzalez, C. (2005). Decision support for real-time, dynamic decision-making tasks. *Organi Behav Hum Dec*, 96, 142–154.

Gonzalez, C., Thomas, R. P., & Vanyukov, P. (2005). The relationships between cognitive ability and dynamic decision making. *Intelligence*, 33, 169–186.

Greig, T. C., Nicholls, S. S., Bryson, G. J., & Bell, M. D. (2004). The Vocational Cognitive Rating Scale: A scale for the assessment of cognitive functioning at work for clients with severe mental illness. *J Voc Rehab*, 21, 71–81.

Guilmette, T. J., & Kastner, M. P. (1996). The prediction of vocational functioning from neuropsychological data. In R. J. Sbordone & C. J. Long (Eds.), *Ecological validity of neuropsychological testing* (pp. 387–411). Delray Beach, FL: Gr Press/St Lucie Press.

Heaton, R. K., Barth, J. T., Crosson, B. A., Larrabee, G. J., & Reynolds, C. R. (2002). Request for review papers on empirical support for areas of neuropsychological practice. *Newsletter 40 (Newsletter of the Division of Clinical Neuropsychology of the American Psychological Association)*, 20, 36–41.

Heaton, R. K., Chelune, G. J., & Lehman, R. A. (1978). Using neuropsychological and personality tests to assess the likelihood of patient employment. *J Nerv Ment Dis*, 166, 408–416.

Heaton, R. K., Marcotte, T. D., Mindt, M. R., Sadek, J., Moore, D. J., Bentley, H., et al. (2004). The impact of HIV-associated neuropsychological impairment on everyday functioning. *J Int Neuropsychol Soc*, 10, 317–331.

Heaton, R. K., Miller, W. S., Taylor, M. J., & Grant, I. (2007). *Revised comprehensive norms for an Expanded Halstead–Reitan Battery: Demographically adjusted neuropsychological norms for African Americans and Caucasian adults.* Lutz, FL: Psychological Assessment Resources.

Heaton, R. K., & Pendleton, M. G. (1981). Use of neuropsychological tests to predict adult patients' everyday functioning. *J Consult Clin Psychol*, 49, 807–821.

Heaton, R. K., Velin, R. A., McCutchan, J. A., Gulevich, S. J., Atkinson, J. H., Wallace, M. R., et al. (1994). Neuropsychological impairment in human immunodeficiency virus–infection: Implications for employment (HNRC Group, HIV Neurobehavioral Research Center). *Psychosom Med*, 56, 8–17.

Hedge, J. W., Borman, W. C., & Lammlein, S. E. (2006). *The aging workforce: Realities, myths, and implications for organizations.* Washington, DC: American Psychological Association.

Iachini, T., Sergi, I., Ruggiero, G., & Gnisci, A. (2005). Gender differences in object location memory in a real three-dimensional environment. *Brain Cognition*, 59, 52–59.

Jensen, J., Lindgren, M., Andersson, K., Ingvar, D. H., & Levander, S. (2000). Cognitive intervention in unemployed individuals with reading and writing disabilities. *Appl Neuropsychol*, 7, 223–236.

Kalechstein, A. D., Newton, T. F., & van Gorp, W. G. (2003). Neurocognitive functioning is associated with employment status: A quantitative review. *J Clin Exp Neuropsychol*, 25, 1186–1191.

Kendall, E., & Terry, D. (1996). Psychosocial adjustment following closed head injury: A model for understanding individual differences and predicting outcome. *Neuropsychol Rehabil*, 6, 101–132.

Klonoff, P. S., Lamb, D. G., & Henderson, S. W. (2001). Outcomes from milieu-based neurorehabilitation at up to 11 years post-discharge. *Brain Inj*, 15, 413–428.

Leblanc, J. M., Hayden, M. E., & Paulman, R. G. (2000). A comparison of neuropsychological and situational assessment for predicting employability after closed head injury. *J Head Trauma Rehabil*, 15, 1022–1040.

Lees-Haley, P. R. (1990). Vocational neuropsychological requirements of U.S. occupations. *Percept Mot Skills*, 70, 1383–1386.

Machamer, J., Temkin, N., Fraser, R., Doctor, J. N., & Dikmen, S. (2005). Stability of employment after traumatic brain injury. *J Int Neuropsychol Soc*, 11, 807–816.

Malloy, P., & Grace, J. (2005). A review of rating scales for measuring behavior change due to frontal systems damage. *Cogn Behav Neurol*, 18, 18–27.

McGurk, S. R., & Mueser, K. T. (2003). Cognitive functioning and employment in severe mental illness. *J Nerv Ment Dis*, 191, 789–798.

McGurk, S. R., & Mueser, K. T. (2004). Cognitive functioning, symptoms, and work in supported employment: A review and heuristic model. *Schizophr Res*, 70, 147–173.

McGurk, S. R., & Mueser, K. T. (2006). Cognitive and clinical predictors of work outcomes in clients with schizophrenia receiving supported employment services: 4-year follow-up. *Adm Policy Ment Health*, 33, 598–606.

Meyer, P. S., Bond, G. R., Tunis, S. L., & McCoy, M. L. (2002). Comparison between the effects of atypical and traditional antipsychotics on work status for clients in a psychiatric rehabilitation program. *J Clin Psychiat*, 63, 108–116.

Newnan, O. S., Heaton, R. K., & Lehman, R. A. (1978). Neuropsychological and MMPI correlates of patients' future employment characteristics. *Percept Mot Skills*, 46, 635–642.

Novack, T. A., Bush, B. A., Meythaler, J. M., & Canupp, K. (2001). Outcome after traumatic brain injury: Pathway analysis of contributions from premorbid, injury severity, and recovery variables. *Arch Phys Med Rehabil*, 82, 300–305.

Nuechterlein, K. H., Barch, D. M., Gold, J. M., Goldberg, T. E., Green, M. F., & Heaton, R. K. (2004). Identification of separable cognitive factors in schizophrenia. *Schizophr Res*, 72, 29–39.

Nybo, T., Sainio, M., & Muller, K. (2004). Stability of vocational outcome in adulthood after moderate to severe preschool brain injury. *J Int Neuropsychol Soc*, 10, 719–723.

Ownsworth, T., & McKenna, K. (2004). Investigation of factors related to employment outcome following traumatic brain injury: A critical review and conceptual model. *Disabil Rehabil*, 26, 765–783.

Ruffolo, C. F., Friedland, J. F., Dawson, D. R., Colantonio, A., & Lindsay, P. H. (1999). Mild traumatic brain injury from motor vehicle accidents: Factors associated with return to work. *Arch Phys Med Rehabil*, 80, 392–398.

Ryan, C. M., Morrow, L. A., Bromet, E. J., & Parkinson, D. K. (1987). Assessment of neuropsychological dysfunction in the workplace: Normative data from the Pittsburgh Occupational Exposures Test Battery. *J Clin Exp Neuropsychol*, 9, 665–679.

Sbordone, R. J. (2001). Limitations of neuropsychological testing to predict the cognitive and behavioral functioning of persons with brain injury in real-world settings. *NeuroRehabilitation*, 16, 199–201.

Sbordone, R. J., & Guilmette, T. J. (1999). Ecological validity: Prediction of everyday and vocational functioning from neuropsychological test data. In J. J. Sweet (Ed.), *Forensic neuropsychology: Fundamentals and practice* (pp. 227–254). Lisse, Netherlands: Swets & Zeitlinger.

Sergi, M. J., Kern, R. S., Mintz, J., & Green, M. F. (2005). Learning potential and the prediction of work skill acquisition in schizophrenia. *Schizophr Bull*, 31, 67–72.

Sherer, M., Novack, T. A., Sander, A. M., Struchen, M. A., Alderson, A., & Thompson, R. N. (2002). Neuropsychological assessment and employment outcome after traumatic brain injury: A review. *Clin Neuropsychol*, 16, 157–178.

Skeel, R. L., Bounds, T., Johnstone, B., Lloyd, J., & Harms, N. (2003). Age differences in a sample of state vocational rehabilitation clients with traumatic brain injury. *Rehabil Psychol*, 48, 145–150.

Tsang, H. W. H. (2003). Augmenting vocational outcomes of supported employment with social skills training. *J Rehabil*, 69, 25–30.

Twamley, E. W., Narvaez, J. M., Sadek, J. R., Jeste, D. V., Grant, I., & Heaton, R. K. (2006). Work-related abilities in schizophrenia and HIV infection. *J Nerv Ment Dis*, 194, 268–274.

U.S. Department of Labor. (1991). *Dictionary of occupational titles* (4th ed.). Washington, DC: Government Printing Office.

U.S. Department of Labor. (2006). O*Net Online: Occupational information network. Available at *online.onetcenter.org*.

van Gorp, W. G., Rabkin, J. G., Ferrando, S. J., Mintz, J., Ryan, E., Borkowski, T., et al. (2007). Neuropsychiatric predictors of return to work in HIV/AIDS. *J Int Neuropsych Soc*, 13, 80–89.

Velligan, D. I., Bow-Thomas, C. C., Mahurin, R. K., Miller, A. L., & Halgunseth, L. C. (2000). Do specific neurocognitive deficits predict specific domains of community function in schizophrenia? *J Nerv Ment Dis*, 188, 518–524.

Wilson, B. A. (1992). Recovery and compensatory strategies in head injured memory impaired people several years after insult. *J Neurol, Neurosur Ps*, 55, 177–180.

Wilson, B. A. (2000). Compensating for cognitive deficits following brain injury. *Neuropsychol Rev*, 10, 233–243.

Wilson, B. A., & Watson, P. C. (1996). A practical framework for understanding compensatory behaviour in people with organic memory impairment. *Memory*, 4, 465–486.

Wilson, J. R. (2006). Interaction with virtual environments. *Int J Hum-Comput St*, 64, 157.

Wood, R. L., & Rutterford, N. A. (2006). Demographic and cognitive predictors of long-term psychosocial outcome following traumatic brain injury. *J Int Neuropsychol Soc*, 12, 350–358.

World Health Organization. (2001). *International classification of functioning, disability, and health*. Geneva: World Health Organization.

CHAPTER 6

Medication Management

Terry R. Barclay, Matthew J. Wright, and Charles H. Hinkin

Medication adherence is broadly defined as the accurate use of medication and refers to proper administration of medicine in the correct dosage, at the appropriate time, and in accordance with any special instructions (Gould, McDonald-Miszczak, & Gregory, 1999). Proper medication adherence can prevent the deleterious effects of many chronic illnesses and is generally associated with improved health over a longer period of time. For example, it has been demonstrated that consistent antihypertensive therapy is associated with a 35–40% lower incidence of stroke, a 20–25% reduction in myocardial infarction, and a more than 50% reduction in heart failure (Neal, MacMahon, & Chapman, 2000). Despite the many benefits associated with adequate medication adherence, however, existing literature suggests that compliance with medication regimens is at best moderate and tends to decline over time in almost all chronic diseases (Dunbar-Jacob, 2002). In fact, although medication adherence is critical to the health maintenance of many individuals, rates of compliance are lower than 50% in most studies (for review, see Dunbar-Jacob et al., 2000; Haynes, McDonald, Garg, & Montague, 2003).

Inadequate compliance with medication regimens has been shown to be associated with a host of untoward consequences, including declines in overall health and increased risk of hospitalization (Col, Fanale, & Kronholm, 1990; Hallas et al., 1992), increased morbidity and mortality (Callahan & Wolinsky, 1995; Ganguli, Dodge, & Mulsant, 2002), and higher health care costs (Gryfe & Gryfe, 1984). Indeed, the estimated financial burden of nonadherence is staggering. The U.S. Department of Health and Human Services (1990) has estimated that approximately 10% of hospital admissions are directly attributable to nonadherence with prescription drug regimens, and 23% of nursing home admissions are seen as secondary to poor compliance with medical regimens. It has been estimated that medication nonadherence alone may have a direct economic cost of at least $100 billion annually. Clearly, determining the causes of poor medication adherence and using that knowledge to structure effective interventions are critically needed.

The existing literature has demonstrated that nonadherence is a complex, multi-dimensional problem. Previous studies have found poor medication adherence to be associated with a host of factors, including neurocognitive status, alcohol and drug use, psychiatric disturbance, insight and judgment, the class of prescribed medication, regimen complexity, drug efficacy, the route of administration, occurrence of negative side effects, type and chronicity of disease/illness, human factors (e.g., packaging and labeling of medication bottles, grade level at which health-related materials are written), physician interaction and communication style, financial resources, level of daily activity, degree of social isolation, family support, beliefs and attitudes regarding one's health, and level of health literacy. Whereas the majority of early studies focused on single constructs as possible determinants of nonadherence, more recent investigations have begun to incorporate broader, and more elaborate, models of medication-taking behavior.

This chapter presents a broad overview of current knowledge regarding the complex nature of adherence to medication regimens and those factors most clearly associated with individuals' medication-taking behavior. In doing so, we begin with a critical review of medication adherence methodologies and measurement techniques, including clinician ratings, self-report measures, pill counts, pharmacy records, electronic monitoring, physiological measurements such as blood tests, and laboratory-based analogue measures. An examination of medication adherence behaviors in select neurocognitive disorders then follows, with special attention paid to research conducted in the areas of normal aging, dementia, HIV/AIDS, and psychiatric illness. These disorders were chosen because they represent well the varied literature in this area and because they illustrate many of the common problems associated with medication nonadherence in those with impaired cognitive abilities. Also included is a brief review of the major psychosocial models that have been used to explain adherence behavior, including theories related to autonomy and self-efficacy, treatment expectancies, the health beliefs model, the theory of reasoned action, and social action theory. The chapter concludes with an evaluation of various medication management interventions and a discussion of future directions in medication adherence research.

Adherence Methodologies and Measurement Techniques

A number of techniques that has been used to measure medication adherence, all of which are characterized by unique strengths and weaknesses. These can be divided into techniques that provide more objective measures, such as plasma drug levels and electronic measuring devices, and those that provide more subjective information, such as patient self-report or clinician ratings.

Biological Markers

Blood levels provide precise quantification of adherence for medications that have a long half-life. For example, blood tests are an excellent means for ascertaining lithium levels and, by extension, whether patients with bipolar disorder are indeed taking their lithium carbonate as prescribed. In contrast, blood tests are not as useful for evaluating adherence rates for medications that are rapidly metabolized. In such cases blood levels can detect whether patients have *recently* taken their medication but cannot assist in determining whether patients *typically* take their medication, as prescribed.

Pill Counts

Pill counts are another technique that have been used to measure adherence rates. The technique is relatively straightforward. If one knows how many pills a patient initially possessed and how many pills he or she should have ingested in the intervening time period, it is easy to calculate the number of pills that should remain at the end of the study period. Excess doses are therefore considered to reflect doses not taken as prescribed. For example, consider a patient on a 3 pills/day regimen who begins with 100 pills and returns to clinic 30 days later. If 10 pills remain, that would be interpreted as perfect adherence ($100 - (30 \times 3) = 10$). While easy for the researcher/clinician to calculate, a decided drawback is that this is also easy for patients to calculate as well. Accordingly, prior to their return to clinic, patients may remove extra doses from their pill bottle and thus appear more adherent than is actually the case.

An innovative approach to overcome this limitation has been introduced by David Bangsberg and colleagues at the University of California at San Francisco (UCSF) (Bangsberg, Hecht, Charlebois, Chesney, & Moss, 2001). They conduct "unannounced pill counts," appearing at participants' residences without warning to conduct adherence assessments. They have found this approach to correlate well with biological outcomes (e.g., HIV viral load, or the amount of virus circulating in the blood). Although this methodology works well in a dense urban community such as San Francisco or New York, it would be excessively cumbersome for use in sparsely populated rural settings or in a sprawling metropolis without public transportation, such as Los Angeles.

Self-Report

Self-report is another widely used methodology. Strengths of self-report include its negligible cost and ease of data collection. Conversely, a weakness of self-report measures is that, for a multitude of reasons, many patients may overstate their actual adherence rates. For example, studies of HIV-infected adults have revealed that patient self-report, relative to electronic monitoring techniques, tends to be accurate among patients who candidly admit to poor adherence but may overestimate actual adherence rates by approximately 10–20% among a large subset of patients who claims perfect or near-perfect adherence (Arnsten et al., 2001; Levine et al., 2005).

Electronic Measuring Devices

The fallibility of self-report may be particularly salient when dealing with individuals who have memory impairment. Individuals with a dementing disorder may encounter considerable difficulty remembering whether or not they took their medication as prescribed. This inability is particularly pronounced when self-reported adherence rates are queried for more distal time periods. For this reason, the utilization of electronic monitoring devices (e.g., Medication Event Monitoring System [MEMS], Aprex Corp, Union City, CA) may better estimate actual adherence. MEMS embeds a computer chip in the cap of a pill bottle that automatically records the date, time, and duration of pill-bottle opening. Although electronic monitoring devices are not a perfect measure of medication adherence, a number of studies has shown that they may be more accurate than pill counts or self-report, both of which appear to significantly overestimate adherence rates. Drawbacks of this method include the bulky nature of the MEMS cap bottle, which precludes inconspicuous transportation of one's medications. This can lead to behavior called "pocket-dosing" in which patients remove an extra dose from their pill bottle to consume at a later point in time rather than carry their pill bottle with them. Also, in the past, the use of MEMS devices has precluded use of daily/weekly pill organizers, although technological advances are now emerging that will overcome this limitation in the future.

Pharmacy Refill Records

Pharmacy refill records have also proven to be a cost-effective proxy for measuring medication adherence. This technique rests on the assumption that if patients are refilling their medication prescriptions in a timely fashion, then they are more likely to be taking their medication as prescribed, as compared to individuals who are tardy in refilling their prescriptions. This approach works best in settings where pharmacy records are centralized and can be easily attained (e.g., in Veterans Administration Medical Centers).

Laboratory-Based Analogue Measures

In addition to attempts to assess real-world medication adherence, several investigators have utilized laboratory-based measures thought to be reflective of individuals' ability to adhere to medical recommendations. Interestingly, two groups (Albert et al., 1999; Gurland, Cross, Chen, & Wilder, 1994) independently developed such analogue measures of medication management skills by the same name: the Medication Management Test (MMT). Gurland and colleagues' (1994) version (MMT-Gurland) was primarily developed to assess the ability of older adults to self-administer medications, whereas Albert and colleagues' (1999) edition (MMT-Albert) was created to assess medication management skills among HIV-infected individuals. Both tests entail sorting, organizing, and making inferences about fictitious medications (e.g., when a prescription would need to be refilled). The MMT-Albert is more in-depth and requires 15–25 minutes to administer; the MMT-Gurland takes approximately 5 minutes to administer.

The MMT-Gurland has been shown to be associated with cognitive decline in older adults (Fulmer & Gurland, 1997; Gurland et al., 1994). The MMT-Albert has been associated with cognitive deficits in HIV-infected individuals, specifically difficulties in memory and executive and motor functioning (Albert et al., 1999, 2003). The MMT-Albert has been further revised by Patterson and colleagues (2002; Medication Management Ability Assessment [MMAA]) and Heaton and colleagues (2004; MMT—Revised [MMT-R]). Heaton and colleagues' adaptation included reordering test items by ascending order of difficulty, rewording some test items and the mock medication insert, as well as reducing the number of fictitious medications (from five to three) and inference items (from fifteen to seven). The MMT-R requires approximately 10 minutes to administer and has been shown to correlate with neuropsychological deficits in executive function and memory in HIV-infected individuals (Heaton et al., 2004).

To better characterize the possible medication management problems faced by individuals suffering from schizophrenia, the MMAA was modified from the MMT-Albert to better mimic interactions between patients and prescribing physicians (Patterson et al., 2002). It also requires examinees to demonstrate how they would self-administer medications after a 1-hour delay. Performance on the MMAA has been associated with memory and executive abilities of participants with schizophrenia (Jeste et al., 2003; Patterson et al., 2002). Interestingly, the MMAA was recently studied in relationship to a virtual reality (VR) task designed to simulate the medication-taking environment of participants with schizophrenia (Baker, Kurtz, & Astur, 2006). Like the MMAA, the experimental VR task correlated with memory and executive functioning, but it also showed significant relationship with sustained attention. Finally, direct observation has also been used (e.g., in tuberculosis programs), but it is prohibitively expensive in all but select cases.

Review of Medication Adherence in Select Neurocognitive Disorders

Normal Aging

Older adults experience more chronic illness and consume more medications than any other age group (see Ball et al., Chapter 10, this volume; Huang et al., 2002; Matteson & McConnell, 1988; Williams & Kim, 2005). In fact, 87–92% of patients over the age of 65 regularly take some form of medication (Gryfe & Gryfe, 1984). The number of drugs taken increases when patients become institutionalized or enter residential care. Between 67 and 80% of noninstitutionalized ambulatory older adults may receive drugs, but in nursing homes, the consumption rate can be as high as 97% (Ray, Federspiel, & Schaffner, 1980). Unfortunately, considerably higher rates of noncompliance have been reported among older patients. Estimates have ranged from 40 to as high as 75% (Ostrum, Hammarlund, Christensen, Plein, & Kethley, 1985), and adherence seems to be particularly problematic for commonly prescribed agents such as antihypertensive medications, lipid-lowering drugs, and antiarthritic medications. As many as 10% of older adults take drugs prescribed for other people, and more than 20% may take medications not currently prescribed and commit drug administration errors that could have serious clinical consequences (Lamy, Salzman, & Nevis-Olesen, 1992). Similarly, inappropriate drug discontinuation may occur up to 40% of the time in this population (Jackson, Ramsdell, Renvall, Smart, & Ward, 1984).

Older adults can experience age-related declines in the cognitive processes necessary for successful medication adherence (Raz, 2000) and therefore may be at higher risk for neglecting to take medications as prescribed. This risk is accentuated for individuals suffering from chronic disease. One of the most prominent causes of nonadherence among older adults is forgetfulness related to medication administration (Col et al., 1990; Leirer, Morrow, Pariante, & Sheikh, 1988). In an adherence study among older adults, Col and colleagues (1990) reported that poor recall had a stronger relationship to treatment nonadherence than did any other predictor (odds ratio = 7.1). Memory failure leading to poor medication adherence likely takes two forms. As elaborated by Morell, Park, and Poon (1990), patients must (1) remember the correct way to take a medication (retrospective memory) and (2) must remember to do so at the proper time (prospective memory). Morell and colleagues have found that (1) older adults have poorer recall of drug instructions than do younger controls; (2) both younger and older individuals have more difficulty recalling medication regimens as they became more complex; and (3) even when given unlimited time to learn medication instructions, older adults often do not study drug instructions sufficiently well to recall them (i.e., they appear to be more prone to metamemory failures).

Comprehension problems have also been shown to be associated with poor adherence to medication instructions among older adults, including comprehension of labels on pill bottles and instructions orally related by the patient's physician (Diehl, Willis, & Schaie, 1995; Kendrick & Bayne, 1982). For example, Kendrick and Bayne (1982) reported that older adults had difficulty translating the instruction "Take every 6 hours" into a specific medication plan, and Hurd and Butkovich (1986) found that most older adults made errors when interpreting prescription labels. Similarly, Morell, Park, and Poon (1989, 1990) found that about 25% of the information in a medication plan was misunderstood by older adults when they were presented with an array of prescription labels and asked to develop a medication schedule based on the instructions. Still other researchers have demonstrated that older adults have difficulty with comprehension of text when inferences are required (Cohen, 1981; Field, Mazor, Briesacher, Debellis, & Gurwitz, 2007; Metlay, 2008). Lower health literacy among older adults has also been implicated in poor comprehension of medication instructions and therefore poor overall adherence (Gazmararian et al., 2006; Morrow et al., 2006). These studies suggest that, as a result of age-related declines in comprehension and memory, older adults tend to have less information available to them, relative to younger individuals, following exposure to medication information and drug administration instructions.

In addition to age-related decrements in memory and comprehension abilities, declines in sensorimotor function, attention, working memory, processing speed, and executive functioning have also been shown to be associated with adherence to medication regimens (Conn, Taylor, & Miller, 1994; Isaac & Tablyn, 1993). At a most basic cognitive level, impairments in sensorimotor function may lead to suboptimal medication adherence. For example, declines in perceptual acuity have been shown to interfere with patient discrimination of basic medication information such as medication tablet color (Hurd & Butkovich, 1986). Impaired motor function has also been shown to be related to problems with opening medication bottles and cutting pills (Isaac & Tablyn, 1993). With regard to attentional abilities, Zacks and Hasher (1997) have found that older adults are deficient in their ability to both direct and to inhibit their attention to irrelevant information. Similarly, older adults have been found to be highly susceptible to both internal and external distraction over delays (Hasher & Zacks, 1988; Rekkas, 2006). Such deficits become particularly problematic when older individuals are faced with the administration of multiple medications and complex drug regimens. Indeed, noncompliance has been shown to increase dramatically among older adults in relation to the number of drugs prescribed (Fernandez et al.,

2006; Wandless & Davie, 1987). For example, dosage errors in one study increased 15-fold among older patients when the number of drugs prescribed was increased from one to four (Parkin, Henney, Quirk, & Crooks, 1986). Similarly, noncompliance was found to be 3.6 times more prevalent among older patients using two or more pharmacies to fill their prescriptions than among those using only one (Col et al., 1990).

Medication adherence also involves working memory, processing speed, and numeric abilities. Working memory is the capacity to process, manipulate, and temporarily store new or recently accessed information (Salthouse & Babcock, 1991). Considerable empirical evidence has demonstrated that working memory functions also decline with age (Craik & Jennings, 1992; Park et al., 1996; Smith, 1996) and therefore negatively impact medication-taking behaviors. In the context of self-medication management, individuals must keep the intention to take medicines in working memory while doing other things and must further rely upon these functions to integrate and develop a medication plan for following multiple drug regimens simultaneously. Salthouse (1996) and others have also demonstrated that older adults are slower at processing information in nearly all situations, relative to younger individuals. Processing speed has been defined as the speed at which mental operations are performed (Salthouse, 1996). Decrements in this domain are thought to compromise medication adherence behaviors by interfering with the complete processing and comprehension of information. For example, if mental operations regarding a medication regimen are performed too slowly, early information might be lost during the subsequent planning process. Finally, declines in numeric abilities, observed as early as age 50 (Schaie, 1996), are also hypothesized to inhibit correct dosage interpretation and to contribute to medication noncompliance.

Although older adults may be more likely to have cognitive deficits that negatively impact adherence, there are, of course, many other factors that predict treatment compliance in this population. Factors contributing to increased medication adherence in this group may include greater stability in lifestyle, less drug and alcohol abuse, and greater familiarity with medication taking and the establishment of routines and regimens to do so successfully. Other predictors include financial status (i.e., can the older patient afford to buy medication?), untoward side effects (e.g., patients often unilaterally discontinue medications that produce intolerable side effects), health beliefs (e.g., increased internal locus of control and greater fatalism regarding health issues), and degree of social integration versus isolation. There is also compelling evidence to suggest that health literacy may play an important role in adherence behaviors among older adults. In fact, previous research has found health literacy to be quite poor in this group as a whole (Council on Scientific Affairs, 1999), and this limitation has significant effects on comprehension and adherence to medical instructions. For example, among 3,260 Medicare patients from a large managed care plan in four cities, 33% of English-speaking and 54% of Spanish-speaking respondents had inadequate to marginal health literacy (Gazmararian et al., 1999). Only 12% of respondents understood the correct timing of dosing medications, and only 16% understood how to take a medication on an empty stomach (Gazmararian et al., 1999). Baker, Parker, Williams, and Clark (1998) demonstrated that patients with inadequate health literacy were at a twofold greater risk of hospital admission, compared with patients with marginal or adequate health literacy.

Research in the field of human factors (see Rogers et al., Chapter 2, this volume, for a comprehensive review), although not limited to older adult populations, has nevertheless contributed a wealth of additional information regarding ways to enhance the comprehension of complex medical information and improve medication compliance in this population. For example, studies have shown that both older and younger adults share preferences for the organization of medication information and tend to understand instructions in terms of what they already know about the task (Morrow, Leirer, Altieri, & Tanke, 1991; Morrow, Leirer, Andrassy, Tanke, & Stine-Morrow, 1996). These preferences suggest a general schema that includes three categories: (1) general information (e.g., name and purpose of the medication), (2) how to take the medication (dose, time, duration, and warnings), and (3) possible outcomes of taking the medication (side effects and what to do in case of an emergency). Interestingly, instructions in these studies were recalled 13–20% more accurately when organized according to this preferred medication-taking schema.

Research in this area has also demonstrated that visual acuity and the presentation and style of written materials has a significant impact on individuals' understanding and retention of information. Age-related declines in visual functioning have been well documented and include reduced visual acuity, contrast sensitivity, diminished perception of peripheral targets, and poorer color discrimination (Kline & Scialfa, 1997). The perception of written information can be enhanced in those with vision problems by increasing contrast (especially for detailed stimuli), avoiding glare, avoiding subtle distinctions among colors, and minimizing the need to discriminate fine detail. Similarly, studies on the effects of aging suggest that larger font sizes (i.e., 12–14 points), conventional font styles, and use of unjustified text are more appropriate for older adults and those with vision impairments (Drummond, Drummond, & Dutton, 2004; Gregory & Poulton, 1970; Vanderplas & Vanderplas, 1980). Instructions can also be improved by adding icons that highlight important information (Wickens, 1992), as such images tend to be more explicit than text, reducing cognitive load and the need for inferential reasoning (Larkin & Simon, 1987). Other studies recommend using relatively short paragraphs, employing active rather than passive voice, avoiding double negatives, and clarifying the structure of text by using summaries, headings, and bullet points.

Despite the wealth of information that has come from studies in the human factors literature, the health care industry has yet to implement many of these findings to enhance the comprehension of medical information among chronically ill patients. For example, as noted by Murray and colleagues (2004), the packaging and labeling of prescription medications has changed very little in the past 50 years; most patients filling prescriptions receive standard orange containers with minimal instructions printed in small font across a curved and glossy white sticker. Clearly, additional work is needed to translate current research findings into everyday, practical enhancements for medication comprehension and compliance.

Dementia

Although considerably fewer in number, relative to studies involving normal older adults, investigations of medication adherence behavior in patients with dementia have recently begun to emerge in the literature. The exclusion of individuals with dementia in earlier studies presumably reflects a general assumption that the neurocognitive mechanisms underlying medication adherence in such individuals may be more obviously deteriorated than in those with other health conditions. Indeed, studies have confirmed that patients with dementing conditions such as Alzheimer's disease typically have difficulty not only remembering which medications they are taking, but also the reason for their use, as a result of disruptions in short-term memory, judgment, and insight (Cooper et al., 2005). More interesting, however, are recent findings related to the association between frontal/executive deficits and poor medication adherence in this population. Results from such studies have implications for work with a variety of other populations, such those with traumatic brain injury and schizophrenia, for whom impairments in executive functions are common.

Executive abilities are the basis for several cognitive processes, including planning, strategizing, maintaining focused attention, and task switching. Studies have found that executively impaired patients are more likely to resist care and are less likely to comply with medication regimens (Allen, Jain, Ragab, & Malik, 2003; Hinkin et al., 2002; Stewart, Gonzalez-Perez, Zhu, & Robinson, 1999). In one study, executive impairment explained 28% of the variance in the performance of activities of daily living in patients with Alzheimer's disease (Boyle et al., 2003).

Adhering to medication regimens requires the involvement of executive functions because taking medicines involves developing and implementing a consistent plan to adhere; remembering to adhere, which typically requires time-based (e.g., at 5:00 P.M.) or event-based (e.g., with food) prospective remembering; and remembering whether the medicine was taken as desired (described as "source monitoring"). Not surprisingly, prospective difficulties are associated with neurological compromise (e.g., HIV-1 infection, Woods et al., 2006; traumatic brain injury, Schmitter-Edgecombe & Wright, 2004). Also, the ability to monitor the source is likely to become more difficult when the action is repetitive (Einstein, McDaniel, Smith, & Shaw, 1998). Recall of an isolated event in this case (e.g., whether or not a dose of medication was taken before bed) can be hampered by the fact that similar events have occurred many times in the past and therefore, as a whole, tend to blur together in memory, due to repetition and reduction in novelty. Indeed, taking medicines for chronic conditions is often repetitive because the same medicine is taken in the same way day after day.

Impaired executive functions may contribute to poor medication adherence in a number of ways. For example, individuals with deficits in such higher-order abilities may fail to take their medications because they cannot maintain the cognitive representation related to the need for medication in the face of other events. Similarly, persons with executive dysfunction may fail to organize their schedule in a manner necessary to accommodate medication taking. On the other hand, such individuals may perseverate on medication taking and unintentionally overdose. Moreover, executive deficits may contribute to faulty reasoning that medication adherence is not necessary or that alternative doses or regimens are acceptable.

Additional studies have demonstrated that, in at least some cases, the functional loss associated with executive impairments may be behaviorally mediated by apathy. Indeed, apathy has been associated with executive impairments in patients with various forms of dementia (Royall, Chiodo, & Polk, 2000). For example, Boyle and colleagues (2003) demonstrated that executive impairment and apathy scores contributed to 44% of the variance in instrumental activities of daily living in patients with Alzheimer's disease. Given that executive functions are involved in behaviors associated with motivation, disruption of the neural circuitry maintaining these higher-order processes may lead to apathy and subsequent functional impairment, resistance to care, and impaired decision-making capacity.

HIV/AIDS

Our group has engaged in several longitudinal investigations designed to identify factors that are associated with medication adherence, with a particular emphasis on neurocognitive factors. Below we present an overview of the primary findings from these studies to illustrate how neurocognitive dysfunction can adversely affect medication adherence.

The introduction of highly active antiretroviral therapy (HAART) has resulted in improved virological, immunological, and clinical outcomes, including improvement in neuropsychological functioning, in HIV-infected adults. Unfortunately, a number of studies has demonstrated that adherence rates of at least 90–95% are required for optimal viral suppression. Lower levels of adherence can lead to increased viral replication and the development of drug-resistant HIV strains with obvious adverse personal and public health consequences.

As previously discussed, cognitive compromise has been found to adversely impact various aspects of compliance with medical directives, including adherence. This relationship has been reported in HIV/AIDS as well as other chronic medical conditions such as diabetes and hypertension. Memory impairment, characterized especially by forgetfulness, motor and psychomotor slowing, attentional disruption, and executive system dysfunction have all been repeatedly observed among HIV-positive individuals.

One recent study, funded by the National Institute of Mental Health (NIMH) and conducted by our group, involved 137 HIV-infected adults who completed a comprehensive battery of neuropsychological tests assessing learning and memory, speed of information processing, attention/working memory, verbal fluency, executive function, and motor speed (Hinkin et al., 2002). Using a methodology employed by Heaton and colleagues at the University of California at San Diego (UCSD) HIV Neurobehavioral Research Center (HNRC), test scores were converted to demographically corrected T-scores and grouped by cognitive domain. A global T-score was also calculated. A liberal cutpoint of one standard deviation below the mean (e.g., $T < 40$) was used to classify participants as cognitively compromised, because this technique allows for an appropriate balance between sensitivity and specificity, particularly in milder disorders. Medication adherence was determined using MEMS caps to measure HAART adherence over a 1-month time frame. Participants who took at least 95% of their prescribed doses were classified as "good adherers."

The mean adherence rate across all 137 participants was 80.2%. Only 34% (46/137) of participants were classified as good adherers, whereas two-thirds of subjects were unable to adequately adhere to their medication regimen. Analyses examining the impact of cognitive compromise on adherence yielded the expected pattern of results. The cognitively impaired subjects' mean adherence rate was only 70%, whereas the neuropsychologically normal subjects evidenced a mean adherence rate of 82%. Logistic regression analyses revealed that neuropsychologically compromised individuals were twice as likely to be classified as poor adherers. Finer-grained examination of the neuropsychological test data revealed that it was executive dysfunction and working memory impairment that drove this relationship. Contrary to our expectations, learning and memory were not significantly associated with medication adherence.

Neuropsychological Dysfunction, Regimen Complexity, and Medication Adherence

Although considerable progress has been made in simplifying HIV medication regimens, historically the effective pharmacological management of HIV/AIDS has involved strict adherence to an extremely demanding, often complex, medication regimen (upwards of 20–30 pills/day, many having specific, compound instructions, such as "Take three times per day on an empty stomach"). Clearly, the relationship between neurocognitive integrity and medication adherence may be mediated by regimen complexity. Medication adherence may then be particularly problematic for the cognitively compromised patient who is on a more complex medication regimen.

Using the above data set, we explored the relationship between neuropsychological dysfunction, regimen complexity, and adherence. As can be seen in Figure 6.1, not only does regimen complexity (defined as a three-times-daily schedule) adversely affect medication adherence, but this effect is particularly pronounced among the cognitively impaired, who were able to successfully adhere to only a little over half of their prescribed doses. Complex medication regimens were not nearly as problematic for the neuropsychologically normal participants.

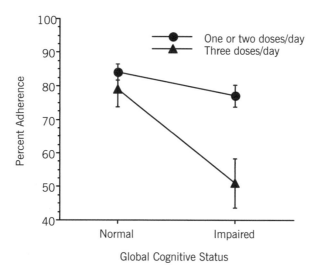

FIGURE 6.1. Relationship between cognitive status, regimen complexity, and medication adherence among HIV-infected adults. ● = one or two doses per day; ▲ = three doses per day. From Hinkin et al. (2002). Reprinted with permission from Lippincott Williams & Wilkins.

Aging, Neuropsychological Impairment, and Adherence

A number of studies has found older HIV-infected adults to be at greater risk for neuropsychological compromise. Because of this heightened risk of cognitive impairment, we posited that older subjects (defined here as over the age of 50) would be less adherent than younger subjects. Contrary to our expectations, we found that the older subjects were actually far more adherent than younger subjects. As can be seen in Figure 6.2, 53% of older subjects were classified as good adherers, whereas only 26% of younger subjects were able to attain a 95% adherence rate. Using a more liberal 90% cutpoint to define good adherence, 71% of older subjects were found to be adherent versus only 37% of younger subjects. It may be that taking medication requires less alteration in lifestyle for older adults or that such alterations are less burdensome for older individuals who may more easily accommodate pill taking into their daily activities. Older adults are also more likely to have prior experiences taking daily medications for other age-related illnesses.

However, a different picture emerges when we look at the interaction between advancing age and neurocognitive compromise. We first grouped the above subjects as a function of their medication adherence (using the 95% adherence cutpoint to dichotomize subjects) and age (using age 50 as a cutpoint) and then compared these groups' performances on neuropsychological testing. For illustrative purposes, Figure 6.3 depicts performance on the Trail Making Test and the California Verbal Learning Test (CVLT). As shown in this figure, there was little difference in cognitive functioning between the two younger groups and the older good adherers. In decided contrast, the older subjects who were poor adherers performed far worse on neuropsychological testing.

These findings suggest that the concomitant presence of both advancing age and neurocognitive impairment poses particular challenges regarding medication management. While we have conceptualized cognitive dysfunction as causing poor adherence, it is equally plausible that poor adherence results in a number of untoward

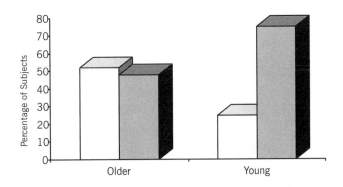

FIGURE 6.2. Medication adherence in younger (< 50 years) and older (≥ 50 years) HIV-infected adults. □ = good adherence (≥ 95%); ■ = poor adherence (< 95%); Older = age 50 or older; Young = less than age 50. From Hinkin et al. (2004). Reprinted with permission from Lippincott Williams & Wilkins.

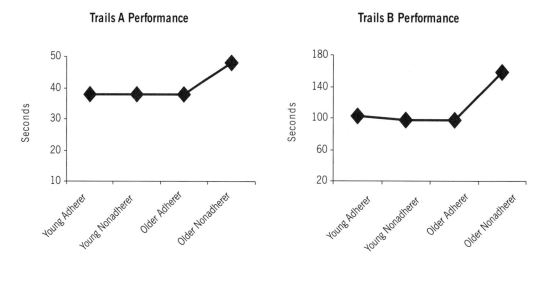

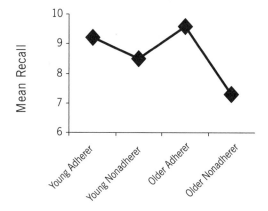

FIGURE 6.3. Trail Making and CVLT performances for younger and older HIV-infected adults as a function of medication adherence. Older = age 50 or older; Younger = less than age 50; CVLT = California Verbal Learning Test.

clinical outcomes, including neuropsychological impairment. In all likelihood, a bidirectional relationship exists, with cognitive impairment adversely affecting patients' ability to adhere to their medication regimen, which in turn results in further disease progression and a worsening of cognitive function. Figure 6.4 depicts the relationship between medication adherence and specific neurocognitive domains among older HIV-infected patients. In addition to higher rates of global neurocognitive impairment, poor adherence was associated with compromised executive function, memory, and speed of information processing.

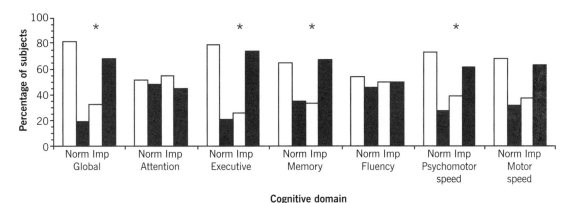

FIGURE 6.4. Medication adherence in older HIV-infected adults as a function of neurocognitive impairment. □ = good adherence (percentage adherence ≥95%); ■ = poor adherence (percentage adherence < 95%); Imp = cognitively impaired; Norm = cognitively normal; Global = a composite of all the individual cognitive domains; * = significant at $p < .05$. From Hinkin et al. (2004). Reprinted with permission from Lippincott Williams & Wilkins.

Drug Use/Abuse and Medication Adherence

Drug use or abuse may also adversely affect medication adherence via several potential mechanisms. Multiple studies have found substance abuse to be a risk factor for the development of neuropsychological impairment. Drug use can also give rise to new-onset psychiatric dysfunction or exacerbate a preexisting condition. Disruptions to sleep and eating patterns and increased psychosocial instability may also contribute to poorer adherence.

In a longitudinal study funded by the National Institute on Drug Abuse (NIDA) and based on a different cohort, we examined the impact of drug use and abuse on medication adherence among 150 HIV-infected individuals, 102 of whom tested urinalysis positive for recent illicit drug use. Medication adherence was tracked over a 6-month period using an electronic monitoring device (MEMS caps). We found that individuals urine-positive for illicit/recreational drugs demonstrated significantly worse medication adherence than did drug-negative participants (63 vs. 79%, respectively). Logistic regression revealed that drug use was associated with over a fourfold greater risk of adherence failure. The use of stimulants (i.e., cocaine or methamphetamine) proved to be particularly disruptive to adherence in this sample of HIV-infected adults. Participants who tested positive for stimulants were seven times more likely to be poor adherers than those who tested negative.

Interestingly, we were able to compare adherence rates for time periods when subjects were not using stimulants to time periods when those same subjects were using stimulants. We computed 3-day adherence rates for visits at which participants tested stimulant positive as well as adherence rates for visits at which the same participants tested stimulant negative. For each participant this yielded two adherence rates corresponding to when he or she was and was not using stimulant drugs. The 3-day mean adherence rate for participants who tested positive for recent stimulant use was 51.3% compared to a 3-day mean adherence rate of 71.7% for the same participants when they had not recently used stimulants. As such, the deleterious impact of drug use on adherence appears to be more a function of state rather than trait. This finding suggests that it is the acute effects of intoxication, rather than stable features that may be characteristic of the drug-using populace, which adversely affect medication adherence.

Psychiatric Status

Studies have reported nonadherence rates among psychiatric patients ranging from 26% (Drake, Osher, & Wallach, 1989) to as high as 73% (Razali & Yahya, 1995), depending on patient characteristics and the technique used to measure medication adherence. In unipolar disorders the 1-year relapse rates are as high as 80% in patients not taking antidepressants, as compared to 30% for those who adhere, yet 60% of patients discontinue their medications within 3 months of beginning treatment (Myers & Brainthwaite, 1992). Similarly, approximately 60% of patients admitted with mania failed to adhere to their medication regimen in the month prior to hospitalization (Keck et al., 1996).

Psychiatric disturbances, including depression and anxiety, have been associated with poorer medication compliance, to varying degrees, in studies using diverse measures and methodologies (Carney, Freedland, Eisen, Rich, & Jaffe, 1995; Edinger, Carwille, Miller, Hope, & Mayti, 1994; Hinkin et al., 2000; Sensky, Leger, & Gilmour, 1996; Shapiro et al., 1995). For example, a small meta-analysis (12 articles) found that depressed patients were three times more likely to be noncompliant with medication and behavioral treatment regimens (Dimatteo, Lepper, & Croghan, 2000). Similarly, patients suffering from coronary artery disease who also had a diagnosis of major depression adhered to their cardiac medication regimen less than 45% of the time during a 3-week adherence monitoring phase, whereas nondepressed patients showed 70% adherence (Carney et al., 1995). Shapiro and colleagues (1995) found psychiatric disturbance to be one of the best predictors of decreased compliance and mortality following heart transplantation. Likewise, Wang and colleagues (2002) demonstrated significant effects of depressive symptomatology on antihypertensive medication regimens, and Ciechanowski, Katon, and Russo (2000) found that depressive symptom severity was associated with poorer diet and medication regimen adherence among diabetics. A study by Sensky and colleagues (1996) found that affective disturbance interacted with other psychosocial variables, including health locus of control and social support, to negatively impact adherence to diet and other health behaviors among patients on chronic hemodialysis. Finally, neuropsychiatric dysfunction, including apathy, depression, and hostility, has been related to decreased adherence among older adults as well (Carney et al., 1995).

Recent studies have revealed that cognitive deficits associated with psychiatric illness may play a role in adherence behaviors. For example, there is increasing evidence that neurocognitive impairment in some patients with bipolar disorder is enduring and may represent a trait rather than a state variable. Deficits in learning and memory (Cavanagh, Van Beck, Muir, & Blackwood, 2002) and executive abilities (Dupont et al., 1990; Goldberg et al., 1993; Morice, 1990) have been found consistently, even during the euthymic phase of the illness. Such impairments may have detrimental effects on patients' ability to remember dosing instructions and to appropriately plan and organize a medication-taking regimen.

In addition to the neurocognitive deficits associated with psychiatric illness, a variety of other factors, such as ethnicity and attitudes and beliefs about psychotropic medication, may play a role in determining adherence behaviors among those with emotional disorders. For example, 78% of 2,000 people surveyed in one study thought that antidepressants were addictive, less than half thought they were effective, and only 16% believed that they should be given to individuals with depression (Priest, Vize, Roberts, Roberts, & Tylee, 1996). These findings suggest that physicians and others mental health practitioners have an important role in educating patients and the general public about the safety and efficacy of available antidepressant agents. With regard to ethnicity, a number of studies has suggested that patients from ethnic/minority groups are less likely to adhere to psychotropic medications than nonminority patients (Fleck, Hendricks, Del Bello, & Strakowski, 2002; Sleath, Rubin, & Huston, 2003). Specifically, previous research has found that both Hispanic and African American primary care patients may be less receptive to antidepressant medications than European Americans (Cooper et al., 2003). Poor adherence in these groups may be due to prohibitive cost, beliefs about depression or other psychiatric illnesses and the importance of its treatment, concerns about antidepressants, treatment preferences, and stigma related to taking psychiatric medication (Bultman & Svarstad, 2000; Maidment, Livingston, & Katona, 2002; Sirey et al., 2001).

The studies reviewed above help to explain medication-taking behaviors in some individuals; factors associated with adherence to medication regimens have also been studied in the context of more severe psychopathology, including those with schizophrenia and other psychotic disorders. Despite the overwhelming evidence that neuroleptic medication is effective in the treatment of schizophrenia, many patients do not take their medications (Dencker & Liberman, 1995; Hale, 1995), and antipsychotic nonadherence is therefore a major barrier to the effective pharmacological treatment of these individuals (Dolder et al., 2004). Several studies have shown that approximately one-third of patients with schizophrenia are fully compliant with medications, one-third are partially compliant, and one-third of patients are entirely noncompliant (Buchanan, 1992; Fleischhacker, Meise, Gunther, & Kurz, 1994; Weiden, Shaw, & Mann, 1995). Moreover, 55% of people with schizophrenia who do not take antipsychotic medication will relapse over the course of a year, compared to only 14% of those who comply with their medication regimen (Stephenson, Rowe, Haynes, Macharia, & Leon, 1993). Not surprisingly, multiple investigations have demonstrated that poor medication adherence among patients with schizophrenia is associated with a variety of poor health outcomes, including increased rehospitalization, repeated emergency room visits, worsening of symptoms, and even homelessness (Marder, 1998; Moore, Sellwood, & Stirling, 2000; Olfson et al., 2000; Weiden & Olfson, 1995).

Several reviews of the literature on medication adherence in schizophrenia (Fenton, Blyler, & Heinssen, 1997; Kampman & Lehtinen, 1999) have identified consistent predictors of poor adherence in this population, including more severe psychopathology, comorbid substance abuse, presence of medication side effects, depressive symptoms, an absence of social support from family or friends, practical barriers (e.g., inability to afford medications), lack of insight, and neurocognitive dysfunction.

Although there is substantial heterogeneity among such individuals with regard to the level and pattern of cognitive impairment, some of the most commonly impaired abilities in schizophrenia include attention, working memory, verbal and nonverbal learning, executive skills, and some psychomotor abilities (Heaton & Drexler, 1987; Heinrichs & Zakzanis, 1998; Schwartz, Rosse, Veazey, & Deutsch, 1996). A major barrier to adherence in this population is related to a lack of insight or an inability to understand one's disorder and the need for treatment (Lacro, Dunn, Dolder, Leckband, & Jeste, 2002). Diminished insight, coupled with other cognitive deficits, may decrease patients' ability to adhere to their treatment regimens (Green, 1996; Green, Kern, Braff, & Mintz, 2000).

Psychosocial Models of Adherence

Although the primary thrust of this chapter has been to highlight the relationship between cognitive abilities and medication adherence, many other intra- and extra-personal factors have been shown to have an impact on adherence behaviors. Qualitative studies have indicated that medication adherence is dynamic and multifactorial in determination (Remien et al., 2003). Several of these studies suggest that medication adherence is influenced by side effects, self-efficacy, lifestyle factors and self-identity, illness ideology, affect, and medication burden (Carrick, Mitchell, Powell, & Lloyd, 2004; Remien et al., 2003; Wilson, Hutchinson, & Holzemer, 2002). Numerous theories developed to explain health-related behaviors have been applied to the study of medication adherence. A detailed review of this work is beyond the scope of this chapter, but, in general, most of these theories deal with external influences (e.g., environmental, social) and/or internal influences (e.g., attitudes/beliefs, motivation) on medication-taking behavior. One such internal influence is self-awareness of bodily sensations and processes. Interestingly, in a sample of patients in hemodialysis ($N = 52$), bodily self-focusing tendencies (i.e., increased attention to physical sensations) were shown to interact with illness-related physical impairment to influence medication and dietary adherence (Christensen, Wiebe, Edwards, Michels, & Lawton, 1996). High body self-focusing and illness-related physical impairments were predictive of poorer adherence, whereas high body self-focusing and low illness-related physical impairments predicted better adherence. These findings suggest an interaction between treatment expectancies (based on illness-related impairment) and body self-focusing in which adherence behavior improves with positive expectancies and high body self-focusing and declines with negative expectancies and high body self-focusing. However, treatment expectancies are likely multifactorial in nature, reflecting current and past health status, real and perceived barriers to adherence, self-efficacy, and motivation (Christensen et al., 1996; Reynolds, 2003; Williams, Rodin, Ryan, Grolnick, & Deci, 1998).

Health Beliefs Model

In order to better predict complex health-related behaviors such as medication compliance, the health beliefs model was proposed (HBM; Rosenstock, 1974). The HBM is derived from a well-established body of psychological and behavioral theory and posits that health behaviors depend mainly on the desire to avoid illness and the belief that certain actions will prevent or alleviate disease. The model consists of a number of dimensions, including perceived susceptibility to illness, perceived illness severity, perceived benefits of treatment, and perceived barriers to treatment compliance. "Perceived susceptibility" refers to an individual's belief that he or she is at risk of contracting an illness or, in the case of a previously established infection, belief in the diagnosis and the vulnerability to illness in general. "Perceived illness severity" describes feelings regarding the seriousness of contracting an illness or of leaving it untreated, and requires evaluation of possible social, occupational, and psychological consequences. "Perceived benefits of treatment" refers to beliefs in the effectiveness of various actions in reducing disease threat. Finally, "perceived barriers to treatment compliance" describes a kind of cost–benefit analysis in which individuals weigh the treatment's effectiveness against potential negative consequences of compliance, such as disruption of daily activities and adverse side effects. HBM theory predicts that individuals are more likely to comply with treatment regimens if they perceive themselves to be potentially vulnerable to the illness, perceive the consequences of illness as severe, are convinced of the efficacy of the proposed treatment regimen, and see relatively few costs associated with adherence (Budd, Hughes, & Smith, 1996; Smith, Ley, Seale, & Shaw, 1987).

In addition to these four dimensions, the HBM also postulates that diverse demographic, psychosocial, and psychological variables may affect individuals' perceptions and thereby indirectly influence health-related behaviors. The model also states that individuals need a prompt (e.g., a reminder either of the threat of illness or the action that must be taken against it) before they will engage in health-related behaviors (Weinstein, 1988). These "cues to action" may be internal (e.g., recognition of prodromal symptoms) or external (e.g., comments made by significant others). The HBM has been shown to explain variation in medical regimen adherence behavior in patients with a variety of diseases and disorders, including HIV (Barclay et al., 2007), hypertension (Brown & Segal, 1996; Mendoza, Munoz, Merino, & Barriga, 2006), diabetes (Harris, Skyler, Linn, et al., 1982), heart disease (Mirotznik, Feldman, & Stein, 1995), epilepsy (Green & Simons-Morton, 1988), end-stage renal disease (Cummings, Becker, Kirscht, & Levin, 1982), and psychiatric illnesses such as depression and schizophrenia (Adams & Scott, 2000; Cohen, Parikh, & Kennedy, 2000).

Autonomy and Self-Efficacy

Others have attempted to explain medication adherence via social determination frameworks in which autonomous (volitional) and controlled (nonvolitional) behavior regulation are distinguished. Whereas "self-efficacy" refers to one's belief in one's own ability to *organize* and *execute* an action, "autonomy" relates to one's *regulation* of actions. In one study, a mixed sample of patients ($N = 126$) that was required to adhere to simple medication regimes ($M = 1.36$ medications, $M = 1.40$ doses daily), a sense of autonomy with regard to health care management accounted for 68% of the variance in medication adherence (Williams et al., 1998). Furthermore, perceived physician support of autonomous health care management was found to significantly mediate this relationship. Interestingly, in this study, perceived barriers did not predict adherence, although they were negatively correlated with autonomy and perceived autonomy support. The authors suggest that autonomy mediates the relationship between perceived barriers and adherence, such that individuals with higher levels of health care autonomy and perceived support for health care autonomy perceive fewer barriers to adherence. It is also possible that increased autonomy facilitates self-efficacy, thereby reducing perceived barriers. Whatever the case may be, this study highlights the role of personal control and social support as important contributors to medication adherence behaviors.

Theory of Reasoned Action

A related psychological model for explaining health-related behaviors is the theory of reasoned action (Ajzen & Fishbein, 1980). The central tenet of this model is that the *intention* to adhere is the best predictor of ultimate adherence, with intentions seen as a function of patients' beliefs and expectations, their values, and the normative pressures exerted by their social referent group. Noting that the best intentions are often thwarted if the requisite abilities or opportunities are lacking, Ajzen (1985), in his theory of planned behavior, incorporated locus of control into the previous model. Research has shown both models to have reasonable predictive utility, with the theory of planned behavior more appropriate for health care situations not entirely under the patient's perceived control (Millstein, 1996).

Social Action Theory

Social action theory (SAT; Ewart, 1991) was formulated to deal with interactions between internal and external factors. SAT holds that contextual influences (physical environment, social/cultural environment, and biological factors) interact and modulate mood and arousal, which impact self-regulatory processes (motivation, problem solving, generative capabilities, and interactive social factors) that, in turn, lead to action states (e.g., medication adherence). A large ($N= 2,765$), multisite (Los Angeles, Milwaukee, New York City, San Francisco) study of HIV-positive individuals on complex antiretroviral therapy (ART) revealed that the contextual factors of African American heritage, number of daily doses, symptom difficulty, being in a primary relationship, having a history of drug use (injection drug use or crack cocaine use), and having a history of homelessness were predictive of poor (< 90%) adherence (Johnson et al., 2003). Additionally, poor adherers also reported higher rates of depressive, anxious, and stress-related symptoms. Self-regulatory factors associated with poor adherence were low adherence self-efficacy, difficulty fitting medication schedule into daily routines, problems managing medication side effects, fatigue related to medication adherence, and disbelief in the efficacy of the prescribed ART regimen. The positive association between being in a primary romantic relationship and nonadherence was surprising. The authors addressed this finding by suggesting that the majority of their participants may have been involved in problematic relationships, although this was not assessed. Others have demonstrated that negative relationships can have a deleterious effect on medication adherence (Dimatteo, 2004; Perlick et al., 2004). That said, Johnson and colleagues' (2003) study supports an association between medication adherence and contextual and self-regulatory factors. Future studies investigating these relationships with structural equation modeling may help to better test the predicted interactions posited by SAT.

Additional Psychosocial Models

One contextual factor that has received considerable research attention to date is social support, which is often differentiated into structural and functional components (Berk, Berk, & Castle, 2004; Dimatteo, 2004; Simoni, Frick, & Huang, 2006; Weaver et al., 2005). Structural components are variables such as marital status, living arrangement, and social network density, whereas functional components describe variables such as practical support, emotional support, and family cohesion. A recent meta-analysis on social support and medical regimen adherence demonstrated that several areas of functional support were highly associated with medical adherence (Dimatteo, 2004), the strongest of these being practical support. Emotional support and family cohesiveness were also associated with adherence, and family conflict was negatively related to medication adherence. Similarly, others have shown that medication adherence suffers when caregivers are overburdened (Perlick et al., 2004). Among structural supports in Dimatteo's meta-analysis, marital status and living with someone were modestly related to adherence. Overall, this meta-analytic review indicates the importance of social support, particularly functional social support, in medical regimen adherence, although it does not specify how this relationship may be moderated.

Recent studies of ART adherence in HIV-positive individuals have attempted to delineate the nature of the relationships between social support, affect, and medication adherence, using structural equation modeling. One such study (Simoni et al., 2006) showed that social support was positively associated with spirituality and negatively associated with negative affect (e.g., depression), which, in turn, predicted adherence self-efficacy in HIV-positive individuals ($N = 136$). Adherence self-efficacy was predictive of self-reported adherence, which, in turn, predicted viral load. Unfortunately, the model only accounted for 8% of the total variance in ART adherence. A more compelling study, also utilizing structural equation modeling, demonstrated that the relationship between medication adherence, social support, and affect was mediated by avoidant coping strategies reported by HIV-infected individuals ($N = 322$; Weaver et al., 2005). More specifically, 20% of the variance in medication adherence (measured via MEMS caps) was predicted by negative affect and poor social support, as moderated by avoidant coping. The same model also accounted for 44% of the variance in viral load.

In sum, many theories have been postulated to explain medication adherence behaviors across a wide range of patient populations. Research generated by these theories has demonstrated that sociodemographic factors (e.g., homelessness, drug use, ethnic/racial minority status), treatment expectancies, health beliefs/attitudes, self-efficacy, a sense of autonomy in health care management, social support, cohesive and positive support networks, emotional functioning, and coping styles seem to play a part in medication adherence. Additionally, many researchers have begun to examine how these factors interact and influence adherence, although the many complexities in this area of investigation have limited our understanding of medication-taking behavior. Moreover, little is known about the interaction between these numerous factors and neurocognitive deficits in attention/concentration, memory, or executive functioning. Beyond their direct effects on medication adherence, such cognitive difficulties may moderate or mediate the influence of predictors such as treatment expectancies, health beliefs, autonomous health care management, coping styles, and social support. Indeed, recent data collected from individuals suffering from schizophrenia have shown that difficulties in sustained attention, verbal memory, and executive functioning correlate with their attitudes and beliefs about medications (Kim et al., 2006; Maeda et al., 2006).

Medication Adherence Interventions

Given the prevalence of suboptimal medication adherence across patients with chronic illnesses and neurocognitive deficits, interventions aimed at improving medication-taking behavior are clearly needed. A wide variety of strategies has been used to increase compliance in such populations, including rehabilitation techniques aimed at improving actual neurocognitive impairments, as well as compensatory mechanisms designed to support limitations in cognitive functioning, such as pillboxes, medication charts, and voice-mail reminder services.

Intervention strategies used to improve medication management in populations with neuropsychological deficits have not been thoroughly investigated to date. Although interventions that do not specifically target cognitive abilities have been shown to improve medication adherence in some individuals with such deficits (e.g., Antoni et al., 2006; Higgins, Livingston, & Katona, 2004), cognitive impairments have nevertheless been demonstrated to interfere with medication adherence in many populations (Chen et al., 2005; Heaton et al., 2004; Park, Morrell, Frieske, & Kincaid, 1992). In the past, these deficits have been treated with restorative (e.g., practice drills to improve memory function) or compensatory interventions (e.g., use of a daily planner to improve memory for daily events) (Wilson, 1999). Restorative techniques are generally used during periods of natural recovery (e.g., in the first 6 months following a traumatic brain injury) but are typically discontinued when improvements in function begin to plateau (Wilson, 2000). Rehabilitation strategies used to target attention, memory, and executive functioning impairments have been used on an individual basis and in combination. Targeting isolated cognitive deficits is obviously most beneficial for individuals who suffer from solitary impairments. Whereas targeting cognitive impairments separately may also enhance medication-taking behaviors in persons with multiple/overlapping cognitive deficits, intervention strategies that approach medication adherence as a more complex neurocognitive operation will likely result in more significant and tangible outcomes.

In addition to cognitive remediation techniques, researchers have evaluated the effectiveness of external aids such as pillboxes and pill bottle alarms (Mackowiak et al., 1994; Park et al., 1992), voice-mail reminders (Andrade et al., 2005; Leirer, Morrow, Tanke, & Pariente, 1991), and organizational charts (Park et al., 1992). Haynes and colleagues have conducted several reviews of medication intervention research (Haynes, McKibbon, & Kanani, 1996; Haynes et al., 2000, 2003) and have consistently observed that successful interventions are often complex and involve some combination of providing more convenient care, education, and reminders to take medication, as well as encouragement to self-monitor and increased support through counseling, family therapy, and/or supervision. However, even the most effective interventions have not led to notable outcomes. In fact, for the most part, adherence interventions have been found to be minimally effective; that is, effect sizes have typically been small ($\leq.25$), indicating that detecting significant change with such strategies would be difficult (Haynes et al., 2003).

Despite limitations in overall effectiveness, a few studies have shown increased adherence with the use of various compensatory strategies. For example, Park and colleagues (1992) found that older adults who used both an organizer and a chart designed to minimize cognitive effort in taking medications made considerably fewer errors in their medication regimens than control subjects (18.3% for controls vs. 1.8% for the intervention group). The use of charts and written instructions to augment verbal communication has also been shown to be beneficial in a number of other studies (Coe, Prendergast, & Psathas, 1984; Lamy et al., 1992). Similarly, color-coded pill bottles matched with a weekly pillbox have been demonstrated to enhance compliance in some patients (Martin & Mead, 1982). Finally, Leirer and colleagues (1991) found a fourfold reduction in episodes of poor adherence when voice-mail reminders were used to cue older subjects about their medication regimen.

Well-designed medication instructions that reduce cognitive demands and motivate the patient may also work to improve adherence (Park, Willis, Morrow, Diehl, & Gaines, 1994). Such instructions may be even more effective if, in addition to explaining how to take medication, they present information that targets incorrect beliefs about the illness or the drug. For example, Carter, Beach, and Inui (1986) found that reminder messages for flu vaccinations improved clinic attendance significantly when they contained information that addressed incorrect beliefs about the side effects and risks of the immunizations.

Some experts have noted that there is a number of interventions that physicians and other health care providers could perform more regularly to potentially increase medication adherence in their patients. These interventions include explaining why particular medicines are being prescribed and what outcome is expected, emphasizing the shared responsibility between physician and patient, and trying to anticipate common barriers to adherence (e.g., economic limitations, cognitive impairment, negative side effects). Other important interventions include providing information about health conditions and medications both orally and in writing at a level understandable to patients, asking patients to explain the consequences of not taking medications or how to cope with adverse side effects, and mobilizing patients' families to assist in providing additional support or supervision of their family members' medication taking. Conducting regular medication reviews has also been associated with improved adherence in some patients. Such reviews may enhance adherence by improving the doctor–patient relationship and/or by emphasizing the relevance and importance of medications. Given the frequency of polypharmacy, particularly in older populations, reviewing and possibly reducing the number of medications may also help to improve adherence. Some researchers have also suggested that the timing of medication taking should be matched to patients' daily schedules when feasible (Coe et al., 1984), because if regimens interfere with normal everyday activities, poor adherence is more likely to occur. Finally, improved detection and treatment of dementia, psychiatric disorders, and alcohol use disorders may also have a positive impact on adherence.

As noted earlier, the field of human factors has the potential to play a major role in the improvement of medication adherence across populations and disease treatment models. Research in this area has demonstrated that the presentation and style of written materials have a significant impact on individuals' understanding and retention of information. Given that both older and younger adults share a preference for medication information presented in an organized format (Morrow et al., 1991, 1996), adherence may be improved if drug instructions are delivered in a way that more closely conforms to this desired schema. For example, studies suggest that use of larger font sizes, conventional font styles, and unjustified text may be more appropriate for older adults and those with vision or cognitive impairments (Drummond et al., 2004; Vanderplas & Vanderplas, 1980). Instructions may also be improved by adding icons that highlight important information (Wickens, 1992), using relatively short paragraphs, and relying more heavily upon summaries, headings, and bullet points.

Future Directions

Most early research on medication-taking behaviors focused on single constructs as possible determinants of poor adherence, such as the demographic features of the patient (e.g., age, race, gender) or aspects of the therapeutic regimen (e.g., number of medications). However, as illustrated in this chapter, medication adherence is an extremely complex behavior, and it is likely that no single variable can account for the rates of poor compliance that have been observed across various diseases and patient populations. Therefore, more research that considers several of these explanatory factors simultaneously is greatly needed. Only by examining complex models of adherence behavior that take into account demographic, medication, disease, psychosocial, and neurocognitive variables will the most important predictors of adherence begin to be identified.

Considering the limited effectiveness of many available medication adherence interventions, greater emphasis should be placed on finding effective techniques to improve medication compliance and clinical outcomes. Interventions are needed to enhance patient education, increase patients' health literacy, encourage the use of drug delivery systems, improve monitoring of medication use, and enhance communication among providers about patients' adherence patterns. Because the factors influencing adherence are many and varied, multifaceted, tailored interventions may be necessary to improve self-administration of medications in most populations. Finally, because physicians frequently underestimate subtle impairment or disability in their patients (Calkins et al., 1991; Canadian Task Force, 1991), clear-cut practice guidelines and suitable methods of measuring those cognitive, motor, and sensory functions required for accurate drug administration are essential for ultimate preventive management.

Acknowledgments

This chapter includes data gathered as part of a National Institute of Mental Health (NIMH)–funded study (No. RO1 MH58552) and a National Institute on Drug Abuse (NIDA)–funded study (No. RO1 DA13799). Support was also provided by the VA Merit Review program. Terry R. Barclay and Matthew J. Wright were supported by an NIMH training grant (No. T32 MH19535).

References

Adams, J., & Scott, J. (2000). Predicting medical adherence in severe mental disorders. *Acta Psychiat Scand*, *101*, 119–124.

Ajzen, I. (1985). From intentions to actions. In J. Kuhl & Beckman (Eds.), *Action control from cognition to behavior*. New York: Springer-Verlag.

Ajzen, I., & Fishbein, M. (1980). *Understanding attitudes and predicting social behavior*. Englewood Cliffs, NJ: Prentice-Hall.

Albert, S. M., Flater, S. R., Clouse, R., Todak, G., Stern, Y., & Marder, K. (2003). Medication management skill in HIV: I. Evidence for adaptation of medication management strategies in people with cognitive impairment. II. Evidence for a pervasive lay model of medication efficacy. *AIDS Behav*, *7*(3), 329–338.

Albert, S. M., Weber, C. M., Todak, G., Polanco, C., Clouse, R., & McElhiney, M., et al. (1999). An observed performance test of medication management ability in HIV: Relation to neuropsychological status and medication adherence outcomes. *AIDS Behav*, *3*(2), 121–128.

Allen, S. C., Jain, M., Ragab, S., & Malik, N. (2003). Acquisition and short-term retention of inhaler techniques require intact executive function in elderly subjects. *Age Ageing*, *32*, 299–302.

Andrade, A. S., McGruder, H. F., Wu, A. W., Celano, S. A., Skolasky, R. L., Selnes, O. A., et al. (2005). A programmable prompting device improves adherence to highly active antiretroviral therapy in HIV-infected subjects with memory impairment. *Clin Infect Dis*, *41*(6), 875–882.

Antoni, M. H., Carrico, A. W., Durán, R. E., Spitzer, S., Penedo, F., & Ironson, G., et al. (2006). Randomized clinical trial of cognitive behavioral stress management on human immunodeficiency virus viral load in gay men treated with highly active antiretroviral therapy. *Psychosom Med*, *68*, 143–151.

Arnsten, J. H., Demas, P. A., Farzadegan, H., Grant, R. W., Gouretvitch, M. N., Chang, C. J., et al. (2001). Antiretroviral therapy adherence and viral suppression in HIV-infected drug users: Comparison of self-report and electronic monitoring. *Clin Infect Dis*, *33*(8), 1417–1423.

Baker, D. W., Parker, R. M., Williams, M. V., & Clark, W. S. (1998). Health literacy and the risk of hospital admission. *J Gen Intern Med*, *13*, 791–798.

Baker, E. K., Kurtz, M. M., & Astur, R. S. (2006). Virtual reality assessment of medication compliance in patients with schizophrenia. *CyberPsychol Behav*, *9*(2), 224–229.

Bangsberg, D. R., Hecht, F. M., Charlebois, E. D., Chesney, M., & Moss, A. (2001). Comparing objective measures of adherence to HIV antiretroviral therapy: Electronic medication monitors and unannounced pill counts. *AIDS Behav*, *5*(3), 275–281.

Barclay, T. R., Hinkin, C. H., Mason, K. I., Reinhard, M. J., Marion, S. D., Levine, A. J., et al. (2007). Age-associated predictors of medication adherence in HIV-positive adults: Health beliefs, self-efficacy, and neurocognitive status. *Health Psychol*, *26*(1), 40–49.

Berk, M., Berk, L., & Castle, D. (2004). A collaborative approach to the treatment alliance in bipolar disorder. *Bipolar Disord*, 6, 504–518.

Boyle, P. A., Malloy, P. F., Salloway, S., Cahn-Weiner, D. A., Cohen, R., & Cummings, J. L. (2003). Executive dysfunction and apathy predict functional impairment in Alzheimer's disease. *Am J Geriatr Psychiat*, 11, 214–221.

Brown, C. M., & Segal, R. (1996). The effects of health and treatment perceptions on the use of prescribed medication and home remedies among African American and white American hypertensives. *Soc Sci Med*, 43(6), 903–917.

Buchanan, A. (1992). A two year prospective study of treatment compliance in patient with schizophrenia. *Psychol Med*, 22, 787–797.

Budd, R. J., Hughes, I. C., & Smith, J. A. (1996). Health beliefs and compliance with antipsychotic medication. *Brit J Clin Psychol*, 35(3), 393–397.

Bultman, D. C., & Svarstad, B. L. (2000). Effects of physician communication style on client medication beliefs and adherence with antidepressant treatment. *Patient Educ Couns*, 40, 173–185.

Calkins, D. R., Rubenstein, L. V., Cleary, P. D., Davies, A. R., Vette, A. M., Fink, A., et al. (1991). Failure of physicians to recognize functional disability in ambulatory patients. *Ann Intern Med*, 114, 451–454.

Callahan, C. M., & Wolinsky, F. D. (1995). Hospitalization for major depression among older Americans. *Gerontol A-Biol*, 50A, M196–M202.

Canadian Task Force on the Periodic Health Examination. (1991). Periodic health examination, 1991 update no. 1: Screening for cognitive impairment in the elderly. *Can Med Assoc J*, 144, 425–431.

Carney, R. M., Freedland, K. E., Eisen, S. A., Rich, M. W., & Jaffe, A. S. (1995). Major depression and medication adherence in elderly patients with coronary artery disease. *Health Psychol*, 14(1), 88–90.

Carrick, R., Mitchell, A., Powell, R. A., & Lloyd, K. (2004). The quest for well-being: A qualitative study of the experience of taking antipsychotic medication. *Psychol Psychother-T*, 77, 19–33.

Carter, W., Beach, L, & Inui, T. S. (1986). The flu shot study: Using multiattribute utility theory to design a vaccination intervention. *Organ Behav Hum Dec*, 38, 378–391.

Cavanagh, J. T., Van Beck, M., Muir, W., & Blackwood, D. H. (2002). Case-control study of neurocognitive function in euthymic patients with bipolar disorder: An association with mania. *Br J Psychiatry*, 180, 293–295.

Chen, E. Y., Hui, C. L., Dunn, E. L., Miao, M. Y., Yeung, W., & Wong, C., et al. (2005). A prospective 3-year longitudinal study of cognitive predictors of relapse in first-episode schizophrenic patients. *Schizophr Res*, 77, 99–104.

Christensen, A. J., Wiebe, J. S., Edwards, D. L., Michels, J. D., & Lawton, W. J. (1996). Body consciousness, illness-related impairment, and patient adherence in hemodialysis. *J Consult Clin Psych*, 64, 147–152.

Ciechanowski, P. S., Katon, W. J., & Russo, J. E. (2000). Depression and diabetes: Impact of depressive symptoms on adherence, function, and costs. *Arch Inter Med*, 160, 3278–3285.

Coe, R. M., Prendergast, C. G., & Psathas, G. (1984). Strategies for obtaining compliance with medication regimens. *J Am Geriatr Soc*, 32, 589–594.

Cohen, G. (1981). Inferential reasoning in old age. *Cognition*, 9, 59–72.

Cohen, N. L., Parikh, S. V., & Kennedy, S. H. (2000). Medication compliance in mood disorders: Relevance of the health belief model and other determinants. *Primary Care Psychia*, 6, 101–110.

Col, N., Fanale, J. E., & Kronholm, P. (1990). The role of medication noncompliance and adverse drug reactions in hospitalizations of the elderly. *Arch Intern Med*, *150*, 841–845.

Conn, V., Taylor, S., & Miller, R. (1994). Cognitive impairment and medication compliance. *J Gerontol Nurs*, *12*, 41–47.

Cooper, B., Carpenter, I., Katona, C., Schroll, M., Wagner, C., Fialova, D., et al. (2005). The AdHOC study of older adults' adherence to medication in 11 countries. *Am J Geriat Psychiat*, *13*(12), 1067–1076.

Cooper, L. A., Gonzales, J. J., Gallo, J. J., Rost, K. M., Meredith, L. S., Rubenstein, L. V., et al. (2003). The acceptability of treatment for depression among African American, Hispanic, and white primary care patients. *Medical Care*, *41*, 479–489.

Council on Scientific Affairs. (1999). Ad Hoc Committee on Health Literacy for the Council on Scientific Affairs, American Medical Association. *JAMA*, *281*, 552–557.

Craik, F. I. M., & Jennings, J. M. (1992). Human memory. In F. I. M. Craik & T. A. Salthouse (Eds.), *The handbook of aging and cognition*. Hillsdale, NJ: Erlbaum.

Cummings, K. M., Becker, M. H., Kirscht, J. P., & Levin, N. W. (1982). Psychosocial factors affecting adherence to medical regimens in a group of hemodialysis patients. *Med Care*, *20*, 567–579.

Dencker, S. J., & Liberman, R. P. (1995). From compliance to collaboration in the treatment of schizophrenia. *Int Clin Psychopharm*, *9*(Suppl. 5), 75–78.

Diehl, M., Willis, S. L., & Schaie, W. (1995). Everyday problem solving in older adults: Observational assessment and cognitive correlates. *Psychol Aging*, *10*(3), 478–491.

Dimatteo, M. R. (2004). Social support and patient adherence to medical treatment: A meta-analysis. *Health Psychol*, *23*, 207–218.

Dimatteo, M. R., Lepper, H. S., & Croghan, T. W. (2000). Depression is a risk factor for non-compliance with medical treatment: Meta-analysis of the effects of anxiety and depression on patient adherence. *Arch Inter Med*, *160*, 2101–2107.

Dolder, C. R., Lacro, J. P., Warren, K. A., Golshan, S., Perkins, D. O., & Jeste, D. V. (2004). Brief evaluation of medication influences and beliefs: Development and testing of a brief scale for medication adherence. *J Clin Psychopharm*, *24*(4), 404–409.

Drake, R. E., Osher, F. C., & Wallach, M. A. (1989). Alcohol use and abuse in schizophrenia: A prospective community study. *J Nerv Ment Dis*, *177*, 408–414.

Drummond, S. R., Drummond, R. S., & Dutton, G. N. (2004). Visual acuity and the ability of the visually impaired to read medication instructions. *Brit J Ophthalmol*, *88*(12), 1541–1542.

Dunbar-Jacob, J. (2002, April). *Adherence: Perspective on the individual*. Master lecture presented at the 23rd annual meeting of the Society of Behavioral Medicine, Washington, DC.

Dunbar-Jacob, J., Erlen, J. A., Schlenk, E. A., Ryan, C. M., Sereika, S. M., & Doswell, W. M. (2000). Adherence in chronic disease. *Annu Rev Nurs Res*, *18*, 48–90.

Dupont, R. M., Jernigan, T. L., Butters, N., Delis, D., Hesselink, J. R., Heindel, W., et al. (1990). Subcortical abnormalities detected in bipolar affective disorder using magnetic resonance imaging. *Arch Gen Psychiat*, *47*, 55–59.

Edinger, J. D., Carwille, S., Miller, P., Hope, V., & Mayti, C. (1994). Psychological status, syndromatic measures, and compliance with nasal CPAP therapy for sleep apnea. *Percept Motor Skill*, *78*, 1116–1118.

Einstein, G. O., McDaniel, M. A., Smith, R., & Shaw, P. (1998). Habitual prospective memory and aging: Remembering instructions and forgetting actions. *Psychol Sci*, *9*, 284–288.

Ewart, C. K. (1991). Social action theory for public health psychology. *Am Psychol*, *46*, 931–946.

Fenton, W. S., Blyler, C. R., & Heinssen, R. K. (1997). Determinants of mediation compliance in schizophrenia: Empirical and clinical findings. *Schizophrenia Bull, 23,* 637–651.

Field, T. S., Mazor, K. M., Briesacher, B., Debellis, K. R., & Gurwitz, J. H. (2007). Adverse drug events resulting from patient errors in older adults. *J Am Geriatr Soc, 55*(2), 271–276.

Fleck, D. E., Hendricks, W. L., Del Bello, M. P., & Strakowski, S. M. (2002). Differential prescription of maintenance antipsychotics to African-American and white patients with new-onset bipolar disorder. *J Clin Psychiat, 63,* 658–664.

Fleischhacker, W. W., Meise, U., Gunther, V., & Kurz, M. (1994). Compliance with antipsychotic drug treatment: Influence of side effects. *Acta Psychiatr Scand, 89,* 11–15.

Fulmer, T., & Gurland, B. (1997). Evaluating the caregiver's intervention in the elder's task performance: Capacity versus actual behavior. *Int J Geriatr Psych, 12*(9), 920–925.

Ganguli, M., Dodge, H. H., & Mulsant, B. H. (2002). Rates and predictors of mortality in an aging, rural, community-based cohort: The role of depression. *Arch Gen Psychiat, 59,* 1046–1052.

Gazmararian, J. A., Baker, D. W., Williams, M. V., Parker, R. M., Scott, T. L., Green, D. C., et al. (1999). Health literacy among Medicare enrollees in a managed care organization. *J Amer Med Assoc, 281,* 545–551.

Gazmararian, J. A., Kripalani, S., Miller, M. J., Echt, K. V., Ren, J., & Rask, K. (2006). Factors associated with medication refill adherence in cardiovascular-related diseases: A focus on health literacy. *J Gen Intern Med, 21*(12), 1215–1221.

Goldberg, T. E., Gold, J. M., Greenberg, R., Griffin, S., Schulz, S. C., Pickar, D., et al. (1993). Contrasts between patients with affective disorders and patients with schizophrenia on a neuropsychological test battery. *Am J Psychiat, 150,* 1355–1362.

Gould, O. N., McDonald-Miszczak, L., & Gregory, J. (1999). Prediction accuracy and medication instructions: Will you remember tomorrow? *Aging Neuropsychol C, 6,* 141–154.

Green, L. W., & Simons-Morton, D. G. (1988). Denial, delay and disappointment: Discovering and overcoming the causes of drug errors and missed appointments. *Epilepsy Res, 1,* 7–21.

Green, M. F. (1996). What are the functional consequences of neurocognitive deficits in schizophrenia? *Am J Psychiat, 153,* 321–330.

Green, M. F., Kern, R. S., Braff, D. L., & Mintz, J. (2000). Neurocognitive deficits and functional outcome in schizophrenia: Are we measuring the "right stuff"? *Schizophrenia Bull, 26,* 119–136.

Gregory, M., & Poulton, E. C. (1970). Even versus uneven right-hand margins and the role of comprehension reading. *Ergonomics, 13*(4), 427–434.

Gryfe, C. I., & Gryfe, B. M. (1984). Drug therapy of the aged: The problem of compliance and roles of physicians and pharmacists. *J Am Geriatr Soc, 32,* 301–307.

Gurland, B. J., Cross, P., Chen, J., & Wilder, D. E. (1994). A new performance test of adaptive cognitive functioning: The medication management (MM) test. *Int J Geriatr Psych, 9*(11), 875–885.

Hale, A. S. (1995). Atypical antipsychotic and compliance in schizophrenia. *Nord J Psychiat, 49*(Suppl. 35), 31–39.

Hallas, J., Gram, L. F., Grodum, E., Damsbo, N., Brøsen, K., Haghfelt, T., et al. (1992). Drug related admissions to medical wards: A population based survey. *Eur J Clin Pharmacol, 20,* 193–200.

Harris, R., Skyler, J. S., & Linn, M. W. (1982). Relationship between the health belief model and compliance as a basis for intervention in diabetes mellitus. In Z. Laron & A. Galatzer (Eds.), *Psychological aspects of diabetes in children and adolescents, pediatric adolescent endocrinology* (Vol. 10). Basel, Switzerland: Karger.

Hasher, L., & Zacks, R. T. (1988). Working memory, comprehension, and aging: A review and a new view. In G. H. Bower (Ed.), *The psychology of learning and motivation: Advances in research and theory.* San Diego, CA: Academic Press.

Haynes, R. B., McDonald, H., Garg, A. X., & Montague, P. (2003). Interventions for helping patients to follow prescriptions for medications. *Cochrane D Syst Rev*, Issue 1 (Article No. CD000011).

Haynes, R. B., McKibbon, K. A., & Kanani, R. (1996). Systematic review of randomized trials of interventions to assist patients to follow prescriptions for medications. *Lancet, 348*, 383–386.

Haynes, R. B., Montague, P., Oliver, T., McKibbon, K. A., Brouwers, M., C., & Keneni, R. (2000). Interventions for helping patients to follow prescriptions for medications. *Cochrane D Syst Rev*, Issue 2 (Article No. CD000011).

Heaton, R. K., & Drexler, M. (1987). Clinical neuropsychological findings in schizophrenia and aging. In N. E. Miller & G. D. Cohen (Eds.), *Schizophrenia and aging.* New York: Guilford Press.

Heaton, R. K., Marcotte, T. D., Rivera-Mindt, M., Sadek, J., Moore, D. J., & HIV Neurobehavioral Research Center (HNRC) Group. (2004). The impact of HIV-associated neuropsychological impairment on everyday functioning. *J Int Neuropsych Soc, 10*, 317–331.

Heinrichs, R. W., & Zakzanis, K. K. (1998). Neurocognitive deficit in schizophrenia: A quantitative review of the evidence. *Neuropsychology, 12*, 426–445.

Higgins, N., Livingston, G., & Katona, C. (2004). Concordance therapy: An intervention to help older people take antidepressants. *J Affect Disorders, 81*, 287–291.

Hinkin, C. H., Barclay, T. R., Castellon, S. A., Levine, A. J., Durvasula, R. S., Marion, S. D., et al. (2007). Drug use and medication adherence among HIV-1 infected individuals. *AIDS Behav, 11*(2), 185–194.

Hinkin, C. H., Castellon, S. A., Durvasula, R. S., Hardy, D. J., Lam, M. N., Mason, K. I., et al. (2002). Medication adherence among HIV+ adults: Effects of cognitive dysfunction and regimen complexity. *Neurology, 59*, 1944–1950.

Hinkin, C. H., Castellon, S. A., Hardy, D. J., Lam, M. N., Stefaniak, M., & Durvasula, R. S. (2000). Neuropsychological predictors of medication adherence in HIV/AIDS: A preliminary report. *J Int Neuropsych Soc, 6*, 135.

Hinkin, C. H., Hardy, D. J., Mason, K. I., Castellon, S. A., Durvasula, R. S., Lam, M. N., et al. (2004). Medication adherence in HIV-infected adults: Effect of patient age, cognitive status, and substance abuse. *AIDS, 18*(1), S19–S25.

Huang, B., Bachmann, K. A., He, X., Chen, R., McAllister, J. S., & Wang, T. (2002). Inappropriate prescriptions for the aging population of the United States: An analysis of the National Ambulatory Medical Care Survey, 1997. *Pharmacoepidem Dr S, 11*(2), 127–134.

Hurd, P. D., & Butkovich, S. L. (1986). Compliance problems and the older patient: Assessing functional limitations. *Drug Intel Clin Phar, 20*, 228–231.

Isaac, L. M., Tablyn, R., & the McGill–Calgary Drug Research Team. (1993). Compliance and cognitive function: A methodological approach to measuring unintentional errors in medication compliance in the elderly. *Gerontologist, 33*, 772–781.

Jackson, J. E., Ramsdell, J. W., Renvall, M., Smart, J., & Ward, H. (1984). Reliability of drug histories in a specialized geriatric outpatient clinic. *J Gen Intern Med, 4*, 39–43.

Jeste, S. D., Patterson, T. L., Palmer, B. W., Dolder, C. R., Goldman, S., & Jeste, D. V. (2003). Cognitive predictors of medication adherence among middle-aged and older outpatients with schizophrenia. *Schizophr Res, 63*(1), 49–58.

Johnson, M. O., Catz, S. L., Remien, R. H., Rotheram-Borus, M. J., Morin, S. F., Charlebois, E., et al. (2003). Theory-guided, empirically supported avenues for intervention on HIV medication nonadherence: Findings from the healthy living project. *AIDS Patient Care ST, 17*, 645–656.

Kampman, O., & Lehtinen, K. (1999). Compliance in psychosis. *Acta Psychiatr Scand*, *100*, 167–175.

Keck, P. E., Jr., McElroy, S. L., Strakowski, S. M., Stanton, S. P., Kizer, D. L., Palistreri, D. M., et al. (1996). Factors associated with pharmacologic non-compliance in patients with mania. *J Clin Psychiat*, *57*, 292–297.

Kendrick, R., & Bayne, J. (1982). Compliance with prescribed medication by elderly patients. *Can Med Assoc J*, *127*, 961–962.

Kim, S., Shin, I., Kim, J., Yang, S., Shin, H., & Yoon, J. (2006). Association between attitude toward medication and neurocognitive function in schizophrenia. *Clin Neuropharmacol*, *29*, 197–205.

Kline, D. W., & Scialfa, C. T. (1997). Sensory and perceptual functioning: Basic research and human factors implications. In A. D. Fisk & W. A. Rogers (Eds.), *Handbook of human factors and the older adult*. New York: Academic Press.

Lacro, J. P., Dunn, L. B., Dolder, C. R., Leckband, S. G., & Jeste, D. V. (2002). Prevalence of and risk factors for medication nonadherence in patients with schizophrenia: A comprehensive review of recent literature. *J Clin Psychiat*, *63*(10), 892–909.

Lamy, P. P, Salzman, C., & Nevis-Olesen, J. (1992). Drug prescribing patterns, risks, and compliance guidelines. In C. Salzman (Ed.), *Clinical geriatric psychopharmacology* (2nd ed., pp. 15–37). Baltimore: Williams & Wilkins.

Leirer, V. O., Morrow, D. G., Pariante, G. M., & Sheikh, J. L. (1988). Elders' non-adherence, its assessment and computer assisted instruction for medication recall training. *J Am Geriatr Soc*, *36*, 877–884.

Leirer, V. O., Morrow, D. G., Tanke, E. D., & Pariante, G. M. (1991). Elders' nonadherence: Its assessment and medication reminding by voice mail. *Gerontologist*, *31*(4), 514–520.

Levine, A. J., Hinkin, C. H., Castellon, S. A., Mason, K. I., Lam, M. N., & Perkins, A., et al. (2005). Variations in patterns of highly active antiretroviral therapy (HAART) adherence. *AIDS Behav*, *9*(3), 355–362.

Mackowiak, E. D., O'Connor, T. W., Jr., Thomason, M., Nighswander, R., Smith, M., Vogenberg, A., et al. (1994). Compliance devices preferred by elderly patients. *Am Pharm*, *NS34*, 47–52.

Maeda, K., Kasai, K., Watanabe, A., Henomatsu, K., Rogers, M. A., & Kato, N. (2006). Effect of subjective reasoning and neurocognition on medication adherence for persons with schizophrenia. *Psychiatr Serv*, *57*, 1203–1205.

Maidment, R., Livingston, G., & Katona, C. (2002). Just keep taking the tablets: Adherence to antidepressant treatment in older people in primary care. *Int J Geriatr Psych*, *17*, 752–757.

Marder, S. R. (1998). Facilitating compliance with antipsychotic medication. *J Clin Psychiat*, *59*, 21–25.

Martin, D. C., & Mead, K. (1982). Reducing medication errors in a geriatric population. *J Am Geriatr Soc*, *4*, 258–260.

Matteson, M., & McConnell, E. (1988). *Gerontological nursing: Concepts of practice*. Philadelphia: Saunders.

McDaniel, M. A., Glisky, E. L., Guynn, M. J., & Routhieaux, B. C. (1999). Prospective memory: A neuropsychological study. *Neuropsychology*, *13*, 103–110.

Mendoza, P. S., Munoz, P. M., Merino, E. J., & Barriga, O. A. (2006). Determinant factors of therapeutic compliance in elderly hypertensive patients. *Rev Med Chile*, *134*(1), 65–71.

Metlay, J. P. (2008). Medication comprehension and safety in older adults. *LDI Issue Brief*, *14*(1), 1–4.

Millstein, S. G. (1996). Utility of the theories of reasoned action and planned behavior for predicting physician behavior: A prospective analysis. *Health Psychol*, *15*, 398–402.

Mirotznik, J., Feldman, L., & Stein, R. (1995). The health belief model and adherence with a community center-based, supervised coronary heart disease exercise program. *J Commun Health, 20*(3), 233–247.

Moore, A., Sellwood, W., & Stirling, J. (2000). Compliance and psychological reactance in schizophrenia. *Brit Psycholog Soc, 39,* 287–295.

Morice, R. (1990). Cognitive flexibility and pre-frontal dysfunction in schizophrenia and mania. *Brit J Psychiat, 157,* 50–54.

Morrell, R. W., Park, D. C., & Poon, L. W. (1989). Quality of instructions on prescription drug labels: Effects on memory and comprehension in young and old adults. *Gerontologist, 29,* 345–354.

Morrell, R. W., Park, D. C., & Poon, L. W. (1990). Effects of labeling techniques on memory and comprehension of prescription information in young and old adults. *Journal of Gerontology, 45,* P166–P172.

Morrow, D., Clark, D., Tu, W., Wu, J., Weiner, M., Steinley, D., et al. (2006). Correlates of health literacy in patients with chronic heart failure. *Gerontologist, 46*(5), 669–676.

Morrow, D. G., Leirer, V. O., Altieri, P., & Tanke, E. D. (1991). Elders' schema for taking medication: Implications for instruction design. *J Gerontol, 48,* P378–P385.

Morrow, D. G., Leirer, V. O., Andrassy, J. M., Tanke, E. D., & Stine-Morrow, E. A. L. (1996). Age differences in schemes for taking medication. *Hum Factors, 38,* 556–573.

Murray, M. D., Morrow, D. G., Weiner, M., Clark, D. O., Tu, W., Deer, M. M., et al. (2004). A conceptual framework to study medication adherence in older adults. *Am J Geriatr Pharmacother, 2*(1), 36–43.

Myers, E., & Brainthwaite, A. (1992). Outpatient compliance with antidepressant medication. *Brit J Psychiat, 160,* 83–86.

Neal, B., MacMahon, S., & Chapman, N. (2000). Effects of ACE inhibitors, calcium antagonists, and other blood-pressure-lowering drugs: Results of prospectively designed overviews of randomized trials. Blood Pressure Lowering Treatment Trialists' Collaboration. *Lancet, 356,* 1955–1964.

Olfson, M., Mechanic, D., Hansell, S., Boyer, C. A., Walkup, J., & Weiden, P. J. (2000). Predicting medication noncompliance after hospital discharge among patients with schizophrenia. *Psychiat Serv, 51,* 216–222.

Ostrum, F. E., Hammarlund, E. R., Christensen, D. B., Plein, J. B., & Kethley, A. J. (1985). Medication usage in an elderly population. *Med Care, 23,* 157–170.

Park, D. C., Morrell, R. W., Frieske, D., & Kincaid, D. (1992). Medication adherence behaviors in older adults: Effects of external cognitive supports. *Psychol Aging, 7,* 252–256.

Park, D. C., Smith, A. D., Lautenschlager, G., Earles, J., Frieske, D., Zwahr, M., et al. (1996). Mediators of long-term memory performance across the life span. *Psychol Aging, 11*(4), 621–637.

Park, D. C., Willis, S. L., Morrow, D., Diehl, M., & Gaines, C. L. (1994). Cognitive function and medication usage in older adults. *J Appl Gerontol, 13,* 39–57.

Parkin, D. M., Henney, C. R., Quirk, J., & Crooks, J. (1986). Deviation from prescribed drug treatment after discharge from hospital. *Brit Med J, 2,* 686–688.

Patterson, T. L., Lacro, J., McKibbin, C. L., Moscona, S., Hughs, T., & Jeste, D. V. (2002). Medication management ability assessment: Results from a performance-based measure in older outpatients with schizophrenia. *J Clin Psychopharm, 22*(1), 11–19.

Perlick, D. A., Rosenheck, R. A., Clarkin, J. F., Maciejewski, P. K., Sirey, J., & Struening, E., et al. (2004). Impact of family burden and affective response on clinical outcome among patients with bipolar disorder. *Psychiatr Serv, 55,* 1029–1035.

Priest, R. G., Vize, C., Roberts, A., Roberts, M., & Tylee, A. (1996). Lay people's attitudes to treatment of depression: Results of opinion poll for Defeat Depression Campaign just before its launch. *Brit Med J, 313,* 858–859.

Ray, W. A., Federspiel, C. F., & Schaffner, W. A. (1980). A study of antipsychotic drug use in nursing homes: Epidemiological evidence suggesting misuse. *Am J Public Health, 70,* 485–491.

Raz, N. B. (2000). Aging of the brain and its impact on cognitive performance: Integration of structural and functional findings. In F. I. M. Craik & T. A. Salthouse (Eds.), *The handbook of aging and cognition.* Mahwah, NJ: Erlbaum.

Razali, M. S., & Yahya, H. (1995). Compliance with treatment in schizophrenia: A drug intervention program in a developing country. *Acta Psychiat Scand, 91,* 331–335.

Rekkas, P. V. (2006). Interference resolution in the elderly: Evidence suggestive of differences in strategy on measures of prepotent inhibition and dual task processing. *Neuropsychology, Development, and Cognition, 13*(3–4), 341–365.

Remien, R. H., Hirky, A. E., Johnson, M. O., Weinhardt, L. S., Whittier, D., & Minh Le, G. (2003). Adherence to medication treatment: A qualitative study of facilitators and barriers among a diverse sample of HIV+ men and women in four U.S. cities. *AIDS Behav, 7,* 61–72.

Reynolds, N. R. (2003). The problem of antiretroviral adherence: A self-regulatory model for intervention. *AIDS Care, 15,* 117–124.

Rosenstock, I. M. (1974). Historical origins of the health belief model. *Health Educ Monog, 2,* 1–8.

Royall, D. R., Chiodo, L. K., & Polk, M. J. (2000). Correlates of disability among elderly retirees with "subclinical" cognitive impairment. *J Gerontol A-Biol, 55,* M541–M546.

Salthouse, T. A. (1996). The processing-speed theory of adult age differences in cognition. *Psychol Rev, 103,* 403–428.

Salthouse, T. A., & Babcock, R. (1991). Decomposing adult age differences in working memory. *Dev Psychol, 27,* 763–776.

Schaie, K. W. (1996). Intellectual development in adulthood: The Seattle longitudinal study. New York: Cambridge University Press.

Schmitter-Edgecombe, M., & Wright, M. J. (2004). Event-based prospective memory following severe closed-head injury. *Neuropsychology, 18,* 353–361.

Schwartz, B. L., Rosse, R. B., Veazey, C., & Deutsch, S. I. (1996). Impaired motor skill learning in schizophrenia: Implications for corticostriatal dysfunction. *Biol Psychiat, 39,* 241–248.

Sensky, T., Leger, C., & Gilmour, S. (1996). Psychosocial and cognitive factors associated with adherence to dietary and fluid restriction regimens by people on chronic hemodialysis. *Psychother Psychosom, 65,* 36–42.

Shapiro, P. A., Williams, D. L., Foray, A. T., Gelman, I. S., Wukich, N., & Sciacca, R. (1995). Psychosocial evaluation and prediction of compliance problems and morbidity after heart transplantation. *Transplantation, 60,* 1462–1466.

Simoni, J. M., Frick, P. A., & Huang, B. (2006). A longitudinal evaluation of a social support model of medication adherence among HIV-positive men and women on antiretroviral therapy. *Health Psychol, 25,* 74–81.

Sirey, J. A., Bruce, M. L., Alexopoulos, G. S., Perlick, D. A., Rave, P., Friedman, S. J., et al. (2001). Perceived stigma and patient-related severity of illness as predictors of antidepressant drug adherence. *Psychiat Serv, 52,* 1615–1620.

Sleath, B., Rubin, R. H., & Huston, S. A. (2003). Hispanic ethnicity, physician–patient communication, and antidepressant adherence. *Compr Psychiat, 44,* 198–204.

Smith, A. D. (1996). Memory. In J. E. Birren (Ed.), *The encyclopedia of gerontology.* New York: Academic Press.

Smith, N. A., Ley, P., Seale, J. P., & Shaw, J. (1987). Health beliefs, satisfaction and compliance. *Patient Educ Couns, 10*(3), 279–286.

Stephenson, B. J., Rowe, B. H., Haynes, R. B., Macharia, W. M., & Leon, G. (1993). Is this patient taking the treatment as prescribed? *J Amer Med Assoc, 269,* 2779–2781.

Stewart, J. T., Gonzalez-Perez, E., Zhu, Y., & Robinson, B. E. (1999). Cognitive predictors of resistiveness in dementia patients. *Am J Geriat Psychiat, 7,* 259–263.

U.S. Department of Health and Human Services. (1990). *Medication regimens: Causes of non-compliance.* Washington, DC: Author.

Vanderplas, J. M., & Vanderplas, J. H. (1980). Some factors affecting legibility of printed materials for older adults. *Percept Motor Skill, 50,* 923–932.

Wandless, I., & Davie, J. W. (1987). Can drug compliance in the elderly be improved? *Brit Med J, 1,* 359–361.

Wang, P. S., Bohn, R. L., Knight, E., Glynn, R. J., Mogun, A., & Arorn, J. (2002). Non-compliance with antihypertensive medications: The impact of depressive symptoms and psychosocial factors. *J Gen Intern Med, 17,* 504–511.

Weaver, K. E., Llabre, M. M., Durán, R. E., Antoni, M. H., Ironson, G., Penedo, F. J., et al. (2005). A stress and coping model of medication adherence and viral load in HIV-positive men and women on highly active antiretroviral therapy (HAART). *Health Psychol, 24,* 385–392.

Weiden, P. J., & Olfson, M. (1995). Cost of relapse in schizophrenia. *Schizophrenia Bull, 21,* 419–429.

Weiden, P. J., Shaw, E., & Mann, J. (1995). Antipsychotic therapy: Patient preferences and compliance. *Curr Approaches Psychosis, 4,* 1–7.

Weinstein, N. D. (1988). The precaution adoption process. *Health Psychol, 7,* 355–386.

Wickens, C. D. (1992). *Engineering psychology and human performance* (2nd ed.). New York: Harper Collins.

Williams, B. R., & Kim, J. (2005). Medication use and prescribing considerations for elderly patients. *Dent Clin N Am, 49*(2), 411–427.

Williams, G. C., Rodin, G. C., Ryan, R. M., Grolnick, W. S., & Deci, E. L. (1998). Autonomous regulation and long-term medication adherence in adult outpatients. *Health Psychol, 17,* 269–276.

Wilson, B. A. (1999). *Case studies in neuropsychological rehabilitation* New York: Oxford University Press.

Wilson, H. S., Hutchinson, S. A., & Holzemer, W. L. (2002). Reconciling incompatibilities: A grounded theory of HIV medication adherence and symptom management. *Quali Health Res, 12,* 1309–1322.

Woods, S. P., Morgan, E. E., Marquie-Beck, J., Carey, C. L., Grant, I., & HIV Neurobehavioral Research Center (HNRC) Group. (2006). Markers of macrophage activation and axonal injury are associated with prospective memory in HIV-1 disease. *Cogn Behav Neurol, 19,* 217–221.

Zacks, R., & Hasher, L. (1997). Cognitive gerontology and attentional inhibition: A reply to Burke and McDowd. *J Gerontol B-Psychol, 52*(6), P274–P283.

CHAPTER 7

The Brain on the Road

Matthew Rizzo and Ida L. Kellison

Automobile driving has become an indispensable activity of daily life, yet vehicular crashes injure millions and regularly kill over 40,000 people in the United States each year at a cost of about $230 billion dollars (National Highway Traffic Safety Administration [NHTSA], 2003). About 1.2 million people die worldwide due to vehicular crashes and tens of millions are injured (Peden & Sminkey, 2004). This is a preventable global disaster that must be urgently addressed.

This chapter examines relationships between cognition and driver safety and tools for discriminating between safe and unsafe drivers. Studies of normal and cognitively impaired operators in controlled circumstances in a driving simulator and in the field (i.e., in natural and naturalistic settings using instrumented vehicles) reveal valuable information on the coordinated activities of neural systems (e.g., attentional, visuomotor, and decision making) required to safely drive a car. The results can inform public policy and help guide the development of in-vehicle safety countermeasures to avert real-world car crashes, injuries, and death.

A host of medical, neurological, and psychiatric disorders (e.g., Alzheimer's disease, Parkinson's disease, sleep disorders, personality disorders, and effects of licit and illicit drugs) can impair the ability to drive. The purpose of this chapter is to outline general principles for approaching these problems rather than to detail a specific approach to each disorder.

Conceptual Framework

The chain of causality in vehicular crashes can be conceived as follows: *Cognitive abilities and impairments determine specific driver behaviors and safety errors, which in turn predict crashes.* In many cases, the causal pathway involves a concatenation of factors or events, some of which can be prevented or controlled (Runyan, 1998). Interventions for injury prevention and control can operate before, during, or after a crash occurs at the levels of driver capacity, vehicular and road design, and public policy (Haddon, 1972; Michon, 1979).

Relationships between driver performance factors and safety errors can be represented by an imaginary triangle (Heinrich, Petersen, & Roos, 1980) or "iceberg" (Maycock, 1997). Visible above the "water line" are safety errors that produce car crashes resulting in fatality, serious injury, mild injury, or (most frequently) only property damage. Submerged below the water line are behaviors that are perhaps more indirectly related to crashes and occur more frequently. These range from relatively innocuous errors, such as failing to adjust a seat belt or check the rearview mirror on a deserted highway, to more serious errors such as choosing to drive while drowsy or distracted. These errors lead to deviations into opposing traffic lanes and produce near crashes (a.k.a., "near misses"). Although crashes produce an overwhelming public health burden, they are statistically infrequent events and tend to follow a Poisson distribution (i.e., a discrete probability distribution expressing the probability of a number of events occurring in a fixed period of time if these events occur with a known average rate and are independent of the time since the last event; e.g., Siskind, 1996; Thomas, 1996).

A key strategy for research on determining crash risk in the real world is to discover the relationships between high-frequency–low-severity events that produce errors or near misses but not crashes, and the low-frequency–high-severity events that lead to reported crashes in states' epidemiological records. It is also important to understand how mental mechanisms and vehicular and road system design features underpin cognitive errors in real-world tasks. The driving task may involve "hidden" strategic, tactical, and operational variables that are simply not tapped by standard neuropsychological probes (Michon, 1979).

Figure 7.1 depicts a simple information-processing model for understanding driver errors that may lead to vehicular crashes and shows where different impairments may interrupt different stages in the model. The driver (1) perceives and attends to stimulus evidence (e.g., through vision, audition, vestibular, and somatosensory inputs) and interprets the situation on the road; (2) formulates a plan based on the particular driving situation and relevant previous experience or memory; (3) executes an action

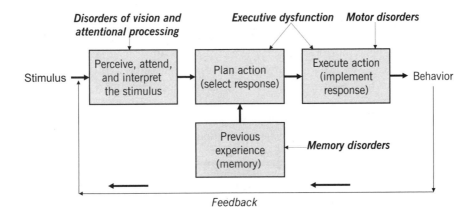

FIGURE 7.1. Information-processing model for understanding driver error.

(e.g., by applying the accelerator, brake, or steering controls); and (4) monitors the outcome of the behavior as a source of potential feedback for subsequent corrective actions. The driver's behavior is either safe or unsafe as a result of errors at one or more of these stages in the driving task.

The risk of driver errors increases with deficits in attention, perception, response selection (which depends on memory and decision making), response implementation (a.k.a., executive functions), and awareness of cognitive and behavioral performance (a.k.a., metacognition). As we shall see, the individual's emotional state, level of arousal (or sleepiness), psychomotor factors, and general mobility (e.g., Marottoli, Cooney, Wagner, Doucette, & Tinetti, 1994; Uc et al., 2006) are also relevant. Individuals with impairments in these domains are more likely than unimpaired drivers to commit errors that cause motor vehicular crashes. Some errors can be detected because drivers normally monitor their performance. When feedback on driving performance fails to match expectations, the discrepancy is often identified "online" (Wickens, 1992) and drivers can take corrective action. Drivers with cognitive deficits are less likely to realize their errors or impaired status.

Sensation and Perception

Automobile driving requires selective processing of a large volume of continuous and often competing sensory and perceptual cues from vision, hearing, vestibular, and somatosensory (tactile or haptic and vibratory) sources. Visual cues are especially important to driving (e.g., Hills, 1980) because they convey long-range information about driver self-trajectory (egomotion), changes in the terrain, and the trajectories of other objects on a potential collision course with the driver.

A host of static and dynamic visual cues provide indispensable information on the structure, distance, and time to contact other objects that may arise unexpectedly across the panorama. We survey the world with binocular visual fields that normally span about 180 degrees. The fovea has the highest acuity and spans about 3 degrees around fixation; the macula spans about 10 degrees and participates in detail-oriented tasks such as map reading and sign localization. The peripheral visual fields have low visual acuity but good temporal resolution and movement detection.

Common patterns of visual loss correspond to different diseases and lesions in visual pathways and create a variety of risks for drivers (Rizzo & Kellison, 2004). Crashes and traffic violations in the 3-year records of 17,500 California driver's license applicants increased with impairments of static visual acuity, dynamic visual acuity (i.e., acuity for moving letter shapes), glare recovery, and visual fields (Burg, 1968).

Common eye disorders cause visual sensitivity loss and visual field impairments that can impair driver safety (American Academy of Ophthalmology Policy Statement, 2006). For example, cataracts are a risk factor for car crashes (Owsley, Stalvey, Wells, Sloane, & McGwin, 2001) and are treatable with surgery. Ubiquitous in aging eyes, they cause a reduction in acuity and the creation of distracting reflections (e.g., halos around lights) or glare. Glaucoma can affect driving by producing both visual impairments and visual field loss. Macular degeneration affects areas of high-detail vision around fixation. Retinitis pigmentosa, an inherited condition that tends to affect younger drivers, constricts the peripheral visual fields, causing inability to detect objects approaching from the side. Even glasses may cause trouble while driving due to reflections, distortions, or discontinuities (e.g., caused by looking across bifocal or trifocal lenses or glare). Glare is a disabling effect of intense light and reflections off object surfaces or ocular media that can veil our perception of critical environmental targets (Stiles & Crawford, 1937). For instance, glare from the headlights of oncoming traffic can mask information on the changing terrain and locations of nearby vehicles.

Drivers with lesions of visual areas in the occipital lobe and adjacent temporal and parietal lobes have various visual field defects (e.g., homonymous hemianopia or quadrantanopia) and may fail to perceive objects or events in the defective fields (Rizzo & Barton, 2005). Search strategies to compensate for the visual defect may create extra work that distracts from the driving task. Lesions in the occipital and parietal lobes (in the dorsal or "where" pathway) may have greater effects on driving performance than do lesions in the occipital and temporal lobes (in the ventral or "what" pathway). Dorsally located lesions produce visual loss in the ventral or lower visual fields that may obscure the view of the vehicular controls and much of the road ahead of the driver. In addition, dorsal visual pathway lesions can impair processing of movement cues, as in cerebral akinetopsia (cerebral motion blindness), and reduce visuospatial processing and attention abilities. Some patients with these types of lesions have impairments in visual search and the useful field of view (UFOV; i.e., the visual area from which information can be acquired without moving the eyes or head) and are clearly unfit to drive. One example is the hemineglect syndrome, which results in the failure to orient to targets in the left visual hemifields in patients with right parietal lobe lesions (Rizzo & Barton, 2005). Another is Bálint's syndrome (simultanagnosia/spatial disorientation, optic ataxia, and ocular apraxia), which generally involves bilateral dorsal visual pathway lesions.

Ventrally located lesions produce upper-visual-field defects that may be less troublesome for driving; however, they may also cause impairments in (1) object recognition (visual agnosia) affecting interpretation of roadway targets, (2) reading (pure alexia) affecting roadway sign and map reading, and (3) color perception (cerebral achromatopsia), impeding use of color cues in decoding traffic signals and road signs and detection of roadway boundaries and objects defined by hue contrast (Rizzo & Barton, 2005).

Drivers with cerebral lesions may have various deficits that affect perception of structure and depth and are not measured by standard clinical tests. The brain employs multiple cues on object structure and depth because this information is so critical for interacting with moving objects and obstacles (Palmer, 1999). Binocular stereopsis (stereo vision) and motion parallax provide unambiguous cues to relative depth. For motion parallax, moving the head along the interaural axis produces relative movement of objects. The orderly relationship between relative velocities of images across the retina and relative distances of objects in the scene provides cues to structure and depth. Motion parallax impairments may contribute to vehicular crashes when impaired drivers must make quick judgments with inaccurate or missing perceptual information on the location of surrounding obstacles (Nawrot, 2001).

Detecting and avoiding potential collisions require information on approaching objects and the driver's vehicle. Objects set to collide with the driver stay at a fixed location in the driver's field of view, whereas "safe" objects move to the left or right. Time to contact (TTC) is estimated from the expanding retinal image of the approaching object. Older drivers are less accurate than younger drivers at detecting an impending collision during braking (Andersen, Cisneros, Atchley, & Saidpour, 1999; Andersen, Cisneros, Saidpour, & Atchley, 2000) and judging if an approaching object will crash into them (Andersen, Saidpour, & Enriquez, 2001). Performance is worse for longer TTC conditions, possibly due to a greater difficulty in detecting the motion of small objects in the road scene ahead of the driver (Andersen, Saidpour, & Enriquez, 2001).

Displacement of images across the retina during travel produces optic flow patterns (Gibson, 1979) that can specify the trajectory of self-motion (egomotion) with accuracy (Warren & Hannon, 1988; Warren, Mestre, & Morris, 1991). Perception of heading from optical flow patterns is optimal in a limited part of the flow field surrounding the future direction of travel (Mestre, 2001). On curved roads, drivers tend to fixate the information flowing from the inside edge of the road where the curve changes direction (Land & Lee, 1994). The findings are relevant to detection of collisions, design of roads, and positioning of traffic warnings within a driver's dynamic visual environment, and may be interpreted in terms of a dynamic UFOV (see the section on attention and driving below).

Perception of structure from motion (SFM; also known as "kinetic depth perception") whereby subjects see the three-dimensional structure of an object defined by motion cues, is a likely real-world use of motion cues that may fail in drivers with cerebral lesions. SFM can be measured using a task in which subjects perceive shapes defined by random dot elements that move among varying amounts of random dot noise (see Figure 7.2); this ability is impaired in akinetopsia and early Alzheimer's disease (Rizzo & Nawrot, 1998). SFM deficits have been associated with greater risk for safety errors and car crashes in driving simulation scenarios (Rizzo, 2001; Rizzo, Reinach, McGehee, & Dawson, 1997).

FIGURE 7.2. Screenshot from the perception of structure from motion (SFM) test.

Executive Functions and Driver Behavior

Executive functions provide control over information processing and are a key determinant of driver strategies, tactics, and safety. These functions include decision making, impulse control, judgment, task switching, and planning (e.g., Benton, 1991; Damasio, 1996, 1999; Rolls, 1999, 2000). Executive functions strongly interact with working memory (i.e., the process of briefly storing information so that it is available for use) and attention, which operates on the contents of working memory (Baddeley & Logie, 1992; Cabeza & Nyberg, 2000; Dias, Robbins, & Roberts, 1996; Norman & Shallice, 1986). The mapping between executive functions measured in laboratory settings and real-life driving performance can be addressed using a set of theoretically motivated tasks. Table 7.1 shows hypothesized relationships between off-road cognitive (executive function) tests and specific driving behaviors.

Decision Making

Decision making requires the evaluation of immediate and long-term consequences of planned actions. Impaired decision making appears to be a critical factor in driver errors that lead to vehicular crashes (van Zomeren, Brouwer, & Minderhoud, 1987). Causes of impaired decision making include acquired brain lesions affecting prefrontal areas (due to stroke, trauma, or neurodegenerative impairment), antisocial personality disorder, effects of drugs and alcohol (Bechara, Tranel, Damasio, & Damasio, 1996; Fuster, 1996; Rizzo, Sheffield, & Stierman, 2003; Rolls, Hornak, Wade, & McGrath, 1994; Stuss, Gow, & Hetherington, 1992), and fatigue (Jones & Harrison, 2001; Paul, Boyle, Rizzo, & Tippin, 2005). Driving outcomes of impaired decision making could include traffic violations (e.g., speeding), unsafe vehicular maneuvers, engaging in extraneous and unsafe behavior while driving, and, of course, crashes.

Go/No-Go Decision Making

Driver strategies include deciding on a sequence of trips or stops (for gas, food, directions, or naps), evaluation of traffic and weather risks, and making go/no-go decisions regarding whether to take a trip. Driving outcomes of go/no-go decisions could include adapting to speed changes near a school, choosing to switch on the headlights at twilight or in rain, changing gears on a hill, and deciding whether and when to overtake another vehicle, change lanes in traffic, or pass through intersections and traffic signals.

Abstract virtual environments can be used to assess go/no-go decision-making behavior in a driving-like task. Using a personal computer equipped with a steering wheel and pedals, subjects (28 with and 22 without cognitive impairments) drove through intersections that had gates that opened and closed (Rizzo, Severson, Cremer, & Price, 2003; Rizzo, Sheffield, et al., 2003). A green "Go" or red "Stop" signal appeared at the bottom of the display as the subject approached the gate, and a gate-closing trigger point was computed. Cognitively impaired drivers who had frontal lobe damage, such as shown in Figure 7.3, had more crashes into closed gates, more failures to go at open gates, and longer times to complete the task. These findings suggest a failure of response selection criteria based on prior experience, as previously

TABLE 7.1. Hypothesized Relationships between Tests of Executive Function and Driving Behaviors

Test name	Ability measured	Driving behavior	Reference
Iowa Gambling Task	Decision making	Traffic violation (e.g., speeding); engaging in behavior extraneous to driving	Bechara et al. (1994)
Go/No-Go	Decision making and response inhibition	Running red light; timing of left turn across traffic; engaging in behavior extraneous to driving; stopping at or continuing through a yellow light	Podsiadlo & Richardson (1991)
Tower of Hanoi	Planning and execution of multistep tasks	Sudden brake application; swerving across lanes; running car near empty; viewing a map while driving (extraneous behavior)	Lezak (1995)
Wisconsin Card Sorting Test	Response to changing contingencies	Failure to adjust speed or following distance in response to changing road conditions	Lezak (1995)
Trail Making Tests A and B	Response alternation	Failure to alternate eye gaze appropriately between road, mirrors, and gauges	Lezak (1995)
Stroop Color and Word Test	Response inhibition, impulse control	Glances of > 2 seconds off road; e.g., with passenger present or while eating; failing to pull over for emergency vehicle or making inappropriate maneuver for emergency vehicle; speeding up to prevent another driver from merging	Lezak (1995)
AX-Continuous Processing Task	Working memory, response inhibition, impulse control	Running red light; following lead car through intersection; following familiar routes even though intending to deviate	Beck et al. (1956)
Controlled Oral Word Association	Cognitive fluency and flexibility (verbal)	Slowed processing of verbal traffic signs; failure to adjust to altered driving conditions (e.g., slowing in response to construction signs)	Lezak (1995)
Design Fluency	Cognitive fluency and flexibility (nonverbal)	Slowed processing of symbolic or pictorial traffic signs; failure to adjust driving in response to such signage	Lezak (1995)

reported in individuals with decision-making impairments on a gambling-related task (e.g., Bechara, Damasio, Tranel, & Damasio, 1997). Drivers who had lesions in areas that did not produce executive dysfunction performed well on the go/no-go task, supporting the specificity of this task in localizing decision-making impairments in a driving-like task.

Surveillance of Driver Decisions at Traffic Intersections

Real-world patterns of driver go/no-go decision making can be evaluated from experimental observations of many drivers as they pass through traffic intersections.

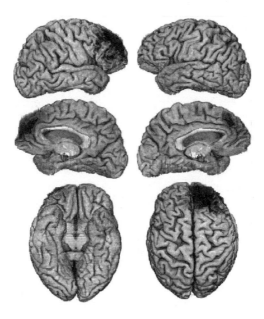

FIGURE 7.3. Three-dimensional magnetic resonance imaging reconstruction of the brain surface shows a right frontal lobe lesion (dark areas) in a subject who participated on the go/no-go decision-making task

Hanowski, Wierwille, Garness, and Dingus (2000) and Wierwille, Hanowski, and Hankey (2002) used video surveillance to assess driver errors at intersections with stop signs or traffic lights during high-volume traffic, providing an evaluation of real-world driver go/no-go decision making. The analyses resulted in the development of probability taxonomies that provide a framework (decision tree) for analyzing critical incidents in large volumes of data. For every 10,000 drivers entering the intersection, 3.3% made some sort of driver error: 1.5% during left turns, 0.5% during right turns, 0.4% going forward, and 0.9% during other activities; 41/10,000 drivers ran through red lights—31 on left turns, 8 going forward, and 2 on right turns. (For similar results, see Bonneson, Zimmerman, & Brewer, 2002; Fakhry & Salaita, 2002; Retting, Ulmer, & Williams, 1999; Retting, Williams, Farmer, & Feldman, 1999.) For intersections with stop signs, there was a 3.0% overall probability of a driver-error critical incident of any type. Most occurred during left turns (1.5%), followed by going forward (0.7%), right turns (0.2%), and other scenarios (0.6%). The overall rate of running the stop sign was 19/10,000 vehicles, and the rate for a rolling stop was similar, at 15/10,000 vehicles, for a total stop sign violation rate of 34/10,000 vehicles. (For higher stop-sign violation rates, see Fakhry & Salaita, 2002; Pietrucha, Opiela, Knoblauch, & Crigler, 1989.) Hanowski and colleagues (2000) and Wierwille, Hanowski, and Hankey (2002) showed that red-light-running events are also common critical incidents, occurring at a rate of about 3%. However, these observations of general traffic do not provide specific insight into the causal mechanisms or the precipitating or contributing factors in impaired drivers. Greater insight is needed into specific decision-making mechanisms in these situations in order to identify possible intervention strategies.

Impulse Control/Response Inhibition

Drivers with impaired decision making may also show impairments in impulse control and response inhibition. Impulse control is related to decision making but does not involve evaluation of immediate and long-term consequences (Barratt, 1994; Evenden, 1999). "Impulsiveness" can be perceptual, cognitive, or motor. Motor impulsiveness may be "nonaffective," as on the Stroop (1935) test, in which subjects must identify the color of ink used to print a conflicting color name by inhibiting the compulsion to read the color name. Affective motor impulsiveness occurs when a person cannot inhibit a habit of responding to a stimulus that predicts a reward with affective value (Zuckerman, 1996), as when a driver impulsively speeds up to prevent another car from merging ahead. In perceptual impulsiveness, failure of inhibition occurs at the level of working memory, before a response can be readied and executed. Observers may have more trouble identifying a visual target among distracters if the distracters are familiar. For instance, a driver traveling in a stable convoy of vehicles may follow the convoy through an intersection without noticing that the signal has turned red. Cognitive impulsiveness reflects inability to evaluate the outcome of a planned action and may give the appearance of failure to perceive or evaluate risk. For example, a driver may embark on a long road trip despite poor weather conditions or an unsound vehicle.

Perceptual impulsiveness resembles "lapses" in the Reason taxonomy (Reason, 1984) of error. Lapses represent failure to carry out an action rather than commission of an incorrect action. Lapses may be caused by the interruption of an ongoing sequence by another task, and they give the appearance of forgetfulness. For example, a driver returning home from work may begin talking on a cell phone and miss ("forget" to take) a highway exit. Disinhibition failures in executive dysfunction may contribute to "slips," errors in which an intention is incorrectly executed because the intended action sequence departs slightly from routine. Slips may resemble inappropriate but more frequent actions and are relatively automated (Norman, 1981). In this case, behavior is guided by a contextually appropriate strong habit due to lack of close monitoring by attention. A driver whose destination requires deviation from a familiar route may make a wrong turn toward a more habitual destination. A driver approaching a tollbooth may be distracted by an onboard warning light, fail to decelerate, and strike a slower lead car.

Drivers with executive dysfunction may commit rule-based errors when they believe they understand a situation and formulate a plan by "if–then" rules, but the "if" conditions are not met, a "bad" rule is applied, or the "then" part of the rule is poorly chosen. For instance, a driver may dismiss an engine temperature warning light, fail to service the vehicle, and suffer a vehicular breakdown in traffic.

Decision-making impairment can occur independently of memory impairment, but memory impairment tends to compromise a driver's decision-making ability because the driver cannot learn or recall all the situational contingencies required to make optimal decisions. Knowledge-based errors signify inappropriate decision making and planning due to failure to comprehend. In this case a driver may be overwhelmed by the complexity of a traffic situation and lack information to interpret it correctly.

In practice it is often difficult to determine unambiguously whether an error leading to a critical incident was due to a driver lapse, slip, rule-based, or knowledge-based error. Accordingly, we use a set of specific operational definitions for detecting critical incidents and empirically derived "decision tree" tools for classifying these unsafe incidents and identifying their likely causes. Such empirically derived tools and models provide taxonomic frameworks for organizing and interpreting data on driver error and for identifying common causes and mitigation strategies from seemingly unrelated instances (Dingus, Hetrick, & Mollenhauer, 1999; Grayson, 1997; Huguenin, 1997; Rizzo, McGehee, Dawson, & Anderson, 2001; Wilde, 1982).

Attention and Working Memory

A critical executive function related to driving is the continuous direction of attention to relevant features of the driving environment. We remember and act upon attended stimuli, not unattended items. There is increasing evidence that specific regions of the prefrontal cortex are essential in directing cognitive resources toward the accomplishment of tasks with a wide range of memory demands (Cabeza et al., 2003: Nyberg et al., 2003). Defects of attention clearly impair driver decisions (e.g., Ball, Owsley, Sloane, Roenker, & Bruni, 1993; Owsley, Ball, Sloane, Roenker, & Bruni, 1991; Parasuraman & Nestor, 1991; Rizzo, McGehee, Dawson, & Anderson, 2001; Rizzo, Reinach, McGehee, & Dawson, 1997) and affect a variety of processes (e.g., Parasuraman & Davies, 1984). Automatic attention processes are fast and involuntary and should contribute to subconscious corrections during driving, including control of steering wheel or accelerator pedal position during uneventful driving on mundane highway segments (Dingus, Hardee, & Wierwille, 1987; McGehee, Lee, Rizzo, Dawson, & Bateman, 2004). Controlled attention processes are slow and operate during capacity-demanding tasks and conscious decision making. Examples include glancing between the road and rearview mirror while maneuvering in and out of a traffic convoy, or the deliberate surveillance of a busy intersection with changing traffic signals, using head and eye movements. This is a "dilemma zone" where critical go/no-go decisions (see above) must be made (Mahelel, Zaidel, & Klein, 1985). The decision to accelerate or brake depends on driving speed and the time for which the green or yellow signal is visible (Allsop, Brown, Groeger, & Robertson, 1991).

Owsley and colleagues (1991) and Ball and colleagues (1993) linked driving impairment with reduction in the useful field of view (UFOV), the visual area from which information can be acquired without moving the eyes or head (Ball, Beard, Roender, Miller, & Griggs, 1988). Performance on the UFOV task depends on speed of processing and divided and selective attention. The UFOV begins to deteriorate by age 20. This deterioration may reveal itself as a shrinking of the field of view or a decrease in efficiency with which drivers extract information from a cluttered scene (Sekuler, Bennett, & Mamelak, 2000). Diminished efficiency in advancing age is worse when attention is divided between central and peripheral visual tasks. Driver performance may also change when attention is divided between the road and an onboard task, and gaps of greater than 2 seconds may interrupt scanning of the road (Wierwille, Hulse, Fischer, & Dingus, 1988).

Focused Attention

Executive functions control the focus of attention (Vecera & Luck, 2003). Without focused attention, we may be unaware of marked changes in an object or a scene made during a saccade, flicker, blink, or movie cut; this is known as "change blindness" (O'Regan, & Rensink, 1999; Rensink, O'Regan, & Clark, 1997, 2000; Simons & Levin, 1997). Traces of retinal images in visual working memory fade without being consciously perceived or remembered ("inattentional amnesia"). The very act of perceiving one item in a rapid series of images briefly inhibits ability to perceive another image, the "attentional blink" (Rizzo, Akutsu, & Dawson, 2001). Focused attention is thought to permit consolidation of information temporarily stored in visual working memory. Perceptual errors are likely if working memory is still occupied by one item when another item arrives, due to interference or limitations in capacity, which at a bottleneck stage admits only one item at a time.

Failure to detect roadway events increases when information load is high, as at complex traffic intersections with high traffic and visual clutter (Batchelder, Rizzo, Vanderleest, & Vecera, 2003; Caird, Edwards, & Creaser, 2001). Driver errors occur when attention is focused away from a critical roadway event in which vehicles, traffic signals, and signs are seen but not acted upon, or are missed altogether (Treat, 1980). Sometimes eye gaze is captured by irrelevant distracters (Kramer, Cassavaugh, Irwin, Peterson, & Hahn, 2001; Theeuwes, 1991), such as "mudsplashes" on a windscreen that prevent a driver from seeing a critical event (e.g., an incurring vehicle or a child chasing a ball; O'Regan et al., 1999). Drivers with cerebral lesions are liable to be "looking but not seeing," even under conditions of low information load (Rizzo & Hurtig, 1987; Rizzo et al., 1997; Risso, Akutsu, & Dawson, 2001) and resembling the effects observed in air-traffic controllers during prolonged, intensive monitoring of radar displays.

Shifting Attention

Safe driving requires executive control to shift the focus of attention among critical tasks such as tracking the road terrain; monitoring the changing locations of neighboring vehicles; reading signs, maps, traffic signals, and dashboard displays; and checking the mirrors (Owsley et al., 1991). These tasks require an ability to shift attention between disparate spatial locations, local and global object details, and different visual tasks. Drivers must also shift attention between modalities when they drive while conversing with other occupants, listening to the radio or tapes, using a cell phone, or interacting with in-vehicle devices (Kantowitz, 2000, 2001). These attentional abilities can fail in drivers with visual processing impairments caused by cerebral lesions (Rizzo et al., 2004; Vecera & Rizzo, 2004).

Functional neuroimaging studies show changes in frontal lobe activity with driver modulation of vehicular speed (Calhoun et al., 2002; Peres, van de Moortele, Lehericy, LeBihan, & Guezennez, 2000) and with alcohol-impaired driving (Calhoun, Pekar, & Pearlson, 2004). These studies also suggest that engaging in conversation distracts the brain from processing information in a visually demanding task such as driving, and vice versa (Just et al., 2001). Cell phone conversation disrupts driving performance by diverting attention to an engaging cognitive context other than the one immediately associated with driving (Strayer & Johnston, 2001). A host of other modern "infotainment" devices also distract cognitive resources away from the driving task (Ehret, Gray, & Kirschenbaum, 2000; Kantowitz, 2000). The interference occurs at the level of central processes that can be disrupted by cerebral lesions. Relevant interactions in aging and brain injury can be measured by administering a controlled auditory verbal processing load during driving tasks (Boer, 2001; Kantowitz, 2001; Rizzo et al., 2004).

Metacognition

Metacognition is the awareness of one's own thought processes and efficacy. This self-awareness of cognitive processes can include specific contexts and strategies to enhance understanding (e.g., "My brain works best before lunchtime"; "I should keep lists") (Fernandez-Duque, Baird, & Posner, 2000; Garner, 1988). Metacognition has been linked with executive functions by cognitive, developmental, and educational psychologists studying control of cognition, the developing awareness of the mind in children, and effects of awareness on learning and academic success (Mazzoni & Nelson, 1998; Shimamura, 1994). Some neuropsychologists and cognitive scientists study the anatomy of self-awareness (Fernandez-Duque et al., 2000; Mazzoni & Nelson, 1998) and awareness of impairments in neurological and psychiatric patients (e.g., with Korsakoff's amnesia, aphasia, schizophrenia, neglect syndrome) (McGlynn, 1998; Shimamura, 1994), in patients with prefrontal lesions (Schacter, 1998; Stuss & Knight, 2002), and in those with alcohol and drug effects or fatigue and sleep deprivation. Metacognition depends on the coordinated activity of multiple brain areas (McGlynn, 1998) and is relevant to driver safety in terms of awareness of (1) cognitive functions, (2) driving behavior; (3) vehicular performance, (4) road conditions, (5) rules of the road, (6) self-impairment, and (7) compensatory strategies to mitigate the effects of impairment. Lack of awareness of impairments (anosognosia) may exacerbate the consequences of impairments in other aspects of cognition (Anderson & Tranel, 1989). Drivers who lack awareness of their impaired cognition and behavior are liable to place themselves and others in harm's way while driving because they fail to take steps that might compensate for their impairments.

Predictions of driver safety may fail because drivers may behave differently in the real world than might be expected based on tests in the clinical laboratory (Reger et al., 2004). The relationships between disease status, clinical measures of cognition and awareness, and driving performance may help clinicians working with patients and families to improve or rehabilitate cognitively impaired drivers (Eby, Molnar, Shope, Vivoda, & Fordyce, 2003). Natural and naturalistic studies in the field (see below) can help describe more accurately how cognitive dysfunction affects everyday behaviors, including automobile driving (Rizzo, Robinson, & Neale, 2006).

Emotions and Personality

Driving a motor vehicle can be a major source of annoyance, especially to aggressive drivers (Sivak, 1983) who may curse, shout, gesticulate, speed, flash their lights, ignore traffic signals, fail to signal, tailgate, drive under the influence of drugs and alcohol, or even use their car to block or strike another car or a pedestrian. "Road rage" is a media-coined term used to describe extremely aggressive and often criminal events (Brewer, 2000). Aggressive drivers are more likely to be young, male, single, use alcohol or drugs, have a premorbid personality disorder, and experience increased levels of stress at home, work, and in a car (Deery & Fildes, 1999; DiFranza, Winters, Goldberg, Cirillo, & Biliouris, 1986; Holzapfel, 1995). Car-related stresses may include crowded roadways, vehicular breakdowns, getting lost, and slow drivers ahead. Stressful life events, such as disruption of personal relationships, may precede some car crashes. Having a gun in the car is a marker for dangerous and aggressive driving behavior (Miller, Azrael, Hemenway, & Solop, 2002). Personality factors associated with aggressive driver crash involvement are thrill seeking, impulsiveness, hostility/aggression, and emotional instability (Beirness, 1993; Dahlen, Martin, Ragan, & Kuhlman, 2005; Jonah, 1997; Schwebel, Severson, Ball, & Rizzo, 2006). Crash-prone drivers have been described as emotionally immature, irresponsible, antisocial, and poorly adjusted, with a history of a traumatic childhood, delinquency, family disruption, and poor work records (Suchman, 1970). Psychiatric factors related to impaired driving ability include alcoholism, antisocial personality disorder, depression, and psychosis (Noyes, 1985; Tsuang, Boor, & Fleming, 1985). A driver with depression may fail to focus attention adequately on the road. A driver with schizophrenia may be distracted by pathological thoughts or hallucinations. Antipsychotic, antidepressant and anxiolytic medications may slow driver reaction times and decrease driver arousal. The impacts of personality and personality disorders, aggression, risk taking, psychiatric disorders, and drugs on driver safety and crash risk require further study.

Arousal, Alertness, and Fatigue

Attention, perception, memory, and executive functions that are crucial to the driving task are critically affected by drugs and fatigue (Dinges, 2000), and many vehicular crashes are caused by sleepy drivers (Horne & Reyner, 1995, 1996; Laube, Seeger, Russi, & Bloch, 1998; Leger, 1994; Lyznicki, Doege, Davis, & Williams, 1998), including busy health care personnel (Barger et al., 2005). Sleep deprivation may cause neurologically normal, high-performing young adult airline pilots to perform as if they have visual constriction or simultanagnosia, as in Bálint's syndrome (Russo, Thorne, & Thomas, 1999; Thorne, Thomas, & Russo, 1999).

Drivers with sleep disorders such as obstructive sleep apnea syndrome (OSAS), are at particular risk for a crash (George & Smiley, 1999; Horstmann, Hess, Bassetti, Gugger, & Mathis, 2000; Young, Blustein, Finn, & Palta, 1997). They may minimize the degree to which they are sleepy (Dement, Carskadon, & Richardson, 1978; Engleman, Hirst, & Douglas, 1997) and fail to recognize that they are having trouble driving. Some drivers in sleep-related crashes deny having felt tired beforehand (Jones, Kelly, & Johnson, 1979), and sleep-deprived truck drivers often underestimate their fatigue (Arnold et al., 1997). Symptom minimization may be intentional or due to unawareness of sleepiness (Stutts, Wilkins, & Vaughn, 1999), possibly due to an altered frame of reference for fatigue.

Sleep disturbances may accompany the hallmark motor, cognitive, psychiatric, and autonomic disturbances in Parkinson's disease (PD), due to varied involvement of noradrenergic, cholinergic, and serotoninergic systems. Excessive daytime sleepiness or "sleep attacks" have been reported secondary to the use of dopaminergic medications for treatment of PD (Ferreira, Galitzky, & Brefel-Courbon, 2000; Ferreira, Galitzky, Montastruc, & Rascol, 2000; Ferreira, Pona, & Costa, 2000; Ferreira, Thalamas, & Galitzky, 2000; Frucht, Greene, & Fahn, 2000; Frucht, Rogers, Greene, Gordon, & Fahn, 1999; Hauser, Gauger, Anderson, & Zesiewicz, 2000; Homan, Wenzy, & Suppan, 2000; Lang & Lozano, 1998a, 1998b; Montastruc, Brefel-Courbon, & Senard, 2000; Paladini, 2000; Ryan, Slevin, & Wells, 2000; Schapira, 2000). The reported lack of warning before falling asleep might actually point to amnesia or lack of awareness for the prodrome of sleepiness (Olanow, Schapira, & Roth, 2000).

The border between wakefulness and sleep is indistinct, and falling asleep can be conceived as a process characterized by decreasing arousal, lengthening response time, and intermittent response failure (Ogilvie, Wilkinson, & Allison, 1989). Gastaut and Broughton (1965) found that 2–4 minutes of electroencephalograph (EEG)-defined sleep must elapse before more than half of subjects recognize that they had actually been sleeping. The EEG may show progression from wakefulness to Stages I and II sleep, or be preceded by "microsleeps" in which the EEG shows 5 or more seconds of alpha dropout and an increase in theta activity (Harrison & Horne, 1996) (Figure 7.4a). These periods of approaching sleep onset have been correlated with subjective sleepiness among long-haul truck drivers (Kecklund & Akerstedt, 1993) and healthy, sleep-deprived drivers (Horne & Reyner, 1996; Reyner & Horne, 1998), and with deteriorating driving simulator performance in healthy, sleep-deprived drivers (Horne & Reyner, 1996; Reyner & Horne, 1998) and OSAS patients (Paul et al., 2005; Risser, Ware, & Freeman, 2000).

Further research is needed to address how cognitive errors in the driving task increase as a function of severity of sleep disturbances, measured by polysonography (PSG) and the Multiple Sleep Latency Test (MSLT). Continuous positive airway pressure (CPAP) therapy in drivers with OSAS should lead to improvement in cognitive function, driving performance, and awareness of impairment, and is an area for further research.

Observed drowsiness can be quantified through physiological and cognitive performance measures (see Figure 7.4b). Self-reported estimates of acute drowsiness can be obtained using the Stanford Sleepiness Scale (Hoddes, Zarcone, Smythe, Phillips, & Dement, 1973) and of chronic drowsiness using the Epworth Sleepiness Scale (Johns, 1991). Physiological indices of impending sleep can be measured aboard a vehicle, using a variety of techniques. These include EEG (e.g., of drowsiness or microsleeps), decreased galvanic skin response (GSR), increased respiratory rate, increased heart rate variability, reduced electromyograph (EMG) activity (e.g., cervical paraspinous muscles), and percent eyelid closure (PERCLOS). PERCLOS scores of 80% or greater are highly correlated with falling asleep (Dinges, 2000). The lid closure can be used to trigger auditory or haptic warning (e.g., vibrating seats in a long-haul truck), which may prevent sleep- or drowsiness-related crashes.

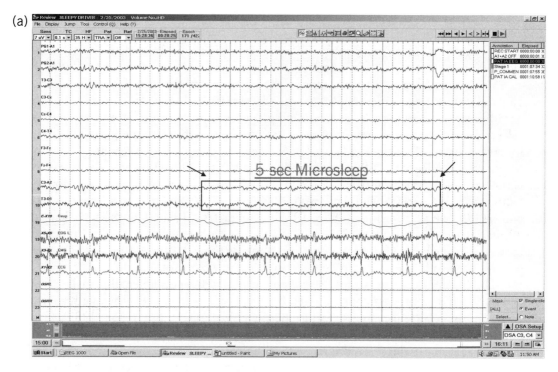

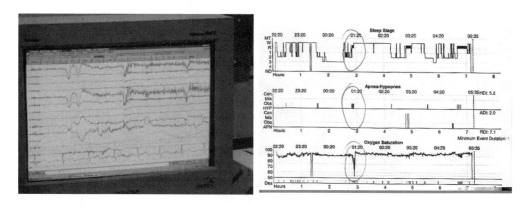

FIGURE 7.4. (a) Segment of EEG depciting a microsleep. (b) EEG recording during simulated driving. EEG surface electrodes are connected to the head of a behaving driver seated within the simulator cab and responding to challenges in an experimental driving scenario.

Drug Effects

Certain medications have been associated with greater relative risk of automobile crashes in the epidemiological record (e.g., Ray, Thapa, & Shorr, 1993). Antidepressants, pain medications, antihistamines, anticonvulsants, antihypertensives, antilipemics, hypoglycemic agents, sedatives, and hypnotics have all been implicated. Aside from general drowsiness, the specific mechanisms whereby these medications impair driving performance, remain unclear. Drug use, including use of prescription medications, may cause as many fatal accidents as alcohol consumption (Centers for Disease Control and Prevention, 2006). Alcohol and illicit drugs such as marijuana (e.g., Lamers & Ramaekers, 2001) and methylenedioxy-*N*-methylamphetamine (MDMA) (e.g., Logan & Couper, 2001) also pose serious driving safety risks. One study examining the effects of alcohol alone, marijuana alone, and their combined effects reported significant impairment in driving ability following administration of alcohol or marijuana alone, whereas combining the two substances resulted in "dramatic" impairments in such driving-related phenomena as time driven out of lane and standard deviation of lateral position (Ramaekers, Robbe, & O'Hanlon, 2000). Driving performance is often impaired at legally defined cutoffs for sobriety (usually 0.8–1.0 mg/dl of ethanol in the United States and 0.5 mg/dl in Europe).

Deleterious effects of drugs on driving seem likely to depend partly on neurotransmitter systems involved in "executive functions" that are known to be critical for driving: decision making and working memory. According to a "somatic marker hypothesis" (Damasio, 1994, 1996), decision making is largely guided by somatic (emotional) signals linked to prior experiences with reward and punishment. The generation of somatic states is linked to a neural system that includes the ventromedial (VM) prefrontal cortex, amygdala, and somatosensory cortices (SI, SII, and insula). Working memory defects result from dysfunction in a neural system in which the dorsolateral prefrontal cortex is a critical region (see above). Elucidation of the chemical substrates (e.g., serotonin, dopamine, acetylcholine) that modulate frontal lobe functions in at-risk older drivers may help guide development of pharmacological interventions that improve cognitive performance in the driving task. Studies of the effects of pharmacological agents on driving performance can be conducted most safely in a driving simulator (Lamers, Bechara, Rizzo, & Ramaekers, 2006).

Assessment of Driving Performance

Road Tests

States generally consider a road test, conducted under the direct observation of a trained expert, to be the "gold standard" of driver fitness. The expert grades driver performance on several driving tasks to calculate a cutoff score to classify a driver as safe or unsafe for licensure. However: (1) Road tests were developed to ensure that novice drivers know and can apply the rules of the road, not to test experienced drivers who may be impaired; (2) road testing carries the risk inherent in the real-world road environment; (3) road test conditions can vary depending on the weather, daylight, traffic, and driving course; (4) driving experts may have different biases and grading criteria; and (5) there are few data to show that road tests are correlated with crash involvement. There have been several attempts to develop empirically based reliable and valid road tests (e.g., Hunt et al., 1997).

State Records

The main data that transportation researchers have on actual collisions and contributing factors are collected post hoc (in forensic or epidemiological research). These data are highly dependent upon eyewitness testimony, driver memory, and police reports, all of which have serious limitations. The best information regarding near collisions generally comes from anecdotal reports by driving evaluators and instructors (usually testing novice drivers) and police reports of moving violations. Most of these potential crash precursors, if they are even recognized, are known only to the involved parties and are never available for further study and subsequent dissemination of safety lessons.

Driving Simulators

Driving simulators have been applied to (1) quantify driver performance in cognitively impaired drivers, (2) study basic aspects of cognition in drivers with brain lesions, (3) probe the effects of information-processing overload on driver safety, and (4) optimize the ergonomics of vehicular design. Driving simulation offers advantages over the use of road tests or driving records in assessments of driver fitness. Simulator studies provide the only means to replicate exactly the experimental road conditions under which driving comparisons are made, and simulations are safe, with none of the risk of the road or test track. Simulation has been successfully applied to assess performance profiles in drivers who are at risk for a crash due to a variety of different conditions, including sleep apnea, drowsiness, alcohol and other drug effects, old age, Alzheimer's disease, Parkinson's disease, HIV, or traumatic brain injury (Brouwer, Ponds, Van Wolffelaar, & Van Zomeren, 1989; Dingus et al., 1987; Guerrier, Manivannan, Pacheco, & Wilkie, 1995; Haraldsson, Carenfelt, Laurell, & Tornros, 1990; Madeley, Hulley, Wildgust, & Mindham, 1990; Marcotte et al., 2006; McMillen & Wells-Parker, 1987; Rizzo et al., 1997). There are several different types of simulators (e.g., film, noninteractive, interactive, fixed vs. motion based, desktop, full cab; cf. Milgram, 1994). Special concerns are often raised about fitness to drive with Alzheimer's disease (AD), the most common cause of abnormal cognitive decline in older adults (Cummings & Cole, 2002). Johansson and Lundberg (1997) raised the important concern that the first manifestation of AD may sometimes be a fatal crash and that preclinical AD raises the risk of a crash several fold. Brain autopsies showed neuropathological evidence of possible or probable AD in over half of 98 older drivers who perished in vehicular crashes, yet none had a diagnosis of AD, and family members were often unaware of a problem (Lundberg, Hakamies-Blomqvist, Almkvist, & Johansson, 1998).

Figure 7.5a shows how driving simulation can be applied to study drivers with mild-to-moderate cognitive impairment due to AD. In this simulation, subjects drive on a virtual highway passing an emergency vehicle (a police car) stopped by the shoulder of the highway. To minimize the chance of contact with the vehicle or nearby

(a)

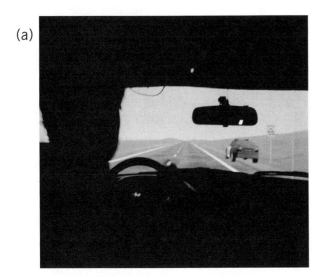

(b)

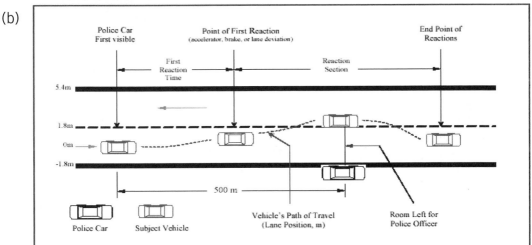

FIGURE 7.5. (a) Driving simulation requiring avoidance of a stopped police car. (b) Avoidance maneuver of an unimpaired simulator driver.

pedestrian, the driver must perceive, attend to, and interpret the roadway situation, formulate an evasive plan, and then exert appropriate action upon the accelerator, brake, or steering controls, all under pressure of time. Figure 7.5b shows the typical response of a normal individual, that is, slowing and steering around the parked police vehicle.

A relative drawback to simulation research is simulator adaptation syndrome (SAS), characterized by autonomic symptoms including nausea and sweating (Stanney, 2002). The discomfort is thought to be due to a mismatch between visual cues of movement, which are plentiful, and inertial cues, which are lacking or imperfect, even in simulators with a motion base (Rizzo, Sheffield, et al., 2003). In our experience SAS is more likely with crowded displays (as in simulated urban traffic), advanced age, female gender, and history of migraine or motion sickness. SAS may also result from conflicts between visual cues that are represented with differing success in modern computer displays. Choice of equipment and scenario design (e.g., avoiding sharp curves, left turns, frequent stops, and crowded scenes) can minimize SAS.

Another issue in simulator-based research is the need to test the validity of the simulation (e.g., Marcotte et al., 2004). This may involve detailed comparisons of driver performance in a simulator with performance in an instrumented vehicle and with state records of crashes and moving violations in each population of drivers being studied (Rizzo, 2004). The apparent face validity of the simulation—that is, that the driver appears to be driving a car and is immersed in the task—does not guarantee a lifelike performance. Drivers may behave differently in a simulator where no injury can occur, compared to real-life driving situations in which life, limb, and licensure are at stake. They may even perform differently when the same scenario is implemented on different simulator platforms, motivating calls for development of standard scenarios by an international Simulator Users Group (*www.engineering. uiowa.edu/simusers*).

Efforts to improve driving simulators have often focused on making the simulations more "lifelike," yet the added cost (e.g., of a mechanical motion base) might not translate to better assessments of driver safety. Abstract versions of reality that enhance some critical environmental cues (e.g., dynamic texture or shading) and minimize others might provide more effective tests (of "functional reality") that correlate even better with actual driver performance (see the description of the go/no-go scenario above). Advances in understanding the role and representations of key visual cues from the environment in dynamic graphical displays should improve the acceptance and measurement characteristics of driving simulator tools.

The future application of driving simulation to study drivers with medical impairments will benefit from a standardized approach to scenario design, certification standards for ecological validity of simulator graphics and vehicular dynamics, uniform definitions of measures of system performance, and cost-effective methods for geo-specific visual database development (Rizzo, Severson, et al., 2003).

Instrumented Vehicles

Instrumented vehicles (IVs) permit quantitative assessments of driver performance in the field, in a real car, under actual road conditions. These natural or naturalistic measurements are not subject to the type of human bias that affects interrater reliability on a standard road test. For these reasons, we developed the multipurpose field research vehicles known as ARGOS (the **A**utomobile for **R**esearch in er**GO**nomics and **S**afety) and NIRVANA (Nissan–Iowa Instrumented Research Vehicle of Advanced Neuroergonomic Assessment; see Figure 7.6). These vehicles are designed to examine objective indices of driving performance in normal and potentially unfit drivers and to assess the safety and usability of prototype automotive technologies. Each consists of a mid-sized vehicle with extensive instrumentation and sensors hidden within its infrastructure.

Internal networks of modern vehicles allow for the continuous communication of detailed information from the driver's own car (Rizzo, Jermeland, & Severson, 2002). Modern vehicles report variables relevant to speed, emissions controls, and

NIRVANA

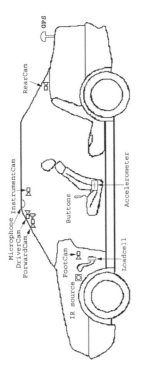

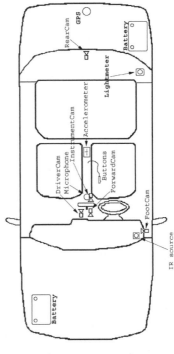

(c)

(a)

(b)

FIGURE 7.6. (a) Exterior view, (b) interior view, and (c) instrumentation of NIRVANA.

vehicular performance, and some vehicles allow more detailed reporting options (e.g., on seatbelt and headlight use, climate and traction control, wheel speed, and antilock brake system activation). Lane-tracking video can be processed with computer algorithms to assess lane-keeping behavior. Radar systems in the vehicle can gather information on the proximity, following distance, and lane-merging behavior of the driver and other neighboring vehicles on the road. Global positioning systems (GPSs) can show where and when a driver drives, takes risks, and commits errors. IVs equipped to detect infrared signals associated with possible cell phone use (without recording conversations) can assess potential driver distraction and risk acceptance. Wireless systems can check the instrumentation and send performance data to remote locations. These developments can provide direct, real-time information on driver strategy, vehicular usage, upkeep, drive lengths, route choices, and decisions to drive during inclement weather and high traffic.

The driving assessment in an IV can incorporate segments of "baseline" driving to assess vehicular control on uneventful segments of highway under conditions of low cognitive loading. The drives can also incorporate essential maneuvers such as left turns, right turns, stopping at a stop sign, and maintaining vehicular control. Kinematic measures of driver control during vehicular maneuvers include speed, lateral and longitudinal acceleration, yaw, and others (Gillespie, 1992; Milliken & Milliken, 2003). For example, large lateral accelerations indicate when a driver has swerved to miss an obstacle, whereas large longitudinal accelerations occur when a driver either braked hard or accelerated hard to avoid an obstacle. High yaw rate can indicate if a driver has swerved or is rapidly turning the steering wheel. The kinematics of driving has been documented extensively in the automotive industry and in race cars (Gillespie, 1992; Milliken & Milliken, 2003).

In addition, standardized challenges can be introduced that stress critical cognitive abilities during the driving task. These tasks are comparable to scenarios implemented in driving simulators and include route-finding tasks (Uc, Rizzo, Anderson, Shi, & Dawson, 2004, 2005), sign identification (Smothers, Rizzo, & Shi, 2003), and multitasking (i.e., driving while performing distracter tasks, as in holding a conversation or using in-vehicle devices such as cell phones and navigation equipment; Rizzo et al., 2004).

The advantage of using IVs to study patients with relatively specific cognitive impairments is exemplified in the recent findings of preserved procedural knowledge for driving skills in drivers with relatively circumscribed and dense amnesia following bilateral hippocampal and parahippocampal lesions caused by herpes simplex encephalitis (Anderson et al., in press). Radar-equipped IVs have also provided insights on traffic entry judgments in older drivers with attention impairments (Pietras, Shi, Lee, & Rizzo, 2006). Drivers pressed a button to indicate the last possible moment they could safely cross a road in front of an oncoming vehicle. The speed and distance of the oncoming vehicles were measured and time to contact was calculated. Each driver's time to cross the roadway was independently measured. Compared to unimpaired drivers, attention-impaired drivers accepted shorter TTC values, took longer to cross the roadway, and showed shorter safety cushions (the difference of time to contact and time to cross the roadway). A Monte Carlo simulation analysis was used to model how potential differences between the attention-impaired and nonimpaired groups might influence traffic dynamics and the potential for crashes. It showed that these performance differences increased the crash risk of the impaired group by up to 17.9 times that of the nonimpaired group. IVs can also be used to assess excessive risk taking in younger drivers (Boyce & Geller, 2002).

Olsen, Lee, and Wierwille (2002) combined IV video and radar data to study lane change decisions in neurologically normal adult drivers. Of 8,667 lane changes, 304 (3.5%) were unsafe because the driver initiated the lane change while a vehicle was nearby in the adjacent lane (e.g., in the blind spot) or was forced to make an evasive maneuver to avoid a crash. Continuous monitoring of radar and video information from the IVs of drivers with a range of cognitive abilities could provide additional insight into mechanisms of error that lead to such critical incidents that car crashes may result ("naturalistic driving").

Naturalistic Driving

Multiple studies have used IVs in traffic safety research (e.g., Dingus et al., 1995; Dingus, Neale, & Garness, 2002; Hanowski et al., 2000; Rizzo et al., 2004). Because an experimenter is present in most cases, drivers are liable to drive in an overly cautious and unnatural manner. Because total data collection times are often less than an hour and crashes and serious safety errors are relatively uncommon, until recently no study has captured precrash or crash data for a police-reported crash or on general vehicular usage.

A person driving his or her own IV is exposed to the usual risk of the real-world road environment without the psychological pressure that may be present when a driving evaluator is in the car. Road test conditions can vary depending on the weather, daylight, traffic, and driving course. However, this is an advantage in naturalistic testing, because repeated observations in varying real-life settings can provide rich information regarding driver risk acceptance, safety countermeasures and adaptive behaviors, and unique insights on the ranging relationships between low-frequency–high-severity driving errors and high-frequency–low-severity driver errors.

Such "brain-in-the-wild" relationships (Rizzo et al., 2006) were explored in detail in a study of naturalistic driving performance and safety errors in 100 neurologically normal individuals, driving 100 total driver years (Dingus et al., 2005; Neale, Dingus, Klauer, Sudweeks, & Goodman, 2005). All enrolled drivers allowed installation of an instrumentation package into their vehicle (78 cars) or drove a new model-year IV provided for their use. Data collection provided almost 43,000 hours of actual driving data, over 2,000,000 vehicular miles. There were 69 crashes, 761 near crashes, and 7,479 other relevant incidents (including 5,568 driver errors) for which data could be completely reduced (see Figure 7.7). Crash severity varied, with 75% being mild impacts, such as when tires strike curbs or other obstacles. Using taxonomy tools to classify all relevant incidents, the majority could be described as "lead vehicle" incidents, however several other conflict types (adjacent vehicle, following vehicle, single vehicle, object/obstacle) occurred at least 100 times each. Driver inattention was deemed to be a factor in most of these incidents.

In summary, IVs can gather continuous data over long periods of time in naturalistic studies of driver behavior. These studies, which hitherto relied on questionnaires completed by individuals who may have unreliable memory and cognition, can offer unique insights on vehicular usage by at-risk drivers.

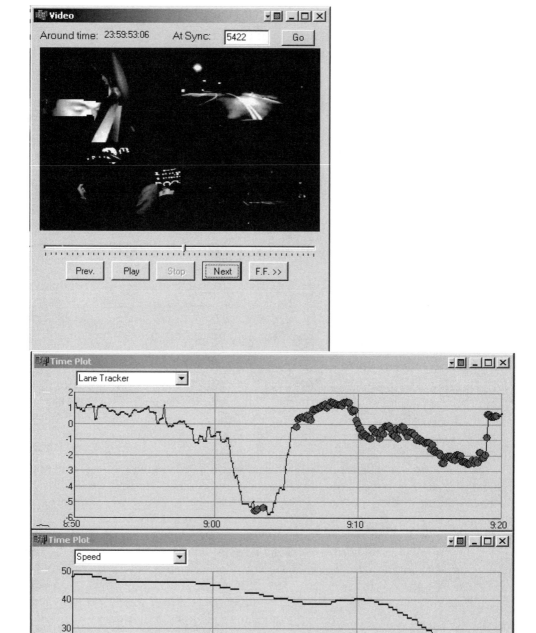

FIGURE 7.7. A drowsy driver loses control and swerves into the lane of oncoming traffic. There is a corresponding change in lane tracking position and a dip in speed, as shown by the electronic data from the IV. Courtesy of Dr. V. Neale.

Countermeasures

Cognitive impairment is an important risk factor for vehicular crashes in older adults. Adverse outcomes include side impact collisions at traffic intersections, inaccurate time-to-contact estimates leading to unsafe traffic entry decisions and rear-end collisions with lead vehicles, and run-off-the-road crashes on curved roads. Cognitive interventions with speed of processing and attention training may help mitigate crash risk in some drivers (see the work of Ball and colleagues, e.g., Ball et al., 1988). Another promising intervention strategy is to develop on-board driver assist and collision warning devices to mitigate the risk of crashes in drivers with cognitive impairments.

Ongoing research in our laboratory aims to determine an optimal set of signals for alerting drivers to unsafe behavior and impending traffic conflicts using a driving simulator and then an IV, and to estimate the benefits of the proposed safety interventions across the United States in terms of crashes averted. A key aspect of this research is to develop collision warning algorithms and display parameters. Effective warning systems must promote a timely and appropriate driver response and minimize annoyance from nuisance warnings (Bliss & Acton, 2003; Kiefer et al., 1999). The system's success depends on how well the algorithm and driver interface match driver capabilities and preferences (Brown, Lee, & McGehee, 2001; Burgett, Carter, Miller, Najm, & Smith, 1998; Lee, McGehee, Brown, & Reyes, 2002; Parasuraman, Hancock, & Olofinboba, 1997; Tijerina, Jackson, Pomerleau, Romano, & Peterson, 1995). Algorithms are calculated to signal when to issue warnings and have strong effects on the safety benefit of collision warning systems. Driver interface is also important because it influences how quickly the driver responds and whether the driver will accept the system. A loud auditory warning might generate a quick response, but frequent loud warnings could undermine driver acceptance by distracting and annoying drivers (Sorkin, 1988). Another key interface characteristic that could affect driver performance and acceptance is the warning modality. Several studies have found that haptic displays (e.g., a vibrating seat, pedals, or steering wheel) improve driver reactions to collision situations (Janssen & Nilsson, 1993; Raby, McGehee, Lee, & Norse, 2000; Tijerina et al., 2000).

Driver alerting systems must communicate urgency and minimize annoyance. To express the immediacy of attention required by the situation and minimize confusion, the alert urgency should map systematically to the degree of hazard (Edworthy & Adams, 1996; Haas & Casali, 1995). Different sounds communicate urgency levels (Hellier & Edworthy, 1999). Perceived urgency of sounds changes predictably with fundamental frequency, amplitude envelope, harmonics, interpulse speed, rhythm, repetition, speed change, pitch range, pitch contour, and musical structure (Edworthy, Loxley, & Dennis, 1991); of these, interpulse speed was found to have the strongest influence. People perceive atonal bursts as more urgent. Increasing the number of burst repetitions increased alert urgency, but also irritation. Annoying alerts may attract attention but lead a driver to ignore or disable them.

Annoyance, like urgency, can be assessed psychophysically and physiologically (Loeb, 1986). Annoyance may signify a reaction to a sound based on its physical nature, emotional content, novelty, or the situation being judged (Fucci, Petrosino, McColl, Wyatt, & Wilcox, 1997; Kryter, 1985). Annoyance depends on sound loudness, noisiness, sharpness, roughness, harmony, and tonality (Berglund & Preis, 1997; Khan, Johansson, & Sundback, 1997). Noisiness increases with sound level, duration, frequency, spectrum, complexity, and abruptness of increase (Kryter, 1985). Increasing loudness slowly and decreasing it rapidly is more annoying than increasing it rapidly and decreasing slowly (Nixon, Von Gierke, & Rosinger, 1969).

Existing studies have focused on visual or auditory cues in operators with normal or corrected-to-normal vision and cognition without considering how response patterns might change for impaired observers. Complementing visual cues with cues in another sensory mode speeds reaction time (Nickerson, 1973; Todd, 1912). Haptic cues may speed response and reduce annoyance and offer a promising cue for alerting drivers to critical events in information-rich domains. Haptic warnings have proved more effective than visual cues in alerting pilots to mode changes in cockpit automation (83 vs. 100%), but the warnings did impede concurrent visual tasks (Sklar & Sarter, 1999). One type of haptic cue (torque-based kinesthetic) reduced reaction times more than auditory cues (Gielen, Schnidt, & Van den Heuvel, 1983), and another type (vibrotactile) enhanced reaction time to visual cues (Diederich, 1995). Older drivers may rely more on alert signals because of reduced self-confidence (Lee & See, 2004) and may use sound and vibration alerts more effectively than visual alerts if they have visual-processing impairments.

Practical Assessment and Public Policy

Demographic and health factors may impact driving ability. Relevant factors are age, education, gender, general health, vision status, mobility, and driving frequency. Frequency of driving can be assessed using a Driving Habits Questionnaire (Ball et al., 1998; Stalvey, Owsley, Sloan, & Ball, 1999). Health status information can be obtained using a checklist of medical conditions (e.g., heart disease, cancer) and when they occurred. Certain medical factors (e.g., use of some medications, having a history of falls, back pain, kidney disease, heart disease, diabetes, stroke, bursitis, visual impairment, sleep apnea) are associated with increased risk of driving errors (see Hu, Trumble, Foley, Eberhard, & Wallace, 1998).

Psychological state of the drivers can be collected using the General Health Questionnaire (GHQ; Goldberg, 1972). Medication use can be assessed by asking drivers to bring all prescription and over-the-counter medication to the clinic. A driver's chronic sleep disturbance can be assessed from the driver's self-report on the Epworth Sleepiness Scale.

A relevant visual assessment can include tests of letter acuity (e.g., the ETDRS chart; Ferris, Kassoff, Bresnick, & Bailey, 1982), contrast sensitivity (Pelli, Robson, & Wilkins, 1988), and visual field sensitivity (which is often assessed using automated perimetry) (Trick, 2003). UFOV reduction in patients who have normal visual fields can be demonstrated using visual tasks under differing attention loads (Ball et al., 1993). Overall visual health can be assessed with the National Eye Institute Visual Function Questionnaire–25 (Mangione et al., 2001).

Several standardized tasks can be used to assess cognitive abilities that are essential to the driving task (see below). Impaired performance on some of these tasks (e.g., CFT, Trail Making Test Part B) may be especially predictive of driving safety risk. Of note, neuropsychological test scores are often corrected (e.g., scaled for age and education) to improve the ability to detect deviations from normative reference groups. However, what matters on the road is pure ability, regardless of demographic characteristics. For example, if a driver exhibits slowed processing speed, it is relevant that he or she is slow compared to all other drivers who might be on the road, not just compared to other drivers in the same demographic group. Consequently, studies that aim to correlate neuropsychological performance with driving performance and to generate predictions of safety in individual drivers should use raw (i.e., not corrected for age, education, or gender) neuropsychological test scores. Alternatively, uncorrected scaled scores could allow for placement of the measures on a common metric and assist in normalizing the distribution. Importantly, though there are some large normative groups that make this approach potentially attractive, evidence suggests that the use of norms based on different normative groups may result in significantly different standard scores (Anderson et al., 2007). It should be noted that no single test is sufficiently reliable to base judgments on fitness to drive, and a variety of sources and approaches are needed (Reger, 2004).

Briefly, Judgment of Line Orientation (JLO) assesses visuospatial perception. Visuoconstructional ability is tested using the Rey–Osterreith Complex Figure Test copy version (CFT-copy) and the block design subtest (Blocks) from the Wechsler Adult Intelligence Scale—Revised (WAIS-R). The CFT-recall version and the Benton Visual Retention Test (BVRT) test nonverbal memory, while the Rey Auditory Verbal Learning Test (AVLT) indexes anterograde verbal memory. The Trail Making Test Part B (TMT-B) and Controlled Oral Word Association (COWA) test aspects of executive function. These tasks are described in detail elsewhere (e.g., Lezak, 1995). Several approaches have been developed to derive an overall estimate of neuropsychological functioning; for example, the global deficit score, which emphasizes number and severity of deficits by assigning more weight to below-average performances (Marcotte et al., 2004). We have also found it useful to calculate a composite measure of cognitive impairment (Adstat; Cogstat) by assigning standard T-scores (mean = 50, SD = 10) to each of the tests from the neuropsychological assessment battery (Rizzo, Anderson, Dawson, & Nawrot, 2000; Uc et al., 2005). Mobility can be assessed using versions of the functional reach task and the get-up-and-go task (e.g., Podsiadlo & Richardson, 1991). There are, of course, many other potentially useful tests of vision, cognition, and mobility, as well as of personality and driving habits to consider, depending on the questions being asked and resources, expertise, and time available for testing.

The Swedish Road Administration (Vägverket) proposed operational guidelines for assessing fitness to drive in motorists with dementia, based on screening measures such as the Clinical Dementia Rating (CDR) and the Mini-Mental State Examination (MMSE). Generally, patients with moderate to severe dementia (e.g., cutoffs: MMSE ≤17; CDR ≥2) should not drive. The American Academy of Neurology (AAN) supports the use of regular testing and optional reporting of cases involving dementia (Dubinsky, Stein, & Lyons, 2000). The American Medical Association/National Highway Traffic Safety Administration (AMA/NHTSA; 2003), American Academy of Ophthalmology (AAO; 2006), American Association of Motor Vehicle Administrators (AAMVA), and the Federal Motor Carrier Safety Administration (FMCSA) have formulated and are revising their own guidelines for at-risk drivers with visual, cognitive, or medical impairments, based on the best available current peer-reviewed evidence. In these policy-making efforts it is critical to consider the relationship between different driver outcomes (such as having a crash) and driver safety (Table 7.2).

The AAN set out to create fair, comprehensive, and accurate guidelines for advising drivers with neurological disease or cognitive impairments as to whether they should continue to drive (Dubinsky et al., 2000). These guidelines searched for well-designed, controlled studies of driving in individuals with AD, using the National Library of Medicine's MEDLINE database and an evidence-based review of the medical literature from 1966 to 1998 with the search terms "aged" or "Alzheimer's" and "automobile." The review did not use the term "driving." The results suggested that drivers with mild dementia (CDR 0.5) had an increased risk of a crash that was not as great as that tolerated in teenage drivers and less than that of drivers operating a vehicle at common lower legal limits of intoxication (0.8 mg/dl). They recommended that these mildly demented drivers be retested at 6-month intervals. Foley, Masaki, Ross, and White (2000) studied driving cessation in older men with incident dementia in the Honolulu Asia Driving Study (HAAS), a population-based longitudinal study of AD and other dementias of over 3-year durations. Only 22% of the participants in incident cases of diagnosed AD or other dementia with a CDR of 1 were still driving at the time of their evaluation, versus 46% of those with a CDR of 0.5 (30% overall). Reduced vision, grip strength, standing balance, and gait speed contributed to driving cessation. (These were not used in AAN guidelines). Foley et al. estimated that, nationwide, about 4% of men $\geq$ 75 years who drive (~175,000 persons) have very mild or mild dementia (i.e., CDR < 2). Rarely do men with moderate or more severe stage dementia (CDR $\geq$ 2) continue to drive. About 1 in 10 of the demented drivers reportedly used a "copilot" to facilitate driving. The wisdom of using a copilot is unclear, as it may increase the passenger's risk for a motor vehicular injury or fatality.

Foley, Masaki, White, Ross, and Eberhard (2001) took issue with the AAN. Whereas the AAN recommended that patients with AD and CDR of 1 should not

TABLE 7.2. Driving Endpoints and Their Prediction of Unsafe Driving

Endpoint	Comment
Reported at-fault accident above baseline rate	Valid, insensitive
Reported at-fault accident without comparison to baseline rate	Less valid, insensitive
License revocation by statute	Valid de factor, insensitive
Driving privileges revoked by family member	Probably valid, insensitive
Self-surrender of license	Probably valid, very insensitive
Failed on-road driving test by blinded professional examiner using statutory criteria	Valid de factor, sensitive, probably the gold standard
Failed on-road driving test by blinded professional examiner using validated research criteria	Valid, sensitive

drive and that their families should be informed of this clinical recommendation, Foley and colleagues (2001) suggested that patients may not accept the physician's advice and family members may have trouble complying with this recommendation. The AAN recommended referring patients for a driving evaluation to determine which patients with AD and a CDR of 0.5 are "appropriate" to continue driving, but Foley and colleagues countered that this assumes that this service is readily available and ideally covered by a patient's health insurance policy; in reality, there are few qualified examiners in the United States, and the charge for an evaluation may not be covered by a typical Medicare-linked supplemental insurance. There are ~ 14 million drivers ≥ 70 years, and the number is growing, so demand for driver evaluation services and insurance coverage will increase. Dubinsky and colleagues (2000) acknowledged that it is difficult to enforce cessation of driving, and adequate testing facilities are lacking. They asserted that the AAN guidelines were developed for health care professionals to point out potential problems associated with allowing even mildly cognitively impaired individuals to drive but were not designed to recommend legislation. State and federal governments are responsible for legislation and enforcement of driving restrictions.

Duchek and colleagues (2003) showed that many drivers with CDR scores of 1 or greater are unsafe to drive within a year of their road tests. However, mandatory reporting of drivers with health complaints is controversial because it may inhibit drivers with treatable conditions from seeking required medical attention. The American Medical Association (AMA) recommended that physicians report their patients' medical conditions when the condition poses a threat and the patient is apparently disregarding the physician's advice not to drive—with liability protections for good-faith reporting.

The AAN supports the development and promotion of better evaluation tools to assess driver safety, to help physicians recognize when a driver should be referred for evaluation, and to help state officials conduct such an evaluation. This is important because state agencies are not equipped to perform complex assessments of performance in drivers with flagged medical conditions for determination of driving safety. Relevant training and diagnostic tools can be developed in collaborations between state transportation officials and other medical expert groups, including physician and patient organizations. Stricter driving and reporting standards may be needed for drivers who provide public transportation or transport hazardous material. State and federal efforts are needed to plan for and provide transportation resources for individuals who are unable to transport themselves. Health care personnel should review the driving laws in their area and be prepared to discuss and document their medical recommendations in light of these regulations (American Academy of Neurology, 2006).

Conclusions

Safe driving requires the coordination of attention, perception, memory, motor and executive functions (including decision making) and self-awareness or metacognition. These abilities may be impaired by fatigue; overwork; illicit drugs and alcohol; advancing age; medical, neurological, personality, or psychiatric disorders; and prescription drug effects. Because age or medical diagnosis alone is often an unreliable criterion for licensure, decisions on fitness to drive should be based on empirical observations of performance, preferably under conditions of optimal stimulus and response control in environments that are challenging yet safe. Real-life crashes are sporadic, uncontrolled events during which few objective observations can be made. Personal accounts and even state crash records may be incomplete, and crashes are underreported. In most cases, state road tests are designed to test if novice drivers know and can apply the rules of the road, not to predict crash involvement in veteran drivers who may now be impaired. Linkages between cognitive abilities measured by neuropsychological tasks and driving behavior assessed using driving simulators and natural and naturalistic observations in IVs can help standardize the assessment of fitness to drive. By understanding the patterns of driver safety errors that cause crashes, it may be possible to design interventions to reduce these errors and injuries and increase mobility. These interventions include driver performance monitoring devices, collision alerting and warning systems, road design, and graded licensure strategies.

Acknowledgments

This research was supported by Grant Nos. AG 15071, AG 17707, and R01 AG026027 from the National Institute on Aging (NIA).

References

Allsop, R. E., Brown, I. D., Groeger, J. A., & Robertson, S. A. (1991). *Approaches to modeling driver behaviour at actual and simulated traffic light signals* (Contractor report no. 264). Crowthorne, UK: Transport and Road Research Laboratory.

American Academy of Ophthalmology. (2006). *Policy statement: Vision requirements for driving.* Retrieved September 25, 2006, from *www.aao.org/aao/member/policy/driving. cfm.*

American Academy of Neurology. (2006). *Position statement on physician reporting of medical conditions that may affect driving competence.* St. Paul, MN: Author. Available at *www.aan.com/advocacy/issues/tools/56.pdf.*

American Medical Association/National Highway Traffic Safety Administration/U.S. Department of Transportation. (2003, June). *Physician's guide to assessing and counseling older drivers.* Retrieved August 31, 2009, from *www.amaassn.org/ama1/pub/upload/ mm/433/chapter1.pdf.*

Andersen, G. J., Cisneros, J., Atchley, P., & Saidpour, A. (1999). Speed, size, and edge-rate information for the detection of collision events. *J Exp Psychol: Hum Percept Perform, 25,* 256–269.

Andersen, G. J., Cisneros, J., Saidpour, A., & Atchley, P. (2000). Age-related differences in collision detection during deceleration. *Psychol Aging, 15,* 241–252.

Andersen, G. J., Saidpour, A., & Enriquez, A. (2001, August). *Detection of collision events by older and younger drivers.* Paper presented at the First International Driving Symposium on Human Factors in Driver Assessment, Training, and Vehicle Design, Aspen, CO.

Anderson, A. M., Skoblar, B. M., White, T., Jacobson, C., Fernandez, H. H., Foote, K. D., et al. (2007, February). *Selection of normative reference data influences clinical considerations*. Paper presented at the annual meeting of the International Neuropsychological Society, Portland, OR.

Anderson, S. W., & Tranel, D. (1989). Awareness of disease states following cerebral infarction, dementia, and head trauma: Standardized assessment. *Clin Neuropsychol*, 3(4), 327–339.

Arnold, P. K., Hartley, L. R., Corry, A., Hochstadt, D., Penna, F., & Feyer, A. M. (1997). Hours of work, and perceptions of fatigue among truck drivers. *Accid Anal Prev*, 29(4), 471–477.

Baddeley, A., & Logie, R. (1992). Auditory imagery and working memory. In D. Reisberg (Ed.), *Auditory imagery* (pp. 179–197). Hillsdale, NJ: Erlbaum.

Ball, K., Beard, B. L., Roenker, D. L., Miller, R. L., & Griggs, D. S. (1988). Age and visual search: Expanding the useful field of view. *J Opt Soc Am A*, 5(12), 2210–2219.

Ball, K., Owsley, C., Sloane, M., Roenker, D., & Bruni, J. (1993). Visual attention problems as a predictor of vehicle crashes in older drivers. *Invest Ophthalmol Vis Sci*, 34, 3110–3123.

Ball, K., Owsley, C., Stalvey, B., Roenker, D. L., Sloane, M. E., & Graves, M. (1998). Driving avoidance and functional impairment in older drivers. *Accid Anal Prev*, 30(3), 313–322.

Barger, L. K., Cade, B. E., Ayas, N. T., Cronin, J. W., Rosner, B., Speizer, F. E., et al. (2005). Extended work shifts and the risk of motor vehicle crashes among interns. *N Engl J Med*, 352(2), 125–34.

Barratt, E. S. (1994). Impulsiveness and aggression. In J. Monahan & H. J. Steadman (Eds.), *Violence and mental disorder: Developments in risk assessment* (pp. 61–79). Chicago: University of Chicago Press.

Batchelder, S., Rizzo, M., Vanderleest, R., & Vecera, S. P. (2003). Traffic scene related change blindness in older drivers. In M. Rizzo, J. D. Lee, & D. McGehee (Eds.), *Proceedings of Driving Assessment 2003: Second International Driving Symposium on Human Factors in Driver Assessment, Training and Vehicle Design* (pp. 177–181). Iowa City: University of Iowa.

Bechara, A., Damasio, A. R., Damasio, H., & Anderson, S. W. (1994). Insensitivity to future consequences following damage to human prefrontal cortex. *Cognition*, 50, 7–15.

Bechara, A., Damasio, H., Tranel, D., & Damasio, A. R. (1997). Deciding advantageously before knowing the advantageous strategy. *Science*, 275, 1293–1295.

Bechara, A., Tranel, D., Damasio, H., & Damasio, A. R. (1996). Failure to respond autonomically to anticipated future outcomes following damage to prefrontal cortex. *Cereb Cortex*, 6(2), 215–225.

Beck, L. H., Bransome, E. D., Jr., Mirsky, A. F., Rosvold, H. E., & Sarason I. (1956). A continuous performance test of brain damage. *Consult Psychol*, 20(5), 343–350.

Beirness, D. J. (1993). Do we really drive as we live?: The role of personality factors in road crashes. *Alcohol, Drugs and Driving*, 9, 129–143.

Benton, A. L. (1974). *The Revised Visual Retention Test: Clinical and experimental applications* (4th ed.) New York: Psychological Corporation.

Benton, A. L. (1991). The prefrontal region: Its early history. In H. S. Harvey, H. M. Eisenberg, & A. L. Benton (Eds.), *Frontal lobe function and dysfunction* (pp. 3–32). New York: Oxford University Press.

Berglund, B., & Preis, A. (1997). Is perceived annoyance more subject-dependent than perceived loudness? *Acoustica*, 83(2), 313–319.

Bliss, J. P., & Acton, S. A. (2003). Alarm mistrust in automobiles: How collision alarm reliability affects driving. *Appl Ergon*, 34(6), 499–509.

Boer, E. R. (2001). Behavioral entropy as a measure of driving performance. In *Proceedings of the First International Driving Symposium on Human Factors in Driver Assessment, Training and Vehicle Design* (pp. 225–229). Iowa City: University of Iowa.

Bonneson, J., Zimmerman, K., & Brewer, M. (2002). *Engineering countermeasures to reduce red-light running* (Report no. 4027-2). College Station: Texas Transportation Institute.

Boyce, T. E., & Geller, E. S. (2002). An instrumented vehicle assessment of problem behavior and driving style: Do younger males really take more risks? *Accid Anal Prev, 34*(1), 51–64.

Brewer, A. M. (2000). Road rage: What, who, when, where and how. *Transport Reviews, 20,* 49–64.

Brouwer, W. H., Ponds, R. W., Van Wolffelaar, P. C., & Van Zomeren, A. H. (1989). Divided attention 5 to 10 years after severe closed head injury. *Cortex, 25*(2), 219–230.

Brown, T. L., Lee, J. D., & McGehee, D. V. (2001). Human performance models and rear-end collision avoidance algorithms. *Hum Factors, 43*(3), 462–482.

Burg, A. (1968). Vision and driving: A summary of research findings. *High Res Rec, 216,* 1–12.

Burgett, A. L., Carter, A., Miller, R. J., Najm, W. G., & Smith, D. L. (1998). *A collision warning algorithm for rear-end collisions* (No. 98-S2-P-31). Washington, DC: National Highway Traffic Safety Administration.

Cabeza, R., Dolcos, F., Prince, S. E., Rice, H. J., Weissman, D. H., & Nyberg, L. (2003). Attention-related activity during episodic memory retrieval: A cross-function fMRI study. *Neuropsychologia, 41,* 390–399.

Cabeza, R., & Nyberg, L. (2000). Neural bases of learning and memory: Functional neuroimaging evidence. *Curr Opin Neurol, 13*(4), 415–421.

Caird, J. K., Edwards, C. J., & Creaser, J. (2001, August). *The effect of time constraints on older and younger driver decisions to turn at intersections using a modified change blindness paradigm.* Paper presented at the First International Driving Symposium on Human Factors in Driver Assessment, Training and Vehicle Design, Aspen, CO.

Calhoun, V. D., Pekar, J. J., McGinty, V. B., Adali, T., Watson, T. D., & Pearlson, G. D. (2002). Different activation dynamics in multiple neural systems during simulated driving. *Hum Brain Mapp, 16*(3), 158–167.

Calhoun, V. D., Pekar, J. J., & Pearlson, G. D. (2004). Alcohol intoxication effects on simulated driving: Exploring alcohol-dose effects on brain activation using functional MRI. *Neuropsychopharmacol, 29*(11), 2097–2117.

Centers for Disease Control and Prevention. (2006). National Drunk and Drunk Driving Prevention Month. *Morbidity and Mortality Weekly Report, 55*(48), 1293–1296.

Cummings, J. L., & Cole, G. (2002). Alzheimer disease. *JAMA, 287*(18), 2335–2338.

Dahlen, E. R., Martin, R. C., Ragan, K., & Kuhlman, M. M. (2005). Driving anger, sensation seeking, impulsiveness, and boredom proneness in the prediction of unsafe driving. *Accid Anal Prev, 37*(2), 341–348.

Damasio, A. R. (1994). *Descartes' error: Emotion, reason, and the human brain.* New York: Putnam.

Damasio, A. R. (1996). The somatic marker hypothesis and the possible functions of the prefrontal cortex. *Philos Trans R Soc Lond B Biol Sci, 351,* 1413–1420.

Damasio, A. R. (1999). *The feeling of what happens: Body and emotion in the making of consciousness.* New York: Harcourt.

Deery, H. A., & Fildes, B. N. (1999). Young novice driver subtypes: Relationship to high-risk behavior, traffic accident record, and simulator driving performance. *Hum Factors, 41*(4), 628–643.

Dement, W. C., Carskadon, M. A., & Richardson, G. (1978). Excessive daytime sleepiness in the sleep apnea syndrome. In C. Guilleminault & W. C. Dement (Eds.), *Sleep apnea syndromes* (pp. 23–46). New York: Liss.

Dias, R., Robbins, T. W., & Roberts, A. C. (1996). Dissociation in prefrontal cortex of affective and attentional shifts. *Nature, 380,* 69–72.

Diederich, A. (1995). Intersensory facilitation of reaction time: Evaluation of counter and diffusion coactivation models. *J Math Psych, 39,* 197–215.

DiFranza, J. R., Winters, T. H., Goldberg, R. J., Cirillo, L., & Biliouris, T. (1986). The relationship of smoking to motor vehicle accidents and traffic violations. *NY State J Med, 86*(9), 464–467.

Dinges, D. (2000). Accidents and fatigue. In *Proceedings of the International Conference: The sleepy driver and pilot.* Stockholm: National Institute for Psychosocial Factors and Health.

Dingus, T. A., Hardee, H. L., & Wierwille, W. W. (1987). Development of models for onboard detection of driver impairment. *Accid Anal Prev, 19,* 271–283.

Dingus, T. A., Hetrick, S., & Mollenhauer, M. (1999). Empirical methods in support of crash avoidance model building and benefits estimation. *ITS Journal, 5,* 93–125.

Dingus, T. A., Klauer, S. G., Neale, V. L., Petersen, A., Lee, S. E., Sudweeks, J. D., et al. (2005). *The 100-car naturalistic driving study: Phase II – Results of the 100-car field experiment* (Interim Project Report for DTNH22-00-C-07007, Task Order 6). Washington, DC: National Highway Traffic Safety Administration.

Dingus, T. A., McGehee, D. V., Hulse, M. C., Jahns, S. K., Manakell, N., Mollenhaust, M. A., et al. (1995). *TravTek evaluation task C-3-Camera Car Study* (Federal Highway Administration Technical Report). Washington, DC: Department of Transportation.

Dingus, T. A., Neale, V. L., & Garness, S. A. (2002). *Impact of sleeper berth usage on driver fatigue* (Final Project Report No. 61-96-00068). Washington, DC: U.S. Department of Transportation, Federal Motor Carriers Safety Administration.

Dubinsky, R. M., Stein, A. C., & Lyons, K. (2000). Practice parameter: Risk of driving and Alzheimer's disease (an evidence-based review): Report of the Quality Standards Subcommittee of the American Academy of Neurology. *Neurology, 54*(12), 2205–2211.

Duchek, J. M., Carr, D. B., Hunt, L., Roe, C. M., Xiong, C., Shah, K., et al. (2003). Longitudinal driving performance in early-stage dementia of the Alzheimer type. *J Am Geriat Soc, 51*(10), 1342–1347.

Eby, D. W., Molnar, L. J., Shope, J. T., Vivoda, J. M., & Fordyce, T. A. (2003). Improving older driver knowledge and self-awareness through self-assessment: The driving decisions workbook. *J Safety Res, 34*(4), 371–381.

Edworthy, J., & Adams, A. (1996). *Warning design: A research perspective.* Bristol, PA: Taylor & Francis.

Edworthy, J., Loxley, S., & Dennis, I. (1991). Improving auditory warning design: Relationship between warning sound parameters and perceived urgency. *Hum Factors, 33*(2), 205–231.

Ehret, B. D., Gray, W. D., & Kirschenbaum, S. S. (2000). Contending with complexity: Developing and using a scaled world in applied cognitive research. *Hum Factors, 42*(1), 8–23.

Engleman, H. M., Hirst, W. S. J., & Douglas, N. J. (1997). Under reporting of sleepiness and driving impairment in patients with sleep apnea/hypopnea syndrome. *J Sleep Res, 6,* 272–275.

Evenden, J. (1999). Impulsivity: A discussion of clinical and experimental findings. *J Psychopharmacol, 13*(2), 180–192.

Fakhry, S. M., & Salaita, K. (2002). Aggressive driving: A preliminary analysis of a serious threat to motorists in a large metropolitan area. *J Trauma, 52*(2), 217–223; discussion 223–214.

Fernandez-Duque, D., Baird, J. A., & Posner, M. I. (2000). Awareness and metacognition. *Conscious Cogn, 9*(2, Pt. 1), 324–326.

Ferreira, J. J., Galitzky, M., & Brefel-Courbon, C. (2000). "Sleep attacks" as an adverse drug reaction of levodopa monotherapy. *Movement Disord, 15*(Suppl. 3), 129.

Ferreira, J. J., Galitzky, M., Montastruc, J. L., & Rascol, O. (2000). Sleep attacks in Parkinson's disease. *Lancet, 355*, 1333–1334.

Ferreira, J. J., Pona, N., & Costa, J. (2000). Somnolence as an adverse drug reaction of antiparkinson drugs: A meta-analysis of published randomized placebo-controlled trails. *Movement Disord, 15*(Suppl. 3), 128.

Ferreira, J. J., Thalamas, C., & Galitzky, M. (2000). "Sleep attacks" and Parkinson's disease: Results of a questionnaire survey in a movement disorders outpatient clinic. *Movement Disord, 15*(Suppl. 3), 187.

Ferris, F. L., III, Kassoff, A., Bresnick, G. H., & Bailey, I. (1982). New visual acuity charts for clinical research. *Am J Ophthalmol, 94*(1), 91–96.

Foley, D. J., Masaki, K. H., Ross, G. W., & White, L. R. (2000). Driving cessation in older men with incident dementia. *J Am Geriatr Soc, 48*(8), 928–930.

Foley, D. J., Masaki, K., White, L., Ross, G. W., & Eberhard, J. (2001). Practice parameter: Risk of driving and Alzheimer's disease. *Neurology, 56*(5), 695.

Frucht, S. J., Rogers, J. D., Greene, P. E., Gordon, M. F., & Fahn, S. (1999). Falling asleep at the wheel: Motor vehicle mishaps in persons taking pramipexole and ropinirole. *Neurology, 52*(9), 1908–1910.

Frucht, S. J., Greene, P. E., & Fahn, S. (2000). Sleep episodes in Parkinson's disease: A wake-up call. *Mov Disord, 15*(4), 601–603.

Fucci, D., Petrosino, L., McColl, D., Wyatt, D., & Wilcox, C. (1997). Magnitude estimation scaling of the loudness of a wide range of auditory stimuli. *Percept Mot Skills, 85*(3), 1059–1066.

Fuster, J. M. (1996). *The prefrontal cortex: Anatomy, physiology, and neuropsychology of the frontal lobe* (3rd ed.). New York: Raven Press.

Garner, R. (1988). *Metacognition and reading comprehension*. Norwood, NJ: Ablex.

Gastaut, H., & Broughton, R. (1965). A clinical and polygraphic study of episodic phenomena during sleep. In J. Wortis (Ed.), *Recent advances in biological psychology* (pp. 197–223). New York: Plenum Press.

George, C. F., & Smiley, A. (1999). Sleep apnea and automobile crashes. *Sleep, 22*(6), 790–795.

Gibson, J. J. (1979). *The ecological approach to visual perception*. Boston: Houghton Mifflin.

Gielen, S. C., Schmidt, R. A., & Van den Heuvel, P. J. (1983). On the nature of intersensory facilitation of reaction time. *Percept Psychophys, 34*(2), 161–168.

Gillespie, T. D. (1992). *Fundamentals of vehicle dynamics*. Warrendale, PA: Society of Automotive Engineers.

Goldberg, D. (1972). *GHQ: The selection of psychiatric illness by questionnaire*. London: Oxford University Press.

Grayson, G. B. (1997). Theories and models in traffic psychology: A contrary view. In V. E. C. T. Rothengatter (Ed.), *Traffic and transport psychology: Theory and application* (pp. 93–96). New York: Pergamon.

Guerrier, J. H., Manivannan, P., Pacheco, A., & Wilkie, F. (1995, October). *The relationship of age and cognitive characteristics of drivers to performance of driving tasks on an interactive driving simulator*. Paper presented at the 39th annual meeting of the Human Factors and Ergonomics Society, San Diego.

Haas, E. C., & Casali, J. G. (1995). Perceived urgency of and response time to multi-tone and frequency-modulated warning signals in broadband noise. *Ergonomics*, *38*(11), 2313–2326.

Haddon, W., Jr. (1972). A logical framework for categorizing highway safety phenomena and activity. *J Trauma*, *12*(3), 193–207.

Hanowski, R. J., Wierwille, W. W., Garness, S. A., & Dingus, T. A. (2000). *Impact of local/ short haul operations on driver fatigue: Final report* (No. DOT-MC-00-203). Washington, DC: U.S. Department of Transportation, Federal Motor Carriers Safety Administration.

Haraldsson, P.-E., Carenfelt, C., Laurell, H., & Tornros, J. (1990). Driving simulator vigilance test. *Acta Otolaryngol (Stockholm)*, *110*, 136–140.

Harrison, Y., & Horne, J. A. (1996). Occurrence of "microsleeps" during daytime sleep onset in normal subjects. *Electroencephalogr Clin Neurophysiol*, *98*(5), 411–416.

Hauser, R. A., Gauger, L., Anderson, W. M., & Zesiewicz, T. A. (2000). Pramipexole-induced somnolence and episodes of daytime sleep. *Mov Disord*, *15*(4), 658–663.

Heinrich, H. W., Petersen, D., & Roos, N. (1980). *Industrial accident prevention*. New York: McGraw-Hill.

Hellier, E., & Edworthy, J. (1999). On using psychophysical techniques to achieve urgency mapping in auditory warnings. *Appl Ergon*, *30*(2), 167–171.

Hills, B. (1980). Vision, visibility and driving. *Perception*, *9*, 183–216.

Hoddes, E., Zarcone, V., Smythe, H., Phillips, R., & Dement, W. C. (1973). Quantification of sleepiness: A new approach. *Psychophysiology*, *10*(4), 431–436.

Holzapfel, H. (1995). Violence and the car. *World Transport Policy and Practice*, *1*, 57–65.

Homan, C. N., Wenzy, L. K., & Suppan, M. (2000). Sleep attacks after acute administration of apomorphine. *Mov Disord*, *15*(Suppl. 3), 108.

Horne, J. A., & Reyner, L. A. (1995). Sleep related vehicle accidents. *BMJ*, *310*, 565–567.

Horne, J. A., & Reyner, L. A. (1996). Counteracting driver sleepiness: Effects of napping, caffeine, and placebo. *Psychophysiology*, *33*(3), 306–309.

Horstmann, S., Hess, C. W., Bassetti, C., Gugger, M., & Mathis, J. (2000). Sleepiness-related accidents in sleep apnea patients. *Sleep*, *23*(3), 383–389.

Hu, P. S., Trumble, D. A., Foley, D. J., Eberhard, J. W., & Wallace, R. B. (1998). Crash risks of older drivers: A panel data analysis. *Accid Anal Prev*, *30*(5), 569–581.

Huguenin, R. D. (1997). Do we need traffic psychology models? In V. E. C. T. Rothengatter (Ed.), *Traffic and transport psychology: Theory and application* (pp. 31–52). New York: Pergamon.

Hunt, L. A., Murphy, C. F., Carr, D., Duchek, J. M., Buckles, V., & Morris, J. C. (1997). Reliability of the Washington University Road Test: A performance-based assessment for drivers with dementia of the Alzheimer type. *Arch Neurol*, *54*(6), 707–712.

Janssen, W., & Nilsson, L. (1993). Behavioural effects of driver support. In A. M. Parkes & S. Franzen (Eds.), *Driving future vehicles* (pp. 147–155). Washington, DC: Taylor & Francis.

Johansson, K., & Lundberg, C. (1997). The 1994 International Consensus Conference on Dementia and Driving: A brief report. Swedish National Road Administration. *Alzheimer Dis Assoc Disord*, *11*(Suppl. 1), 62–69.

Johns, M. W. (1991). A new method for measuring daytime sleepiness: The Epworth Sleepiness Scale. *Sleep*, *14*(6), 540–545.

Jones, K., & Harrison, Y. (2001). Frontal lobe function, sleep loss and fragmented sleep. *Sleep Med Rev*, *5*(6), 463–475.

Jones, T. O., Kelly, A. H., & Johnson, D. R. (1979). Half a century and a billion kilometres safely. *Trans Soc Automotive Eng*, *87*, 2271–2302.

Just, M. A., Carpenter, P. A., Keller, T. A., Emery, L., Zajac, H., & Thulborn, K. R. (2001).

Interdependence of nonoverlapping cortical systems in dual cognitive tasks. *Neuroimage*, *14*(2), 417–426.

Kantowitz, B. H. (2000, October). *Effective Utilization of the in-vehicle information: Integrating attractions and distractions*. Paper presented at the Convergence 2000 International Congress on Transportation Electronics, Society of Automotive Engineers, Detroit, MI.

Kantowitz, B. H. (2001). Using microworlds to design intelligent interfaces that minimize driver distraction. In *Proceedings of the First International Driving Symposium on Human Factors in Driver Assessment, Training and Vehicle Design* (pp. 42–57). Iowa City: University of Iowa.

Kecklund, G., & Akerstedt, T. (1993). Sleepiness in long distance truck driving: An ambulatory EEG study of night driving. *Ergonomics*, *36*(9), 1007–1017.

Khan, M. S., Johansson, O., & Sundback, U. (1997). Development of an annoyance index for heavy-duty diesel engine noise using multivariate analysis. *Noise Control Eng J*, *45*(4), 157–167.

Kiefer, R., LeBlanc, D., Palmer, M., Salinger, J., Deering, R., & Shulman, M. (1999). *Development and validation of functional definitions and evaluation procedures for collision warning/avoidance systems* (No. DOT HS 808 964). Washington, DC: Crash Avoidance Metrics Partnership.

Kramer, A. F., Cassavaugh, N. D., Irwin, D. E., Peterson, M. S., & Hahn, S. (2001). Influence of single and multiple onset distractors on visual search for singleton targets. *Percept Psychophys*, *63*(6), 952–968.

Kryter, K. D. (1985). *The effects of noise on man*. London: Academic Press.

Lamers, C. T., Bechara, A., Rizzo, M., & Ramaekers, J. G. (2006). Cognitive function and mood in MDMA/THC users, THC users and non-drug using controls. *J Psychopharmacol*, *20*(2), 302–311.

Lamers, C. T., & Ramaekers, J. G. (2001). Visual search and urban driving under the influence of marijuana and alcohol. *Hum Psychopharmacol*, *16*(5), 393–401.

Land, M. F., & Lee, D. N. (1994). Where we look when we steer. *Nature*, *369*, 742–744.

Lang, A. E., & Lozano, A. M. (1998a). Parkinson's disease. *N Engl J Med*, *339*(15), 1044–1053.

Lang, A. E., & Lozano, A. M. (1998b). Parkinson's disease. *N Engl J Med*, *339*(16), 1130–1143.

Laube, I., Seeger, R., Russi, E. W., & Bloch, K. E. (1998). Accidents related to sleepiness: Review of medical causes and prevention with special reference to Switzerland. *Schweiz Med Wochenschr*, *128*(40), 1487–1499.

Lee, J. D., McGehee, D. V., Brown, T. L., & Reyes, M. L. (2002). Collision warning timing, driver distraction, and driver response to imminent rear-end collisions in a high-fidelity driving simulator. *Hum Factors*, *44*(2), 314–334.

Lee, J. D., & See, K. A. (2004). Trust in automation: Designing for appropriate reliance. *Hum Factors*, *46*(1), 50–80.

Leger, D. (1994). The cost of sleep-related accidents: A report for the National Commission on Sleep Disorders Research. *Sleep*, *17*(1), 84–93.

Lezak, M. D. (1995). *Neuropsychological assessment* (3rd ed.). New York: Oxford University Press.

Loeb, M. (1986). *Noise and human efficiency*. Chichester, UK: Wiley.

Logan, B. K., & Couper, F. J. (2001). 3, 4-methylenedioxymethamphetamine (MDMA, ecstasy) and driving impairment. *J Forensic Sci*, *46*(6), 1426–1433.

Lundberg, C., Hakamies-Blomqvist, L., Almkvist, O., & Johansson, K. (1998). Impairments of some cognitive functions are common in crash-involved older drivers. *Accid Anal Prev*, *30*(3), 371–377.

Lyznicki, J. M., Doege, T. C., Davis, R. M., & Williams, M. A. (1998). Sleepiness, driving, and motor vehicle crashes. Council on Scientific Affairs, American Medical Association. *JAMA, 279*(23), 1908–1913.

Madeley, P., Hulley, J. L., Wildgust, H., & Mindham, R. H. (1990). Parkinson's disease and driving ability. *J Neurol Neurosur Ps, 53*(7), 580–582.

Mahelel, D., Zaidel, D., & Klein, T. (1985). Driver's decision process on termination of the green light. *Accid Anal Prev, 17*, 373–380.

Mangione, C. M., Lee, P. P., Gutierrez, P. R., Spritzer, K., Berry, S., & Hays, R. D. (2001). Development of the 25-item National Eye Institute Visual Function Questionnaire. *Arch Ophthalmol, 119*(7), 1050–1058.

Marcotte, T. D., Lazzaretto, D., Scott, J. C., Roberts, E., Woods, S. P., & Letendre, S. (2006). Visual attention deficits are associated with driving accidents in cognitively-impaired HIV-infected individuals. *J Clin Exp Neuropsychol, 28*(1),18–28.

Marcotte, T. D., Wolfson, T., Rosenthal, T. J., Heaton, R. K., Gonzalez, R., Ellis, R. J., et al. (2004). A multimodal assessment of driving performance in HIV infection. *Neurology, 63*(8), 1417–1422.

Marottoli, R. A., Cooney, L. M., Wagner, D. R., Doucette, J., & Tinetti, M. (1994). Predictors of automobile crashes and moving violations among elderly drivers. *Ann Intern Med, 121*, 842–846.

Maycock, G. (1997). Accident liability: The human perspective. In E. T. Rothengatter & V. E. Carbonell (Eds.), *Traffice and transport psychology: Theory and application* (pp. 65–76). New York: Pergamon.

Mazzoni, G., & Nelson, T. O. (1998). *Metacognition and cognitive neuropsychology: Monitoring and control processes.* Mahwah, NJ: Erlbaum.

McGehee, D. V., Lee, J. D., Rizzo, M., Dawson, J., & Bateman, K. (2004). Quantitative analysis of steering adaptation on a high performance fixed-base driving simulator. *Transport Res, 7*(3), 181–196.

McGlynn, S. M. (1998). Impaired awareness of deficits in a psychiatric context: Implications for rehabilitation. In D. J. Hacker, J. Dunlosky, & A. C. Graesser (Eds.), *Metacognition in educational theory and practice* (pp. 221–248). Mahwah, NJ: Erlbaum.

McMillen, D. L., & Wells-Parker, E. (1987). The effect of alcohol consumption on risk-taking while driving. *Addict Behav, 12*(3), 241–247.

Mestre, D. R. (2001). Dynamic evaluation of the useful field of view in driving. In *Proceedings of Driving Assessment 2001, Human Factors in Driver Assessment, Training and Vehicle Design* (pp. 234–239). Iowa City: University of Iowa.

Michon, J. A. (1979). Dealing with danger: Summary report of a workshop in the Traffic Research Center, State University Groningen, The Netherlands.

Milgram, P. (1994). A taxonomy of mixed reality visual displays. *IEICE Transactions on Information Systems, 77-D*, 1321–1329.

Miller, M., Azrael, D., Hemenway, D., & Solop, F. I. (2002). "Road rage" in Arizona: Armed and dangerous. *Accid Anal Prev, 34*(6), 807–814.

Milliken, W. F., & Milliken D. L. (2003). *Race car vehicle dynamics.* Warrendale, PA: SAE International.

Montastruc, J. L., Brefel-Courbon, C., & Senard, J. M. (2000). Sudden sleep attacks and antiparkinsonian drugs: A pilot prospective pharmacoepidemiological study. *Movement Disord, 15*(Suppl. 3), 130.

National Highway Traffic Safety Administration (NHTSA). (2003). *Early assessment.* Washington, DC: National Center for Statistics and Analysis. Retrieved May 13, 2004, from *www.nhtsa.dot.gov/nhtsa/announce/press/pressdisplay.cfm?year=2004&filename=FF ARSrls404.html.*

Nawrot, M. (2001, August). *Depth perception in driving: Alcohol intoxication, eye move-*

ment changes, and the disruption of motion parallax. Paper presented at the First International Driving Symposium on Human Factors in Driver Assessment, Training and Vehicle Design, Aspen, CO.

Neale, V. L., Dingus, T. A., Klauer, S. G., Sudweeks, J., & Goodman, M. J. (2005). An overview of the 100-Car Naturalistic Study and findings. In (Ed.), *International Technical Conference on the Enhanced Safety of Vehicles.* Washington, DC: National Highway Traffic Safety Administration.

Nickerson, R. S. (1973). Intersensory facilitation of reaction time: Energy summation or preparation enhancement? *Psychol Rev, 80,* 489–509.

Nixon, C. W., Von Gierke, H. D., & Rosinger, G. (1969). Comparative annoyances of "approaching" versus "receding" sound sources. *J Acoust Soc Am, 45,* 843–853.

Norman, D. A. (1981). Categorization of action slips. *Psychological Review, 88*(1), 1–15.

Norman, D. A., & Shallice, T. (1986). Attention to action: Will and automatic control of behavior. In R. J. Davidson, G. E. Schwartz, & D. Shapiro (Eds.), *Consciousness and self-regulation: Advances in research and theory* (Vol. 4, pp. 1–18): New York: Plenum Press.

Noyes, R., Jr. (1985). Motor vehicle accidents related to psychiatric impairment. *Psychosomatics, 26*(7), 569–572, 575–566, 579–580.

Nyberg, L., Marklund, P., Persson, J., Cabeza, R., Forkstam, C., Petersson, K. M., et al. (2003). Common prefrontal activations during working memory, episodic memory, and semantic memory. *Neuropsychologia, 41,* 317–377.

Ogilvie, R. D., Wilkinson, R. T., & Allison, S. (1989). The detection of sleep onset: Behavioral, physiological, and subjective convergence. *Sleep, 12*(5), 458–474.

Olanow, C. W., Schapira, A. H., & Roth, T. (2000). Waking up to sleep episodes in Parkinson's disease. *Mov Disord, 15*(2), 212–215.

Olsen, E. C. B., Lee, S. E., & Wierwille, W. W. (2002). Analysis of distribution, frequency, and duration of naturalistic Lane Changes. In (Ed.), *Proceedings of the Human Factors and Ergonomics Society 46th annual meeting* (pp. 1789–1793). Santa Monica, CA: Human Factors and Ergonomics Society.

O'Regan, J. K., Rensink, R. A., & Clark, J. J. (1999). Change-blindness as a result of "mudsplashes." *Nature, 398,* 34.

Owsley, C., Ball, K., Sloane, M. E., Roenker, D. L., & Bruni, J. R. (1991). Visual/cognitive correlates of vehicle accidents in older drivers. *Psychol Aging, 6,* 403–415.

Owsley, C., Stalvey, B. T., Wells, J., Sloane, M. E., & McGwin, G., Jr. (2001). Visual risk factors for crash involvement in older drivers with cataract. *Arch Ophthalmol, 119,* 881–887.

Paladini, D. (2000). Sleep attacks in two Parkinson's disease patients taking ropinirole. *Movement Disord, 15*(Suppl. 3), 130–131.

Palmer, S. E. (1999). *Vision science: Photons to phenomenology.* Cambridge, MA: MIT Press.

Parasuraman, R., Hancock, P. A., & Olofinboba, O. (1997). Alarm effectiveness in driver-centred collision-warning systems. *Ergonomics, 40*(3), 390–399.

Parasuraman, R., & Nestor, P. G. (1991). Attention and driving skills in aging and Alzheimer's disease. *Hum Factors, 33*(5), 539–557.

Paul, A., Boyle, L., Rizzo, M., & Tippin, J. (2005, June). *Variability of driving performance during microsleeps.* Paper presented at the 3rd International Driving Symposium on Human Factors in Driving Assessment, Training, and Vehicle Design, Rockport, ME.

Pelli, D. G., Robson, J. G., & Wilkins, A. J. (1988). The design of a new letter chart for measuring contrast sensitivity. *Clin Vision Sci, 2,* 187–199.

Peres, M., van de Moortele, P. F., Lehericy, S., LeBihan, D., & Guezennez, C. Y. (2000). fMRI of mental strategy in a simulated aviation performance task. *Aviat, Space Envir Md, 71,* 1218–1231.

Pietras, T. A., Shi, Q., Lee, J. D., & Rizzo, M. (2006). Traffic-entry behavior and crash risk for older drivers with impairment of selective attention. *Percept Motor Skill, 102*(3), 632–644.

Pietrucha, M. T., Opiela, K. S., Knoblauch, R. L., & Crigler, K. L. (1989). *Motorist compliance with standard traffic control devices* (No. FHWA-RD-89-103). Washington, DC: U.S. Department of Transportation.

Podsiadlo, D., & Richardson, S. (1991). The timed "Up and GO" test: A test of basic functional mobility for frail elderly persons. *J Am Geriatr Soc, 39*(2), 142–148.

Raby, M., McGehee, D. V., Lee, J. D., & Norse, G. E. (2000). Defining the interface for a snowplow lane tracking device using a systems-based approach. *Proc Hum Factors Ergon Soc, 3*, 369–372.

Ramaekers, J. G., Robbe, H. W. J., & O'Hanlon, J. F. (2000.) Marijuana, alcohol and actual driving performance. *Hum Psychopharm Clin, 15*(7), 551–558.

Ray, W. A., Thapa, P. B., & Shorr, R. I. (1993). Medications and the older driver. *Clin Geriatr Med, 9*(2), 413–438.

Reason, J. (1984). Lapses of attention. In R. Parasuraman & D. R. Davies (Eds.), *Varieties of attention* (pp. 515–549). New York: Academic Press.

Reger, M. A., Welsh, R. K., Watson, G. S., Cholerton, B., Baker, L. D., & Craft, S. (2004). The relationship between neuropsychological functioning and driving ability in dementia: A meta-analysis. *Neuropsychology, 18*(1), 85–93.

Rensink, R. A., O'Regan, J. K., & Clark, J. J. (1997). To see or not to see: The need for attention to perceive changes in scenes. *Psychol Sci, 8*, 368–373.

Rensink, R. A., O'Regan, J. K., & Clark, J. J. (2000). On the failure to detect changes in scenes across brief interruptions. *Vis Cog, 7*, 127–145.

Retting, R. A., Ulmer, R. G., & Williams, A. F. (1999). Prevalence and characteristics of red light running crashes in the United States. *Accid Anal Prev, 31*(6), 687–694.

Retting, R. A., Williams, A. F., Farmer, C. M., & Feldman, A. F. (1999). Evaluation of red light camera enforcement in Oxnard, California. *Accid Anal Prev, 31*(3), 169–174.

Reyner, L. A., & Horne, J. A. (1998). Falling asleep whilst driving: Are drivers aware of prior sleepiness? *Int J Legal Med, 111*(3), 120–123.

Risser, M. R., Ware, J. C., & Freeman, F. G. (2000). Driving simulation with EEG monitoring in normal and obstructive sleep apnea patients. *Sleep, 23*(3), 393–398.

Rizzo, M. (2001, June). *Eye, brain, and performance in at-risk older drivers.* Paper presented at the 2nd Research Colloquium, The Eye and The Auto 2001, Detroit Institute of Ophthalmology, Detroit, MI.

Rizzo, M. (2004). Safe and unsafe driving. In M. Rizzo & P. J. Eslinger (Eds.), *Principles and practice of behavioral neurology and neuropsychology* (pp. 197–222). Philadelphia: Saunders.

Rizzo, M., Akutsu, H., & Dawson, J. (2001). Increased attentional blink after focal cerebral lesions. *Neurology, 57*(5), 795–800.

Rizzo, M., Anderson, S. W., Dawson, J., Myers, R., & Ball, K. (2000). Visual attention impairments in Alzheimer's disease. *Neurology, 54*(10), 1954–1959.

Rizzo, M., Anderson, S. W., Dawson, J., & Nawrot, M. (2000). Vision and cognition in Alzheimer's disease. *Neuropsychologia, 38*(8), 1157–1169.

Rizzo, M., & Barton, J. J. S. (2005). Central disorders of visual function. In N. R. Miller & N. J. Newman (Eds.), *Walsh and Hoyt's Neuro-ophthalmology* (6th ed.). Baltimore: Williams & Wilkins.

Rizzo, M., & Hurtig, R. (1987). Looking but not seeing: Attention, perception, and eye movements in simultanagnosia. *Neurology, 37*(10), 1642–1648.

Rizzo, M., Jermeland, J., & Severson, J. (2002). Instrumented vehicles and driving simulators. *Gerontechnology, 1*(4), 291–296.

Rizzo, M., & Kellison, I. L. (2004). Eyes, brains, and autos. *Arch Ophthalmol, 122*(4), 641–647.

Rizzo, M., McGehee, D. V., Dawson, J. D., & Anderson, S. N. (2001). Simulated car crashes at intersections in drivers with Alzheimer disease. *Alzheimer Dis Assoc Disord, 15*(1), 10–20.

Rizzo, M., & Nawrot, M. (1998). Perception of movement and shape in Alzheimer's disease. *Brain, 121*(Pt. 12), 2259–2270.

Rizzo, M., Reinach, S., McGehee, D., & Dawson, J. (1997). Simulated car crashes and crash predictors in drivers with Alzheimer's disease. *Arch Neurol, 54*, 545–553.

Rizzo, M., Robinson, S., & Neale, V. (2006). The brain in the wild: Tracking human behavior in natural and naturalistic settings. In R. Parasuraman & M. Rizzo (Eds.), *Neuroergonomics: The brain at work* (pp. 113–128). New York: Oxford University Press.

Rizzo, M., Severson, J., Cremer, J., & Price, K. (2003). An abstract virtual environment tool to assess decision-making in impaired drivers. In *Proceedings of the 2nd International Driving Symposium on Human Factors in Driver Assessment, Training and Vehicle Design* (pp. 40–47). Iowa City: University of Iowa.

Rizzo, M., Sheffield, R., & Stierman, L. (2003). Demographic and driving performance factors in simulator adaptation syndrome. In M. Rizzo, J. D. Lee, & D. McGehee (Eds.), *Proceedings of driving assessment 2003: The Second International Driving Symposium on Human Factors in Driver Assessment, Training and Vehicle Design* (pp. 201–208). Iowa City: University of Iowa.

Rizzo, M., Shi, Q., Dawson, J., Anderson, S. W., Kellison, I., & Pietras, T. A. (2005). Stops for cops: Impaired response implementation in older drivers with cognitive decline. *Journal of the Transportation Research Board, 1922*, 1–8.

Rizzo, M., Stierman, L., Skaar, N., Dawson, J., Anderson, S. W., & Vecera, S. P. (2004). Effects of a controlled auditory–verbal distraction task on older driver vehicle control. *Transp Res Board, 1865*, 1–6.

Rolls, E. T. (1999). *The brain and emotion*. Oxford, UK: Oxford University Press.

Rolls, E. T. (2000). The orbitofrontal cortex and reward. *Cereb Cortex, 10*, 284–294.

Rolls, E. T., Hornak, J., Wade, D., & McGrath, J. (1994). Emotion-related learning in patients with social and emotional changes associated with frontal lobe damage. *J Neurol Neurosurg Psychiatry, 57*(12), 1518–1524.

Runyan, C. W. (1998). Using the Haddon matrix: Introducing the third dimension. *Inj Prev, 4*(4), 302–307.

Russo, M., Thorne, D., & Thomas, M. (1999). Sleep deprivation induced Bálint's syndrome (peripheral visual field neglect): A hypothesis for explaining driving simulator accidents in awake but sleepy drivers. *Sleep, 22*(Suppl. 1), 327.

Ryan, M., Slevin, J. T., & Wells, A. (2000). Non-ergot dopamine agonist-induced sleep attacks. *Pharmacotherapy, 20*(6), 724–726.

Schapira, A. H. (2000). Sleep attacks (sleep episodes) with pergolide. *Lancet, 355*, 1332–1333.

Schwebel, D. C., Severson, J., Ball, K. K., & Rizzo, M. (2006). Individual difference factors in risky driving: The roles of anger/hostility, conscientiousness, and sensation-seeking. *Accid Anal Prev, 38*(4), 801–810.

Sekuler, A. B., Bennett, P. J., & Mamelak, M. (2000). Effects of aging on the useful field of view. *Exp Aging Res, 26*(2), 103–120.

Shimamura, A. P. (1994). The neuropsychology of metacognition. In J. Metcalfe & A. P. Shimamura (Eds.), *Metacognition* (pp. 253–276). Cambridge, MA: MIT Press.

Simons, D. L., & Levin, D. T. (1997). Change blindness. *Trends in Cogn Sci, 1*, 261–267.

Siskind, V. (1996). Does license disqualification reduce reoffence rates? *Accid Anal Prev, 28*(4), 519–524.

Sivak, M. (1983). Society's aggression level as a predictor of traffic fatality rate. *J Safety Res*, *14*, 93–99.

Sklar, A. E., & Sarter, N. B. (1999). Good vibrations: Tactile feedback in support of attention allocation and human–automation coordination in event-driven domains. *Hum Factors*, *41*(4), 543–552.

Stalvey, B., Owsley, C., Sloan, M. E., & Ball, K. (1999). The Life Space Questionnaire: A measure of the extent of mobility of older adults. *J Appl Gerontol*, *18*, 479–498.

Stanney, K. M. (Ed.). (2002). *Handbook of virtual environments: Design, implementation, and applications*. Mahwah, NJ: Erlbaum.

Stiles, W. S., & Crawford, B. H. (1937). The effect of a glaring light source on extrafoveal vision. *Roy Soc Lond B. Bio*, *122*, 225.

Strayer, D. L., & Johnston, W. A. (2001). Driven to distraction: Dual-task studies of simulated driving and conversing on a cellular telephone. *Psychol Sci*, *12*(6), 462–466.

Stroop, J. R. (1935). Studies of interference in serial verbal reactions. *J Exp Psychol*, *18*, 643–662.

Stuss, D. T., Gow, C. A., & Hetherington, C. R. (1992). "No longer Gage": Frontal lobe dysfunction and emotional changes. *J Consult Clin Psychol*, *60*(3), 349–359.

Stuss, D. T., & Knight, R. T. (2002). *Principles of frontal lobe function*. New York: Oxford University Press.

Stutts, J. C., Wilkins, J. W., & Vaughn, B. V. (1999). Why do people have drowsy driving crashes?: Input from drivers who just did. Washington, DC: AAA. Retrieved October 9, 1999, from *www.aaafoundation.org/pdf/sleep/pdf*.

Suchman, E. A. (1970). Accidents and social deviance. *J Health Soc Behav*, *11*(1), 4–15.

Theeuwes, J. (1991). Exogenous and endogenous control of attention: The effect of visual onsets and offsets. *Percept Psychophys*, *49*(1), 83–90.

Thomas, I. (1996). Spatial data aggregation: Exploratory analysis of road accidents. *Accid Anal Prev*, *28*(2), 251–264.

Thorne, D., Thomas, M., & Russo, M. (1999). Performance on a driving-simulator divided attention task during one week of restricted nightly sleep. *Sleep*, *22*(Suppl. 1), 301.

Tijerina, L., Jackson, J. L., Pomerleau, D. A., Romano, R. A., & Peterson, A. (1995). *Run-off road collision avoidance using IVHS countermeasures: Task 3 Report—Volume II* (No. DTNH22-93-07023). Washington, DC: U.S. Department of Transportation.

Tijerina, L., Johnston, S., Parmer, E., Pham, H. A., Winterbottom, M. D., & Barickman, F. S. (2000). *Preliminary studies in haptic displays for rear-end collision avoidance system and adaptive cruise control applications*. Washington, DC: National Highway Transportation Safety Administration.

Todd, J. W. (1912). Reaction time to multiple stimuli. *Archives of Psychology*, *3*, 1–65.

Treat, J. R. (1980). A study of precrash factors involved in traffic accidents. *HRSI Res Rev*, *10*, 1–35.

Trick, G. (2003). Beyond visual acuity: New and complementary tests of visual function. In J. J. S. Barton & M. Rizzo (Eds.), *Neuro-ophthalmology: Vision and brain* (pp. 363–386). Philadelphia: Saunders.

Tsuang, M. T., Boor, M., & Fleming, J. A. (1985). Psychiatric aspects of traffic accidents. *Am J Psychiatry*, *142*(5), 538–546.

Uc, E. Y., Rizzo, M., Anderson, S. W., Shi, Q., & Dawson, J. D. (2004). Driver route-following and safety errors in early Alzheimer disease. *Neurology*, *63*(5), 832–837.

Uc, E. Y., Rizzo, M., Anderson, S. W., Shi, Q., & Dawson, J. D. (2005). Driver landmark and traffic sign identification in early Alzheimer's disease. *J Neurol Neurosur Ps*, *76*(6), 764–768.

Uc, E. Y., Rizzo, M., Anderson, S. W., Sparks, J., Rodnitzky, R. L., & Dawson, J. D. (2006). Impaired visual search in drivers with Parkinson's disease. *Ann Neurol*, *60*(4), 407–413.

van Zomeren, A. H., Brouwer, W. H., & Minderhoud, J. M. (1987). Acquired brain damage and driving: A review. *Arch Phys Med Rehabil, 68*(10), 697–705.

Vecera, S. P., & Luck, S. J. (2003). Attention. In V. S. Ramachandran (Ed.), *Encyclopedia of the human brain* (Vol. 1, pp. 269–284). San Diego, CA: Academic Press.

Vecera, S. P., & Rizzo, M. (2004). What are you looking at?: Impaired "social attention" following frontal-lobe damage. *Neuropsychologia, 42*(12), 1657–1665.

Warren, W. H., & Hannon, D. J. (1988). Direction of self-motion is perceived from optical flow. *Nature, 336*, 162–163.

Warren, W. H. J., Mestre, D. R., & Morris, M. W. (1991). Perception of circular heading from optical flow. *J Exp Psychol: Human, 17*, 28–43.

Wechsler, D. (1981). *Wechsler Adult Intelligence Scale—Revised*. New York: Psychological Corporation.

Wickens, C. D. (1992). *Engineering psychology and human performance* (2nd ed.). New York: HarperCollins.

Wierwille, W. W., Hanowski, R. J., & Hankey, J. M. (2002). *Identification and evaluation of driver errors: Overview and recommendations* (Final report for contract DTFH 61-97-C-00051). Washington, DC: Federal Highway Administration.

Wierwille, W. W., Hulse, M. C., Fischer, T. J., & Dingus, T. A. (1988). *Effects of variation in driving task attentional demand on in-car navigation system usage*. Warren, MI: General Motors Research Laboratories.

Wilde, G. J. S. (1982). The theory of risk homeostasis: Implications for safety and health. *Risk Anal, 2*, 249–258.

Young, T., Blustein, J., Finn, L., & Palta, M. (1997). Sleep-disordered breathing and motor vehicle accidents in a population-based sample of employed adults. *Sleep, 20*(8), 608–613.

Zuckerman, M. (1996). The psychobiological model for impulsive unsocialized sensation seeking: A comparative approach. *Neuropsychobiology, 34*(3), 125–129.

CHAPTER 8

Considerations in the Cross-Cultural Assessment of Functional Abilities

Mariana Cherner

The need to assess disability in persons of diverse cultural backgrounds continues to increase, both as a result of immigration patterns around the world as well as the impetus to transfer available technologies from developed countries to more resource-limited settings. Occupational scientists have devoted significant effort to developing awareness about the delivery of culturally competent rehabilitation services, making care providers cognizant of potential mismatches between the professional and the patient with regard to health-related views, generalizability of activities of daily living, nonverbal communication, and cultural norms (see, e.g., Jezewski & Sotnik, 2001, for a listing of issues and resources pertinent to rehabilitation settings). Similarly, work in cultural psychology and psychiatry, as well as medical anthropology, highlights cultural and sociodemographic differences in the understanding of health, disease, and disability (James & Foster, 1999; Reynolds Whyte & Ingstad, 1995; Truscott, 2000; van der Geest & Reis, 2002). In neuropsychology we have been concerned with the applicability of cognitive assessment methods that were developed and validated primarily in the Western world, and most often in English, to other populations. Increasingly, neuropsychologists have also been interested in the correspondence between performance on cognitive tests and "real-world" functioning, as the latter is not only of practical interest but also a requisite for diagnosing most types of dementing disorders.

Efforts to adapt functional assessment instruments for use across different populations have led investigators to address certain basic dimensions that determine equivalence between the original instrument and the adapted one. These dimensions pertain primarily to aspects of construct validity. Once construct validity can be reasonably demonstrated, then the resulting instrument is ready for pilot testing, which may lead to further adjustments. Next, the psychometric properties of the instrument should be examined, leading to other potential adjustments, and finally the instrument can be subjected to norming with representative samples of interest.

209

The Adaptation Process

Effective adaptations are accomplished by successive approximation. "Adaptation," in this context, is the overall process of making an instrument appropriate for use in a setting that is different from its original. This may involve translation into another language, translation into regional variants of the same language, and/or replacing certain concepts in an instrument to harmonize with a different cultural, regional, or linguistic context. The section that follows uses translation into a new language to detail the iterative process required to achieve a sound instrument, but the steps involved apply to other mentioned aspects of adaptation and are reflected in the subsequent sections on construct validity.

Translation

When translation is required, the method of forward translation into the new language or variant followed by back translation into the original language (typically English) had been advocated by many as necessary to achieve an accurate translation (Brislin, 1970). However, arguably more critical steps are required in order to obtain a usable instrument. First, the translation needs to be performed and subsequently examined by truly bilingual individuals with relevant expertise (e.g., neuropsychologists, medical professionals, occupational therapists) who can determine linguistic and conceptual equivalence and make adjustments to the original translation, as needed. Bonomi and colleagues (Bonomi et al., 1996) exemplify the use of these strategies in their translation of the English version of the Functional Assessment of Cancer Therapy (FACT) into six European languages. In this case, two professional translators produced the first translation to the target language. Then a third independent translator was used to reconcile the two versions, and a fourth translator performed the back translation into English. Next, a panel of three to four bilingual health professionals evaluated the translations and resolved any discrepancies. Finally, the newly translated scales were pretested on a small cohort of the target population to ensure their comprehensibility and make any final changes. These methods are echoed in the findings of a task force appointed by the International Society for Pharmacoeconomics and Outcomes Research (ISPOR), which reviewed a number of methods employed by several organizations and distilled a 10-step set of guidelines for the translation and adaptation of patient-reported outcome measures (Wild et al., 2005): (1) preparation, (2) forward translation, (3) reconciliation, (4) back translation, (5) back-translation review, (6) harmonization among multiple language versions and the original instrument, (7) "cognitive debriefing" by testing the instrument on a relevant target group, (8) review of the cognitive debriefing results and finalization, (9) proofreading, and (10) producing a final report detailing the adaptation process. In their review of standards for the development of cross-cultural quality-of-life instruments, Schmidt and Bullinger (2003) also add that the preparation stage should include literature review and focus groups with the aim of arriving at suitable test items, which are then pared down after pilot testing and cognitive debriefing. Additionally, the interval properties and item response characteristics of the resulting scales need to be ascertained, along with their psychometric properties of reliability and validity. Finally, these authors advocate norming the instrument with a representative sample of the target population.

A great deal of literature already exists regarding the translation of psychological instruments, the details of which are beyond the scope of this chapter. The reader is referred to the International Test Commission (*www.intestcom.org*) and the associated *International Journal of Testing* (*www.leaonline.com/loi/ijt*) to keep abreast of developing guidelines on cross-cultural test adaptation and administration, as well as discussions on statistical methods derived from item response theory, such as Rasch analysis (Lundgren-Nilsson et al., 2005; Tennant, McKenna, & Hagell, 2004), designed to address the psychometric equivalence of adapted instruments. These issues are not covered in the present chapter, which instead focuses on construct validity.

Ascertaining Construct Validity

Construct validity is paramount in the application of instruments that assess daily functioning. If our goal is to determine the level of specific functional abilities, say, for vocational placement, then we would be interested in knowing whether a person has the requisite skills in an absolute sense. In such a case, cultural differences are not of interest. For example, does the person have sufficient manual dexterity and visuospatial skills to work in an assembly line? The criterion for what constitutes sufficient ability will be indexed by the specific requirements of the job and (ideally) by the minimum level of ability of others already performing that job successfully. On the other hand, if we are interested in understanding whether someone with acquired cognitive deficits is suffering declines in his or her ability to live independently, then we need methods for capturing everyday functioning that are culturally and sociodemographically relevant for that individual.

In their adaptation of the Functional Assessment of Chronic Illness Therapy (FACIT), Lent, Hahn, Eremenco, Webster, and Cella (1999) suggested five components of instrument equivalency: (1) *semantic*: the meaning of stimulus items is the same; (2) *content*: the items' relevance to each culture is intact; (3) *concept*: the items measure the same theoretical construct; (4) *criterion*: the adapted and original items show similar properties when compared against a standardized measurement; and (5) *technical*: the method of assessment results in comparable cultural measurement. A variation of this scheme refers to component 4 as "item equivalence" and divides component 5 into "operational equivalence," referring to the comparability of the measurement methods across cultures, and "measurement equivalence," referring to the interpretability of results across cultures (Schmidt & Bullinger, 2003). In a similar vein, a cross-cultural applicability research (CAR) effort led by the World Health Organization (WHO) and the U.S. National Institutes of Health (NIH) addressed both the cultural relativity of disability constructs and the psychometric requirements for the development of cross-cultural instruments to measure disability and adaptive functioning (Üstün, Chatterji, Bickenbach, Trotter, & Saxena, 2001). This group focused on obtaining equivalency in three dimensions for a revision of the WHO International Classification of Impairments, Disabilities, and Handicaps (ICIDH; WHO, 1980), now called the International Classification of Functioning, Disability, and Health (ICF; WHO, 2001). The dimensions identified were (1) *functional equivalence*: the degree to which domains of activities can be identified that serve similar functions across different cultures; (2) *conceptual equivalence*: whether concepts of disability are understood similarly across cultures; and (3) *metric equivalence*: the degree to which measured constructs exhibit similar measurement characteristics in different cultures. In order to arrive at these components of cultural applicability, CAR investigators from 15 different countries attempted to identify (1) whether the domains, subdomains, and individual items of the original English-language instrument corresponded to concepts in the local culture; (2) whether the domains, subdomains, and individual items were readily translatable, or whether a new English term needed to be adopted to facilitate translation; (3) whether the instrument's components were applicable across sociodemographic groups within a culture; and (4) whether the instrument fit the needs and practices of institutions in the culture.

Although the language used to describe components of instrument adaptation differ somewhat across authors, all point to ascertaining construct validity by ensuring that instruments applied cross-culturally make sense linguistically, are conceptually understood, and have practical relevance in the culture, starting with whether the assessment process itself is comprehended in the culture. In large measure these aspects of instrument construction apply not only to determining equivalency between an existing instrument and its cross-culturally adapted counterpart, but also when attempting to construct new instruments to measure adaptive functioning in a particular cultural context.

Linguistic Appropriateness

One aspect of cultural and sociodemographic relevance, and among the first steps in the adaptation process, is accomplishing linguistic appropriateness. At its most basic, linguistic appropriateness requires that the words used in instructions and stimulus items be understandable by the person being evaluated. This requirement obliges those constructing or adapting a measure to be familiar with language use in the target population across educational level, social class, gender, geographic region, or any other stratification that may apply to that group. For example, the meaning of words can vary among Spanish speakers of different national origin. If a task required following instructions to bake a cake, the translation of "cake" for an Argentine population would be "*torta*." However, this means "sandwich" in Mexico, so for that group the translation would have to be "*pastel*." In addition, regional, educational, or social class differences in language use also typically exist within the same country. For instance, because the names of food and dishes are often regionally bound, it may be challenging to construct a linguistically neutral and generalizable activities of daily living (ADL) instrument that uses food-related stimuli. This can also be the case with the names of medical conditions that a patient may be required to report. The case of food and illness names additionally illustrates possible influences of formal education and life experience within the same country or ethnic group, as it can be expected that individuals with greater education and affluence would be familiar with a broader range of food choices, formal medical terms, and other mainstream experiences. Thus, special care needs to be taken to accomplish translations and adaptations that are linguistically neutral and generalizable to as many variants of the target population as possible. Loewenstein and colleagues (Loewenstein, Arguelles, Barker, & Duara, 1993) give good examples of this process in their adaptation of neuropsychological and functional assessments for Spanish speakers in South Florida, where the investigators had to be aware of idioms that are prevalent, for example, among Spanish speakers of Cuban descent but unfamiliar to Hispanics from other parts of the world. For instance, the term *"moros y cristianos"* (Moors and Christians) is the name of a typical Cuban dish of rice and beans. In Spain, however, this term denotes the holiday commemorating the *Reconquista*, or the Moorish occupation of the Iberian peninsula that began in the 8th century and their eventual ouster by the Christians lasting through the 15th century.

Conceptual Equivalence

The other challenge of linguistic appropriateness when adapting existing instruments is achieving conceptual equivalence in the translation. Often, words that correspond to a literal translation from the English do not convey the intended meaning. As an example, when translating the FACT, Bonomi and colleagues (1996) found that in the item "I am proud of how I am coping with my illness," the expression of pride was viewed negatively by Norwegian respondents. As a result of input from physicians and patients, the phrase "proud of" was instead translated as the more acceptable "satisfied with." Equally, certain concepts or expressions that are common in English may not have close equivalents in another language, such as the item "I am full of pep" from the Profile of Mood Scales (McNair, Lorr, Heuchert, & Droppleman, 1971). For the interested reader, the vicissitudes of achieving conceptual equivalence are demonstrated in the efforts to adapt the SF-36, which are detailed in a special issue of the *Journal of Clinical Epidemiology* (Wagner et al., 1998; *www.SF-36.org*). The SF-36 is the short form of the Medical Outcomes Study (MOS) Health Survey (Stewart, Ware, Sherbourne, & Wells, 1992), a self-report health symptom inventory that has been translated for use in more than a dozen countries and multiple languages. During the process of adapting this questionnaire, teams of investigators in each country rated the difficulty of translating every item and offered their final wording for discussion within a panel of SF-36 experts to determine that conceptual equivalence was accomplished.

Ecological Validity

As demonstrated by the WHO adaptation of the ICF (Üstün et al., 2001), conceptual equivalence does not apply only to language use, but is also dependent on conceptions of health and illness as well as mental and physical limitations across cultures. Thus, the construct validity of an instrument is threatened if it requires respondents to make judgments or attributions about their cognitive or physical capacities that they are not accustomed to making. Whether the instrument measures dependence in ADLs by self- or other-report, clinician's observation, or direct assessment of performance, the items being measured need to be representative of individuals' experience in order to be meaningful. Therefore, in addition to the linguistic aspects mentioned, the construct validity of a measure of everyday functioning depends also on its ecological validity.

In developing an ADL scale for use with Thai older adults with dementia, Senan-arong and colleagues (2003) included certain culturally specific items that exemplify ecological validity, such as hiring a taxi-boat, bicycling, and walking to the village. Fillenbaum and colleagues (1999) similarly included culturally relevant components of daily functioning when creating an ADL scale for a rural older adult Indian population, such as the ability to remember important local festivals. Some examples of cultural differences in the relevance of items assessing everyday functioning were encountered by Jitapunkul, Kamolratanakul, and Ebrahim (1994) when attempting to use the Office of Population Censuses and Surveys (OPCS) England disability scale with an older adult Thai population. They noted that certain subscales of the OPCS resulted in extremely large proportions of disability in this group. In particular, the face validity of certain items such as "feels the need to have someone present all the time" and "sometimes sits for hours doing nothing" could not be interpreted in the same way as with English populations, since these can be normal aspects of Thai life. Additionally, certain items that were meant to assess basic ADLs in Western cultures corresponded to extended ADLs in Thai culture. For instance, "climbing a flight of stairs" is considered a basic ambulation activity in Western scales, but since traditional Thai homes contain difficult-to-navigate ladders instead of stairs, this item needs to be considered an extended ADL.

Ecological or face validity can require attention even when the adaptation is between relatively similar cultures. During the adaptation of the SF-36 International Quality of Life Assessment into Swedish, certain items from the original English-language version had to be changed to improve face validity. These included changing "playing golf" to "walking in the forest or gardening," adapting the notion of "walking a block" to a distance in kilometers for rural populations, and noting that the effort and complexity of dressing oneself differs depending on the climate that is typical for that population (Wagner et al., 1998). To determine the ecological validity of items in measures of adaptive functioning, it is therefore also important to establish the degree of familiarity with the tasks or items to which a person is being asked to respond. This is critical when attempting to document declines in ADL independence and their relationship to cognitive functioning, as task familiarity is likely to affect responses independently of acquired neuropsychological impairment. For example, in certain traditional households, men across the socioeconomic spectrum may be unfamiliar with cooking or grocery shopping. The same may be true of women of very high socioeconomic status (SES) who might have service personnel to perform these tasks. Thus, persons fitting these descriptions might perform more poorly on a laboratory task of everyday functioning that requires preparing a meal, despite intact cognitive status. Similarly, very healthy people may have few opportunities to take medications; thus, sicker people may do better at a medication management task. SES could also influence performance on such a task, as indigent people may have had fewer opportunities to take medications.

Another aspect of ecological validity pertains to familiarity with the manner in which responses are to be obtained. A clear and simple example of this is the inappropriateness of requiring an illiterate person to select a response from a number of written questionnaire items. A less obvious instance of adjustments required to maintain ecological validity is demonstrated by the work Baltussen and colleagues (Baltussen, Sanon, Sommerfeld, & Wurthwein, 2002), who found the need to adapt a visual analog scale (VAS) to measure burden of disease among low-educated residents in rural Burkina Faso, West Africa. As the metric properties of the traditional VAS were unfamiliar in this population, the authors employed a finite number of wooden blocks with which respondents could express their valuation of a number of disease states.

Finally, after considering linguistic appropriateness, conceptual equivalence, and ecological validity, the resulting instrument needs to be tested with a pilot sample from the target population to ensure that it is understood and received as intended. At this stage, additional adjustments can be made based on feedback from the respondents. Only then should the other psychometric properties of the final instrument be subjected to examination, such as criterion validity, internal consistency, and reliability. Figure 8.1 summarizes the goals and steps required for the successful adaptation of measures for use across diverse cultural or linguistic settings.

Experiences in Adapting Direct Observation Measures of Daily Functioning from English to Spanish

Direct observation of ADL performance requires measuring everyday behaviors in the individual's environment or recreating common activities in a laboratory setting. The latter is more amenable to standardization and quantification, making it more useful for research and outcomes-based clinical care. This section illustrates the application of the concepts discussed earlier by showing the process of adaptation of laboratory measures of daily functioning for use with Spanish speakers from the U.S.–Mexico border region.

Faced with the need to evaluate functional status in monolingual Spanish speakers with HIV in San Diego, California, my colleagues and I at the HIV Neurobehavioral Research Center (HNRC) undertook the adaptation of a battery of tests of everyday functioning that has shown relationships to HIV-associated cognitive impairment among English speakers (Heaton et al., 2004; Marcotte et al., 1999). This battery assesses a number of instrumental activities of daily living (IADLs) by direct observation in the laboratory and also includes reports of everyday functioning outside of the laboratory, ranging from subjective ratings of disability and life quality to verifiable information such as automobile driving record. The direct assessment measures conducted in the laboratory include basic (e.g., identifying currency, making change) and advanced (e.g., paying bills, staying within a budget) financial management, grocery shopping, cooking, ordering and paying for a meal at a restaurant, medication management exercises, a manualized and computerized assessment of job aptitude. With the exception of tests borrowed from the Direct Assessment of Functional Status (DAFS—Loewenstein & Bates, 1992; Loewenstein, Rubert, Arguelles, & Duara, 1995), which were already available in Spanish, all of our functional measures were first translated into Spanish by a master's level linguist and experienced psychometrist under the supervision of a bilingual neuropsychologist. Then they back-translated by another bilingual neuropsychologist. Next, the translated measures were circulated among Spanish speakers with neuropsychological experience (psychologists and psychometricians) from five different regions (Argentina, Colombia, Mexico, Puerto Rico, and Spain; these were selected by convenience, but additional input would be

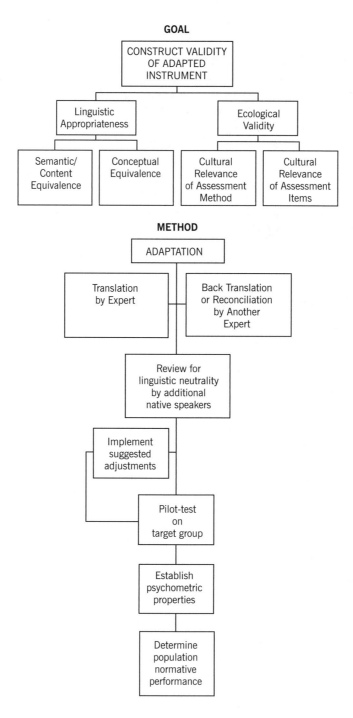

FIGURE 8.1. Schematic of the goals and methods for accomplishing appropriate cross-cultural and cross-linguistic adaptations. The goal is to accomplish construct validity by ensuring that adapted instruments are linguistically equivalent and have cultural relevance. The methodology to accomplish these goals requires adaptation by experts, which may include translation, with iterative adjustment and harmonization by additional experts as well as feedback from pilot testing. Psychometric properties and equivalence with the original instrument need to be established before the adapted instrument is applied. Normative performance in the population also needs to be determined to interpret performance in patient groups.

sought if the measures were to be used in countries not represented) to elicit appropriate refinements so that we could make the final measures as linguistically neutral as possible. At this step in the adaptation we also made certain contextual changes to fit our target population, which, in this case were comprised Spanish-speaking immigrants of Mexican origin. As a simple example, for a task that requires ordering a meal at a restaurant, we replaced the English menu items with items listed on the menu of an actual Mexican restaurant in the area.

The next step in our adaptation process was to pilot the resulting measures on a group of Spanish-speaking study participants to gather feedback about the quality of the translation as well as the ecological validity of the exercises and questionnaires in the battery. Based on this feedback, we made a number of modifications to the original measures in order to make the functional assessments more culturally relevant and appropriate. The modifications were designed to change the cultural context of the task without altering the requisite abilities (Rivera Mindt et al., 2003).

For example, we discovered that few participants used checks or checkbooks in their daily lives; therefore, for a section on financial management, we changed the task such that "utility bills" were paid in cash rather than with checks, and the checkbook balancing task was replaced with having to figure the balance remaining on a phone card. For a cooking task, we learned from our pilot participants that few used a microwave oven, as was required in the original English-language exercise. We therefore modified the task to use a hotplate as a stove top, and it had a positive reception. Although the details of the tasks were adapted, the calculations or abilities required to complete each exercise remained the same. Likewise, the scoring schemes and ranges of possible scores for the various measures were unchanged in order to preserve equivalence with the English versions, as much as possible, and facilitate comparisons.

In certain clinical or research settings, it is of interest to identify economic losses associated with unemployment or job changes related to an illness or disability. Among immigrant or displaced populations, factors other than disability may account for changes to lower levels of vocational functioning. These might include lack of language proficiency, unavailability of documentation pertaining to professional qualifications or permission to work, and barriers to the transference of professional degrees and licenses obtained abroad. Thus, in our adaptation of a self-report employment questionnaire that includes a complete work history, highest vocational attainment, earned income, and degree of responsibility at work, we make a distinction between employment in the United States *versus* in the country of origin. Additionally, we obtain the participants' own assessments of whether they are employed in accordance with their capabilities, and if not, their perception of reasons for this.

Because participants are likely to have different levels of familiarity with certain activities, each task in our battery is followed by a graded 5-point classification of familiarity to determine the frequency with which the task is encountered in daily life. This information can then be used to examine the influence of familiarity on task performance. Additionally, since our target population is an immigrant sample, we have also included a multidimensional acculturation scale (Hazuda, Haffner, Stern, & Eifler, 1988) to help discern the influence of acculturative factors on task performance. Such information helps to confirm the ecological validity of the battery in this population. In addition to the laboratory tasks, we also included self-report measures of daily functioning, from which we can derive information on concurrent validity. As of the writing of this chapter, this validation and standardization study was still in the data-gathering phase. The performance of healthy Spanish speakers is to be used to describe the psychometric properties of the battery, such as test–retest reliability, and an HIV-positive group will serve to partially validate the battery by showing its sensitivity to HIV-associated dysfunction. Preliminary results suggest that performance on the resulting functional battery is related to cognitive status among Spanish speakers with HIV (Cherner et al., 2006; Suarez et al., 2008).

Conclusions

Awareness of the need for culturally appropriate instruments is becoming widespread among the various disciplines that deal with measurement of disability and functional independence. Substantial gains have been made in the development of parameters to guide the adaptation and construction of instruments for use across diverse cultural contexts, all with the aim of creating measures that have sound construct and psychometric properties. A number of widely used instruments, primarily self-report questionnaires that survey ADLs within other aspects of disability and health functioning, have been systematically adapted for use in multiple linguistic and cultural contexts, and their psychometric properties have been investigated. Such work is invaluable because it allows for potential comparisons of the functional impact of various health-related states across the world. A number of less well-known instruments has also been created for use with specific populations, with methodologies and validation procedures that are not as consistently described. In order to compare the relationship between cognitive status and everyday functioning in diverse populations, not only do the ADL measurements need to be standardized and subjected to psychometric rigor, but also neuropsychological tests need to be appropriately adapted and normed for the groups on which they will be used.

Significant work remains in the area of direct assessment of function. This method has intrinsic appeal, as it yields the most proximal observation of actual ability. A number of standardized batteries exists (Moore, Palmer, Patterson, & Jeste, 2007), but very little has been reported on the applicability of these measurements in diverse populations, either across the world or among ethnocultural groups within the same country (Jeste et al., 2005; Loewenstein et al., 1992). With this type of assessment, it may be challenging to create instruments that are universally equivalent. There may in fact be few activities of everyday functioning that can be standardized across cultures or sociodemographic groups with vastly different daily living experiences, such as, say, Japanese business executives and indigenous residents of the Orinoco river region. Such cross-group comparisons may need to be restricted to populations with similar ranges of industrialization and literacy, but the challenge is open to tackle the creation of these kinds of measurements. In principle, it should be possible to arrive at conceptual-level categories of daily functioning (e.g., procuring nourishment, maintaining shelter, engaging in commerce) that could be agreed are universally applicable to humans. The WHO ICF (2001) is an example of such an attempt.

In sum, the generation of culturally appropriate and equivalent instruments is possible and desirable for the purpose of comparing effects of interest across populations. There will be cases where the human experience is so dissimilar that sufficient equivalence among instruments cannot be accomplished. Conceptually, however, ecologically valid methods can be devised to measure the functional impact of illness and brain dysfunction *within* a population, even when cross-group comparisons are challenging.

Moreover, although this perspective remains to be tested empirically, I would like to suggest that direct assessment of functional abilities may be the best indicator of cognitive status in persons with little or no formal education, where our traditional neuropsychological tests may be less informative, as long as tasks can be designed that are ecologically valid for the individual.

Acknowledgments

I wish to acknowledge the contributions of Daniel Barron, BS, Monica Rivera Mindt, PhD, Paola Suárez, MA, Margarita Padilla-Vélez, PhD, and Carolina Posada, BA, in the writing of this chapter.

References

Baltussen, R. M., Sanon, M., Sommerfeld, J., & Wurthwein, R. (2002). Obtaining disability weights in rural Burkina Faso using a culturally adapted visual analogue scale. *Health Econ*, 11(2), 155–163.

Bonomi, A. E., Cella, D. F., Hahn, E. A., Bjordal, K., Sperner-Unterweger, B., Gangeri, L., et al. (1996). Multilingual translation of the Functional Assessment of Cancer Therapy (FACT) quality of life measurement system. *Qual Life Res*, 5(3), 309–320.

Brislin, R. W. (1970). Back-translation for cross-cultural research. *J Cross Cult Psychol*, 1, 185–216.

Cherner, M., Suarez, P. A., Dawes, S. E., Rivera Mindt, M., Marcotte, T. D., Heaton, R. K., et al. (2006). Relationship between cognitive deficits and performance on tests of everyday functioning in HIV+ Spanish speakers: Preliminary results. *J Int Neuropsychol Soc*, S1, 57.

Fillenbaum, G. G., Chandra, V., Ganguli, M., Pandav, R., Gilby, J. E., Seaberg, E. C., et al. (1999). Development of an activities of daily living scale to screen for dementia in an illiterate rural older population in India. *Age Ageing*, 28(2), 161–168.

Hazuda, H. P., Haffner, S. M., Stern, M. P., & Eifler, C. W. (1988). Effects of acculturation and socioeconomic status on obesity and diabetes in Mexican Americans. The San Antonio Heart Study. *Am J Epidemiol*, 128(6), 1289–1301.

Heaton, R. K., Marcotte, T. D., Mindt, M. R., Sadek, J., Moore, D. J., Bentley, H., et al. (2004). The impact of HIV-associated neuropsychological impairment on everyday functioning. *J Int Neuropsychol Soc*, 10(3), 317–331.

James, K. C., & Foster, S. D. (1999). Weighing up disability. *Lancet*, 354, 87–88.

Jeste, N. D., Moore, D. J., Goldman, S. R., Bucardo, J., Davila-Fraga, W., Golshan, S., et al. (2005). Predictors of everyday functioning among older Mexican Americans vs. Anglo-Americans with schizophrenia. *J Clin Psychiatry*, 66(10), 1304–1311.

Jezewski, M. A., & Sotnik, P. (2001). *Culture brokering: Providing culturally competent rehabilitation services to foreign-born persons.* Buffalo: Center for International Rehabilitation Research Information and Exchange, State University of New York at Buffalo.

Jitapunkul, S., Kamolratanakul, P., & Ebrahim, S. (1994). The meaning of activities of daily living in a Thai elderly population: Development of a new index. *Age Ageing, 23*(2), 97–101.

Lent, L., Hahn, E., Eremenco, S., Webster, K., & Cella, D. (1999). Using cross-cultural input to adapt the Functional Assessment of Chronic Illness Therapy (FACIT) scales. *Acta Oncol, 38*(6), 695–702.

Loewenstein, D., Ardila, A., Rosselli, M., Hayden, S., Duara, R., Berkowitz, N., et al. (1992). A comparative analysis of functional status among Spanish- and English-speaking patients with dementia. *J Gerontol, 47*(6), P389–P394.

Loewenstein, D., Arguelles, T., Barker, W., & Duara, R. (1993). A comparative analysis of neuropsychological test performance of Spanish-speaking and English-speaking patients with Alzheimer's disease. *J Gerontol, 48*(3), P142–P149.

Loewenstein, D., & Bates, B. (1992). *Manual for administration and scoring the Direct Assessment of Functional Status scale for older adults (DAFS).* Miami Beach, FL: Mount Sinai Medical Center.

Loewenstein, D., Rubert, M. P., Arguelles, T., & Duara, R. (1995). Neuropsychological test performance and prediction of functional capacities among Spanish-speaking and English-speaking patients with dementia. *Arch Clin Neuropsychol, 10*(2), 75–88.

Lundgren-Nilsson, A., Grimby, G., Ring, H., Tesio, L., Lawton, G., Slade, A., et al. (2005). Cross-cultural validity of functional independence measure items in stroke: A study using Rasch analysis. *J Rehabil Med, 37*(1), 23–31.

Marcotte, T. D., Heaton, R. K., Wolfson, T., Taylor, M. J., Alhassoon, O., Arfaa, K., et al. (1999). The impact of HIV-related neuropsychological dysfunction on driving behavior. The HNRC Group. *J Int Neuropsychol Soc, 5*(7), 579–592.

McNair, D. M., Lorr, M., Heuchert, J. W. P., & Droppleman, L. F. (1971). *Profile of Mood States (POMS).* North Tonawanda, NY: Multi-Health Systems.

Moore, D. J., Palmer, B. W., Patterson, T. L., & Jeste, D. V. (2007). A review of performance-based measures of functional living skills. *J Psychiatr Res, 41,* 97–118.

Reynolds Whyte, S., & Ingstad, B. (Eds.). (1995). *Disability and culture.* Berkeley and Los Angeles: University of California Press.

Rivera Mindt, M., Cherner, M., Marcotte, T. D., Moore, D. J., Bentley, H., Esquivel, M. M., et al. (2003). The functional impact of HIV-associated neuropsychological impairment in Spanish-speaking adults: A pilot study. *J Clin Exp Neuropsychol, 25*(1), 122–132.

Schmidt, S., & Bullinger, M. (2003). Current issues in cross-cultural quality of life instrument development. *Arch Phys Med Rehabil, 84*(4 Suppl. 2), S29–S34.

Senanarong, V., Harnphadungkit, K., Prayoonwiwat, N., Poungvarin, N., Sivasariyanonds, N., Printarakul, T., et al. (2003). A new measurement of activities of daily living for Thai elderly with dementia. *Int Psychogeriatr, 15*(2), 135–148.

Stewart, A. L., Ware, J. E., Sherbourne, C. D., & Wells, K. B. (1992). Psychological distress/well-being and cognitive functioning measures. In A. L. Stewart & J. E. Ware (Eds.), *Measuring functioning and well-being: The medical outcomes study approach* (pp. 102–142). Durham, NC: Duke University Press.

Suarez, P., Dawes, S., Rivera Mindt, M., Marcotte, T., Grant, I., Heaton, R., et al. (2008). Performance on tests of everyday functioning in Spanish speakers with and without HIV infection. *J Int Neuropsych Soc, 14*(S1), 68. Retrieved from *http://journals.cambridge. org/action/displayIssue?jid=INS&volumeId=14&issueId=S1.*

Tennant, A., McKenna, S. P., & Hagell, P. (2004). Application of Rasch analysis in the development and application of quality of life instruments. *Value Health, 7*(Suppl. 1), S22–S26.

Truscott, D. J. (2000). Cross-cultural ranking of IADL skills. *Ethn Health, 5*(1), 67–78.

Üstün, T. B., Chatterji, S., Bickenbach, J. E., Trotter, R. T., & Saxena, S. (2001). Disability and cultural variation: The ICIDH-2 cross-cultural applicability research study. In T. B. Üstün, S. Chatterji, J. Bickenbach, R. Trotter, R. Room, & S. Saxena (Eds.), *Disability and culture: Universalism and diversity* (pp. 3–19). Seattle, WA: Hogrefe & Huber for the World Health Organization.

van der Geest, S., & Reis, R. (2002). Ethnocentrism and medical antrhopology. In S. v. d. Geest & R. Reis (Eds.), *Ethnocentrism: Reflections on medical antrhopology* (pp. x–23). Amsterdam: Aksant.

Wagner, A. K., Gandek, B., Aaronson, N. K., Acquadro, C., Alonso, J., Apolone, G., et al. (1998). Cross-cultural comparisons of the content of SF-36 translations across 10 countries: Results from the IQOLA Project. International Quality of Life Assessment. *J Clin Epidemiol, 51*(11), 925–932.

Wild, D., Grove, A., Martin, M., Eremenco, S., McElroy, S., Verjee-Lorenz, A., et al. (2005). Principles of good practice for the translation and cultural Adaptation Process for Patient-Reported Outcomes (PRO) Measures: Report of the ISPOR Task Force for Translation and Cultural Adaptation. *Value Health, 8*(2), 94–104.

World Health Organization. (1980). *International Classification of Impairment, Disability and Handicap: ICIDH*. Geneva: Author.

World Health Organization. (2001). *International Classification of Functioning, Disability and Health: ICF*. Geneva: Author. Retrieved from *http://apps.who.int/classifications/icfbrowser/*.

PART II

EVERYDAY IMPACT OF NORMAL AGING AND NEUROPSYCHIATRIC DISORDERS

CHAPTER 9

The Impact of Cognitive Impairments on Health-Related Quality of Life

Robert M. Kaplan, Brent T. Mausbach, Thomas D. Marcotte, and Thomas L. Patterson

Diseases and their consequent disabilities are important for two reasons. First, illness may cause premature death. Second, diseases may cause dysfunctions, as well as other symptoms, that lead to disabilities in an individual's performance of usual activities of daily living. Biomedical studies typically refer to health outcomes in terms of mortality (death) and morbidity (dysfunction) and sometimes of symptoms (Kaplan, 1990). Cognitive dysfunction is an important form of disability that has been understudied in relation to quality of life. We focus on cognitive issues in this chapter. Although the effects of cognitive dysfunction can occur in many conditions, we focus on neurocognitive impairments resulting from human immunodeficiency virus (HIV), psychosis, and Alzheimer's disease.

Over the last 30 years, medical and health services researchers have developed new quantitative methods to assess health status. These measures are often called quality-of-life (QOL) measures. Since they are generally used exclusively to evaluate health status, we prefer the more descriptive term "health-related quality of life" (Kaplan & Bush, 1982).

Measurement of Health-Related QOL

Figure 9.1 summarizes the number of papers on quality of life identified in PubMed between 1972 and 2007. In 1972, PubMed did not identify any publications under the QOL topic heading. However, over the next 35 years, the number of articles that use the QOL key word grew dramatically. In 2007, PubMed identified 7,551 such articles. In 1 year, from 2006 to 2007, the number of articles listed under the QOL keyword grew by 16% (or 1,046 articles).

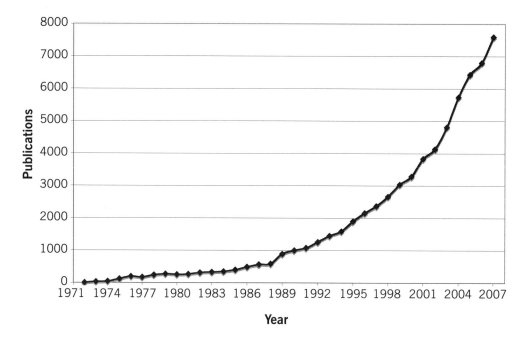

FIGURE 9.1. Quality-of-life publications in PubMed between 1972 and 2007.

There are a least three reasons for measuring QOL in clinical studies. First, QOL measures are used to quantify the impact of a condition and to compare the effects of diseases with the consequences of other chronic medical problems. Second, these measures can be used to evaluate changes resulting from clinical intervention over the course of disease. Third, QOL measures are necessary as a central component of cost-effectiveness analysis.

A wide variety of measures has been used to quantify health-related QOL (Bourbeau, Maltais, Rouleau, & Guimont, 2004; Dimitrov & Rumrill, 2005; Kaplan, Ries, Reilly, & Mohsenifar, 2004; Schmier, Halpern, Higashi, & Bakst, 2005). These measures are similar in that each expresses the effects of medical care in terms that can be reported directly by a patient. However, the rationales for the methods differ considerably.

Distinctions between Health QOL Measures

Table 9.1 lists some of the many methods for evaluating QOL outcomes and makes several distinctions between measures. There are two major approaches to QOL assessment: psychometric and decision theory. The psychometric approach is used to offer a profile summarizing different dimensions of QOL. The best known example of the psychometric tradition is the Medical Outcomes Study 36-Item Short Form (SF-36; Ware & Gandek, 1998). The decision theory approach attempts to weight the different dimensions of health in order to provide a single expression of health status. Supporters of this approach argue that psychometric methods fail to consider that different health problems are not of equal concern. A minor itch is a symptom, for example, as is coughing up blood. However, the importance of a minor itch and coughing blood is not equal. Simple symptom counts may miss the severity or impact of more serious complaints.

In an experimental trial using the psychometric approach, some aspects of QOL may improve whereas others get worse. For example, a medication might reduce coughing but increase skin problems or reduce energy. When components of outcome change in different directions, an overall subjective evaluation is often used to integrate the components and offer a summary of whether the patient is better or worse off. The decision theory approach provides an overall measure of QOL that integrates subjective function states, preferences for these states, morbidity, and mortality.

In addition to the distinction between psychometric and decision theory approaches, measures can be classified as either generic (top of Table 9.1) or disease targeted (bottom of Table 9.1). Generic measures can be used with any population, whereas disease-targeted measures are used with patients who have a particular diagnosis.

TABLE 9.1. Summary of Quality-of-Life Measures Used to Evaluate Outcomes in Adults

Measure	Type	Purposes
Generic measures		
SF-36 (Ware & Gandek, 1998)	Profile	Descriptive studies, clinical change
Sickness Impact Profile (SIP; Bergner, Bobbitt, Carter, & Gilson, 1981)	Profile	Descriptive studies, clinical change
Nottingham (Kaplan et al., 1998) Health Profile (NHP; Baro et al., 2006)	Profile	Descriptive studies, clinical change
Health Utilities Index (HUI; Feeny et al., 1999)	Decision theory	Descriptive studies, clinical change, cost effectiveness
EuroQol (EQ-5D; Kind, 1997)	Decision theory	Descriptive studies, clinical change, cost effectiveness
Quality of Well-Being Scale (QWB; Kaplan et al., 1989, 1998)	Decision theory	Descriptive studies, clinical change, cost effectiveness
Health and Activities Limitations Index (HALex; Gold, Franks, & Erickson, 1996)	Decision theory	Descriptive studies, clinical change, cost effectiveness
Disease-targeted measures		
National Eye Institute–25 Item Visual Functioning Questionnaire (NEI-VFQ-25; Mangione et al., 2001)	Profile	Descriptive studies, clinical change studies in vision and eye disease
Heart Failure Symptom Check list (HFSC; Grady, Jalowiec, Grusk, White-Williams, & Robinson, 1992; Grady & Lanuza, 2005)	Profile/symptom-specific	Descriptive studies, clinical change studies in heart failure
St. Georges Respiratory Questionnaire (SGRQ; Jones, Quirk, & Baveystock, 1991)	Profile	Descriptive studies, clinical change studies in chronic lung disease

Finally, measures can be divided by their uses. Most measures can be used to characterize populations and to study clinical changes. However, only generic, decision theory–based measures can be used to evaluate cost effectiveness. This chapter concentrates on a generic decision-based method that has been applied in a variety of studies, and, in particular, we address the potential impact of neuropsychological dysfunction on QOL.

Quality of Well-Being Scale

The general health policy model grew out of substantive theories in economics, psychology, medicine, and public health. This model includes components for mortality (death), morbidity (health-related QOL), and time. The rationale for the model is that diseases and disabilities are important for two reasons. First, illness may cause the life expectancy to be shortened. Second, illness may make life less desirable at times prior to death (health-related QOL) (Kaplan et al., 1995; Kaplan, Bush, & Berry, 1976; Kaplan & Groessl, 2002; Kaplan, Groessl, Sengupta, Sieber, & Ganiats, 2005; Kaplan & Ries, 2005).

Central to the general health policy model is a general conceptualization of QOL. The Quality of Well-Being (QWB) Scale is one method of measuring QOL for calculations in the model. The QWB is a preference-weighted measure combining three scales of functioning with a measure of symptoms and problems to produce a point-in-time expression of well-being that runs from 0 (for death) to 1.0 (for asymptomatic full function) (Kaplan, Ganiats, Sieber, & Anderson, 1998). The model separates health outcomes into distinct components. These are life expectancy (mortality), functioning (morbidity), preference for observed functional states (utility), and duration of stay in health states (prognosis). The morbidity component is the core of the QWB measures. In addition to classification into observable levels of function, individuals are also classified by their symptoms or problems. Symptoms, such as fatigue or a sore throat, might not be directly observable by others, whereas problems, such as a missing limb, might be noticeable by others. On any particular day, nearly 80% of the general population is optimally functional. However, over an interval of 7 days, only 12% experience no symptoms. Symptoms or problems may be severe, such as painful neuropathy, or minor, such as mild stomach discomfort after taking medication.

In order to obtain preference weights for observable health states, peer judges place the observable states of health and functioning onto a preference continuum ranging from 0 for death to 1.0 for completely well (Kaplan, Bush, & Berry, 1979). A quality-adjusted life year (QALY) is defined as the equivalent of a completely well year of life, or a year of life free of any symptoms, problems, or health-related disabilities (Kaplan et al., 1976). The well-life expectancy is the current life expectancy adjusted for diminished QOL associated with dysfunctional states and the durations of stay in each state (Bush & Zaremba, 1971). The model quantifies the health activity or treatment program in terms of the QALYs that it produces or saves.

The General Health Policy Model integrates components to express outcomes in a common measurement unit. Using information on current functioning and duration, it is possible to express the health outcomes in terms of QALYs. The model for point-in-time QWB is:

$$QWB = 1 - (\text{observed mobility} \times \text{mobility weight})$$
$$- (\text{observed physical activity} \times \text{physical activity weight})$$
$$- (\text{observed social activity} \times \text{social activity weight})$$
$$- (\text{observed symptom/problem} \times \text{symptom/problem weight})$$

$$QALY = QWB \times \text{duration in years}$$

The net cost–utility ratio is defined as

$$\frac{\text{Net cost}}{\text{Net QALYs}} = \frac{\text{Cost of treatment} - \text{cost of alternative}}{QALYsT - QALYdsC}$$

where QALYsT and QALYsC are the QALYs produced by treatment (T) and control (C) groups, respectively.

Alternative Versions of the QWB

There are currently two versions of the QWB, an interviewer-administered version and self-reported version. In 1996 the QWB was adapted to a self-administered form (QWB-SA). The current version of the QWB-SA can be printed on two sides of a single page and takes about 10 minutes to complete (Kaplan et al., 1998).

The development of new forms for the QWB has gone through several stages. First, a new list of symptoms and problems was developed. The current version of the QWB uses a list of 26 symptoms or problems; the QWB-SA has 59 symptoms. The improved symptoms assessment not only better reflects health status, it also more closely resembles a clinical review of symptoms, thus increasing the clinical utility of the QWB-SA. The QWB-SA has been shown to be highly correlated with the interviewer-administered QWB and to retain the psychometric properties (Kaplan, Sieber, & Ganiats, 1997). The QWB-SA should provide a better representation of HIV signs and symptoms; in addition, QWB preference weights have been validated in HIV-infected populations.

The QWB has been used in numerous clinical trials and studies to evaluate medical and surgical therapies in conditions such as chronic obstructive pulmonary disease (Kaplan, Atkins, & Timms, 1984), HIV (Kaplan et al., 1995; Kaplan, Patterson, et al., 1997), cystic fibrosis (Orenstein & Kaplan, 1991; Orenstein, Pattishall, Nixon, Ross, & Kaplan, 1990), diabetes mellitus (Kaplan, Hartwell, Wilson, & Wallace, 1987), atrial fibrillation (Ganiats, Palinkas, & Kaplan, 1992), lung transplantation (Squier et al., 1995), arthritis (Kaplan, Alcaraz, Anderson, & Weisman, 1996; Kaplan, Schmidt, & Cronan, 2000), end-stage renal disease (Rocco, Gassman, Wang, & Kaplan, 1997), cancer (Kaplan, 1993), depression (Pyne, Patterson, Kaplan, & Gillin, 1997; Pyne, Patterson, Kaplan, & Ho, 1997), and several other conditions (Kaplan et al., 1998). Furthermore, the method has been used for health resource allocation modeling and has served as the basis for an innovative experiment on the rationing of health care by the state of Oregon (Kaplan, 1994; Kaplan & California Policy Seminar, 1993). Studies have also demonstrated that the QWB is responsive to clinical change derived from surgery (Squier et al., 1995) and from medical conditions such as rheumatoid arthritis (Bombardier et al., 1986), AIDS (Kaplan et al., 1995), and cystic fibrosis (Orenstein et al., 1990).

General information about the QWB can be found at *qwbsa.ucsd.edu*.

The Relationship between Neurocognitive Dysfunction and Health-Related QOL

Generic QOL measures, such as the QWB, can be used with any patient group. Indeed such measures are now used to evaluate patients with nearly all medical conditions. In the following sections we offer three examples (HIV, schizophrenia, Alzheimer's disease) relating cognitive functioning to general QOL in clinical populations.

HIV-Related Neurocognitive Impairment

The diverse impacts of both HIV disease and its treatment require a general approach to assessment. Although there have been several previous attempts to evaluate QOL in HIV-infected patients, most focused only on psychological outcomes. A number of studies has attempted to characterize the health status and economic impacts of HIV infection, although we are aware of only a few studies that have applied general health-related QOL scales (Lorenz, Cunningham, Spritzer, & Hays, 2006; Wu & Bailey, 1988; Wu, Hays, Kelly, Malitz, & Bozzette, 1997). There have been many studies on QOL in HIV (Crystal, Fleishman, Hays, Shapiro, & Bozzette, 2000; Cunningham, Crystal, Bozzette, & Hays, 2005; Lorenz et al., 2006), and many of these papers have appeared recently (Bolge, Mody, Ambegaonkar, McDonnell, & Zilberberg, 2007; Howland et al., 2007; Maserati et al., 2007; Preau et al., 2007; Protopopescu et al., 2007; Shalit, True, & Thommes, 2007). However, few of the studies use measures appropriate for the evaluation of new therapies, including highly active antiretroviral therapy (HAART) (Maserati et al., 2007). Aggressive new therapies require new approaches to evaluation because they may cause short-term reductions in QOL in order to enhance long-term survival. Few assessment methods consider the effects of treatment over the course of time.

Diverse Effects of HIV on Everyday Functioning

We examined data from 400 HIV-positive and 114 HIV-uninfected men enrolled in a longitudinal study at the University of California, San Diego (UCSD) HIV Neurobehavioral Research Center (HNRC), a collaborative investigation of UCSD Naval Hospital in San Diego and the San Diego Veterans Affairs Medical Center. Demographic characteristics of the participants are summarized in Table 9.2. The controls were slightly better educated, and there were fewer African Americans in the control group. No member of the control group had an HIV-related diagnosis.

All participants received a comprehensive medical, neurological, and neuropsychological evaluation (see Heaton et al., 1994, for details). The information from the neurological examinations (sensation, motor function, reflexes, alertness, and concentration) was grouped into summary clinical ratings for central nervous system (CNS) and peripheral nervous system functioning, ranging from 1 for unimpaired to

TABLE 9.2. Summary of Demographic Characteristics for Controls and HIV-Positive Participants

	Controls (n = 114)		HIV-positive (n = 400)		p-value
Socioeconomic status (5-point scale, 1 lowest, 5 highest)	Mean	(SD)	Mean	(SD)	
	3.7	(1.1)	3.8	(1.0)	$p < .6$
Education (years)	Mean	(SD)	Mean	(SD)	
	14.8	(2.1)	14.1	(2.1)	$p < .01$
Income (in U.S. dollars)	Mean	(SD)	Mean	(SD)	
	22,560	(20,785)	22,049	(16,047)	$p < .9$
Ethnicity	n	(%)	n	(%)	
American Indian	2	(1.8)	1	(0.3)	
African American	4	(3.5)	49	(12.3)	
Cuban			2	(0.5)	
Filipino			5	(1.3)	
Hispanic	6	(5.3)	21	(5.3)	
Latin American			1	(0.3)	
Mexican American			8	(2.0)	
Asian	2	(1.8)	1	(0.3)	
Pacific Islander			5	(1.3)	
Puerto Rican	2	(1.8)	1	(0.3)	
White	98	(86.0)	306	(76.5)	$p < .01$

Note. From Kaplan et al. (1995). Adapted with permission from the American Psychosomatic Society.

5 for high levels of impairment (Gulevich et al., 1992). In addition, the ratings of central (i.e., brain) impairment were studied. A psychiatric evaluation assessed emotional well-being both historically and currently using standardized measures, including the Profile of Mood States (POMS; NcNair, Lorr, & Droppleman, 1980) and the Beck Depression Scale (Beck, 1976).

Relation between Health-Related QOL and Neurological and Functional Status in HIV Infection

The QWB was associated with a variety of neurological ratings of CNS impairment. These ratings were provided by a clinical neurologist on the basis of structured neurological evaluations and nerve conduction studies. Higher ratings by the neurologist represent more impairment. There was a systematic relationship indicating that neurologist ratings of greater severity were associated with lower (closer to death) QWB scores (Figure 9.2).

HIV infection may have a wide variety of effects upon everyday functioning. One of the most important impacts is the inability or diminished ability to maintain gainful employment. One study in the pre-HAART era suggested that transition from HIV asymptomatic to HIV symptomatic status was associated with an estimated reduction in the rate of employment from 74 to 26%. Among the employed asymptomatic subjects, 44% earned more than $30,000 per year, whereas only 21% of the employed patients with AIDS earned $30,000 or more (Wachtel et al., 1992).

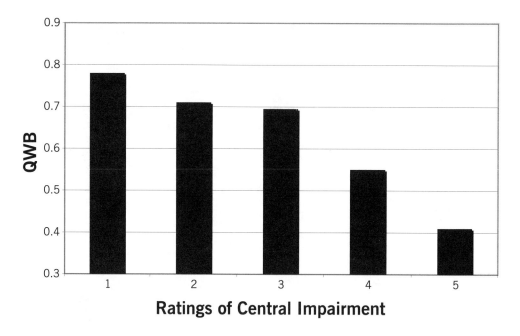

FIGURE 9.2. Relationship between neurologist global ratings of impairment and QWB scores. Based on Kaplan et al. (1995).

The disabling aspects of HIV disease become increasingly important as they affect work. In particular, it is important to allow the person with AIDS to continue to be productive in the workplace as long as he or she has the functional capacity to do so; some studies have indicated that once HIV-infected individuals stop working, they are unlikely to return to work (Rabkin, 2004).

The HNRC study offered some of the first evidence suggesting that neurocognitive impairment is associated with employment status. Compared to cognitively normal HIV-positive participants, HIV-positive participants with neuropsychological impairment had higher rates of unemployment and subjective decreases in job-related abilities and work productivity, even after controlling for medical status (Heaton et al., 1994). Figure 9.3 shows the differences between estimated wages for HNRC participants who were unimpaired versus those who were impaired.

The relationship between neurocognitive functioning, employment, and the QWB is complex. Figure 9.4 summarizes the relationship between a neuropsychologist's global rating of functioning and a QWB score, indicating that as impairment increases, QOL is reduced. In further pilot investigation, a random sample of 100 HNRC participants was evaluated for recent changes in work status. The purpose of the study was to find real-life correlates of neuropsychological deficits. A group of 11 had a recent reduction in work time or had lost a job. These 11 were not different from the rest of the cohort on their most recent neuropsychological or blood chemistry measures. There were, however, significant differences on the QWB, but in the unexpected direction. Those who had reduced work or lost a job scored higher in QOL at the 1-year follow-up than the cohort as a whole (.850 vs. .735; $p < .003$) and

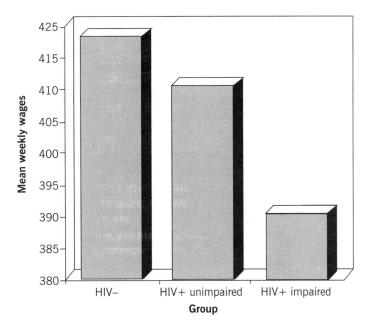

FIGURE 9.3. Differences between estimated wages for HNRC patients who were unimpaired versus those who were impaired. Error bars not shown because data are estimates.

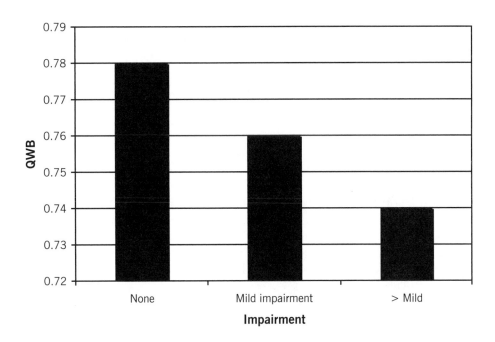

FIGURE 9.4. Relationship between a neuropsychologist's global rating of functioning and QWB score.

had improved QWB scores over the last year (+ .063), whereas the total cohort had declined slightly (–.009; $p < .07$). These findings may suggest that reducing demands associated with work may have some health benefits. We are hesitant to place much importance on these findings because there were only 11 patients in this group, and we are unable to determine whether other clinical or demographic characteristics might explain the differences in the QWB scores (Pyne et al., 2003).

Relationship between QOL and Psychological Functioning in HIV Infection

A variety of studies has demonstrated the validity of the QWB for assessing depression in patients with HIV disease. In one study ratings of depression using the Hamilton Depression Scale (HAM-D) were obtained from 285 HIV patients and 84 HIV-negative men who participated in the HNRC cohort. The data were obtained at baseline and 6 months later. Depression was defined as HAM-D scores greater than 10. The study demonstrated a systematic relationship between HAM-D scores and QWB scores at baseline ($t = 8.74$, $p < .001$). In addition, 22 HIV-positive subjects experienced increases of 10 points on the HAM-D Scale between 1- and 6-month evaluations. Significant reductions in QWB scores were observed for these individuals ($t = 2.62$, $p < .02$). Analyses of QWB symptoms suggested greater symptom severity among those whose HAM-D scores increased (Kaplan et al., 1997). In addition, there was a greater reduction in physical activity component of the QWB among those experiencing an increase in depression. In other words, mood was associated with both symptoms and physical function. One interpretation is that the physical symptoms of HIV/AIDS prevent or restrict people from engaging in preferred activities, which in turn causes depression. This model is supported among persons undergoing chemotherapy or radiation therapy for cancer (Williamson, 2000).

HIV-Associated Neurocognitive Disorders and Health-Related QOL

HIV-associated neurocognitive disorders (HAND) can range from subtle, "asymptomatic" deficits that do not affect everyday functioning to HIV-associated dementia (HAD), a severe and debilitating dementia that significantly affects activities of daily living (Antinori et al., 2007; Grant & Atkinson, 1995). In 2006 a workgroup ("Frascati Workgroup") was organized by the National Institute of Mental Health and National Institute of Neurological Diseases and Stroke, with the goal of revisiting the diagnostic criteria originally proposed by an American Academy of Neurology AIDS Task Force (American Academy of Neurology AIDS Task Force, 1991) to determine whether the criteria should be revised (based on clinical research and possible phenotypic changes seen over the last 15 years). The final criteria proposed by this group (Antinori et al., 2007) were consistent with those originally proposed by Grant, Heaton, and Atkinson (1995) and in use at the HNRC.

In order to examine the relationship between neurocognitive status and health-related QOL, we classified HIV-positive study participants into diagnostic categories consistent with the schema proposed by the Frascati Workgroup. To be considered "impaired," individuals must show cognitive impairment in at least two cognitive domains, such that a focal deficit in a single cognitive ability domain does not qualify as having "global" neurocognitive impairment. The primary criteria for determining whether an individual has a HAND (1) the presence of neuropsychological impairment and (2) whether these impairments impact everyday activities. In brief, a diagnosis of *asymptomatic neurocognitive impairment* (ANI) involves the presence of cognitive impairment, objectively determined via cognitive tests, which does not affect everyday functioning. *Mild neurocognitive disorder* (MND) requires objective evidence of neuropsychological impairments that cause noticeable difficulty in the execution of everyday activities. The criteria for HAD are similar, but require more severe cognitive impairment and marked disruption in everyday functions. In each of these diagnostic categories, the impairment, in the opinion of the diagnosing clinician, cannot be attributable to a comorbid condition and must represent a decline from previous functioning.

Figure 9.5 shows the relationship between diagnostic classification and QWB score. As the figure shows, the impact on health-related QOL is greatest in those who meet criteria for syndromic impairment; MND and HAD.

Self-Reported Cognitive Functioning and QWB in HIV Infection

Participants also completed the Patient's Assessment of Own Functioning Inventory (PAOFI; Chelune, Ferguson, Koon, & Dickey, 1986), a 41-item questionnaire in which participants report the frequency with which they experience problems with memory, language/communication, use of hands, sensory perception, and higher-level cognition. The questionnaire focuses on cognition. As seen in Figures 9.6–9.8, health-related QOL decreases as the number of cognitive problems increases. Figure 9.6

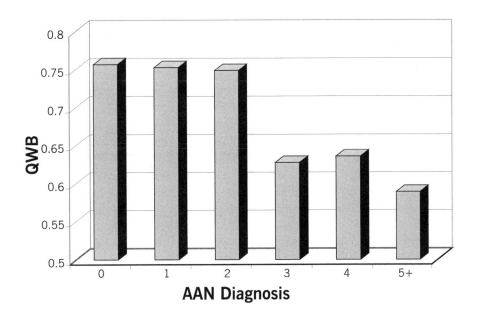

FIGURE 9.5. QWB by American Academy of Neurology diagnosis.

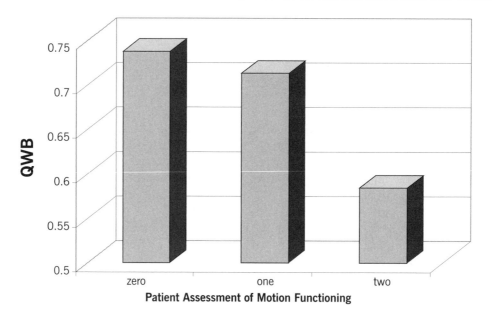

FIGURE 9.6. QWB patient assessment of motion functioning.

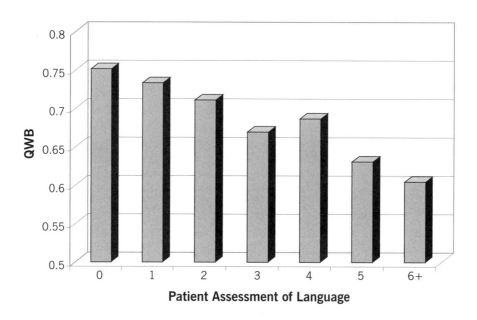

FIGURE 9.7. QWB by patient assessment of language.

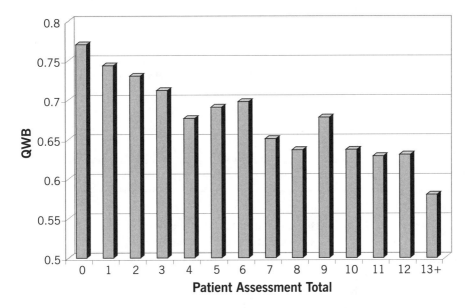

FIGURE 9.8. QWB by patient assessment total.

shows the relationship between self-reported motor functioning (difficulty feeling objects with one's hands and seeing things) and QWB scores. As seen in the figure, there is a systematic relationship between problems in perceptual–motor functioning and QWB, in that participants with two or more problems lose more than 15% of their QOL.

Figure 9.7 shows the relationship between language problems and QWB. Language was assessed using 10 items that asked about difficulties in understanding language, spoken communications, reading, and speaking, as well as thinking of names, retrieving names, writing, and spelling. There was a systematically negative correlation between these variables. Patients with no problems in language achieved QWB scores of nearly 0.75. As language problems increased, QWB scores decreased. For those reporting six or greater language problems, QWB scores were 0.60. In other words, there was nearly a 0.15 difference compared to those without problems. For each 6 years a person lives with a 0.15 deficit in self-assessed language, the equivalent of 1 year of life is lost.

Overall, there were 5 self-assessment scales and 33 individual items on the PAOFI. Figure 9.8 shows the relationship between total number of self-assessed problems and QWB scores. Those with no self-assessed problems have QWB scores of 0.77, whereas those with 13 or more self-assessed problems have QWB scores of only 0.57.

Relationship between Neurocognition and Overall Functioning in Middle-Aged and Older Adults with Psychosis

Atypical antipsychotic medications may have an important role in the management of symptoms in patients with schizophrenia. The overall importance of schizophrenia deserves attention because the disease is expensive in terms of treatment costs, loss of productivity, and public assistance expenditures (Ganguly, Kotzan, Miller, Kennedy, & Martin, 2004; Miller & Martin, 2004). Improved care of schizophrenia symptoms has resulted in a greater number of patients living in the community rather than in institutions. However, reductions in symptoms do not automatically result in an improved ability to function in the real world. In order to assess these issues, we used data from a specialized center at UCSD and the San Diego Veterans Affairs Medical Center. The center focuses on late-onset schizophrenia.

We conducted an analysis of the relationship between cognitive functioning and QWB scores among 240 middle-aged and older adults (mean age = 52.6 ± 7.4 years; range = 37–79 years) with schizophrenia or schizoaffective disorder. To be eligible, patients had to be 40 years or older and have a DSM-IV-based diagnosis of schizophrenia or schizoaffective disorder. Patients were excluded if they (1) had a DSM-IV diagnosis of dementia, (2) represented a serious suicide risk, (3) could not complete the assessment battery, or (4) were participating in any other psychosocial intervention or drug research at the time of intake. Participants were primarily male (64.4%) and residing in an assisted-living setting such as a board and care, nursing facility, or skilled nursing facility (71%). The remainder of participants resided in the community either alone (9%) or with a friend or family member (20%). At the time of their assessments, all participants were receiving medication treatment with typical and/ or atypical neuroleptics.

Functional outcomes were assessed using three measures. The first, called the UCSD Performance-Based Skills Assessment (Mausbach et al., 2007), requires participants to role-play a variety of complex situations involving management of finances, social and communications skills, transportation, and household chores. Participants are given a score in each functional area, and the sum of scores from each domain is the total score. Higher scores indicate better functioning. Global cognitive functioning was assessed using the Dementia Rating Scale (DRS). Symptoms of psychosis were assessed via the Positive and Negative Syndrome Scale (PANSS).

An analyses of 236 participants revealed a significant correlation between total DRS scores and the QWB scores ($r = .25$, $p < .001$), with lower QWB scores associated with worse cognition. Mean QWB scores by tertile of DRS are shown in Figure 9.9.

The QWB was significantly correlated with four of the DRS domains: attention ($r = .17$, $p = .009$), initiation ($r = .24$, $p < .001$), conceptualization ($r = .14$, $p = .032$), and memory scores ($r = .22$, $p = .001$). The correlation between DRS construction scores and QWB scores was not significant ($r = .07$, $p = .3$). Figure 9.10 shows QWB scores by tertiles of the initiation component of the DRS. As with the total score, there is a strong relationship between initiation–preservation scores and QWB.

Estimating the Overall Impact of Neurocognitive Consequences in Alzheimer's Disease

Alzheimer's disease is a degenerative brain disorder that results in gradual atrophy of higher cortical regions. It is marked by gradual onset and a deteriorating course. The first symptoms of Alzheimer's disease include forgetfulness, anomia, irrationality,

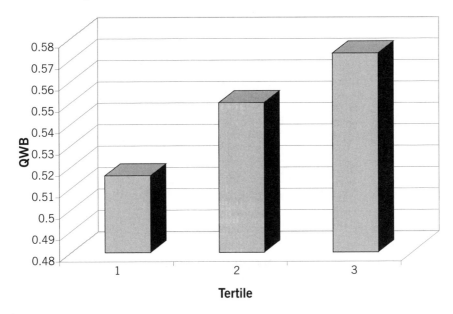

FIGURE 9.9. Mean QWB scores by tertile of Dementia Rating Scale in patients with late-onset schizophrenia.

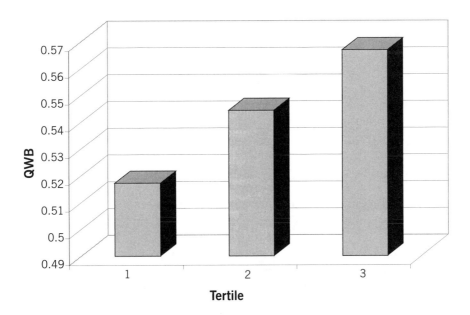

FIGURE 9.10. Mean QWB scores by tertile of the initiation component of the Dementia Rating Scale in patients with late-onset schizophrenia.

loss of initiative, and disorientation. These initial symptoms progress to widespread dementia, loss of functioning, and death. An amnesic syndrome is most prominent in many patients with Alzheimer's disease; in others, naming and spatial difficulties are primary (Loewenstein, Acevedo, Agron, Martinez, & Duara, 2007). Alzheimer's disease is more common than previously believed, affecting about 15% of adults over age 64 and contributing significantly to health care costs (Kirby et al., 2006). In the general population, this risk rises to 25% at age 90. In first-degree relatives of patients with Alzheimer's disease, the risk at age 90 is 50% (Breitner, Silverman, Mohs, & Davis, 1988).

We have attempted to quantify the impact of Alzheimer's disease. In contrast to diseases that cause early death, those affected by Alzheimer's disease gradually lose function over an extended period of time. Focusing only on mortality fails to recognize the serious impact Alzheimer's disease has upon health-related QOL. In order to understand the full impact of Alzheimer's disease, it is necessary to develop models that consider the effects on both mortality and life quality. Similarly, new interventions developed for the treatment of Alzheimer's disease need to be evaluated with measures that consider side effects as well as the benefits.

To evaluate this issue we studied 159 patients with the diagnosis of probable or possible Alzheimer's disease and their spousal caregivers, along with 52 control nonpatient–spousal dyads ($N = 211$) recruited as part of a longitudinal study on Alzheimer's disease caregiving. In addition to the QWB, the subjects completed several other measures. The Mattis Dementia Rating Scale (MDRS; Miller & Pliskin, 2006) consists of a mental status examination that assesses basic cognitive functions such as recent and remote memory, attention, orientation, mental control, and language. The Memory and Behavior Problem Checklist (MBPC; Zarit, Reever, & Bach-Peterson, 1980) consists of 29 common problems encountered in dementia. The spousal caregiver (or, in the case of controls, the spousal noncaregiver) completed these items by proxy for the reference subject. This measure assesses both the frequency of the dementia problems in the patient and the degree of stress that the caregivers experience. The Brief Symptom Inventory (BSI) is a 53-item self-report inventory taken from the Hopkins Symptom Checklist (Derogatis, Yevzeroff, & Wittelsberger, 1975). It measures five dimensions of psychiatric symptom distress that are commonly associated with Alzheimer's disease: anxiety, depression, obsessive–compulsiveness, somatization, and interpersonal difficulty.

Measures of respite time taken by patient caregivers were also obtained. "Respite time" refers to the amount of relief that caregivers took from the burden of caring for the patients with Alzheimer's disease. Respite time taken may increase as the disease progresses, making it an indirect measure of the severity of the disease. However, other factors, such as the health of the caregiver and the availability of resources, also may influence the amount of respite time taken. Not much is known about the reliability and validity of respite time as a marker of disease progression in Alzheimer's disease. Therefore, results concerning a relationship between respite time and the QWB must be interpreted with caution.

Parametric tests were used to evaluate the relationships between the QWB and the other measures. Subjects who completed each measure of interest were included in the analysis. Scores on the QWB were found to be strongly associated with measures of different aspects of impairment resulting from Alzheimer's disease.

Patients with poorer cognitive functioning in areas such as recent and remote memory, attention, orientation, mental control, and language, as measured by the MDRS, tended to have lower QWB scores ($r = .52$, $p < .01$). Lower QWB scores were also associated with greater behavioral impairment, as measured by the MBPC ($r = .64$, $p < .01$). Strong relationships were found between the QWB and MBPC items. Mean QWB scores were calculated for each of the five MBPC response options, and the means were compared by analysis of variance. Differences were found for many items, such as Asks Repeatedly ($F(4,123) = 15.49$, $p < .001$), Forgets Day ($F(4,122) = 36.43$, $p < .001$), Loses Things ($F(4,125) = 11.32$, $p < .001$), Unable to Cook ($F(4,124) = 10.54$, $p < .001$), Unable to Shop ($F(4,123) = 10.23$, $p < .001$), and Unable to Do Simple Tasks ($F(4,124) = 13.27$, $p < .001$). The correlations obtained were highly significant: lower QWB scores were associated with poorer reported functioning (see Figure 9.11). Follow-up analyses indicated that in most cases, the significant results obtained were a reflection of large differences in QWB between items scored as "never" or "not at all" and items indicating that the poorer functioning was present to at least some degree.

QWB scores were also associated with self-reported psychiatric distress: The relationship between the QWB and the BSI, although weaker than the relationship between the QWB and the measures of cognitive and behavioral functioning, was nevertheless still statistically significant ($r = -.26$, $p < .01$).

Caregivers of patients with lower QWB scores received a greater amount of respite time ($F(4,123) = 25.26$, $p < .01$) and needed it more often ($F(4,108) = 13.42$, $p < .01$) than did caregivers of patients with higher QWB scores

It might be argued that the analyses were biased because some nonaffected patients were included. Contrasts between patients and controls provide estimates of the impact of disease in comparison to persons roughly matched by age, sex, socio-economic status, and living conditions. For a more stringent test we compared QWB scores against MBPC scores, with analysis limited to those carrying a diagnosis of Alzheimer's disease. For this analysis there were significant linear contrasts for several MBPC scales, including Unable to Dress ($F(1,95) = 4.65$, $p < .03$), Unable to Feed ($F(1,95) = 3.87$, $p < .05$), Unable to Bathe ($F(1,95) = 3.63$, $p = .05$), Unable to Shave ($F(1,95) = 6.16$, $p < .01$), Incontinent ($F(1,95) = 9.23$, $p < .01$), and Unable to Cook ($F(1,95) = 6.79$, $p < .01$).

Results from this study suggest that the general QWB is significantly associated with measures of dementia, memory and behavior problems, psychiatric symptoms, and respite time. These variables were selected for study because of their presumed relationship with QOL (Kerner, Patterson, Grant, & Kaplan 1998).

Summary

Cognitive dysfunction can significantly impact many aspects of everyday functioning, and as such can also profoundly affect overall QOL. Data from a variety of studies at UCSD have demonstrated a systematic relationship between cognitive dysfunction and overall health-related QOL. There is a variety of different ways to measure health-related QOL. This chapter has focused on a general method known as the QWB scale. This is one of several approaches to estimate health outcome on a con-

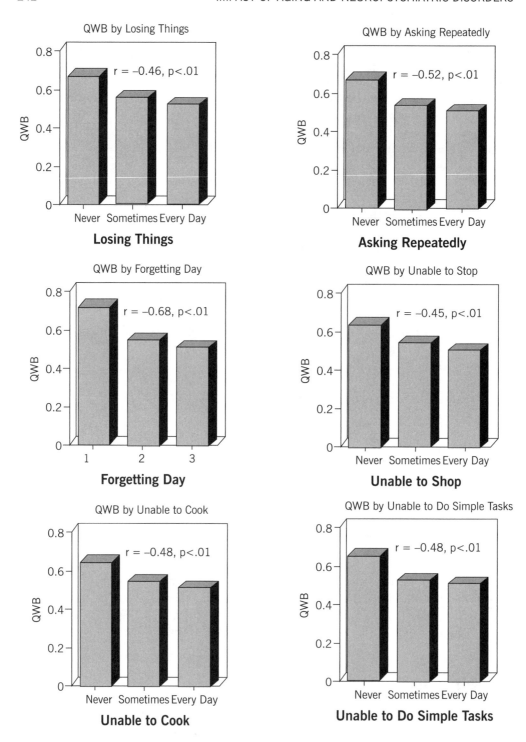

FIGURE 9.11. Mean QWB score for patients who have problems never, sometimes, or every day in losing things (*upper left*), asking repeatedly (*upper right*), forgetting day (*middle left*), shopping (*middle right*), cooking (*lower left*), and doing simple things (*lower right*).

tinuum ranging from death (0) to optimum function (1.0). Several other methods are available to estimate a similar metric. The advantage of these kinds of methods is that they can be combined with survival analysis. Those who are deceased are scored as 0.0. The combined index allows adjustment for life expectancy by QOL among survivors. These generic methods are used to provide overall estimates of treatment effectiveness. A new treatment for cognitive impairment, for example, might be reflected in improvements in overall functioning. The benefit, as estimated in these generalized units, can be compared with the benefit of treatments in very different areas of medicine and health care. Ultimately, these measures can be used for cost-effectiveness analysis.

The relationship between cognitive impairment and overall functioning has received relatively little study. The utility-based measures described in this chapter are among a wide variety of techniques used to estimate health-related QOL. We encourage the use of different methods in new studies evaluating cognitive impairment. We look forward to an evolving literature that includes overall assessment of the effects of cognitive impairment on everyday life.

In summary, the neurocognitive deficits observed in HIV disease, schizophrenia, and Alzheimer's disease are associated with measurable reductions in general health status. These neuropsychological deficits were identified through professional evaluation and by simple patient self-reports. In each case differences between well-functioning and poorly functioning patents can be as large as 0.15, or 15% of the difference between wellness and death. Accumulated over time, these deficits amount to the loss of a year of life for each 6 years of illness. Another way to state this: Each year that six patients experience this difficulty for 1 year, they collectively lose a year of life. General measures of health outcome are useful for studies evaluating new approaches to remediate the effects of cognitive impairment. Using generic outcome measures allows for the assessment of the relative cost effectiveness of the new treatments and may inform reimbursement decisions.

Acknowledgments

Dr. Robert M. Kaplan was supported by the National Institutes of Health (NIH) Grant No. 1 P01 AG020679-01A2, UCLA Claude D. Pepper Older Americans Independence Center, NIH/National Institute on Aging Grant No. 5P30AG028748, and Centers for Disease Control and Prevention Grant No. U48 DP000056-04. The HIV studies were supported by National Institute of Mental Health Grant No. 5 P50 MH45294 (HIV Neurobehavioral Research Center).

References

Antinori, A., Arendt, G., Becker, J. T., Brew, B. J., Byrd, D. A., Cherner, M., et al. (2007). Updated research nosology for HIV-associated neurocognitive disorders. *Neurology, 69,* 1789–1799.

Baro, E., Ferrer, M., Vazquez, O., Miralles, R., Pont, A., Esperanza, A., et al. (2006). Using the Nottingham Health Profile (NHP) among older adult inpatients with varying cognitive function. *Qual Life Res, 15*(4), 575–585.

Beck, A. T. (1976). *Cognitive therapy and the emotional disorders.* New York: Hoeber.

Bergner, M., Bobbitt, R. A., Carter, W. B., & Gilson, B. S. (1981). The sickness impact profile: Development and final revision of a health status measure. *Med Care, 19*(8), 787–805.

Bolge, S. C., Mody, S., Ambegaonkar, B. M., McDonnell, D. D., & Zilberberg, M. D. (2007). The impact of anemia on quality of life and healthcare resource utilization in patients with HIV/AIDS receiving antiretroviral therapy. *Curr Med Res Opin, 23*(4), 803–810.

Bombardier, C., Ware, J., Russell, I. J., Larson, M., Chalmers, A., & Read, J. L. (1986). Auranofin therapy and quality of life in patients with rheumatoid arthritis: Results of a multicenter trial. *Am J Med, 81*(4), 565–578.

Bourbeau, J., Maltais, F., Rouleau, M., & Guimont, C. (2004). French-Canadian version of the chronic respiratory and St George's Respiratory Questionnaires: An assessment of their psychometric properties in patients with chronic obstructive pulmonary disease. *Can Respir J, 11*(7), 480–486.

Breitner, J. C., Silverman, J. M., Mohs, R. C., & Davis, K. L. (1988). Familial aggregation in Alzheimer's disease: Comparison of risk among relatives of early- and late-onset cases, and among male and female relatives in successive generations. *Neurology, 38*(2), 207–212.

Bush, J. W., & Zaremba, J. (1971). Estimating health program outcomes using a Markov equilibrium analysis of disease development. *Am J Public Health, 61*(12), 2362–2375.

Chelune, G. J., Ferguson, W., Koon, R., & Dickey, T. O. (1986). Frontal lobe disinhibition in attention deficit disorder. *Child Psychiatry Hum Dev, 16*(4), 221–234.

Crystal, S., Fleishman, J. A., Hays, R. D., Shapiro, M. F., & Bozzette, S. A. (2000). Physical and role functioning among persons with HIV: Results from a nationally representative survey. *Med Care, 38*(12), 1210–1223.

Cunningham, W. E., Crystal, S., Bozzette, S., & Hays, R. D. (2005). The association of health-related quality of life with survival among persons with HIV infection in the United States. *J Gen Intern Med, 20*(1), 21–27.

Derogatis, L. R., Yevzeroff, H., & Wittelsberger, B. (1975). Social class, psychological disorder, and the nature of the psychopathologic indicator. *J Consult Clin Psychol, 43*(2), 183–191.

Dimitrov, D., & Rumrill, P. D. (2005). Multivariate methods in rehabilitation. *Work, 24*(2), 205–212.

Ganguly, R., Kotzan, J. A., Miller, L. S., Kennedy, K., & Martin, B. C. (2004). Prevalence, trends, and factors associated with antipsychotic polypharmacy among Medicaid-eligible schizophrenia patients, 1998–2000. *J Clin Psychiatry, 65*(10), 1377–1388.

Ganiats, T. G., Palinkas, L. A., & Kaplan, R. M. (1992). Comparison of Quality of Well-Being scale and functional status index in patients with atrial fibrillation. *Med Care, 30*(10), 958–964.

Gold, M., Franks, P., & Erickson, P. (1996). Assessing the health of the nation: The predictive validity of a preference-based measure and self-rated health. *Med Care, 34*(2), 163–177.

Grady, K. L., Jalowiec, A., Grusk, B. B., White-Williams, C., & Robinson, J. A. (1992). Symptom distress in cardiac transplant candidates. *Heart Lung, 21*(5), 434–439.

Grady, K. L., & Lanuza, D. M. (2005). Physical functional outcomes after cardiothoracic transplantation. *J Cardiovasc Nurs, 20*(5, Suppl.), S43–S50.

Grant, I., Heaton, R. K., & Atkinson, J. H. (1995). Neurocognitive disorders in HIV-1 infection. *Curr Top Microbiol Immunol, 202*, 11–32.

Gulevich, S. J., Kalmijn, J. A., Thal, L. J., Iragui-Madoz, V., McCutchan, J. A., Kennedy, C., et al. (1992). Sensory testing in human immunodeficiency virus type 1-infected men. HIV neurobehavioral research center group. *Arch Neurol, 49*(12), 1281–1284.

Heaton, R. K., Velin, R. A., McCutchan, J. A., Gulevich, S. J., Atkinson, J. H., Wallace, M. R., et al. (1994). Neuropsychological impairment in human immunodeficiency virus-infection: Implications for employment. *Psychosom Med, 56*(1), 8–17.

Howland, L. C., Storm, D. S., Crawford, S. L., Ma, Y., Gortmaker, S. L., & Oleske, J. M. (2007). Negative life events: Risk to health-related quality of life in children and youth with HIV infection. *J Assoc Nurses AIDS Care*, 18(1), 3–11.

Jones, P. W., Quirk, F. H., & Baveystock, C. M. (1991). The St George's Respiratory Questionnaire. *Resp Med*, 85 Suppl. B(5), 25–31; discussion, 33–27.

Kaplan, R. M. (1990). Behavior as the central outcome in health care. *Am Psychol*, 45(11), 1211–1220.

Kaplan, R. M. (1993). Quality of life assessment for cost/utility studies in cancer. *Cancer Treat Rev*, 19 Suppl. A(1), 85–96.

Kaplan, R. M. (1994). Value judgment in the Oregon Medicaid experiment. *Med Care*, 32(10), 975–988.

Kaplan, R. M., Alcaraz, J. E., Anderson, J. P., & Weisman, M. (1996). Quality-adjusted life years lost to arthritis: Effects of gender, race, and social class. *Arthrit Care Res*, 9(6), 473–482.

Kaplan, R. M., Anderson, J. P., Patterson, T. L., McCutchan, J. A., Weinrich, J. D., Heaton, R. K., et al. (1995). Validity of the Quality of Well-Being scale for persons with human immunodeficiency virus infection. HNRC group, HIV Neurobehavioral Research Center. *Psychosom Med*, 57(2), 138–147.

Kaplan, R. M., Anderson, J. P., Wu, A. W., Mathews, W. C., Kozin, F., & Orenstein, D. (1989). The Quality of Well-Being scale: Applications in AIDS, cystic fibrosis, and arthritis. *Med Care*, 27(3, Suppl.), S27–S43.

Kaplan, R. M., Atkins, C. J., & Timms, R. (1984). Validity of a Quality of Well-Being scale as an outcome measure in chronic obstructive pulmonary disease. *J Chron Dis*, 37(2), 85–95.

Kaplan, R. M., & Bush, J. W. (1982). Health-related quality of life for evaluation research and policy analysis. *Health Psychol*, 1(1), 621–680.

Kaplan, R. M., Bush, J. W., & Berry, C. C. (1976). Health status: Types of validity and the index of well-being. *Health Serv Res*, 11(4), 478–507.

Kaplan, R. M., Bush, J. W., & Berry, C. C. (1979). Health status index: Category rating versus magnitude estimation for measuring levels of well-being. *Med Care*, 17(5), 501–525.

Kaplan, R. M., & California Policy Seminar. (1993). *Allocating health resources in California: Learning from the Oregon experiment*. Berkeley, CA: California Policy Seminar.

Kaplan, R. M., Ganiats, T. G., Sieber, W. J., & Anderson, J. P. (1998). The quality of well-being scale: Critical similarities and differences with SF-36. *Int J Qual Health Care*, 10(6), 509–520.

Kaplan, R. M., & Groessl, E. J. (2002). Applications of cost/effectiveness methodologies in behavioral medicine. *Journal of Consulting and Clinical Psychology*, 70, 482–493.

Kaplan, R. M., Groessl, E. J., Sengupta, N., Sieber, W. J., & Ganiats, T. G. (2005). Comparison of measured utility scores and imputed scores from the SF-36 in patients with rheumatoid arthritis. *Med Care*, 43(1), 79–87.

Kaplan, R. M., Hartwell, S. L., Wilson, D. K., & Wallace, J. P. (1987). Effects of diet and exercise interventions on control and quality of life in non-insulin-dependent diabetes mellitus. *Journal of General Internal Medicine*, 2(4), 220–228.

Kaplan, R. M., Patterson, T. L., Kerner, D. N., Atkinson, J. H., Heaton, R. K., & Grant, I. (1997). The Quality of Well-Being scale in asymptomatic HIV-infected patients. HNRC Group, HIV Neural Behavioral Research Center. *Quality of Life Research*, 6(6), 507–514.

Kaplan, R. M., & Ries, A. L. (2005). Quality of life as an outcome measure in pulmonary diseases. *J Cardiopulm Rehabil*, 25(6), 321–331.

Kaplan, R. M., Ries, A. L., Reilly, J., & Mohsenifar, Z. (2004). Measurement of health-related quality of life in the national emphysema treatment trial. *Chest*, 126(3), 781–789.

Kaplan, R. M., Schmidt, S. M., & Cronan, T. A. (2000). Quality of well-being in patients with fibromyalgia. *Journal of Rheumatology, 27*(3), 785–789.

Kaplan, R. M., Sieber, W. J., & Ganiats, T. G. (1997). The Quality of Well-Being scale: Comparison of the interviewer-administered version with a self-administered questionnaire. *Psychol Health, 12*(6), 783–791.

Kerner, D. N., Patterson, T. L., Grant, I., & Kaplan, R. M. (1998). Validity of the Quality of Well-Being scale for patients with Alzheimer's disease. *J Aging Health, 10*(1), 44–61.

Kirby, J., Green, C., Loveman, E., Clegg, A., Picot, J., Takeda, A., et al. (2006). A systematic review of the clinical and cost-effectiveness of memantine in patients with moderately severe to severe Alzheimer's disease. *Drug Aging, 23*(3), 227–240.

Loewenstein, D. A., Acevedo, A., Agron, J., Martinez, G., & Duara, R. (2007). The use of amnestic and nonamnestic composite measures at different thresholds in the neuropsychological diagnosis of MCI. *J Clin Exp Neuropsychol, 29*(3), 300–307.

Lorenz, K. A., Cunningham, W. E., Spritzer, K. L., & Hays, R. D. (2006). Changes in symptoms and health-related quality of life in a nationally representative sample of adults in treatment for HIV. *Qual Life Res, 15*(6), 951–958.

Mangione, C. M., Lee, P. P., Gutierrez, P. R., Spritzer, K., Berry, S., & Hays, R. D. (2001). Development of the 25-item National Eye Institute Visual Function Questionnaire. *Arch Ophthalmol, 119*(7), 1050–1058.

Maserati, R., Foli, A., Tomasoni, L., Sighinolfi, L., Maggiolo, F., Sacchini, D., et al. (2007). Effects of structured treatment interruptions on metabolic, anthropometric, immunologic, and quality of life outcomes in HIV-positive adults on haart. *Curr HIV Res, 5*(3), 337–343.

Mausbach, B. T., Bowie, C. R., Harvey, P. D., Twamley, E. W., Goldman, S. R., Jeste, D. V., et al. (2007). Usefulness of the UCSD performance-based skills assessment (UPSA) for predicting residential independence in patients with chronic schizophrenia. *J Psychiatr Res, 42*(4), 320–327.

Miller, J. M., & Pliskin, N. H. (2006). The clinical utility of the Mattis Dementia Rating Scale in assessing cognitive decline in Alzheimer's disease. *Int J Neurosci, 116*(5), 613–627.

Miller, L. S., & Martin, B. C. (2004). Current and future forecasts of service use and expenditures of Medicaid-eligible schizophrenia patients in the state of Georgia. *Schizophr Bull, 30*(4), 983–995.

NcNair, D., Lorr, M., & Droppleman, L. (1980). *Profile of Mood States (POMS) manual.* San Diego, CA: Educational and Industrial Testing Services.

Orenstein, D. M., & Kaplan, R. M. (1991). Measuring the quality of well-being in cystic fibrosis and lung transplantation: The importance of the area under the curve. *Chest, 100*(4), 1016–1018.

Orenstein, D. M., Pattishall, E. N., Nixon, P. A., Ross, E. A., & Kaplan, R. M. (1990). Quality of well-being before and after antibiotic treatment of pulmonary exacerbation in patients with cystic fibrosis. *Chest, 98*(5), 1081–1084.

Preau, M., Protopopescu, C., Spire, B., Sobel, A., Dellamonica, P., Moatti, J. P., et al. (2007). Health related quality of life among both current and former injection drug users who are HIV-infected. *Drug Alcohol Depend, 86*(2–3), 175–182.

Protopopescu, C., Marcellin, F., Spire, B., Preau, M., Verdon, R., Peyramond, D., et al. (2007). Health-related quality of life in HIV-1-infected patients on HAART: A five-years longitudinal analysis accounting for dropout in the Aproco-Copilote Cohort (ANRS co-8). *Qual Life Res, 16*(4), 577–591.

Pyne, J. M., Patterson, T. L., Kaplan, R. M., Gillin, J. C., Koch, W. L., & Grant, I. (1997). Assessment of the quality of life of patients with major depression. *Psychiatr Serv, 48*(2), 224–230.

Pyne, J. M., Patterson, T. L., Kaplan, R. M., Ho, S., Gillin, J. C., Golshan, S., et al. (1997).

Preliminary longitudinal assessment of quality of life in patients with major depression. *Psychopharmacol Bull*, *33*(1), 23–29.

Pyne, J. M., Sieber, W. J., David, K., Kaplan, R. M., Rapaport, M. H., & Williams, D. K. (2003). Use of the Quality of Well-Being Self-Administered version (QWB-SA) in assessing health-related quality of life in depressed patients. *J Affect Disorders*, *76*, 237–247.

Rabkin, J. (2004). Depression and HIV. *Focus*, *19*, 1–5.

Rocco, M. V., Gassman, J. J., Wang, S. R., & Kaplan, R. M. (1997). Cross-sectional study of quality of life and symptoms in chronic renal disease patients: The modification of diet in renal disease study. *Am J Kidney Dis*, *29*(6), 888–896.

Schmier, J. K., Halpern, M. T., Higashi, M. K., & Bakst, A. (2005). The quality of life impact of acute exacerbations of chronic bronchitis (AECB): A literature review. *Qual Life Res*, *14*(2), 329–347.

Shalit, P., True, A., & Thommes, J. A. (2007). Quality of life and tolerability after administration of enfuvirtide with a thin-walled needle: QUALITE study. *HIV Clin Trials*, *8*(1), 24–35.

Squier, H. C., Ries, A. L., Kaplan, R. M., Prewitt, L. M., Smith, C. M., Kriett, J. M., et al. (1995). Quality of well-being predicts survival in lung transplantation candidates. *Am J Resp Crit Care*, *152*(6, Pt. 1), 2032–2036.

Wachtel, T., Piette, J., Mor, V., Stein, M., Fleishman, J., & Carpenter, C. (1992). Quality of life in persons with human immunodeficiency virus infection: Measurement by the medical outcomes study instrument. *Ann Intern Med*, *116*(2), 129–137.

Ware, J. E., Jr., & Gandek, B. (1998). Overview of the SF-36 health survey and the International Quality of Life Assessment (IQOLA) project. *Journal of Clinical Epidemiology*, *51*(11), 903–912.

Williamson, G. M. (2000). Extending the activity restriction model of depressed affect: Evidence from a sample of breast cancer patients. *Health Psychol*, *19*(4), 339–347.

Wu, A. W., Hays, R. D., Kelly, S., Malitz, F., & Bozzette, S. A. (1997). Applications of the medical outcomes study health-related quality of life measures in HIV/AIDS. *Qual Life Res*, *6*(6), 531–554.

Wu, M. C., & Bailey, K. (1988). Analysing changes in the presence of informative right censoring caused by death and withdrawal. *Stat Med*, *7*(1–2), 337–346.

Zarit, S. H., Reever, K. E., & Bach-Peterson, J. (1980). Relatives of the impaired elderly: Correlates of feelings of burden. *Gerontologist*, *20*(6), 649–655.

CHAPTER 10

Normal Aging and Everyday Functioning

Karlene Ball, Lesley A. Ross, and Sarah Viamonte

The boundaries between what is considered "normal" aging and the early stages of disease can become difficult to draw as people grow older and the prevalence of cognitive decline and age-related pathologies increases. Normal age-related cognitive changes may have very slight or a more pronounced impact on functional abilities, similarly blurring these boundaries. Some changes may be minor, such as having difficulty remembering where you put your keys, whereas others may have a greater impact on daily functioning and independence, such as repeatedly failing to take medications properly. This chapter focuses on what is typically considered normal age-related cognitive changes. Current research on structural changes found within the brain, cognitive changes and their impact on daily activities, and interventions to promote and maintain cognition and everyday function is discussed. Finally, we address some current and future directions for research efforts in cognitive aging.

The Physiology of Aging

All bodily systems are ultimately affected by age. Although age-related changes in physical, sensory, and skeletal–motor systems may be more visible, with an obvious impact on daily functioning, numerous changes within the brain, illuminated by recent animal, behavioral, and imaging research, also have an impact on cognition and daily functioning.

Although research in cognitive neuroscience has greatly advanced in recent years, there is still debate regarding the mechanisms, causes, and consequences of aging within the brain. Neural and cognitive research is often confounded by cohort effects, study design, repeated exposure of participants to many cognitive assessments in longitudinal studies, and participant attrition, resulting in the possibility of sample bias (Small, 2001). In addition to these general difficulties, there is a great amount of heterogeneity in the aging process, with both interindividual and intraindividual differences. The numerous interindividual differences found among older adults has cast some doubt on the generalization and inevitability of neurological declines, suggesting that some commonly held beliefs regarding age-related declines in cognitive abilities, such as memory loss as a result of nonpathological aging, may not be a part of normal aging (Small, 2001). Additionally, there is also great intraindividual variability in the aging process. This variability has been discussed in terms of cognitive plasticity (Nyberg, 2005), or the ability of the brain to change throughout the lifespan. Although it is generally accepted that plasticity is maintained throughout the lifespan, there is also some evidence of reduced plasticity in older adults. Such reductions in plasticity may be due to both processing deficits (e.g., decreased cognitive speed), associated with frontal cortex changes, and production deficits (e.g., language, behavioral initiation), where neural correlates appear to be specific to the task at hand (Nyberg, 2005).

Until recently, it was widely believed that impairments found during the normal aging process were due to neuronal loss, usually found in the hippocampus and neocortical areas. However, recent development of sterological techniques and more accurate counting methods have revealed that there is no widespread neuronal loss throughout the brain (for a review, see Keller, 2006); rather, decreases in brain matter are more likely the result of reduced gray matter volume (Abe et al., 2008). In addition, research has also demonstrated that age-related reductions in gray matter are associated with decreased cognitive function, specifically in the domains of attention and executive function (Zimmerman et al., 2006).

The advancement of the cognitive reserve theory helps account for some of the heterogeneity related to normal cognitive aging, as well as the differing presentations observed in persons with the same pathology (i.e., not every case of Alzheimer's disease is cognitively, behaviorally, or functionally the same) (Satz, 1993; Stern, 2002; Whalley, Deary, Appleton, & Starr, 2004). This theory postulates that a greater number of novel environmental interactions (e.g., education, work, or leisure activities) results in greater neuronal development—including neurogenesis, migration, differentiation, arborization, synaptogenesis, synaptic sculpting, and myelination—throughout the lifespan (Perry, 2002). Early imaging research supports a neural basis for cognitive reserve (Stern et al., 2003). As such, if pathology occurs that damages the neural structure within the brain, persons with a greater reserve may not demonstrate the same cognitive impact as others with the same pathology but less reserve, or observable deficits may not be manifest until a later time point when greater pathological damage has occurred.

A recent review of this theory demonstrates additional support for the protective nature of cognitive enrichment, through behavioral, nutritional, and pharmacological experiences, upon neural structures and functions (Milgram, Siwak-Tapp, Araujo, & Head, 2006). For example, Wilson and colleagues (2002) investigated the impact of cognitively stimulating activities and physical activities on the risk for developing Alzheimer's disease. They found that persons who had higher levels of cognitively stimulating activities had a smaller risk of developing the disease (odds ratio [OR] .36; 95% confidence interval [CI] .20–.65), thus supporting the concept of cognitive reserve.

Upon evaluating some of the enrichment and intervention research, Salthouse (2006) concluded that there is no solid evidence that cognitive stimulation actually slows the rate of cognitive decline. Other researchers would argue that previous experiences and interventions do have an impact on the cognitive abilities of trained participants relative to control groups (Ball et al., 2002; Scarmeas & Stern, 2003; Willis et al., 2006), in part due to the fact that boosting cognitive ability results in potential longitudinal declines originating from a higher level of cognitive function. However, even researchers who are not completely convinced by the evidence that increased cognitive activity slows cognitive decline have noted that adults should still be engaging in challenging activities, as they are not harmful and can be enjoyable (Salthouse, 2006), thereby resulting in a higher quality of life.

Another commonly espoused theory that complements the construct of cognitive reserve is the frontal lobe theory (see Phillips & Sala, 1998, for a review). Although other areas of the brain may also exhibit deterioration, such as that found in the hippocampus, many researchers have targeted the frontal lobes as particularly relevant for cognitive function. That is, the frontal lobes appear to be particularly relevant for executive function (as described below), and age-related changes are typically more advanced in this area of the brain. Several researchers have furthered explored this theory and have begun to define the specific areas of the frontal lobes important to cognition. For example, the dorsolateral prefrontal cortex regions, involved in fluid intelligence tasks, appear to be a key contributor to age-related cognitive decline (Phillips & Sala, 1998), rather than some other areas falling under the "frontal lobes" umbrella, such as the ventromedial prefrontal area (MacPherson, Phillips, & Sala, 2002).

Cognitive Changes

Cognitive abilities provide us with the flexibility to negotiate the world in which we live. Whether we are reading and following directions in order to cook a meal or program a DVR, preparing our tax returns, learning and remembering new information presented in a class, or driving a car, our cognitive skills allow us to engage in many unique and challenging situations. As a result, age-related decline in cognitive function can potentially impact the daily function of older adults.

Intelligence

In the absence of disease, such as dementia, age-related declines in intelligence tend to be minimal until the eighth decade of life (Schaie, 1996b). Although the incidence of dementia increases with age, affecting between 5 and 10% of people over the age of 65, dementia is not an inevitable outcome of aging even into the tenth decade of life (Anderson-Ranberg, Vasegaard, & Jeune, 2001). Intellectual functioning has been categorized into two domains: crystallized and fluid abilities. Crystallized abilities, which include vocabulary and simple arithmetic, have been found to increase or remain stable into middle age, and any declines in these abilities tend to occur very late in life, if at all. In contrast, fluid abilities, which include memory, reasoning, speed of processing, and higher-order thought processes (Horn, 1982), may begin to decline in young adulthood, according to findings from the Seattle Longitudinal Study of Adult Intelligence (Schaie, 1994). However, age-related declines in fluid abilities are not inevitable. Higher education and continued intellectual activity, as well as expertise in a particular area, may protect against age-related decline in this broad domain (Compton, Bachman, & Logan, 1997; Hoyer & Rybash, 1994).

Memory

Memory loss is one of the most frequent cognitively related complaints of older adults. One reason for this frequency may be that memory is fundamental to most everyday activities, and the inability to remember something can be embarrassing and quite obvious. Although some normal age-related memory decline occurs, these changes typically do not have a severe impact on daily function. Intact memory functioning requires activation of both cortical and subcortical areas of the brain. When the hippocampus is damaged in Alzheimer's disease, profound memory loss occurs. Regardless of disease presence, research has linked memory decline to self-reported impairment in many instrumental activities of daily living (IADLs), including shopping, preparing meals, managing finances, and managing complex medication regimens (Pathy, Sinclair, & Morley, 2006).

Changes in the aging brain also occur in the temporal cortex, hippocampus, and limbic system, all of which are associated with memory (Eustache et al., 1995). Schofield and colleagues (1997) found that 31% of cognitively intact community-residing elders reported memory complaints. Given that there may be declines in metamemory as well (i.e., people forget that they forget), the prevalence of those with memory impairments may be even greater than reported.

It is believed that many age-related changes in memory are due to declines in short-term memory. The phrase "short-term memory" has been used to denote both the immediate recall of information as well as working memory. Working memory can be described as the ability to simultaneously store and manipulate information temporarily. Although the ability to immediately recall relatively simple information remains intact in normal aging, working memory is poorer, on the average, in older adults (Foos & Wright, 1992; Salthouse, 1992). For example, the ability to retain increasingly long strings of digits presented aurally, mentally manipulate those digits so that they are in reverse sequence, and recite them aloud is a classic working memory task, the performance of which declines with age. Although normal declines in working memory are expected with age, frank deficits in working memory may be suggestive of dementia and have been associated with early IADL impairments in Alzheimer's disease (Earnst et al., 2001).

Long-term memory consists of two broad classes of memory—declarative (episodic and semantic) and nondeclarative (procedural)—which are differentially affected by aging. The primary distinction between declarative and nondeclarative memory is that declarative (explicit) memory refers to conscious learning and nondeclarative (implicit) memory refers to unconscious learning. Nondeclarative memory can be described as unintentional, automatic, or without awareness, and it relies upon familiarity rather than deliberate study (Kausler, 1994; Smith, 1996). Use of nondeclarative memory occurs when one performs automatic skills such as flipping a light switch (Light & Albertson, 1989; Poon, 1985). Nondeclarative memory remains intact in normal aging as well as in the early stages of Alzheimer's disease (Kuzis et al., 1999). Older adults more often have difficulty with declarative memory as they age, and age-related impairments can be seen in both types of declarative memory: episodic and semantic. Episodic memory involves the recall of temporal (e.g., when) and spatial (e.g., where) information associated with past personal experiences/ events. Semantic memory involves language and world knowledge, which are reinforced throughout the lifespan and thus more resistant to age-related decline. Alternatively, episodic memory involves discrete occurrences and generally declines with age (Hooyman & Kiyak, 2005).

Executive Function

Executive function is one of the most complex cognitive functions and includes the ability to plan, sequence, organize, inhibit responses, think abstractly, monitor the self, and reallocate mental resources. As noted previously, these abilities are primarily associated with the frontal lobes of the brain, as demonstrated by the deficits in these skills observed in younger adults with acquired frontal lobe lesions. Some researchers have argued that the executive function impairments observed in normal aging are similar to those observed in younger individuals with frontal lobe lesions (Moscovitch & Winocur, 1992). Executive function is needed to complete tasks that require complex behavior or involve multiple steps. Many investigators have demonstrated age-related decline in prefrontal and frontal lobe function, associated with executive functioning (Glisky, Polster, & Routhieaux, 1995; Parkin & Java, 1999; Souchay, Isingrini, & Espagnet, 2000; West & Alan, 2000). Inhibition is one key aspect of executive function that declines with age. The ability to inhibit responses is as important as initiating them. Inhibition allows one to access, delete, or restrain cognitive behaviors (Hasher, Zacks, & Rahhal, 1999) and prevents "mental clutter," distraction, and interference, thereby facilitating the allocation of mental resources to the task at hand. Perhaps one of the most salient examples of successful inhibition is the ability to refrain from making hurtful or socially inappropriate comments.

Reasoning

Reasoning is a cognitive ability that uses logic, knowledge, and principles to find solutions to a problem. It is a sophisticated problem-solving ability, used in a variety of real-world tasks and requiring both memory and executive functioning. Age-related declines may become apparent when the task is unfamiliar or complex (Hayslip & Sterns, 1979). Not surprisingly, declines in reasoning can impair successful decision making in everyday situations such as financial investment or medical treatment.

Attention

Attention encompasses a rather broad spectrum of abilities that range from automatic orientation toward a loud noise to remaining vigilant for long periods of time (i.e., sustained attention). Divided attention is quite commonly used in everyday contexts and occurs when people try to do two or more things at once ("multitasking"). This ability may or may not decline with age, depending on the individual and the difficulty of the tasks being performed. The use of a cell phone while driving is an example of a task requiring divided attention that can be difficult for all age groups. Selective attention is the ability to attend to relevant information while ignoring irrelevant information or distraction. This executive-function-based ability is another area in which age-related decline has been documented (Parasuraman & Greenwood, 1998).

Speed of Processing

Speed of processing refers to the rate at which information is perceived and processed. Facility in processing speed is one of the first cognitive abilities to decline with age (Schaie, 1994). Age-related decrements in speed of processing vary depending on task complexity (Allen, Madden, & Slane, 1995; Bashore, Ridderinkhof, & van der Molen, 1998; Fisher, Fisk, & Duffy, 1995). Over the past decade, many studies have demonstrated relationships between cognitive processing speed and everyday function in older adults. Various indices of mobility have been linked to processing speed impairments in older adults, including number of falls (Vance, Ball, et al., 2006), performance mobility via the Performance Oriented Mobility Assessment (Owsley & McGwin, 2004), life space (a measure of the extent of movement within an individual's environment) (Stalvey, Owsley, Sloane, & Ball, 1999), and driving outcomes such as on-road driving performance, driving simulator performance, and crash risk (Clay et al., 2005). Slower processing speed is also related to slower performance of IADLs (Edwards, Ball, et al., 2002).

Daily Functioning and Aging

There is substantial evidence that cognitive abilities are important predictors of individual differences in the ability to function in everyday life; in this way age-related cognitive decline can jeopardize independence. However, the ability to perform everyday activities relies on many functions (e.g., physical, sensory, and cognitive), and these functions are better predictors of real-world abilities than age per se. It is undoubtedly the case that a critical level of cognitive decline must occur before that decline begins to affect everyday abilities. It is not surprising that age-related cognitive declines are observable in a clinical or laboratory environment much earlier than are real-world functional declines. There is, for example, a considerable difference between someone's ability to perform an unfamiliar cognitive test in a laboratory and his or her ability to shop, balance a checkbook, drive a vehicle, or prepare a meal. It is perhaps because of the multiple determinants of everyday ability and the possibility of compensation in everyday life that decline in functional competence occurs at a later chronological age then declines in associated cognitive abilities (Allaire & Marsiske, 1999; Diehl, Willis, & Schaie, 1995; Willis et al., 1998). Furthermore, older adults who have had lifelong disadvantages (e.g., low education, low income) may be at increased risk (Willis, 1996b) for both cognitive and functional decline, and may exhibit decline at an earlier chronological age.

   Much recent research in the area of cognition and functional abilities has focused on the development of assessments that are predictive of difficulty in performing everyday activities, as well as the determination of those critical cutpoints in cognitive function that define impaired and nonimpaired function in everyday life. In the development of such measures, the emphasis has been to determine the bases of age-related functional problems (e.g., which cognitive abilities are relevant), as well as the development of interventions that would potentially maintain everyday function and independence. With an increasing number of older adults continuing to work and drive, the long-term goal is to identify how assessment can be improved to better address older adults' difficulties in performing everyday activities. We now summarize some examples of linking cognitive assessment to everyday ability in relation to aging, followed by a brief discussion of cognitive training.

Self-Reported ADL/IADL Function

Self-report is a common way of assessing everyday abilities among older adults. With age, older adults may begin to report increased difficulty, especially with the performance of daily activities that rely on cognitive function. Lawton and Brody (1969) defined specific categories of daily activities essential to maintaining an independent lifestyle. These include abilities such as financial management, medication management, ability to use the telephone, ability to prepare meals, and housekeeping (Fillenbaum, 1987). Because the performance of these *instrumental activities of daily living* (IADLs) is necessary to maintain one's household and therefore independence in the community, disability in IADLs typically precedes disability in the more basic *activities of daily living* (ADLs; self-care such as dressing, feeding oneself, and toileting). In the United States in 1995, 32% of community-dwelling women and 24% of men age 70 and over reported difficulty or inability to perform at least one ADL (Kramarow, Lentzer, Rooks, Weeks, & Saydah, 1999). For those age 85 and over, 55% of women and 42% of men reported ADL loss.

Performance-Based ADL/IADL Function

Research has shown that some older adults may not be able to validly evaluate their everyday abilities (Friedman et al., 1999; Rubenstein, Schairer, Wieland, & Kane, 1984). For example, it has been reported that older adults with mild cognitive impairment, as well as healthy older adults, tend to overestimate their abilities (Rubenstein et al., 1984). In contrast, older adults suffering from depression tend to underestimate their abilities (Kiyak, Teri, & Borson, 1994). Because of these discrepancies there has been an emphasis on developing performance-based measures of everyday abilities rather than relying solely on self-report of IADL ability (Diehl et al., 1995). Some of these measures—for example, those evaluated in the ACTIVE clinical trial; see section on training—include measures of everyday problem solving (Jobe et al., 2001; Schaie, 1996b; Willis, Jay, Diehl, & Marsiske, 1992), and measures of everyday speed such as the timed IADL (TIADL). For example, the TIADL measure assesses IADL task completion accuracy and time for activities such as looking up a phone number, finding food items on a crowded shelf, making change, finding ingredient information on cans of food, and finding relevant information on medication bottles (Edwards, Ball, et al., 2002; Owsley, McGwin, Sloane, Stalvey, & Wells, 2001; Owsley, Sloane, McGwin, & Ball, 2002).

Mobility

One everyday ability that has been evaluated by self-report, performance measures, and multiple outcomes is mobility. Mobility is extremely important to older adults since it ensures access to social contacts and health care, and is important for independence and a satisfying quality of life. Mobility has been broadly defined as "a person's intentional movement throughout his or her environment" (Owsley & McGwin, 2004, p. 1901), and it can be assessed in a variety of ways. With increasing age, mobility limitations become more prevalent and are associated with impairments in sensory, cognitive, and/or physical functioning (Barberger & Fabrigoule, 1997). Mobility limitations negatively impact quality of life by increasing the need for formal care and decreasing independence in nearly 20% of adults age 65 or older (Guralnik, Fried, & Salive, 1996). In addition, mobility limitations are associated with acute medical conditions (Branch & Meyers, 1987), depression (Seeman, 1996), and declining independence (Manton, 1988).

Some of the ways in which mobility is assessed as an IADL include a count of negative events (e.g., falls, vehicle crashes), actual performance (e.g., rapid pace walk or driving performance), and self-report (e.g., regarding driving difficulty or driving habits). A brief description of some of the research linking cognitive ability with these outcomes follows as an example of one area in which cognitive research is being translated into everyday applications.

Useful Field of View

One cognitive assessment that has been studied extensively with respect to its relationship to mobility outcomes is the Useful Field of View (UFOV) test. This test measures the speed with which information of increasing complexity is processed by an individual (Ball, Edwards, & Ross, 2007). The past 10–20 years have been marked by technological advances in both evaluation and intervention approaches aimed at enhancing UFOV; cutpoints predictive of everyday outcomes and norms for older populations are now available (Ball, Wadley, Vance, & Edwards, 2007; Clay et al., 2005; Edwards et al., 2006). For example, speed of processing training, which targets the speed with which complex visual information is processed, is one method by which the UFOV can be enhanced (Ball et al., 2002; Willis et al., 2006).

Falls

Falls are one of the leading causes of injury among older adults and can be life-threatening. Nearly one-third of adults age 65 and older fall at least once each year (Bergland, Pettersen, & Laake, 2000; Stalenhoef, Diederiks, de Witte, Schiricke, & Crebolder, 1999). The result can be severe mobility restriction, as a result of a broken hip, or even death (Cummings et al., 1995; Tinetti, Speechley, & Ginter, 1988). Falls relate to quality of life by limiting or eliminating one's ability to leave home for social events or even bathe and dress in more serious situations (Sicard-Rosenbaum, Light, & Behrman, 2002; Stalenhoef et al., 1999; Tinetti, Williams, & Gill, 2000).

Although some falls are caused by extrinsic agents (e.g., slippery floors), many can be linked to declining cognitive function (Fuller, 2000; Tinetti et al., 1988). Recent results from a large sample study indicate that impaired UFOV test performance is associated with an increased risk of falls, suggesting that interventions to improve cognitive function may be helpful in reducing falls among older adults (Vance, Roenker, et al., 2006).

Driving

Driving is a vital means of maintaining mobility in many countries, and older adults in the United State report strong reliance upon the personal vehicle for their transportation, and thus independence, needs (Jette & Branch, 1992). As individuals age, however, their driving skills may become compromised by declining visual and/or cognitive processing. Driving cessation poses a severe threat to mobility and can lead to decreased volunteerism, employment opportunities, social activities, and access to health care (Marottoli et al., 2000). Public concerns call for both effective evaluation of driving risk and proven rehabilitative programs, whenever available, for those at risk. There is a large literature relating visual and cognitive function to driving competence (Ball, Owsley, Sloane, Roenker, & Bruni, 1993). A recent meta-analysis evaluated the relationship between the UFOV and objective measures of driving performance (Clay et al., 2005). Results showed converging evidence from multiple sites and investigators that the UFOV test is strongly related to driving competence among older adults.

With respect to driving habits, many older adults begin to avoid specific driving situations, begin to limit their driving, or stop driving altogether in response to declining visual and cognitive abilities. Significant changes in all these driving habits are detected after age 75 (Ball & Owsley, 1991, 1993, 2000; Ball et al., 1993; Marottoli, Cooney, Wagner, Doucetter, & Tinetti, 1994; Owsley, Ball, Sloane, Roenker, & Bruni, 1991; Owsley et al., 1998a, 1998b, 2001; Schaie, 1994; Sims, Owsley, Allman, Ball, & Smoot, 1998; Stalvey et al., 1999). Cognitive losses have been associated with many of these outcomes. Specifically, deficiencies in executive function, mental status, speed of processing, and memory have been associated with decreased driving exposure, increased driving avoidance, increased self-reported driving difficulty, and driving cessation among older adults (Ball, Owsley, et al., 1998; Foley, Wallace, & Eberhard, 1995; Johansson, Bronge, Lundberg, Persson, & Viitanen, 1996; Stutts, 1998).

In summary, it is important to note that the performance of "real-life" tasks relies upon multiple complex cognitive abilities (Allaire & Marsiske, 1999; Willis, 1996a) as well as an individual's overall health, social skills, and social networks. Even so, the identification of specific cognitive skills that are related to specific functional declines has led to effective interventions.

Training

Rather than recommending general activities that are cognitively stimulating, such as crossword puzzles and reading, which may or may not challenge the brain in a systematic fashion, some researchers have gone a step further and developed specific training protocols designed to enhance particular cognitive abilities. There have been a variety of exercise, pharmacological, vitamin-based, and cognitive training programs, focusing on either particular fluid abilities or general strategies for daily living. For a recent review of interventions and their possible impact on cognitive aging, see Kramer and Willis (2003).

One of the most recent and controlled studies has been the Advanced Cognitive Training for Independent and Vital Elderly (ACTIVE) study. ACTIVE was a clinical, randomized, single-blind trial investigating the long-term effects of cognitive training on mental abilities and possible translation to everyday activities in older adults (N = 2,802; Jobe et al., 2001). Specifically, the effects of standardized memory, reasoning, and speed-of-processing interventions that required up to ten 60- to 75-minute training sessions initially, and booster training for half of the participants, were investigated for over 5 years. Memory and reasoning training involved teaching participants strategies such as mnemonic memory devices (Rasmusson, Rebok, Bylsma, & Brandt, 1999; Rebok & Balcerak, 1989) and finding patterns in series of words and letters that benefit reasoning abilities (Willis, 1987; Willis & Schaie, 1986). Training to improve processing speed used a computerized practice involving more complex and challenging identification and localization of targets at increasingly faster paces (Ball et al., 2007; Edwards et al., 2002). All three interventions were found to be effective at improving the targeted cognitive ability for up to 5 years, and reasoning training was found to improve self-reported IADLs. For those who received booster training, speed-of-processing training was found to transfer to everyday speed outcome measures at 5 years (Ball et al., 2002; Willis et al., 2006).

Speed-of-processing training has been more extensively evaluated relative to everyday outcomes, as well as in populations where more impairment was present at baseline. Older participants who have undergone such training have been found to have faster processing speed (i.e., cognitive laboratory tasks; Edwards, Wadley, Vance, Roenker, & Ball, 2005), faster everyday processing speed (i.e., everyday life tasks; Willis et al., 2006), better performance on TIADLs; Edwards et al., 2002, 2005), faster complex reaction time (Roenker, Cissell, Ball, Wadley, & Edwards, 2003), reductions in dangerous driving maneuvers (Roenker et al., 2003), and were less likely to experience extensive and clinically relevant declines in health-related quality of life (Wolinsky et al., 2006). For a detailed review of the training procedures and outcomes, see Ball and colleagues (2007).

Future Directions

In light of the recently published results from the ACTIVE clinical trial and other studies, a great deal of media attention has been focused on the findings that cognitive abilities can be maintained, to some extent, with practice. This publicity has resulted in the marketing of many training programs, many of which have not yet been scientifically evaluated. Future directions in this area will involve field studies that evaluate the impact of assessment and training programs conducted in real-world settings (e.g., senior centers, medical offices) on clinical and everyday outcomes. Further work is also needed in evaluating the combined impact of programs with different domain emphases (e.g., what is the impact of combining aerobic exercise with a focused cognitive training program?). Questions related to who is most likely to benefit from such programs, how much, and for how long will need to be addressed in a systematic fashion. Finally, an understanding of changes that occur in the brain as a result of training (via imaging or other neurological studies) will undoubtedly help to address some of these issues and solidify approaches to cognitive training in the future.

Authors' Note

Karlene Ball owns stock in the Visual Awareness Research Group (formerly Visual Awareness, Inc.) and Posit Science, Inc., the companies that market the Useful Field of View Test and speed of processing training software. Posit Science acquired Visual Awareness, and Dr. Ball continues to collaborate on the design and testing of these assessment and training programs as a member of the Posit Science Scientific Advisory Board.

References

Abe, O., Yamasue, H., Aoki, S., Suga, M., Yamada, H., Kassai, K., et al. (2008). Aging in the CNS: Comparison of gray/white matter volume and diffusion tensor data. *Neurobiol Aging, 29,* 102–116.

Allaire, J. C., & Marsiske, M. (1999). Everyday cognition: Age and intellectual ability correlates. *Psychol Aging, 14*(4), 627–644.

Allen, P. A., Madden, D. J., & Slane, S. (1995). Visual and word encoding and the effect of adult age and word frequency. In P. A. Allen & T. R. Bashore (Eds.), *Age differences in word and language processing* (pp. 30–71). Amsterdam: North Holland.

Anderson-Ranberg, K., Vasegaard, L., & Jeune, B. (2001). Dementia is not inevitable: A population-based study of Danish Centenarians. *J Gerontol B-Psychol, 56B,* P152–P159.

Ball, K., Beard, B. L., Roenker, D. L., Miller, R. L., & Griggs, D. S. (1998). Age and visual search: Expanding the useful field of view. *J Opt Soc Am A, 5*(12), 2210–2219.

Ball, K., Berch, D. B., Helmers, K. F., Jobe, J. B., Leveck, M. D., Marsiske, M., et al. (2002). Effect of cognitive training interventions with older adults: A randomized controlled trial. *JAMA, 288*(18), 2271–2281.

Ball, K., Edwards, J. D., & Ross, L. A. (2007). The impact of speed of processing training on cognitive and everyday functions. *J Gerontol: Psychol Sci, 62*(Special Issue 1), 19–31.

Ball, K., & Owsley, C. (1991). Identifying correlates of accident involvement for the older driver. *Hum Factors, 33*(5), 583–595.

Ball, K., & Owsley, C. (1993). The Useful Field of View test: A new technique for evaluating age-related declines in visual function. *J Am Optom Assoc, 64*(1), 71–79.

Ball, K., & Owsley, C. (2000). Increasing mobility and reducing accidents of older drivers. In K. W. Schaie & M. Pietrucha (Eds.), *Mobility and transportation in the elderly* (pp. 213–251). New York: Springer.

Ball, K., Owsley, C., Sloane, M. E., Roenker, D. L., & Bruni, J. R. (1993). Visual attention problems as a predictor of vehicle crashes in older drivers. *Invest Ophth Vis Sci, 34*(11), 3110–3123.

Ball, K., Owsley, C., Stalvey, B., Roenker, D. L., Sloane, M. E., & Graves, M. (1998). Driving avoidance and functional impairment in older drivers. *Accident Anal Prev, 30*(3), 313–322.

Ball, K., Wadley, V. G., Vance, D. E., & Edwards, J. D. (2007). Does driving benefit quality of life among older drivers? In H.-W. Wahl (Ed.), *New dynamics in old age: Individual, environmental, and societal perspectives* (pp. 199–212). Amityville, NY: Baywood.

Barberger, G. P., & Fabrigoule, C. (1997). Disability and cognitive impairment in the elderly. *Disabil Rehabil, 19*(5), 175–193.

Bashore, T. R., Ridderinkhof, K. R., & van der Molen, W. W. (1998). The decline of cognitive processing speed in old age. *Current Directions in Psychological Science, 6*, 163–169.

Bergland, A., Pettersen, A. M., & Laake, K. (2000). Functional status among elderly Norwegian fallers living at home. *Physiother Res Int: J Res Clin Phys Ther, 51*(3), 33–45.

Branch, L. G., & Meyers, A. R. (1987). Assessing physical function in the elderly. *Clin Geriatr Med, 3*(1), 29–51.

Clay, O. J., Wadley, V. G., Edwards, J. E., Roth, D. L., Roenker, D. L., & Ball, K. K. (2005). Cumulative meta-analysis of the relationship between useful field of view and driving performance in older adults: Current and future implications. *Optometry Vision Sci, 82*(8), 724–731.

Compton, D. M., Bachman, L. D., & Logan, J. A. (1997). Aging and intellectual ability in young, middle-aged, and older educated adults: Preliminary results from a sample of college faculty. *Psychol Rep, 81*(1), 79–90.

Cummings, S. R., Nevitt, M. C., Browner, W. S., Stone, K., Fox, K. M., Ensrud, K. E., et al. (1995). Risk factors for hip fracture in white women: Study of osteoporotic fractures research group [see comments]. *New Engl J Med, 332*(12), 767–773.

Diehl, M., Willis, S. L., & Schaie, K. W. (1995). Everyday problem solving in older adults: Observational assessment and cognitive correlates. *Psychol Aging, 10*, 478–490.

Earnst, K. S., Wadley, V. G., Aldridge, T. M., Steenwyk, A. B., Hammond, A. E., Harrell, L. E., et al. (2001). Loss of financial capacity in Alzheimer's disease: The role of working memory. *Aging, Neuropsych C, 8*(2), 109–119.

Edwards, J. D., Ball, K., Wadley, V. G., & Wood, K. M. (2002). SKILL: Impact of speed of processing training on cognitive and everyday performance [abstract]. *Gerontologist, 42*, 308.

Edwards, J. D., Ross, L. A., Wadley, V. G., Clay, O. J., Crowe, M. G., Roenker, D. L., et al. (2006). The Useful Field of View test: Normative data for older adults. *Arch Clin Neuropsych, 21*, 275–286.

Edwards, J. D., Wadley, V. G., Myers, R. S., Roenker, D. L., Cissell, G. M., & Ball, K. (2002). Transfer of a speed of processing intervention to near and far cognitive functions. *Gerontology, 48*, 329–340.

Edwards, J. D., Wadley, V. G., Vance, D. E., Roenker, D. L., & Ball, K. K. (2005). The impact of speed of processing training on cognitive and everyday performance. *Aging Ment Health, 9*(3), 262–271.

Eustache, F., Rioux, P., Desgranges, B., Marchal, G., Petit-Taboue, M. C., Dary, M., et al. (1995). Healthy aging, memory subsystems and regional cerebral oxygen consumption. *Neuropsychologia, 33*(7), 867–887.

Fillenbaum, G. G. (1987). Activities of daily living. In G. L. Maddox (Ed.), *The encyclopedia of aging* (pp. 3–4). New York: Springer.

Fisher, D. L., Fisk, A. D., & Duffy, S. A. (1995). Why latent models are needed to test hypotheses about slowing of word and language processes in older adults. In P. A. Allen & T. R. Bashore (Eds.), *Age differences in word and language processing* (pp. 1–29). Amsterdam: North Holland.

Foley, D. J., Wallace, R. B., & Eberhard, J. (1995). Risk factors for motor vehicle crashes among older drivers in a rural community. *J Am Geriatr Soc, 43*, 776–781.

Foos, P. W., & Wright, L. (1992). Adult age differences in the storage of information in working memory. *Exp Aging Res, 2*, 51–57.

Friedman, S. M., Munoz, B., Rubin, G. S., West, S. K., Bandeen-Roche, K., & Fried, L. P.

(1999). Characteristics of discrepancies between self-reported visual function and measured reading speed: Salisbury Eye Evaluation Project Team. *Invest Ophth Vis Sci*, *40*(5), 858–864.

Fuller, G. F. (2000). Falls in the elderly. *Am Fam Physician*, *61*(7), 2159–2168, 2173–2154.

Glisky, E. L., Polster, M. R., & Routhieaux, B. C. (1995). Double dissociation between item and source memory. *Neuropsychology*, *9*, 229–235.

Guralnik, J. M., Fried, L. P., & Salive, M. E. (1996). Disability as a public health outcome in the aging population. *Annu Rev Publ Health*, *17*, 25–46.

Hasher, L., Zacks, R. T., & Rahhal, T. A. (1999). Timing, instructions, and inhibitory control: Some missing factors in the age and memory debate. *Gerontology*, *45*, 355–357.

Hayslip, B., Jr., & Sterns, H. L. (1979). Age differences in relationships between crystallized and fluid intelligence and problem solving. *J Gerontol*, *34*, 404–414.

Hooyman, N. R., & Kiyak, H. A. (2005). Cognitive changes with aging. In N. R. Hooyman & H. A. Kiyak (Eds.), *Social gerontology: A multidisciplinary perspective* (7th ed., pp. 164–193). Boston: Allyn & Bacon.

Horn, J. L. (1982). The theory of fluid and crystallized intelligence in relation to concepts of cognitive psychology and aging in adulthood. In F. I. M. Craik & S. Trehub (Eds.), *Aging and cognitive processes* (Vol. 8, pp. 237–278). New York: Plenum Press.

Hoyer, W. J., & Rybash, J. M. (1994). Characterizing adult cognitive development. *J Adult Dev*, *1*(1), 7–12.

Jette, A. M., & Branch, L. G. (1992). A ten-year follow up of driving patterns among the community dwelling elderly. *Hum Factors*, *34*, 25–31.

Jobe, J. B., Smith, D. M., Ball, K., Tennstedt, S. L., Marsiske, M., Willis, S. L., et al. (2001). ACTIVE: A cognitive intervention trial to promote independence in older adults. *Control Clin Trials*, *22*(4), 453–479.

Johansson, K., Bronge, L., Lundberg, C., Persson, S. M., & Viitanen, M. (1996). Can a physician recognize an older driver with increased crash potential? *J Am Geriatr Soc*, *44*, 1198–1204.

Kausler, D. H. (1994). *Learning and memory in normal aging*. New York: Springer.

Keller, J. N. (2006). Age-related neuropathology, cognitive decline, and Alzheimer's disease. *Ageing Res Rev*, *5*, 1–13.

Kiyak, H. A., Teri, L., & Borson, S. (1994). Physical and functional health assessment in normal aging and in Alzheimer's disease: Self-reports vs. family reports. *Gerontologist*, *34*, 324–330.

Kramarow, E., Lentzer, H., Rooks, R., Weeks, J., & Saydah, S. (1999). *Health and aging chartbook: Health, United States, 1999*. Hyattsville, MD: National Center for Health Statistics.

Kramer, A. F., & Willis, S. L. (2003). *Cognitive plasticity and aging* (Vol. 43). San Diego, CA: Academic Press.

Kuzis, G., Sabe, L., Tiberti, C., Merello, M., Leiguarda, R., & Starkstein, S. E. (1999). Explicit and implicit learning in patients with Alzheimer disease and Parkinson disease with dementia. *Neuropsychiatry Neuropsychol Behav Neurol*, *12*(4), 265–269.

Lawton, M. P., & Brody, E. M. (1969). Assessment of older people: Self-maintaining and instrumental activities of daily living. *Gerontologist*, *9*(3), 179–186.

Light, L. L., & Albertson, S. A. (1989). Direct and indirect tests of memory for category exemplars in young and older adults. *Psychol Aging*, *4*, pp. 487–492.

MacPherson, S. E., Phillips, L. H., & Sala, S. D. (2002). Age, executive function, and social decision making: A dorsolateral prefrontal theory of cognitive aging. *Psychol Aging*, *17*(4), 598–609.

Manton, K. G. (1988). A longitudinal study of functional change and mortality in the United States. *J Gerontol A-Biol*, *43*, M5153–M5161.

Marottoli, R. A., Cooney, L. M., Wagner, D. R., Doucetter, J., & Tinetti, M. E. (1994). Predictors of automobile crashes and moving violations among elderly drivers. *Ann Intern Med, 121,* 842–846.

Marottoli, R. A., Mendes de Leon, C. F., Glass, T. A., Williams, C. S., Cooney, L. M., & Berkman, L. F. (2000). Consequences of driving cessation: Decreased out-of-home activity levels. *J Gerontol B-Psychol, 55,* S334–S340.

Milgram, N. W., Siwak-Tapp, C. T., Araujo, A., & Head, E. (2006). Neuroprotective effects of cognitive enrichment. *Ageing Res Rev, 5,* 354–369.

Moscovitch, M., & Winocur, G. (1992). The neuropsychology of memory and aging. In F. I. M. Craik & T. A. Salthouse (Eds.), *The handbook of aging and cognition* (pp. 315–372). Hillsdale, NJ: Erlbaum.

Nyberg, L. (2005). Cognitive training in healthy aging: A cognitive neuroscience perspective. In R. Cabeza, L. Nyberg, & D. Park (Eds.), *Cognitive neuroscience of aging: Linking cognitive and cerebral aging* (pp. 309–321). New York: Oxford University Press.

Owsley, C., Ball, K., McGwin, G., Jr., Sloane, M. E., Roenker, D. L., White, M. F., et al. (1998a). Predicting future crash involvement in older drivers: Who is at risk ? *JAMA, 279,* 1083–1088.

Owsley, C., Ball, K., McGwin, G., Jr., Sloane, M. E., Roenker, D. L., White, M. F., et al. (1998b). Visual processing impairment and risk of motor vehicle crash among older adults. *JAMA, 279*(14), 1083–1088.

Owsley, C., Ball, K., Sloane, M. E., Roenker, D. L., & Bruni, J. R. (1991). Visual perceptual/cognitive correlates of vehicle accidents in older drivers. *Psychol Aging, 6*(3), 403–415.

Owsley, C., & McGwin, G., Jr. (2004). Association between visual attention and mobility in older adults. *J Am Gerontol Soc, 52,* 1901–1906.

Owsley, C., McGwin, G., Jr., Sloane, M. E., Stalvey, B. T., & Wells, J. (2001). Timed instrumental activities of daily living tasks: Relationship to visual function in older adults. *Optometry Vision Sci, 78*(5), 350–359.

Owsley, C., Sloane, M., McGwin, G., Jr., & Ball, K. (2002). Timed instrumental activities of daily living tasks: relationship to cognitive function and everyday performance assessments in older adults. *Gerontology, 48,* 254–265.

Owsley, C., Stalvey, B., Wells, J., & Sloane, M. E. (1999). Older drivers and cataract: Driving habits and crash risk. *J Gerontol A-Biol, 54A*(4), M203–M211.

Parasuraman, R., & Greenwood, P. M. (1998). Selective attention in aging and dementia. In R. Parasuraman (Ed.), *The attentive brain* (pp. 461–487). Cambridge, MA: MIT Press.

Parkin, A. J., & Java, R. I. (1999). Deterioration of frontal lobe function in normal aging: Influences of fluid intelligence versus perceptual speed. *Neuropsychology, 13*(4), 539–545.

Pathy, M. S. J. (Ed.). (2006). *Principles and practice of geriatric medicine* (4th ed.). Chichester, UK: Wiley.

Pathy, M. S. J., Sinclair, A. T., & Morley, J. E. (Eds.). (2006). *Principles and practice of geriatric medicine* (4th ed.). Hoboken, NJ: Wiley.

Perry, B. D. (2002). Childhood experience and the expression of genetic potential: What childhood neglect tells us about nature and nurture. *Brain Mind, 3,* 79–100.

Phillips, L. H., & Sala, S. D. (1998). Aging, intelligence, and anatomical segregation in the frontal lobes. *Learning and Individual Differences, 10*(3), 217–243.

Poon, L. W. (1985). Differences in human memory with aging: Nature, causes, and clinical implications. In J. Birren & K. W. Schaie (Eds.), *Handbook of the psychology of aging* (pp. 427–462). New York: van Nostrand Reinhold.

Rasmusson, D. X., Rebok, G. W., Bylsma, F. W., & Brandt, J. (1999). Effects of three types of memory training in normal elderly. *Aging, Neuropsychol C, 6*(1), 56–66.

Rebok, G., & Balcerak, L. J. (1989). Memory self-efficacy and performance differences in young and old adults: Effects of mnemonic training. *Dev Psychol, 25,* 714–721.

Roenker, D. L., Cissell, G. M., Ball, K. K., Wadley, V. G., & Edwards, J. D. (2003). Speed-of-processing and driving simulator training result in improved driving performance. *Hum Factors*, *45*(2), 218–233.

Rubenstein, L. Z., Schairer, C., Wieland, G. D., & Kane, R. (1984). Systematic biases in functional status assessment of elderly adults: Effects of different data sources. *J Gerontol*, *39*, 686–691.

Salthouse, T. A. (1992). What do adult age differences in the digit symbol substitution test reflect? *J Gerontol*, *47*(3), P121–P128.

Salthouse, T. A. (2006). Mental exercise and mental aging: Evaluating the validity of "use it or lose it" hypothesis. *Perspect Psychol Sci*, *1*(1), 68–87.

Satz, P. (1993). Brain reserve capacity on symptom onset after brain injury: A formulation and review of evidence for threshold theory. *Neuropsychology*, *7*(3), 273–295.

Scarmeas, N., & Stern, Y. (2003). Cognitive reserve and lifestyle. *J Clin Exp Neuropsyc*, *25*(5), 625–633.

Schaie, K. W. (1994). The course of adult intellectual development. *Am Psychol*, *49*(4), 304–313.

Schaie, K. W. (1996a). Intellectual development in adulthood. In J. E. Birren & K. W. Schaie (Eds.), *Handbook of the psychology of aging* (4th ed., pp. 266–286). San Diego, CA: Academic Press.

Schaie, K. W. (1996b). *Intellectual development in adulthood. The Seattle Longitudinal study*. New York: Cambridge University Press.

Schofield, P. W., Marder, K., Dooneief, G., Jacobs, D. M., Sano, M., & Stern, Y. (1997). Association of subjective memory complaints with subsequent cognitive decline in community-dwelling elderly individuals with baseline cognitive impairment. *Am J Psychiatr*, *154*(5), 609–615.

Seeman, T. E. (1996). Social ties and health: The benefits of social integration. *Ann Epidemiol*, *6*(5), 442–451.

Sicard-Rosenbaum, L., Light, K. E., & Behrman, A. L. (2002). Gait, lower extremity strength, and self-assessed mobility after hip arthoroplasty. *J Gerontol B-Psychol*, *57*(1), M47–M51.

Sims, R. V., Owsley, C., Allman, R. M., Ball, K., & Smoot, T. M. (1998). A preliminary assessment of the medical and functional factors associated with vehicle crashes by older adults. *J Am Geriatr Soc*, *46*(5), 556–561.

Small, S. A. (2001). Age-related memory decline: Current concepts and future directions. *Arch Neurol*, *58*, 360–364.

Smith, A. D. (1996). Memory. In J. E. Birren & K. W. Schaie (Eds.), *Handbook of the psychology of aging* (4th ed., pp. 236–250). San Diego, CA: Academic Press.

Souchay, C., Isingrini, M., & Espagnet, L. (2000). Aging, episodic memory, feeling-of-knowing, and frontal functioning. *Neuropsychology*, *14*(2), 299–309.

Stalenhoef, P. A., Diederiks, J. P., de Witte, L. P., Schiricke, K. H., & Crebolder, H. F. (1999). Impact of gait problems and falls on functioning in independent living persons of 55 years and over: A community survey. *Patient Educ Couns*, *36*(1), 23–31.

Stalvey, B. T., Owsley, C., Sloane, M. E., & Ball, K. (1999). The Life Space Questionnaire: A measure of the extent of mobility of older adults. *J Appl Gerontol*, *18*(4), 460–478.

Stern, Y. (2002). What is cognitive reserve?: Theory and research application of the reserve concept. *J Int Neuropsych Soc*, *8*, 448–460.

Stern, Y., Zarahn, E., Hilton, H. J., Flynn, J., DeLaPaz, R., & Rakitin, B. (2003). Exploring the neural basis of cognitive reserve. *J Clin Exp Neuropsyc*, *25*(5), 691–701.

Stutts, J. C. (1998). Do older drivers with visual and cognitive impairments drive less? *J Am Geriatr Soc*, *46*, 854–861.

Tinetti, M. E., Speechley, M., & Ginter, S. F. (1988). Risk factors for falls among elderly persons living in the community. *New Engl J Med, 319*, 1701–1707.

Tinetti, M. E., Williams, C. S., & Gill, T. M. (2000). Health, functional, and psychological outcomes among older persons with chronic dizziness. *J Am Geriatr Soc, 48*(4), 417–421.

Vance, D. E., Ball, K., Roenker, D. L., Wadley, V. G., Edwards, J. D., & Cissell, G. M. (2006). Predictors of falling in older Maryland drivers: A structural-equation model. *J Aging Phys Activ, 14*, 254–269.

Vance, D. E., Roenker, D. L., Cissell, G. M., Edwards, J. D., Wadley, V. G., & Ball, K. (2006). Predictors of driving exposure and avoidance in a field study of older drivers from the state of Maryland. *Accident Anal Prev, 38*(4), 823–831.

West, R., & Alan, C. (2000). Age-related decline in inhibitory control contributes to the increased Stroop effect observed in older adults. *Psychophysiology, 37*, 179–189.

Whalley, L. J., Deary, I. J., Appleton, C. L., & Starr, J. M. (2004). Cognitive reserve and the neurobiology of cognitive aging. *Ageing Res Rev, 3*, 369–382.

Willis, S. L. (1987). Cognitive training and everyday competence. *Ann Rev Gerontol Geriatr, 25*, 714–721.

Willis, S. L. (1996a). Everyday cognitive competence in elderly persons: Conceptual issues and empirical findings. *Gerontologist, 36*(5), 595–601.

Willis, S. L. (1996b). Everyday problem solving. In J. E. Birren & K. W. Schaie (Eds.), *Handbook of the psychology of aging* (4th ed., pp. 287–307). San Diego, CA: Academic Press.

Willis, S. L., Allen-Burge, R., Dolan, M., Bertrand, R., Yesavage, J., & Taylor, J. (1998). Everyday problem solving among individuals with Alzheimer's disease. *Gerontologist, 38*, 569–577.

Willis, S. L., Jay, G. M., Diehl, M., & Marsiske, M. (1992). Longitudinal change and prediction of everyday task competence in the elderly. *Res Aging, 14*(1), 68–91.

Willis, S. L., & Schaie, K. W. (1986). Training the elderly on the ability factors of spatial orientation and inductive reasoning. *Psychol Aging, 1*, 239–247.

Willis, S. L., Tennstedt, S., Marsiske, M., Ball, K., Elias, J., Koepke, K. M., et al. (2006). Long-term effects of cognitive training on everyday functional outcomes in older adults. *JAMA, 296*(23), 2805–2814.

Wilson, R. S., Bennett, D. A., Bienias, J. L., Aggarwal, N. T., Mendes de Leon, C. F., Morris, J. C., et al. (2002). Cognitive activity and incident AD in a population-based sample of older persons. *Neurology, 59*, 1910–1914.

Wolinsky, F. D., Unverzagt, F. W., Smith, D. M., Jones, R., Wright, E., & Tennstedt, S. L. (2006). The effects of the ACTIVE cognitive training trial on clinically relevant declines in health-related quality of life. *J Gerontol: Soc Sci, 61B*(5), S281–S287.

Zimmerman, M. E., Brickman, A. M., Paul, R. H., Grieve, S. M., Tate, D. F., Gunstad, J., et al. (2006). The relationship between frontal gray matter volume and cognition varies across the healthy adult lifespan. *Am J Geriat Psychiat, 14*(10), 823–833.

CHAPTER 11

Everyday Functioning in Dementia and Mild Cognitive Impairment

Paul Malloy and Nicole C. R. McLaughlin

Dementia is defined by the presence of acquired deficits in memory and other cognitive domains. It must be distinguished from more localized brain impairment (e.g., aphasia following focal stroke) and from delirium or confusional states. Some research diagnostic criteria for dementia also require that the patient display impairment in activities of daily living (ADLs; see below).

With new medical advancements extending the average human lifespan, there has also been a growing proportion of the population with dementia. As of 2005 there were 24.3 million individuals with dementia across the world; that number is expected to increase by 4.6 million every year, with 81.8 million cases estimated by the year 2040. In the Western world, the prevalence of dementia is below 1% in individuals ages 60–64 years, but it increases to 24–33% in people 85 years of age and older (Ferri et al., 2005). The number of individuals with dementia is expected to grow 100% between 2001 and 2040 in developed countries, with a 300% increase in Asia, China, and the western Pacific regions.

Given this overall incidence of dementia in the world, Alzheimer's disease has become a growing concern in society, as it is generally regarded as the most common type of dementia in older adults. Given the dramatic cognitive and functional declines caused by this neurodegenerative disease, there are ramifications for patients, caregivers, and society. Multiple functional areas are impacted in dementia of the Alzheimer's type (DAT), including driving, medication management, and other basic ADLs (BADLs) and instrumental ADLs (IADLs).

Diagnostic Criteria for DAT

DAT can be definitively diagnosed only through identification of neuropathological changes in the brain (see below). It is clinically diagnosed by ruling out other possible diagnoses (e.g., vascular dementia) and by assessment of the clinical features displayed by the patient. Several groups have provided research diagnostic criteria for clinical diagnosis of DAT.

According to the DSM-IV criteria, DAT is characterized by multiple cognitive deficits, including memory impairment and impairment in at least one other cognitive domain (i.e., aphasia, apraxia, agnosia, disturbance in executive functioning). To receive a diagnosis, the deficits must cause significant impairment in social or occupational functioning and represent a decline from previous functioning. Alternative causes for the decline should be ruled out, such as other central nervous system conditions that cause dementia (American Psychiatric Association, 1994).

According to the National Institute for Neurological and Communicative Diseases and Stroke—Alzheimer's Disease and Related Disorders Association (NINCDS-ADRDA) criteria (McKhann et al., 1984), to receive a diagnosis of probable Alzheimer's disease, an individual must have (1) dementia, as established by a clinical examination and documented by a rating scale and neuropsychological testing; (2) deficits in two or more areas of cognition; (3) progressive worsening of memory and other cognitive functions; (4) no disturbance of consciousness; (5) onset between ages 40 and 90; and (6) absence of systemic disorders or other brain diseases.

Diagnostic Criteria for Mild Cognitive Impairment

According to criteria from the Mayo Clinic (Petersen et al., 2001), the diagnosis of mild cognitive impairment (MCI) is made when an individual has (1) a memory complaint, preferably corroborated by an informant; (2) an objective memory impairment (for age and education) demonstrated on examination; (3) preserved general cognitive function; (4) intact ADLs; and (5) is not demented. MCI is distinguished from dementia by the absence of deficits in everyday functioning and by less severe or widespread cognitive impairment. Three types of MCI have been described: amnestic, multiple-domain (e.g., memory plus language impairment), and single nonmemory. Differential diagnosis for MCI should include psychiatric disease (e.g., depression), medications, sleep disturbance, and/or metabolic disturbance (Graham et al., 1997).

Conversion from MCI to DAT

Researchers have become increasingly concerned about how to diagnosis and treat Alzheimer's disease early in the disease process (i.e., MCI rather than DAT), in order to retard or prevent progression and minimize disability and health care costs. Studies have shown that individuals with MCI are at increased risk for development of a dementia. Three-year conversion rates of older adults with MCI at baseline range from 27 to 46% (Ganguli, Dodge, Shen, & DeKosky, 2004; Tschanz et al., 2006), as compared to a rate of 3.3% of older adults without cognitive impairment converting in the same 3-year period (Tschanz et al., 2006). It is likely that patients with the amnestic subtype of MCI will progress to DAT, whereas other subtypes may reflect other etiologies such as vascular dementia or "normal aging" (Levey, Lah, Goldstein, Steenland, & Bliwise, 2006; Portet et al., 2006). Greater than 50% of individuals with amnestic MCI have been shown to develop dementia within 3 years (Busse, Bischkopf, Riedel-Heller, & Angermeyer, 2003).

Clinical Assessment of Dementia and MCI

Memory clinics commonly employ a multidisciplinary approach to the diagnosis of dementia. A neurologist or other physician takes a medical history and conducts physical and neurological examinations. The neurological exam is often normal in the early stages of DAT but abnormal in the early stages in other dementias, such as movement disorders (e.g., Parkinson's disease) and cerebrovascular disease. The physician will usually order laboratory tests such as B12/folate, RPR (rapid plasma reagin; the screening test for syphilis), liver function tests, and thyroid panels to iden-tify treatable medical conditions that may be contributing to cognitive change. A computed tomography (CT) or magnetic resonance imaging (MRI) scan will usu-ally be ordered to rule out structural lesion (e.g., brain tumor, stroke) and to assess the localization and severity of cerebral atrophy. If the dementia is not too severe at presentation, a neuropsychologist will conduct an assessment. Neuropsychological assessment can be helpful in early detection of cognitive deficits, differential diag-nosis, and in tracking changes over time in response to treatment or progression of disease. Because the earliest deficits in DAT are typically in the domains of memory, naming, and construction abilities, a neuropsychological battery should, at minimum, assess these areas of cognition. In addition, most neuropsychologists will include tests of orientation, attention, executive, and motor functions. Ratings scales completed by family members to measure neuropsychiatric problems (Cummings et al., 1994; Grace & Malloy, 2001) and ADLs can also be useful diagnostic tools. As is discussed below, noncognitive problems are often important determinants of real-world failure in patients with dementia.

Neuropsychological Testing in DAT

Individuals with DAT generally show rapid forgetting on delayed recall tasks (Braaten, Parsons, McCue, Sellers, & Burns, 2006), resulting from decreased con-solidation of both verbal and visual information (Kramer et al., 2003). The pattern of memory deficits can also differentiate DAT from other dementias. Individuals with DAT have more susceptibility to distractors in visual search tasks and more diffi-culty with dual-task performance (Baddeley, Baddeley, Bucks, & Wilcock, 2001). Deficits in semantic (or category) fluency tasks are evident early in the disease pro-cess, especially when compared with performance on phonemic (or letter) fluency tasks (Greenaway et al., 2006; Murphy, Rich, & Troyer, 2006; Rascovsky, Salmon, Hansen, Thal, & Galasko, 2007). In comparison, individuals with frontotemporal dementia (FTD) are more likely to demonstrate increased impairment on phonemic, as compared to semantic, fluency, or similar impairment on both tasks (Rascovsky et al., 2007). Another prominent deficit in DAT is in confrontation naming (Braaten et al., 2006; Greenaway et al., 2006), and individuals with DAT may present early on with complaints of difficulties in word finding. However, individuals with semantic dementia may perform worse than individuals with DAT on naming, and deficits on this task alone (as with any neuropsychological task) are not sufficient to diagnose a specific disease process (Kramer et al., 2003). Visuospatial functioning impairments are also common in DAT. Deficits may show on construction tasks (Malloy, Belanger, Hall, Aloia, & Salloway, 2003), in visual perception tasks (Ska, Poissant, & Joanette, 1990), or in visuospatial organization (Greenaway et al., 2006). Deficits in visuospatial abilities may contribute to difficulties in real-world functioning, such as driving (Uc, Rizzo, Anderson, Shi, & Dawson, 2005).

Neuroimaging in DAT

Individuals with amnestic MCI display significant hippocampal atrophy on CT or MRI early in the disease process (Becker et al., 2006), but with a lesser severity than that shown in later Alzheimer's disease (AD). Quantified structural neuroimaging has shown greater gray matter loss in converters to DAT relative to nonconverters in the hippocampal area, inferior and middle temporal gyrus, posterior cingulate, and precuneus (Chetelat et al., 2005). Volume loss in the medial temporal lobe has been shown to be the most sensitive measure to identify DAT (Zakzanis, Graham, & Campbell, 2003). Using functional imaging such as positron emission tomography (PET), both early- and late-onset DAT groups display hypometabolism in the bilateral parietotemporal regions when compared with controls. Research has shown predominant posterior cortical association area involvement in early-onset DAT, with involvement of the medial temporal lobes in late-onset DAT (Kemp et al., 2003).

Rating Scales

Most clinical trials for dementia have two primary outcome measures: an experienced clinician rating of functioning using a structured interview, and one or more neuropsychological tests. Some clinician ratings measure severity and others measure change. The scales that have been most commonly used include the Clinical Dementia Rating (CDR) scale and the related CDR—Sum of Boxes (CDR-SB), the Global Deterioration Scale (GDS), the Functional Assessment Staging Test (FAST) procedure, Clinical Global Impressions of Change (CGIC), and Clinician's Interview-Based Impression of Change Plus Caregiver Input (CIBIC-Plus) (Reisberg, 2007). These scales measure functional decline or improvement, but vary in the domains assessed: ADLs (CDR, FAST, CIBIC-Plus), cognition (CDR, GDS, CIBIC-Plus), and behavioral deficits (CIBIC-Plus). In addition, some require the examiner to assess change from baseline functioning (CIBIC-Plus), whereas others (CDR, FAST, GDS) provide a cross-sectional rating of dementia severity.

　　The CDR, for example, is a structured interview that is rated on a 5-point scale ranging from "no cognitive impairment" to "severe dementia" (Morris, 1993, 1997). The global score is derived from individual scores in six domains, including memory, orientation, judgment and problem solving, community affairs, home and hobbies, and personal care. Information is collected from both a collateral source and the presenting patient, and level of ability is rated for each domain. Individuals using the CDR should be trained according to a specific protocol, in order to increase reliability, but some subjectivity is unavoidable in the application of all these scales. A particular challenge for the examiner is determining how to combine discrepant information from different sources (e.g., good rating of everyday memory by the informant but poor performance by the patient on interview items assessing memory).

Neuropathology and Genetics of MCI/DAT

Neuropathological hallmarks of DAT include plaques composed of amyloid ß and tangles composed of hyperphosphorylated tau (Blennow, de Leon, & Zetterberg, 2006). Compared with neurofibrillary tangles (NFTs), neuritic plaques (NPs) are a less common occurrence of normal aging. Accumulation of NPs, not NFTs, occurs early in the course of DAT (Tiraboschi, Hansen, Thal, & Corey-Bloom, 2004). However, NFTs appear to be the major determinants of cognitive decline after the early stages of dementia (Tiraboschi et al., 2004). In amnestic MCI neuropathological findings suggest a transitional stage of evolving DAT (Petersen et al., 2006) characterized by elevated NPs (Markesbery et al., 2006). In regard to cognition, a correlation between plaque and tangle burden and cognitive status has been found in younger patients, but not in older patients with DAT (Prohovnik et al., 2006).

The apolipoprotein E (ApoE) gene has been implicated as a genetic marker for DAT. Individuals with at least one ApoE 4 allele are at higher risk of developing AD than those with ApoE 2 or 3 alleles (Tschanz et al., 2006). Each allele copy has been shown to lower the age of onset by almost 10 years (Corder et al., 1993). Familial DAT is a rare autosomal disease with early onset (deficits appearing even as early as the third decade of life), caused by mutations in several genes linked to amyloid ß metabolism. Mutations on the presenilin genes account for most cases of familial disease (Sherrington et al., 1995). The prevalence of familial DAT is below 0.1% (Harvey, Skelton-Robinson, & Rossor, 2003).

There continues to be significant research into the causes of DAT. For example, the amyloid cascade hypothesis suggests that there is an imbalance between the production and clearance of amyloid ß in the brain, which is the initiating event that leads to neuronal degeneration and dementia (Hardy & Selkoe, 2002). Additionally, given the relationship between cerebrovascular disease and DAT, there has been a suggestion that neurovascular dysfunction contributes to the decline in DAT. The neurovascular hypothesis states that dysfunctional blood vessels may contribute to cognitive dysfunction by impairing delivery of nutrients to neurons and reducing amyloid ß clearance from the brain (Iadecola, 2004). Some research has suggested that, rather than tau and amyloid ß being precursors to neuronal degeneration and dementia in the brain, they are a byproduct of an earlier pathological event. Oxidative stress causes the buildup of oxidative damage in molecules and may contribute to DAT (Mariani, Polidori, Cherubini, & Mecocci, 2005). In addition to the theories involving oxidative stress, other researchers have indicated that other changes (along with oxidative stress), such as mitogenic changes, may have a role in DAT (Zhu, Raina, Perry, & Smith, 2004).

Activities of Daily Living

Basic ADLs (BADLs) include such self-care behaviors as grooming and bathing. Instrumental IADLs (IADLs) include more complex interactions with the environment such as cooking, bill paying, and medication management. These behaviors can be evaluated by direct observation or via informant rating scales. It might be argued that observation in a standard environment is the superior method, not being subject to caregiver biases. However, the advantage of informant ratings is that it takes into consideration performance over an extended period in the relatively unstructured home environment. In the home the patient often needs to initiate and organize an activity, unlike in the laboratory situation where the materials may be laid out and tasks prompted by the examiner. As is discussed below, it is deficits in executive functioning, including the ability to initiate an action, that often cause ADL failures.

With regard to cognition, research has demonstrated that moderate dementia (Mini-Mental State Examination [MMSE] score of 16 or below) seems to be a point at which most IADLs are lost, and many BADLs decline throughout the following year (Feldman, Van Baelen, Kavanagh, & Torfs, 2005). But it is common to observe some decline in IADLs in patients with milder cognitive impairment. It might be expected that memory dysfunction is the cause of failures in ADLs (as measured by informant rating), and indeed memory and ADL deficits are related (Farias et al., 2006). However, executive functioning has also been shown to be significantly related to performance of ADLs. Frontal lobe systems are disproportionately affected by aging, possibly resulting in deficits in planning, organization, self-control, and awareness of problems that affect the ability to care for oneself. In a study of community-dwelling individuals without dementia, we found that executive function and depression severity accounted for a significant proportion of variance in IADLs, with executive function making the greatest contribution. Tests measuring other cognitive functions, such as memory, language, and spatial skills, did not contribute significantly to the prediction of functional status. Furthermore, executive measures accounted for more variance than other demographic characteristics such as general health status, age, and educational level (Cahn-Weiner, Boyle, & Malloy, 2002). In another study of patients with mild to moderate DAT, frontal systems dysfunction accounted for 44% of the variance in IADLs and 28% of the variance in BADLs (as measured by informant ratings), independent of memory problems (Boyle, Malloy, et al., 2003). Similar strong relationships between executive dysfunction and functional deficits have been demonstrated in vascular dementia (Boyle, Paul, et al., 2003).

There is also a strong relationship between the presence of behavioral disturbance and poor performance of ADLs, especially IADLs, in dementia. Both MMSE scores and neuropsychiatric symptoms have been shown to be related to ADL performance (Tekin, Fairbanks, O'Connor, Rosenberg, & Cummings, 2001). Neuropsychiatric symptoms (e.g., apathy and disinhibition) related to frontal lobe dysfunction are particularly disruptive to ADLs. In fact, a stronger relationship has been found between ADL function and scores on the Frontal Systems Behavior Scale (FrSBe) than between ADLs and cognitive measures in patients with dementia (Norton, Malloy, & Salloway, 2001). We have shown that behavioral disturbance affects performance of ADLs (independent of cognitive deficits) in DAT (Boyle, Malloy, et al., 2003).

In regard to the relationship between neuropathological changes and ADLs, there is a positive correlation between total ADL scores (as measured by informant rating) and NP and NFT counts in DAT patients. Hippocampal NP and NFT counts, right and left orbital frontal NP counts, and occipital NP counts are all related to ADL scores. ADL performance did not correlate with age at death, age at symptom onset, dementia duration, gender, or education (Marshall, Fairbanks, Tekin, Vinters, & Cummings, 2006).

Falls

Researchers have predicted that three-quarters of older people with cognitive impairment or dementia may fall each year (Shaw et al., 2003). Individuals with DAT have a higher frequency of falls than other older adults (Morris, Rubin, Morris, & Mandel, 1987), and the number increases with dementia severity (Ganguli et al., 2006). Falls have been found to occur in 7.4% of community-residing patients with DAT studied for a 2-week period (Bassiony et al., 2004).

Being able to get up from a chair, previous falls, needing a helper when walking, and hyperactive symptoms are risk factors for falls (Kattin, Gustafson, & Sandman, 2005). In elderly community residents with cognitive impairment, sedative use was associated with a high risk of falling (Tinetti & Williams, 1998). Of 336 people (75 years and older), 108 had fallen at least once, and 24% had experienced fall serious fall-related injuries. In a nursing home, 240 older adults with dementia suffered 1,343 falls in a 2-year period, which was estimated to be 4.1 falls per year, per person. Falls occurred primarily after admission or transfer to another unit. Men displayed twice the risk as women. Inadequate use of materials, stumbling/slipping, and gait and equilibrium disturbances also contribute to falls (van Dijk, Meulenberg, van de Sande, & Habbema, 1993).

Living Alone/Wandering

Individuals with cognitive impairment are at higher risk for harm due to wandering, which often occurs in response to disorientation or confusion (Tierney et al., 2004). "Critical wandering" has been defined as wandering away from supervised care or a controlled environment or being unable to locate (Butler & Barnett, 1991). The Alzheimer's Association estimates that 60% of people with DAT will wander and become lost in the community at some point (Rowe, 2003; Rowe & Bennett, 2003). These incidents may result in injury or even death due to hypothermia, drowning, dehydration (Rowe & Bennett, 2003). In Virginia, for example, 16% of lost person cases reported to search-and-rescue (SAR) personnel were individuals with DAT, second in rate only to lost children. Extrapolating from previous research, SAR estimated that over 125,000 critical wandering incidents by individuals with DAT occur every year. To reduce wandering, the SAR recommends that caregivers use behavioral measures (e.g., avoid changing the schedule or leaving the patient alone), environmental modifications (e.g., keep the person oriented, design an interesting walking path), and control the exits (lock windows, gate stairs) (Alzheimer's Disease and Related Disorders SAR Research, 2000–2007).

Driving

Review of research based on crash statistics and performance studies of drivers with DAT has shown mild driving impairment in individuals with probable DAT (CDR = 0.5), similar to drivers ages 16–21 years and those with blood alcohol concentration greater than 0.08%. Drivers with a CDR scale equal to 1 (mild dementia) are a significant problem with regard to crashes and driving performance measures (Dubinsky, Stein, & Lyons, 2000). If patients with dementia continue to drive for 5 years, 47% will be involved in accidents, as compared to 10% of healthy controls (Friedland et al., 1988).

In one on-road driving study, drivers with mild DAT identified fewer landmarks and traffic signs and made more at-fault safety errors (i.e., erratic steering, lane deviation, unsafe intersection behavior), as compared to controls. Ability to identify roadside targets was predicted by scores on tests of visual abilities and cognitive functioning (executive, memory, and spatial tasks). Safety errors were predicted by performance on memory and visual perception tasks (Uc et al., 2005). Another study also demonstrated that individuals with DAT frequently make operational errors on a real-world driving test, including hesitant driving, diminished awareness of traffic environment, tactical errors such as problems with changing lanes smoothly, and judgment errors such as making a turn onto a one-way street (Grace et al., 2005). Unsafe drivers (as determined through an on-road driving test) with mild DAT were impaired across all neuropsychological measures (Hopkins Verbal Learning Test [HVLT], Rey–Osterrieth Complex Figure [ROCF], Neuropsychological Assessment Battery [NAB] driving scenes, Trail Making Test [TMT], computerized mazes), except for finger tapping. Spatial (ROCF) and executive functioning tasks (TMT-B) distinguished safe from unsafe drivers. Other research studies have also shown that driving abilities are related to nonverbal executive functioning skills (Porteus mazes, computerized mazes, clock drawing; Ott et al., 2000, 2003), as well as visual attention skills (Whelihan, DiCarlo, & Paul, 2005).

Clinicians are fair in their prediction of actual driving performance only if they base their judgment on standard road testing. In individuals with very mild to mild dementia, clinician accuracy ranged from 62 to 78%, with dementia specialists ranging from 72 to 78% and general practitioners from 62 to 64% (Ott et al., 2005).

Prediction of driving safety by clinicians is poor; even patients with mild dementia tend to make errors while driving, and the risk of serious accidents increases greatly as dementia progresses. Hence, the cautious clinician should encourage patients with dementia to stop driving or greatly curtail their driving. This can be a contentious issue with patients and their families, but safety must be a primary concern.

Medication Adherence

Older adults with cognitive impairment are at higher risk for nonadherence to a medication regimen (Cooper et al., 2005). In a study of 1,107 community-dwelling elders, Ganguli and colleagues (2006) found that inadvertent medication nonadherence increased with dementia severity. The levels of discrepancy between information patients provided to their physicians and information they provided in response to detailed, standardized assessments also varied with dementia severity. Clinicians should therefore be alert to the possibility of receiving unreliable health information from patients with even mild dementia, as there can be serious consequences. Underuse of prescribed medications can result in exacerbation of a medical condition (e.g., hypothyroidism) or further brain damage (e.g., stroke in an untreated patient with hypertension). Overuse can precipitate a toxic confusional state, a common reason for hospitalization in older adults with dementia.

In other chronic illnesses, adherence interventions have included home visits (Johnson, Taylor, Sackett, Dunnett, & Shimizu, 1978), simplifying the medication regimen (Girvin, McDermott, & Johnston, 1999), use of special medication containers (Rehder, McCoy, Blackwell, Whitehead, & Robinson, 1980), use of electronic alarm reminders (Safren, Hendriksen, Desousa, Boswell, & Mayer, 2003), use of telephone reminders (Friedman et al., 1996), and psychoeducation (Bailey et al., 1990). Home visits to facilitate medication compliance are often impractical for real-world application in dementia clinics. While simplifying the medication regimen would benefit individuals with dementia, this is not always possible, as many such patients have multiple medical conditions requiring concurrent treatment. Several studies have advised customizing treatment to meet patients' special needs and cognitive capabilities (e.g., Cohen-Mansfield, 2001; Gerdner, 2000). Thus, interventions to improve medication adherence in patients with dementia are more likely to succeed if they focus on environmental modifications and mnemonic aids, rather than focusing on the patients' skills and knowledge. A multifaceted intervention utilizing an electronic reminder system, special medication containers, structuring of the home environment, and psychoeducation for caregivers is likely to be most helpful.

Caregiver Burden

As the severity of dementia progresses, caregivers of the individual with dementia must increase the amount of support they provide for their loved one. Not unexpectedly, the demands placed on the caregiver may lead to an increase in emotional, physical, and financial stress. Sixty-eight percent of caregivers have been shown to be highly burdened, with no difference between caregivers of individuals with dementia who were institutionalized and those living in the community (Papastavrou, Kalokerinou, Papacostas, Tsangari, & Sourtzi, 2007). Caregivers show an increase in symptoms of depression (Papastavrou et al., 2007; Sink, Covinsky, Barnes, Newcomer, & Yaffe, 2006), and even severe depression appears to worsen as the dementia progresses (Berger et al., 2005). The majority of caregivers, with estimates at almost three-quarters of all caregivers, are women (Ory, Hoffman, Yee, Tennstedt, & Schulz, 1999). Women tend to show a higher level of burden, including higher levels of depression, as compared to men (Gallicchio, Siddiqi, Langenberg, & Baumgarten, 2002; Papastavrou et al., 2007; Thompson et al., 2004). Although there may be gender biases in reporting mental health symptoms (World Health Organization, 2002), as in other disorders, other factors may contribute to the increased burden experienced by women as compared to men, such as the manner in which women and men cope with the increased stress (i.e., men tend to use more problem-solving strategies) (Thompson et al., 2004).

Sources of caregiver burden include (1) patient variables, such as severity and duration of the dementia, patient psychopathology, behavior problems, and ADL limitations; (2) caregiver variables, such as age and health of caregiver, level of education, gender, caregiver's time demands, religious beliefs, problem-solving skills, and perception of disease; and (3) environmental variables, such as financial resources, social support, and the quality of caregivers' prior relationship with the care recipient (Papastavrou et al., 2007; Rymer et al., 2002).

There is minimal research thoroughly examining the relationship between degree of patient cognitive deficit and caregiver burden. Most studies have not demonstrated that measures of general cognitive status predict burden (Coen, Swanwick, O'Boyle, & Coakley, 1997), although the severity of the dementia overall may show a relationship with caregiver burden (Donaldson, Tarrier, & Burns, 1998). Other research has indicated that the care recipient's perception of memory deficits is associated with level of caregiver burden (Rymer et al., 2002).

Over and above cognitive deficits, associated behavioral disturbances in the patient add significantly to caregiver burden. Disinhibition and apathy in the individual with dementia are particularly troublesome problems for caregivers (Boyle, Malloy, et al., 2003; Davis & Tremont, 2007; Rymer et al., 2002). Caregivers with a high desire to institutionalize their care recipients may have greater knowledge of dementia but also a higher burden, more family dysfunction, and decreased social support (Spitznagel, Tremont, Davis, & Foster, 2006). Less burdened relatives tend to use more problem-solving approaches to cope with the increased demands (i.e., quickly resolving emotional upsets, confronting problems, discussing whether a proposed solution to a problem was effective). High premorbid relationship satisfaction with the care recipient has been shown to decrease level of burden as well as reactivity to memory and behavior problems (Steadman, Tremont, & Davis, 2007). Taking into account all of these factors is especially important in providing supports for these caregivers within the community.

Summary and Future Directions

As the world population ages, dementia is becoming an increasing public health crisis. AD is the most common cause of dementia, and although we have learned much about the genetics and molecular basis of this disease, to date no cure for this condition has been found. Patients with dementia display progressive deficits in ADLs that are caused by both decline in cognition and increases in behavioral problems. Dementia is also associated with increased risk of falls, wandering, automobile accidents, and medication errors that may be fatal. Interventions focusing on modifying the environment, providing mnemonic aids, and assisting caregivers are likely to be most helpful in reducing real-world problems in patients with dementia.

In terms of future research, studies are likely to identify other genes associated with risk for DAT and other dementias, allowing for more accurate assessment of risk and differential diagnosis. New medications are being developed to arrest or reverse the AD process by reducing amyloid burden, rather than merely improving symptoms by boosting neurotransmitter availability. Other mechanisms (e.g., oxidative stress) contributing to cell death in dementia are being investigated, and this research may lead to new forms of treatment. In addition to pharmacological treatments for DAT, there may be promise in continuing to explore cognitive and behavioral treatments, both in the laboratory and real-world settings.

In the realm of everyday functioning, better algorithms are needed to predict functional decline on an individual basis. Studies combining quantified neuroimaging with cognitive and behavioral measures are likely to make this prediction process more accurate. Neuropsychologists need to further parse those aspects of memory and executive functioning that are most strongly related to everyday functioning, and to identify the brain systems underlying these abilities. Standardized, psychometrically sound assessment tools for assessing everyday functioning are also needed. Such instruments would allow clinicians to better discriminate changes in functioning due to dementia versus normal aging and to accurately track such changes over time. There is a scarcity of research examining medical adherence rates, both in regard to adherence to medications for treating DAT and to other medications for emotional and physical health. In the public health sector, greater awareness is needed in both clinicians and the general public of the dangers faced by cognitively impaired older adults who try to live independently, manage their own finances, or drive. There also should be greater emphasis placed on support of caregivers, who often suffer from stress and depression while attempting to maintain the everyday functioning of their loved one with dementia.

References

American Psychiatric Association. (1994). *Diagnostic and statistical manual of mental disorders* (4th ed.). Washington, DC: Author.

Alzheimer's disease and related disorders SAR research. (2000–2007). Charlottesville, VA: dbS Productions. Retrieved July 12, 2007, from *www.dbs-sar.com/SAR_Research/alzheimer_research.htm.*

Baddeley, A. D., Baddeley, H. A., Bucks, R. S., & Wilcock, G. K. (2001). Attentional control in Alzheimer's disease. *Brain, 124*(Pt. 8), 1492–1508.

Bailey, W. C., Richards, J. M., Jr., Brooks, C. M., Soong, S. J., Windsor, R. A., & Manzella, B. A. (1990). A randomized trial to improve self-management practices of adults with asthma. *Arch Intern Med, 150*(8), 1664–1668.

Bassiony, M. M., Rosenblatt, A., Baker, A., Steinberg, M., Steele, C. D., Sheppard, J. M., et al. (2004). Falls and age in patients with Alzheimer's disease. *J Nerv Ment Dis, 192*(8), 570–572.

Becker, J. T., Davis, S. W., Hayashi, K. M., Meltzer, C. C., Toga, A. W., Lopez, O. L., et al. (2006). Three-dimensional patterns of hippocampal atrophy in mild cognitive impairment. *Arch Neurol, 63*(1), 97–101.

Berger, G., Bernhardt, T., Weimer, E., Peters, J., Kratzsch, T., & Frolich, L. (2005). Longitudinal study on the relationship between symptomatology of dementia and levels of subjective burden and depression among family caregivers in memory clinic patients. *J Geriatr Psychiatry Neurol, 18*(3), 119–128.

Blennow, K., de Leon, M. J., & Zetterberg, H. (2006). Alzheimer's disease. *Lancet, 368,* 387–403.

Boyle, P. A., Malloy, P. F., Salloway, S., Cahn-Weiner, D. A., Cohen, R., & Cummings, J. L. (2003). Executive dysfunction and apathy predict functional impairment in Alzheimer disease. *Am J Geriatr Psychiatry, 11*(2), 214–221.

Boyle, P. A., Paul, R., Moser, D., Zawacki, T., Gordon, N., & Cohen, R. (2003). Cognitive and neurologic predictors of functional impairment in vascular dementia. *Am J Geriatr Psychiatry, 11*(1), 103–106.

Braaten, A. J., Parsons, T. D., McCue, R., Sellers, A., & Burns, W. J. (2006). Neurocognitive differential diagnosis of dementing diseases: Alzheimer's dementia, vascular dementia, frontotemporal dementia, and major depressive disorder. *Int J Neurosci*, *116*(11), 1271–1293.

Busse, A., Bischkopf, J., Riedel-Heller, S. G., & Angermeyer, M. C. (2003). Subclassifications for mild cognitive impairment: Prevalence and predictive validity. *Psychol Med*, *33*(6), 1029–1038.

Butler, J. P., & Barnett, C. A. (1991). Window of wandering. *Geriatr Nurs*, *12*(5), 226–227.

Cahn-Weiner, D. A., Boyle, P. A., & Malloy, P. F. (2002). Tests of executive function predict instrumental activities of daily living in community-dwelling older individuals. *Appl Neuropsychol*, *9*(3), 187–191.

Chetelat, G., Landeau, B., Eustache, F., Mezenge, F., Viader, F., de la Sayette, V., et al. (2005). Using voxel-based morphometry to map the structural changes associated with rapid conversion in MCI: A longitudinal MRI study. *Neuroimage*, *27*(4), 934–946.

Coen, R. F., Swanwick, G. R., O'Boyle, C. A., & Coakley, D. (1997). Behaviour disturbance and other predictors of carer burden in Alzheimer's disease. *Int J Geriatr Psychiatry*, *12*(3), 331–336.

Cohen-Mansfield, J. (2001). Nonpharmacologic interventions for inappropriate behaviors in dementia: A review, summary, and critique. *Am J Geriatr Psychiatry*, *9*(4), 361–381.

Cooper, C., Carpenter, I., Katona, C., Schroll, M., Wagner, C., Fialova, D., et al. (2005). The AdHOC study of older adults' adherence to medication in 11 countries. *Am J Geriatr Psychiatry*, *13*(12), 1067–1076.

Corder, E. H., Saunders, A. M., Strittmatter, W. J., Schmechel, D. E., Gaskell, P. C., Small, G. W., et al. (1993). Gene dose of apolipoprotein E type 4 allele and the risk of Alzheimer's disease in late onset families. *Science*, *261*, 921–923.

Cummings, J. L., Mega, M., Gray, K., Rosenberg-Thompson, S., Carusi, D. A., & Gornbein, J. (1994). The Neuropsychiatric Inventory: Comprehensive assessment of psychopathology in dementia. *Neurology*, *44*(12), 2308–2314.

Davis, J. D., & Tremont, G. (2007). Impact of frontal systems behavioral functioning in dementia on caregiver burden. *J Neuropsychiatry Clin Neurosci*, *19*(1), 43–49.

Donaldson, C., Tarrier, N., & Burns, A. (1998). Determinants of carer stress in Alzheimer's disease. *Int J Geriatr Psychiatry*, *13*(4), 248–256.

Dubinsky, R. M., Stein, A. C., & Lyons, K. (2000). Practice parameter: Risk of driving and Alzheimer's disease (an evidence-based review). Report of the Quality Standards Subcommittee of the American Academy of Neurology. *Neurology*, *54*(12), 2205–2211.

Farias, S. T., Mungas, D., Reed, B. R., Harvey, D., Cahn-Weiner, D., & Decarli, C. (2006). MCI is associated with deficits in everyday functioning. *Alzheimer Dis Assoc Disord*, *20*(4), 217–223.

Feldman, H. H., Van Baelen, B., Kavanagh, S. M., & Torfs, K. E. (2005). Cognition, function, and caregiving time patterns in patients with mild-to-moderate Alzheimer disease: A 12-month analysis. *Alzheimer Dis Assoc Disord*, *19*(1), 29–36.

Ferri, C. P., Prince, M., Brayne, C., Brodaty, H., Fratiglioni, L., Ganguli, M., et al. (2005). Global prevalence of dementia: A Delphi consensus study. *Lancet*, *366*, 2112–2117.

Friedland, R. P., Koss, E., Kumar, A., Gaine, S., Metzler, D., Haxby, J. V., et al. (1988). Motor vehicle crashes in dementia of the Alzheimer type. *Ann Neurol*, *24*(6), 782–786.

Friedman, R. H., Kazis, L. E., Jette, A., Smith, M. B., Stollerman, J., Torgerson, J., et al. (1996). A telecommunications system for monitoring and counseling patients with hypertension. Impact on medication adherence and blood pressure control. *Am J Hypertens*, *9*(4, Pt. 1), 285–292.

Gallicchio, L., Siddiqi, N., Langenberg, P., & Baumgarten, M. (2002). Gender differences in burden and depression among informal caregivers of demented elders in the community. *Int J Geriatr Psychiatry*, *17*(2), 154–163.

Ganguli, M., Dodge, H. H., Shen, C., & DeKosky, S. T. (2004). Mild cognitive impairment, amnestic type: An epidemiologic study. *Neurology, 63*(1), 115–121.

Ganguli, M., Du, Y., Rodriguez, E. G., Mulsant, B. H., McMichael, K. A., Vander Bilt, J., et al. (2006). Discrepancies in information provided to primary care physicians by patients with and without dementia: The Steel Valley Seniors Survey. *Am J Geriatr Psychiatry, 14*(5), 446–455.

Gerdner, L. A. (2000). Effects of individualized versus classical "relaxation" music on the frequency of agitation in elderly persons with Alzheimer's disease and related disorders. *Int Psychogeriatr, 12*(1), 49–65.

Girvin, B., McDermott, B. J., & Johnston, G. D. (1999). A comparison of enalapril 20 mg once daily versus 10 mg twice daily in terms of blood pressure lowering and patient compliance. *J Hypertens, 17*(11), 1627–1631.

Grace, J., Amick, M. M., D'Abreu, A., Festa, E. K., Heindel, W. C., & Ott, B. R. (2005). Neuropsychological deficits associated with driving performance in Parkinson's and Alzheimer's disease. *J Int Neuropsychol Soc, 11*(6), 766–775.

Grace, J., & Malloy, P. F. (2001). *Frontal Systems Behavior Scale (FrSBe): Professional manual.* Lutz, FL: Psychological Assessment Resources.

Graham, J. E., Rockwood, K., Beattie, B. L., Eastwood, R., Gauthier, S., Tuokko, H., et al. (1997). Prevalence and severity of cognitive impairment with and without dementia in an elderly population. *Lancet, 349*, 1793–1796.

Greenaway, M. C., Lacritz, L. H., Binegar, D., Weiner, M. F., Lipton, A., & Munro Cullum, C. (2006). Patterns of verbal memory performance in mild cognitive impairment, Alzheimer disease, and normal aging. *Cogn Behav Neurol, 19*(2), 79–84.

Hardy, J., & Selkoe, D. J. (2002). The amyloid hypothesis of Alzheimer's disease: Progress and problems on the road to therapeutics. *Science, 297*, 353–356.

Harvey, R. J., Skelton-Robinson, M., & Rossor, M. N. (2003). The prevalence and causes of dementia in people under the age of 65 years. *J Neurol Neurosurg Psychiatry, 74*(9), 1206–1209.

Iadecola, C. (2004). Neurovascular regulation in the normal brain and in Alzheimer's disease. *Nat Rev Neurosci, 5*(5), 347–360.

Johnson, A. L., Taylor, D. W., Sackett, D. L., Dunnett, C. W., & Shimizu, A. G. (1978). Self-recording of blood pressure in the management of hypertension. *Can Med Assoc J, 119*(9), 1034–1039.

Kattin, K., Gustafson, Y., & Sandman, P. (2005). Factors associated with falls among older, cognitively impaired people in geriatric care settings. *Am J Geriatr Psychiatry, 13*(6), 501–509.

Kemp, P. M., Holmes, C., Hoffmann, S. M., Bolt, L., Holmes, R., Rowden, J., et al. (2003). Alzheimer's disease: Differences in technetium-99m HMPAO SPECT scan findings between early onset and late onset dementia. *J Neurol Neurosurg Psychiatry, 74*(6), 715–719.

Kramer, J. H., Jurik, J., Sha, S. J., Rankin, K. P., Rosen, H. J., Johnson, J. K., et al. (2003). Distinctive neuropsychological patterns in frontotemporal dementia, semantic dementia, and Alzheimer disease. *Cogn Behav Neurol, 16*(4), 211–218.

Levey, A., Lah, J., Goldstein, F., Steenland, K., & Bliwise, D. (2006). Mild cognitive impairment: An opportunity to identify patients at high risk for progression to Alzheimer's disease. *Clin Ther, 28*(7), 991–1001.

Malloy, P., Belanger, H., Hall, S., Aloia, M., & Salloway, S. (2003). Assessing visuoconstructional performance in AD, MCI and normal elderly using the Beery Visual–Motor Integration Test. *Clin Neuropsychol, 17*(4), 544–550.

Mariani, E., Polidori, M. C., Cherubini, A., & Mecocci, P. (2005). Oxidative stress in brain aging, neurodegenerative and vascular diseases: An overview. *J Chromatogr B Analyt Technol Biomed Life Sci, 827*(1), 65–75.

Markesbery, W. R., Schmitt, F. A., Kryscio, R. J., Davis, D. G., Smith, C. D., & Wekstein, D. R. (2006). Neuropathologic substrate of mild cognitive impairment. *Arch Neurol, 63*(1), 38–46.

Marshall, G. A., Fairbanks, L. A., Tekin, S., Vinters, H. V., & Cummings, J. L. (2006). Neuropathologic correlates of activities of daily living in Alzheimer disease. *Alzheimer Dis Assoc Disord, 20*(1), 56–59.

McKhann, G., Drachman, D., Folstein, M., Katzman, R., Price, D., & Stadlan, E. M. (1984). Clinical diagnosis of Alzheimer's disease: Report of the NINCDS-ADRDA Work Group under the auspices of Department of Health and Human Services Task Force on Alzheimer's Disease. *Neurology, 34*(7), 939–944.

Morris, J. C. (1993). The Clinical Dementia Rating (CDR): Current version and scoring rules. *Neurology, 43*(11), 2412–2414.

Morris, J. C. (1997). Clinical Dementia Rating: A reliable and valid diagnostic and staging measure for dementia of the Alzheimer type. *Int Psychogeriatr, 9*(Suppl. 1), 173–178.

Morris, J. C., Rubin, E. H., Morris, E. J., & Mandel, S. A. (1987). Senile dementia of the Alzheimer's type: An important risk factor for serious falls. *J Gerontol, 42*(4), 412–417.

Murphy, K. J., Rich, J. B., & Troyer, A. K. (2006). Verbal fluency patterns in amnestic mild cognitive impairment are characteristic of Alzheimer's type dementia. *J Int Neuropsychol Soc, 12*(4), 570–574.

Norton, L. E., Malloy, P. F., & Salloway, S. (2001). The impact of behavioral symptoms on activities of daily living in patients with dementia. *Am J Geriatr Psychiatry, 9*(1), 41–48.

Ory, M. G., Hoffman, R. R., III, Yee, J. L., Tennstedt, S., & Schulz, R. (1999). Prevalence and impact of caregiving: A detailed comparison between dementia and nondementia caregivers. *Gerontologist, 39*(2), 177–185.

Ott, B. R., Anthony, D., Papandonatos, G. D., D'Abreu, A., Burock, J., Curtin, A., et al. (2005). Clinician assessment of the driving competence of patients with dementia. *J Am Geriatr Soc, 53*(5), 829–833.

Ott, B. R., Heindel, W. C., Whelihan, W. M., Caron, M. D., Piatt, A. L., & DiCarlo, M. A. (2003). Maze test performance and reported driving ability in early dementia. *J Geriatr Psychiatry Neurol, 16*(3), 151–155.

Ott, B. R., Heindel, W. C., Whelihan, W. M., Caron, M. D., Piatt, A. L., & Noto, R. B. (2000). A single-photon emission computed tomography imaging study of driving impairment in patients with Alzheimer disease. *Dement Geriatr Cogn Disord, 11*(3), 153–160.

Papastavrou, E., Kalokerinou, A., Papacostas, S. S., Tsangari, H., & Sourtzi, P. (2007). Caring for a relative with dementia: Family caregiver burden. *J Adv Nurs, 58*(5), 446–457.

Petersen, R. C., Doody, R., Kurz, A., Mohs, R. C., Morris, J. C., Rabins, P. V., et al. (2001). Current concepts in mild cognitive impairment. *Arch Neurol, 58*(12), 1985–1992.

Petersen, R. C., Parisi, J. E., Dickson, D. W., Johnson, K. A., Knopman, D. S., Boeve, B. F., et al. (2006). Neuropathologic features of amnestic mild cognitive impairment. *Arch Neurol, 63*(5), 665–672.

Portet, F., Ousset, P. J., Visser, P. J., Frisoni, G. B., Nobili, F., Scheltens, P., et al. (2006). Mild cognitive impairment (MCI) in medical practice: A critical review of the concept and new diagnostic procedure. Report of the MCI Working Group of the European Consortium on Alzheimer's Disease. *J Neurol Neurosurg Psychiatry, 77*(6), 714–718.

Prohovnik, I., Perl, D. P., Davis, K. L., Libow, L., Lesser, G., & Haroutunian, V. (2006). Dissociation of neuropathology from severity of dementia in late-onset Alzheimer disease. *Neurology, 66*(1), 49–55.

Rascovsky, K., Salmon, D. P., Hansen, L. A., Thal, L. J., & Galasko, D. (2007). Disparate letter and semantic category fluency deficits in autopsy-confirmed frontotemporal dementia and Alzheimer's disease. *Neuropsychology, 21*(1), 20–30.

Rehder, T. L., McCoy, L. K., Blackwell, B., Whitehead, W., & Robinson, A. (1980). Improving medication compliance by counseling and special prescription container. *Am J Hosp Pharm, 37*(3), 379–385.

Reisberg, B. (2007). Global measures: Utility in defining and measuring treatment response in dementia. *Int Psychogeriatr, 19*(3), 421–456.

Rowe, M. A. (2003). People with dementia who become lost. *Am J Nurs, 103*(7), 32–39.

Rowe, M. A., & Bennett, V. (2003). A look at deaths occurring in persons with dementia lost in the community. *Am J Alzheimer's Dis Other Demen, 18*(6), 343–348.

Rymer, S., Salloway, S., Norton, L., Malloy, P., Correia, S., & Monast, D. (2002). Impaired awareness, behavior disturbance, and caregiver burden in Alzheimer disease. *Alzheimer Dis Assoc Disord, 16*(4), 248–253.

Safren, S. A., Hendriksen, E. S., Desousa, N., Boswell, S. L., & Mayer, K. H. (2003). Use of an on-line pager system to increase adherence to antiretroviral medications. *AIDS Care, 15*(6), 787.

Shaw, F. E., Bond, J., Richardson, D. A., Dawson, P., Steen, I. N., McKeith, I. G., et al. (2003). Multifactorial intervention after a fall in older people with cognitive impairment and dementia presenting to the accident and emergency department: Randomised controlled trial. *Brit Med J, 326*, 73.

Sherrington, R., Rogaev, E. I., Liang, Y., Rogaeva, E. A., Levesque, G., Ikeda, M., et al. (1995). Cloning of a gene bearing missense mutations in early-onset familial Alzheimer's disease. *Nature, 375*, 754–760.

Sink, K. M., Covinsky, K. E., Barnes, D. E., Newcomer, R. J., & Yaffe, K. (2006). Caregiver characteristics are associated with neuropsychiatric symptoms of dementia. *J Am Geriatr Soc, 54*(5), 796–803.

Ska, B., Poissant, A., & Joanette, Y. (1990). Line orientation judgment in normal elderly and subjects with dementia of Alzheimer's type. *J Clin Exp Neuropsychol, 12*(5), 695–702.

Spitznagel, M. B., Tremont, G., Davis, J. D., & Foster, S. M. (2006). Psychosocial predictors of dementia caregiver desire to institutionalize: Caregiver, care recipient, and family relationship factors. *J Geriatr Psychiatry Neurol, 19*(1), 16–20.

Steadman, P. L., Tremont, G., & Davis, J. D. (2007). Premorbid relationship satisfaction and caregiver burden in dementia caregivers. *J Geriatr Psychiatry Neurol, 20*(2), 115–119.

Tekin, S., Fairbanks, L. A., O'Connor, S., Rosenberg, S., & Cummings, J. L. (2001). Activities of daily living in Alzheimer's disease: Neuropsychiatric, cognitive, and medical illness influences. *Am J Geriatr Psychiatry, 9*(1), 81–86.

Thompson, R. L., Lewis, S. L., Murphy, M. R., Hale, J. M., Blackwell, P. H., Acton, G. J., et al. (2004). Are there sex differences in emotional and biological responses in spousal caregivers of patients with Alzheimer's disease? *Biol Res Nurs, 5*(4), 319–330.

Tierney, M. C., Charles, J., Naglie, G., Jaglal, S., Kiss, A., & Fisher, R. H. (2004). Risk factors for harm in cognitively impaired seniors who live alone: A prospective study. *J Am Geriatr Soc, 52*(9), 1435–1441.

Tinetti, M. E., & Williams, C. S. (1998). The effect of falls and fall injuries on functioning in community-dwelling older persons. *J Gerontol A Biol Sci Med Sci, 53*(2), M112–119.

Tiraboschi, P., Hansen, L. A., Thal, L. J., & Corey-Bloom, J. (2004). The importance of neuritic plaques and tangles to the development and evolution of AD. *Neurology, 62*(11), 1984–1989.

Tschanz, J. T., Welsh-Bohmer, K. A., Lyketsos, C. G., Corcoran, C., Green, R. C., Hayden, K., et al. (2006). Conversion to dementia from mild cognitive disorder: The Cache County study. *Neurology, 67*(2), 229–234.

Uc, E. Y., Rizzo, M., Anderson, S. W., Shi, Q., & Dawson, J. D. (2005). Driver landmark and traffic sign identification in early Alzheimer's disease. *J Neurol Neurosurg Psychiatry*, *76*(6), 764–768.

van Dijk, P. T., Meulenberg, O. G., van de Sande, H. J., & Habbema, J. D. (1993). Falls in dementia patients. *Gerontologist*, *33*(2), 200–204.

Whelihan, W. M., DiCarlo, M. A., & Paul, R. H. (2005). The relationship of neuropsychological functioning to driving competence in older persons with early cognitive decline. *Arch Clin Neuropsychol*, *20*(2), 217–218.

World Health Organization. (2002). *Gender and mental health*. Geneva: Author. Retrieved July 12, 2007, from *www.who.int/gender/other_health/en/*.

Zakzanis, K. K., Graham, S. J., & Campbell, Z. (2003). A meta-analysis of structural and functional brain imaging in dementia of the Alzheimer's type: A neuroimaging profile. *Neuropsychol Rev*, *13*(1), 1–18.

Zhu, X., Raina, A. K., Perry, G., & Smith, M. A. (2004). Alzheimer's disease: The two-hit hypothesis. *Lancet Neurol*, *3*(4), 219–226.

CHAPTER 12

Everyday Functioning in Vascular Dementia

Robert H. Paul, Susan E. Maloney, and Patricia Boyle

Dementia secondary to cerebrovascular disease (referred to herein as "vascular dementia") is a form of dementia that remains a scientific and clinical paradox. Vascular dementia (VaD) is relatively straightforward in terms of the known mechanisms and ultimate etiology (i.e., one or more cerebral strokes), yet the evolution of the condition and the expression of clinical symptoms are notably complex. Further complicating this picture are the lack of universally accepted methods for clinical diagnosis, the heterogeneity of the condition, the identification of multiple subtypes, and neuropathological findings suggesting that pure vascular pathology might be rare compared to the frequency of comorbid vascular and Alzheimer's pathology.

For these reasons one may question the value of reviewing activities of daily living (ADLs) in the context of VaD. However, we believe that four factors render VaD a particularly important focus for the study of ADLs. These factors are (1) the pathophysiology of the most common VaD subtype and the consequent impact on clinical symptoms; (2) the nearly ubiquitous presence of vascular disease with advanced age; (3) the heterogeneous progression and clinical outcomes associated with the condition; and (4) the common (albeit not universal) cognitive profile of VaD. In the present chapter we review these four topic areas in terms of how each may impact the individual's ability to execute ADLs in clinically important and unique ways. We also discuss opportunities to support the performance of ADLs in this population and areas of future research.

VaD Nomenclature (Terms and Conditions)

Given the somewhat tumultuous history of VaD (for a recent review, see Libon, Price, Garrett, & Giovannetti, 2004), it is worthwhile to briefly visit the historic and current nomenclature and diagnostic challenges associated with the condition before devoting serious text to the four major topic areas noted above. For the purpose of the present chapter we refer to VaD as a significant cognitive impairment resulting from vascular disturbances (Jellinger, 2005), usually of ischemic or hemorrhagic origin. For diagnostic purposes, the cognitive impairment must be sufficiently severe to interfere with the independent execution of daily activities. The latter criterion is consistent with current criteria for diagnosis of dementia as outlined in common diagnostic schemes (e.g., DSM-IV, NINDS-AIRENS; Roman, 2005).

Until recently, VaD was termed poststroke dementia or, more commonly, multi-infarct dementia (MID). These terms have been used less consistently in recent years, but a number of additional terms has been introduced into the scientific literature, including "strategic infarct dementia," "subcortical ischemic vascular dementia," and "lacunar state." Less severe cognitive impairment resulting from vascular dysfunction has been referred to as "vascular cognitive impairment" or "mild vascular impairment" (Erkinjuntti, Roman, Gauthier, Feldman, & Rockwood, 2004). It is worth clarifying, however, that the term "vascular cognitive impairment" was originally introduced to capture the entire spectrum of cognitive dysfunction from "brain at risk," to "mild impairment," and eventually "dementia," but the term has gained popularity recently to refer more specifically to the *mild* stages of cognitive impairment associated with a cerebrovascular etiology (analogous to the prodromal stage of Alzheimer's disease, referred to as "mild cognitive impairment"). This confusion in nomenclature has hampered communication efforts across research studies. In response, Roman and colleagues (2004) have recently suggested that the term "vascular cognitive disorder" replace "vascular cognitive impairment" to refer to the broader spectrum of impairment. We have adopted the latter nomenclature in this chapter.

Diagnosis of VaD

The primary factor for the diagnosis of VaD is the association between the observed cognitive impairment and vascular-related brain injury (Erkinjuntti et al., 2000; Merino & Hachinski, 2005). This can be relatively straightforward in the case of large-vessel cortical stroke, when patients develop sudden major neurological symptoms typical of stroke syndromes such as aphasia, amnesia, or neglect. This subtype of VaD may be encountered commonly in acute inpatient and rehabilitation settings and less commonly in general medical clinics (with the exception of chronic cases). However, as described in greater detail below, a large-vessel stroke that has a clear temporal relationship between the onset of the stroke and symptom(s) is not the most common scenario. More commonly, VaD results from the progressive development of smaller strokes in subcortical regions of the brain, and these lesions may develop slowly and insidiously. To the clinician, this disease profile can present a considerable diagnostic challenge given the absence of a clear-cut temporal relationship between the vascular injury and the onset of clinical symptoms. Further complicating this scenario is the observation that the vascular pathology is heterogeneous. Although some regions of the brain are more vulnerable to stroke than others, strokes can occur virtually anywhere in the brain. Perhaps, then, it should not be surprising that a standard diagnostic scheme for VaD has not been universally accepted.

A number of diagnostic schemes have been developed to assist the clinician in the diagnostic process, though none has been without criticism (see Table 12.1 and

TABLE 12.1. Diagnostic Criteria for VaD

According to DSM-IV-TR[a]

A. The development of multiple cognitive deficits manifested by both
   (1) memory impairment (impaired ability to learn new information or to recall previously learned information)
   (2) one (or more) of the following cognitive disturbances:
       (a) aphasia
       (b) apraxia
       (c) agnosia
       (d) disturbance in executive functioning

B. The cognitive deficits in Criteria A1 and A2 each cause significant impairment in social or occupational functioning and represent a significant decline from a previous level of functioning.

C. Focal neurological signs and symptoms or laboratory evidence indicative of cerebrovascular disease that is/are judged to be etiologically related to the disturbance.

D. The deficits do not occur exclusively during the course of a delirium.

According to the State of California Alzheimer's Disease Diagnostic and Treatment Centers[b]

I. Dementia is deterioration from a known or estimated prior level of intellectual function sufficient to interfere broadly with the conduct of the patient's customary affairs of life, which is not isolated to a single narrow category of intellectual performance, and which is independent of level of consciousness.
   This deterioration should be supported by historical evidence and documented by either bedside mental status testing or ideally by more detailed neuropsychological examination, using tests that are quantifiable, reproducible, and for which normative data are available.

II. Probable IVD (ischemic vascular dementia)
    A. Criteria for the clinical diagnosis of probable IVD include all of the following:
       1. Dementia
       2. Evidence of two or more ischemic strokes by history, neurologic signs, and/or neuroimaging studies; or occurrence of a single stroke with a clearly documented temporal relationship to the onset of dementia
       3. Evidence of at least one infarct outside the cerebellum by neuroimaging scans
    B. The diagnosis of probable IVD is supported by
       1. Evidence of multiple infarcts in brain regions known to affect cognition
       2. A history of multiple transient ishemic attacks
       3. History of vascular risk factors
       4. Elevated Hachinski Ischemia Scale

III. Possible IVD
     A. Criteria for the clinical diagnosis of possible IVD include the following:
        1. Dementia
        and one or more of the following:
        2a. A history or evidence of a single stroke (but not multiple strokes) without a clearly documented temporal relationship to the onset of dementia
        2b. Binswanger's syndrome (without multiple strokes) that includes all of the following:
            i. Early-onset urinary incontinence not explained by urologic disease, or gait disturbance not explained by peripheral cause
            ii. Vascular risk factors
            iii. Extensive white matter changes on neuroimaging

IV. Definite IVD
    A. Criteria for the clinical diagnosis of definite IVD requires histopathic examination of the brain, as well as:
       1. Clinical evidence for dementia
       2. Pathological confirmation of multiple infarcts, some outside of the cerebellum

[a]American Psychiatric Association (2000).
[b]Chui et al. (1992).

Consentino et al., 2004). The *Diagnostic and Statistical Manual of Mental Disorders* (4th ed.; DSM-IV) and the *International Classification of Diseases* provide general guidelines for classifying patients with dementia into diagnostic groups, including VaD. Brain imaging evidence of cerebrovascular disease (CVD) is not required by either diagnostic scheme. That is, a diagnosis of VaD can be rendered as long as the patient exhibits physical symptoms consistent with stroke (e.g., paresis, gait abnormality) in addition to the cognitive criteria (Merino & Hachinski, 2005).

In practice, clinicians regularly rely on the use of structural magnetic resonance imaging (MRI) as the sole evidence of CVD because the physical signs may not be present in the absence of cortical involvement or strategic strokes. This reliance on MRI poses several challenges, most notably because the sensitivity of MRI, although better than computerized tomography (CT), is not a perfect proxy for brain pathology. Use of specific acquisition sequences, such as fluid attenuated inversion recovery (FLAIR), increases the sensitivity of MRI to stroke (Brandt-Zawadski, Atkinson, Detrick, Bradley, & Scidmore, 1996); however, studies using diffusion tensor imaging (DTI) have revealed greater sensitivity to CVD compared to traditional structural MRI (O'Sullivan et al., 2004). As such, the clinical utility of MRI to identify stroke and support diagnoses of VaD in the clinical setting is still evolving. A second challenge regarding the clinical reliance on MRI is the lack of clarity regarding the degree of vascular burden evident on MRI required to warrant a diagnosis of VaD. As described in greater detail later in the chapter, evidence of CVD on MRI is extremely common in advanced age, and therefore clinicians are required to define "how much is too much" when reviewing evidence of CVD on MRI. As it turns out, making this determination is not a straightforward task.

Two additional diagnostic schemes for VaD include the criteria developed by the State of California Alzheimer's Disease Diagnostic and Treatment Centers (SCADDTC) and the criteria of the National Institute of Neurological Disorders and Stroke—Association Internationale pour la Recherche et l'Enseignement en Neurosciences (NINDS-AIREN). Both of these sets of criteria were developed specifically to identify VaD (Merino & Hachinski, 2005). SCADDTC and NINDS-AIREN define dementia based on a platform of criteria initially set forth for the identification of Alzheimer's disease (AD). These criteria rely more heavily on brain CT or MRI to determine the presence of cerebrovascular pathology, and, as such, remain vulnerable to the limitations of MRI described above (Erkinjuntti et al., 2004).

The SCADDTC criteria for a definite diagnosis of VaD focus more on ischemic vascular dementia. These criteria require evidence of CVD, including evidence of CVD outside of the cerebellum. In addition, clinical evidence of dementia must be observed, which may include the early appearance of gait disturbance and urinary incontinence. If there is clinical or pathological evidence of a significant second disorder, the case should be classified as a mixed dementia (Chui et al., 1992). According to the report of the NINDS-AIREN International Workshop, VaD is a complex disorder characterized by cognitive impairment resulting from ischemic or hemorrhagic stroke or from ischemic-hypoxic brain lesions. The clinical criteria for the diagnosis of definite VaD include the early presence of a gait disturbance; history of unsteadiness and frequent, unprovoked falls; early urinary frequency, urgency; pseudobulbar palsy; and personality and mood changes or other subcortical deficits, including psychomotor retardation and abnormal executive function. Dementia is defined as cognitive decline that manifests as impairment of memory and deficits in at least two other domains, such as attention, executive functions, or language, among others. The criteria also rule out any other clinical or pathological disorders capable of producing dementia (Roman et al., 1993).

Pathophysiology of VaD

Common areas of the brain affected by stroke include the white matter of the cerebral hemispheres and the subcortical nuclei, especially the striatum and the thalamus. This distinctive targeting of subcortical tissue has prompted some to classify VaD as a type of subcortical dementia, but, again, heterogeneity is the rule, and it is important to recall that some individuals experience devastating cortical damage secondary to arterial territorial infarcts and distal field infarcts (Erkinjuntti et al., 2000, 2004). Components of subcortical injury also include lacunar infarcts and white matter lesions (Erkinjuntti et al., 2004), with possible loss of myelin and/or axons, reduced number of oligodendrocytes, and reactive astrocytosis (Wallin, Milos, Sjorgren, Pantoni, & Erkinjuntti, 2003). The lesions can affect the frontothalamic circuits that connect the prefrontal cortex to the striatum and thalamus, which may explain the common executive profile historically assigned to VaD and described in greater detail later in the chapter.

Interestingly, cholinergic deficits may occur in VaD because the basal forebrain nuclei are permeated by arterioles that are susceptible to arterial hypertension (Erkinjuntti et al., 2004). Lesions can disrupt the cholinergic connections involved in neurotransmission between the basal forebrain and the cortex and amygdala, thereby disrupting the spread of cholinergic input to the cortex (Erkinjuntti et al., 2004; Tomimoto, Ohtani, & Ihara, 2005). These processes may underlie the modest clinical efficacy of acetylcholinergic therapies in the treatment of VaD (Demaerschalk & Wingerchuk, 2007). It should also be noted, however, that vascular damage is often reported in the medial temporal lobe, and hippocampal atrophy may occur in VaD (albeit without plaques and tangles observed with AD). When involvement of the medial temporal lobe occurs, the clinical expression may differ substantially compared to cases where the pathology is restricted to subcortical white matter (Erkinjuntti et al., 2004). This complicated picture of pathophysiology helps to explain the heterogeneous nature of VaD. However, one important message is that although heterogeneity is the rule, subcortical ischemic vascular disease remains the most common subtype of VaD, and this presentation may have significant implications regarding the impact of vascular disease on ADLs.

A pure genetic form of VaD is cerebral autosomal dominant arteriopathy with subcortical infarcts and leukoencephalopathy (CADASIL). This rare genetic disease is associated with mutations in the NOTCH3 gene and the development of multiple small-vessel strokes that usually begin in the fourth decade of life. As a genetic disease, CADASIL could potentially provide a powerful model for the study of cognitive and functional deficits associated with vascular disease; however, success in that regard has been fairly modest at best. In part, this lack of success could be associated with the observation that patients diagnosed with CADASIL often experience an enormous burden of cerebral strokes before the associated symptoms become clinically expressed (i.e., before cognitive and behavioral deficits become evident; Scheid et al., 2006). As such, the relationships between observed vascular damage and cognitive/behavioral deficits are more tenuous than what is typically seen in other forms of VaD (as discussed later in the chapter).

Frequency of VaD and CVD

Clinical data reveal that VaD is one of the most common forms of dementia, constituting about 15–20% of prevalent dementia cases worldwide (Roman, 2005), and it frequently co-occurs with AD, the most common cause of dementia. In the Western world VaD accounts for about 10% of all dementia cases (Jellinger, 2005). VaD is more prevalent in ethnic populations most affected by cerebral small-vessel disease, and, in contrast to AD, VaD is slightly more common in men than women (Roman, 2005). One-third of dementia autopsies show vascular pathology, but some estimates of pure VaD at autopsy are as low as 2–11% (Hachinski et al., 2006; Jellinger, 2005). Although the relatively low percentage of VaD at autopsy suggests a near absence of the condition in the general population (particularly in reference to AD), it is important to note that many cases of AD also present with notable vascular burden at autopsy (Fernando, Ince, & MRC study group, 2004), and therefore it is unclear whether results from autopsy best reflect the frequency of pure vascular impairment experienced by patients when they first enter (or ideally, *should* enter) the clinical setting. For example, clinical stroke is widely recognized as a risk factor for incident dementia, including AD, and cerebral infarctions detected at autopsy are associated with a more than two-fold increase in the risk of dementia (Schneider, Wilson, Bienias, Evans, & Bennett, 2004). Thus, it is possible that individuals develop vascular disease as the sentinel event that signals the onset of additional degenerative processes. Alternatively, individuals predisposed to vascular disease may develop an additional degenerative disease unrelated to the vascular damage (i.e., true independent comorbidity). In either example, the final result at autopsy would suggest multiple pathologies, but that would not be reflective of the actual clinical picture that initially developed years before the autopsy. This mystery will not be easy to untangle, but the general message is that the frequency of vascular impairment among older adults may be greater than currently recognized.

Much of the older adult population suffers from vascular disease, and although this is a risk factor for cognitive decline and dementia, it is prevalent independent of dementia. White matter hyperintensities (WMH) observed on MRI are evident in up to 70% of the population suffering from VaD or AD (Jeerakathil et al., 2004). MRI studies have also reported a high prevalence of WMH in clinically asymptomatic older adults. Tupler, Coffey, Logue, Djang, and Fagan (1992) used MRI to find WMH in 48 of 66 healthy adults ages 45–84 years. The subjects with WMH tended to be older and show greater risk factors for vascular disease compared to those without WMH. The frequency with which WMH are observed on MRI suggests that age may be a powerful risk factor for WMH (Garde, Mortensen, Rostrup, & Paulson, 2005; Jeerakathil et al., 2004). Enzinger and colleagues (2005) found continued brain volume loss at a mean rate of 0.4% of global brain atrophy annually in older individuals in the absence of clinical symptoms, and more importantly, the higher the severity of WMH independently predicted a higher rate of brain atrophy. These data suggest that vascular damage negatively impacts overall brain integrity, and this may lower the threshold for the expression of dementia.

The frequency of CVD in older adults is likely associated with its staggering impact on this population. Seventy-three percent of men and women in the United States ages 55–64 are likely to have one or more risk factors for vascular disease (National Center for Health Statistics, 2005). The primary risk factors for CVD are age, hypertension, smoking, diabetes mellitus, hyperhomocysteinemia, hyperlipidemia, congestive heart failure, cardiac arrhythmias, atrial fibrillation, transient ischemic attacks, obstructive sleep apnea, and coronary artery bypass graft surgery (Hachinski & Munoz, 2000; Meyer, Rauch, Rauch, Haque, & Crawford, 2000; Roman, 2005). A study using the Farmingham Stroke Risk Profile found a significant relationship between cardiovascular risk factors and WMH, with hypertension raising the risk of WMH by 70% (Jeerakathil et al., 2004). Both treated and untreated hypertension can result in decreased white matter volume, supporting a role for subclinical cerebrovascular risk in accelerating brain pathology (Salat et al., 2005). This finding is notable considering that about 30% of the U.S. population suffers from elevated blood pressure (National Center for Health Statistics, 2005). The vascular mechanisms behind these relationships are now becoming clearer. For example, in a recent study conducted by members of our group, a strong relationship ($r = -.63$) was identified between endothelial-dependent vasodilation and subcortical hyperintensities on MRI in a sample of older adults with CVD. These findings suggest that alterations in mechanisms that regulate vascular tone may be associated with the development of microvascular strokes in the brain as people age.

Heterogeneous Outcome of VaD

Tissue injury responsible for dementia in VaD can be irreversible, partially reversible, or progressive (Groves et al., 2000), making VaD a condition with diverse outcomes. For example, a sudden cortical or thalamic stroke may induce an acute change in cognitive and behavioral function that produces considerable functional loss but does not progress over time in the absence of subsequent infarcts. By contrast, strategic infarcts may cause severe acute cognitive symptoms, but the symptoms may improve significantly over 1 year, and function may remain stable in the absence of additional infarcts (Selnes & Vinters, 2006). Finally, subcortical ischemic strokes may begin as clinically silent infarcts but may continue to occur until a threshold has been exceeded and cognitive impairment is expressed clinically. In these cases, function typically continues to deteriorate over time with additional infarcts.

Unfortunately, the risk of mortality is greater in VaD than other dementias, and length of survival after the onset of VaD is shorter than that of individuals diagnosed with AD (Groves et al., 2000). For example, one study examined the risk of mortality in more than 3,500 participants of the Cardiovascular Health Cognition Study (Fitzpatrick, Kuller, Lopez, Kawas, & Jagust, 2005). After controlling for age, sex, and race, persons with VaD were more than four times more likely to die during follow-up than those with normal cognition, and those with AD were twice more likely to die than those with normal cognition. Median survival from dementia onset to death was about 4 years among those with VaD and about 7 years among those with AD, as compared to 11 years for those with normal cognition. It is important to emphasize, however, that prevention of subsequent strokes and management of existing vascular risk factors (e.g., hypertension) may slow or eliminate progression of cognitive decline. This is very different from AD and other forms of dementia, where further deterioration is effectively certain and the available pharmacological interventions have shown only modest efficacy in altering the rate of subsequent decline.

Cognitive Profile of VaD

As outlined above, VaD is complex in part because of the variability of cerebrovascular pathology and resulting clinical symptoms (Roman, 2005). Not surprisingly then, the cognitive profile of VaD is also remarkably heterogeneous. Given the importance of location in determining stroke outcome, it stands to reason that cerebrovascular lesions that occur in the hippocampus will have a much different clinical consequence than lesions that occur in the occipital association cortex. However, the cognitive profile may also be highly influenced by other stroke factors such as the number and volume of infarcts as well as host factors, including premorbid function (Sachdev et al., 2006). In our own studies, we have also found that overall brain volume is an important determinant of global cognitive function in VaD (Paul et al., 2003).

Despite the existence of multiple determinants of cognitive impairment in VaD, there is some evidence of a common cognitive profile associated with the condition. Many studies describe the cognitive profile of VaD as it compares to that of AD. For the most part, these studies have demonstrated that VaD is characterized by more prominent impairments in executive function and psychomotor speed, whereas AD is characterized by more striking impairment in delayed memory and semantic language. A frequently cited review of the literature published by Looi and Sachdev (1999) noted that executive dysfunction was the cognitive domain that most consistently differentiated VaD from AD. Similarly Tierney and colleagues (2001) reported that performance on verbal fluency and recognition memory best discriminated patients with VaD from those with AD. In this study 31 individuals diagnosed with probable AD and 31 individuals diagnosed with subcortical ischemic VaD completed a battery of 10 neuropsychological tests intended to assess multiple primary domains of cognitive function. Logistic regression analyses revealed that only performances on letter fluency (FAS) and recognition memory on the Rey Auditory Verbal Learning Test differentiated the two groups, with poor performance on letter fluency and relatively better performance on recognition memory consistent with vascular disease.

As noted by Bowler (2000) a limitation of most of the available studies examining the cognitive profile of VaD is that the cognitive domains contrasted in statistical analyses may also have been involved in the initial diagnosis of VaD; thus, there is the potential problem of tautology inherent in these studies. When neuropsychological scores are not involved in the diagnostic process, the differences between dementia types may be less prominent. For example, our group (Paul et al., 2000) examined the pattern of cognitive function among patients with VaD who were diagnosed without reference to individual cognitive test scores. For this study, patients were classified on the basis of MRI findings of white matter ischemic disease only, or white matter ischemic disease plus cortical stroke. When we compared the two subgroups, we found significant impairments in both groups across cognitive domains, including language (Boston Naming Test), visual integration (Hooper Visual Organization Test), immediate and delayed memory (logical memory), and psychomotor speed/response fluency (Trail Making Test Part A, grooved pegboard). Interestingly, although the addition of cortical strokes increased the severity of cognitive impairment, the overall pattern did not change; that is, both groups exhibited impairments across cognitive domains. Similarly, Reed and colleagues (2004) examined cognitive patterns of autopsy-confirmed cases of VaD and found only a modest correlation between cerebrovascular pathology and neuropsychological deficits.

The results described above suggest that executive impairment may not be the "fingerprint" of VaD. With that caveat noted, there is evidence that deficits in this cognitive domain are very common among patients diagnosed with the condition. As described by Jefferson, Brickman, Aloia, and Paul (2004), it is possible that executive dysfunction is a common but not universal deficit in VaD (i.e., a common thread akin to amnestic memory dysfunction associated with AD). This possibility would fit with the subcortical ischemic subtype of VaD that is now recognized as the most common variant. If true, this would suggest that executive dysfunction may be present in most cases of VaD, but that impairment in other cognitive domains (as shown in our studies) may also coexist, as determined by the distribution of vascular damage. The emphasis on an executive profile has enormous ramifications regarding the ability of patients to execute ADLs (as described in the next section).

Relationships between VaD and ADLs

Prior to a full discussion regarding ADLs it is useful to provide some clarification regarding terminology. Below we refer to overall ability to perform activities of daily living as ADLs (including all types of activities), whereas the specific ability to perform instrumental activities of daily living is referred to as IADLs (e.g., shopping, financial management, laundry, telephone use) and the specific ability to perform basic activities of daily living as BADLs (e.g., bathing, grooming, dressing, toileting). The studies below review cognitive and neuropsychiatric predictors of all three aspects of everyday functioning. We have divided the following discussion into two sections, the first focused on frequency and course of ADL impairment associated with vascular disease and the second focused on predictors of ADL impairment in this population.

Frequency of ADL Impairment Associated with VaD

Clavier, Hommel, Besson, Noelle, and Perret (1994) reported that 26% of patients with lacunar infarction exhibited significant ADL loss within 1 year of the stroke. Similarly, Samuelsson, Soderfeldt, and Olsson (1996) reported longitudinal data on cohorts of individuals with first-ever stroke and no significant premorbid impairment in ADL function. Six months following their initial strokes, 23% were significantly impaired (i.e., fully dependent) in IADL function, and 12% were dependent on both ADL and IADL function. The latter percentage doubled 3 years poststroke. These findings suggest that ADL impairment is relatively common following first-ever stroke, and that ADL impairments progress over time.

Course of ADL Decline among Patients with VaD

Although the course of ADL decline has been extensively studied in individuals with AD, surprisingly few studies have examined this issue in patients with VaD. The paucity of research likely reflects the challenges associated with studying a disorder with multiple subtypes that may be associated with different trajectories of decline. For example, individuals with VaD due to large-vessel strokes may be expected to follow a stepwise course of deterioration in functioning, whereas individuals with VaD due to small-vessel disease may be expected to show a more gradual, progressive decline. Understanding the course of ADL declines in VaD may be difficult because a careful evaluation of the subpopulation of VaD patients being studied is required; however, understanding the potential course of decline is critically important for patient management and the development of supportive or rehabilitative interventions.

Placebo-controlled, randomized clinical trials investigating the efficacy of pharmacological agents for treating the cognitive symptoms of dementia provide some data regarding the course of ADL declines in VaD. Such trials typically include mildly to moderately impaired patients with VaD due to multiple strokes, and rates of functional decline often are compared to those of patients with AD. In one study Erkinjuunti and colleagues (2002) evaluated ADLs in placebo-treated, mildly to moderately impaired patients with VaD (Mini-Mental State Examination [MMSE] scores 10–25) enrolled in a 6-month clinical trial. Untreated persons with VaD were found to decline slowly, showing an ADL decline of 4.5% over 6 months. In two comparable studies of patients with AD (Feldman et al., 2001; Raskind, Mintzer, Mehnert, & Ferris, 2001) untreated patients were found to show a decline of about 6% over 6 months and about 12% over 1 year. The relatively slower ADL decline among patients with VaD as compared to patients with AD has been corroborated in additional studies, and it is generally accepted that the rate of functional decline is slower in VaD as compared to AD (Kitter, 1999; Nyenhuis, Gorelick, Freels, & Garron, 2002).

Recently, some investigators have begun to evaluate ADLs in patients with VaD due to small-vessel disease and/or chronic ischemia. As is the case with VaD due to stroke, VaD due to small-vessel disease is associated with a progressive decline in IADLs that is slower than, or equivalent with, that reported among individuals with AD. We recently reported a 20% decline in IADLs over 1 year in 30 patients with VaD of moderate severity (Boyle, Paul, Moser, & Cohen, 2004). This decline translates to the complete loss of a single IADL or the partial loss of two IADLs. It is important to acknowledge that the loss of even one skill (e.g., medication management) results in an increased need for care and may even precipitate nursing home placement. Taken together, the available studies suggest that there is a progressive deterioration of ADLs among patients with VaD. Although the rate of ADL decline appears to be somewhat slower among patients with VaD than among patients with AD, the available findings suggest that the nature of ADL declines is similar. IADLs tend to decline earlier than do BADLs in both groups, and ultimately all patients with dementia are at risk for functional dependence. It's worth reiterating that this course of decline is fairly specific to individuals with a diagnosis of VaD, and the course does not apply directly to individuals who have experienced an acute stroke (since only about one-third of these individuals meet diagnostic criteria for dementia).

Cognitive and Neuropsychiatric Correlates of ADL Impairment in VaD

Some hints at what to expect regarding cognitive predictors of ADLs in VaD can be taken from the literature that has focused on other populations. One interesting study was conducted by Royall, Palmer, Chiodo, and Polk (2005). In this large longitudinal study of 547 retired older adults living independently in the community, performance on tests of executive function but not performance on tests of memory function predicted ADL performance. More interestingly, the investigators found that individuals diagnosed with amnestic mild cognitive impairment (MCI; the presumed prodromal stage of AD) were *unlikely* to convert to dementia until the development of executive impairments. In short, this study found that executive impairments mediated change in ADL status (and consequently dementia diagnosis).

Boyle, Malloy, and colleagues (2003) reported a similar result when executive function was assessed in a cohort of patients diagnosed with AD. In this study executive dysfunction and severity of apathy accounted for more than 40% of the variance in IADLs, and executive dysfunction and frontal-behavioral impairment accounted for nearly 30% of the variance in BADLs. Again the relationship between executive function and ADLs makes intuitive sense, as the ability to plan, organize, sequence, and other aspects of executive function are critical for the management of ADLs. It is interesting, however, that executive function plays such an important role in both basic and instrumental ADLs. Collectively, it appears that the executive profile of VaD may impact ADLs more dramatically in this population as compared to other dementias characterized more prominently by memory loss early in the dementia process.

Generally speaking, there are relatively few publications in the area of ADLs and VaD, and much of the work that has been completed has focused on a few cohorts of patients. As such, some caution should be exercised when drawing conclusions from the extant literature. Nevertheless, the information available from the published studies completed in the last 10 years has significantly improved our understanding of ADLs in this population, and we review these studies in this section. Specifically, we review cognitive and neuropsychiatric correlates of ADLs in VaD and biomarker correlates of cerebrovascular disease and ADLs. The specific cognitive and neuropsychiatric predictors of ADLs are summarized in Table 12.2.

In one of the earlier studies, Boyle, Cohen, Paul, Moser, and Gordan (2002) examined 32 individuals diagnosed with VaD according to NINDS-AIREN criteria. All subjects completed a neuropsychological battery, and ADLs were assessed with the Lawton and Brody scale. Not unexpectedly, in this sample IADLs were more impaired than ADLs. Separate regressions were conducted to identify the strongest predictors of BADLs and IADLs. For the latter, performance on the grooved pegboard, Digit Span, Trail Making Part B, and FAS were entered into the regression, and only performance on the grooved pegboard was retained as a significant predictor of BADLs (accounting for 51% of the variance). By contrast, when the same variables were entered into the regression to predict IADLs, performance on Digit

TABLE 12.2. Cognitive and Neuropsychiatric Predictors of Basic and Instrumental Activities of Daily Living

Study	BADL predictors	IADL predictors
Boyle et al. (2002)	Fine motor speed, and dexterity	Attention span, fine motor speed, and dexterity
Boyle et al. (2004)	Not examined	Cognitive flexibility, response inhibition
Bennet et al. (2002)	Attention span, verbal retention[a]	Block Design[a]
Jefferson, Cahn-Weiner, et al. (2006)	Memory decline[a]	Initiation–Perseveration from the Dementia Rating Scale[a]
Zawacki et al. (2002)	Apathy accounted for 27%[b]	Apathy accounted for 51%[b]
Fitten et al. (1995)	N/A	The Sternberg short-term memory task, sustained attention, visual tracking, total MMSE[c]

[a]These cognitive predictors were examined longitudinally and reflect the relationship between cognitive performance and decline in the ADL domain over time.
[b]In this study apathy was the primary predictor variable; cognitive tests were not included in the study.
[c]This study investigated predictors for driving impairment, not overall IADLs.

Span and the grooved pegboard were retained in the final model, with Digit Span accounting for 29% of the variance, and grooved pegboard providing an additional 14% to the model. Results from this study suggest that attentional/executive functions are most important for IADLs, and fine motor speed and dexterity may be most important for BADLs.

In follow-up studies (Boyle et al., 2004; Jefferson, Cahn-Weiner, et al., 2006), members of our group examined the cognitive predictors of ADL decline over a 12-month period; the same cohort described above was reevaluated after 12 months. In the first study, Boyle and colleagues (2004) identified a statistically significant decline in IADL scores over the 12-month period for the cohort. In addition, performance on tests of executive function, including Initiation–Perseveration, Stroop interference, and Trail Making B, all correlated with baseline IADL performance, and baseline performance on the Initiation–Perseveration test predicted IADL scores at the 12-month follow-up. Importantly, this finding held after accounting for global cognitive impairment as measured by the MMSE.

In the second study (Jefferson, Cahn-Weiner, et al., 2006) we examined both IADLs and BADLs, and again examined the relationships between changes in performances on Initiation–Perseveration and Memory subscales of the Dementia Rating Scale (DRS) with changes in IADL and BADL scores across the 12-month window. Results from this study revealed that change in Initiation–Perseveration uniquely predicted change in IADLs, whereas change in Memory uniquely predicted change in BADLs. When considered in light of the studies referenced above, it appears that executive function is significantly related to baseline and subsequent declines in IADLs, whereas motor function and memory performance may account for more variance in BADLs at baseline and over time, at least within a 12-month time frame.

Studies that have examined decline in ADLs over a longer time period have reported similar findings. Bennet and colleagues (2002) examined cognitive and noncognitive predictors of change in ADLs over an extended period of time in a sample of patients initially diagnosed with subcortical ischemic vascular disease. Participants underwent neuroimaging with CT, neurological exam, and neuropsychological evaluations, including IADL and BADL assessment at baseline and four times over nearly 6 years. A total of 77 individuals were enrolled, but only 36 were available for the final assessment. Results revealed that 24% of the group converted to dementia during the follow-up periods, with a relatively equal number diagnosed with mixed dementia compared to VaD. Predictors of IADL decline (defined as decline greater than 25% or more on the Lawton and Brody scale) included age, years of education (possibly reflecting increased cognitive reserve), ventricular enlargement, MMSE score, paratonia, and performances on Digit Span and delayed verbal memory test. Interestingly, the number of infarcts, severity of leukoaraiosis, and cortical atrophy did not predict decline in ADLs. Predictors of decline in BADLs (defined as a reduction in two or more points on the Katz scale of ADLs) included ventricular enlargement, coordination, snout reflex, MMSE score, and performance on Block Design. As noted by these authors, one important finding from this study is that decline in IADLs among patients with VaD is most strongly correlated with cognitive variables, whereas decline in BADLs is correlated with both cognitive and physical variables. This finding is generally similar to the conclusion drawn by Boyle and colleagues (2002), who noted that motor symptoms associated with VaD influence independent living abilities. It is important to note that motor functions also become impaired in other forms of dementias, such as in AD; however, the expression may occur much earlier in the disease process among patients with VaD.

The absence of relationships between CVD on CT and decline in ADLs in the study described above is surprising, but may have been influenced by the use of CT and visual ratings of leukoaraiosis, both of which are less sensitive than MRI and computerized programs to quantitate vascular lesion load (Davis Garrett et al., 2004). In a study conducted by our group (Boyle, Paul, et al., 2003), 29 individuals with VaD, diagnosed according to NINDS-AIREN criteria, underwent neuropsychological evaluation and brain MRI using a FLAIR acquisition sequence. FLAIR produces a very strong T-2 weighted image with suppression of cerebrospinal fluid (CSF) signal, resulting in superior sensitivity to acute and chronic stroke compared to other conventional MRI methods (Brandt-Zawadski et al., 1996). The severity of subcortical hyperintensities (SH) was defined using a semiautomated thresholding technique to quantify pixel intensity values identified a priori as consistent with subcortical ischemic disease. A ratio of SH to total brain volume was calculated to control for possible differences in SH secondary to smaller or larger overall brain size. Overall cortical volume was also determined. Results of this study revealed that performance on the Initiation–Perseveration subscale ($r = -.53$) of the DRS and total score on the DRS ($r = -.54$) correlated with IADL function. In addition, SH ratio ($r = .58$) but not total cortical volume ($r = .18$) correlated with IADL score. When these variables were entered into a multiple regression, performance on the Initiation–Perseveration accounted for 28% of the variance in IADL score, whereas SH ratio accounted for an additional 14% of the variance. These findings suggest that cognitive factors are more closely related to ADL performance than neuroimaging markers of CVD, but the imaging markers may provide additional explanatory power.

One limitation of many previous studies examining ADLs in dementia, and VaD in particular, is the reliance on caregiver-reported declines in functional capacity. This can be problematic in cases where primary caregivers spend limited time with affected patients (e.g., in some cases of adult caregivers or out-of-home living placements), or when participants have had limited exposure to specific types of ADLs (e.g., older males with no recent history cooking, cleaning, laundry). The subjective scales are also prone to recall and accuracy errors. One approach to circumvent these issues is to ask subjects to complete aspects of ADLs as part of the assessment process; this step has been accomplished in a study of subcortical ischemic VaD (Giovannetti, Schmidt, Gallo, Sestito, & Libon, 2006).

Giovannett and colleagues (2006) administered the Natural Action Test (NAT; Schwartz et al., 2003) to 23 individuals with probable AD and 25 individuals with VaD diagnosed according to the California criteria for ischemic VaD. Completion of the NAT requires subjects to perform tasks of increasing difficulty level (e.g., make toast, wrap a gift while avoiding distracters, and pack a multi-item lunchbox using items not in view). An Accomplishment Score was computed for each item and for the overall test; this score reflected the percentage of steps completed without error. In addition to completing the NAT, subjects also underwent a neuropsychological assessment, including tests that tapped executive functions, language, and memory. Results of the study revealed no significant differences in total NAT score between the two groups, with both groups falling in the impaired range, on average. Examination of the individual items revealed that the patients with VaD obtained significantly lower accomplishment scores and committed more errors on the gift-wrapping-with-distracters task compared to the patients with AD. These findings indicate that the ability to complete everyday aspects of living may be compromised to a greater degree among individuals with VaD, compared to those with AD, after controlling for severity of dementia.

Apathy

The studies above describe strong and consistent relationships between neuropsychological capacity and ability to execute ADLs. It is important to note, however, that studies have also implicated specific neuropsychiatric symptoms as determinants of ADL performance in VaD. For example, our group examined the relationship between severity of apathy and ADL performance among the cohort of patients with VaD described in the studies by Boyle, Paul, and colleagues (2003; Boyle, 2002). Apathy is an interesting neuropsychiatric sequelae of VaD because it is common and it is a possible manifestation of the disruption in the frontal-subcortical circuits initially described by Alexander, Crutcher, and DeLong (1990). Five of these frontal-subcortical circuits have received considerable research attention, including the anterior cingulate loop, which, via vascular pathology, may underlie the expression of apathy in VaD. A similar relationship has been described to explain apathy in other conditions that predominately affect subcortical brain circuits (e.g., see Paul et al., 2005).

Considering that apathy reflects a loss of cognitive, behavioral, or emotional iner-
tia, it makes intuitive sense that significant symptoms of apathy would interfere with
the execution of ADLs among patients with dementia. Zawacki and colleagues (2002)
examined this possibility formally by measuring apathy using a symptom checklist of
frontal-type deficits completed by caregivers of the patients enrolled in our previous
studies. The checklist provided indices of three frontal behavioral syndromes: apathy,
disinhibition, and dysexecutive function. Ratings were based on severity of behavioral
problems that patients exhibited in each of these domains. Results revealed that apathy accounted for 27% of the variance in BADLs, and dementia severity and apathy
accounted for 51% of the variance in IADLs. These findings are intriguing because
they demonstrate that neuropsychiatric symptoms may contribute independently to
ADL dysfunction, but it should be remembered that the expression of apathy is likely
closely related to the overall severity of subcortical dysfunction in key cognitive–
emotional circuits. As such, even though behavioral ratings of apathy are correlated
with ADL impairment, it is important to consider the likely interdependence between
apathy and subcortical dysfunction in this population.

Impairment in Driving and Other Specific IADLs

To our knowledge very few studies have examined specific functional skills such as
driving, medication management, vocational status, or related IADLs in the VaD
population, though a few studies have focused on these issues in nondemented individuals with stroke and in populations at risk for VaD. One highly relevant study was
conducted by Fitten and colleagues (1995). In this study 12 individuals with diagnoses of VaD of mild severity (MMSE > 19) completed a six-stage, 2.7-mile driving road
test on a closed course that was scored for accuracy. The group was also administered
tests of sustained attention, divided attention, and working memory, and comparisons
were made to a cohort of patients diagnosed with probable AD, a cohort of healthy
older adults, a cohort of older adults with diabetes, and a cohort of healthy younger
controls. Patients with VaD and those with AD performed significantly more poorly
on the road test compared to the control groups. Furthermore, the two patient groups
performed more poorly on the tests of working memory and visual tracking/search.
Collapsed across groups, driving performance correlated significantly with performance on the working memory task, sustained attention, visual tracking, and total
MMSE. Results from this study reveal that driving ability is significantly impaired in
patients with VaD, and the degree of driving difficulties is directly correlated with the
severity of cognitive impairment.

Heikkila, Korpelainen, Turkka, Kallanranta, and Summala (1999) evaluated the
driving ability of nondemented stroke patients using multidisciplinary clinical evaluations and driving-related laboratory tests. Twenty male stroke patients participated,
half of whom had experienced infarctions in the dominant hemisphere (DH) and the
other half infarctions in the nondominant hemisphere (NDH). Twenty age-matched
controls also participated. Patients' ability to drive was estimated by a neurologist
based on a clinical examination and findings from a team comprised of an occupational therapist, physiotherapist, speech therapist, and clinical neuropsychologist. All
individuals completed tests of visual short-term memory, perceptual flexibility and

decision making, vigilance, and complex choice reaction time. The stroke patients had noticeable deficiencies on all measures. The DHD patients responded significantly faster than the NDHD patients on the visual memory test, and the NDHD patients were more likely to be incapable of driving a car than the DHD patients. When the patients and their spouses evaluated patient driving capability, both made overestimations, and patients' own personal evaluations of their laboratory tests did not correlate with the neurologist's evaluations. This study identifies the impact of stroke on driving abilities and highlights the importance of evaluating driving capabilities following a stroke.

Jefferson, Paul, Ozonoff, and Cohen (2006) completed a more detailed item analysis of IADL impairment in community older adults enrolled in a study of cardiac function and cognition. In this study, relationships were examined between executive dysfunction and performance on specific IADL items from the Lawton and Brody scale. A number of executive measures were included, but the only significant correlate of IADL score was performance on the Delis–Kaplan Executive Functioning System (D-KEFS) Color–Word Interference test. Interestingly, follow-up analyses revealed that performance on the Color–Word test was most strongly related to ability to shop independently, complete laundry, use transportation, and manage finances. By contrast, there were no significant relationships between executive function and ability to independently complete housekeeping or meal preparation, comply with medication regimen, or use the telephone. These findings are important because the participants enrolled in the study were not demented, but they possessed multiple risk factors for VaD.

Summary

VaD is a common and complex disorder that is a major contributor to disability among older adults and provides a useful target for studies examining the cognitive and neuropsychiatric determinants of functional status. Despite the complexities of the condition, VaD demonstrates unique relationships between dementia and ADLs because of the (1) pathophysiology of the most common subtype of VaD; (2) the frequency of the disorder (including the milder cases); (3) the heterogeneous outcomes that patients may experience; and (4) the predominant but not universal dysexecutive profile associated with the disorder. Although relatively few studies have examined the cognitive and other predictors of ADL dysfunction in patients with VaD, the available evidence suggests that executive dysfunction may be an important determinant of IADL impairments, and motor and other cognitive functions may subserve BADLs. Furthermore, the finding that noncognitive symptoms such as apathy also predict ADL impairment in this population raises the possibility that symptoms specifically associated with VaD should be considered when rendering clinical decisions about the capacity of patients to maintain independence in ADLs. For example, Shiau, Yu, Yuan, Lin, and Liu (2006) recently demonstrated that among patients with VaD, bathing, upper and lower dressing, grooming, and executive dysfunction predicted scores on the Functional Independence Measure (FIM), a common outcome tool used in rehabilitation settings. By contrast, among patients with AD, stairs, lower dressing, tub/shower, and memory impairment predicted FIM scores. These findings underscore our position that unique cognitive and noncognitive factors contribute to ADL impairment in VaD, as compared to other conditions. The observation that executive dysfunction occurs early in the course of VaD and that the presence of executive impairments predict ADL decline may explain the greater degree of caregiver burden associated with VaD compared to AD, when examined in the early stages of the disease (Vetter et al., 1999).

Given the importance of executive functions in maintaining ADLs and the prominence of executive impairment early in the course of VaD, particularly among those with the common subcortical ischemic subtype, it is possible that functional decline begins much earlier in VaD than in other forms of dementia. We believe these findings highlight the importance of assessing cognitive and ADL status in routine clinical exams. Moreover, given the frequency of vascular risk factors, small-vessel disease, and vascular lesions in older adults, even in those without known cognitive impairment, it may be appropriate to begin functional assessments as part of routine clinical evaluations in the primary care setting. In short, cognitive and functional status should be considered as the next important "vital sign" among older patients. A number of screening tools has been developed for use in the primary care setting, and utilization of these tools could help identify individuals at risk for ADL decline earlier in the clinical process.

One cognitive screening method that appears promising is the Montreal Cognitive Assessment screening test developed by Nasreddine and colleagues (2004). The 10-minute screen includes brief measures of verbal learning and memory, naming, construction, executive function, orientation, and attention. Initial results revealed outstanding sensitivity and specificity in the identification of both MCI and dementia, and the screen has been adopted by the NINDS neuropsychology working group for a brief screen of vascular cognitive impairment (Hachinski et al., 2006). When combined with an evaluation of ADL performance using the Lawton and Brody, the Alzheimer's Disease Cooperative Study scale, among others, the primary care physician will be better equipped to shepherd patients into specialized clinical care.

Future Directions

Additional research is greatly needed to further clarify the nature and course of ADL dysfunction in VaD and to examine the extent to which pharmacological and nonpharmacological interventions may slow the course of ADL declines. Prospective studies that evaluate well-characterized subpopulations of patients with VaD over several years; assess a wider array of cognitive, motor, neurological, and behavioral features; and utilize comprehensive ADL evaluations will provide much needed knowledge about the natural history of VaD. Information regarding the nature of ADL declines is essential for effective patient management, particularly with regard to rehabilitative and other efforts to maintain functional status. In addition, functional status is an important outcome in studies examining the potential benefits of both pharmacological and nonpharmacological interventions.

Importantly, because the factors associated with functional impairment in VaD may change over time as vascular lesions accumulate, future investigations should seek to clarify *specific* predictors of ADL impairment among patients with VaD of varying degrees of severity. As noted above, relatively few studies have examined specific cognitive and neuropsychiatric predictors of ADL impairment in subpopulations of these patients, and identifying these predictors represents an important research goal. Moreover, the threshold of vascular burden required to produce functional loss is unknown, although the available imaging techniques may be well suited to examine this issue. In particular, new techniques such as DTI and magnetization transfer imaging may provide measures of tissue damage that very closely related to clinical status. Importantly, there are no currently approved treatments for VaD. However, the ability to identify those patients at increased risk for functional disability early in the course of the disease will promote the implementation of targeted interventions to maintain independent living. Furthermore, functional status is arguably the most important outcome for research examining the efficacy of the pharmacological agents currently used for the symptomatic treatment of VaD. Moreover, new pharmacological agents are under investigation, and knowledge of the natural course of VaD is a prerequisite for the future adequate design and powering of double-blind drug trials. One ongoing study is investigating the efficacy of a cholinesterase inhibitor, Aricept (donepezil), specifically for improving functional status in patients with VaD. In addition, memantine, a moderate-affinity N-methyl-D-aspartic acid (NMDA) receptor antagonist, is under investigation, as are dietary supplements, including B12 and folate. Thus, the increased awareness of the natural history of VaD and the resulting ability to identify high-risk patients may have significant emotional, financial, and public health implications. Understanding the specific predictors of ADL dysfunction ultimately may significantly improve treatment options and reduce the high cost of health care for patients with VaD.

References

Alexander, G. E., Crutcher, M. D., & DeLong, M. R. (1990). Basal ganglia–thalamocortical circuits: Parallel substrates for motor, oculomotor, "prefrontal" and "limbic" functions. *Progr Brain Res*, 85, 119–146.

American Psychiatric Association. (2000). *Diagnostic and statistical manual of mental disorders* (text rev.). Washington, DC: Author.

Bennett, H. P., Corbett, A. J., Gaden, S., Grayson, D. A., Kril, J. J., & Broe, G. A. (2002). Subcortical vascular disease and functional decline: A 6-year predictor study. *J Am Geriatr Soc*, 50, 1969–1977.

Bowler, J. V. (2000). Criteria for vascular dementia: Replacing dogma with data. *Arch Neurol*, 57(2), 170–171.

Boyle, P. A., Cohen, R. A., Paul, R., Moser, D., & Gordon, N. (2002). Cognitive and motor impairments predict functional declines in patients with vascular dementia. *Int J Geriatr Psych*, 17, 164–169.

Boyle, P. A., Malloy, P. F., Salloway, S., Cahn-Weiner, D. A., Cohen, R., & Cummings, J. L. (2003). Executive dysfunction and apathy predict functional impairment in Alzheimer's disease. *Am J Geriat Psychiat*, 11, 214–221.

Boyle, P. A., Paul, R., Moser, D., Zawacki, T., Gordon, N., & Cohen, R. (2003). Cognitive and neurologic predictors of functional impairment in vascular dementia. *Am J Psychiat*, 11 (1), 103–106.

Boyle, P. A., Paul, R. H., Moser, D. J., & Cohen, R. A. (2004). Executive impairments predict functional declines in vascular dementia. *Clin Neuropsychol*, *18*(1), 75–82.

Brandt-Zawadski, M., Atkinson, D., Detrick, M., Bradley, W. G., & Scidmore, G. (1996). Fluid-attenuated inversion recovery (FLAIR) for assessment of cerebral infarction. *Stroke*, *27*, 1187–1191.

Chui, H. C., Victoroff, J. I., Margolin, D., Jagust, W., Shankle, R., & Katzman, R. (1992). Criteria for the diagnosis of ischemic vascular dementia proposed by the State of California Alzheimer's Disease Diagnostic and Treatment Centers. *Neurology*, *42*, 473–480.

Clavier, I., Hommel, M, Besson, G., Noelle, B., & Perret, J. E. (1994). Long-term prognosis of symptomatic lacunar infarcts: A hospital-based study. *Stroke*, *25*, 2005–2009.

Consentino, S. A., Jefferson, A. L., Carey, M., Price, C. C., Davis Garrett, K., Swenson, R., et al. (2004). The clinical diagnosis of vascular dementia: A comparison among four classification systems and a proposal for a new paradigm. *Clin Neuropsychol*, *18*(1), 6–21.

Davis Garrett, K., Cohen, R. A., Paul, R. H., Moser, D. J., Malloy, P. F., Shah, P., et al. (2004). Computer-mediated measurement and subjective ratings of white matter hyperintensities in vascular dementia: relationships to neuropsychological performance. *Clin Neuropsychol*, *18*(1), 50–62.

Demaerschalk, B. M., & Wingerchuk, D. M. (2007). Treatment of vascular dementia and vascular cognitive impairment. *Neurologist*, *13*(1), 37–41.

Enzinger, C., Fazekas, F., Matthews, P. M., Ropele, S., Schmidt, H., Smith, S., et al. (2005). Risk factors for progression of brain atrophy in aging. *Neurology*, *64*, 1704–1711.

Erkinjuntti, T., Inzitari, D., Pantoni, L., Wallin, A., Scheltens, P., Tockwood, K., et al. (2000). Limitations of clinical criteria for the diagnosis of vascular dementia in clinical trials. *Ann N Y Acad Sci*, *903*, 262–272.

Erkinjuntti, T., Kurz, A., Gauthier, S., Bullock, R., Lillienfeld, S., & Damaraju, C. V. (2002). Efficacy of galantamine in probable vascular dementia and Alzheimer's disease combined with cerebrovascular disease: A randomized clinical trial. *Lancet*, *359*, 1283–1290.

Erkinjuntti, T., Roman, G., Gauthier, S., Feldman, H., & Rockwood, K. (2004). Emerging therapies for vascular dementia and vascular cognitive impairment. *Stroke*, *35*, 1010–1017.

Feldman, H., Sauter, A., Donald, A., Gélinas, I., Gauthier, S., Torfs, K., et al. (2001). The Disability Assessment for Dementia Scale: A 12-month study of functional ability in mild–moderate severity Alzheimer's disease. *Alz Dis Assoc Dis* , *15*, 89–95.

Fernando, M. S., Ince, P. G., & MRC study group. (2004). Vascular pathologies and cognition in a population-based cohort of elderly people. *J Neurol Sci*, *226*(1–2), 13–7.

Fitten, J. L., Perryman, K. M., Wilkinson, C. J., Little, R. J., Burns, M. M., Pachana, N., et al. (1995). Alzheimer and vascular dementias and driving: A prospective road and laboratory study. *JAMA*, *273(17), 1360–1365*.

Fitzpatrick, A. L., Kuller, L. H., Lopez, O. L., Kawas, C. H., & Jagust, W. (2005). Survival following dementia diagnosis: Alzheimer's disease and vascular dementia. *J Neurol Sci*, *229–230*, 43–49.

Garde, E., Mortensen, E. L., Rostrup, E., & Paulson, O. B. (2005). Decline in intelligence is associated with progression in white matter hypertensity volume. *J Neurosurg Psychiatr*, *76*, 1289–1291.

Giovannetti, T., Schmidt, K. S., Gallo, J. L., Sestito, N., & Libon, D. J. (2006). Everyday action in dementia: Evidence for differential deficits in Alzheimer's disease versus subcortical vascular dementia. *J Int Neuropsych So*, *12*, 45–53.

Groves, W. C., Brandt, J., Steinberg, M., Warren, A., Rosenblatt, A., Baker, A., et al. (2000). Vascular dementia and Alzheimer's disease: Is there a difference? A comparison of symptoms by disease duration. *J Neuropsych Clin N*, *12*(3), 305–315.

Hachinski, V., Iadecola, C., Peterson, R. C., Breteler, M. M., Nyenhuis, D. L., Black, S., et al. (2006). National Institute of Neurological Disorders and Stroke—Canadian Stroke Network Vascular Cognitive Impairment harmonization standards. *Stroke, 37,* 2220–2241.

Hachinski, V., & Munoz, D. (2000). Vascular factors on cognitive impairment: Where are we now? *Ann N Y Acad Sci, 903,* 1–5.

Heikkila, V., Korpelainen, J., Turkka, J., Kallanranta, T., & Summala, H. (1999). Clinical evaluation of the driving ability in stroke patients. *Acta Neurol Scand, 99*(6), 349–355.

Jeerakathil, T., Wolf, P. A., Beiser, A., Massaro, J., Seshadri, S., D'Agostino, R. B., et al. (2004). Stroke risk profile predicts white matter hyperintensity volume. *Stroke, 35,* 1857–1861.

Jefferson, A. L., Brickman, A. M., Aloia, M. S., & Paul, R. H. (2004). The cognitive profile of vascular dementia. In R. H. Paul, R. Cohen, B. R. Ott, & S. Salloway (Eds.), *Vascular dementia: Cerebrovascular mechanisms and clinical management* (pp. 131–144). Totowa, NJ: Humana Press.

Jefferson, A. L., Cahn-Weiner, D., Boyle, P., Paul, R. H., Moser, D. J., Gordon, N., et al. (2006). Cognitive predictors of functional decline in vascular dementia. *Int J Geriatr Psych, 21,* 752–754.

Jefferson, A. L., Paul, R. H., Ozonoff, A., & Cohen, R. A. (2006). Evaluating elements of executive functioning as predictors of instrumental activities of daily living (IADLs). *Arch Clin Neuropsych, 21,* 311–320.

Jellinger, K. A. (2005). The neuropathological substrates of vascular-ischemic dementia. In R. H. Paul, R. Cohen, B. R. Ott, & S. Salloway (Eds.), *Vascular dementia: Cerebrovascular mechanisms and clinical management* (pp. 23–56). Totowa, NJ: Humana Press.

Kitter, B., for the European/Canadian Propentofylline study group. (1999). Clinical trials of propentofylline in vascular dementia. *Alz Dis Assoc Dis, 13*(Suppl. 3), S166–S171.

Libon, D. J., Price, C. C., Garrett, K. D., & Giovannetti, T. (2004). From Binswanger's disease to leuokoaraiosis: What have we learned about subcortical vascular dementia? *Clin Neuropsychol, 18*(1), 83–100.

Looi, J. C., & Sachdev, P. S. (1999). Differentiation of vascular dementia from AD on neuropsychological tests. *Neurology, 53*(4), 670–678.

Merino, J. G., & Hachinski, V. (2005). Diagnosis of vascular dementia: Conceptual challenges. In R. H. Paul, R. Cohen, B. R. Ott, & S. Salloway (Eds.), *Vascular dementia: Cerebrovascular mechanisms and clinical management* (pp. 57–72). Totowa, NJ: Humana Press.

Meyer, J. S., Rauch, G. M., Rauch, R. A., Haque, A., & Crawford, K. (2000). Cardiovascular and other risk factors for Alzheimer's disease and vascular dementia. *Ann N Y Acad Sci, 903,* 411–423.

Nasreddine, Z. S., Phillips, N. A., Bédirian, V., Charbonneau, S., Whitehead, V., Collin, I., et al. (2005). The Montreal Cognitive Assessment, MoCA: A brief screening tool for mild cognitive impairment. *J Am Geriatr Soc, 53*(4), 695–699.

National Center for Health Statistics. (2005). *Health, United States, 2005, with chartbook on trends in the health of Americans.* Hyattsville, MD: Author.

Nyenhuis, D. L., Gorelick, P. B., Freels, S., & Garron D. (2002). Cognitive and functional decline in African Americans with VaD, AD, and stroke without dementia. *Neurology, 58*(1), 56–61.

O'Sullivan, M., Morris, R. G., Huckstep, B., Jones, D. K., Williams, S. C., & Markus, H. S. (2004). Diffusion tensor MRI correlates with executive dysfunction in patients with ischaemic leuokoaraiosis. *J Neurol, Neurosur, and Ps, 75*(3), 441–447.

Paul, R. H., Brickman, A. M., Navia, B., Hinkin, C., Malloy, P. F., Jefferson, A. L., et al. (2005). Apathy is associated with volume of the nucleus accumbens in patients infected with HIV. *J Neuropsych Clin N, 17*(2), 167–171.

Paul, R. H., Cohen, R. A., Moser, D. J., Ott, B. R., Sethi, M., Sweet, L., et al. (2003). Clinical correlates of cognitive decline in vascular dementia. *Cogn Behav Neurol, 16*(1), 40–46.

Paul, R. H., Cohen, R. A., Ott, B. R., Zawacki, T., Moser, D. J., Davis, J., et al. (2000). Cognitive and functional status in two subtypes of vascular dementia. *Neurorehabilitation, 15,* 199–205.

Raskind, M., Mintzer, J., Mehnert, A., & Ferris, S. H. (2001). Decline in ability to perform ADLs in patients with Alzheimer's disease not receiving treatment. *J Neurol Sci, 187,* S140–S141.

Reed, B., Mungas, D. M., Kramer, J. H., Betz, B. P., Ellis, W., Vinters, H. V., et al. (2004). Clinical and neuropsychological features in autopsy-defined vascular dementia. *Clin Neuropsychol, 18*(1), 63–74.

Roman, G. C. (2005). Clinical forms of vascular dementia. In R. H. Paul, R. Cohen, B. R. Ott, & S. Salloway (Eds.), *Vascular dementia: Cerebrovascular mechanisms and clinical management* (pp. 7–22). Totowa, NJ: Humana Press.

Roman, G. C., Sachdev, P., Royall, D. R., Bullock, R. A., Orgogozo, J. M., Lopez-Pousa, S., et al. (2004). Vascular cognitive disorder: A new diagnostic category updating vascular cognitive impairment and vascular dementia. *J Neurol Sci, 226,* 81–87.

Roman, G. C., Tatemichi, T. K., Erkinjuntti, T., Cummings, J. L., Masdeu, J. C., Garcia, J. H., et al. (1993). Vascular dementia: Diagnostic criteria for research studies. Report of the NINDS-AIREN International Workshop. *Neurology, 43,* 250–260.

Royall, D. R, Palmer, R., Chiodo, L. A., & Polk, M. J. (2005). Executive control mediates memory's association with change in instrumental activities of daily living: The Freedom House study. *J Am Geriatr Soc, 53,* 11–17.

Sachdev, P. S., Brodaty, H., Valenzuela, M. J., Lorentz, L., Looi, J. C., Berman, K., et al. (2006). Clinical determinants of dementia and mild cognitive impairment following ischaemic stroke: The Sydney stroke study. *Dement: Geriatr Cogn, 21*(5–6), 275–283.

Salat, D. H., Tuch, D. S., Hevelone, N. D., Fischl, B., Corkin, S., Rosas, H. D., et al. (2005). Age related changes in prefrontal white matter measured by diffusion tensor imaging. *Ann N Y Acad Sci, 1064,* 37–49.

Samuelsson, M., Soderfeldt, B., & Olsson, G. B. (1996). Functional outcome in patients with lacunar infarction. *Stroke, 27,* 842–846.

Scheid, R., Preul, C., Lincke, T., Matthes, G., Schroeter, M. L., Guthke, T., et al. (2006). Correlation of cognitive status, MRI- and SPECT-imaging in CADASIL patients. *Eur J Neurol, 13*(4), 363–370.

Schneider, J. A., Wilson, R. S., Bienias, J. L., Evans, D. A., & Bennett, D. A. (2004). Cerebral infarctions and the likelihood of dementia from Alzheimer's disease pathology. *Neurology, 62*(7), 1148–1155.

Selnes, O. A., & Vinters, H. V. (2006). Vascular cognitive impairment. *Nat Clin Pract, 2*(10), 538–547.

Shiau, M. Y., Yu, L., Yuan, H. S., Lin, J. H., & Liu, C. K. (2006). Functional performance of Alzheimer's disease and vascular dementia in southern Taiwan. *Kaohsiung J Med Sci, 22*(9), 437–446.

Tierney, M. C., Black, S. E., Szalai, J. P., Snow, W. G., Fisher, R. H., Nadon, G., et al. (2001). Recognition memory and verbal fluency differentiate probable Alzheimer's disease from subcortical ischemic vascular dementia. *Arch Neurol, 58*(10), 1654–1659.

Tomimoto, H., Ohtani, R., & Ihara, M. (2005). Absence of cholinergic deficits in "pure" vascular dementia. *Neurology, 65*(1), 179.

Tupler, L. A., Coffey, C. E., Logue, P. E., Djang, W. T., & Fagan, S. M. (1992). Neuropsychological importance of subcortical white matter hyperintensity. *Arch Neurol, 49*(12), 1248–1252.

Vetter, P. H., Krauss, S., Steiner, O., Kropp, P., Moller, W. D., Moises, H. W., et al. (1999). Vascular dementia versus dementia of Alzheimer's type: Do they have differential effects on caregivers' burden? *J Gerontol: Br Psychol Sci Soc Sci, 54*(2), S93–S98.

Wallin, A., Milos, V., Sjorgren, M., Pantoni, L., & Erkinjuntti, T. (2003). Classification and subtypes of vascular dementia. *Int Psychogeriatr, 15*(1), 27–37.

Zawacki, T., Grace, J., Paul, R., Moser, D. J., Ott, B. R., Gordon, N., et al. (2002). Behavioral problems as predictors of functional abilities of vascular dementia patients. *J Neuropsych Clin N, 14*(3), 296–302.

CHAPTER 13

Everyday Impact of Traumatic Brain Injury

Rema A. Lillie, Kristina Kowalski, Brigitte N. Patry, Claire Sira, Holly Tuokko, and Catherine A. Mateer

Traumatic brain injury (TBI) is not a misnomer as the "traumatic" effects of such an injury can be long-lasting and profound. TBI most often results in diffuse injury to the brain, which can lead to a varied pattern of disruption in an individual's everyday life. Following a TBI, many individuals struggle with meeting the everyday demands of their household such as paying bills, caring for children, preparing meals, or attending appointments. Often, individuals with TBI struggle with returning to employment at the same level of performance as prior to the injury. Direct effects of the injury, such as damage to brain structures, are most often coupled with additional obstacles, such as frustration, anxiety, or mood disturbances, which exacerbate cognitive difficulties and create new challenges. The physical effects of injury, such as pain and spasticity, can interfere with completing daily tasks.

This chapter begins with an introduction to brain injury and its resulting sequelae, including the impact on various domains of cognition. A discussion follows of the relationship between TBI and performance of everyday activities, including instrumental activities of daily living (IADLs), financial management, driving performance, and vocational functioning. An integrative section identifies common links in everyday dysfunction and provides general recommendations for assessment and intervention.

Overview of TBI and Its Sequelae

Pathophysiology

There are numerous potential sources of brain injury in cases of TBI, and they typically occur in two stages. In the first stage, primary injuries are caused by mechanical forces. Linear acceleration–deceleration forces usually generate focal lesions when a moving skull is suddenly decelerated or when a stationary head is abruptly accelerated. As the brain continues its trajectory, damage incurred at its point of compression against the skull is called a "*coup* injury." A "*contre-coup* injury" refers to (hemorrhagic) contusions sustained to the opposite side of the brain when it rebounds. Orbitofrontal and anterior temporal regions are highly vulnerable because they are propelled over bony protrusions and cavities of the skull below. "Diffuse axonal injury" refers to microscopic damage caused by widespread stretching and shearing of axons deep in the brain. It occurs when a head movement is abruptly stopped and the brain continues to rotate within the skull (rotational forces).

Within 24 hours a cascade of negative events can produce secondary injuries. Brain tissue may swell and become displaced, thereby causing further shearing and tearing of blood vessels. Consequently, blood clots may form either in the space surrounding the brain (e.g., extradural and subdural hematomas) or within the brain itself (intracerebral hematomas). Hematomas can force portions of brain tissue to shift into nearby spaces (herniation). Bleeding, edema, and development of hydrocephalus due to impaired circulation of cerebrospinal fluid may result in increased intracranial pressure. Limbic structures are particularly vulnerable to hypoxia and ischemia caused by metabolic and vascular disturbances, and by systemic complications that interfere with oxygen or blood supply to the brain (e.g., crushing and choking injuries, extensive blood loss). Tissue scarring can lead to delayed onset of seizures.

Levels of Severity

The level of coma upon hospital admission (Glasgow Coma Scale or GCS; Teasdale & Jennett, 1974) and the duration of posttraumatic amnesia (PTA) are most commonly employed to classify the severity of TBI. PTA is defined as a period postinjury marked by confusion and an inability to consistently and accurately recall ongoing events. Classification guidelines are provided in Table 13.1; note that there is some variability in the criteria used to rate the severity of an injury. These guidelines are based on data from the American Congress of Rehabilitation Medicine (1993) and from Lezak (1995).

Epidemiology

The incidence of TBI in the United States is 200 cases per 100,000 persons (Sorenson & Kraus, 1991). A recent report by the Centers for Disease Control and Prevention (Langlois, Rutland-Brown, & Thomas, 2006), based on 1995–2001 data, revealed that at least 1.4 million people sustain a TBI each year. Moderate and severe TBI

TABLE 13.1. Guidelines for Rating Severity of Brain Injury

TBI severity	GCS score	Length of unconsciousness	Duration of PTA
Mild	13–15	30 minutes or less[a]	< 1 hour (or < 24 hours[a])
Moderate	9–12	< 6 hours	1–24 hours
Severe	3–8	> 6 hours	> 24 hours

[a]American Congress of Rehabilitation Medicine (1993) and Lezak (1995).

make up 20–30% of cases; the rest are mild. Men outnumber women by a 1.5 ratio, and incidence is highest for children and for people between the ages of 15 and 24 or over the age of 75. It is estimated that 80,000–90,000 of these individuals are permanently disabled due to their injury. The leading causes of TBI are falls (28%), motor vehicle collisions (MVCs; 20%), and being "struck by/against" an object (19%). Most TBI-related hospitalizations (235,000/year) and deaths (55,000/year) are due to MVCs.

Psychopathology

Psychopathology has been implicated both as a contributing factor to the risk for TBI as well as a complicating factor in rehabilitation following injury. Substance misuse is a common problem, with data suggesting that 44–66% of individuals hospitalized for TBI have some history of alcohol abuse. Between one-third and one-half of individuals affected by TBI are intoxicated at the time of the injury. Intoxication at the time of the injury can lead to more complications and longer acute hospital stays; a history of alcohol abuse is strongly associated with increased morbidity and mortality, perhaps due to a history of multiple injuries (Corrigan, 1995).

The most commonly diagnosed mental health disorders following brain injury are depression and specific anxiety disorders, with a significant proportion of individuals having two or more diagnoses (Hibbard, Uysal, Kepler, Bogdany, & Silver, 1998). Prevalence of depression following injury (Kreutzer, Seel, & Gourley, 2001) has been reported at nearly nine times the rate found in community samples. Rates of suicide are also higher in this group, with suicide three to four times more likely as compared to the general population (Teasdale & Engberg, 2001). Due to the life-altering affects of brain injury and the traumatic nature of many injuries (e.g., car crashes, falls, assaults), some mental health distress has been suggested to be normative for this population (Williams, Evans, & Fleminger, 2003). Clinically significant anxiety disorders, such as posttraumatic stress disorder and obsessive–compulsive disorder, are common in this population (Epstein & Ursano, 1994). Even mild injuries can play a role in the emergence and expression of anxiety (Moore, Terryberry-Spohr, & Hope, 2006). In fact, those with milder injuries have at times been shown to have more mental health concerns than those with more severe injuries (Rapoport, McCauley, Levin, Song, & Feinstein, 2002; Van Reekum, Cohen, & Wong, 2000), perhaps due to a higher level of insight.

Cognitive Profiles Associated with TBI

Attention

Attention is particularly vulnerable to dysfunction following a TBI. Difficulties with concentration, multitasking, and speed of thinking are among the most common complaints of TBI survivors (de Guise, Feyz, LeBlanc, Richard, & Lamoureux, 2005; van Zomeren & Brouwer, 1994).

On objective testing, slowed speed of processing is almost universally reported, even 2–5 years after a severe injury (e.g., Perbal, Couillet, Azouvi, & Pouthas, 2003; Ponsford & Kinsella, 1992; Ríos, Periáñez, & Muñoz-Céspedes, 2004; Spikman,

Deelman, & van Zomeren, 2000; van Zomeren & Brouwer, 1994). A meta-analytic study on mild TBI documented the largest effect size for speed-of-processing tests compared to other cognitive domains (Frencham, Fox, & Maybery, 2005).

Other than speed of processing, complex attention is also frequently impacted by TBI. This effect is reflected in a difficulty dividing attention between stimuli and may occur regardless of injury severity (Bate, Mathias, & Crawford, 2001; Cicerone, 1997; Ponsford & Kinsella, 1992). It may be related to impairment of control and executive mechanisms (McDowell, Whyte, & D'Esposito, 1997; Serino et al., 2006), to slowed speed of processing (Ponsford & Kinsella, 1992; van Zomeren & Brouwer, 1994), and/or to working memory deficits (Park, Moscovitch, & Robertson, 1999). An inability to mentally manipulate several sources of information simultaneously (working memory) is common (Perbal et al., 2003; Ríos et al., 2004; Serino et al., 2006) and may persist for years (Vanderploeg, Curtiss, & Belanger, 2005).

Disruptions of selective attention (Bate et al., 2001; Robertson, Ward, Ridgeway, & Nimmo-Smith, 1996; Schmitter-Edgecombe & Kibby, 1998) have been reported. Sustained attention (Loken, Thornton, Otto, & Long, 1995; Robertson et al., 1996) may also be susceptible to dysfunction after TBI, particularly in cases of diffuse damage (Riccio, Reynolds, Lowe, & Moore, 2002). By contrast, attention span is relatively robust to the effects of mild or chronic injury (Cicerone, 1997; Leclercq et al., 2000).

Memory

Decline of anterograde memory (difficulty learning new information) is often reported by TBI survivors, regardless of injury severity (Alves, 1992; de Guise et al., 2005). Whether these deficits persist beyond a few months in mild cases has not been unequivocally established (Dikmen, Machamer, & Temkin, 2001; Leininger, Gramling, & Farrell, 1990), but several people with severe TBI experience lasting memory impairments (Goldstein & Levin, 1995; Zec et al., 2001). Injury-related variables have been associated with the level (Wiegner & Donders, 1999), but not the pattern (Curtiss, Vanderploeg, Spencer, & Salazar, 2001), of memory performance.

Residual learning difficulties are rare with a mild TBI (Iverson, Lovell, & Smith, 2000; Ogden & Wolfe, 1998). By contrast, there are multiple reports of reduced verbal and visual learning following more severe injuries (e.g., Blachstein, Vakil, & Hoofien, 1993; Crosson, Novack, & Trennery, 1988; Shum, Harris, & O'Gorman, 2000).

There are conflicting reports regarding retention of information over a delay (Fork et al., 2005; Shum et al., 2000; Zec et al., 2001). A retrieval deficit may explain the weaker performance on free-recall tasks compared to cued-recall and recognition measures (Crosson et al., 1988; Curtiss et al., 2001; Nolin, 2006). After TBI, memory performance may be characterized by reduced semantic clustering during learning (Blachstein et al., 1993; Crosson et al., 1988; Nolin, 2006) and by a high number of intrusions upon recall or recognition (retrieval of items that were not presented or positive response to items not previously encountered) (Crosson et al., 1988; Nolin, 2006; Shum et al., 2000; Zec et al., 2001). Prospective memory, or memory for actions to be performed in the future, can be disrupted (Shum, Valentine, & Cutmore, 1999); implicit memory is relatively intact (Shum, Sweeper, & Murray, 1996).

Executive Functioning

The term "executive functions" refers to a set of higher-order cognitive skills necessary to successfully formulate and execute independent, goal-directed behaviors. Such skills may be impaired, even in chronic cases of TBI, and may be associated with some of the daily struggles experienced by people with moderate to severe injury (Hart, Whyte, Kim, & Vaccaro, 2005; Kim et al., 2005).

Verbal fluency deficits are common following mild to severe TBI, likely because of compromise in processing speed and initiation (Brooks, Fos, Greve, & Hammond, 1999; Cockburn, 1995; Kersel, Marsh, Havill, & Sleigh, 2001; Leclercq et al., 2000). Individuals may be slower to retrieve words (Raskin & Rearick, 1996). Verbal abstract reasoning (Fork et al., 2005) and planning may be impaired, although inefficient planning is more noticeable on relatively unstructured measures requiring a self-generated strategy (Spikman et al., 2000) than on structured tasks (Cockburn, 1995; Ponsford & Kinsella, 1992; Spikman et al., 2000). Severe injuries and diffuse axonal injury may be more likely to disrupt problem solving and mental flexibility (Cockburn, 1995; de Guise et al., 2005; Fork et al., 2005; Ríos et al., 2004). Greater susceptibility to distraction and interference is also reported (Ríos et al., 2004; Stuss et al., 1985). However, clinical observations of disinhibition postinjury have not been empirically supported using tests requiring inhibition of prepotent or ongoing responses (Bate et al., 2001; Ponsford & Kinsella, 1992; Rieger & Gauggel, 2002; Stuss et al., 1985).

It is important to keep in mind that, as noted by Wilson, Herbert, and Shiel (2003), neuropsychological evaluation provides an indirect link to treatment because it identifies the underlying substrates involved in completing daily activities, but it does not provide a direct sample of different behaviors in naturalistic environments. Inclusion of more ecologically valid tests, such as the Behavioural Assessment of the Dysexecutive Syndrome (BADS), the Test of Everyday Attention (TEA), and the Rivermead Behavioural Memory Test (RBMT), can help bridge this gap, but these tests can at times be plagued by ceiling effects for individuals who have subtler difficulties, and they may have less than ideal psychometric properties. Standardized measures can also be limited by the provision of structure, rules, and organization—the very types of skills that may challenge individuals with TBI in their everyday lives (see Manchester, Priestley, & Jackson, 2004).

Awareness

Impairment of self-awareness has been related to TBI severity (Prigatano, Bruna, & Mataro, 1998; Sherer, Boake, et al., 1998) and this impairment persists in approximately 30% of survivors with severe TBI (Prigatano & Altman, 1990). It is unclear whether self-awareness deficits relate to other neuropsychological disturbances (Prigatano, 2005). In a recent study an executive function composite score, derived from eight measures tapping cognitive flexibility, working memory, and response inhibition, was associated with the degree of self-awareness post-TBI (Hart et al., 2005), suggesting that some neuropsychological measures may be sensitive to alterations in self-awareness.

Comparison of self-ratings with those made by significant others indicates that persons with TBI may underestimate the extent or the impact of deficits pertaining to selective aspects of their overall functioning. Although they may lack insight into their cognitive and behavioral difficulties, they can report physical limitations and problems with activities of daily living (ADLs) and overt emotional responses (Fleming & Strong, 1999; Hart, Sherer, Whyte, Polansky, & Novack, 2004; Hart et al., 2005; Roche, Fleming, & Shum, 2002; Sherer, Boake, et al., 1998).

Impaired self-awareness is associated with rehabilitation-related variables, including poorer compliance with participation (Lam, McMahon, Priddy, & Gehred-Schultz, 1998), increased length of rehabilitation stay (Malec, Buffington, Moessner, & Degiorgio, 2000), reduced functional independence at discharge (Sherer, Hart, & Nick, 2003), and less employability (Sherer, Bergloff, et al., 1998).

IADLs in TBI

Limitations in completing ADLs, especially instrumental activities of daily living (IADLs), are common following TBI (Olver, Ponsford, & Curran, 1996; Pagulayan, Temkin, Machamer, & Dikmen, 2006), with the specific impact on everyday life dependent on the type and severity of injury as well as the timing postinjury.

Impairments in daily living are most commonly seen following moderate to severe injuries (Sohlberg & Mateer, 2001). Difficulties in performing basic ADLs (e.g., dressing, bathing, eating) occur early following injury and are impacted by physical sequelae such as paresis, incoordination, and balance problems. These types of limitations are often addressed by physical therapy geared toward strengthening and normalizing muscle tone, working on balance and postural control, and restituting gait patterns. Compensatory training in using an unimpaired limb or assistive devices may be implemented with occupational therapy. Over time, difficulties with basic self-care skills most often improve. In one study of nearly 1,800 individuals with TBI, only 3.2% of responders identified a persistent need for increasing independence in basic self-care skills at 1-year postinjury (Corrigan, Whiteneck, & Mellick, 2004).

In contrast to marked improvements seen in basic ADLs in the TBI population, difficulties in performing IADLs, such as shopping, cooking, housework, and management of medication and finances, have been shown to persist over time (Colantonio et al., 2004; Corrigan et al., 2004; Dikmen, Machamer, Powell, & Temkin, 2003; Farmer & Eakman, 1995; Pagulayan et al., 2006). For example, in one study of 210 individuals with moderate to severe brain injuries (Dikmen et al., 2003), approximately 60% of participants reported cognitive problems in performing daily activities 3–5 years postinjury. In comparison, 70% reported no problems in completing personal care activities. Of the domains polled, personal care and ambulation were rated as least affected at 3–5 years postinjury. Similarly, in a study of long-term outcomes post-TBI (Colantonio et al., 2004) that included participants up to 24 years postinjury, 88% of the 306 persons interviewed could bathe, dress, eat, transfer, use the toilet, and telephone independently. More limitations were reported for IADLs. Even with assistance, 10% of the sample reported an inability to complete a variety of daily tasks such as shopping, meal preparation, housework, money management, and navigating in the community.

Distinctions between recovery of ADLs with continued difficulty on IADLs are important because independence in basic self-care does not translate directly into independent living. In terms of the long-term disability associated with TBI, the continued difficulty in completing daily tasks negatively impacts an individual's day-to-day life. Although only a small percentage of persons with TBI require restricted living situations in the long term (approximately 10%) (Colantonio et al., 2004; Dikmen et al., 2003), difficulty in completing daily tasks suggests increased burden on others, including family and caregivers, for a substantial portion of survivors with TBI. Management of finances has consistently been identified as a key problem area post-TBI (e.g., Colantonio et al., 2004). Due to its importance both in independent living and as identified in this population, financial management is addressed in a separate section below.

IADLs are, by definition, more cognitively demanding than ADLs and can be negatively impacted by a variety of brain injury sequelae. A task as seemingly simple as preparing a meal, for example, requires organization of materials, sequencing of steps, memory, and focused attention, among other skills. Add a distracting environment (e.g., background noise, telephone ringing) and the task can become nearly impossible for someone who has difficulty managing competing goals (e.g., divided attention or working memory problems).

The pathophysiology of TBI tends to impair the very cognitive substrates necessary for completing daily tasks. Diffuse damage leads to difficulties with attention and executive control skills, both of which are crucial for completing IADLs. Slowed speed of processing, common in this population, can impair one's ability to make the quick, on-the-spot decisions necessary for many daily activities. One can imagine how challenging it would be for an individual with slowed speed of processing and difficulty multitasking to listen to a salesperson in a store, with competing background noise, and make a decision about which dog food to purchase or which over-the-counter medication would best treat cold symptoms.

Memory problems can also have a profound impact on one's ability to complete IADLs. Problems with prospective memory, or the ability to remember an upcoming event, can interfere with making/keeping appointments (which can be costly) or remembering to place a phone call or pick up a prescription at the pharmacy. Memory problems can also lead to safety concerns in everyday tasks, such as leaving the iron on or a pot on the stove.

Impairments in self-awareness that have been reported in the TBI population (e.g., Prigatano & Altman, 1990) can interfere with a person's willingness to accept help with everyday tasks or use external aids. At times, families express concern over leaving an individual with TBI at home alone because he or she may attempt to complete a task, not recognizing limitations (e.g., making tea but leaving the kettle on, leaving to run an errand and getting lost).

Assessment of IADLs is most often completed by an occupational therapist. There are a vast array of tools available for assessment, ranging from questionnaire data, rating scales, or interviews (both self-report and report by a significant other), to observation of activities performed in realistic environments (see Law, Baum, &

Dunn, 2005). In most rating scales or questionnaires, assessment of IADLs is incorporated into a more general evaluation of overall functioning. Although there are many to choose from (e.g., Neurobehavioral Functioning Inventory [NFI], Mayo-Portland Adaptability Inventory [MPAI], Sickness Impact Profile [SIP], Medical Outcomes Study 36-Item Short-Form Health Survey), a commonly used scale is the Community Integration Questionnaire (CIQ; Willer, Rosenthal, Kreutzer, Gordon, & Rempel, 1993) consisting of 15 items related to home integration, social integration, and productive activities. Other more general ratings scales are often used to reach conclusions about the ability to complete daily tasks (e.g., Functional Independence Measure + Functional Assessment Measure [FIM+FAM], Disability Rating Scale, Glasgow Outcome Scale), but these scales are intended for use as summary outcome measures and do not capture subtler difficulties on the performance of IADLs in particular. As individual variability impacts the pattern of IADL performance, interviews with patients and, ideally, a significant other, can provide valuable insight into where problems arise on a daily basis.

Although time-consuming, direct observation of IADL performance in a realistic environment is one of the best indicators of day-to-day functioning. Individuals can be rated on standard scales while completing IADLs (e.g., Farmer & Eakman, 1995) or can be asked to complete a standard inventory of measures (e.g., Multiple Errands Test; Shallice & Burgess, 1991). The benefit of this type of observation is that, as compared to a dichotomous rating of able/not able, the clinician can observe where in the process a breakdown occurs. Identifying the source of disrupted performance is crucial to intervention attempts.

Neuropsychological evaluation has also been used to predict performance of IADLs, with mixed results (Farmer & Eakman, 1995; Johnston, Shawaryn, Malec, Kreutzer, & Hammond, 2006). Some reviews suggest that up to 85% of the variance in levels of functional abilities can be reflected in test scores (Acker, 1990). Others have argued (Manchester et al., 2004) that the very nature of neuropsychological evaluation (e.g., testing in a quiet environment, provision of rules and structure, clear task demands, no multitasking) limits the applicability of neuropsychological test performance to everyday environments, where individuals are faced with distractions, noise, and a need for self-direction and planning. As neuropsychology has evolved as a profession from delineating isolated components of cognitive functioning and localizing lesions to providing a broader picture of an individual's ability to function in real-world environments, the need for ecologically valid tests has increased and that challenge is currently being addressed. In the meantime, neuropsychological evaluation remains a vital component in the assessment of IADLs because it complements more real-world observations by providing hypotheses for *why* a breakdown in task completion is occurring (e.g., problems with memory, attention). Such information can suggest direct avenues for intervention.

Other factors that seriously impact completion of IADLs post-TBI are beyond the scope of the current discussion but require mention. For example, fatigue is common following TBI, with reported rates as high as 73% in some samples (Olver et al., 1996), and can significantly impact a person's ability to complete household tasks. Pain and headaches are often ongoing following brain injury (Nicholson & Martelli, 2004) and can impact the number and type of activities one can complete on a daily basis. Rates of depression and anxiety are high in this population and can negatively affect day-to-day functioning years postinjury (Morton & Wehman, 1995). One large study of 722 individuals with brain injuries reported a prevalence rate of 42% for major depressive disorder 2½ years postinjury (Kreutzer et al., 2001). A population-based study reported increased suicide rates in individuals with brain injury as compared to the general public (Teasdale & Engberg, 2001). A study of 76 individuals approximately 14 years following brain injury suggests that anxiety remains a significant problem for 44% of the group (Hoofien, Gilboa, Vakil, & Donovick, 2001). Although the diversity of potential sources of impairment can be overwhelming, considering each in a thorough assessment of limiting factors for IADL performance can provide multiple options for intervention. Often, a multifaceted approach leads to the best outcome.

Perhaps most important to consider is the impact that difficulties in performing IADLs has both on affected individuals and their families. The personal toll of not being able to manage household responsibilities can be huge. Additionally, family members and caregivers are often faced with picking up the slack in an already challenging situation, which can increase pressure within the household and within relationships. As the TBI population is a relatively young group (NIH Consensus Conference, 1999), the cost of limitations in completing daily activities, both to the individuals involved and to society, is extensive. Assessment and treatment of IADL performance in individuals with TBI is essential to improve long-term outcomes.

Money Management

Managing money and handling one's finances are crucial to independent living and have been found to be among the factors most salient to success in the transition to independent living after TBI. Money management incorporates a broad range of tasks, from relatively simple ones, such as currency identification or calculating the correct change, to those that are more complex, such as interpreting bank statements, completing tax returns, and negotiating bank loans. In addition, money management requires planning and monitoring of financial actions in relation to personal resources and values if the numerous risks involved in poor financial decision making are to be avoided.

Given the complex, cognitively demanding nature of money management, it is not surprising that people with brain damage of various etiologies (e.g., traumatic or degenerative) may experience difficulty with at least some aspects of handling finances. For example, individuals may struggle with completing monetary transactions due to problems with attention (e.g., sustaining attention when calculating), comprehension (e.g., interpreting bills and statements), perception (e.g., visual recognition problems with currency), memory (e.g., paying bills on time), or executive functions (e.g., planning and monitoring expenses).

It has been estimated that at least 30% of people with traumatic brain dysfunction, including those who are institutionalized, exhibit some money management problems (Australian Bureau of Statistics, 1996; Dawson & Chipman, 1995; Ponsford, Olver & Curran, 1995). However, as yet, relatively little is known about the specific types or severity of money management problems faced by these individuals.

Researchers from La Trobe University in Australia have begun to investigate the types of money management deficits seen in people with TBI and their relation to neuropsychological measures of cognitive functions. Hoskin, Jackson, and Crowe (2005a) compared responses on a Money Management Survey (MMS) for a group of 35 people with acquired brain dysfunction (ABD) of heterogeneous etiologies to 15 control participants without ABD matched on age, gender, and socioeconomic status. Of note, the control participants reported money management problems such as not paying the rent or bills on time (47%), spending all their money before the next pay day (20%), needing to borrow money because they had run out (20%), and not checking their change (18%). However, the control participants reported significantly fewer problems in comparison to the participants with ABD or case managers' reports of the ABD participants. In addition to the problems experienced by the control subjects, people with ABD also exhibited other problems such as impulse buying (56%), not leaving money for essentials (47%), and difficulty using automated teller machines (ATMs).

These researchers also noted that people with ABD have difficulty using automatic machines more generally. Crowe, Mahony, O'Brien, and Jackson (2003) compared 90 people with ABD (30 mild, 30 moderate, and 30 severe) with 30 nonimpaired individuals of similar age, gender, and educational attainment on a questionnaire measure of ATM use. The ABD sample consistently confirmed that they had difficulty using automated transport ticketing machines, ATMs, and automatic telephone answering and responding devices. Understanding and remembering the instructions for these tasks appeared to be the major impediment to successful usage. In a related study, Crowe, Mahony, and Jackson (2003) showed that level of competence with automated machines for 45 people with ABD and 15 age- and gender-matched control participants was related to overall performance on a neuropsychological test battery.

Similarly, in addition to examining differences in performance of money management tasks between participants with and without ABD, Hoskin, Jackson, and Crowe (2005b) examined the relations between responses on the MMS and performance on a battery of neuropsychological tests. Specifically, measures of general intelligence, memory, attention/executive functions, and mood were included. When the relation between these neuropsychological measures and the MMS staff report for the ABD participants was examined, only three individual neuropsychological measures emerged as relevant. All were measures of memory, and the correlations were relatively small (prospective memory, $r = -.44$; word list total recall, $r = -.33$; and word list delayed recall, $r = -.41$). However, when logistic regression was used to examine the relations between neuropsychological measures of specific domains and specific money management difficulties, prediction success was good. Measures of impulse control were significantly predictive of problematic impulse spending, and measures of memory were significantly predictive of late payment of bills or rent. Using a similar neuropsychological battery, Hoskin, Jackson, and Crowe (2005a) were able to discriminate between people with ABD who were independently managing their personal finances from those who had been appointed an administrator to assist in financial management. The measures of attention/executive functions were most useful in classifying group membership, with 83.7% of individuals being correctly classified.

Other insights into money management skills after TBI come from a study of self-awareness where participants were asked to perform tasks, two of which were related to money management (i.e., simple math calculations used in daily activities and checkbook reconciliation) and answer self-awareness questions related to the performance of these tasks (Abreu et al., 2001). Performance on the two money management items was highly correlated and was collapsed into one measure. The largest discrepancy between the self-rating by the people with TBI and the therapists, a measure of impaired self-awareness, was consistently associated with money management performance. Self-awareness is a complex construct and mediated by many factors (e.g., executive functions such as anticipation, goal selection, preplanning, and monitoring; Stuss, 1991). Moreover, it has been argued that individuals must be able to recognize where and when difficulties exist if they are to access or request help in these areas (Diehl, 1998). A deficit in self-awareness, then, particularly within the money management domain, leaves a person with TBI vulnerable to experiencing financial difficulties or financial abuse.

Issues relevant to money management have been the focus of a number of studies conducted with other groups of people highly vulnerable to experiencing financial difficulties or financial abuse, such as older adults with degenerative brain diseases (e.g., Alzheimer's disease), and may inform this growing area of research in TBI. Many of the dementia studies adopt a performance-based definition of impairment that focuses on discovering where and when performance deficits occur on specific money management tasks. For example, Marson and colleagues (2000) developed the Financial Capacity Instrument (FCI) to assess domain-level financial activities and task-specific financial abilities in people with dementia. The FCI was found to reliably discriminate between healthy older adult control participants and people with mild to moderate Alzheimer's disease. Yet, as noted earlier, money management involves tasks of differing levels of complexity as well as other skills. For example, the ability to make decisions or direct others in managing one's affairs is critically important to financial management. In our research on awareness of financial skills in people with dementia (Cramer, Tuokko, Mateer, & Hultsch, 2004; Van Wielingen, Cramer, & Tuokko, 2004; Van Wielingen, Tuokko, Cramer, Mateer, & Hultsch, 2004), we developed the Measure of Awareness of Financial Skills (MAFS) to examine performance on money-related tasks as well as reports of difficulties with tasks (of varying levels of complexity) provided by individuals with dementia (self) and people who know them well (other). Discrepancy between the reports of self and others can be examined as a measure of awareness. In our research, individuals with mild dementia lacked awareness of difficulties performing complex tasks, whereas people with moderate/severe dementia lacked awareness concerning the difficulties they experienced across tasks, regardless of complexity. Similarly, those people with dementia who experienced executive dysfunction were more likely than those without executive dysfunction to be unaware of impairment in performing simple as well as complex tasks. These findings echo the executive dysfunction observed by Hoskin and colleagues (2005a) in people with TBI who had been appointed an administrator to assist in financial management, suggesting that lack of awareness of impairments may have been central to their need for supervision.

This brief examination of money management in TBI indicates that many different types of cognitive deficits may affect successful performance on money management tasks, but that deficits in self-awareness and/or other executive functions appear pivotal in terms of increased vulnerability. There is also evidence to suggest that specific types of cognitive deficits (e.g., memory, impulse control) relate to specific types of money management problems (e.g., remembering to pay bills, impulse spending). Though money management research is in its infancy, it is being conducted in groups of people with different types of brain dysfunction (e.g., traumatic, degenerative). The application and comparison of measures, approaches, and findings across these groups may be particularly useful for clarifying the types and nature of money management deficits that place people at risk, their relation to neuropsychological measures of cognitive functions, and strategies for maximizing independent functioning within this domain of everyday functioning.

Driving

Driving is a complex behavior that, like financial management, is cognitively demanding. For many recovering from a TBI, the ability to drive is an indicator of regained independence and normality. The complexity of the driving task relates both to the number of abilities, cognitive and otherwise, that influence an individual's ability to drive safely and to the complexity inherent in a dynamic, unpredictable driving environment. Fitness to drive and return to driving after TBI are issues of significant concern for individuals with TBI and for other drivers, alike. Substantial literature has investigated driving and the influence of various impairments on driving performance in TBI.

Many cognitive abilities, including attention, speed of information processing, memory, executive functioning, and awareness, influence an individual's ability to drive safely and contribute to the complexity of the driving task. For example, attention is required for many aspects of driving, such as focusing on important aspects of the driving environment; staying vigilant for traffic signs, other traffic, and road conditions; and performing secondary nondriving tasks while driving (e.g., talking on the phone, adjusting radio controls). In addition, speed of information processing influences how quickly one can process information and make rapid decisions and responses to unpredictable driving situations. Memory also influences many driving tasks, including the ability to remember traffic regulations, navigate through familiar areas, maintain and operate a car, and remember where the car is parked. Executive functions, such as decision making and planning, also impact driving performance (e.g., how to maneuver in traffic, select a route, plan a trip, avoid challenging driving situations). Self-awareness is essential to safe driving; knowledge of one's own physical/motor, sensoriperceptual, and/or cognitive deficits and the influence of these impairments on driving ability is necessary to implement appropriate compensation strategies (e.g., avoiding challenging situations, such as driving at night) and to know when it is necessary to stop driving altogether.

There is widespread agreement that individuals recovering from TBI may possess residual impairments (e.g., cognitive, sensoriperceptual, motor, behavioral, or emotional) that could compromise their ability to drive safely (e.g., Hawley, 2001;

Lengenfelder, Schultheis, Al-Shihabi, Mourant, & DeLuca, 2002; Leon-Carrion, Dominguez-Morales, & Barroso Y Martin, 2005; Wald, Liu, & Reil, 2000). We acknowledge the influence of all these areas on driving performance, but in the interest of space, we focus primarily on the cognitive disturbances (e.g., attention, information-processing speed, memory, executive function, awareness) in TBI that are especially relevant as possible barriers to successful driving performance.

A large proportion of individuals suffering from TBI returns to driving, with percentages ranging across studies from approximately 32 to 80% (Fisk, Schneider, & Novack, 1998; Formisano et al., 2005; Hawley, 2001; Lew et al., 2005; Olver et al., 1996; Pietrapiana et al., 2005; Priddy, Johnson, & Chow, 1990; Schultheis, Matheis, Nead, & DeLuca, 2002), and many do so without assessment or advice from driving experts (Christie, Savill, Buttress, Newby, & Tyerman, 2001; Leon-Carrion et al., 2005). Returning to driving can be an important factor in successful functional recovery and resumption of normal lifestyle after TBI (Pietrapiana et al., 2005; Rapport, Hanks, & Bryer, 2006; Schultheis, Hillary, & Chute, 2003). For example, studies using the FIM+FAM have shown that drivers with TBI are rated as significantly more functionally independent by clinicians than are ex-drivers with TBI (Fisk et al., 1998; Hawley, 2001).

Few would dispute that a return to driving is integral to maintaining independence and successful community integration, and research has supported this notion. In brain-injured populations, in particular, research has demonstrated that driving independence is associated with employment and job stability (Devani Serio & Devens, 1994; Kreutzer et al., 2003), confidence, quality of life, resumption of previous activities (Hawley, 2001), and social integration (Dawson & Chipman, 1995; Rapport et al., 2006). Moreover, it has been shown that *not driving* is particularly socially (Mazaux et al., 1997) and functionally disabling (Rapport et al., 2006) in individuals recovering from TBI. In addition, substantial literature has documented the negative consequences of driving cessation in older non-brain-injured populations (e.g., decreased independence, isolation, loneliness) (Harrison & Ragland, 2003; Marottoli et al., 2000; Ragland, Satariano, & MacLeod, 2005). In TBI, these negative consequences are compounded by the possibility of underlying emotional and behavioral disturbances, as well as lack of insight, making it harder for individuals to appreciate the potential need to adjust their driving or stop driving altogether.

There is considerable controversy regarding the optimal method of assessing driving performance by people with TBI. Studies of fitness to drive in TBI have utilized diverse evaluation methods, including on-road or closed-circuit/off-road evaluations, driving simulations, neuropsychological assessment of driving-relevant abilities, and objective or subjective measurement of accident and violation rate. For a discussion of the strengths and weaknesses of these methods, the reader is directed to Fox, Bowden, and Smith (1998), the British Psychological Society (2001), Rizzo, McGehee, Dawson, and Anderson (2001), as well as Rizzo, Reinach, McGehee, and Dawson (1997).

It is difficult to estimate how an individual recovering from TBI will behave in real-world driving situations due to the heterogeneity of TBI (e.g., nature and extent of damage, driving skill, preinjury driving experience, driving-related attitudes, personality, and rate of recovery); the difficulty of observing some types of cognitive, emotional and behavioral disturbances; and the undetermined ecological validity of driving outcome measures. Even the most ecologically valid method, an on-road driving assessment, has several important weaknesses, such as increased safety risk for the driver, examiner, and other road users; the subjectivity of the driving evaluation (Fox et al., 1998; McKenna, Jefferies, Dobson, & Frude, 2004; Schultheis et al., 2003); and the less demanding environmental conditions and decision-making processes found in on-road tests (e.g., predetermined routes, less busy times, instructions/cues provided by examiner) compared to the real world (British Psychological Society, 2001; Schultheis et al., 2003). Moreover, behavior during driving testing may not accurately represent an individual's behavior in everyday driving situations (e.g., more caution, motivation to drive safely) (British Psychological Society, 2001; Fox et al., 1998; Pietrapiana et al., 2005).

Much of the research investigating driving following TBI has been described in terms of Michon's (1985) hierarchical model of driving. According to this model, driving is a cognitive problem-solving task composed of three levels of driving skill: (1) strategic (i.e., goal formation, such as trip planning, route selection, and the associated evaluation of risks and benefits), (2) tactical (i.e., maneuvering to negotiate within the driving environment), and (3) operational (i.e., perceptual processing of the driving environment and performing behaviors required to control the vehicle).

Many individuals with TBI exhibit operational deficits (e.g., difficulty performing secondary in-car tasks, steering, and speed control) (Brouwer & Withaar, 1997; Haikonen et al., 1998; Lew et al., 2005; Lundqvist & Ronnberg, 2001). It has been proposed that individuals displaying impairments at the operational level of driving skill may still drive safely by compensating for their impairments through decisions they make at the strategic and tactical levels of skill (Brouwer, Withaar, Tant, & van Zomeren, 2002; Haikonen et al., 1998). Some individuals recovering from TBI have been found to drive safely by employing strategic (e.g., avoiding challenging situations) and tactical (e.g., slowing down) adjustments to compensate for their operational deficits (Priddy et al., 1990; van Zomeren, Brouwer, Rothengatter, & Snoek, 1988). Since lack of awareness may result from TBI, assessment of self-knowledge of one's deficits and the awareness of the need to compensate for one's driving impairments is of utmost importance in predicting driving safety in this population. Individuals with TBI will most likely return to driving if their physical functioning is greater than 80%, as measured by the FIM-FAM, regardless of their cognitive problems and against doctors' advice (Leon-Carrion et al., 2005).

The links between cognitive deficits, self-awareness, and use of compensatory behaviors in safe driving are important ones that have received, as yet, relatively little attention. For example, speed in information processing is necessary for quick decision making and prompt responses to the unpredictable driving environment, and a TBI-related impairment in this area can be compensated for by slowing speed, thereby reducing time pressure at the operational level (Schmidt, Brouwer, Vanier, & Kemp, 1996). However, in a study by Haikonen and colleagues (1998), people with mixed brain damage had difficulty dividing their attention between secondary in-car tasks (e.g., adjusting the radio, dialing a phone number) and driving, resulting in prolonged glances away from the road. These participants did not reduce their speed or refuse to perform the secondary tasks, suggesting lack of awareness of the safety risk associated with taking their attention off the road. Performance on neuropsychological measures supported impairments in executive functions, which are required to control the safety risks associated with taking one's eyes off the road during second-ary tasks, and in the visuospatial and motor abilities necessary for secondary task performance.

Other studies examining associations between specific aspects of cognitive func-tions and driving performance have reported inconsistent results. Some studies have failed to find associations between driving and neuropsychological test performance in TBI samples (e.g., Pietrapiana et al., 2005), whereas others have found support (Coleman, 2001; Coleman et al., 2002). It has been suggested that those studies fail-ing to find associations did not use cognitive measures specifically relevant to the driving context, such as higher-order executive functions (Coleman et al., 2002). Executive functions may be particularly relevant to both the tactical and strategic levels of driving (Schmidt et al., 1996). Behaviors such as anticipating, planning, decision making, and self-monitoring, viewed as executive functions, are necessary for drivers to monitor and adapt to the complex driving environment (Christie et al., 2001). Several studies (Brooke, Questad, Patterson, & Valois, 1992; Coleman, 2001), but not all (Schmidt et al., 1996), have found significant relationships between mea-sures of executive functions and driving performance in TBI. Schmidt and colleagues (1996) found that when speed of information processing was controlled, patients with closed-head injury were unimpaired both on their ability to adapt flexibly to chang-ing task demands in a driving simulator and on neuropsychological tests requiring planning and flexibility. Performance on the Useful Field of View (UFOV) test—a measure of speed of information processing (subtest 1), divided attention (subtest 2), and selective attention (subtest 3)—has been associated with driving performance in TBI. For example, Fisk, Novack, Mennemeier, and Roenker (2002) found that in a TBI sample, performance on the UFOV was correlated with the results of the Trail Making Test Part B, a measure of visuomotor tracking skills, on which poor performance has often been associated with driving impairment in previous research. Compared to young adult controls, individuals with TBI had slower visual process-ing, greater difficulty detecting stimuli throughout the peripheral field (e.g., at all eccentricities) in UFOV subtests 2 and 3, and significantly greater impairment on UFOV subtests 2 and 3 (Fisk et al., 2002). In another study, Novack and colleagues (2006) found that younger age and poorer performance on Trail Making Test Part B and UFOV subtest 2 significantly predicted failure ratings on an on-road driving test in a moderate to severe TBI sample, and younger age and poor performance on UFOV subtest 2 significantly predicted poorer scores on the Driving Assessment Scale (DAS; e.g., a checklist of 25 safe driving behaviors). Criticisms of the UFOV test include the suggestion that subtest 1 (information-processing speed) may not be sufficiently demanding of attentional resources to predict poor driving, that subtest 3 (selective attention) may be too demanding for individuals with TBI (Novack et al., 2002), and that the UFOV has less utility for predicting driving impairment and crash risk in individuals with mild TBI than for individuals with moderate to severe TBI (Schneider & Gouvier, 2005).

Research on driving performance and cognitive impairments in TBI has suffered from several limitations. Comparison between studies is difficult due to differences in samples (e.g., location, severity, and type of brain damage) and measurements (e.g., outcome measures, neuropsychological tests) (Brouwer et al., 2002; Coleman et al., 2002). For example, many studies assess cognitive functions that are nonspecific to the driving task (McKenna, 1998). Stronger relationships may be found if the relationships between specific driving behaviors (e.g., impairments in divided attention) and specific aspects of driving skill (e.g., multitasking while driving, such as adjusting controls on the dashboard) are studied.

Many of the cognitive impairments in TBI may compromise the ability to drive safely. Despite methodological concerns and inconsistent findings, most of the research on driving in TBI suggests that a comprehensive assessment involving multiple types of driving assessment, specifically, is warranted. It is important to maintain respect for a patient's autonomy while protecting the safety of other road users, who may be at increased risk of harm if incompetent drivers are permitted to drive. For this reason, it is crucial to adequately assess abilities that influence safe driving, including self-awareness and ability to compensate for deficiencies, and it is equally crucial that future research continue efforts to improve evaluation methods. The influence of cognitive impairments on driving has been studied extensively in both normal and cognitively impaired (e.g., demented) older adult populations. Findings from these studies may be useful in informing TBI research on the relation between specific types of cognitive impairments and specific types of driving problems.

Vocational Functioning

TBI often has a significant negative impact on vocational outcome. Cognitive deficits and emotional disturbances associated with TBI interact with a host of other factors to determine clients' ability to return to competitive employment. The vocational rehabilitation literature reveals a number of both environmental and person-related factors that are associated with the likelihood of returning to work after TBI. We have briefly summarized findings from that literature below.

With respect to environmental factors, brain-injured individuals are more likely to return to work if they are supported in the workplace. Support may take the form of formal and informal fringe benefits, health insurance availability, opportunities for advancement, opportunities for social interaction with coworkers, a socially inclusive atmosphere, and decision-making latitude (Ponsford, Sloan, & Snow, 1995; Wehman, Targett, West, & Kregel, 2005). In addition, job coaches or vocational rehabilitation specialists have been found to be a cost-effective way to help brain-injured workers maintain their employment (Wehman et al., 2005).

Person-related factors that impact return to work include a number of demographic, injury-related, and social–emotional variables. The age of the person at the time of the brain injury is related to whether or not he or she will successfully return to work. Individuals who are severely brain injured prior to age 7 are unlikely to obtain competitive employment in their lives (Ownsworth & McKenna, 2004). These clients have sustained a TBI during a formative time in both brain development and social learning. They are doubly disadvantaged in that they have experienced not only an extremely disruptive event, but also must learn to negotiate life's challenges with a damaged brain. This observed effect is much weaker for mild to moderate injuries than it is for severe injuries. Interestingly, individuals age 40 or older at the time of the study (regardless of their age when they were injured) share this disadvantage; these individuals may have more trouble returning to work because of internal variables. They may experience, for example, reduced ability to adapt to changes in the workplace or changes in their own abilities, or they may experience discrimination in the workplace manifesting as employer unwillingness to hire a person with both cognitive deficits and a reduced capacity for long-term employment (Ownsworth & McKenna, 2004). Instead, employers are likely more willing to invest resources in younger employees.

The type of work a person does prior to a brain injury is also relevant to outcome postinjury. Brain-injured clients with higher preinjury qualifications are more likely to return to work (Ownsworth & McKenna, 2004). For example, in one study (Fleming, Tooth, Hassell, & Chan, 1999) individuals employed premorbidly in more "upper-status" occupations (e.g., managers, professionals, tradespersons, clerks) were more likely to return to work postinjury as compared to those in lower-status occupations (e.g., laborers, plant/machine operators). This may be due to vocational assets including greater occupational stability prior to the injury and more work experience. In addition, having occupational training prior to injury allows the client to return to work in an area that is well learned, such that the challenge of learning a new job may not be as necessary. As noted previously, individuals who are 40 years or older, have less preinjury education, and work in unskilled occupations are less likely to return to work following a TBI. Of note, younger individuals, despite not have a long work history or stable employment prior to the brain injury, are more likely to return to work. Clearly there is an interaction between the advantages of youth and the disadvantage of lower preinjury qualifications.

Injury variables such as severity (e.g., length of time in coma or length of PTA), cause of injury, and the presence of lesions on computerized tomography (CT) scan are also related to likelihood of returning to work, though there are methodological difficulties surrounding the research in this area (Wehman et al., 2005). It has been reported that the highest rates of return to work occur between 1 and 6 months postinjury. Moreover, clients who return to work within 2 years of injury are more likely to still be working at follow-up than clients who have not yet returned 2 years postinjury. Since sufficient recovery to allow for return to work would be unlikely in the first 6 months following a moderate to severe injury, these findings suggest that return to work is most likely following mild injuries. It is uncertain whether duration of coma or duration of PTA is directly related to return to work. It may be that these variables are strongly related to survival and neuropsychological deficits following brain injury and in this way they predict return to work indirectly (Ownsworth & McKenna, 2004). Along these same lines, one might expect a longer duration of acute rehabilitation to predict a poorer vocational outcome. The literature is mixed in this regard, however. Still, a longer hospital stay may be associated with a poorer employment outcome. Nevertheless, it is important to recognize that in the current fiscal climate, length of hospital stay may be more related to staffing and bed shortages than it is to patient readiness for discharge.

The most reliable predictor of vocational outcome with respect to severity of injury is not an injury variable at all—it is the client's functional status at the time of discharge. However, functional status is closely related to such factors as type and severity of injury. In addition, clients' status in physical, cognitive, and behavioral domains as well as their functional impairment and community participation are strongly related to the likelihood of returning to work postinjury (Ownsworth & McKenna, 2004). Clearly functional status can differ widely in clients who have had a similar length of stay in hospital; therefore this measure is much more sensitive to both obvious and subtle differences between clients with TBI.

As might be expected, poor awareness is a negative predictor of returning to work; interestingly, some authors contend that increased insight is best achieved through trial and error in a real working environment, rather than through counseling (Wehman et al., 2005). At the opposite end of the awareness spectrum are clients who are exquisitely aware of their deficits following a TBI. These clients are at risk of ruminative thoughts and depression (see below), which also may interfere with their ability to return to work postinjury.

Postacute emotional adjustment following TBI is known to be related to the likelihood of returning to work. Clients who are depressed at 6–12 months postinjury are less likely to return to work. This time period corresponds with increased awareness of the nature and degree of deficits associated with the incurred brain injury (Ownsworth & McKenna, 2004). Similarly, clients who exhibit symptoms of anxiety and/or helplessness are less likely to return to work. Finally, as might be expected, clients who have a diagnosis of posttraumatic stress disorder (more common in samples with mild traumatic brain injury) are less likely to return to work. It is useful to know that emotional indicators are related to likelihood of returning to work, as this is an area where rehabilitation professionals can intervene. TBI clients may become depressed, withdrawn, and anxious as a reaction to the disruption in their lives, their losses, and the chronic frustration associated with acquired disabilities (Rosenthal & Bond, 1990). Although it is not yet known whether the emotional disturbance is the antecedent or consequence of the difficulties experienced returning to work, it is important to adequately assess and treat the emotional distress, as it most likely is a bidirectional effect.

An associated variable in the search for predictors of vocational outcome is coping skills. TBI clients who show less effective coping and higher levels of hopelessness are less likely to be employed. As with the discussion of emotional disturbances above, it is not known whether a client's poor coping and feelings of hopelessness are an antecedent to lack of work or a result of not being able to find stable employment (Ownsworth & McKenna, 2004). Coping problems may be present prior to a brain injury, but are likely exacerbated by the stress associated with a TBI.

A client's preinjury psychological adjustment is strongly related to his or her employment status years postinjury (MacMillon, Hart, Martelli, & Zasler, 2002). In particular, a history of substance abuse often reflects psychological vulnerability (i.e., more limited premorbid coping skills) and biological vulnerability (e.g., alcohol-related brain damage) and may lead to an impaired ability to cope with the demands imposed by a TBI (MacMillon, Hart, Martelli, & Zasler, 2002). If a client with TBI has a preinjury history of substance abuse, he or she is less likely to return to work postinjury.

A neuropsychological assessment can be a moderately good predictor of whether or not a client is likely to return to work. In a study of 293 adults with nonpenetrating TBI, Boake and colleagues (2001) found that productivity, defined as competitive employment or full-time student status at 1–4 years postinjury (93% of sample was

1–2 years postinjury), was predicted by early neuropsychological testing. Specifically, these researchers found that long-term productivity was predicted by completion of at least one neuropsychological test before discharge from inpatient rehabilitation, by an injury–test interval of less than 2 months, and by normal-range scores on 10 of the 15 neuropsychological tests administered. As individuals in this study were not tested until PTA had resolved, there may be a link to injury severity variables. However, given that early test scores predicted those individuals who would reach a productive outcome, the findings support early administration of neuropsychological testing as a useful tool in determining whether a given patient will or will not reach a productive outcome.

While long-term prognosis soon after injury can be difficult and, hence, early test scores should not be used as a definitive statement regarding long-term functioning, such early testing can identify those individuals most at risk for future difficulties in productivity and can direct rehabilitative efforts and support services early in treatment. Such information can also be invaluable in anticipating financial compensation needs and changes in family roles (Boake et al., 2001).

Whereas the Boake and colleagues (2001) study supported a comprehensive assessment of various cognitive domains, a meta-analysis by Ownsworth and McKenna (2004) found that although attention/processing speed, memory, and visuospatial skills showed mixed results in predicting outcome, a client's executive functioning, including concept formation, complex attentional skills (divided and selective attention), mental flexibility, mental programming, and planning ability were reliable predictors of whether or not that client returned to work. As noted, the most common cognitive and behavioral difficulties following brain injury include poor memory, concentration difficulties, irritability and impatience, fatigue, slowness of thinking, problems with initiation, and reduced awareness (Sherer, Bergloff, et al., 1998). These changes in cognitive and emotional functioning impact return to work directly and also interact with each other and other variables, including those discussed above.

Summary

TBI involves diffuse insult to the brain and a variety of consequences that may negatively impact daily living. Individuals with moderate to severe injuries, approximately 20–30% of the TBI population (Langlois et al., 2006), tend to experience the most impact on daily functioning, though even individuals with mild injuries can be affected (Rizzo & Tranel, 1996). Although the exact pattern of impairment will vary from individual to individual, most often some aspects of daily living are affected following injury, with more substantial difficulties experienced in the early stages of recovery. TBI leads to permanent and pervasive impairments in daily living in a small proportion of cases, with approximately 10% of affected individuals requiring long-term assisted care environments (Colantonio et al., 2004; Dikmen et al., 2003).

The cognitive sequelae of TBI often affect the skills necessary for completing everyday tasks, including IADLs, financial management, and driving, as well as the ability to return to work. Measures of executive functions often serve as the best neuropsychological predictors of everyday abilities across domains of function because they tap the underlying skills (e.g., planning, sequencing, and organization) vital to completing daily tasks. Measures of executive functioning and verbal memory have been linked to functional outcome over and above other neuropsychological indices (Hanks, Rapport, Millis, & Deshpande, 1999). Speed in processing information and complex attentional skills are crucial for driving and rapid decision making across tasks and are often negatively impacted by TBI. Memory impairments can limit one's ability to learn new skills (e.g., vocational training), keep in mind appointments, or remember errands that need to be completed. A thorough evaluation of a person's cognitive strengths and weaknesses can help the clinician formulate hypotheses regarding which particular part of a task is creating difficulty for a given individual. Such information is important in planning intervention strategies.

For a subset of individuals with TBI, disturbances in self-awareness can negatively impact rehabilitation outcome. When considering the possible consequences of driving without compensating for possible difficulties or attempting to manage finances without the requisite skills, it becomes clear that impairments in self-awareness warrant early assessment and intervention. In treatment settings insight is not a unitary phenomenon and may emerge over time such that different problem areas may be acknowledged at different times (Wilson, Herbert, & Shiel, 2003). A lack of insight or self-awareness can be related to a variety of factors, including lack of information, an inability to integrate information, or an inability to make appropriate inferences with the information (e.g., "My thinking is slowed, which may affect my ability to drive") (Langer & Padrone, 1992). Deficits in self-awareness can be impacted by both neurological and emotional factors (Prigatano, 2005). The decision to challenge impairments in awareness must be made on an individual basis and will include such factors as the nature of the problem and expected outcome. At times, high levels of insight can be associated with depression and a lack of motivation, leading the clinician to avoid pushing for increased understanding (often involving feedback on failures) in certain contexts. In contrast, in situations where safety to self or others may be concerned, a clinician may be more likely to challenge unawareness of deficits. (For a discussion of factors impacting self-awareness and rehabilitation of deficits, see Prigatano, 2005.)

As noted previously, neuropsychological evaluation provides only an indirect link to everyday functioning. For intervention purposes, it is vital to obtain additional information on behaviors as they occur in more naturalistic environments. An interview with the affected individual and a significant other can identify the types of situations in which difficulties are likely to arise and can provide direct targets for intervention. Functional assessment, involving the direct observation of the client in different situations or completing everyday tasks, can also be a useful tool. Neuropsychological test performance and behavioral data provide complementary information and lead to a more clearly defined view of a person's abilities and disabilities. Identifying when a breakdown in functioning occurs (behavioral data) and for what reason (neuropsychological data) can help tailor a more individualized rehabilitation regimen that is most likely to benefit the client. For a review of some of the factors to consider in an assessment of performance on everyday tasks post-TBI, see Table 13.2.

TABLE 13.2. Factors Impacting Completion of Everyday Tasks Post-TBI

- Cognitive skills
- Pain
- Fatigue
- Self-awareness
- Physical limitations
- Psychosocial/emotional functioning
- Impulsivity
- Sensoriperceptual problems
- Preinjury abilities, attitudes, personality
- Environmental demands (e.g., degree of support, structure)
- Severity of injury

Conclusions

Each year in the United States it is estimated that approximately 280,000–420,000 people suffer a moderate to severe brain injury (Langlois et al., 2006; Rutland-Brown, Langlois, Thomas, & Xi, 2006) and the Centers for Disease Control and Prevention (CDC) estimates that over 5.3 million Americans currently have a long-term or life-long need for help in daily living due to a TBI (Thurman, Alverson, Dunn, Guerrero, & Sniezek, 1999). Given that the population of affected individuals is relatively young, the ongoing disabilities will have a lasting impact on the affected individuals, their families and caregivers, as well as society as a whole. Assessment and treatment of individuals with TBI is crucial to minimizing the long-term impact of such injuries on their daily functioning.

References

Abreu, B. C., Seale, G., Scheibel, R. S., Huddleston, N., Zhang, L., & Ottenbacher, K. J. (2001). Levels of self-awareness after acute brain injury: How patients' and rehabilitation specialists; perceptions compare. *Arch Phys Med Rehabil, 82,* 49–56.

Acker, M. B. (1990). A review of the ecological validity of neuropsychological tests. In D. E. Tupper & K. D. Cicerone (Eds.), *The neuropsychology of everyday life: Assessment and basic competencies* (pp. 19–55). Boston: Kluwer.

Alves, W. M. (1992). Natural history of post-concussive signs and symptoms. *Phys Med Rehab: State of the Art Rev, 6,* 21–32.

American Congress of Rehabilitation Medicine. (1993). Definition of mild traumatic brain injury. *J Head Trauma Rehab, 8*(3), 86–87.

Australian Bureau of Statistics. (1996). *Disability, ageing and careers: Brain injury and stroke.* Australia 1993 (Cat. No. 4437.0). Canberra, Australia: Author.

Bate, A. J., Mathias, J. L., & Crawford, J. R. (2001). Performance on the Test of Everyday Attention and standard tests of attention following severe traumatic brain injury. *Clin Neuropsychol, 15*(3), 405–422.

Blachstein, H., Vakil, E., & Hoofien, D. (1993). Impaired learning in patients with closed-head injuries: An analysis of components of the acquisition process. *Neuropsychology,* 7(4), 530–535.

Boake, C., Millis, S. R., High, W. M., Jr., Delmonico, R. L., Kreutzer, J. S., Rosenthal, M., et al. (2001). Using early neuropsychologic testing to predict long-term productivity outcome from traumatic brain injury. *Arch Phys Med Rehab,* 82(6), 761–768.

British Psychological Society. (2001). *Fitness to drive and cognition: A document of the Multi-disciplinary Working Party on acquired neuropsychological deficits and fitness to drive 1999.* Leicester, UK: British Psychological Society.

Brooke, M. M., Questad, K. A., Patterson, D. R., & Valois, T. (1992). Driving evaluation after traumatic brain injury. *Am J Phys Med Rehabil,* 71(3), 177–182.

Brooks, J., Fos, L. A., Greve, K. W., & Hammond, J. S. (1999). Assessment of executive function in patients with mild traumatic brain injury. *J Trauma: Inj, Infect, Crit Care,* 46(1), 159–163.

Brouwer, W. H., & Withaar, F. K. (1997). Fitness to drive after traumatic brain injury. *Neuropsychol Rehabil,* 7(3), 177–193.

Brouwer, W. H., Withaar, F. K., Tant, M. L. M., & van Zomeren, A. H. (2002). Attention and driving in traumatic brain injury: A question of coping with time-pressure. *J Head Trauma Rehab,* 17(1), 1–15.

Christie, N., Savill, T., Buttress, S., Newby, G., & Tyerman, A. (2001). Assessing fitness to drive after head injury: A survey of clinical psychologists. *Neuropsychol Rehabil,* 11(1), 45–55.

Cicerone, K. D. (1997). Clinical sensitivity of four measures of attention to mild traumatic brain injury. *Clin Neuropsychol,* 11(3), 266–272.

Cockburn, J. (1995). Performance on the Tower of London test after severe head injury. *J Int Neuropsych Soc,* 1(6), 537–544.

Colantonio, A., Ratcliff, G., Chase, S., Kelsey, S., Escobar, M., & Vernich, L. (2004). Long term outcomes after moderate to severe traumatic brain injury. *Disabil Rehabil,* 26(5), 253–261.

Coleman, R. D. (2001). Awareness and fitness to drive in a TBI sample. *Diss Abstr Int,* 61(10), 5556B. (UMI No. 9992182)

Coleman, R. D., Rapport, L. J., Ergh, T. C., Hanks, R. A., Ricker, J. H., & Millis, S. R. (2002). Predictors of driving outcome after traumatic brain injury. *Arch Phys Med Rehabil,* 83(10), 1415–1422.

Corrigan, J. D. (1995). Substance abuse as a mediating factor in outcome from traumatic brain injury. *Arch Phys Med Rehabil,* 76(4), 302–309.

Corrigan, J. D., Whiteneck, G., & Mellick, D. (2004). Perceived needs following traumatic brain injury. *J Head Trauma Rehab,* 19(3), 205–216.

Cramer, K., Tuokko, H., Mateer, C., & Hultsch, D. (2004). Measuring awareness of financial skills: Reliability and validity of a new measure. *Aging Ment Health,* 8, 161–171.

Crosson, B., Novack, T. A., & Trennery, M. R. (1988). California Verbal Learning Test (CVLT) performance in severely head-injured and neurologically normal adult males. *J Clin Exp Neuropsych,* 10(6), 754–768.

Crowe, S. F., Mahony, K., & Jackson, M. (2003). Predicting competency in automated machine use in an acquired brain injury population using neuropsychological measures. *Arch Clin Neuropsych,* 19, 673–691.

Crowe, S. F., Mahony, K., O'Brien, A., & Jackson, M. (2003). An evaluation of the usage patterns and competence in dealing with automated delivery of services in an acquired head injury sample. *Neuropsychol Rehabil,* 13, 497–515.

Curtiss, G., Vanderploeg, R. D., Spencer, J., & Salazar, A. M. (2001). Patterns of verbal learning and memory in traumatic brain injury. *J Int Neuropsych Soc,* 7(5), 574–585.

Dawson, D. R., & Chipman, M. (1995). The disablement experienced by traumatically brain-injured adults living in the community. *Brain Injury*, *9*, 339–353.

De Guise, E., Feyz, M., LeBlanc, J., Richard, S.-L., & Lamoureux, J. (2005). Overview of traumatic brain injury patients at a tertiary trauma centre. *Can J Neurol Sci*, *32*(2), 186–193.

Devani Serio, C., & Devens, M. (1994). Employment problems following traumatic brain injury: Families assess the cause. *NeuroRehabilitation*, *4*, 53–57.

Diehl, M. (1998). Everyday competence in later life: Current status and future directions. *Gerontologist*, *38*(4), 422–433.

Dikmen, S., Machamer, J., & Temkin, N. (2001). Mild head injury: Facts and artifacts. *J Clin Exp Neuropsyc*, *23*(6), 729–738.

Dikmen, S. S., Machamer, J. E., Powell, J. M., & Temkin, N. R. (2003). Outcome 3 to 5 years after moderate to severe traumatic brain injury. *Arch Phys Med Rehab*, *84*, 1449–1457.

Epstein, R. S., & Ursano, R. J. (1994). Anxiety disorders. In J. M. Silver, S. C. Yudofsky, & R. E. Hales (Eds.), *Neuropsychiatry of traumatic brain injury* (pp. 285–311). Washington, DC: American Psychiatric Association.

Farmer, J. E., & Eakman, A. M. (1995). The relationship between neuropsychological functioning and instrumental activities of daily living following acquired brain injury. *Appl Neuropsychol*, *2*, 107–115.

Fisk, G. D., Novack, T., Mennemeier, M., & Roenker, D. (2002). Useful field of view after traumatic brain injury. *J Head Trauma Rehab*, *17*(1), 16–25.

Fisk, G. D., Schneider, J. J., & Novack, T. A. (1998). Driving following traumatic brain injury: Prevalence, exposure, advice and evaluations. *Brain Injury*, *12*(8), 683–695.

Fleming, J., & Strong, J. (1999). A longitudinal study of self-awareness: Functional deficits underestimated by persons with brain injury. *Occup Ther J Res*, *19*(1), 3–17.

Fleming, J. M., Tooth, L., Hassell, M., & Chan, W. (1999). Prediction of community integration and vocational outcome 2–5 years after traumatic brain injury rehabilitation in Australia. *Brain Injury*, *6*, 417–431.

Fork, M., Bartels, C., Ebert, A. D., Grubich, C., Synowitz, H., & Wallesch, C.-W. (2005). Neuropsychological sequelae of diffuse traumatic brain injury. *Brain Injury*, *19*(2), 101–108.

Formisano, R., Bivona, U., Brunelli, S., Giustini, M., Longo, E., & Taggi, F. (2005). A preliminary investigation of road traffic accident rate after severe brain injury. *Brain Injury*, *19*(3), 159–163.

Fox, G. K., Bowden, S. C., & Smith, D. S. (1998). On-road assessment of driving competence after brain impairment: Review of current practice and recommendations for a standardized examination. *Arch Phys Med Rehab*, *79*(10), 1288–1296.

Frencham, K. A. R., Fox, A. M., & Maybery, M. T. (2005). Neuropsychological studies of mild traumatic brain injury: A meta-analytic review of research since 1995. *J Clin Exp Neuropsyc*, *27*, 334–351.

Goldstein, F. C., & Levin, H. S. (1995). Post-traumatic and anterograde amnesia following closed head injury. In A. D. Baddeley, B. A. Wilson, & F. N. Watts (Eds.), *Handbook of memory disorders* (pp. 187–209). New York: Wiley.

Haikonen, S., Wikman, A.-S., Kalska, H., Summala, H., Hietanen, M., Nieminen, T., et al. (1998). Neuropsychological correlates of duration of glances at secondary tasks while driving. *Appl Neuropsychol*, *5*(1), 24–32.

Hanks, R. A., Rapport, L. J., Millis, S. R., & Deshpande, S. A. (1999). Measures of executive functioning as predictors of functional ability and social integration in a rehabilitation sample. *Arch Phys Med Rehab*, *80*(9), 1030–1037.

Harrison, A., & Ragland, D. R. (2003). Consequences of driving reduction or cessation for older adults. *Transport Res Rec*, *1843*, 96–104.

Hart, T., Sherer, M., Whyte, J., Polansky, M., & Novack, T. (2004). Awareness of behavioral, cognitive, and physical deficits in acute traumatic brain injury. *Arch Phys Med Rehab*, *85*, 1450–1456.

Hart, T., Whyte, J., Kim, J., & Vaccaro, M. (2005). Executive function and self-awareness of "real-world" behavior and attention deficits following traumatic brain injury. *J Head Trauma Rehab*, *20*(4), 333–347.

Hawley, C. A. (2001). Return to driving after head injury. *J Neurol, Neurosur Ps*, *70*(6), 761–766.

Hibbard, M. R., Uysal, S., Kepler, K., Bogdany, J., & Silver, J. (1998). Axis I psychopathology in individuals with traumatic brain injury. *J Head Trauma Rehabil*, *13*(4), 24–39.

Hoofien, D., Gilboa, A., Vakil, E., & Donovick, P. J. (2001). Traumatic brain injury (TBI) 10–20 years later: A comprehensive outcome study of psychiatric symptomatology, cognitive abilities and psychosocial functioning. *Brain Injury*, *15*(3), 189–209.

Hoskin, K. M., Jackson, M., & Crowe, S. F. (2005a). Can neuropsychological assessment predict capacity to manage personal finances?: A comparison between brain impaired individuals with and without administrators. *Psychiat, Psychol Law*, *12*, 56–67.

Hoskin, K. M., Jackson, M., & Crowe, S. F. (2005b). Money management after acquired brain dysfunction: The validity of neuropsychological assessment. *Rehabil Psychol*, *50*, 355–365.

Iverson, G. L., Lovell, M. R., & Smith, S. S. (2000). Does brief loss of consciousness affect cognitive functioning after mild traumatic brain injury? *Arch Clin Neuropsych*, *15*(7), 643–648.

Johnston, M. V., Shawaryn, M. A., Malec, J., Kreutzer, J., & Hammond, F. M. (2006). The structure of functional and community outcomes following traumatic brain injury. *Brain Injury*, *20*(4), 391–407.

Kersel, D. A., Marsh, N. V., Havill, J. H., & Sleigh, J. W. (2001). Neuropsychological functioning during the year following severe traumatic brain injury. *Brain Injury*, *15*(4), 283–296.

Kim, J., Whyte, J., Hart, T., Vaccaro, M., Polansky, M., & Coslett, H. B. (2005). Executive function as a predictor of inattentive behavior after traumatic brain injury. *J Int Neuropsych Soc*, *11*(4), 434–445.

Kreutzer, J. S., Marwitz, J. H., Walker, W., Sander, A., Sherer, M., Bogner, J., et al. (2003). Moderating factors in return to work and job stability after traumatic brain injury. *J Head Trauma Rehab*, *18*(2), 128–138.

Kreutzer, J. S., Seel, R. T., & Gourley, E. (2001). The prevalence and symptom rates of depression after traumatic brain injury: A comprehensive examination. *Brain Injury*, *15*(7), 563–576.

Lam, C. S., McMahon, B. T., Priddy, D. A., & Gehred-Schultz, A. (1998). Deficit awareness and treatment performance among traumatic brain injury adults. *Brain Injury*, *2*, 235–242.

Langer, K. G., & Padrone, F. J. (1992). Psychotherapeutic treatment of awareness in acute rehabilitation of traumatic brain injury. *Neuropsychol Rehabil*, *2*, 59–70.

Langlois, J. A., Rutland-Brown, W., & Thomas, K. E. (2006). *Traumatic brain injury in the United States: Emergency department visits, hospitalizations, and deaths*. Atlanta, GA: Centers for Disease Control and Prevention, National Center for Injury Prevention and Control.

Law, M., Baum, C., & Dunn, W. (Eds.). (2005). *Measuring occupational performance: Supporting best practice in occupational therapy* (2nd ed.). Thorofare, NJ: Slack.

Leclercq, M., Couillet, J., Azouvi, P., Marlier, N., Martin, Y., Strypstein, E., et al. (2000). Dual task performance after severe diffuse traumatic brain injury or vascular prefrontal damage. *J Clin Exp Neuropsyc*, *22*(3), 339–350.

Leininger, B. E., Gramling, S. E., & Farrell, A. D. (1990). Neuropsychological deficits in symptomatic minor head injury patients after concussion and mild concussion. *J Neurol, Neurosur Ps, 53*(4), 293–296.

Lengenfelder, J., Schultheis, M. T., Al-Shihabi, T., Mourant, R., & DeLuca, J. (2002). Divided attention and driving: A pilot study using virtual reality technology. *J Head Trauma Rehab, 17*(1), 26–37.

Leon-Carrion, J., Dominguez-Morales, M. R., & Barroso Y Martin, J. M. (2005). Driving with cognitive deficits: Neurorehabilitation and legal measures are needed for driving again after severe traumatic brain injury. *Brain Injury, 19*(3), 213–219.

Lew, H. L., Poole, J. H., Ha Lee, E., Jaffe, D. L., Huang, H.-C., & Brodd, E. (2005). Predictive validity of driving-simulator assessments following traumatic brain injury: A preliminary study. *Brain Injury, 19*(3), 177–188.

Lezak, M. D. (1995). *Neuropsychological assessment* (3rd ed.). New York: Oxford University Press.

Loken, W. J., Thornton, A. E., Otto, R. L., & Long, C. J. (1995). Sustained attention after severe closed head injury. *Neuropsychology, 9*(4), 592–598.

Lundqvist, A., & Ronnberg, J. (2001). Driving problems and adaptive driving behaviour after brain injury: A qualitative assessment. *Neuropsychol Rehabil, 11*(2), 171–185.

MacMillon, P. J., Hart, R. P., Martelli, M. F., & Zasler, N. D. (2002). Pre-injury status and adaptation following traumatic brain injury, *Brain Injury, 16*(1), 41–49.

Malec, J. E., Buffington, A. L. H., Moessner, A. M., & Degiorgio, L. (2000). A medical/vocational case coordination system for persons with brain injury: An evaluation of employment outcomes. *Arch Phys Med Rehab, 81*, 1007–1015.

Manchester, D., Priestley, N., & Jackson, H. (2004). The assessment of executive functions: Coming out of the office. *Brain Injury, 18*(11), 1067–1081.

Marottoli, R. A., de Leon, C. F. M., Glass, T. A., Williams, C. S., Cooney, L. M., Jr., & Berkman, L. F. (2000). Consequences of driving cessation: Decreased out-of-home activity levels. *J Gerontol: Soc Sci, 55*(6), S334–S340.

Marson, D. C., Sawries, S. M., Snyder, S., McInturff, B., Stalvey, T., Boothe, A., et al. (2000). Assessing financial capacity in patients with Alzheimer's disease. *Arch Neurol, 57*, 877–884.

Mazaux, J., Masson, F., Levin, H. S., Alaoui, P., Maurette, P., & Barat, M. (1997). Long term neuropsychological outcome and loss of social autonomy after traumatic brain injury. *Arch Phys Med Rehabil, 78*, 1316–1320.

McDowell, S., Whyte, J., & D'Esposito, M. (1997). Working memory impairments in traumatic brain injury: Evidence from a dual-task paradigm. *Neuropsychologia, 35*(10), 1341–1353.

McKenna, P. (1998). Fitness to drive: A neuropsychological perspective. *J Ment Health (UK), 7*(1), 9–18.

McKenna, P., Jefferies, L., Dobson, A., & Frude, N. (2004). The use of a cognitive battery to predict who will fail an on-road driving test. *Brit J Clin Psychol, 43*(3), 325–336.

Michon, J. A. (1985). A critical view of driver behaviour models: What do we know; what should we do? In L. Evans & R. C. Schwing (Ed.), *Human behaviour and traffic safety* (pp. 485–520). New York: Plenum Press.

Moore, E. L., Terryberry-Spohr, L., & Hope, D. A. (2006). Mild traumatic brain injury and anxiety sequelae: A review of the literature. *Brain Injury, 20*(2), 117–132.

Morton, M. V., & Wehman, P. (1995). Psychosocial and emotional sequelae of individuals with traumatic brain injury: A literature review and recommendations. *Brain Injury, 9*(1), 91–92.

Nicholson, K., & Martelli, M. F. (2004). The problem of pain. *J Head Trauma Rehab, 19*(1), 2–9.

NIH Consensus Conference. (1999). Rehabilitation of persons with traumatic brain injury. *JAMA*, *282*(10), 974–983.

Nolin, P. (2006). Executive memory dysfunctions following mild traumatic brain injury. *J Head Trauma Rehab*, *21*(1), 68–75.

Novack, T. A., Baños, J. H., Alderson, A. L., Schneider, J. J., Weed, W., Blankenship, J., et al. (2006). UFOV performance and driving ability following traumatic brain injury. *Brain Injury*, *20*(5), 455–461.

Ogden, J. A., & Wolfe, M. (1998). Post-concussional syndrome: A preliminary study comparing young and middle-aged adults. *Neuropsychol Rehabil*, *8*, 413–431.

Olver, J. H., Ponsford, J. L., & Curran, C. A. (1996). Outcome following traumatic brain injury: A comparison between 2 and 5 years after injury. *Brain Injury*, *10*(11), 841–848.

Ownsworth, Y., & McKenna, K. (2004). Investigation of factors related to employment outcome following traumatic brain injury: A critical review and conceptual model. *Disabil Rehabil*, *26*(13), 765–784.

Pagulayan, K. F., Temkin, N. R., Machamer, J., & Dikmen, S. S. (2006). A longitudinal study of health-related quality of life after traumatic brain injury. *Arch Phys Med Rehab*, *87*, 611–618.

Park, N. W., Moscovitch, M., & Robertson, I. H. (1999). Divided attention impairments after traumatic brain injury. *Neuropsychologia*, *37*(10), 1119–1133.

Perbal, S., Couillet, J., Azouvi, P., & Pouthas, V. (2003). Relationships between time estimation, memory, attention, and processing speed in patients with severe traumatic brain injury. *Neuropsychologia*, *41*, 1599–1610.

Pietrapiana, P., Tamietto, M., Torrini, G., Mezzanato, T., Rago, R., & Perino, C. (2005). Role of premorbid factors in predicting safe return to driving after severe TBI. *Brain Injury*, *19*(3), 197–211.

Ponsford, J. L., & Kinsella, G. (1992). Attentional deficits following closed-head injury. *J Clin Exp Neuropsyc*, *14*(5), 822–838.

Ponsford, J. L., Olver, J. H., & Curran, C. (1995). A profile of outcome two years following traumatic brain injury. *Brain Injury*, *9*, 1–10.

Ponsford, J. L., Sloan, S., & Snow, P. (1995). *Traumatic brain injury: Rehabilitation for everyday adaptive living*. Hillsdale, NJ: Erlbaum.

Priddy, D. A., Johnson, P., & Chow, S. L. (1990). Driving after severe head injury. *Brain Injury*, *4*, 267–272.

Prigatano, G. P. (2005). Disturbances of self-awareness and rehabilitation of patients with traumatic brain injury: A 20-year perspective. *J Head Trauma Rehab*, *20*(1), 19–29.

Prigatano, G. P., & Altman, I. M. (1990). Impaired awareness of behavioral limitations after traumatic brain injury. *Arch Phys Med Rehab*, *71*, 1058–1064.

Prigatano, G. P., Bruna, O., & Mataro, M. (1998). Initial disturbances of consciousness and resultant impaired awareness in Spanish patients with traumatic brain injury. *J Head Trauma Rehab*, *13*(5), 29–38.

Ragland, D. R., Satariano, W. A., & MacLeod, K. E. (2005). Driving cessation and increased depressive symptoms. *J Gerontol A-Biol*, *60A*(3), 399–403.

Rapoport, M., McCauley, S., Levin, H., Song, J., & Feinstein, A. (2002). The role of injury severity in neurobehavioral outcome 3 months after traumatic brain injury. *Neuropsychiatry Neuropsychol Behav Neurol*, *15*(2), 123–132.

Rapport, L. J., Hanks, R. A., & Bryer, R. C. (2006). Barriers to driving and community integration after traumatic brain injury. *J Head Trauma Rehab*, *21*(1), 34–44.

Raskin, S. A., & Rearick, E. (1996). Verbal fluency in individuals with mild traumatic brain injury. *Neuropsychology*, *10*(3), 416–422.

Riccio, C. A., Reynolds, C. R., Lowe, P., & Moore, J. J. (2002). The continuous performance test: A window on the neural substrates for attention? *Arch Clin Neuropsych, 17*(3), 235–272.

Rieger, M., & Gauggel, S. (2002). Inhibition of ongoing responses in patients with traumatic brain injury. *Neuropsychologia, 40*(1), 76–85.

Ríos, M., Periáñez, J. A., & Muñoz-Céspedes, J. M. (2004). Attentional control and slowness of information processing after severe traumatic brain injury. *Brain Injury, 18*(3), 257–272.

Rizzo, M., McGehee, D. V., Dawson, J. D., & Anderson, S. N. (2001). Simulated car crashes at intersections in drivers with Alzheimer disease. *Alz Dis Assoc Dis, 15*(1), 10–20.

Rizzo, M., Reinach, S., McGehee, D., & Dawson, J. (1997). Simulated car crashes and crash predictors in drivers with Alzheimer disease. *Arch Neurol, 54*(5), 545–551.

Rizzo, M., & Tranel, D. (1996). Overview of head injury and postconcussive syndrome. In M. Rizzo & D. Tranel (Eds.), *Head injury and postconcussive syndrome* (pp.1–18). New York: Churchill Livingstone.

Robertson, I. H., Ward, T., Ridgeway, V., & Nimmo-Smith, I. (1996). The structure of normal human attention: The test of everyday attention. *J Int Neuropsych Soc, 2*(6), 525–534.

Roche, N. L., Fleming, J. M., & Shum, D. H. K. (2002). Self-awareness of prospective memory failure in adults with traumatic brain injury. *Brain Injury, 16*(11), 931–945.

Rosenthal, M., & Bond, M. R. (1990). Behavioral and psychiatric sequelae. In M. Rosenthal, E. R. Griffith, J. S. Kreutzer, J. D. Miller, & M. R. Bond (Eds.), *Rehabilitation of the adult and child with traumatic brain injury* (2nd ed., pp. 179–192). Philadelphia: Davis.

Rutland-Brown, W., Langlois, J. A., Thomas, K. E., & Xi, Y. L. (2006). Incidence of traumatic brain injury in the United States, 2003. *J Head Trauma Rehabil, 21*(6), 544–548.

Schmidt, I. W., Brouwer, W. H., Vanier, M. V., & Kemp, F. (1996). Flexible adaptation to changing task demands in severe closed head injury patients: A driving simulator study. *Appl Neuropsychol, 3*(4), 155–165.

Schmitter-Edgecombe, M., & Kibby, M. K. (1998). Visual selective attention after severe closed head injury. *J Int Neuropsych Soc, 4*(2), 144–159.

Schneider, J. J., & Gouvier, W. D. (2005). Utility of the UFOV test with mild traumatic brain injury. *Appl Neuropsychol, 12*(3), 138–142.

Schultheis, M. T., Hillary, F., & Chute, D. L. (2003). The neurocognitive driving test: Applying technology to the assessment of driving ability following brain injury. *Rehabil Psychol, 48*(4), 275–280.

Schultheis, M. T., Matheis, R. J., Nead, R., & DeLuca, J. (2002). Driving behaviors following brain injury: Self-report and motor vehicle records. *J Head Trauma Rehab, 17*(1), 38–47.

Serino, A., Ciaramelli, E., Di Santantonio, A., Malagù, S., Servadei, F., & Làdavas, E. (2006). Central executive system impairment in traumatic brain injury. *Brain Injury, 20*(1), 23–32.

Shallice, T., & Burgess, P. W. (1991). Deficits in strategy application following frontal lobe damage in man. *Brain, 114*(2), 727–741.

Sherer, M., Bergloff, P., Levin, E., High, W. J., Oden, K. E., & Nick, T. G. (1998). Impaired awareness and employment outcome after traumatic brain injury. *J Head Trauma Rehab, 13*(5), 52–61.

Sherer, M., Boake, C., Levin, E., Silver, B. V., Ringholz, G. M., & High, W. M. (1998). Characteristics of impaired awareness after traumatic brain injury. *J Int Neuropsych Soc, 4*, 380–387.

Sherer, M., Hart, T., & Nick, T. G. (2003). Measurement of impaired self-awareness after traumatic brain injury: A comparison of the Patient Competency Rating Scale and the Awareness Questionnaire. *Brain Injury, 17*(1), 25–37.

Shum, D., Sweeper, S., & Murray, R. (1996). Performance on verbal implicit and explicit memory tasks following traumatic brain injury. *J Head Trauma Rehab, 11*(2), 43–53.

Shum, D., Valentine, M., & Cutmore, T. (1999). Performance of individuals with severe long-term traumatic brain injury on time-, event-, and activity-based prospective memory tasks. *J Clin Exp Neuropsyc, 21*(1), 49–58.

Shum, D. H., Harris, D., & O'Gorman, J. G. (2000). Effects of severe traumatic brain injury on visual memory. *J Clin Exp Neuropsyc, 22*(1), 25–39.

Sohlberg, M. M., & Mateer, C. A. (2001). *Cognitive rehabilitation: An integrative neuropsychological approach.* New York: Guilford Press.

Sorenson, S. B., & Kraus, J. F. (1991). Occurrence, severity, and outcomes of brain injury. *J Head Trauma Rehab, 6*(2), 1–10.

Spikman, J. M., Deelman, B. G., & van Zomeren, A. H. (2000). Executive functioning, attention and frontal lesions in patients with chronic CHI. *J Clin Exp Neuropsyc, 22*(3), 325–338.

Stuss, D. T. (1991). Disturbances of self-awareness after frontal system damage. In G. P. Prigatano & D. L. Schacter (Eds.), *Awareness for deficits after brain injury* (pp. 63–83). New York: Oxford University Press.

Stuss, D. T., Ely, P., Hugenholtz, H., Richard, M. T., Larochelle, S., Poirier, C. A., et al. (1985). Subtle neuropsychological deficits in patients with good recovery after closed head injury. *Neurosurgery, 17*, 41–46.

Teasdale, G., & Jennett, B. (1974). Assessment of coma and impaired consciousness: A practical scale. *Lancet, 2*, 81–84.

Teasdale, T. W., & Engberg, A. W. (2001). Suicide after traumatic brain injury: A population study. *J Neurol, Neurosur Ps, 71*, 436–440.

Thurman, D. J., Alverson, C., Dunn, K. A., Guerrero, J., & Sniezek, J. E. (1999). Traumatic brain injury in the United States: A public health perspective. *J Head Trauma Rehabil, 14*(6), 602–615.

Vanderploeg, R. D., Curtiss, G., & Belanger, H. G. (2005). Long-term neuropsychological outcomes following mild traumatic brain injury. *J Int Neuropsyc Soc, 11*(3), 228–236.

Van Reekum, R., Cohen, T., & Wong, J. (2000). Can traumatic brain injury cause psychiatric disorders? *J Neuropsychiatry Clin Neurosci, 12*(3), 316–327.

Van Wielingen, L. E., Cramer, K., & Tuokko, H. (2004). *Measure of Awareness of Financial Skills (MAFS) administration and scoring manual.* Competency Workgroup, Centre on Aging, Department of Psychology, University of Victoria, Victoria, BC.

Van Wielingen, L. F., Tuokko, H., Cramer, K., Mateer, C., & Hultsch, D. (2004). Awareness of financial skills in dementia. *Aging Ment Health, 8*, 374–380.

van Zomeren, A. H., & Brouwer, W. H. (1994). *Clinical neuropsychology of attention.* New York: Oxford University Press.

van Zomeren, A. H., Brouwer, W. H., Rothengatter, J. A., & Snoek, J. W. (1988). Fitness to drive a car after recovery from severe head-injury. *Arch Phys Med Rehab, 69*(2), 90–96.

Wald, J. L., Liu, L., & Reil, S. (2000). Concurrent validity of a virtual reality driving assessment for persons with brain injury. *CyberPsychol Behav, 3*(4), 643–654.

Wehman, P., Targett, P., West, M., & Kregel, J. (2005). Productive work and employment for persons with traumatic brain injury: What have we learned after 20 years? *J Head Trauma Rehab, 20*(2), 115–127.

Wiegner, S., & Donders, J. (1999). Performance on the California Verbal Learning Test after traumatic brain injury. *J Clin Exp Neuropsyc, 21*(2), 159–170.

Willer, B., Rosenthal, M., Kreutzer, J., Gordon, W., & Rempel, R. (1993). Assessment of community integration following rehabilitation for TBI. *J Head Trauma Rehab, 8*, 75–87.

Williams, W. H., Evans, J. J., & Fleminger, S. (2003). Neurorehabilitation and cognitive-behaviour therapy of anxiety disorders after brain injury: An overview and a case illustration of obsessive–compulsive disorder. *Neuropsychol Rehabil, 13*(1–2), 133–148.

Wilson, B. A., Herbert, C. A., & Shiel, A. (2003). *Behavioural approaches in neuropsychological rehabilitation: Optimising rehabilitation procedures.* New York: Psychology Press.

Zec, R. F., Zellers, D., Belman, J., Miller, J., Matthews, J., Ferneau-Belman, D., et al. (2001). Long-term consequences of severe closed head injury on episodic memory. *J Clin Exp Neuropsyc, 23*(5), 671–691.

CHAPTER 14

Neuropsychological Assessment and Sports-Related Mild Traumatic Brain Injury (Concussion)

Mark R. Lovell and Jamie E. Pardini

Neuropsychological assessment has rapidly become an indispensable component of the return-to-play decision-making process following a sports-related concussion. Indeed, several recent international consensus conferences have highlighted neuropsychological assessment as a key element of the return-to-sport evaluation process. This chapter examines the evolving field of sports neuropsychology with specific reference to the clinical application of neuropsychological evaluation technology in both professional and amateur athletics. In addition to reviewing the neurophysiological substrata of sports-related concussion, this chapter presents a scientifically based return-to-play protocol that emphasizes the application of neuropsychological assessment tools.

Definition of Concussion and Pathophysiology of Injury

Despite numerous published studies and years of research, there is currently no universally accepted definition of concussion in sports. As early as 1966 the Committee on Head Injury Nomenclature of Neurological Surgeons (Congress of Neurosurgeons, 1966) defined concussion as "a clinical syndrome characterized by the immediate and transient post-traumatic impairment of neural function such as alteration of consciousness, disturbance of vision or equilibrium, etc., due to brain stem dysfunction" (p. 392). More recently, however, other definitions have been put forth. For example, the American Academy of Neurology (AAN; 1997) defines concussion as "any trauma induced alteration in mental status that may or may not include a loss of consciousness" (p. 392). Authors of the AAN definition felt that the Committee on Head Injury Nomenclature definition may be too limiting given the assumption of brainstem involvement. Furthermore, authors of the AAN guidelines highlighted the currently accepted fact that concussion often occurs without a loss of consciousness.

Most recently, an international Concussion in Sports (CIS) panel convened in Vienna in 2001 and again in Prague in 2004 to reevaluate existing definitions of concussion and to suggest new return-to-play guidelines (Aubry et al., 2002; McCrory et al., 2005). Both meetings were sanctioned by the Federation Internationale de Football Association (FIFA) in conjunction with the International Olympic Committee (IOC) and the International Ice Hockey Federation (IHF). The CIS group adopted a broad-based definition of concussion and defined the injury as "a complex pathophysiological process affecting the brain, induced by traumatic biomechanical forces" (p. 6). The authors further defined the injury by the following features:

1. Concussion may be caused by either a direct blow to the head or elsewhere in the body with an "impulsive" force transmitted to the head.
2. Concussion typically results in the rapid onset of short-lived impairment of neurological function that resolves spontaneously.
3. Concussion may result in neuropathological changes, but the acute clinical symptoms largely reflect a functional disturbance rather than structural injury.
4. Concussion results in a graded set of clinical syndromes that may or may not involve loss of consciousness.
5. Concussion is typically associated with normal, gross structural imaging studies.

The Vienna and Prague CIS groups' directives represented an important improvement on previous guidelines for several reasons. First, these statements emphasized the complexity of the disorder and the wide variety of signs/symptoms that characterize it. Second, these statements reflected more contemporary thought regarding the *neurometabolic* (as opposed to structural) changes that occur with injury.

Epidemiology of Concussion in Sports

Contemporary estimates of concussion in sports have been undergoing almost constant revision over the past decade. Although a figure of 300,000 injuries per year was utilized for many years as an estimate of injuries (Thurman & Guerro, 1997), recent revised figures from the Centers for Disease Control and Prevention (CDC) have suggested that sports-related concussion may be much more common, occurring in upward of 4 million athletes per year (Langlios, Gioia, & Collins, 2007). This dramatic change in estimates of injury reflect a realistic understanding that prior estimates did not take into account the fact that most injuries were previously either unrecognized or not reported to medical or team personnel (Delaney, Lacroix, Gagne, & Antoniou, 2001). Although significant attention has been given to the occurrence of concussion in professional athletics, including the National Football League (Pellman, Lovell, Viano, & Casson, 2006) and National Hockey League (Lovell & Burke, 2000), the vast majority of injuries is thought to occur at the high school level or below. Concussions may also occur within the context of recreational activities such as skiing, skateboarding, and cycling.

Pathophysiology of Concussion

Research into the subtle metabolic effects of concussion has resulted in new insights into its pathophysiology. This line of research has been a relatively recent development. Utilizing a rodent model, David Hovda and his colleagues (Hovda, Prins, & Becker, 1998) initially described a metabolic dysfunction that occurs when cells, immediately injured upon concussive insult, are exposed to dramatic changes at both the intracellular and extracellular levels. These changes are the result of excitatory amino acid (EAA)-induced ionic shifts with increased Na/KATP-ase activation and resultant hyperglycolysis (Bergschneider, Hovda, & Shalmon, 2003). Thus, there is a high-energy demand within the brain shortly after concussive injury that is accompanied by a decrease in cerebral blood flow. Although the exact mechanism is not completely understood, research suggests that an accumulation of endothelial Ca++ may lead to widespread cerebral neurovascular constriction. The resulting "metabolic mismatch" between energy demand and energy supply within the brain has been postulated to produce cellular vulnerability during the acute recovery period. Animal models have indicated that this dysfunction can last up to 2 weeks or theoretically longer in the human model (Hovda et al., 1998).

The metabolic rather than structural basis of concussion provides an explanation of why traditional neurodiagnostic techniques such as computed tomography (CT) and magnetic resonance imaging (MRI) are almost invariably normal following injury (Johnston, Pitto, Chankowsky, & Chen, 2001). It should be stressed, however, that these techniques are invaluable in ruling out more serious pathology (e.g., cerebral bleed, skull fracture) that may also occur with head trauma.

As suggested above, our understanding of the metabolic process of concussion in the human model is currently far from complete. However, this model of pathology has raised many questions regarding the danger of concussion in athletes of all ages. It has been suggested that metabolic dysfunction, until fully resolved, may lead to significantly increased neurological vulnerability if a subsequent trauma (even minor) is sustained. Such metabolic dysfunction is theoretically linked to "second-impact syndrome" (Cantu & Voy, 1995) and may also form the basis for the less severe, though occasionally incapacitating, "postconcussion syndrome." Second-impact syndrome is a rare but usually fatal condition that occurs only in children and adolescents.

Although long-term deficits in the form of postconcussion syndrome have been observed in athletes of all ages, it is generally presumed that proper management of concussion leads to optimum prognosis and minimal cumulative effects with regard to cognitive processes. Conversely, returning an athlete to participation prior to *complete* recovery may greatly increase the risk of lingering, long-term, or even catastrophic neurological sequelae. As such, acute assessment of concussion and determination of any existing signs/symptoms of injury prove critical to the safe management of the athlete.

On-Field and Sideline Management of Concussion

The diagnosis of sports-related concussion is complex and can be tricky under the best of circumstances. There may be no direct trauma to the head, and the concussed athlete is infrequently rendered unconscious. The athlete may be unaware that he or she has been injured immediately after the injury and may not show any obvious signs of concussion, such as clumsiness, gross confusion, or obvious amnesia. Under these circumstances, the athlete may continue to play, thereby exposing him- or herself to additional injury. To complicate this situation, athletes at all levels of competition may minimize or hide symptoms in an attempt to prevent their removal from the game, thus creating the potential for exacerbation of their injury (Lovell et al., 2002).

Initial Sideline Signs and Symptoms of Evaluation and Return to Play

Table 14.1 provides a summary of common on-field signs and symptoms of concussion. It should be stressed that sideline presentation may vary widely form athlete to athlete, depending on the biomechanical forces involved, specifically affected brain areas, prior history of injury, and numerous other factors. In reviewing the common signs and symptoms of concussion, it is important to note that an athlete may present with as few as one symptom of injury or potentially a constellation of symptomatology. A thorough assessment of *all* common symptoms associated with concussion should be conducted with the concussed athlete.

Headache is the most commonly reported symptom of injury and may be seen in up to 70% of athletes who sustain a concussion (Collins, Field, et al., 2003). Although it is true that musculoskeletal headaches and other preexisting headache syndromes may complicate the assessment of postconcussion headache, any presentation of headache following a blow to the head or body should be managed conservatively and should lead to removal from the field, court, or ice, pending more formal evaluation. Most frequently, a concussion headache is described as a sensation of pressure in the skull that may be localized to one region of the head or may be generalized in nature. In some athletes (particularly athletes with a history of migraine), the headache may take the form of a vascular headache, may be unilateral, and is often described as

TABLE 14.1. University of Pittsburgh Signs and Symptoms of Concussion

Signs observed by staff	Symptoms reported by athlete
• Appears to be dazed or stunned	• Headache
• Is confused about assignment	• Nausea
• Forgets plays	• Balance problems or dizziness
• Is unsure of game, score, or opponent	• Double or fuzzy/blurry vision
• Moves clumsily	• Sensitivity to light or noise
• Answers questions slowly	• Feeling sluggish or slowed down
• Loses consciousness	• Feeling "foggy" or groggy
• Shows behavior or personality change	• Concentration or memory problems
• Forgets events prior to play (retrograde)	• Change in sleep pattern (appears later)
• Forgets events after hit (posttraumatic)	• Feeling fatigued or tired

throbbing or pulsating. The headache may develop immediately after injury, or take minutes to hours to emerge. Therefore it is essential to question the potentially concussed athlete regarding the development of symptoms beyond the first few minutes after injury. Commonly, a postconcussion headache is worsened by physical exertion. Thus, if the athlete complains of worsening headache during exertive testing or return to play, a postconcussion headache should be suspected, and conservative management is indicated. Although headache following a concussion does not necessarily constitute a medical emergency, a severe headache, particularly when accompanied by vomiting or rapidly declining mental status, may signal a life-threatening situation such as a subdural hematoma or intracranial bleed. This situation recently occurred with the death of actress Natasha Richardson. This should prompt immediate transport to hospital and a CT scan of the brain.

Although headache is the most common symptom of concussion, there may be no accompanying headache, and other signs or symptoms of injury should be carefully assessed. For example, athletes commonly experience blurred or "fuzzy" vision, changes in peripheral vision, or other visual disturbance. These visual changes, in addition to photosensitivity and/or dizziness or balance problems, are also common. Furthermore, an athlete may report increased fatigue, "feeling a step slow," or feeling sluggish. Fatigue is especially prominent in concussed athletes in the days following injury, and this symptom may be as prominent as headache in this regard. In addition to these symptoms, cognitive or mental status changes are commonly seen immediately following injury. Athletes with any degree of mental status change should be managed conservatively, and a thorough discussion of these issues is warranted. Table 14.2 provides a model for assessment of acute or on-field cognitive changes that may accompany concussion.

TABLE 14.2. University of Pittsburgh Sideline Mental Status Testing Card

On-field cognitive testing

Orientation (ask the athlete the following questions)

- What stadium is this?
- What city is this?
- Who is the opposing team?
- What month is it?
- What day is it?

Posttraumatic amnesia (ask the athlete to repeat the following words)
- *Girl, dog, green*

Retrograde amnesia (ask the athlete the following questions)
- What happened in the prior quarter or half?
- What do you remember just prior to the hit?
- What was the score of the game prior to the hit?
- Do you remember the hit?

Concentration (ask the athlete to do the following)
- Repeat the days of the week backward, starting with today
- Repeat these numbers backward: *63, 419*

Word list memory
- Ask the athlete to repeat the three words from earlier (*girl, dog, green*)

Return to Sport Following Concussion

Return-to-Play Guidelines

During the past 30 years, over 20 concussion management guidelines have been published with the intent of providing guidance and direction for the sports medicine practitioner in making complex return-to-play decisions (Collins, Lovell, & McKeag, 1999). These guidelines have typically been accompanied by grading scales designed to reflect and characterize the severity of the injury. Although these guidelines have no doubt resulted in improved care of the athlete, the multiplicity of directives also has created significant confusion and sparked almost continuous debate. A historical review of all past and current concussion guidelines is beyond the scope of this chapter; however, a brief review of four of the more recent and popular guidelines is provided in Table 14.3.

Cantu was the first to propose a grading scale and accompanying management guidelines based on his own clinical experience as a neurosurgeron (Cantu, 1992). However, Cantu was careful to emphasize that these guidelines were intended to sup-

TABLE 14.3. Recent Concussion Grading Scales

Guideline	Grade 1	Grade 2	Grade 3
Cantu (1992)	1. No loss of consciousness 2. Posttraumatic amnesia lasts less than 30 minutes	1. Loss of consciousness lasts longer than 5 minutes *or* 2. Posttraumatic amnesia lasts longer than 30 minutes	1. Loss of consciousness lasts longer than 5 minutes *or* 2. Posttraumatic amnesia lasts longer than 24 hours
Colorado Guidelines (Kelly, Nichols, & Filley, 1991)	1. Confusion without amnesia 2. No loss of consciousness	1. Confusion with amnesia 2. No loss of consciousness	1. Loss of consciousness (of any duration
AAN (1997)	1. Transient confusion 2. No loss of consciousness 3. Mental status changes from concussion symptoms resolve in less than 5 minutes	1. Transient confusion 2. No loss of consciousness 3. Concussion symptoms or mental status change lasts longer than 15 minutes	1. Loss of consciousness (brief or prolonged)
Cantu (2001)	1. No loss of consciousness *or* 2. Posttraumatic amnesia *or* signs/symptoms last longer than 30 minutes	1. Loss of consciousness lasts less than 1 minute *or* 2. Posttraumatic amnesia lasts longer than 30 minutes but less than 24 hours	1. Loss of consciousness lasts more than 1 minute *or* 2. Posttraumatic amnesia lasts longer than 24 hours *or* 3. Postconcussion signs or symptoms last longer than 7 days

Note. AAN, American Academy of Neurology.

plement rather than replace clinical judgment. The original Cantu guidelines allowed return to play the day of injury if the athlete were symptom free both at rest and following physical exertion. For athletes who experienced any loss of consciousness (e.g., grade 3 concussion), a restriction of contact for 1 month was recommended. Athletes who had suffered a grade 2 concussion were allowed to return to play in 2 weeks *if* asymptomatic for a period of 7 days.

More recently, Cantu has amended his guidelines (Cantu, 2001) to emphasize the duration of posttraumatic symptoms in grading the severity of the concussion and making return-to-play decisions. Grade 1 concussion was redefined by an *absence* of loss of consciousness and postconcussion signs or symptoms lasting less than 30 minutes. Same-day return to competition was allowed only if the athlete was completely asymptomatic following the injury.

The Colorado Guidelines (Kelly, Nichols, & Filley, 1991) were published in 1991 following the death of a high school athlete due to second-impact syndrome (SIS) and were drafted under the auspices of the Colorado Medical Society. These guidelines allowed for same-day return to play if symptoms cleared within 20 minutes of injury. For more severe injury (grade 3 concussion), these guidelines recommended immediate transport to a hospital for further evaluation. These guidelines were later revised under the sponsorship of the AAN (1997). The AAN guidelines allowed return to competition the same day of injury if the athlete's signs and symptoms cleared within 15 minutes of injury. Grade 2 concussion was managed in a manner similar to the Colorado Guidelines, with return to competition within 1 week, if asymptomatic.

Although management guidelines reached their zenith of popularity during the 1980s and 1990s, in the late 1990s sports medicine practitioners and organizations began to question both the scientific basis of the guidelines as well as their clinical utility. This questioning subsequently led to an international effort to articulate concussion management that took place in 2002 under the auspices of FIFA in conjunction with the IOC and the IHF. The organizers of this meeting assembled a group of physicians, neuropsychologists and sports administrators in Vienna, Austria, as noted at the beginning of the chapter, to explore methods of reducing morbidity secondary to sports-related concussion. These deliberations led to the publication of a document outlining recommendations for both the diagnosis and management of concussion in sports (Aubrey et al., 2002). One of the most important conclusions of this meeting was that none of the previously published concussion management guidelines was adequate to assure proper management of every concussion. One of the most important directives to arise from this meeting was the recognition of neuropsychological assessment as the "cornerstone" of postinjury management and return-to-play decision making.

The recognition of neuropsychological assessment as a key element of the postconcussion evaluation process represented a particularly important development in the diagnosis and management of the concussed athlete. The use of baseline neuropsychological testing was specifically recommended whenever possible. In addition, a graduated return-to-play protocol was emphasized. The recommendations of the CIS group are presented in Table 14.4. It was specifically recommended that each step would, in most circumstances, be separated by 24 hours. Furthermore, any recurrence of concussive symptoms should lead to the athlete dropping back to the previous level. In other words, if an athlete is asymptomatic at rest but develops a

TABLE 14.4. Vienna Concussion Conference: Return-to-Play Recommendations

Athletes should complete the following stepwise process prior to return to play following concussion.

1. Removal from contest following any signs/symptoms of concussion
2. No return to play in current game
3. Medical evaluation following injury
   a. Rule out more serious intracranial pathology
   b. Neuropsychological testing considered "cornerstone" or proper postinjury assessment
4. Stepwise return to play
   a. No activity and rest until asymptomatic
   b. Light aerobic exercise
   c. Sport-specific training
   d. Noncontact drills
   e. Full-contact drills
   f. Game play

headache following light aerobic exercise, then he or she should return to complete rest for at least 24 hours or until the athlete is once again asymptomatic. The Vienna group further recognized that conventional structural neuroimaging studies (e.g., computed tomography [CT], magnetic resonance imaging [MRI], electroencephalography [EEG]) are typically unremarkable following concussive injury and should be employed only when a structural lesion is suspected. The group further noted that functional imaging techniques are in the early stages of development but may provide valuable information in the future.

Individual Factors Determining Return to Play

Once a concussed athlete has been removed from a game, the medical team is faced with the often challenging decision of determining when the athlete is safely able to return to play. Decisions regarding return to sports following concussion are typically made based on a number of factors, such as the severity of the injury (as measured by duration of loss of consciousness, amnesia, and confusion), the athlete's reported symptoms (e.g., lingering headache, fatigue, photosensitivity), and performance on neuropsychological testing. In addition to these variables that relate to clinical recovery, a number of other factors may play a role in the decision-making process. With the advent of neuropsychological assessment in sports and an accompanying increase in research, data are rapidly emerging to shed light on individual factors that may play a role in the incidence, severity, and length of recovery in concussion.

Age

Current concussion guidelines assume identical return-to-play criteria for athletes regardless of age. Based on these guidelines, it has traditionally been assumed that the speed of recovery is the same at all age groups and athletic levels. Unfortunately, prior to 2003, there was no published study examining outcome from concussion in the high school athlete or younger populations. Recent research has begun to expose potentially different age-related responses to concussive injury.

Based on research examining individuals with more complicated mild traumatic brain injury (MTBI), several theories have emerged that might explain age-related differences to recovery from MTBI. One such theory is that children undergo more prolonged and diffuse cerebral swelling after TBI, which suggests that they may be at an increased risk for secondary injury (Pickles, 1950). Furthermore, the immature brain may be up to 60 times more sensitive to glutamate (McDonald & Johnston, 1990), a neurotransmitter involved in the metabolic cascade following concussion. These factors may lead to a longer recovery period and could increase the likelihood of permanent or severe neurological deficit should reinjury occur during the recovery period. Such a theory may help account for the finding that SIS has been found to occur only in adolescent athletes (Cantu & Voy, 1995).

One published study has directly examined recovery from concussion in college versus in high school (Field, Collins, Lovell, & Maroon, 2003). Specifically, baseline and postconcussion neurocognitive functioning was measured in a sample of 53 athletes. Even though the college sample had a greater prior incidence of concussion, high school athletes were found to take longer to recover from concussion. Another study (Lovell et al., 2003) reveals the apparent heightened vulnerability to concussion in the high school athlete. Specifically, the issue of the "ding" or "very mild" concussion was examined in high school athletes ages 13–17 years. This study revealed that high school athletes with less than 15 minutes of on-field symptoms required at least 7 days for full neurocognitive and symptom recovery. This study and a follow-up analysis (Lovell, Collins, Iverson, Johnston, & Bradley, 2004) call into question the validity of the grading systems for management of mild concussion. These findings indicate that all high school athletes diagnosed with concussion should be removed from play during that contest.

The Vienna meeting also recommended that all concussed athletes be removed from the playing contest if concussion is diagnosed (Aubry et al., 2002). It should be stressed that no prospective data have examined the issue of the grade 1 concussion in college or professional-age athletes. As noted above, there may be significant age-related differences in response to a concussive injury. Furthermore, intangibles such as level of competition and overall risk–benefit analysis for return to play are also likely to differ at different levels (e.g., professional vs. amateur). Professional athletes may be willing to assume greater risk, given obvious monetary and other considerations. Conversely, few parents would risk injury in a high school athlete who is unlikely to compete beyond high school.

Concussion History

In addition to the age of the athlete, the *concussion history* of the athlete may potentially be an important factor in determining return-to-play suitability. A growing body of evidence suggests that there may be cumulative detrimental effects from multiple concussions. These effects have typically been associated with the neuropsychological impairment and neurological abnormalities that have been documented primarily in boxers (Jordan, Relkin, & Ravdin, 1997; Roberts, Allsop, & Bruton, 1990). Lately, however, this topic has been of rising concern among other athletic populations. In a study of almost 400 college football players, Collins and colleagues (1999) revealed long-term subtle neurocognitive deficits in those suffering two or more concussions. As well, Matser, Kessels, and Lezak (1999) suggest that cumulative long-term consequences in response to repetitive blows to the head are being seen in professional soccer players. In addition, high school and collegiate athletes suffering three or more concussions appear to be more vulnerable to subsequent injury than athletes with no history of injury (Collins et al., 2002). Even though data are emerging, no conclusive determinations can yet be made regarding how many concussions should force retirement from sports, in general.

Time between Injuries

Yet another issue that is often evaluated in making return-to-play decisions is the *time between injuries*. Although no current research has formally investigated this factor, most concussion management guidelines contain a provision that restricts play following multiple concussions within a given season (AAN, 1997; Cantu, 1992, 2001; Wojyts et al., 1999). This recommendation appears to be based on the well-established clinical experience of many sports medicine personnel, who have observed that recently concussed athletes are prone to reinjury (often additional concussions) if they play too soon following an initial injury.

Given the complexity of the factors contributing to recovery and outcome following sports-related concussion, individualized evaluation is essential. Over the past decade, neurocognitive testing has been repeatedly demonstrated as a sensitive, valid, and practical assessment tool for helping practitioners make more quantified and data-driven decisions regarding postinjury concussion management.

Current Models of Neuropsychological Assessment in Sports

The use of neuropsychological testing as a diagnostic tool in sports medicine is a relatively recent development that began in the mid-1980s within the context of a large multisite research project undertaken by Barth and his colleagues (1989) at the University of Virginia. This study demonstrated the potential utility of neuropsychological test procedures to document cognitive recovery within the first week following concussion. However, this study did not immediately result in the widespread adoption of neuropsychological testing in organized athletics at the clinical level. In the early 1990s, a series of events transpired that shifted the use of neuropsychological testing in sports to the clinical arena. First, injuries to a number of high-profile professional athletes resulted in the implementation of baseline neuropsychological testing by a number of National Football League (NFL) teams (Lovell, 1998). Similarly, following career-ending injuries for members of the National Hockey League (NHL), the league mandated baseline neuropsychological testing for all athletes (Lovell & Burke, 2000). In addition to the increased use of neuropsychological testing in professional sports, several large-scale studies of collegiate athletes were undertaken. These studies (Collins et al., 1999; Echemendia, Putukian, & Macklin, 2001; Hinton-Bayre, Geffen, & Geffen, 1999; Macciocchi, Barth, & Alves, 1996) further verify that neuropsychological testing yields useful clinical information. Specifically, neuropsychological testing allowed a baseline–postinjury analysis of the subtle aspects of cognitive function likely affected by concussive injury, thus providing objective data with which to make more informed decisions regarding return to play.

The use of traditional neuropsychological assessment has resulted in a rapid expansion of our knowledge regarding concussions and has become a popular clinical tool within both collegiate and professional ranks. For instance, both the NFL and NHL utilize traditional neuropsychological tasks such as the Hopkins Verbal Leaning Test (Brandt & Benedict, 2001) and the Symbol Digit Modalities Test (Smith, 1982). These tests were also utilized by Echemendia and his colleagues (2001) at Penn State University. However, the more widespread application of testing within the college ranks has been limited due to practical and economic constraints. Furthermore, neuropsychological testing at the high school level had been extremely limited prior to the year 2000. This latter fact is disturbing given that the vast majority of at-risk athletes fall within high school ranks and below. Traditional neuropsychological testing has proven to be too time-consuming and costly for many amateur organizations, and the expansion of testing has also been limited by a shortage of trained neuropsychologists to oversee the administration and interpretation of the assessment process. As a result of these inherent limitations of traditional assessment and in parallel to the widespread proliferation of the microcomputer, several researchers have begun to develop computer-based neuropsychological testing procedures.

Computer-based neuropsychological testing procedures have a number of advantages and relatively few disadvantages when compared to more traditional neuropsychological testing methods. First, the use of computers allows the evaluation of large numbers of student athletes with minimal manpower. For example, through our program at the University of Pittsburgh, we routinely evaluate up to 20 athletes simultaneously within a high school or college computer laboratory. This ease of administration promotes the assessment of an entire football team within a reasonable time period and with minimal human resources. Second, data acquired through testing can be easily stored in a specific computer or computer network and can therefore be accessed at a later date (e.g., following injury). This system promotes the efficient clinical evaluation of athletes and also greatly expands the possibilities for research. Third, the use of the microcomputer promotes the more accurate measurement of cognitive processes such as reaction time and information-processing speed. In fact, computerized assessment allows for the evaluation of response times that are accurate to 1/100th of a second, whereas traditional testing allows for accuracy within only to 1–2 seconds. This increased accuracy no doubt increases the *validity* of test results in detecting subtle changes in neurocognitive processes. Fourth, the utilization of the computer allows for the randomization of test stimuli that should help to improve *reliability* across multiple administration periods, minimizing the "practice effects" that naturally occur with multiple exposures to the stimuli. These practice effects have clouded the interpretation of research studies and have also presented an obstacle for the clinician evaluating the true degree of neurocognitive deficit following injury. Limiting the influence of practice effects on testing allows for a direct interpretation of postinjury data in relation to the athlete's baseline to determine whether full cognitive recovery has occurred. Lastly, computer-based approaches allow for the rapid dissemination of clinical information into a coherent clinical report that can be easily interpreted by the sports medicine clinician. In summary, there are many benefits derived from a computer-based approach insofar as the technology has appropriate sensitivity, reliability, and validity in measuring the subtle aspects of concussive injury.

Approaches to Computer-Based Neuropsychological Testing

There are several computer-based management approaches under development to help provide the sports medicine clinician with neurocognitive data to better determine return to play and other management issues following concussive injury (Schnirring, 2001). Specifically, four computer-based models have been detailed in the scientific literature (Schatz & Zillmer, 2003). These include ImPACT (Immediate Post-Concussion Assessment and Cognitive Testing) CogState, Headminders, and ANAM (Automated Neuropsychological Assessment Metric). Differences do exist between these test batteries, and each program is at different stages of validation. Clearly, issues such as *sensitivity*, *reliability*, and *validity* of the respective test batteries should be given careful scrutiny before implementation is adopted. In addition, issues regarding test selection, cognitive domains measured, details of the clinical report, and consultation options for each instrument should be given careful review prior to implementation. A detailed review of these critical issues for each computerized battery is beyond the scope of this chapter. The reader is urged, however, to adequately explore the published literature pertaining to each of these test batteries prior to adopting one particular approach clinically. Again, it is imperative that clinicians understand that the cognitive data derived from these instruments are not a panacea to concussion management. Rather, these tools provide one piece of clinical datum with which to make complicated decisions regarding clinical management and eventual return to play options for the concussed athlete.

Computerized neuropsychological testing is beginning to create heated interest within the sports medicine arena. The ability to collect objective, sensitive, and detailed neurobehavioral information pertaining to athletes' postconcussive status is of obvious merit and transcends standard levels of care. For example, such an approach to concussion management is systematic and individually tailored, rather than applying general standards (e.g., grading systems) that lack empirical validation. To familiarize the reader with a computerized approach to concussion management, we review our program at the University of Pittsburgh Medical Center (UPMC).

A Clinical Model for Computerized Neuropsychological Testing

The UPMC Sports Medicine Concussion Program is a specialized clinical and research protocol that utilizes neurocognitive testing to assist in general concussion management issues (e.g., determining return to play, retirement decisions). This program utilizes the ImPACT computer-based neuropsychological testing program (Collins et al., 2002; Collins, Iverson, et al., 2003; Lovell et al., 2003, 2004), which was developed to address the inherent limitations of traditional neuropsychological assessment and that has allowed our program to provide consultative services to many colleges, high schools, and professional sports organizations. Although the development and construction of this computer program is detailed elsewhere (Lovell et al., 2004;

Maroon, Lovell, & Norwig, 2000), a brief review is provided below. We should emphasize that other computer-based approaches to assessment are currently in use, and our program represents only one such approach.

The ImPACT neuropsychological battery is comprised of seven modules that assess multiple neurocognitive abilities. In the interest of gathering as much neuropsychological data within an approximate 20-minute administration time, several modules are designed to evaluate multiple cognitive domains simultaneously. To aid in the clinical interpretation of test performance, select module scores are combined to yield *Composite Indices*. These composite scores were constructed to better isolate test performance within the cognitive domains of *reaction time*, *verbal memory*, *visual memory*, *processing speed*, and *impulse control*. These domains were chosen based on evidence from earlier neuropsychological research involving paper-and-pencil testing and clinical experience that have revealed both individualized and, at times, diffuse difficulties following concussion.

As an adjunct to the neurocognitive scores provided by the clinical report, a symptom self-report inventory is also included within the ImPACT program (see Table 14.5). This 21-item scale (Lovell & Collins, 1998) requires the athlete to subjectively rank symptoms such as headache, dizziness, photosensitivity, and so on. Each symptom is rated on a 0 (no complaint) to 6 (severe symptom) scale. This inventory

TABLE 14.5. The Postconcussion Symptom Scale

Symptom	None	Minor		Moderate		Severe	
Headache	0	1	2	3	4	5	6
Nausea	0	1	2	3	4	5	6
Vomiting	0	1	2	3	4	5	6
Balance problems	0	1	2	3	4	5	6
Dizziness	0	1	2	3	4	5	6
Fatigue	0	1	2	3	4	5	6
Trouble falling asleep	0	1	2	3	4	5	6
Sleeping more than usual	0	1	2	3	4	5	6
Sleeping less than usual	0	1	2	3	4	5	6
Drowsiness	0	1	2	3	4	5	6
Sensitivity to light	0	1	2	3	4	5	6
Sensitivity to noise	0	1	2	3	4	5	6
Irritability	0	1	2	3	4	5	6
Sadness	0	1	2	3	4	5	6
Nervousness	0	1	2	3	4	5	6
Feeling more emotional	0	1	2	3	4	5	6
Numbness or tingling	0	1	2	3	4	5	6
Feeling slowed down	0	1	2	3	4	5	6
Feeling mentally "foggy"	0	1	2	3	4	5	6
Difficulty concentrating	0	1	2	3	4	5	6
Difficulty remembering	0	1	2	3	4	5	6
Visual problems	0	1	2	3	4	5	6

Note. Data from Lovell and Collins (1998).

allows for the direct comparison of postconcussion symptoms to preinjury symptom reporting and promotes a more comprehensive understanding of the recovery process for athletes, health care professionals, and other interested individuals such as parents and coaches. It is important to note that subjective symptoms and neurocognitive test results do not always correlate, and the evaluation of both aspects of recovery is essential.

The University of Pittsburgh Protocol for Return to Play

Based on recent research regarding recovery from concussion and the Vienna international consensus statement (Aubry et al., 2002), the UPMC return-to-play protocol involves the graduated return-to-play of the athlete to competition based on his or her progression through several steps in the recovery process. First and foremost, we feel strongly that athletes who have either abnormal neuropsychological testing results or are symptomatic should not be returned to play following injury until they are asymptomatic at rest and with exertion and any cognitive difficulties have resolved.

As reviewed earlier in the chapter, we also strongly suggest that younger athletes (e.g., high school age and below) should not be returned to play during the game in which they were injured. This restriction allows for closer evaluation of evolving signs and symptoms and will help to prevent more severe injury. We recommend formal neuropsychological testing (e.g., ImPACT) the day after injury to assess initial neurocognitive status. Although some clinicians do not feel it necessary to evaluate athletes until they are symptom free, we feel that understanding the severity of injury acutely, with respect to both symptoms and cognitive dysfunction, allows for better patient care and injury management. For example, if an athlete demonstrates severe symptoms of injury, it may be best for him or her to remain out of school or participate in a modified schedule until symptoms improve. If the athlete experiences significant memory problems, attentional dysfunction, or fatigue, it may be necessary for him or her to be granted temporary academic accommodations until the injury resolves. Such accommodations may include untimed testing, shorter homework or classroom assignments, open-book tests, tutoring, multiple modality instruction, and so on. We also feel that it is important to reevaluate the athlete regularly with regard to reported at-rest symptoms and cognitive functioning so that management recommendations can be adjusted according to progress in recovery, and so that necessary referrals can be made in cases where symptoms become chronic (e.g., referral to a neurologist specializing in headache management; referral for balance therapy; referral for a physical medicine and rehabilitation specialist for fatigue and dizziness). Given the significant variability in severity and presentation of concussion, the regularity with which follow-up evaluations are conducted is often based on the clinician's judgment. For example, if acute symptoms and cognitive difficulties are mild and require no accommodations, it may be reasonable to see the athlete a second time once he or she becomes asymptomatic, then again at the end of the exertional trials for final testing. For more complex and chronic cases, the second evaluation may be completed 2–4 weeks after the first evaluation, even though the athlete may remain symptomatic, so that the clinician can determine the need for adjustments to accommodations and referral recommendations.

Once the athlete is symptom free at rest, we suggest graduated aerobic exertional testing to check for the return of symptoms such as headache, dizziness, nausea, or fogginess. As suggested by the CIS group, at least 24 hours should separate each exertional step (e.g., low to moderate to high exertion). When the athlete becomes asymptomatic following exertion, neuropsychological testing should also be completed, and the athlete's test results should be compared to his or her baseline. In our protocol, determining when an athlete has truly returned to baseline levels of cognitive functioning involves examining any discrepancy between final testing and baseline testing. A test score is considered significantly different from baseline if it exceeds the reliable change index (RCI) that has been developed for each subtest (Iverson, Lovell, & Collins, 2003). An RCI is an estimate of measurement error that can occur between test–retest sessions for a variety of reasons. Stability coefficients for this test are similar to other noncomputerized neuropsychological tests. Only the Visual Motor Speed Composite was found to have a practice effect on test–retest, which was relatively modest (1.7 points; see Iverson et al., 2003). Other subtests were not determined to have practice effects, primarily due to alternate forms and randomization of stimuli. If preinjury baseline neuropsychological testing has not been previously completed, the athlete's test performance should be compared to normative standards for his or her age and gender. As with conventional models of neuropsychological testing, the clinician will need to form an estimation of preinjury functioning based on the athlete's demographic, academic, and other relevant histories. If an athlete has previously been tested for special education (e.g., gifted, learning disability), then prior testing may be used for forming preinjury estimates of functioning, and repeating some of the prior paper-and-pencil testing may be a useful adjunct in determining if the athlete has returned to baseline.

Finally, it should be emphasized that this protocol is based on research with primarily high school subjects, and the management of the older athlete (e.g., college or professional) may vary. Hopefully, recent large-scale research projects within the NFL and NHL will shed additional light on the management of concussion in professional athletes. See the case example in the appendix at the end of this chapter for an illustration of poor concussion management and its consequences.

New Frontiers in Concussion Assessment in Sports

Although neuropsychological testing has increasingly been utilized as both a research and clinical tool, the past several years have witnessed the emergence of an intense focus on the development of sophisticated brain imaging techniques. This interest grew out of new technological advances in brain imaging in addition to frustration regarding the well-known lack of sensitivity of more traditional anatomic imaging techniques such as CT and MRI. Although useful in identifying brain injury in more severe cases, CT and MRI scans are not often helpful in identifying subtler brain-related changes that are thought to occur on a metabolic rather than anatomical level (Lovell et al., 2004).

For example, recent research has examined the potential utility of functional magnetic resonance imaging (fMRI) as a viable tool for the assessment of neural processes following MTBI. The technology is based on the measurement of specific correlates of brain activation, such as cerebral blood flow and oxygenation (McAllister, Sparling, & Flashman, 2001). The use of fMRI also promotes the study of brain activation (or lack thereof) through the "in-scanner" implementation of specific neuropsychological tasks. The administration of specific neuropsychological tests to nonconcussed individuals during the fMRI scanning process reveals measurable and predictable changes in brain activity that can be contrasted with the performance of athletes following concussion. In addition, fMRI involves no exposure to radiation and can be safely utilized in children, and repeat evaluations can be undertaken with minimal risk. These advantages promote the assessment of changes in neural substrata that may occur with mild concussion and make it possible to track the recovery process. Potentially, one of the most important uses of fMRI scanning is the ability to provide validity data regarding the sensitivity and specificity of neuropsychological testing to detect subtle changes in brain function.

Although a promising tool, fMRI has yet to be widely implemented in clinical settings. This is no doubt a function of the sophisticated technology needed to acquire and analyze the images and the considerable expense of the procedure. At the current time, only a few laboratories are actively investigating the use of fMRI in sports-related head injury, although this is likely to change within the next few years. Notably, Johnston and her colleagues at McGill University in Montreal have developed an fMRI protocol that assesses several components of working memory (Johnston et al., 2001). In the United States, our laboratory at the University of Pittsburgh is one of only a handful of research programs structured to collect both neuropsychological and fMRI data in athletes and thereby equipped to participate in this multiyear prospective study. Prior neuropsychological testing (ImPACT) of a large cohort (over 1,500) of male and female high school and college athletes provides our baseline profiles. In the event of an injury, the athletes undergo repeat testing within 24 hours to 1 week and also undergo fMRI scanning within this time frame. An additional fMRI scan as well as neuropsychological testing "in scanner" and "out of scanner" is completed as the patient recovers, allowing us to track the relationship between regional fMRI activation and neuropsychological test results. Through this study, we have now evaluated approximately 210 athletes with concussion as well as a group 50 noninjured athletes who serve as a control group.

Figure 14.1A provides a graphic depiction of averaged fMRI data on a sample of 13 concussed high school athletes who had undergone fMRI evaluation. The areas of illumination show hyperactivation in the dorsolateral prefrontal cortex (DLPFC) as the memory task becomes more difficult through increased memory load on the n-back test (Ernst, Chang, Jovicich, Ames, & Arnold, 2002; Owen, 1997). The DLPFC is highly involved in working memory (e.g., the capacity of the athlete to recall information in the face of interference and distraction) (Owen, McMillan, Laird, & Bullmore, 2005). Therefore, this pattern of hyperactivation appears to reflect a need for the concussed brain to increase its metabolic activity in response to the task becoming more difficult. Figure 14.1B shows activation to the n-back task for 13 control (not concussed) athletes for comparison.

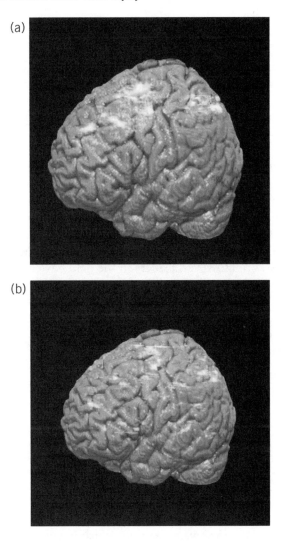

FIGURE 14.1. fMRI and sports-related concussion. (a) Group activation map for concussed athletes. Illuminated areas indicate increased activation in concussed group with increased memory load on in-scanner n-back test. (b) Group activation map for control athletes. Less activation to the n-back test is evident when visually compared to the concussed group map.

In addition to investigating changes in cerebral blood flow through fMRI, the University of Pittsburgh is also in the process of investigating other noninvasive brain imaging protocols that may increase our base of knowledge regarding recovery from concussion. More specifically, we have recently launched a project to evaluate the correlations between changes in neuropsychological testing (the ImPACT evaluation) and magnetoencephalography (MEG) data. MEG may provide a sophisticated picture of subtle changes in brain electrical activity and has better temporal resolution than fMRI, making it ideal for brain activation studies that utilize *in vivo* (in-scanner) neuropsychological testing.

Conclusions and Future Directions

This chapter has focused on new developments in the management of sports-related concussion. Specifically, we have emphasized that the clinical management of concussion is evolving rapidly, and we still have much to learn about both the short- and long-term consequences of injury. As increasingly more research studies are designed to investigate the biomechanics, pathophysiology, and clinical course of sports-related concussion, our management strategies will continue to evolve over the next 5–10 years. Although the future of concussion management remains somewhat uncertain at the current time, one trend has become particularly clear over the past 2 years: Concussion management has become increasingly individualized. This trend is likely to continue in the near future. The 1980s and 1990s were characterized by the publication of multiple concussion "guidelines," which made specific return-to-play recommendations based on duration of concussion markers such as loss of consciousness, amnesia, and so on. However, leaders in the field have acknowledged that these guidelines may have limited utility, and the focus has shifted to a more individualized approach based on an absence of any clinical symptomatology and establishment of normal brain function prior to return to play (Grindel, Lovell, & Collins, 2001). The diagnostic techniques outlined in this article will likely play an important role the clinical management of concussion.

Appendix: Case Illustration

Case Description

Brad Groves, a star football player at his college, was referred to us following events related to a seemingly benign "ding to the head" during a game against a rival school. According to many people in this small community, Brad was a "sure thing" to enter the NFL draft once he completed his degree.

Brad and his mother arrived in our office after their attorney contacted me to schedule an independent medical evaluation. Brad and his parents were very concerned that his health, his season, and perhaps his career were in serious jeopardy due to a potentially mishandled concussive injury. It is not uncommon for us to evaluate concussed athletes who appear to have received bad advice, lack of treatment, or mismanagement of a concussive injury, though lawsuits are relatively infrequent. During our initial evaluation, Brad told me his story.

This game was an early game, and it was quite a hot day. Brad dropped back to receive a pass and was "blindsided" by the opposing team's defensive back. Brad stated that he did not even see the player coming before he was hit. According to his teammates, coaches, and his father, who was present for the game, Brad lay on the field unconscious for approximately 30 seconds. By the time he had awakened, he was reportedly surrounded by a coach and a few athletic trainers and student trainers. In the initial few seconds following his arousal, Brad appeared confused and was uncertain of what had happened. After about a minute's time he was reoriented and able to correctly answer questions about the game prior to the hit, as well as report correctly his location and the approximate time of day. However, Brad did not recall, and still does not remember, being in the huddle immediately prior to the play, the actual play in which he was injured, or the hit. Review of the game tape as well as reports from others would indicate that he was struck from his right side with great force, which seemed to whip his head back and forth before he fell to the ground, striking the left side of his body and the back and left sides of his head.

Brad was escorted to the sideline and was able to walk on his own, showing no difficulty with coordination or balance. As he sat on the bench to watch the remaining half hour of the game, he remembers complaining of a significant "pounding" headache that was present "all over [his] head." He was informally assessed by his athletic trainer, who took notes on his symptom presentation. For the rest of the game, he reported nausea (but no vomiting), mild dizziness, headache as described above, and feeling "worn out." Brad reports that his coach and athletic trainer told him to "take it easy" when he returned to his dorm room, and to report to practice to see how he was doing on Monday.

Knowing that there is extreme variability in how sideline evaluations are conducted, I asked Brad about his immediate symptoms in more detail. *In addition to the above-described symptoms, Brad also revealed that his experience of feeling "worn out" appeared to be above and beyond how he would feel after playing a difficult game and getting "knocked around a little." Upon my query, he did report feeling bothered by the sunlight and crowd noise during the game, which was unusual for him. When asked, he stated he did feel mentally "foggy" and "slowed down" as well. The night of the hit, Brad reported difficulty sleeping, stating that although he fell asleep quickly and early, he had a very restless sleep. As the weekend progressed, he reported continued difficulty with all of the above-described symptoms and having a "short fuse" when interacting with his roommates. Brad attended classes on Monday, prior to going to football practice in the afternoon. He reported feeling drowsy during class and had difficulty paying attention enough to take notes. He also reported "bombing" a calculus quiz, which he would normally pass with an "A or B."*

When he arrived at practice late in the afternoon, he reported to his athletic trainer to talk about how he was recovering. Brad told the trainer that he continued to have a "constant headache, which was getting less intense every day," as well as having continued problems with feeling sick to his stomach, a little dizzy when he stood up, and feeling irritated by other people. He then told his athletic trainer about his difficulty with sleeping and paying attention in class. The trainer stated that Brad did get "dinged pretty hard" and that he should probably "take it a little easy for the next few days." His practice schedule was modified to include only jogging and weightlifting, but not practicing, until Thursday. It was the hope of his athletic trainer and coach, as well as the hope of Brad, that he could return to full practice before the end of the week, as an important game was coming up.

Over the next few days Brad worked out each day for about 1 hour with the team, then watched practices. He described feeling a little better by the end of the week. The athletic trainer had discussed Brad's training regimen with the coach, and both had agreed that if he was feeling better by the end of the week, he should play. For Thursday afternoon's practice, Brad participated in an "in one, out one" situation, where he would rest every other play, as he still had headaches and tired out more quickly. On game day (the following Saturday), Brad did not start, but was kept as a "reserve" player in case his replacement was not performing well or if there was a "crunch" situation. Brad was sent in the in final quarter, because the game was tied with 10 minutes on the clock. He proudly reports that though he did not feel "all that good," he was still able to catch the pass that eventually allowed his team to win the game. His total playing time was approximately 6 minutes, and he states he did not get "hit hard" that game.

I watched Brad revel in the glory of his accomplishment, then decided to probe further his reaction to playing that first game. Based on his report, he was clearly not fully recovered or back to his normal self when he returned to play. However, he was at least showing improvement and a drive to compete that allowed for the decision to be made (by Brad, his trainer, and his coach) that he would return only for a "crunch" situation that game. I asked Brad how his symptoms changed (or didn't) when he exercised during practice and played in the game.

Overall, Brad reported noticing that he felt worse at the end of a workout or following his 6 minutes of play, compared to how he typically felt over this past week, as well as com-

pared to how he typically felt following exertional activity. There appeared to be a general trend whereby he would physically exert himself and feel fine, even better for a short time, then feel his symptoms "kick in." He reported a spike in his headaches, dizziness, and nausea that would typically last until he went to bed. When he awoke the next day, his symptoms would return to their typical mild levels, which he did not believe interfered significantly with his daily life.

After winning the Saturday game, Brad stated that he rested for the remainder of the weekend and then returned to practice on Monday, resuming a regular class and football schedule. Although he continued to have headaches, some dizziness, mild irritability, and restless sleep, he believed he could "work through it" so that he could finish the season. Because he resumed regular activities and generally performed well during practice and play, Brad's trainers and coaches never followed up with Brad regarding his concussion.

Brad played and practiced without incidence for 2 weeks. He reported to me that he knew he was more tired and could never "shake" his headache or the other symptoms that worsened after he exerted himself, though he continued to play well and earn praise for his abilities.

Approximately 1 month postinjury, he played in the final game of the season and sustained a new injury, very similar to his original concussion. Brad states that he hit the back of his head on the ground when he was tackled after attempting to catch a pass. He describes the injury as occurring from a "typical tackle," whereby he was hit from the front just fractions of a second after he caught the pass, which caused him to fall backward and strike the back of his helmet on the ground. He remembers the incident in full, including catching the pass, the sensation of falling, and feeling his head strike the ground. He says he felt "stung . . . dizzy," but he arose right away and walked to the sideline on his own, knowing that his dropped pass had resulted in a fourth-down situation. Brad reports that no one asked him about the fall, and he believes that this is because it appeared on the game tape to be nothing of consequence. As he sat on the sideline during the following defensive sequence, Brad reported that his headache became throbbing and painful to the extent that he felt dizzy and nauseated and eventually vomited on the sideline. He was not returned to play. The day after the game, he informed his parents about what had happened during the game, and his mother insisted he go to the emergency room. Once there, Brad received an MRI scan, which was unremarkable. He attended a few final team meetings, and then did not have contact with the trainer or coach over the holiday break.

I saw Brad toward the beginning of the spring semester, about 2 months following his last injury. At the time he reported for this initial evaluation, he was having continued difficulty with some of his concussion symptoms, including frequent headaches, intermittent dizziness (especially when rising quickly), intermittent sleep difficulties, and problems with irritability ("having a short fuse"). In addition, he reported that his grades and academic performance, from the time of the first incident, had worsened since the second incident. His grade point average had dropped from a 3.2 to a 2.7. When I inquired about Brad's explanation for the drop in grades, he stated that he was not "partying more"; in fact, he felt he was studying for longer periods of time, yet earning lower grades. There was no evidence that his class schedule for the most recent semester was any more rigorous than previous semesters' schedules. Brad believed that he was having problems both in and out of the classroom, with difficulty paying attention in class, focusing on his homework, and learning and recalling information on which he was to be tested. He said that his academic difficulties, memory problems, and irritability had been noticed by his roommates and closest friends, who affectionately gave him the nickname "Zombie."

My task, then, was to determine if there were any observable cognitive deficits that might be linked to Brad's three concussions. Unfortunately, Brad had never received any type of baseline cognitive testing, which can often be found if the athlete's school participates in baseline testing of its athletes in high-risk sports, or if the athlete has ever received psychological testing as part of an evaluation for attention-deficit/hyperactivity disorder (ADHD), learning disability (LD), or a gifted program. However, based on Brad's overall preinjury college (3.65) and high school (3.95) grade-point average (GPA), as well as his Scholastic Aptitude Test (SAT) score of 1310, I believed his estimated premorbid functioning to be in the average to high average ranges.

Neuropsychological Testing and Results

For the duration of our next visit, I administered a neuropsychological test battery in order to objectively assess Brad's memory, attention, speed, and executive functioning. I used a combination of paper-and-pencil and computerized tests in order to obtain a thorough assessment of this athlete's current cognitive abilities. Table 14.6 reports the battery used, as well as the standard scores for Brad's performance on each measure.

Overall, Brad demonstrated performance consistent with estimates of his premorbid functioning, with a few noted areas of neurocognitive deficit. First, most tests measuring complex attention/working memory functions appeared to be attenuated. He demonstrated significantly more difficulty on Trail Making Test B when compared to Trail Making Test A, making one sequencing and one set error. In addition, his performance on the simpler part of the Auditory Consonant Trigrams test was within normal limits, but his performance on the 18-second-delay condition of the test was in the low average range. Brad also exhibited more difficulty with backward span compared to forward span on the Digit Span subtest of the Wechsler Adult Intelligence Scale–III (WAIS-III).

Secondly, Brad demonstrated initial difficulty with learning efficiency; his first three learning trials fell in the borderline range. However, he was able to learn all but 2 of 15 words on a list-learning task by the end of five trials. He did not exhibit any difficulty with retrieval of encoded information. In addition, his score on the verbal memory composite of a computerized test battery fell in the low average range. Although he did not have difficulty with learning or retrieval of visual information on the Brief Visuospatial Memory Test—Revised (BVMT-R), he did demonstrate low average performance on the visual memory composite of a computerized neuropsychological test battery, suggesting difficulty encoding and retrieving more complex visual stimuli.

Despite these demonstrated cognitive difficulties, many of Brad's performances were within expected levels, including reaction time, processing speed, verbal fluency, and some executive functions.

Regarding his symptom presentation, Brad endorsed (both in the clinical interview and on the Post-Concussion Symptom Scale) several symptoms consistent with postconcussion syndrome. Specifically, he endorsed moderate difficulty with headaches, attention/concentration, short-term memory, irritability, and insomnia, as well as mild difficulties with dizziness, fatigue, drowsiness, feeling "slowed down," and feeling "foggy" (total symptom score = 26).

At the completion of the testing session, I knew I would not likely see Brad and his family again, unless I was called to testify in court. Therefore, I imparted a few suggestions to assist in his recovery. I instructed him to cease physical exertion until his symptoms began to resolve. When he did exercise, he was to do so at a light intensity and was to stop any activity that caused an increase in his postconcussion syndrome. When his headaches resolved, he could begin to increase his activity level, though he should never engage in any activity that would place him at risk for additional head injury (e.g., biking, skateboarding, pick-up basketball games). Regarding his academic functioning, I encouraged him to seek academic accommodations so that his grades would not continue to suffer. This can typically be accomplished by informing the school medical professional or guidance counselor. In addition, I encouraged him to study in an even-paced manner, taking frequent breaks, as well as using compensa-

TABLE 14.6.Neuropsychological Test Battery for Brad

Test administered	Raw score	Standard score
Rey Auditory Verbal Learning Test (RAVLT)		
RAVLT List A Learning Trial 1	5	$Z = -1.5$
RAVLT List A Learning Trial 2	6	$Z = -1.95$
RAVLT List A Learning Trial 3	8	$Z = -1.89$
RAVLT List A Learning Trial 4	10	$Z = -.95$
RAVLT List A Learning Trial 5	13	$Z = 0.40$
RAVLT List B	5	$Z = -.89$
RAVLT Immediate Recall of List A	13	$Z = .83$
RAVLT Delayed Recall of List A	13	$Z = .79$
RAVLT List A Recognition	15	$Z = 1.0$
Brief Visual Spatial Memory Test—Revised (BVMT-R)		
BVMT-R Learning Trial 1	7	$T = 48$
BVMT-R Learning Trial 2	10	$T = 49$
BVMT-R Learning Trial 3	12	$T = 58$
BVMT-R Total Recall	29	$T = 51$
BVMT-R Delayed Recall	11	$T = 52$
Symbol Digit Modalities Test (SDMT)		
SDMT Total Correct	57	$Z = 0.24$
Trail Making Test (TMT)		
TMT A	21	$T = 53$
TMT B	79; 2 errors	$T = 37$
ImPACT Computerized Test Battery		
ImPACT Verbal Memory Composite	81	17th–18th %ile
ImPACT Visual Memory Composite	68	23rd %ile
ImPACT Processing Speed Composite	38.45	56th–57th %ile
ImPACT Reaction Time Composite	.50	83rd %ile
Controlled Oral Word Association Test (COWAT)		
FAS	46	$Z = .12$
Animals	25	$Z = .58$
Grooved Pegboard		
Dominant (right) hand	58	$T = 55$
Nondominant (left) hand	60	$T = 54$
Auditory Consonant Trigrams (ACT)		
9 seconds	12	$Z = -.13$
18 seconds	8	$Z = -1.20$
WAIS-III Digit Span Subtest		
Total Score		$AS = 9$
Forward Span	7	$Z = .16$
Backward Span	4	$Z = -.73$
Wisconsin Card Sorting Test (WCST)		
Categories Completed	6	WNL
Failures to Maintain Set	0	WNL
Post-Concussion Symptom Scale (PCSS)		
Total Score	26	Moderate

tory strategies such as repetition and associations to help with memory functioning. Lastly, I informed Brad and his parents that he should not return to sports until he was symptom-free at rest, symptom-free during exertion, and normal on cognitive testing. He should certainly be cleared by a medical professional before returning to high-risk activity.

Clinical Interpretation

Overall, it was my impression that Brad was indeed experiencing postconcussion syndrome that was the direct product of his concussions. I also felt that the concussion and its symptoms did not resolve in a timely fashion because the initial injury was not properly managed. Clearly, Brad should not have returned to physically exertional activity while he was still experiencing significant symptoms of the concussion. When he was returned to contact practice and competition the Thursday and Friday following the injury and every game and practice thereafter, he was still experiencing symptoms, and thus was placing himself at high risk for a compounding injury, or even more catastrophic outcome, such as SIS. Luckily, Brad's second concussion did not lead to SIS; however, it certainly exacerbated his preexisting concussion symptoms and caused him significant physical difficulties as well as problems in school.

As I have often observed in cases of an initially mismanaged concussion and premature return to play that is followed by a second concussion, less biomechanical force seemed to cause the second injury. Brad had reported to me, as noted above, that the second injury resulted from what seemed like a "typical tackle" and did not seem to be a strike of significant force. It is likely that, because Brad's brain was still recovering and trying to reach metabolic homeostasis, he was at increased vulnerability to sustaining a new injury.

Regarding the specific question posed to me in the independent medical evaluation, which asked if there were any observable cognitive deficits that might be linked to Brad's concussions, I believed, with a strong degree of medical certainty, that Brad was exhibiting at least mild difficulties with cognitive functioning in the areas of learning efficiency for verbal information, encoding and retrieval of complex verbal information, and working memory/complex attention. In addition, based on his academic achievement as documented through grades and test scores, I estimated his premorbid functioning to be in the average to high average range; thus, some of his average-range performances may also reflect slight attenuations in cognitive functioning, but without baseline information, this would be difficult to determine with much certainty.

Case Outcome

After approximately 1 year had passed, I was asked to participate in a deposition concerning my findings on the case. I reported the details of the case and test results, as well as my interpretation of the information. Attorneys from both sides asked mostly typical and expected questions in this sort of case. One line of questioning probed the meaning of low average scores (as opposed to "impaired" scores) on neuropsychological testing in an individual who is likely average or high average in premorbid ability. Another line of questioning explored how I arrived at my determination that the concussion had been improperly managed. Though I did not identify who I believed to have improperly managed the concussion, I did point to the recently published Vienna guidelines for concussion management (Aubry et al., 2002), which recommend that athletes are not returned to play until they are symptom-free at rest and during exertion, as well as normal on cognitive testing (if available).

Many months after the deposition was completed, I was called to testify in court by the plaintiff's attorneys. At the completion of the trial, Brad's college athletic department was found to be negligent in managing Brad's concussion, since he was reporting symptoms throughout the period that he was returned to exertion as well as returned to play.

References

American Academy of Neurology. (1997). Practice parameter: The management of concussion in sports (summary statement). Report of the Quality Standards Subcommittee. *Neurology, 48,* 581–585.

Aubry, M., Cantu, R., Dvorak, J., Graf-Bauman, T., Johnston, K. M., Kelly, J., et al. (2002). Summary of the first international conference on concussion in sport. *Clin J Sports Med, 12,* 6–11.

Barth, J. T., Alves, W. M., Ryan, T. V., Macciocchi, S. N., Rimel, R. W., & Jane, J. A. (1989). Mild head injury in sports. In H. S. Levin, H. Eisenberg, & A. Benton (Eds.), *Mild head injury* (pp. 257–275). Oxford, UK: Oxford University Press.

Bergschneider, M., Hovda, D. A., & Shalmon, E. (2003). Cerebral hyperglycolsis following severe human traumatic brain injury: A positron emission tomography study. *J Neurosurg, 86,* 241–251.

Brandt, J., & Benedict, R. H. B. (2001). *Hopkins Verbal Learning Test—Revised: Professional manual.* Lutz, FL: Psychological Assessment Resources.

Cantu, R. C. (1992). Cerebral concussion in sport: Management and prevention. *Phys Sports Med, 14,* 64–74.

Cantu, R. C. (2001). Posttraumatic retrograde and anterograde amnesia: Pathophysiology and implications in grading and safe return to play. *J Athl Training, 36,* 244–248.

Cantu, R. C., & Voy, R. (1995). Second impact syndrome: A risk in any sport. *Phys Sports Med, 23,* 27–36.

Collins, M. W., Field, M., Lovell, M. R., Iverson, G. L., Johnston, K. M., Maroon, J., et al. (2003). Relationship between post-concussion headache and neuropsychological test performance in high school athletes. *Am J Sports Med, 31,* 168–173.

Collins, M. W., Grindel, S. H., Lovell, M. R., Dede, D. E., Moser, D. J., Phalin, B. R., et al. (1999). Relationship between concussion and neuropsychological performance in college football players. *J Amer Med Assoc, 282,* 964–970.

Collins, M. W., Iverson, G. L., Lovell, M. R., McKeag, D. B., Norwig, J., & Maroon, J. C. (2003). On-field predictors of neuropsychological and symptom deficit following sports-related concussion. *Clin J Sport Med, 13,* 222–229.

Collins, M. W., Lovell, M. R., Iverson, G. L., Cantu, R. C., Maroon, J. C., & Field, M. (2002). Cumulative effects of sports concussion in high school athletes. *Neurosurgery, 51,* 1175–1181.

Collins, M. W., Lovell, M. R., & McKeag, D. B. (1999). Current issues in managing sports concussion. *J Amer Med Assoc, 282,* 2283–2285.

Congress of Neurological Surgeons. (1966). Committee on head injury nomenclature: Glossary of head injury. *Clin Neurosurg, 12,* 386–394.

Delaney, J. S., Lacroix, V. J., Gagne, C., & Antoniou, J. (2001). Concussions among university football and soccer players: A pilot study. *Clin J Sport Med, 11,* 23–31.

Echemendia, R. J. (20060. *Sports neuropsychology: Assessment and management of traumatic brain injury.* New York: Guilford Press.

Echemendia, R. J., Putukian, M., & Macklin, R. S. (2001). Neuropsychological test performance prior to and following sports-related mild traumatic brain injury. *Clin J Sport Med, 11,* 23–31.

Ernst, T., Chang, L., Jovicich, J., Ames, N., & Arnold, S. (2002). Abnormal brain activation on functional MRI in cognitively asymptomatic HIV patients. *Neurology, 59*, 1343–1349.

Field, M., Collins, M. W., Lovell, M. R., & Maroon, J. C. (2003). Does age play a role in recovery from sports-related concussion?: A comparison of high school and collegiate athletes. *J Pediatr, 142*, 546–553.

Grindel, S. H., Lovell, M. R., & Collins, M. W. (2001). The assessment of sports-related concussions: The evidence behind neuropsychological testing and management. *Clin J Sport Med, 11*, 134–143.

Hinton-Bayre, A. D., Geffen, G. M., & Geffen, L. B. (1999). Concussion in contact sports: Reliable change indices of impairment and recovery. *J Clin Exp Neuropsychol, 21*, 70–86.

Hovda, D. A., Prins, M., & Becker, D. P. (1998). Neurobiology of concussion. In J. E. Bailes, M. R. Lovell, & J. C. Maroon (Eds.), *Sports related concussion* (pp. 12 –51). St. Louis, MO: Quality Medical Publishing.

Iverson, G. L., Lovell, M. R., & Collins, M. W. (2003). Interpreting change on ImPACT following sport concussion. *Clin Neuropsychol, 17*, 460–467.

Johnston, K. M., Pitto, A., Chankowsky, I., & Chen, J. K. (2001). New frontiers in diagnostic imaging in concussive head injuries. *Clin J Sport Med, 11*, 166–175.

Jordan, B. D., Relkin, N. R., & Ravdin, L. D. (1997). Apolipoprotein E epsilon4 associated with chronic traumatic brain injury in boxing. *J Amer Med Assoc, 278*, 136–140.

Kelly, J. P., Nichols, J. S., Filley, C. M. (1991). Concussion in sports: Guidelines for the prevention of catastrophic outcome. *J Amer Med Assoc, 266*, 2867–2869.

Langlios, J., Gioia, G., & Collins, M. W. (2007). *CDC physician's toolkit*. Atlanta, GA: Centers for Disease Control and Prevention.

Lovell, M. R. (1998). Evaluation of the professional athlete. In J. E. Bailes, M. R. Lovell, & J. C. Maroon (Eds.), *Sports-related concussion* (pp. 200–214). St. Louis, MO: Quality Medical Publishing.

Lovell, M. R., & Burke, C. J. (2000). Concussion management in professional hockey. In R. E. Cantu (Ed.), *Neurologic athletic head and spine injury* (pp. 221–231). Philadelphia: Saunders.

Lovell, M. R., & Collins, M. W. (1998). Neuropsychological assessment of the college football player. *J Head Trauma Rehab, 13*, 9–26.

Lovell, M. R., Collins, M. W., Iverson, G. L., Field, M., Maroon, J. C., Cantu, R., et al. (2003). Recovery from mild concussion in high school athletes. *J Neurosurg, 98*, 296–301.

Lovell, M. R., Collins, M. W., Iverson, G. L., Johnston, K. L., & Bradley, J. (2004). Grade 1 or "ding" concussions in high school athletes. *Am J Sports Med, 32*, 47–54.

Lovell, M. R., Collins, M. W., Maroon, J. C., Cantu, R., Hawn, K., Burke, C., et al. (2002). Inaccuracy of symptom reporting following concussion in athletes. *Med Sci Sports Exerc, 34*, S298.

Macciocchi, S. N., Barth, J. T., & Alves, W. (1996). Neuropsychological functioning and recovery after mild head injury in collegiate athletes. *Neurosurgery, 39*, 510–514.

Maroon, J. C., Lovell, M. R., & Norwig, J. (2000). Cerebral concussion in athletes: Evaluation and neuropsychological testing. *Neurosurgery, 47*, 659–672.

Matser, E., Kessels, A., & Lezak, M. (1999). Neuropsychological impairment in amateur soccer players. *J Amer Med Assoc, 282*, 971–974.

McAllister, T. W., Sparling, M. B., & Flashman, L. A. (2001). Differential working memory load effects after mild head injury. *NeuroImage, 14*, 1004–1012.

McCrory, P., Johnston, K., Meeuwisse, W., Aubry, M., Cantu, R., Dvorak, T., et al. (2005). Summary and agreement statement of the 2nd International Conference on Concussion in Sport, Prague 2004. *Brit J Sports Med, 39*, 196–204.

McDonald, J. W., & Johnston, M. V. (1990). Physiological and pathophysiological roles of excitatory amino acids during central nervous system development. *Brain Res Rev, 15,* 41–70.

Owen, A. M. (1997). The functional organization of working memory processes within human lateral frontal cortex: The contribution of functional neuroimaging. *Eur J Neurosci, 9,* 1329–1339.

Owen, A. M., McMillan, K. M., Laird, A. R., & Bullmore, E. (2005). N-Back working memory paradigm: A meta-analysis of normative functional neuroimaging studies. *Hum Brain Map, 25,* 46–59.

Pellman, E. J., Lovell, M. R., Viano, D. C., & Casson, I. R. (2006). Concussions in professional football: Recovery of NFL and high school athletes assessed by computerized neuropsychological testing—Part 12. *Neurosugery, 58,* 263–274.

Pickles, W. (1950). Acute general edema of the brain in children with head injuries. *New Engl J Med, 242,* 607–611.

Roberts, G. W., Allsop, B., & Bruton, C. (1990). The occult aftermatch of boxing. *J Neurol Neurosurg Psychiatry, 53,* 373–378.

Schatz, P., & Zillmer, E. (2003). Computer-based assessment of sports concussion. *Appl Neuropsychol, 10*(1), 42–47.

Schnirring, L. (2001). How effective is computerized concussion management? *Phy Sports Med, 29,* 11–16.

Smith, A. (1982). *The Symbol Digit Modalities Test manual.* Los Angeles: Western Psychological Services.

Thurman, D., & Guerro, J. (1997). Trends in hospitalization associated with traumatic brain injury. *J Amer Med Assoc, 282,* 954–967.

Wojyts, E. D., Hovda, D., Landry, G., Boland, A., Lovell, M. R., McCrea, M., et al. (1999). Concussion in sports. *Am J Sports Med, 27,* 676–686.

CHAPTER 15

Cognitive Functioning and Everyday Tasks in Multiple Sclerosis

Peter A. Arnett and Megan M. Smith

Ecological validity is a central issue for the field of clinical neuropsychology. Neuropsychologists routinely extrapolate the neuropsychological test results of their patients to real-world activities, yet, in many cases the actual empirical data supporting such an extrapolation is limited or nonexistent. If patients are impaired on tasks such as the Wisconsin Card Sorting Test or the California Verbal Learning Test, will they have difficulty with real-world tasks that purportedly require the cognitive functions measured by these tasks? As a more specific example, if patients perform poorly on tasks measuring information processing speed and attention, such as the Symbol Digit Modalities Test or the Paced Auditory Serial Addition Test (PASAT), will their driving skill or their ability to carry out daily household tasks such as cooking be impaired? The goal of the present chapter is to provide a review of some of the existing data relating to the ecological validity of neuropsychological tests in patients with multiple sclerosis (MS). Cognitive problems are very common in MS, and there is a growing body of literature suggesting that such cognitive difficulties have consequences for important real-world tasks. Before reviewing this literature, we summarize what is known about some of the basic characteristics of MS, including pathophysiology, symptom profile and diagnostic issues, epidemiology and disease characteristics, and cognitive functioning and depression. We turn to these issues now.

General Characteristics of MS

Pathophysiology

MS is thought to be caused by an autoimmune process that results in demyelination in the central nervous system; a slow-acting virus or a delayed reaction to a common virus is also considered as a possible cause of this demyelination (Arnett, 2003; Brassington & Marsh, 1998; Compston et al., 2005; Paty & Ebers, 1998; Tröster &

Arnett, 2006). Multiple discrete plaques are formed, in part, by proliferating astrocytes that result in demyelination. Myelin sheaths within plaques are either destroyed or swollen and fragmented. This process disrupts neural transmission by limiting the saltatory conduction process whereby the nerve impulse jumps between gaps in the myelin sheaths. In the normal brain, myelin encloses intact nerves, and the nerve impulse moves fluidly across the gaps in myelin. MS plaques appear as ill-defined, pale, pink-yellow lesions in the untreated brain. Axons and cell bodies of neurons often remain intact, though some cell death is thought to occur with progression of the disease (Brass, Benedict, Weinstock-Guttman, Munschauer, & Bakshi, 2006). MS plaques can occur in the brain and/or spinal cord, and their location is highly variable among patients. Within the brain, plaques near the lateral and third ventricles are most common. The frontal lobes are the next most commonly affected, even when the size of the frontal lobes, relative to the rest of the brain, is taken into account. Plaques are also frequently observed in other major lobes of the brain, the optic nerves, optic chiasm, or optic tracts, as well as the corpus callosum, the brainstem, and the cerebellum. Plaques are also found in white matter regions of the thalamus, hypothalamus, and basal ganglia. The majority of plaques (about 75%) are observed in the white matter, but some occur in the gray matter and in the juncture between the gray and white matter (Pittock & Lucchinetti, 2007).

Symptom Profile and Diagnosis

Symptoms from demyelination in MS most often reflect functions associated with the affected areas. The most common symptoms at MS onset are muscle weakness, paresthesias, gait/balance problems, and visual disturbances. Urinary disturbance, fatigue, problems with balance, and paresthesias (usually numbness and tingling in the limbs, trunk, or face) are also common (Arnett, 2003; Paty & Ebers, 1998). Significant cognitive difficulties and problems with depression are very common symptoms as well. These latter difficulties are discussed in more detail below. Symptom onset is typically acute or subacute, with many MS symptoms being transient and unpredictable. For example, visual disturbances and paresthesias may last for seconds or hours. Because of the short-lived and sometimes unusual nature of symptoms, it is not uncommon for patients in the early stages, prior to formal diagnosis, to be labeled with somatoform disorders.

Up until about 6 years ago, the diagnosis of MS was most often based on Poser and colleagues' (1983) criteria. In this system, there are four categories of diagnosis. "Clinically definite" MS requires two discrete disease attacks and clinical evidence of two separate lesions, or two attacks, clinical evidence of one lesion, and paraclinical evidence of another, separate lesion. "Laboratory-supported definite" MS requires two attacks and either clinical or paraclinical evidence of two separate lesions, and cerebrospinal fluid (CSF) oligoclonal bands or abnormal IgG synthesis rate. "Clinically probable" MS requires two attacks and clinical evidence of one lesion. Finally, "laboratory-supported probable" MS requires two attacks and CSF oligoclonal bands or abnormal IgG synthesis rate.

Currently, however, diagnosis guidelines published by McDonald and colleagues (2001) and Polman and colleagues (2005) are considered the gold standard for the diagnosis of MS. Under these new criteria, lesions should be separated in both time and space. More specifically, patients must have had two or more discrete attacks of the disease lasting at least 24 hours. These attacks, or episodes of neurological change, should also implicate the presence of lesions in at least two different sites in the central white matter. An additional criterion is that at least 30 days should separate the onset of each attack. McDonald and colleagues also lay out specific criteria for defining lesions detected on MRI as abnormal and characteristic of MS. With this new diagnostic system, MRI data are considered preferable to other paraclinical tests; however, additional tests are considered useful when clear-cut MRI findings are not evident or in the case of atypical clinical presentations. In particular, the presence of oligoclonal IgG bands in the CSF different from those in the serum, or elevated IgG, can be used. Furthermore, visual evoked potentials (VEPs) are considered an acceptable supplement to the clinical examination to reveal evidence of additional lesions. In cases of insidious MS progression that do not involve discrete disease attacks, abnormal CSF findings that reflect inflammation and abnormal immune functioning are necessary. Evidence of lesions being separated in space, established by MRI or abnormal VEP, is considered essential. Lastly, there should be evidence indicating separation in time as reflected by the onset of new MRI lesions or increased level of disability over the course of at least 1 year.

New attacks, relapses, or exacerbations commonly occur in MS and imply new disease activity. MS was previously classified under two major types of disease course: relapsing–remitting and chronic progressive. A new system that includes four course types developed by Lublin and Reingold (1996) has been widely adopted. The most common course type is *relapsing–remitting*. Approximately 85% of patients have this type at initial diagnosis. It is characterized by clearly defined disease relapses. Recovery is highly variable, ranging from complete recovery back to prerelapse baseline to sequelae and residual deficit. A central feature of this course type is the absence of disease progression between relapses. *Secondary progressive* is the next most common type of MS. It begins as a relapsing–remitting course, but progression of the disease is evident even between relapses. It is important to note, however, that relapses and remissions may or may not occur once patients enter a secondary progressive course, but disease progression occurs. Before the relatively recent development of disease-modifying drugs, approximately 50% of patients with relapsing–remitting MS developed this course of the disease within 10 years. Long-term data are not yet available to allow for an evaluation of whether such drugs delay this progression. The *primary progressive type* is the next most common course type, affecting approximately 10% of patients and involving an unremitting disease progression for most patients. That said, occasional stabilization and even improvement in functioning can occur, but there are no clear relapses. The least common type of MS is *progressive relapsing*, affecting about 5% of patients. It involves disease progression from onset that is punctuated by acute relapses from which patients may or may not fully recover. The term "chronic progressive" formerly encompassed all progressive types (Tröster & Arnett, 2006).

Complete remission is common following the initial episode of symptoms for relapsing–remitting MS. Subsequent episodes are unpredictable, occurring weeks to years later, and symptoms associated with them remit less completely or not at all.

Relapses are highly variable, lasting days to weeks, and more rarely, hours or months (Compston et al., 2005; Paty & Ebers, 1998).

Epidemiology/Disease Characteristics

MS is about twice as likely to affect women compared to men, and symptom onset occurs in most (about two-thirds of) patients between the ages of 20 and 40. Onset before age of 15 in MS is rare; late onset after age 40 is also relatively uncommon and typically characterized by a quicker progression and greater morbidity. Following disease onset, the average life expectancy of patients is estimated to be greater than 30 years, but as with many aspects of this disease, variability is great (Arnett, 2003).

The incidence and prevalence of MS are quite variable geographically. Relatively few cases occur near the equator, with the greatest number of cases found in the northern and southern latitudes (from about 60 to 300 per 100,000). Thus, although it is estimated that approximately 350,000 persons have MS in the United States and another approximately 400,000 in Europe (Rotstein, Hazan, Barak, & Achiron, 2006), individuals who live north of 40 degrees latitude are approximately three times more likely to have MS compared with residents living in southern regions. Such a discrepant geographic pattern implicates an environmental contribution to the disease. Nonetheless, there appears to be a likely significant genetic contribution to MS, as well, something suggested by the 30–40% concordance in identical twins but only 1–13% in fraternal twins (Poser, 1994; Tröster & Arnett, 2006).

Cognitive Sequelae/Profiles

Since Rao and colleagues' (Rao, Leo, Bernardin, & Unverzagt, 1991) seminal study on the prevalence of cognitive deficits in MS, other investigators have supported their finding of close to a 45% prevalence in community-based samples (Amato, Zipoli, & Portaccio, 2006; Jonsson et al., 2006; McIntosh-Michaelis et al., 1991). Over half of patients in clinically based samples (about 55–65%) have typically been shown to have significant cognitive problems (Amato et al., 2006; Bertrando, Maffei, & Ghezzi, 1983; Feinstein, 2004). In their study, Rao and colleagues (1991) compared 100 community-based patients with MS with 100 matched healthy controls on an extensive neuropsychological battery. They found that memory and complex attention/speeded information processing were the cognitive domains most affected in MS; this finding has been supported by subsequent work. Other domains commonly affected include verbal fluency, working memory, and executive functions involving problem solving and abstract reasoning (Amato et al., 2006; Benedict et al., 2002; Bobholz & Rao, 2003; Feinstein, 2004; Rao, Leo, Bernardin, & Unverzagt, 1991; Wishart et al., 2004).

As Rao and others have noted, however, about 80% of patients with cognitive deficits are relatively mildly affected. Only approximately 5% of patients experience global cognitive deficits that would be consistent with dementia. Even mild cognitive problems, however, have been shown to be associated with difficulty in everyday activities in MS (e.g., work, homemaking, personal care activities, social activities)

(Higginson, Arnett, & Voss, 2000). Thus, even mild cognitive difficulties in MS are a concern in a context of ecological validity.

Nature of Neuropsychological Deficits

In the following sections the percentage of patients with deficits in a particular domain is noted. This determination is based on the percentage of patients who fell below the fifth percentile of controls in Rao, Leo, Bernardin, and Unverzagt's (1991) seminal study. We chose this study because it is the representative community sample of patients with MS and provides one of the best samples of control participants in the literature.

Memory. Difficulties encoding and/or retrieving both verbal and visual information are the most common type of memory deficit in MS. On neuropsychological testing these problems are typically manifested as immediate and delayed recall memory deficits. About 30% of patients have substantial problems, another 30% have moderate problems, and the remaining 40% have mild or no problems with this type of memory (Brassington & Marsh, 1998). Delayed recall deficits are usually a function of deficient immediate recall, not forgetting. The learning curve across repeated trials is similar in slope in MS compared with controls, but is lower in magnitude. Percent retention, recognition, and incidental memory following a delay, and remote memory are usually intact in MS (Arnett, 2003).

Working Memory/Attention/Information-Processing Speed. Working memory deficits and problems with speeded information processing are nearly as common in MS as long-term memory problems. Working memory, defined as the ability to maintain and manipulate information "online," is commonly impaired in MS (D'Esposito et al., 1996; Foong et al., 1999; Grigsby, Ayarbe, Kravcisin, & Busenbark, 1994; Grigsby, Busenbark, Kravcisin, Ayarbe, & Kennedy, 1999) in patients with relapsing–remitting (Grigsby et al., 1999) as well as progressive (Grigsby et al., 1994) subtypes. It can be difficult to separate speeded information processing from working memory/attention because attention is typically necessary for performing any speeded cognitive task. Of note is that DeLuca and colleagues (DeLuca, Chelune, Tulsky, Lengenfelder, & Chiaravalotti, 2004) have reported that processing speed deficits, as measured by the Processing Speed index from the Wechsler Adult Intelligence Scale–III (WAIS-III), are common to both relapsing-remitting and secondary progressive MS subtypes. In contrast, working memory deficits, as measured by the Working Memory index from the WAIS-III, only emerge in patients with a secondary progressive course. One limitation of their study is that the Processing Speed index requires fine motor speed, something that is commonly impaired in patients with MS. The authors did attempt to control for this potential confound by covarying out Finger Tapping test speed, but motor writing impairments may still have exacerbated differences with controls. Using the Sternberg task, an experimental measure that controls for perceptual and motor difficulties, Archibald and Fisk (2000) showed that both relapsing–remitting and secondary progressive MS course types demonstrated significantly slower processing speed compared with controls as the working memory demands of the task increased. Generally, patients with MS show significant difficulty on tasks requiring rapid and complex information processing, like those requiring swift application of working memory operations, attentional switching, or rapid visual scanning. About 20–25% of patients with MS have impairments in this cognitive domain (Rao, Leo, Bernardin, & Unverzagt, 1991). Simple attention span is usually intact, but mild impairments are sometimes found.

Executive Functioning. The next most common cognitive domain typically affected in MS is executive functioning, with approximately 15–20% of individuals with MS showing impairments here (Rao, Leo, Bernardin, & Unverzagt, 1991). Deficits in cognitive flexibility, concept formation, verbal abstraction, problem solving, and planning are commonly found (Amato et al., 2006; Benedict et al., 2002; Bobholz & Rao, 2003; Feinstein, 2004).

Verbal/Linguistic Function. Aphasias are unusual in MS (Arnett, Hussain, Rao, Swanson, & Hammeke, 1996), but mild confrontation naming difficulties are sometimes seen. Similarly, alexia, agraphia, and apraxia are very rare (Mahler, 1992). With that said, speech abnormalities such as dysarthria and hypophonia are common in MS (Hartelius, Runmarker, & Andersen, 2000; Hartelius, Runmarker, Andersen, & Nord, 2000), as are deficits in verbal fluency. A recent meta-analysis suggested that letter–word and semantic fluency tasks are equally sensitive to verbal fluency problems in MS (Henry & Beatty, 2006). Recent data from our lab indicate that the later parts of verbal fluency tasks may be most sensitive to cognitive problems in MS. In particular, we found that patients with MS did not differ significantly from controls in the first 15-second interval of the task, but robust differences were found for the overall task (Smith & Arnett, 2007). We speculated that the initial, more automatic part of the tasks, wherein examinees often produce a large proportion of their words, is not sensitive to fluency deficits in MS, but the more effortful later parts of the task requiring more controlled cognitive processing are sensitive. Overall, 20–25% of patients typically show deficits on verbal fluency tasks (Rao, Leo, Bernardin, & Unverzagt, 1991).

Visuospatial Function. Visuospatial deficits occur with reasonable frequency in MS, with 10–20% of patients showing substantial difficulty with higher-order visuospatial skills involving angle matching or face recognition (Rao, Leo, Bernardin, & Unverzagt, 1991).

Intellectual Function. Although verbal intellectual functioning is impaired in about 20% of patients with MS (Rao, Leo, Bernardin, & Unverzagt, 1991), most patients score within the broad normal range on general measures of intelligence.

Possible Causes of Cognitive Deficits

Cognitive deficits are primarily a direct consequence of the location and extent of brain damage. Because most research in cognition in MS is conducted on participants who are not experiencing acute attacks, there are limited data on cognition during a clinical exacerbation. However, Foong and colleagues (1998) examined memory and attentional performance in a small sample of patients with MS tested during and after an acute exacerbation. They report that, in a subgroup of patients in whom gadolinium-enhanced lesion load decreased following remission, attentional performance improved during recovery, whereas memory performance remained consistently impaired. These findings suggest that some limited aspects of cognitive dysfunction observed during acute exacerbation may be reversible. However, there is clear evidence that overall cognitive impairment is associated with total white matter lesion burden in MS, as measured by T1 magnetic resonance imaging (MRI) lesion volume (Brass et al., 2006; Rao, Leo, Haughton, St. Aubin-Faubert, & Bernardin, 1989). There is also more recent evidence that subcortical gray matter deterioration is associated with overall neuropsychological functioning in MS (Brass et al., 2006), in some cases more highly than lesion volume (Sanfilipo, Benedict, Weinstock-Guttman, & Bakshi, 2006). Thus, cognitive problems caused by primary influences are generally not reversible. Additionally, there is some evidence that frontal lobe lesions are associated with deficits on executive tasks such as the Wisconsin Card Sorting Test (WCST) (Arnett et al., 1994); however, the association between lesions in other brain areas and specific cognitive deficits is less clear (Brassington & Marsh, 1998).

There is also evidence that cognitive problems can appear very early on in the disease course. Jonsson and colleagues (2006) found that 44–48% of patients with MS displayed cognitive impairments within the first year of their diagnosis. Feuillet and colleagues (2007) even found significant evidence of cognitive impairment in over 50% of patients with clinically isolated syndromes suggestive of MS. It has also been demonstrated that once cognitive problems are present, they are likely to progress. Two longitudinal studies have now shown that patients who initially display cognitive problems are most likely to show progression of such difficulties. Kujala, Portin, and Ruutiainen (1997) demonstrated this outcome in a 3-year longitudinal study, and Bergendal, Fredrikson, and Almkvist (2007) showed evidence for such progression over an 8-year follow-up period.

Secondary causes of cognitive impairment arise from factors/conditions associated with the disease, such as depression, anxiety, or fatigue. Cognitive problems caused by a secondary influence are potentially reversible if the secondary influence is successfully treated. There has been less emphasis in the MS literature on these possible secondary causes of cognitive dysfunction. Although many early studies often reported null findings in this realm (Good, Clark, Oger, Paty, & Klonoff, 1992; Krupp, Sliwinski, Masur, Friedberg, & Coyle, 1994; Moller, Wiedemann, Rohde, Backmund, & Sonntag, 1994; Schiffer & Caine, 1991), there is some evidence from a few older studies, but especially from more recent work, that depression is associated with impairments in speeded attentional functioning, working memory, and executive functions (Aikens, Fischer, Namey, & Rudick, 1997; Arnett, Higginson, & Randolph, 2001; Arnett, Higginson, Voss, Bender, et al., 1999; Arnett, Higginson, Voss, Wright, et al., 1999; Denney, Lynch, Parmenter, & Horne, 2004; Fischer, 1988; Landro, Celius, & Sletvold, 2004). One factor that may account for some of the discrepancies in the literature, on which we have focused in our lab, is the variable definitions of depression. We define depression more narrowly as mood disturbance (Arnett et al., 2001; Arnett, Higginson, Voss, Bender, et al., 1999; Arnett, Higginson, Voss, Wright, et al., 1999) or as a combination of mood disturbance and negative evaluative symptoms of depression (Arnett, 2005; Arnett, Higginson, Voss, & Randolph, 2002). We have done this because of the possible overlap theorized between neurovegetative symptoms of depression and MS symptoms (e.g., sleep disturbance, sexual dysfunction, fatigue) (Mohr, Goodkin, Likosky, Beutler, et al., 1997; Randolph, Arnett, Higginson, & Voss, 2000). Nonetheless, some studies have still found associations using depression measures such as the Beck Depression Inventory (BDI) and Center for Epidemiological Studies Depression Scale (CES-D), which also include neurovegetative depression symptoms (Aikens et al., 1997; Beatty, Goodkin, Monson, Beatty, & Hertsgaard, 1988; Denney et al., 2004; Fischer, 1988; Gottberg, Einarsson, Fredrikson, von Koch, & Holmqvist, 2007; Landro et al., 2004).

The presence of unmeasured moderators might also explain some of the discrepancies in the literature on cognitive problems and depression in MS. In a recent theoretical review paper (Arnett, Barwick, & Beeney, 2008), we articulated a comprehensive model that explains how the relationship between cognitive dysfunction and depression may be moderated by factors such as stress, social support, cognitive schema, and coping. In one empirical study we found that coping strategies significantly moderated the relationship between cognitive dysfunction and depression (as measured by the combined Mood and Evaluative scales from the Chicago Multiscale Depression Inventory (CMDI; Nyenhuis et al., 1995). Specifically, patients with MS and cognitive difficulties were at risk for depression only if they used high levels of avoidance coping or low levels of active coping (Arnett et al., 2002; Rabinowitz & Arnett, in press). The influence of moderators such as coping style might explain some of the discrepancies in the literature outlined above. Longitudinally, we have found that negative evaluative depression symptoms are more consistently associated with cognitive dysfunction than mood symptoms (Arnett, 2005).

Besides depression impacting cognitive functioning or cognitive functioning resulting in depression, it is also possible that both common problems in MS could result from some third variable, for example, a common neurobiological factor such as inflammation in the basal ganglia and white matter. We have also previously proposed (Arnett et al., 2001) that, given that left frontal hypoactivation is common in depression in general (e.g., Davidson, 1992; Niemiec & Lithgow, 2005), and the left frontal brain region appears to be important in performance on executive and working memory/speeded processing tasks associated with depression in MS, differential white matter lesion damage and/or hypoactivation in this region could result in both depression and cognitive problems.

Primary problems with visual acuity as well as problems with output modalities (e.g., fine motor skills, oral–motor speed) can also compromise performance on higher-level cognitive tasks requiring these outputs and thereby confound interpretation of test results. It is unclear whether higher-order visual deficits are a function of primary visual disturbances involving blurred vision and diplopia (Rao, Leo, Bernardin, & Unverzagt, 1991), though a recent study from our lab suggests that such factors may play an important role (Bruce, Bruce, & Arnett, 2007). Recent research from our lab also suggests that rudimentary problems with oral–motor speed differentially contribute to performance on commonly used cognitive tasks in evaluating MS, such as the oral version of the Symbol Digit Modalities Test (Smith & Arnett, 2007). Such problems in oral–motor speed appear to magnify the relatively poorer performance of patients with MS on such tasks.

Depression

The prevalence of depression is high in patients with MS (Arnett, 2003; Brassington & Marsh, 1998; Dalton & Heinrichs, 2005; Fischer et al., 1994; Goldman Consensus Group, 2005; Minden & Schiffer, 1990). The lifetime risk for depression has been estimated at around 50% (Patten & Metz, 1997; Sadovnick et al., 1996), compared with a lifetime risk in the general population of around 10–15% (American Psychiatric Association, 1994). Because of its high prevalence, importance to quality of life and patients' well-being (Kenealy, Beaumont, Lintern, & Murrell, 2000), and possible influence on the disease course itself (Ackerman et al., 2000; Dalos, Rabins, Brooks, & O'Donnell, 1983; Franklin, Nelson, Heaton, Burkes, & Thompson, 1988; Mohr et al., 2000), depression has been intensively studied in MS. The significance of depression in MS is also underscored by the fact that depression scores are highly predictive of suicidal intent in patients with MS (Feinstein, O'Conner, & Feinstein, 2002).

Depression in MS has been shown to be treatable through brief and even telephone-based cognitive-behavioral therapy (CBT; Mohr et al., 2000) as well as group therapy. In addition, cognitive-behavioral stress management training has been shown to reduce emotional distress in patients with MS (Fischer et al., 1994), and psychopharmacological treatments have been shown to be effective in treating depression in these patients (Mohr & Goodkin, 1999). Nonetheless, depression has been historically undertreated in MS, despite the fact that successful treatment of depression is associated with greater adherence to immunotherapy (Mohr, Likosky, et al., 1999).

A number of factors has been found to have a strong association with depression, including reduced social support (McCabe, McKern, & McDonald, 2004; McIvor, Riklan, & Reznikoff, 1984), dysfunctional attitudes and negative cognitive schema (Bruce & Arnett, 2005; Shnek, Foley, LaRocca, Smith, & Halper, 1995), stress and maladaptive coping (Jean, Paul, & Beatty, 1999; Pakenham, 1999), and the extent of lesion damage in the brain (Bakshi et al., 2000; Feinstein et al., 2004; Pujol, Bello, Dues, Marti-Vilalta, & Capdevila, 1997; Zorzon et al., 2002). Not surprisingly, depression has also been shown to be related to sexual dysfunction in MS (Demirkiran, Sarica, Uguz, Yerdelen, & Aslan, 2006; Zivadinov et al., 2003). Additionally, research has consistently demonstrated that depression is highly negatively correlated with quality of life in MS (D'Alisa et al., 2006; Janardhan & Bakshi, 2002; Janssens et al., 2003; Patti et al., 2003; Wang, Reimer, Metz, & Patten, 2000) and that effective treatment of depression may alleviate this effect (Hart, Fonareva, Merluzzi, & Mohr, 2005). Effective treatment of depression in patients with MS has also been found to improve adherence to disease-modifying treatment (Mohr, Goodkin, Gatto, & Van Der Wende, 1997).

There is no consensus regarding the nature of depression in the MS literature. Some investigators have presented evidence that neurovegetative symptoms of depression are not valid indicators because of their overlap with MS symptoms (e.g., sleep disturbance, fatigue, sexual dysfunction) (Beeney & Arnett, 2008; Mohr, Goodkin, Likosky, Beutler, et al., 1997; Randolph et al., 2000), whereas others have provided evidence to the contrary (Aikens et al., 1999; Moran & Mohr, 2005). This debate suggests that caution is warranted in interpreting neurovegetative symptoms of depression as such in any individual patient with MS.

Ecological Validity of Cognitive Tests in MS

Perhaps the seminal study examining the ecological validity of cognitive tests in MS was Rao, Leo, Ellington, and colleagues' (1991) comprehensive examination of the impact of cognitive dysfunction on employment and social functioning. These investigators divided their sample of 100 patients with MS into groups of 52 "cognitively intact" and 48 "cognitively impaired" patients. To demarcate their groups, they first determined the mean number of "failed" tests from a comprehensive neuropsychological battery of 31 test indices that a matched control group of 100 participants had taken. These investigators determined that less than 5% of controls failed (scored below the fifth percentile) four or more tests in the battery. Thus, failing four or more tests was operationalized as failing the entire battery. Participants were then administered a number of measures pertaining to real-world skills, including the Expanded Disability Status Scale (EDSS; Kurtzke, 1983), the Incapacity Status Scale (ISS; Kurtzke, 1981), and the Environmental Status Scale (ESS; Mellerup, Fog, & Raun, 1981). The EDSS is a standard measure of physical/neurological disability in MS that focuses primarily on ambulation; the ISS measures basic activities of daily living (ADLs) such as stair climbing, dressing, and bed and chair transfers; the ESS assesses degree of social handicap from illness in seven domains, including employment, social activities, personal assistance required, community assistance required, financial status, need for transportation, and modifications to personal residence. An occupational therapist also conducted a 2-hour evaluation in patients' homes. Patients were rated on the Barthel Index (BI; Mahoney & Barthel, 1965), the Klein–Bell ADL (Activities of Daily Living) Scale (Klein & Bell, 1982), and a homemaking evaluation. In the latter assessment patients performed three tasks: cooking a simple dessert, demonstrating the operation of household appliances, and making a bed. The Klein–Bell scale includes ratings in six ADL domains (i.e., dressing, elimination, mobility, bathing/hygiene, eating, and communication). Finally, the BI provides an overall summary score reflecting level of dependence on others for ADLs. Patients and significant others also completed various self-report measures pertaining to emotional functioning, as well as a measure of sickness-related disability. Because of its relevance to the topic at hand, the results of Rao and colleagues' seminal study are variously described in the relevant sections that follow.

Independent Activities of Daily Living

ADLs involve a variety of basic functions such as dressing oneself, bathing and hygiene, eating, and communicating, among others. Impairments in ADLs are extremely common in MS. In one of the most representative samples of patients with MS reported in the literature to date, Sarah Minden and her colleagues (2006) noted that almost two-thirds of over 2,000 patients with MS in the Sonya Slifka Longitudinal MS Study needed help from another person to perform routine or instrumental activities of daily living. Several studies have now examined the relationship between cognitive dysfunction and ADLs in MS; Rao, Leo, Ellington, and colleagues' 1991 study is perhaps the first in the literature to examine this relationship. They found that the cognitively impaired and cognitively intact groups were not significantly different in EDSS scores or for noncognitive scales from the ISS. Compared with cognitively intact patients, cognitively impaired patients required more personal assistance, as rated on the ESS; were significantly more dependent in their ADLs on the BI; and in the homemaking evaluation displayed significantly greater difficulty following recipes and demonstrating proper utensil use. Of note, the finding regarding utensil use was not statistically significant when differences between the groups in upper extremity incoordination were covaried out of the analysis.

In a study examining 31 cognitively and functionally impaired patients with MS, Higginson and colleagues (2000) used standard clinical neuropsychological tests of memory and attention in addition to two batteries of memory and attentional tests designed to be more ecologically valid, to predict ADLs in MS. The standard clinical tests included the California Verbal Learning Test (CVLT; Delis, Kramer, Kaplan, & Ober, 1987), 7/24 Spatial Recall Test (Rao, Leo, Bernardin, & Unverzagt, 1991), PASAT, and oral Symbol Digit Modalities Test (Smith, 1982); the ecologically valid batteries were the Rivermead Behavioural Memory Test (RBMT; Wilson, Cockburn, & Baddeley, 1985) and the Test of Everyday Attention (TEA; Robertson, Ward, Ridgeway, & Nimmo-Smith, 1994). The ESS (described earlier) was used to measure ADLs. The standard neuropsychological tests were quantified into one index based on the number of scores below the 16th percentile of the MS sample; a comparable strategy was conducted using the subtests from the ecologically valid batteries. These investigators found that both summary indices were significantly ($\geq .40$) correlated with the ESS. More specifically, the following standard subtests were significantly ($p < .05$) correlated with the ESS: CVLT Long-Delay Free Recall, PASAT, and Symbol Digit; on the RBMT, the Name, Belonging, and Story-Delayed subtests; and on the TEA, the Elevator Counting with Distraction, Elevator Counting with Reversal, and Time per Switch from the Visual Elevator task. In a stepwise regression analysis including the two summary indices, only the ecologically valid cognitive index significantly predicted ESS score after level of physical disability (EDSS score) was controlled for.

Grasso, Troisi, Morelli, and Paolucci (2005) examined the relationship between two measures of ADLs (the BI and the Rivermead Mobility Index [RMI]) and cognitive functioning in a group of 230 patients with primary and secondary progressive MS who had undergone a 3-day-a-week, 8-week rehabilitation treatment program. Cognitive functioning was categorized in EDSS format for functional systems (none, minimal, moderate, and severe impairment) by using the results of a neuropsychological evaluation. These investigators found that worse overall scores on the BI were significantly associated with worse cognitive performance. They also found that patients who were not severely impaired cognitively had a probability of improvement on the RMI that was almost twice as high as that of the severely impaired group. These authors speculated that cognitively impaired patients with MS may not be able to benefit from rehabilitation treatment because they may be unable to collaborate with the rehabilitative team in an effective way. One limitation of this study is that, given the broad-based nature of a measure such as the BI, it is unclear which aspects of ADLs were associated with cognitive impairments. Also, the authors did not describe the neuropsychological battery used, nor did they attempt to examine the association between ADLs and specific types of cognitive difficulties.

In a study with implications for rehabilitation, Basso and colleagues (Basso, Lowery, Ghormley, Combs, & Johnson, 2006) examined whether self-generated encoding improved memory for names, appointments, and object locations in a sample of patients with MS and moderate to severe memory problems. They found that, compared with a didactic procedure for encoding information, even patients with moderate–severe memory problems had better recall in ADLs when the information was self-generated. As these authors speculate, it may be that memory-impaired patients with MS would be able to improve their ability to remember names, appointments, and object locations—basic ADLs—if they developed strategies to encode this information themselves.

One limitation of the studies that have been conducted on cognitive dysfunction and ADLs in patients with MS is that most have used subjective reports of ADLs (but cf. Rao, Leo, Ellington, et al., 1991). As Goverover and her colleagues (2005) have noted, subjective reports may be limited in their accuracy, in that the relationship between subjective and objective indicators of ADLs is often weak. In response to this gap in the literature, Goverover et al. conducted a study that examined instrumental ADLs using subjective (Functional Assessment of Multiple Sclerosis [FAMS] and Functional Behavior Profile questionnaire completed by both patients and significant others), and objective measures (Executive Function Performance Test [EFPT]). In the EFPT patients carry out six ADLs, including hand washing, simple cooking, telephone use, medication management, and bill paying (a more complex cooking task was also included). These investigators found that self-reported measures of ADLs were not significantly correlated with EFPT scores. These results suggest caution in interpreting self-reported ADLs in MS, because they may not accurately reflect patients' ability to actually perform various ADLs. However, it is also notable that the authors failed to find significant correlations between self-reported ADLs and EFPT scores in the healthy controls, suggesting that self-report measures and the EFPT measures may be tapping into different aspects of ADL functioning. It may also be the case that the novelty of the environment in which the EFPT tasks were completed provided an additional executive challenge that the participants do not experience in their home environments (e.g., using an unfamiliar stove and utensils to prepare a casserole vs. preparing a familiar recipe at home with frequently used appliances and utensils). This additional executive demand may result in poorer performance and a discrepancy between participants' self-ratings and their performance on the objective measure.

Overall, the existing data on the association between cognitive dysfunction and performance of ADLs in patients with MS indicate that there is a consistent relationship whether ADLs are measured via actual performance or self-report, despite the fact that there may be little association between objective and subjective measures of these ADLs. The data also suggest intriguing clues regarding what might be helpful to patients in rehabilitation. Patients with mild–moderate (but not severe) cognitive impairments appear to show some benefit from rehabilitation programs, even if the outcome measure for the rehabilitation is not cognitive (i.e., mobility). That said, even patients with more severe memory impairments appear to be able to improve their memory of important everyday activities if they self-generate the information that needs to be remembered. Caution is warranted with such an extrapolation, however, because in each of these latter cases, only one study reports the finding.

Driving Ability

Several studies on the relationship between cognitive functioning and driving in MS have been published in recent years. Schultheis, Garay, and DeLuca (2001) appear to have published the first empirical study examining this issue. These investigators compared 13 patients with MS and cognitive impairments with 15 cognitively normal patients with MS and 17 healthy controls on two computerized measures of driving ability. Most of the patients with MS had a relapsing–remitting course type, though of note, a definitive course type could not be ascertained for almost 30% of the sample. Cognitive functioning was assessed with a brief battery of commonly used neuropsychological tests. Participants with MS were included in the cognitively impaired group if they scored below the 5th percentile of controls on at least two of the neuropsychological tasks. The computerized driving tasks included the Neurocognitive Driving Test (NDT) and the Useful Field of Vision (UFOV) test. The UFOV quantifies the visual field area in which drivers rapidly process visual information; it consists of three subtests involving visual information processing, divided attention, and selective attention. The UFOV generates an overall score and also categorizes participants according to risk level (low, moderate, high). The NDT is also computerized and assesses driving-related skills in an ecologically valid format. There are five sections to the NDT that are quantified into two composite scores, with one composite involving response latency and the other involving errors. Schultheis and colleagues found that cognitively impaired patients with MS performed significantly more slowly than both cognitively intact patients with MS and healthy controls on the response latency score from the NDT, and the effect size for the comparison between MS groups was very large (Hedge's g for effect size = 1.84). The groups did not differ on errors on the NDT. On the UFOV test, significantly more cognitively impaired patients with MS (29%) were classified in the high-risk group for probability of driving difficulties compared with both the cognitively intact participants with MS and the healthy controls (0% for both). The cognitively impaired group with MS also performed significantly worse than the other two groups on the central vision and processing section of the UFOV; additionally, cognitively impaired patients with MS performed significantly worse than healthy controls on the selective attention subtest of the UFOV. Thus, these investigators reported the first clear evidence that cognitive impairment in MS was associated with driving difficulties on a simulated test, especially on driving-related activities involving rapid information processing. These findings dovetail nicely with the numerous studies that have demonstrated that deficits in information processing speed are one of the most commonly observed cognitive problems in patients with MS.

Kotterba, Orth, Eren, Fangerau, and Sindern (2003) extended Schultheis and colleagues' (2001) work by comparing the performances of 31 patients with relapsing–remitting MS in a driving simulator with those of 10 healthy matched controls. The driving simulation, conducted using the computer-aided risk (CAR) simulator, involved participants driving for 60 minutes on a "highway." Various obstacles were presented to the drivers, as well as a variety of driving conditions. Concentration errors were identified, including errors of omission—disregarding the speed limit, traffic lights, or the right of way—as well as of commission—turning too far to the right or left or touching curbstones or the opposite lane. Finally, accidents were tallied. Participants were also administered the MS Functional Composite (MSFC) and the EDSS. As noted earlier, the latter is primarily a measure of ambulation that has been most commonly used to quantify disability in MS. The MSFC is a more recently developed measure of disability that measures ambulatory function, arm–hand function, and cognition. Kotterba and colleagues found that the accident rate and the number of concentration faults were significantly higher in patients with MS compared with controls. Interestingly, neither the EDSS nor the two physical components of the MSFC were correlated with either of these difficulties; however, the cognitive index from the MSFC was significantly correlated with concentration errors on the CAR. One important finding from the study that the authors noted is that most accidents occurred during the daytime and in sunny conditions. They reasoned that such situations may have been monotonous, leading to low arousal levels in the participants with MS, and thus making them differentially susceptible to accidents.

One limitation of Kotterba and colleagues' (2003) study is that differential levels of fatigue may have played a role in the poorer performance of patients with MS; however, the authors did not report on fatigue levels of the sample. Another limitation of this study is that the authors used only one test to measure cognitive dysfunction, the PASAT, which is the only measure used to assess cognition on the MSFC. Though the PASAT is conceptualized as a measure of working memory and speeded information processing, it draws upon a number of other cognitive abilities as well. Thus, it is difficult to identify the kinds of cognitive mechanisms that might underlie the driving difficulties of patients with MS in this type of study—a limitation that a future study could rectify by including a broader-based assessment of cognitive functioning that would allow for more precise quantification of the specific types of cognitive problems that were the primary contributors to driving difficulties.

Shawaryn, Schultheis, Garay, and DeLuca (2002) conducted a study similar to Kotterba's (2003) investigation in that they examined the relationship between MSFC scores and driving indices in 29 mostly relapsing–remitting patients with MS. In addition to using the NDT and UFOV measures described above, these investigators included number of self-reported motor vehicle collisions (MVCs), as well as the number of violations and crashes formally reported to the Department of Motor Vehicles (DMV) from the states in which participants lived. These investigators found that the cognition index from the MSFC was significantly inversely correlated with all three UFOV indices, in addition to the response latency index from the NDT. The hand and leg/ambulation components of the MSFC were significantly correlated with the measure of selective attention from the UFOV, and the MSFC hand index was also significantly associated with response latency on the NDT. These authors also found that the overall MSFC (but none of the subcomponents) was inversely correlated with number of reported DMV crashes. One limitation of this study is that they found that education was significantly correlated with overall UFOV score. It was unclear from their follow-up analyses whether this overall UFOV score would still have been significantly predicted by the cognitive component of the MSFC if education had been covaried out of the equation. Other limitations (acknowledged by the authors) included relatively small sample size, in addition to a limited range of physical disability in the sample.

Schultheis, Garay, Millis, and DeLuca (2002) compared 13 cognitively impaired and 14 cognitively intact patients with MS with 17 healthy controls on the numbers of formal MVCs and motor vehicle violations (MVVs) during the previous 5-year period. Most of the patients had relapsing–remitting MS. The cognitively impaired group with MS showed a significantly greater incidence of one or more MVCs compared with both other groups; the groups did not differ on the number of MVVs. The authors' findings on MVCs were especially striking in that the cognitively impaired group with MS also reported driving fewer days per week than the other groups. One potential limitation of this study is that the cognitively impaired group with MS also had significantly less education than the cognitively intact group with MS; however, the cognitively impaired group was very similar to the healthy control group in this regard, so educational differences among the groups in the study are less likely to explain the authors' findings. Another limitation with this study is that a fairly high proportion (almost 30%) of the patients' diagnoses could not be confirmed.

Marcotte and colleagues (2007) evaluated the relative influence of physical versus cognitive difficulties on driving in 17 patients with MS who had some complaints of spasticity and 14 healthy matched controls. Using spasticity as an index of physical difficulties and a battery of commonly used neuropsychological tests to measure cognitive problems, these investigators examined participants' performance on lane-tracking and car-following tasks in a driving simulator. The patients with MS performed significantly worse on both driving tasks. Additionally, the number of impairments on neuropsychological tests was most predictive of difficulty attending to multiple stimuli in the simulator, as well as slowed reaction to speed changes in the car that patients were following. The Trail Making Test Part B, Hopkins Verbal Learning Test—Revised, and Symbol Digit Modalities Test were the most predictive of deviations in lateral position while driving in the simulator. Spasticity was most predictive of difficulties making pedal movements in the simulator. The authors concluded that both cognitive impairments and spasticity could undermine patients' driving performance and that clinicians should attend to both when evaluating patients' suitability for continued driving.

These recent studies examining the ecological validity of neuropsychological tests in the context of driving are provocative. One limitation is that the sample sizes for all of the studies have been relatively small and, with the exception of Marcotte and colleagues' (2007) study, usually limited to patients with minimal physical disabilities. Most of these studies intentionally screened their samples for such patients so that the investigators could more clearly examine the influence of cognitive dysfunction uncontaminated by serious physical problems. Nonetheless, as these authors acknowledge, such an approach limits the generalizability of their findings. With that said, Marcotte and colleagues' study shows that, even in patients with physical problems, cognitive difficulties still make some independent contribution to particular driving problems. Another limitation is that two of the five existing studies used only one task (the PASAT) to measure cognitive dysfunction. Reliance on one task such as this does not allow for a thorough examination of the different cognitive factors that may be critical for an adequate driving performance that is relatively free of driving errors and MVCs. Two of the other three studies, though using more comprehensive cognitive batteries, nonetheless used approaches whereby it was not possible to discern which cognitive impairments (e.g., in memory, attention, information-processing speed, executive functioning) identified on testing were most predictive of driving difficulties.

A final limitation in these studies is that the possible mediating role of depression was not examined. In fact, depression was not reported in any of the above studies. As noted earlier, data published in recent years shows that depression is associated with cognitive dysfunction in some MS samples (e.g., Arnett, 2005; Denney et al., 2004; Landro et al., 2004). This issue has important treatment implications, because if depression results in cognitive dysfunction in some patients with MS, which in turn leads to driving problems, then treatment of depression could improve cognitive functioning and lead to improvements in driving. Of course, such a scenario is speculative, but nonetheless, not implausible. A follow-up study examining the possible role of depression in this equation thus seems warranted.

Medication Management/Adherence

Individuals with MS often have complicated medication regimens, including disease-modifying medications as well as multiple symptom-specific agents such as those for bladder dysfunction or spasticity. Four of the disease-modifying treatments (Avonex, Betaseron, Copaxone, and Rebif) are self-injectable, and dosing varies from daily to once a week. Maintaining adherence to variable medication schedules places demands on executive, attentional, memory, and to some degree, motor skills. Given that the efficacy of disease-modifying treatments has been well established (Burks, 2005; Coppola et al., 2006; Sandberg-Wollheim, 2005), as has the long-term nature of damage done by increasing lesion loads, it is critical to examine any factors that negatively impact treatment adherence. This issue is particularly important when one considers that disease-modifying treatments such as Interferon beta-1a and 1b not only prevent deterioration, but may actually improve cognitive functioning in patients with MS (Barak & Achiron, 2002; Fischer et al., 2000; Pliskin et al., 1996). Investigators have examined psychological factors that contribute to treatment adherence, such as self-efficacy, hope, and perception of physician support (Fraser, Hadjimichael, & Vollmer, 2001; Fraser, Morgante, Hadjimichael, & Vollmer, 2004); perception of medical staff empathy (Mohr, Goodkin et al., 1999); therapeutic expectations (Mohr et al., 1996); and depression (Mohr, Goodkin, Likosky, Gatto, et al., 1997). However, to our knowledge, there are no published reports of empirical studies of the relationship between cognitive functioning and medication adherence in MS.

Examination of other literatures reveals a similar dearth of empirical research. However, some recent work has examined this question in medical populations such as hyperlipidemia, hypertension, and HIV/AIDS. Stilley, Sereika, Muldoon, Ryan, and Dunbar-Jacob (2004) found, in a sample of 158 adults with hyperlipidemia, that higher IQ, mental flexibility, and visuospatial–constructional ability predicted better adherence to a cholesterol-lowering drug. It is worth noting that overall, this sample was not cognitively impaired. In a study of adherence in 48 adults with hypertension, Morrell, Park, Kidder, and Martin (1997) found that working memory was not a significant predictor of total antihypertensive adherence errors in regression analyses, but was correlated with treatment nonadherence for other (nonantihypertensive) medications. In a study of medication adherence in 57 adults who were HIV-positive Albert and colleagues (1999) found that cognitive functioning significantly predicted performance on a test of medication management. More specifically, the researchers reported that poorer performance on an executive functioning measure and a test of fine motor speed and coordination was associated with poorer performance in a test of pill dispensing. Poorer scores on a test of memory predicted poorer performance on a "medication inference" component of the medication management test that involved figuring out whether a mock dose had been missed and predicting how long a prescription would last.

Although these studies may offer clues as to the relationship between cognitive functioning and medication adherence in MS, it is important to note that patients with hypertension, hypercholesterolemia, or HIV face different challenges and experiences than patients with MS. It will be important for future research to address which elements, if any, of cognitive functioning are related to medication adherence and to address possible methods of remediation of deficits that are associated with nonadherence. Adapting a paradigm such as that used by Albert and colleagues (1999) might provide a good starting point in this regard.

Vocational Status

Unemployment rates in MS populations have been reported as high as 80% (Scheinberg et al., 1980), with some research showing that 70–80% of patients with MS are unemployed within 5 years following diagnosis (Kornblith, LaRocca, & Baum, 1986). Because MS affects many individuals in the early stages of their careers, work disability due to MS may affect attainment of life goals, worsen financial difficulties, and exacerbate caregiver stress. In addition to its obvious financial importance, employment has also been found to be related to quality-of-life ratings in MS (Koch, Rumrill, Roessler, & Fitzgerald, 2001). Considering the immense importance of mitigating disability due to MS, clinicians should be aware of factors that reliably predict change in employment status in order to assist patients with treatment planning and better focus rehabilitation efforts.

Several studies have examined factors associated with work status change in MS. Greater physical disability (Beatty, Blanco, Wilbanks, Paul, & Hames, 1995; Edgley, Sullivan, & Dehoux, 1991; Kornblith et al., 1986; LaRocca, Kalb, Scheinberg, & Kendall, 1985; Smith & Arnett, 2005), increased age (Beatty et al., 1995; Edgley et al., 1991; Kornblith et al., 1986), and less education (Edgley et al., 1991; Kornblith et al., 1986; LaRocca et al., 1985) have been found to be related consistently to unemployment in MS. Factors that have less consistent support include gender (males more likely to be employed) (LaRocca et al., 1985) and longer diagnosis duration (Bauer & Firnhaber, 1965; Beatty et al., 1995). Depression has been found to be related consistently to unemployment in general population samples (Dooley, Catalano, & Wilson, 1994; Üstün, 2001) but not in MS (Beatty et al., 1995; Smith & Arnett, 2005).

Due to the cognitive challenges that many people encounter as a part of their work, one might expect cognitive impairment to be a contributing factor to unemployment in individuals with MS. Additionally, Kalechstein, Newton, and van Gorp

(2003) have reported that cognitive functioning is associated with employment status in neurological populations, though patients with MS were not included in this review.

In published empirical studies examining neuropsychological test data and their relationship to unemployment in MS (Beatty et al., 1995; Benedict et al., 2005; Smith & Arnett, 2005), results have been mixed. In the study described earlier, Rao, Leo, Ellington, and colleagues (1991) reported that, compared with cognitively intact patients, the cognitively impaired patients with MS were less likely to be employed. Beatty and colleagues (1995) examined 38 employed patients with MS and 64 patients with MS who had retired due to their illness. The authors reported that, in addition to age and physical disability, memory (as measured by the verbal Selective Reminding Test [SRT] and the Brown–Peterson Test of Short-Term Memory) and verbal fluency (as measured by the Controlled Oral Word Association Test [COWAT]) significantly predicted employment status in a regression model. The employed participants also performed significantly better on neuropsychological measures than those who were no longer employed. Benedict and colleagues (2005), in a study utilizing a clinic sample of 120 patients with MS, found that performance on three cognitive tests (the Judgment of Line Orientation test, Symbol Digit Modalities Test, and the perseverations index on the WCST) significantly predicted employment status (employed vs. unemployed due to MS) in a regression model that included disease duration and a measure of conscientiousness.

We reported findings that were inconsistent with these results (Smith & Arnett, 2005). In a community-based sample of 50 individuals with MS, we controlled for the effect of participants' education levels, depression levels, medication effects, and age on their test performance. After doing this in a multivariate analysis, we found that participants who cut back on their hours due to MS, participants who left their jobs due to MS, and participants who remained employed full time were not significantly different on a variety of cognitive measures commonly found to detect impairment in MS (the PASAT, the oral Symbol Digit, the SRT, the Tower of Hanoi, the COWAT, and the 7/24 Spatial Recall Task). Additionally, when asked what MS symptoms precipitated their employment status change, only a relatively small percentage (10% of the group that cut back on hours, and 29% of the group that left jobs) of participants reported that cognitive symptoms were responsible. This finding is consistent with the results of Edgley and colleagues (1991), who found that only 12% of their unemployed sample reported cognitive symptoms (when asked in an open-ended format) as a primary reason for having discontinued employment. It may be that, although cognitive impairment is common in patients with MS who have had to stop working, it is not the deciding factor for patients who are considering leaving their jobs. This hypothesis is supported by the finding that the majority (86%) of the unemployed patients with MS in our (Smith & Arnett, 2005) sample reported that they left their jobs due to physical or neurological symptoms. It may be that, although patients with MS experience difficulties at work due to their cognitive symptoms, physical symptoms pose the greatest challenge and result in the most disability.

There are many areas for future research to explore in this area. The extent of the impact of cognitive impairment on employment in MS is still unclear, though most studies support a relationship. Additionally, to our knowledge no published empirical studies have examined which cognitive domains may be most influential in affecting employment in individuals with MS. Further investigations into these questions will improve our understanding of the impact of cognitive symptoms in MS and may help cognitively impaired individuals with MS decide between struggling to maintain employment or facing early retirement on disability.

Social Functioning and Quality of Life

Quality of life (QOL) is a somewhat vague concept that often includes a person's life satisfaction, happiness, and standard of living. Within the health sciences, health-related quality of life (HRQOL) is frequently the focus of investigation. The concept of HRQOL specifically refers to the amount a person or group is affected by physical or mental health problems. HRQOL is distinct from QOL, which is decidedly "more difficult to conceptualize and operationalize because it is affected by economic, political, cultural, and spiritual factors that are not the primary focus for health-care providers" (Shawaryn, Schiaffino, LaRocca, & Johnston, 2002, p. 310). "Social functioning" represents another difficult-to-define concept, closely related to QOL. In the current review, we explore the literature regarding the relationship between cognitive dysfunction, social functioning, and HRQOL in MS.

In an exploration of the relationship between cognitive functioning, fatigue, depression, and dyadic adjustment in MS, King and Arnett (2005) found that neither patient nor significant-other ratings of dyadic adjustment were significantly correlated with performance on measures of speeded attention/working memory or long-term memory. However, they reported that executive dysfunction was a significant predictor of significant-other-rated dyadic adjustment, indicating that the significant others of patients experiencing greater executive dysfunction rated the quality of their relationships more negatively. It is important to note that in this investigation, cognitive dysfunction was found to be a weaker predictor of poor dyadic adjustment than fatigue or depression.

Overall, individuals with MS experience poorer QOL when compared with neurologically healthy individuals (Benedict et al., 2005; Shawaryn, Schiaffino, et al., 2002) and individuals with other chronic illnesses (Rudick, Miller, Clough, Gragg, & Farmer, 1992). However, QOL has often been neglected as an outcome measure for treatment of MS (Janardhan & Bakshi, 2000) in favor of physical disability as measured by the EDSS. More recently, investigators have attended to QOL measures as a better reflection of the true impact of MS on an individual's life and, more specifically, research has examined the effect of cognitive dysfunction on HRQOL.

Benedict and colleagues (2005) found that performance on the Brief Visual Memory Test—Revised (BVMT-R) Recognition index was a significant predictor of QOL as measured by the MSQOL-54P, an expansion of the Short Form Health Survey 36 (SF-36) questionnaire, though performance on a variety of other measures sensitive to deficits typically seen in MS (the COWAT, the Judgment of Line Orientation test, the CVLT-II, the Symbol Digit Modalities Test, the PASAT, and the WCST) was not significant. Additionally, the BVMT-R Recognition index was no longer a significant predictor when noncognitive variables were entered into the regression model. In contrast, Shawaryn, Schiaffino, and colleagues (2002) reported that performance on the PASAT was a significant predictor of HRQOL as measured by the SF-36 Mental Component Summary, a measure of mental and emotional aspects of

HRQOL. However, despite the authors' assertion that depression has not been found to be related to measures of cognitive functioning, our earlier review on this topic illustrates that many studies have now demonstrated that depression is significantly associated with worse performance on measures of complex information processing, such as the PASAT. These data suggest that Shawaryn and colleagues' results should be interpreted with caution, as depression may be partially driving the effect in the relationship they reported between HRQOL and the PASAT. The researchers also found that verbal memory (as measured by the CVLT) was a significant predictor of "physical aspects" of HRQOL, along with EDSS scores. In a similar study including a sample of 52 patients with MS, Barker-Collo (2006) found that a composite score of information-processing speed measures (PASAT, Stroop, COWAT, and the Computerized Test of Information Processing) was not a significant predictor of scores on the SF-36. However, the author reports that the effect size indicates that information-processing speed does influence QOL ratings. Unfortunately, Barker-Collo did not consider the possibility of depression influencing this relationship. In other words, if the patients who are experiencing more depression are also experiencing more information-processing dysfunction, then it may be that depression is a moderator in this relationship, as depression has, not surprisingly, been found to be significantly negatively correlated with HRQOL (Amato et al., 2001; Spain, Turbridy, Kilpatrick, Adams, & Holmes, 2007).

Cutajar and colleagues (2000) found that performance on the Rivermead Behavioral Memory Test was significantly negatively correlated with the emotional subscale of the SF-36 in 40 patients with MS. The authors also report that performance on the Luria Frontal Lobe Syndrome Test (LFST) was significantly negatively correlated with scores for physical functioning and life satisfaction on the SF-36. However, LFST performance was also positively correlated with depression, which was not controlled for in the analyses. In another study using the SF-36, Spain and colleagues (2007) found that performance on the Symbol Digit Modalities Test did not predict overall physical and mental health subscale scores in a regression model when other disease variables (e.g., EDSS, depression, fatigue, pain) were entered.

Ryan and colleagues (2007) examined predictors of psychological distress, global life satisfaction, and HRQOL in a sample of 74 individuals with MS. They found that cognitive functioning (as measured by a composite score based on performance on the SDMT, the Brief Test of Attention, Judgment of Line Orientation—Short Form, WAIS-III Letter–Number Sequencing, a Stroop test, the COWAT, the CVLT-II, and the WCST) was a significant predictor of life satisfaction and HRQOL (i.e., more cognitive impairment was related to poorer life satisfaction and HRQOL), though the effect size was small. The authors report that psychological distress and cognition were not significantly related in their sample and note that this is in contrast to previous findings suggesting that patients with MS with higher levels of depression tend to perform more poorly on neuropsychological measures. However, rather than using a measure assessing depression symptoms such as the BDI, they examined the relationship between cognition and psychological distress in general, which may explain the discrepancy in their findings.

In a large sample of MS patients, Benito-Leon, Morales, and Rivera-Navarro (2002) examined the relationship between cognitive dysfunction and HRQOL using the FAMS QOL questionnaire. This 52-item measure has six subscales that measure mobility, symptoms, emotional well-being, general contentment, thinking/fatigue, and family/social well-being. Cognition was measured by the Mini-Mental State Examination (MMSE) and the clock-drawing test. The researchers reported that both cognitive tests were significantly negatively correlated with all six subtests of the FAMS, indicating that low HRQOL was associated with higher levels of cognitive impairment. The authors also found that physical disability, as measured by the EDSS, and depression and anxiety, as measured by the Hamilton Depression Rating Scale and the Hamilton Anxiety Rating Scale, were significantly correlated to the FAMS, with increased physical disability, depression, and anxiety associated with decreased HRQOL. A positive aspect of this study is that as a cognitive screening tool, performance on the clock-drawing test is typically not affected by an individual's level of depression (Herrmann, Kidron, & Shulman, 1998; Wolf-Klein, Silverstone, & Levy, 1989), and it may be therefore concluded that the association between performance on this test and HRQOL was not likely due to depression.

In a sample of 30 extremely impaired patients with MS, Kenealy and colleagues (2000) found that patients with intact autobiographical memory, as measured by the Autobiographical Memory Interview, reported the highest levels of depression, as measured by the Hospital Anxiety and Depression Scale, and the lowest levels of HRQOL, as measured by the SF-36. Surprisingly, the patients with impaired autobiographical memory (60% of the sample) reported higher levels of HRQOL than their intact counterparts. The authors interpreted these findings to suggest that severe cognitive impairment may affect the ability to accurately judge one's own HRQOL. This study suggests that cognitive impairment may not only negatively affect QOL, but also, in cases of severe impairment, might affect the ability of patients with MS to make accurate self-ratings.

The results of the research summarized above are difficult to interpret, given that most studies did not employ consistent measures of cognitive functioning. Additionally, a number of researchers did not control for the possibly confounding effects of comorbid depression on the relationship between cognitive dysfunction and HRQOL. However, it is clear that cognitive dysfunction has some negative impact on HRQOL, though the magnitude of this relationship, the role of depression, and the specific cognitive domains involved remain unclear.

Sexual Dysfunction

Sexuality is influenced by a complex interplay of psychological and physiological factors. Recent functional imaging research has indicated that sexual arousal and response are linked to activity in many areas of the brain, including the cerebellum, limbic system, and multiple other cortical and subcortical regions (Rees, Fowler, & Maas, 2007). In general, people with MS experience lower levels of sexual activity, sexual relationship satisfaction, and sexual satisfaction (McCabe, McKern, McDonald, & Vowels, 2003). Disruption of sexual functioning in MS may be influenced by a variety of symptoms such as impaired mobility, depression, spasticity, impaired sensation, and bowel and bladder functioning. Demirkiran and colleagues (2006) assert that spinal cord lesions are considered to be the major cause of sexual dysfunction in MS; however, Zivadinov and colleagues (2003) found that in a magnetic resonance imaging (MRI) study of 31 patients with MS, sexual dysfunction was predicted only by T1 lesion load of the pons. Not surprisingly, rates of sexual dysfunction are high in MS populations and have been reported at 50–90% (Dupont, 1995). Iatrogenic sexual dysfunction is also seen in MS, typically associated with antidepressants and antispastic agents (Dupont, 1995). In McCabe and colleagues' (2003) sample of 120 men with MS, the top three sexual problems reported were erectile problems (37.3%), lack of sensation (35.9%), and lack of sexual interest (31.7%), all of which were significantly higher than the rates reported by their sample of 79 neurologically healthy men. In the same investigation, the 201 female participants with MS reported the top three sexual problems was anorgasmia (45.1%), lack of sexual interest (42.9%), and lack of sensation (36.2%). Out of these problems, only lack of sensation occurred at a statistically significantly higher rate in the women with MS compared to the 160 neurologically healthy participants.

Because sexuality is often considered a sensitive topic, it has been historically underresearched. This problem is compounded by the fact that the sexuality of women with MS (who are disproportionately affected) and people with disabilities has typically been neglected (Dupont, 1995; Schmidt, Hofmann, Niederwieser, Hapfhammer, & Bonelli, 2005). More recently, however, investigators have begun to explore this issue in MS.

Despite Rao, Leo, Ellington, and colleagues' (1991) finding that cognitively impaired patients with MS reported more sexual dysfunction relative to healthy controls, to our knowledge, there are few empirical studies of the relationship between objective cognitive measures and sexual dysfunction in MS and little research in this area in neurological populations in general. Demirkiran and colleagues (2006) found that, out of a clinic-based sample of 67 patients with MS, 41 reported sexual dysfunction. Although the groups did not differ on MMSE scores, the patients with sexual dysfunction were more likely to report memory and concentration problems. This self-report of cognitive problems was significantly correlated with decreased libido, impaired genital sensation, and decreased lubrication or difficulties with erection. However, it is difficult to interpret whether these groups were truly different in terms of memory and concentration functioning. Given that the MMSE is a screening measure and not sensitive to the cognitive deficits typically seen in MS, the finding that the groups were not different on this measure does not indicate that there are no cognitive differences to be found. However, self-report of cognitive dysfunction has been demonstrated to be associated with depression (Bruce & Arnett, 2004; Carone, Benedict, Munschauer, Fishman, & Weinstock-Guttman, 2005; Maor, Olmer, & Mozes, 2001; Randolph, Arnett, & Freske, 2003), a common correlate of sexual dysfunction. This finding indicates that the correlation between sexual dysfunction and self-reported cognitive impairment may be due, at least in part, to level of depression. Such an inference is supported by findings that depression in MS is associated with negative cognitive biases (Bruce & Arnett, 2005), something that might result in both differentially high self-reports of both sexual dysfunction and cognitive difficulties.

Zivadinov and colleagues (2003) found that sexual dysfunction had a significant, large, negative correlation with performance on the MMSE in a sample of 31 patients with relapsing–remitting MS. However, in this investigation, the patients with sexual dysfunction were also significantly older, more depressed and anxious, and had longer disease durations than the patients who did not report sexual dysfunction, and these factors were not controlled for in the analyses.

In the traumatic brain injury (TBI) literature, Crowe and Ponsford (1999) reported that, in a sample of 14 men with TBI who reported sexual dysfunction subsequent to their injury and 14 age- and education-matched healthy controls, the TBI group scored lower on the Sexual Imagery subscale of the Imaginary Processes Inventory, after controlling for differences in depression as measured by the BDI. The authors interpreted this result as suggesting that cognitive impairment secondary to brain injury was inhibiting sexual imagery required for arousal. If this can be assumed to be the case, it provides a hint to possible relationships between complex cognition and sexual functioning.

As noted previously, many questions remain as to the relationship between cognitive dysfunction in MS and sexual dysfunction. Although an investigation of this relationship would certainly be complicated by the myriad psychosocial and physiological factors that also contribute to sexual functioning, the studies noted above suggest that this may be a fruitful avenue of exploration.

Summary and Conclusions

Research over the past 15–20 years has produced evidence to support the ecological validity of neuropsychological measures commonly employed to measure cognitive dysfunction in individuals with MS. These measures have been shown to predict driving difficulties, impairments in ADLs, reduced HRQOL, and work/vocational difficulties. The literature on sexual dysfunction is sparse and inconclusive at this point, and there are as yet no published reports on the relationship between cognitive functioning and medication adherence in MS. Overall, however, the weight of existing research suggests that the tests most often used in assessing cognitive status in patients with MS are predictive of important real-world behaviors. As research moves toward a greater understanding of the pattern and prevalence of cognitive impairments seen in MS, it is important for our field to understand how these impairments affect patients in their daily lives. Future work is needed to replicate some findings, fill in some of the gaps outlined above, and define more precisely the kinds of dysfunctional cognitive operations that are problematic for specific daily tasks and activities. Such latter work should aid rehabilitation efforts that could be oriented toward circumventing the specific impaired cognitive functions necessary to perform everyday tasks, and developing alternative strategies that allow patients with MS to function more effectively as they attempt to cope with what can be a devastating disease. Additionally, more work examining the possible role that treatable factors such as depression may play in the relationship between cognitive dysfunction and everyday activities is likely to be fruitful.

Author Note

This chapter represents an equal contribution by both authors.

References

Ackerman, K. D., Rabin, B., Heyman, R., Anderson, B. P., Houch, P. R., & Frank, E. (2000). Stressful life events preceded multiple sclerosis disease exacerbations. *Psychosom Med*, *62*, 147.

Aikens, J. E., Fischer, J. S., Namey, M., & Rudick, R. A. (1997). A replicated prospective investigation of life stress, coping, and depressive symptoms in multiple sclerosis. *J Behav Med*, *20*(5), 433–445.

Aikens, J. E., Reinecke, M. A., Pliskin, N. H., Fischer, J. S., Wiebe, J. S., McCracken, L. M., et al. (1999). Assessing depressive symptoms in multiple sclerosis: Is it necessary to omit items from the original Beck Depression Inventory? *Behav Med*, *22*, 127–142.

Albert, S. M., Weber, C. M., Todak, G., Polanco, C., Clouse, R., McElhiney, M., et al. (1999). An observed performance test of medication management ability in HIV: Relation to neuropsychological status and medication adherence outcomes. *AIDS Behav*, *3*(2), 121–128.

Amato, M. P., Ponziani, G., Rossi, F., Liedl, C. L., Stefanile, C., & Rossi, L. (2001). Quality of life in multiple sclerosis: The impact of depression, fatigue, and disability. *Mult Scler*, *7*, 340–344.

Amato, M. P., Zipoli, V., & Portaccio, E. (2006). Multiple sclerosis-related cognitive changes: A review of cross-sectional and longitudinal studies. *J Neurol Sci*, *245*, 41–46.

American Psychiatric Association. (1994). *Diagnostic and statistical manual of mental disorders* (4th ed.). Washington, DC: Author.

Archibald, C. J., & Fisk, J. D. (2000). Information processing efficiency in patients with multiple sclerosis. *J Clin Exp Neuropsyc*, *22*, 686–701.

Arnett, P. A. (2003). Neuropsychological presentation and treatment of demyelinating disorders. In P. Halligan, U. Kischka, & J. Marshall (Eds.), *Handbook of clinical neuropsychology* (pp. 528–543). Oxford, UK: Oxford University Press.

Arnett, P. A. (2005). Longitudinal consistency of the relationship between depression symptoms and cognitive functioning in multiple sclerosis. *CNS Spectr: Int J Neuropsyc Med*, *10*, 372–382.

Arnett, P. A., Barwick, F. H., & Beeney, J. E. (2008). Depression in multiple sclerosis: Review and theoretical proposal. *J Int Neuropsyc Soc*, *14*, 691–724.

Arnett, P. A., Higginson, C. I., & Randolph, J. J. (2001). Depression in multiple sclerosis: Relationship to planning ability. *J Int Neuropsyc Soc*, *7*, 665–674.

Arnett, P. A., Higginson, C. I., Voss, W. D., Bender, W. I., Wurst, J. M., & Tippin, J. (1999). Depression in multiple sclerosis: Relationship to working memory capacity. *Neuropsychology*, *13*, 546–556.

Arnett, P. A., Higginson, C. I., Voss, W. D., & Randolph, J. J. (2002). Relationship between coping, depression, and cognitive dysfunction in multiple sclerosis. *Clin Neuropsychol*, *16*, 341–355.

Arnett, P. A., Higginson, C. I., Voss, W. D., Wright, B., Bender, W. I., Wurst, J. M., et al. (1999). Depressed mood in multiple sclerosis: Relationship to capacity-demanding memory and attentional functioning. *Neuropsychology*, *13*, 434–446.

Arnett, P. A., Hussain, M., Rao, S., Swanson, S., & Hammeke, T. (1996). Conduction aphasia in multiple sclerosis: A case report with MRI findings. *Neurology*, *47*, 576–578.

Arnett, P. A., Rao, S. M., Bernardin, L., Grafman, J., Yetkin, F. Z., & Lobeck, L. (1994). Relationship between frontal lobe lesions and Wisconsin Card Sorting Test performance in patients with multiple sclerosis. *Neurology*, *44*, 420–425.

Bakshi, R., Czarnecki, D., Shaikh, Z. A., Priore, R. L., Janardhan, V., Kaliszky, Z., et al. (2000). Brain MRI lesions and atrophy are related to depression in multiple sclerosis. *NeuroReport*, *11*(6), 1153–1158.

Barak, Y., & Achiron, A. (2002). Effect of interferon-beta-1b on cognitive functions in multiple sclerosis. *Eur Neurol, 47*(1), 11–14.

Barker-Collo, S. L. (2006). Quality of life in multiple sclerosis: Does information-processing speed have an independent effect? *Arch Clin Neuropsych, 21,* 167–174.

Basso, M. R., Lowery, N., Ghormley, C., Combs, D., & Johnson, J. (2006). Self-generated learning in people with multiple sclerosis. *J Int Neuropsyc Soc, 12,* 640–648.

Bauer, H. J., & Firnhaber, W. (1965). Prognostic criteria in multiple sclerosis. *Ann N Y Acad Sci, 122,* 542–551.

Beatty, W. W., Blanco, C. R., Wilbanks, S. L., Paul, R. H., & Hames, K. A. (1995). Demographic, clinical, and cognitive characteristics of multiple sclerosis patients who continue to work. *J Neurol Rehabil, 9,* 167–173.

Beatty, W. W., Goodkin, D. E., Monson, N., Beatty, P. A., & Hertsgaard, D. (1988). Anterograde and retrograde amnesia in patients with chronic progressive multiple sclerosis. *Arch Neurol, 45,* 611–619.

Beeney, J. E., & Arnett, P. A. (2008). Endorsement of self-report neurovegetative items of depression is associated with multiple sclerosis disease symptoms. *Journal of the International Neuropsychological Society, 14,* 1057–1062.

Benedict, R. H. B., Fischer, J. S., Archibald, C. J., Arnett, P. A., Beatty, W. W., Bobholz, J., et al. (2002). Minimal neuropsychological assessment of MS patients: A consensus approach. *Clin Neuropsychol, 16,* 381–397.

Benedict, R. H. B., Wahlig, E., Bakshi, R., Fishman, I., Munschauer, F., Zivadinov, R., et al. (2005). Predicting quality of life in multiple sclerosis: Accounting for physical disability, fatigue, cognition, mood disorder, personality, and behavior change. *J Neurol Sci, 231,* 29–34.

Benito-Leon, J., Morales, J. M., & Rivera-Navarro, J. (2002). Health-related quality of life and its relationship to cognitive and emotional functioning in multiple sclerosis patients. *Eur J Neurol, 9*(5), 497–502.

Bergendal, G., Fredrikson, S., & Almkvist, O. (2007). Selective decline in information processing in subgroups of multiple sclerosis: An 8-year longitudinal study. *Eur Neurol, 57,* 193–202.

Bertrando, P., Maffei, C., & Ghezzi, A. (1983). A study of neuropsychological alterations in multiple sclerosis. *Acta Psychiat Bel, 83,* 13–21.

Bobholz, J., & Rao, S. (2003). Cognitive dysfunction in multiple sclerosis: A review of recent developments. *Curr Opin Neurol, 16,* 283–288.

Brass, S. D., Benedict, R. H. B., Weinstock-Guttman, B., Munschauer, F., & Bakshi, R. (2006). Cognitive impairment is associated with subcortical magnetic resonance imaging grey matter T2 hypointensity in multiple sclerosis. *Mult Scler, 12,* 437–444.

Brassington, J. C., & Marsh, N. V. (1998). Neuropsychological aspects of multiple sclerosis. *Neuropsychol Rev, 8,* 43–77.

Bruce, J. M., & Arnett, P. A. (2004). Self-reported everyday memory and depression in patients with multiple sclerosis. *J Clin Exp Neuropsyc, 26,* 200–214.

Bruce, J. M., & Arnett, P. A. (2005). Depressed MS patients exhibit affective memory biases during and after a list learning task that suppresses higher-order encoding strategies. *J Int Neuropsyc Soc, 11,* 514–521.

Bruce, J. M., Bruce, A. S., & Arnett, P. A. (2007). Mild visual acuity disturbances are associated with performance on tests of complex visual attention in MS. *J Clin Exp Neuropsyc, 13,* 544–548.

Burks, J. (2005). Interferon-beta 1b for multiple sclerosis. *Exp Rev Neurother, 5*(2), 153–164.

Carone, D. A., Benedict, R. H. B., Munschauer, F. E., Fishman, I., & Weinstock-Guttman, B. (2005). Interpreting patient/informant discrepancies of reported cognitive symptoms in MS. *J Int Neuropsyc Soc, 11,* 574–583.

Compston, A., McDonald, I. R., Noseworthy, J., Lassmann, H., Miller, D. H., Smith, K. J., et al. (2005). *McAlpine's multiple sclerosis* (4th ed.). London: Churchill Livingstone.

Coppola, G., Lanzillo, R., Florio, C., Orefice, G., Vivo, P., Ascione, S., et al. (2006). Long-term clinical experience with weekly interferon beta-1a in relapsing multiple sclerosis. *Eur J Neurol, 13*(9), 1014–1021.

Crowe, S. F., & Ponsford, J. (1999). The role of imagery in sexual arousal disturbances in the male traumatically brain injured individual. *Brain Injury, 13*(5), 347–354.

Cutajar, R., Ferriani, E., Scandellari, C., Sabattini, L., Trocino, C., Marchello, L. P., et al. (2000). Cognitive function and quality of life in multiple sclerosis patients. *J NeuroVirol, 6*(Suppl. 2), S186–S190.

D'Alisa, S., Miscio, G., Baudo, S., Simone, A., Tesio, L., & Maurio, A. (2006). Depression is the main determinant of quality of life in multiple sclerosis: A classification-regression (CART) study. *Disabil Rehabil, 28*(5), 307–314.

Dalos, N. P., Rabins, P. V., Brooks, B. R., & O'Donnell, P. (1983). Disease activity and emotional state in multiple sclerosis. *Ann Neurol, 13*, 573–577.

Dalton, J. E., & Heinrichs, R. W. (2005). Depression in multiple sclerosis: A quantitative review of the evidence. *Neuropsychology, 19*, 152–158.

Davidson, R. J. (1992). Anterior brain asymmetry and the nature of emotion. *Brain Cognition, 20*, 125–151.

Delis, D. C., Kramer, J. H., Kaplan, E., & Ober, B. A. (1987). *The California Verbal Learning Test* (research ed.). New York: Psychological Corporation.

DeLuca, J., Chelune, G., Tulsky, D., Lengenfelder, J., & Chiaravalotti, N. D. (2004). Is speed of processing or working memory the primary information processing speed deficit in multiple sclerosis? *J Clin Exp Neuropsyc, 26*, 550–562.

Demirkiran, M., Sarica, Y., Uguz, S., Yerdelen, D., & Aslan, K. (2006). Multiple sclerosis patients with and without sexual dysfunction: Are there any differences? *Mult Scler, 12*, 209–214.

Denney, D. R., Lynch, S. G., Parmenter, B. A., & Horne, N. (2004). Cognitive impairment in relapsing and primary progressive multiple sclerosis: Mostly a matter of speed. *J Int Neuropsyc Soc, 10*, 948–956.

D'Esposito, M., Onishi, K., Thompson, H., Robinson, K., Armstrong, C., & Grossman, M. (1996). Working memory impairments in multiple sclerosis: Evidence from a dual-task paradigm. *Neuropsychology, 10*, 51–56.

Dooley, D., Catalano, R., & Wilson, G. (1994). Depression and unemployment: Panel findings from the Epidemiological Catchment Area study. *Am J Commun Psychol, 22*(6), 745–765.

Dupont, S. (1995). Multiple sclerosis and sexual functioning: A review. *Clin Rehabil, 9*, 135–141.

Edgley, K., Sullivan, M. J. L., & Dehoux, E. (1991). A survey of multiple sclerosis: Part 2. Determinants of employment status. *Can J Rehabil, 4*, 127–132.

Feinstein, A. (2004). The neuropsychiatry of multiple sclerosis. *Can J Psychiat, 49*, 157–163.

Feinstein, A., O'Conner, P., & Feinstein, K. (2002). Multiple sclerosis, interferon beta 1b, and depression. *J Neurol, 24*(9), 815–820.

Feinstein, A., Roy, P., Lobaugh, N., Feinstein, K., O'Connor, P., & Black, S. (2004). Structural brain abnormalities in multiple sclerosis patients with major depression. *Neurology, 62*, 586–590.

Feuillet, L., Reuter, F., Audoin, B., Malikova, I., Barrau, K., Cherif, A. A., et al. (2007). Early cognitive impairment in patients with clinically isolated syndrome suggestive of multiple sclerosis. *Mult Scler, 13*, 124–127.

Fischer, J. S. (1988). Using the Wechsler Memory Scale—Revised to detect and characterize memory deficits in multiple sclerosis. *Clin Neuropsychol, 2*, 149–172.

Fischer, J. S., Foley, F. W., Aikens, J. E., Ericson, D. G., Rao, S. M., & Shindell, S. (1994). What do we *really* know about cognitive dysfunction, affective disorders, and stress in multiple sclerosis?: A practitioner's guide. *J Neurol Rehabil*, *8*(3), 151–164.

Fischer, J. S., Priore, R. L., Jacobs, L. D., Cookfair, D. L., Rudick, R. A., Herndon, R. M., et al. (2000). Neuropsychological effects of interferon beta-1a in relapsing multiple sclerosis. *Ann Neurol*, *48*, 885–892.

Foong, J., Rozewicz, L., Davie, C. A., Thompson, A. J., Miller, D. H., & Ron, M. A. (1999). Correlates of executive function in multiple sclerosis: The use of magnetic resonance spectroscopy as an index of focal pathology. *J Neuropsych Clin N*, *11*, 45–50.

Foong, J., Rozewicz, L., Quaghebeur, G., Thompson, A. J., Miller, D. H., & Ron, M. A. (1998). Neuropsychological deficits in multiple sclerosis after acute relapse. *J Neurol Neurosur Ps*, *64*, 529–532.

Franklin, G. M., Nelson, L. M., Heaton, R. K., Burkes, J. S., & Thompson, D. S. (1988). Stress and its relationship to acute exacerbations of multiple sclerosis. *J Neurol Rehabil*, *2*, 7–11.

Fraser, C., Hadjimichael, O., & Vollmer, T. (2001). Predictors of adherence to Copaxone therapy in individuals with relapsing–remitting multiple sclerosis. *J Neurosci Nur*, *33*(5), 231–239.

Fraser, C., Morgante, L., Hadjimichael, O., & Vollmer, T. (2004). A prospective study of adherence to glatiramer acetate in individuals with multiple sclerosis. *J Neurosci Nur*, *36*(3), 120–129.

Goldman Consensus Group. (2005). The Goldman Consensus statement on depression in multiple sclerosis. *Mult Scler*, *11*, 328–337.

Good, K., Clark, C. M., Oger, J., Paty, D., & Klonoff, H. (1992). Cognitive impairment and depression in mild multiple sclerosis. *J Nerv Ment Dis*, *180*(11), 730–732.

Gottberg, K., Einarsson, U., Fredrikson, S., von Koch, L., & Holmqvist, L. W. (2007). A population-based study of depressive symptoms in multiple sclerosis in Stockholm County: Association with functioning and sense of coherence. *J Neurol, Neurosur Ps*, *78*, 60–65.

Goverover, Y., Kalmar, J., Gaudino-Goering, E., Shawaryn, M. A., Moore, N. B., Halper, J., et al. (2005). The relation between subjective and objective measures of everyday life activities in persons with multiple sclerosis. *Arch Phys Rehab Med*, *86*, 2303–2308.

Grasso, M. G., Troisi, E., Morelli, D., & Paolucci, S. (2005). Prognostic factors in multidisciplinary rehabilitation treatment in multiple sclerosis: An outcome study. *Mult Scler*, *11*, 719–724.

Grigsby, J., Ayarbe, S. D., Kravcisin, N., & Busenbark, D. (1994). Working memory impairment among persons with chronic progressive multiple sclerosis. *J Neurol*, *241*, 125–131.

Grigsby, J., Busenbark, D., Kravcisin, N., Ayarbe, S. D., & Kennedy, P. M. (1999). *Working memory impairment in relapsing–remitting multiple sclerosis*. Unpublished manuscript.

Hart, S., Fonareva, I., Merluzzi, N., & Mohr, D. C. (2005). Treatment for depression and its relationship to improvement in quality of life and psychological well-being in multiple sclerosis patients. *Qual Life Res*, *14*, 695–703.

Hartelius, L., Runmarker, B., & Andersen, O. (2000). Prevalence and characteristics of dysarthria in a multiple-sclerosis incidence cohort: Relation to neurological data. *Folia Phoniatr Log*, *52*, 160–177.

Hartelius, L., Runmarker, B., Andersen, O., & Nord, L. (2000). Temporal speech characteristics of individuals with multiple sclerosis and ataxia dysarthria: "Scanning speech" revisited. *Folia Phoniatr Logo*, *52*, 228–238.

Henry, J. D., & Beatty, W. W. (2006). Verbal fluency deficits in multiple sclerosis. *Neuropsychologia, 44*, 1166–1174.

Herrmann, N., Kidron, D., & Shulman, K. I. (1998). Clock tests in depression, Alzheimer's disease, and elderly controls. *Int J Psychiat Med: Bio Aspects of Patient Care, 28*(4), 437–447.

Higginson, C. I., Arnett, P. A., & Voss, W. D. (2000). The ecological validity of clinical tests of memory and attention in multiple sclerosis. *Arch Clin Neuropsych, 15*, 185–204.

Janardhan, V., & Bakshi, R. (2000). Quality of life and its relationship to brain lesions and atrophy on magnetic resonance images in 60 patients with multiple sclerosis. *Arch Neurol, 57*, 1485–1491.

Janardhan, V., & Bakshi, R. (2002). Quality of life in patients with multiple sclerosis: The impact of fatigue and depression. *J Neurol Sci, 205*(1), 51–58.

Janssens, A. C. J. W., van Doorn, P. A., de Boer, J. B., Kalkers, N. F., van der Merche, F. G. A., Passchier, J., et al. (2003). Anxiety and depression influence the relation between disability status and quality of life in multiple sclerosis. *Mult Scler, 9*, 397–403.

Jean, V., Paul, R. H., & Beatty, W. (1999). Psychological and neuropsychological predictors of coping patterns by patients with multiple sclerosis. *J Clin Psychol, 55*, 21–26.

Jonsson, A., Andresen, J., Storr, L., Tscherning, T., Sorensen, P. S., & Ravnborg, M. (2006). Cognitive impairment in newly diagnosed multiple sclerosis patients: A 4-year follow-up study. *J Neurol Sci, 245*, 77–85.

Kalechstein, A. D., Newton, T. F., & van Gorp, W. G. (2003). Neurocognitive functioning is associated with employment status: A quantitative review. *J Clin Exp Neuropsyc, 25*(8), 1186–1191.

Kenealy, P. M., Beaumont, G. J., Lintern, T., & Murrell, R. (2000). Autobiographical memory, depression and quality of life in multiple sclerosis. *J Clin Exp Neuropsyc, 22*(1), 125–131.

King, K. E., & Arnett, P. A. (2005). Predictors of dyadic adjustment in multiple sclerosis. *Mult Scler, 11*, 700–707.

Klein, R. M., & Bell, B. (1982). Self-care skills: Behavioral management with Klein–Bell ADL scale. *Arch Phys Med Rehab, 63*, 335–338.

Koch, L. C., Rumrill, P. D., Roessler, R. T., & Fitzgerald, S. (2001). Illness and demographic correlates of quality of life among people with multiple sclerosis. *Rehabil Psychol, 46*(2), 154–164.

Kornblith, A. B., LaRocca, N. G., & Baum, H. M. (1986). Employment in individuals with multiple sclerosis. *Int J Rehabil Res, 9*, 155–165.

Kotterba, S., Orth, M., Eren, E., Fangerau, T., & Sindern, E. (2003). Assessment of driving performance in patients with relapsing–remitting multiple sclerosis by a driving simulator. *Eur Neurol, 50*, 160–164.

Krupp, L. B., Sliwinski, M., Masur, D. M., Friedberg, F., & Coyle, P. K. (1994). Cognitive functioning and depression in patients with chronic fatigue syndrome. *Arch Neurol, 51*, 705–710.

Kujala, P., Portin, R., & Ruutiainen, J. (1997). The progress of cognitive decline in multiple sclerosis: A controlled 3-year follow-up. *Brain, 120*, 289–297.

Kurtzke, J. F. (1981). A proposal for a uniform minimal record of disability in multiple sclerosis. *Acta Neurol Scand, 64*, 110–129.

Kurtzke, J. F. (1983). Rating neurologic impairment in multiple sclerosis: An Expanded Disability Status Scale (EDSS). *Neurology, 33*, 1444–1452.

Landro, N. I., Celius, E. G., & Sletvold, H. (2004). Depressive symptoms account for deficient information processing speed but not for impaired working memory in early phase multiple sclerosis (MS). *J Neurol Sci, 217*, 211–216.

LaRocca, N., Kalb, R., Scheinberg, L., & Kendall, P. (1985). Factors associated with unemployment of patients with multiple sclerosis. *J Chron Disabil, 38*(2), 203–210.

Lublin, F. D., & Reingold, S. C. (1996). Defining the clinical course of multiple sclerosis: Results of an international survey. *Neurology, 46*, 907–911.

Mahler, M. E. (1992). Behavioral manifestations associated with multiple sclerosis. *Psychiat Clin N Am, 15*, 427–438.

Mahoney, F. I., & Barthel, D. W. (1965). Functional evaluation: Barthel Index. *Maryland State Med J, 14*, 61–65.

Maor, Y., Olmer, L., & Mozes, B. (2001). The relation between objective and subjective impairment in cognitive function among multiple sclerosis patients: The role of depression. *Mult Scler, 7*, 131–135.

Marcotte, T., Rosenthal, T. J., Robers, E., Lampinen, S., Scott, J., Allen, R., et al. (2007, February 9). *Driving performance in multiple sclerosis.* Paper presented at the annual meeting of the International Neuropsychological Society, Portland, Oregon.

McCabe, M. P., McKern, S., & McDonald, E. (2004). Coping and psychological adjustment among people with multiple sclerosis. *J Psychosom Res, 56*, 355–361.

McCabe, M. P., McKern, S., McDonald, E., & Vowels, L. (2003). Changes over time in sexual and relationship functioning of people with multiple sclerosis. *J Sex Marital Ther, 29*(4), 305–321.

McDonald, W. I., Compston, A., Edan, G., Goodkin, D., Hartung, H.-P., Lublin, F. D., et al. (2001). Recommended diagnostic criteria for multiple sclerosis: Guidelines from the international panel on the diagnosis of multiple sclerosis. *Ann Neurol, 50*, 121–127.

McIntosh-Michaelis, S. A., Wilkinson, S. M., Diamond, I. D., McLellan, D. L., Martin, J. P., & Spackman, A. J. (1991). The prevalence of cognitive impairment in a community survey of multiple sclerosis. *Brit J Clin Psychol, 30*, 338–348.

McIvor, G. P., Riklan, M., & Reznikoff, M. (1984). Depression in multiple sclerosis as a function of length and severity of illness, age, remissions, and perceived social support. *J Clin Psychol, 40*, 1028–1033.

Mellerup, E., Fog, T., & Raun, N. (1981). The socio-economic scale. *Acta Neurol Scand, 64*, 130–138.

Minden, S. L., Frankel, D., Hadden, L., Pefloff, J., Srinath, K. P., & Hoaglin, D. C. (2006). The Sonya Slifka Longitudinal Multiple Sclerosis Study: Methods and sample characteristics. *Mult Scler, 12*, 24–38.

Minden, S. L., & Schiffer, R. B. (1990). Affective disorders in multiple sclerosis. *Arch Neurol, 47*, 98–104.

Mohr, D. C., & Goodkin, D. E. (1999). Treatment of depression in multiple sclerosis: Review and meta-analysis. *Clin Psychol: Sci Pr, 6*(1), 1–9.

Mohr, D. C., Goodkin, D. E., Bacchetti, P., Boudewyn, A. C., Huang, L., & Marrietta, P. (2000). Psychological stress and the subsequent appearance of new brain MRI lesions in MS. *Neurology, 55*, 55–61.

Mohr, D. C., Goodkin, D. E., Gatto, N., & Van Der Wende, J. (1997). Depression, coping and level of neurological impairment in multiple sclerosis. *Mult Scler, 3*, 254–258.

Mohr, D. C., Goodkin, D. E., Likosky, W., Beutler, L., Gatto, N., & Langan, M. K. (1997). Identification of Beck Depression Inventory items related to multiple sclerosis. *J Behav Med, 20*, 407–414.

Mohr, D. C., Goodkin, D. E., Likosky, W., Gatto, N., Baumann, K., & Rudick, R. A. (1997). Treatment of depression improves adherence to interferon beta-1b therapy for multiple sclerosis. *Arch Neurol, 54*, 531–533.

Mohr, D. C., Goodkin, D. E., Likosky, W., Gatto, N., Neilley, L. K., Griffin, C., et al. (1996).

Therapeutic expectations of patients with multiple sclerosis upon initiating interferon beta-1b: Relationship to adherence to treatment. *Mult Scler, 2*(5), 222–226.

Mohr, D. C., Goodkin, D. E., Masuoka, L., Dick, L. P., Russo, D., Eckhardt, J., et al. (1999). Treatment adherence and patient retention in the first year of a phase-III clinical trial for the treatment of multiple sclerosis. *Mult Scler, 5*(3), 192–197.

Mohr, D. C., Likosky, W., Dwyer, P., Van Der Wende, J., Boudewyn, A. C., & Goodkin, D. E. (1999). Course of depression during the initiation of interferon beta-1a treatment for multiple sclerosis. *Arch Neurol, 56,* 1263–1265.

Moller, A., Wiedemann, G., Rohde, U., Backmund, H., & Sonntag, A. (1994). Correlates of cognitive impairment and depressive mood disorder in multiple sclerosis. *Acta Psychiat Scand, 89,* 117–121.

Moran, P. J., & Mohr, D. C. (2005). The validity of Beck Depression Inventory and Hamilton Rating Scale for Depression items in the assessment of depression among patients with multiple sclerosis. *J Behav Med, 28,* 35–41.

Morrell, R. W., Park, D. C., Kidder, D. P., & Martin, M. (1997). Adherence to antihypertensive medications across the life span. *Gerontologist, 37*(5), 609–619.

Niemiec, A., & Lithgow, B. (2005). Alpha-band characteristics in EEG spectrum indicate reliability of frontal brain asymmetry measures in diagnosis of depression. *Conference Proceedings of the IEEE in Engineering Medicine and Biology Society, 7,* 7517–7520.

Nyenhuis, D. L., Rao, S. M., Zajecka, J., Luchetta, T., Bernardin, L., & Garron, D. (1995). Mood disturbance versus other symptoms of depression in multiple sclerosis. *J Int Neuropsyc Soc, 1,* 291–296.

Patten, S. B., & Metz, L. M. (1997). Depression in multiple sclerosis. *Psychother Psychosom, 66,* 286–292.

Patti, F., Cacopardo, M., Palmero, F., Ciancio, M. R., Lopes, R., Restivo, D., et al. (2003). Health-related quality of life and depression in an Italian sample of multiple sclerosis patients. *J Neurol Sci, 211,* 55–62.

Paty, D. W., & Ebers, G. C. (1998). *Multiple sclerosis.* Philadelphia: Davis.

Pittock, S. J., & Lucchinetti, C. F. (2007). The pathology of MS: New insights and potential clinical applications. *Neurologist, 13,* 45–56.

Pliskin, N. H., Hamer, D. P., Goldstein, D. S., Towle, V. L., Reder, A. T., Noronha, A., et al. (1996). Improved delayed visual reproduction test performance in multiple sclerosis patients receiving interferon beta-1b. *Neurology, 47*(6), 1463–1468.

Polman, C. H., Reingold, S. C., Edan, G., Filippi, M., Hartung, H. P., Kappos, L., et al. (2005). Diagnostic criteria for multiple sclerosis: 2005 revisions to the "McDonald Criteria." *Ann Neurol, 58*(6), 840–846.

Poser, C. M. (1994). The epidemiology of multiple sclerosis: A general overview. *Ann Neurol, 36*(S2), S180–S193.

Poser, C. M., Paty, D. W., Scheinberg, L., McDonald, I. W., Davis, F. A., Ebers, G. C., et al. (1983). New diagnostic criteria for multiple sclerosis: Guidelines for research protocols. *Ann Neurol, 13,* 227–231.

Pujol, J., Bello, J., Dues, J., Marti-Vilalta, J. L., & Capdevila, A. (1997). Lesions in the left arcuate fasciculus region and depressive symptoms in multiple sclerosis. *Neurology, 49,* 1105–1110.

Rabinowitz, A. R., & Arnett, P. A. (in press). A longitudinal analysis of cognitive dysfunction, coping, and depression in multiple sclerosis. *Neuropsychology.*

Randolph, J. J., Arnett, P. A., & Freske, P. (2003). Metamemory in multiple sclerosis: Exploring affective and executive contributors. *Arch Clin Neuropsych, 19,* 1–21.

Randolph, J. J., Arnett, P. A., Higginson, C. I., & Voss, W. D. (2000). Neurovegetative symptoms in multiple sclerosis: Relationship to depressed mood, fatigue, and physical disability. *Arch Clin Neuropsych, 15*(5), 387–398.

Rao, S. M., Leo, G. J., Bernardin, L., & Unverzagt, F. (1991). Cognitive dysfunction in multiple sclerosis: 1. Frequency, patterns, and prediction. *Neurology, 41*, 685–691.

Rao, S. M., Leo, G. J., Ellington, L., Nauertz, T., Bernardin, L., & Unverzagt, F. (1991). Cognitive dysfunction in multiple sclerosis: II. Impact on employment and social functioning. *Neurology, 41*, 692–696.

Rao, S. M., Leo, G. J., Haughton, V. M., St. Aubin-Faubert, P., & Bernardin, L. (1989). Correlation of magnetic resonance imaging with neuropsychological testing in multiple sclerosis. *Neurology, 39*, 161–166.

Rees, P. M., Fowler, C. J., & Maas, C. P. (2007). Sexual function in men and women with neurological disorders. *Lancet, 369*, 512–525.

Robertson, I. H., Ward, T., Ridgeway, V., & Nimmo-Smith, I. (1994). *The Test of Everyday Attention*. Suffolk, UK: Thames Valley Testing.

Rotstein, Z., Hazan, R., Barak, Y., & Achiron, A. (2006). Perspectives in multiple sclerosis health care: Special focus on the costs of multiple sclerosis. *Autoimmun Rev, 5*, 511–516.

Rudick, R. A., Miller, D. H., Clough, J. D., Gragg, L. A., & Farmer, R. G. (1992). Quality of life in multiple sclerosis: Comparison with inflammatory bowel disease and rheumatoid arthritis. *Arch Neurol, 49*, 1237–1242.

Ryan, K. A., Rapport, L. J., Sherman, T. E., Hanks, R. A., Lisak, R., & Khan, O. (2007). Predictors of subjective well-being among individuals with multiple sclerosis. *Clin Neuropsychol, 21*, 239–262.

Sadovnick, A. D., Remick, R. A., Allen, J., Swartz, E., Yee, I. M. L., Eisen, K., et al. (1996). Depression and multiple sclerosis. *Neurology, 46*, 628–632.

Sandberg-Wollheim, M. (2005). Interferon-beta 1a treatment for multiple sclerosis. *Exp Rev Neurotherap, 5*(1), 25–34.

Sanfilipo, M. P., Benedict, R. H. B., Weinstock-Guttman, B., & Bakshi, R. (2006). Gray and white matter brain atrophy and neuropsychological impairment in multiple sclerosis. *Neurology, 66*, 685–692.

Scheinberg, L., Holland, N., LaRocca, N., Laitin, P., Bennett, A., & Hall, H. (1980). Multiple sclerosis: Earning a living. *New York State J Med, 80*, 1395–1400.

Schiffer, R. B., & Caine, E. D. (1991). The interaction between depressive affective disorder and neuropsychological test performance in multiple sclerosis patients. *J Neuropsych Clin N, 3*, 28–32.

Schmidt, E. Z., Hofmann, P., Niederwieser, G., Hapfhammer, H.-P., & Bonelli, R. M. (2005). Sexuality in multiple sclerosis. *J Neural Transm, 112*, 1201–1211.

Schultheis, M. T., Garay, E., & DeLuca, J. (2001). The influence of cognitive impairment on driving performance in multiple sclerosis. *Neurology, 56*, 1089–1084.

Schultheis, M. T., Garay, E., Millis, S. R., & DeLuca, J. (2002). Motor vehicle crashes and violations among drivers with multiple sclerosis. *Arch Phys Rehab Med, 83*, 1175–1178.

Shawaryn, M. A., Schiaffino, K. M., LaRocca, N. G., & Johnston, M. V. (2002). Determinants of health-related quality of life in multiple sclerosis: The role of illness intrusiveness. *Mult Scler, 8*, 310–318.

Shawaryn, M. A., Schultheis, M. T., Garay, E., & DeLuca, J. (2002). Assessing functional status: Exploring the relationship between the multiple sclerosis functional composite and driving. *Arch Phys Rehab Med, 83*, 1123–1129.

Shnek, Z. M., Foley, F. W., LaRocca, N. G., Smith, C. R., & Halper, M. S. N. (1995). Psychological predictors of depression in multiple sclerosis. *J Neurol Rehabil, 9*(1), 15–23.

Smith, A. (1982). *Symbol Digit Modalities Test (SDMT) manual (revised)*. Los Angeles: Western Psychological Services.

Smith, M. M., & Arnett, P. A. (2005). Factors related to employment status change in individuals with multiple sclerosis. *Mult Scler, 11*, 602–609.

Smith, M. M., & Arnett, P. A. (2007). Dysarthria predicts poorer performance on cognitive tasks requiring a speeded oral response in an MS population. *J Clin and Exp Neuropsyc*, *29*, 804–812.

Spain, L. A., Turbridy, N., Kilpatrick, T. J., Adams, S. J., & Holmes, A. C. N. (2007). Illness perception and health-related quality of life in multiple sclerosis. *Acta Neurol Scand*, *116*, 293–299.

Stilley, C. S., Sereika, S., Muldoon, M. F., Ryan, C. M., & Dunbar-Jacob, J. (2004). Psychological and cognitive functioning: Predictors of adherence with cholesterol lowering treatment. *Ann Behav Med*, *27*(2), 117–124.

Tröster, A. I., & Arnett, P. A. (2006). Assessment of movement and demyelinating disorders. In P. J. Snyder, P. D. Nussbaum, & D. L. Robins (Eds.), *Clinical neuropsychology: A pocket handbook for assessment* (2nd ed., pp. 243–293). Washington, DC: American Psychological Association.

Üstün, T. B. (2001). The worldwide burden of depression in the 21st century. In M. Weissman (Ed.), *Treatment of depression: Bridging the 21st century* (pp. 35–46). Washington, DC: American Psychiatric Association.

Wang, J. L., Reimer, M. A., Metz, L. M., & Patten, S. B. (2000). Major depression and quality of life in individuals with multiple sclerosis. *Int J Psychiat Med: Bio Aspects of Patient Care*, *30*(4), 307–317.

Wilson, B. A., Cockburn, J., & Baddeley, A. (1985). *The Rivermead Behavioural Memory Test*. Reading, UK: Thames Valley Testing.

Wishart, H. A., Saykin, A. J., McDonald, B. C., Mamourian, A. C., Flashman, L. A., Schuschu, K. R., et al. (2004). Brain activation patterns associated with working memory in relapsing–remitting MS. *Neurology*, *62*, 234–238.

Wolf-Klein, G. P., Silverstone, F. A., & Levy, A. P. (1989). Screening for Alzheimer's disease by clock drawing. *J Am Geriatr Soc*, *37*(8), 730–734.

Zivadinov, R., Zorzon, M., Locatelli, L., Stival, B., Monti, F., Nasuelli, D., et al. (2003). Sexual dysfunction in multiple sclerosis: A MRI, neurophysiological and urodynamic study. *J Neurol Sci*, *210*(1–2), 73–76.

Zorzon, M., Zivadinov, R., Nasuelli, D., Ukmar, M., Bratina, A., Tommasi, M. A., et al. (2002). Depressive symptoms and MRI changes in multiple sclerosis. *Eur J Neurol*, *9*, 491–496.

CHAPTER 16

Everyday Impact of HIV-Associated Neurocognitive Disorders

J. Cobb Scott and Thomas D. Marcotte

Human immunodeficiency virus (HIV) is a retrovirus that causes acquired immuno-deficiency syndrome (AIDS), a disease in which the immune system begins to fail, leading to the appearance of life-threatening opportunistic infections. It is estimated that 38.6 million people worldwide are living with HIV, and in 2005, approximately 4.1 million people became newly infected with HIV, while an estimated 2.8 million people died of AIDS-related illnesses (Joint United Nations Programme on HIV/AIDS, 2006). In the United States the rate of infection has stabilized since 1998, with approximately 40,000 AIDS cases diagnosed annually since that time. The World Health Organization (2006) estimates that 1.2 million people are living with AIDS in the United States. Although HIV is more commonly thought of as an illness attacking the immune system, historically approximately 30–50% of individuals infected with HIV experienced some form of cognitive impairment (e.g., Heaton et al., 1995) due to the effects of the virus in the central nervous system (CNS).

Potent medications that dramatically reduce the amount of virus in the body (highly active antiretroviral therapy [HAART]) became the standard of care in 1996, and since that time the estimated survival time after HIV infection has increased substantially, as has the time between HIV infection and AIDS diagnosis, transforming HIV from an almost uniformly fatal illness into a chronic but somewhat stable condition for individuals with access to treatment (Centers for Disease Control and Prevention, 2006). However, HAART has not eliminated HIV-related neurocognitive disorders, and these impairments remain a significant clinical concern (e.g., Clifford, 2008; Sacktor et al., 2002). Recent cross-sectional data from a multisite study of 1,555 HIV-infected individuals (the CNS HIV Antiretroviral Therapy Effects Research [CHARTER] project) suggest that approximately 50% of HIV-positive individuals still have some form of neurocognitive impairment (Heaton et al., 2009).

In recent years, increasing attention has focused on the everyday, "real-world" effects of HIV-associated neurocognitive disorders (HAND; see below), given that individuals are living longer than ever with HIV, and many individuals are experiencing a "second life" with the advent of HAART therapy (Rabkin & Ferrando, 1997). These everyday outcomes are the focus of this chapter, but in order to understand these effects, background information on the neurological and systemic impact of HIV infection is helpful.

Structural and Neurobiological Aspects of HIV

Life Cycle of the Virus

HIV infection exerts pathogenic effects on both the immune system and the nervous system. HIV belongs to the family of retroviruses, which means that its replication cycle includes a step of reverse transcriptase-mediated conversion of the viral ribonucleic acid (RNA) genome into a deoxyribonucleic acid (DNA) copy. Because HIV is a retrovirus, any drug used to combat HIV infection is referred to as an "antiretroviral." There are currently four classes of antiretrovirals in general use: nucleoside analogue reverse transcriptase inhibitors (NRTIs), nonnucleoside reverse transcriptase inhibitors (NNRTIs), protease inhibitors (PIs), and fusion inhibitors. These current HIV therapies inhibit the viral replication process at various stages (described below): the binding and entry stage (fusion inhibitors), the reverse transcription stage (NRTIs and NNRTIs), or the protein cleavage stage (PIs). New classes of antiretrovirals that focus on inhibiting the virus at other stages are also becoming available, including integrase inhibitors, which aim to block the insertion of the viral DNA into the host cell's DNA, and chemokine (C-Cmotif) receptor 5 (CCR5) inhibitors.

HIV infection of a host cell occurs when an HIV particle encounters a target cell with a cluster of differentiation 4 (CD4) surface molecules. T4-lymphocyte cells (also known as "T-helper" cells, or T-cells) are generally thought to be the main target receptor for HIV due to their abundance of CD4 receptors. HIV also binds to specific chemokine receptors (i.e., CCR5 or C-X-C motif chemokine receptor 4 [CXCR4], among others) on the surface of the host cell, which pull the virus and host cell membranes together, allowing fusion to occur. The HIV RNA, proteins, and enzymes then enter into the cytoplasm of the target cell, and viral RNA is converted to DNA by a viral enzyme called "reverse transcriptase." This DNA then enters the cell nucleus, where the viral DNA is inserted into the host chromosomal DNA via another viral enzyme called "integrase." The resulting integrated DNA virus (called a "provirus") may remain latent for hours to years before becoming active through transcription, in which the cell creates new HIV via copying of DNA into RNA. Each RNA strand is processed, and a corresponding string of proteins is transformed or "translated" into various new viral proteins that are needed to make new virus. In the final step, the new virus is assembled in a complex process involving the cleaving of proteins into smaller proteins by a viral enzyme called "protease," followed by the budding of the new viral particles off the host cell, creating a new virus. Once this virus is assembled and matures, it can then infect new cells and create new virus (for more thorough reviews, see Stevenson, 2003; Trkola, 2004). Thus, the clinical course of HIV infection is associated with a progressive decline in CD4 T-cell levels and an increase in the amount of the virus in the body (i.e., viral load). When the CD4 cell count drops below a critical level, the T-cell mediated immunity begins to fail, and opportunistic infections occur. A diagnosis of AIDS is therefore determined by either a CD4 cell count dropping below $200/mm^3$ or the presence of an AIDS-defining medical condition such as an opportunistic infection.

HIV and the Central Nervous System

HIV enters the brain early after infection (Sonnerborg et al., 1988), and although it is generally not thought to productively infect neurons (Wiley, Schrier, Nelson, Lampert, & Oldstone, 1986), it promotes an inflammatory response in the CNS that is characterized by chronic activation in perivascular macrophages and microglia and related accumulation of neurotoxic cellular byproducts (e.g., Transactivator [Tat] protein and cytokines). As a result, widespread neuronal and glial pathology occurs, particularly in the basal ganglia and the frontal–striatal–thalamocortical circuits (for a more thorough review, see Langford, Everall, & Masliah, 2005). Nonetheless, the neuropathological damage due to HIV infection is evident in both subcortical (e.g., Kure et al., 1991) and neocortical (e.g., Everall, Luthert, & Lantos, 1991; Masliah et al., 1992) structures. In addition, encephalitis (a pathology-based diagnosis characterized by brain inflammation and the presence of multinucleated giant cells and microglial nodules) and neuronal apoptosis (programmed cell death) both commonly occur in HIV infection, particularly with severe dementia. Neuropsychological (NP) assessment appears to be sensitive to HIV encephalitis (Cherner et al., 2002), although the association of virological markers with antemortem NP data have not been consistent (e.g., Brew, Rosenblum, Cronin, & Price, 1995). Synaptodendritic changes, or the pathological processes of pruning and loss of dendritic complexity that affect synaptic functioning, are also evident and may be more useful neural substrates of HIV-associated damage, as these changes correlate closely with the presence and severity of cognitive impairment (Everall et al., 1999; Masliah et al., 1997).

The neurodegenerative changes associated with HIV are also reflected in neuroimaging findings. Computed tomography (CT) and magnetic resonance imaging (MRI) investigations have shown increased ventricular and sulcal spaces, reduced gray and white matter volumes, and white matter signal abnormalities, with findings generally more prominent in the basal ganglia and white matter (e.g., Jernigan et al., 1993; Levin et al., 1990; Post, Berger, & Qeuncer, 1991). White matter hyperintensities seen on MRI have been related to dendritic loss in the frontal cortex (Archibald, 1998), as well as HIV encephalitis (Miller et al., 1997). In addition, increased atrophy is seen across more advanced disease stages (Stout et al., 1998). Investigations using magnetic resonance spectroscopy (MRS), a methodology that measures concentrations of metabolites in the brain, have generally found subtle increases in concentrations of myoinositol and choline in the white matter of individuals in the early stages of HIV infection, ostensibly reflecting glial activation and an inflammatory process that could lead to HIV-associated neurotoxic effects. Decreases in N-acetyl aspartate (a neuronal marker) and additional increases in myoinositol and choline occur in more severe stages of HIV, suggesting increased glial activation and further neuronal damage with HIV progression (see Chang & Ernst, 2005, for a more thorough review).

Neurocognitive Impairment

Diagnostic Criteria

Neurocognitive disorders associated with HIV range from subtle deficits to a severe and incapacitating dementia. The diagnostic terms in common use are based on (1) the presence of neuropsychological impairment and (2) whether these impairments impact everyday activities. Historically, most studies used the diagnostic criteria proposed by either the American Academy of Neurology (AAN) AIDS Task Force (1991) or Grant and Atkinson (1995). "Asymptomatic (or subsyndromic) impairment" refers to the presence of mild cognitive deficits as determined by NP testing, but to a degree that is not severe enough to interfere with everyday functioning (Grant & Atkinson, 1995). Minor cognitive motor disorder (MCMD) or minor neurocognitive disorder (MND; Grant & Atkinson, 1995) require deficits in two or more domains of cognitive functioning and a modest degree of limitation in daily functioning. HIV-associated dementia (HAD) is the most severe form of impairment, with more marked impairment in a number of domains and moderate to severe interference with daily activities.

Given the apparent changes in HAND during the HAART era, the National Institute of Mental Health and National Institute of Neurological Diseases and Stroke tasked a work group to revisit the AAN criteria (Antinori et al., 2007). This group established a revised nosology, consistent with the Grant and Atkinson (1995) approach. The new criteria emphasize the *neurocognitive* complications of these conditions, excluding the motor, social/personality, and emotional abnormalities that were part of the AAN criteria. As with the Grant and Atkinson schema, the revised nosology now includes the mildest ("asymptomatic") form of impairment, in which individuals evidence objective cognitive impairment, but the impairment does not significantly affect everyday functioning (Grant & Atkinson, 1995). This classification is important to include because such impairments still predict mortality (Ellis et al., 1997) and brain pathology, and thus individuals with asymptomatic impairments may warrant close monitoring for potential worsening, perhaps requiring a change in treatment approaches.

The revised criteria for HAND were also more specific than previous criteria in terms of defining cognitive impairment. For each diagnosis, the cognitive impairment cannot be explained by other comorbidities, nor can it be the result of a delirium:

- *Asymptomatic neurocognitive impairment (ANI).* Performance needs to be at least 1 standard deviation (*SD*) below the mean of demographically adjusted normative scores in at least two cognitive domains (attention/information processing, language, abstraction/executive, complex perceptuomotor skills, memory [including learning and recall], simple motor skills, or sensory perceptual abilities). At least 5 cognitive domains need to be assessed.
- *Minor neurocognitive disorder (MND).* MND meets the ANI criteria above. In addition, the neurocognitive abnormality must result in at least mildly impaired everyday functioning and cannot meet criteria for dementia.
- *HIV-associated dementia (HAD).* HAD requires (1) acquired moderate to severe cognitive impairment (at least two *SD* below demographically corrected

normative means in at least two different cognitive areas [see above]), and (2) marked difficulty in everyday functioning due to the cognitive impairment.

The work group also added the qualifier of *in remission* for all three diagnoses, since there is evidence that the neurocognitive impairment may fluctuate in some individuals. The impact of the cognitive impairments is a critical feature of the diagnoses and reinforces the need for robust and standardized methods of assessing real-world functioning.

NP Functioning and Treatment

As noted earlier, in the era preceding HAART, neurobehavioral complications were found in approximately 30–50% of individuals infected with HIV, with greater proportions of cognitive impairments emerging in late disease stages (Heaton et al., 1995; McArthur & Grant, 1998; White, Heaton, & Monsch, 1995). HAART has provided substantial improvements in the systemic health of HIV-infected individuals since its advent in 1996, and there has been a dramatic increase in the time from infection to a diagnosis of AIDS, as well as survival time (Detels et al., 1998; Porter et al., 2003). In addition, evidence has been mounting that initiation of HAART may improve neurocognitive performance in HIV-infected individuals (Ferrando et al., 1998; Letendre et al., 2004; McCutchan et al., 2007; Parsons, Braaten, Hall, & Robertson, 2006; Sacktor et al., 2006; Tozzi et al., 1999), with the most consistent finding being improvement in psychomotor speed (Ferrando, Rabkin, van Gorp, Lin, & McElhiney, 2003; Suarez et al., 2001). Neuroimaging findings also appear to generally support improvement with initiation of HAART (e.g., Chang et al., 1999; Stankoff et al., 2001). There are indications, however, that this treatment benefit may not equal that seen for other AIDS conditions (Dore et al., 1999; Sacktor et al., 2002), and HAND continue to persist, albeit in a less severe form (Tozzi et al., 2001). Moreover, although the incidence of HAD has declined (Deutsch et al., 2001), the prevalence has not (McArthur, 2004; Tozzi et al., 2005), with up to 50% of HIV-positive individuals in the HAART era demonstrating some level of impairment (Heaton et al., 2009), potentially due to their increased longevity and, possibly, to the development of antiretroviral drug resistance (Cysique, Maruff, & Brew, 2004; Dore et al., 1999; Sacktor et al., 2002).

Consistent with its frontostriatal neuropathogenesis, NP deficits in HIV infection are seen in domains that are highly dependent upon these circuits, such as attention/working memory, learning, motor skills, speed of information processing, and executive functioning (Becker et al., 1995; Heaton et al., 1995; Hinkin, Hardy, et al., 2002; Peavy et al., 1994; Reger, Welsh, Razani, Martin, & Boone, 2002). Even the mildest forms of HAND can have substantial effects on the everyday life of affected individuals. Given the continued prevalence of neurocognitive disorders, there is reason to suspect that individuals may be living longer with HIV-related cognitive impairments, highlighting the importance of research into the ramifications of these impairments on daily functioning. Although the literature still leaves much to be explored, a significant amount of evidence suggests that HIV-related neurocognitive dysfunction significantly affects both laboratory and real-world measures of everyday functioning, as well as survival time, in a subset of individuals.

Everyday Impact of HIV Infection

Research to date indicates that HIV-associated functional impairments have significant implications for HIV-infected individuals, caregivers, and potentially society as a whole, including reducing the available workforce, amplifying the economic burden of government-supported health care coverage, and increasing the prevalence of drug-resistant viral strains via inadequate medication adherence (Marcotte, Heaton, & Albert, 2005; van Gorp, Baerwald, Ferrando, McElhiney, & Rabkin, 1999). In order to more thoroughly investigate these functional impairments, researchers in recent years have developed methods specifically tailored for individuals with HIV infection that more directly assess real-world functioning (e.g., Albert et al., 1999; Heaton et al., 2004; Marcotte et al., 1999), as traditional NP tests have limitations as measures of daily functioning (Heaton et al., 2004).

Instrumental Activities of Daily Living

Although a subset of individuals experiences declines in everyday abilities due to the CNS effects of HIV infection, these declines are not universal and are generally only evident in more complex everyday tasks, known as instrumental activities of daily living (IADLs). These include skills such as money management, meal preparation, medication management, and job-related skills. Declines in basic activities of daily living (BADLs), such as bathing, grooming, and dressing, are typically the result of advanced physical symptoms, and a cognitive etiology is only evident in severe HAD. Given that the neurocognitive deficits associated with HIV are more likely to be subtle, especially in the era of HAART treatment, assessing complex IADL functioning is of increasing importance.

In an attempt to objectively investigate the effects of HIV on IADL functioning, Heaton and colleagues (2004) examined 267 HIV-infected individuals on a comprehensive functional battery, including standardized instruments assessing grocery shopping, cooking, financial management, medication management, and vocational functioning. On these assessments, participants performed the required tasks with mock scenarios and items just as if they were carrying out the tasks in everyday life. For example, the cooking task required individuals to follow recipes and coordinate the timing of a meal, using mock food items and a microwave and hot plate.

Cognitively impaired HIV-positive participants performed significantly worse on all functional measures when compared to HIV-positive participants without NP impairment; this difference was particularly evident on a global measure comprised of test results from the entire functional battery (i.e., Functional Deficit Score [FDS]). The largest group differences were reported in vocational skills, followed by finances and medication management. Impairments in executive functioning, learning, verbal abilities, and attention/working memory were most predictive of performance on the functional measures. Importantly, both the NP and functional battery performances were independent predictors of real-world functional status, based on complaints of cognitive difficulties, level of dependence/independence in IADLs, and employment status (see Figure 16.1). Thus, although the NP impairment was generally in the mild or mild-to-moderate range in the cognitively impaired group, the impairment resulted in a substantially increased risk for IADL dependence. These results also suggest,

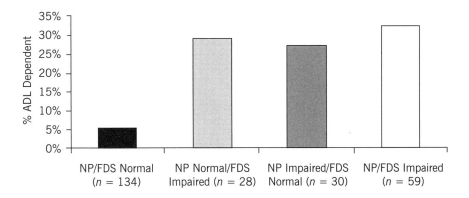

FIGURE 16.1. Rate of ADL dependence by neuropsychological and functional impairment status. From Heaton et al. (2004). Copyright 2004 by the International Neuropsychological Society. Reprinted by permission from Cambridge University Press.

however, that even though neuropsychological assessments provide valuable information regarding functioning outside of the laboratory, they may not capture all of the components that are involved in successful execution of these tasks in real life. Therefore, more direct, functional tests may complement traditional cognitive testing in accurately determining everyday outcomes.

This study also highlights the potential importance of considering affective status in assessing everyday functioning capacity. The authors found that depressed mood was an independent, significant predictor of both objective (i.e., functional battery) and subjective (i.e., cognitive complaints and IADL dependence) everyday functioning, suggesting that some individuals may have had the ability to function at higher levels, but they failed to do so because of their affective symptoms. This finding is consistent with other studies of psychiatric illness and everyday outcomes, such as medication management (see below), as well as with reports that depression results in significant reductions in quality of life (see Moore et al., Chapter 17, this volume).

Quality of Life

Increasing attention has been focused on quality of life (QOL) in the age of HAART. Advanced HIV disease stage and disease-related medical symptoms, such as opportunistic infections and constitutional symptoms, have been consistently shown to be predictive of worse QOL, especially in the pre-HAART era (e.g., Burgess, Dayer, Catalan, Hawkins, & Gazzard, 1993; Revicki, Wu, & Murray, 1995). Comorbid substance abuse and psychiatric disorders, including depression, have also been associated with significantly worse QOL outcomes in HIV-infected individuals (e.g., Liu, Johnson, et al., 2006; Sherbourne et al., 2000). In addition, HIV-associated cognitive impairment can significantly impact one's QOL, even after controlling for relevant medical factors (Kaplan et al., 1995, 1997; Parsons et al., 2006; Revicki et al., 1995; Tozzi et al., 2004; Trepanier et al., 2005). The effects of HAART use on QOL, however, have been surprisingly inconsistent. With successful long-term HAART treatment, improvement may be seen in QOL (e.g., Carrieri et al., 2003; Parsons et

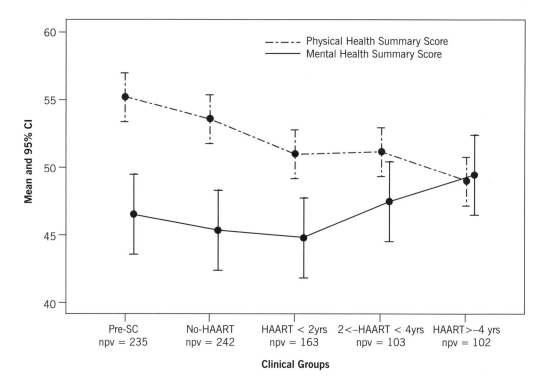

FIGURE 16.2. Physical and Mental Health Quality of Life Summary Score change by HIV and HAART group. *Pre-SC*, preseroconversion; *No-HAART*, HIV infected but no HAART use; *HAART < 2*, on HAART for less than 2 years; *2 HAART < 4*, on HAART for 2–4 years; *HAART 4*, on HAART for 4 and more years; *npv*, number of person visits for each group. From Liu, Ostrow, et al. (2006). Reprinted by permission from Springer Science & Business Media.

al., 2006), although the effect may be greater for mental health QOL than physical health QOL (Liu, Ostrow, et al., 2006; see Figure 16.2). However, a number of studies has shown that HAART regimen can also have detrimental effects on QOL due to adverse side effects and toxicity associated with the drugs (Liu, Ostrow, et al., 2006; Rabkin, Ferrando, Lin, Sewell, & McElhiney, 2000). With the continued increase in life expectancy for individuals with HIV, greater attention will likely be focused on maximizing life quality by developing more efficient and less toxic medication regimens (Wu, 2000).

Survival

In the pre-HAART era, opportunistic infections (e.g., cryptococcus, cytomegalovirus) and cancers (e.g., Kaposi's sarcoma) commonly occurred because of the gradual decline of the body's immune system due to AIDS, and these conditions often led to functional decline and ultimately death because of the body's loss of immune competence. However, HIV-associated neurocognitive impairments are also associated with an increased risk for death, independent of other disease or medical factors. Before effective HAART therapy, HIV-infected individuals who were diagnosed with dementia had an average survival time of 6 months after diagnosis (McArthur et al., 1993), although a subset of patients exhibited a survival period of a year or longer in one study (Bouwman et al., 1998). After controlling for relevant biological variables, even milder neurocognitive impairments increased an individual's risk for death (Mayeux et al., 1993; Wilkie et al., 1998). For example, Ellis and colleagues (1997) found elevated mortality risk for individuals with MCMD (relative risk [RR], 2.2; $p < .01$) and asymptomatic NP impairment (RR, 1.6; $p = .06$) when compared to NP normal participants, even after adjusting for other significant predictors of mortality. One study that examined specific NP predictors of mortality found that a sustained decline in psychomotor performance was predictive of mortality in the follow-up period (Sacktor et al., 1996).

Since the introduction of HAART in 1996, estimated survival time with HIV has significantly increased, and the presence of risk factors for mortality (e.g., elevated viral loads) has concurrently decreased. At the same time, a dramatic increase has occurred in survival time following a diagnosis of dementia, increasing from 1 to 4 years in an Australian cohort (Dore, McDonald, Li, Kaldor, & Brew, 2003). It has been suggested that the relationship between NP impairment and survival may now depend on level of virological response to HAART, as Tozzi and colleagues (2005) found a significant association between neurocognitive impairment and risk of death in participants with inadequate viral suppression, but no such relationship in those with adequate viral suppression due to successful HAART treatment.

The cause of decreased survival in cognitively impaired individuals is still unclear. One potential mechanism may be a more virulent strain of the disease in impaired individuals, although this virulence is not being captured by standard disease markers, which are normally controlled for in analyses. Alternatively, there may be particular host biological features that make some individuals more susceptible to the virus. Cognitive deficits might also affect patients' abilities to manage their disease (e.g., resulting in less effective medication adherence) or effectively use their available resources and support, as HIV treatment and maintenance are complex processes (see below).

Medication Management

It is critical that HIV-infected individuals effectively manage their antiretroviral medications. Deviations from the prescribed dosing and dietary instructions decrease the drug concentrations, lower the likelihood of viral suppression, and increase the risk for progression to AIDS (Bangsberg et al., 2001; Chesney et al., 2000). Moreover, suboptimal adherence may lead to development of a drug-resistant strain of the virus; in fact, transmission of drug-resistant HIV strains has been documented, and there is evidence of increasing rates of drug resistance among newly diagnosed patients both in Europe and the United States (Wensing et al., 2005). Adherence rates need to be at a minimum of 80% (but preferably 90%) of prescribed doses in order to avoid adverse clinical and virological outcomes (Bangsberg, 2006; Haubrich et al., 1999). Unfortunately, studies of adherence by self-report, surprise pill counts, and medication diaries have revealed surprisingly high levels of suboptimal adherence, with up to 40% of individuals failing to take medications in accordance with dosage, time, and dietary instructions (Chesney et al., 2000; Maher et al., 1999; Nieuwkerk et al.,

2001; Singh et al., 1996). Thus, adherence still remains a significant clinical concern, despite reductions in the complexity of antiretroviral dosing (including a triple-drug combination formulated in one pill to be taken once daily).

Approaches to adherence assessment include self-report questionnaires, performance tests of medication management, and electronic pill bottle caps that record when participants open the bottle to take their medications (i.e., Medication Event Monitoring System [MEMS] caps). Relatively consistent predictors of nonadherence have emerged, including adverse side effects of a drugs due to toxicity (e.g., Mocroft et al., 2005), negative health beliefs regarding treatment (e.g., Horne et al., 2004), comorbid psychiatric disorders (e.g., Starace et al., 2002), comorbid substance abuse (e.g., Hinkin et al., 2006), and younger age (e.g., Hinkin et al., 2004). In addition, neurocognitive impairments appear to be a risk factor for medication nonadherence. Overall, studies have suggested that HIV-infected individuals with impairments in memory, executive function, and psychomotor functioning may demonstrate significant difficulties with medication management.

In a series of studies Albert and colleagues (1999, 2003) examined how much of the nonadherence seen in HIV-infected individuals reflects the *inability* to adhere, and the extent to which individuals with the inability to adhere (i.e., cognitive impairment) may adjust the way in which they manage their medications. The authors used a standardized, performance-based test of medication management skill, the Medication Management Test (MMT), which assessed the ability of participants to interpret prescription label information and dispense medications from prespecified prescription medication bottles. They found that individuals with impairments in memory, psychomotor speed, and executive functions displayed performance decrements on this test, as evidenced by difficulties following label information and correctly pouring different medications. Interestingly, they also found that cognitively impaired individuals reported more "fixed" medication regimens (i.e., taking their medications on the same schedule for 3 days), suggesting that these impaired individuals had compensated, to some degree, for their cognitive deficits. Heaton and colleagues (2004) also reported significant differences on a modified version of the MMT between HIV-positive individuals with and without NP impairment, finding that impairments in learning and abstraction/executive functioning were the strongest predictors of failing the task.

In another series of studies Hinkin and colleagues (Hinkin et al., 2004, 2006; Hinkin, Castellon, et al., 2002; Levine et al., 2006) studied adherence to medication regimens as measured by bottle cap openings (MEMS caps), potentially providing a more objective estimate of adherence in everyday life. They found that HIV-positive individuals with impairments in attention, memory, executive functioning, and psychomotor speed were more likely to have lower adherence rates across all age groups. Importantly, the impact of cognitive impairment was most significant in those individuals with complex medication regimens (three or more doses per day; see Figure 16.3). Furthermore, younger HIV-positive individuals (under 50 years of age) and those currently abusing substances were less likely to be adherent, regardless of cognitive status.

Interventions to improve adherence to HAART medications have also recently emerged. Notably, a study using the Disease Management Assistance System (Andrade et al., 2005) suggests that partial remediation of medication management deficits may

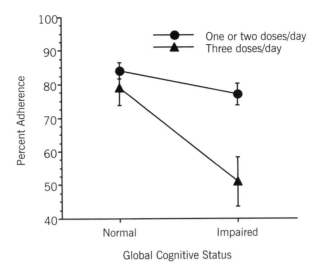

FIGURE 16.3. Relationship between cognitive status, regimen complexity, and medication adherence among HIV-infected adults. From Hinkin, Castellon, et al. (2002). Reprinted with permission from Lippincott Williams & Wilkins.

be possible. This study was a randomized trial in which the treatment group received simple auditory reminding devices that notified individuals of the timing and dosing of their medications. Adherence rates did not significantly differ between the treatment group (80%) and the control group (65%), although an analysis of a subgroup of individuals with memory impairment revealed significantly greater adherence in the treatment group (77%) when compared to the control subjects (57%). The success in this subgroup may be due to remediation of prospective memory impairment (see Other Factors section below), as these devices are aimed at helping individuals with memory deficits "remember to remember." However, the use of such a reminding program may have unintended effects, including reductions in QOL for some individuals (Wu et al., 2006). Although an intervention with robust and enduring effects on adherence and clinical outcomes has not yet been identified, psychosocial and educational interventions are being developed to improve adherence by adjusting health beliefs and providing problem-solving skills and support for overcoming barriers such as psychiatric symptoms (e.g., Golin et al., 2006; Wagner et al., 2006).

Vocational Functioning

Unlike most dementing disorders, the prevalence of HIV tends to be highest in younger individuals who, prior to their illness, had many years of possible work life ahead of them. In the mid-1990s, many HIV-infected individuals experienced a "second life" (Rabkin & Ferrando, 1997) as a result of available HAART treatments, including a dramatic change in their health and functional outlook. It has been proposed that this change has created new opportunities for individuals to return to work, even for those who have been unemployed or on disability for years (Martin, Steckart, & Arns, 2006). However, the complex symptom constellation associated with HIV infection, including opportunistic infections, physical limitations, fatigue, and/or cognitive impairment, may still provide a multitude of reasons for work-related disability, and it is still unclear whether this change in outlook has resulted in a shift in functional outcomes, including employment. Given that studies have estimated the productivity loss due to HIV infection may cost as much as $22,000 per person, per year (Liu, Guo, & Smith, 2004), it has become particularly important to examine the factors that contribute to vocational decline as well as the successful return to work.

Early investigations examined trends in HIV-infected groups and group differences in employment status and job performance between HIV-positive and HIV-negative groups. According to results from the AIDS Cost and Services Survey in the United States, conducted in 1991 and 1992, 52% of HIV-infected individuals were unemployed and had quit the labor force entirely, and an additional 11% were looking for suitable full-time work (Sebesta & LaPlante, 1996). Only 29% were employed full-time, with an additional 9% working part time. Employed individuals with AIDS also worked fewer hours than both HIV-infected individuals without AIDS and HIV-negative individuals (Leigh, Lubeck, Farnham, & Fries, 1995). Furthermore, Kass, Munoz, Chen, Zucconi, and Bing (1994) reported that individuals with AIDS were 2.7 times more likely to lose full-time employment over a 6-month follow-up period than demographically similar HIV-negative individuals. In all studies, those with symptomatic HIV were more likely to be unemployed than asymptomatic individuals.

Neurocognitive status is also an important consideration in prediction of disability status in HIV-infected individuals. Albert and colleagues (1995) reported a relative risk ratio of work disability of 2.76 for initially asymptomatic HIV-positive participants when compared to HIV-negative participants during 4.5 years of follow-up. This increased risk was largely the result of a much higher risk (RR, 8.47) for a subset of participants who developed severe NP impairment, as HIV-infected individuals who did not evidence NP impairment at follow-up did not have an elevated risk of disability (RR, 2.21). Heaton and colleagues (1994) found unemployment to be almost three times higher in HIV-positive, neurocognitively impaired individuals than in HIV-positive, neurocognitively normal individuals (26.9 vs. 9.7%, respectively), even in those with only mild impairment (22% reported unemployment). After removing participants with potentially disabling medical conditions, this relationship still held (17.5 vs. 7.9%, respectively). In employed participants, those with NP impairment evidenced a higher rate of difficulty performing their jobs (29.6 vs. 5.9%). Similarly, in a study of advanced HIV disease, unemployed participants were twice as likely to be NP impaired as employed participants (22 vs. 11%), with physical limitations and performance on the Trail Making Test Part B significantly predicting employment status (van Gorp et al., 1999).

It is possible that HIV-positive individuals may stop working due to physical decline or because they are eligible for disability based on an AIDS diagnosis (i.e., developing an AIDS-defining medical condition or a CD4 cell count below 200/mm^3). This limitation can be addressed by using objective measures of vocational functioning. Heaton and colleagues (1996) utilized a standardized battery of vocational-related tasks (Valpar International Corporation, 1986, 1992) that provided ability estimates of 13 job abilities as identified by the U.S. Department of Labor (1991). Participants completed both manual (e.g., placing wires through loops) and computerized (e.g., size discrimination, tracking) tasks, including work samples. This battery enables a comparison of current performance (on the work-sample battery) with previous ability, as specified by jobs that individuals have held throughout their work history.

In this study, the HIV-positive, NP normal; HIV-positive, NP impaired; and HIV-negative, cognitively normal groups were matched on prior work history, indicating that the groups were likely equivalent on premorbid vocational functioning. However, the HIV-positive, NP impaired group performed significantly worse on the work sample than the HIV-positive, NP normal and HIV-negative groups; furthermore, although the latter two groups demonstrated higher current functioning than expected, given their work history (a person's work often doesn't require his or her highest ability levels), the HIV-positive, NP impaired group had reduced abilities compared to their prior work history, suggesting a decline from previous functioning. A similar pattern of results was found in a larger cohort from the HAART era, with the discrepancy between prior work ability and current vocational functioning being almost three times greater in the NP impaired group (Heaton et al., 2004). In this study, the presence of an AIDS diagnosis, high levels of depression, and NP deficits in abstraction/executive functioning, verbal function, and attention/working memory abilities were the strongest predictors of work-sample performance.

Recently, studies have examined predictors of returning to work, since successful HAART treatment may give HIV-infected individuals the potential to be productively employed, even after years of being out of the labor force. Although HAART increases the probability that HIV-positive individuals will remain employed (Goldman & Bao, 2004), longitudinal studies (e.g., Lem et al., 2005; Martin, Arns, Batterham, Afifi, & Steckart, 2006; Rabkin, McElhiney, Ferrando, van Gorp, & Lin, 2004) following individuals on HAART have found that only a small proportion of individuals who was unemployed at baseline was employed at follow-up. The strongest predictor of employment and amount of hours worked in these studies was the receipt of disability payments (those receiving payments were less likely to return to work), with past or current diagnosis of depressive disorder, physical limitations, and worse performance on NP measures also significantly predicting change in employment and amount of hours worked. The link between disability benefits and unemployment is consistent with survey results that have found that the most significant barriers to returning to work for individuals infected with HIV are the potential loss of disability benefits and publicly funded health insurance (Brooks, Martin, Ortiz, & Veniegas, 2004). This reluctance to endanger benefits, although controversial, likely reflects fear that benefits may not be reinstated once taken away, even with worsening health (Razzano, Hamilton, & Perloff, 2006); moreover, treatment of HIV/AIDS is quite expensive, and health insurance agencies are often reluctant to pay for the high costs of medical care. In addition, many HIV-positive individuals may enter the workforce after many years of being unemployed, whereupon they are more likely to land low-wage or part-time positions that are more likely to provide inadequate or minimal health insurance (Lem et al., 2005). In contrast to previous reports, a recent study examining a number of predictors for returning to work found that 52% of individuals unemployed at baseline found some sort of employment during 2 years of follow-up (van Gorp et al., 2007). Only performance on a measure of learning (California Verbal Learning Test [CVLT]) predicted finding employment; older age, presence of an AIDS diagnosis, and length of unemployment comprised barriers to finding work.

Although a number of programs aimed at helping HIV-infected individuals return to work have been described (e.g., Kohlenberg & Watts, 2003), few studies have examined the effectiveness of an occupational rehabilitation program with HIV-infected individuals. Kielhofner and colleagues (2004) employed a program that combined psychoeducation with occupational therapy services, addressing a range of physical, psychosocial, and environmental issues. The authors reported that of 90 participants who completed the return-to-work program, 60 (66.7%) returned to work. Despite these promising initial results, more prospective studies are needed to thoroughly examine the predictors of successful reentry into the workforce for HIV individuals, especially as increasing numbers of individuals may participate in vocational rehabilitation or assistance programs (McGinn, Gahagan, & Gibson, 2005).

Automobile Driving

Similar to employment, driving an automobile is a task that younger persons afflicted with HIV would be expected to undertake frequently. Driving is a complex activity, requiring intact attention, perception, tracking, choice reactions, sequential movements, judgment, and planning. Assessment of driving abilities is challenging, as there is currently no clear standard for the concept of "impaired driving skills" (Marcotte & Scott, 2004). However, there is growing evidence, via a number of methodologies for assessing driving abilities, that a subset of HIV-infected individuals with cognitive impairment experience an overall reduction in driving abilities.

Based on a self-report survey, 29% percent of 146 HIV-positive participants at the HIV Neurobehavioral Research Center (HNRC) reported a decline in their driving ability since becoming infected and were less likely to drive than NP normal individuals (odds ratio [OR] = 2.9; p = .02), even after controlling for Centers for Disease Control and Prevention (CDC) stage and employment status (Marcotte et al., 2000). In addition, cognitively impaired individuals were more likely than cognitively intact individuals to have a moving violation (33 vs. 10%; p = .003) in the prior year. These relationships held even after controlling for demographic, disease, and driving history (e.g., miles driven in the past year; proportion admitting to driving while intoxicated). Violation and crash history provide an extended sample of behavior that may offer the most realistic impression of how individuals perform under conditions in which they actually drive. On the other hand, this information is not always reliable, particularly with cognitively impaired individuals, and crashes and tickets are both rare occurrences that may not capture impairments, especially since a crash may be avoided because of the defensive behavior of other drivers (or, conversely, could be the fault of other drivers).

Investigations of driving ability in cognitively impaired HIV-positive individuals using objective laboratory tests have yielded a more detailed picture of the deficits associated with a subset of these patients. Our group (Marcotte et al., 1999) utilized an interactive, computer-based driving simulator to study 68 HIV-infected individuals at varying disease stages, assessing lane tracking, divided attention, driving in traffic, and crash avoidance. We found that cognitively impaired individuals had an increased propensity to "swerve" in their lane, resulting in a five times higher likelihood of failing the lane-tracking task. In addition, participants with cognitive impairment displayed a significantly higher number of simulator crashes on a city driving simulation compared to cognitively intact individuals (2.3 crashes vs. 1.5 crashes), with those diagnosed with MND having the highest number of crashes. Impairments in the domains of abstraction/executive functioning and attention/speed of information processing were most often associated with poor performance on the simulations.

We later extended these findings by using a multimodal assessment that included a 35-minute on-road driving evaluation, computer-based simulations that emulated city driving and assessed navigation skills, and NP testing (Marcotte et al., 2004). The on-road evaluation was designed to be lengthy enough to obtain an adequate sampling of behaviors (e.g., both residential and highway driving) without being overly taxing to participants. The simulations were designed to capture abilities not normally assessed in driving evaluations, such as quick decision making (i.e., in emergency or novel situations) and the ability to effectively navigate using a map.

Forty HIV-positive and 20 HIV-negative control participants were tested with these assessments. The HIV-positive, NP impaired participants, in contrast to the HIV-negative and HIV-positive, NP normal groups, were classified as unsafe in the on-road evaluation at a higher rate (36 vs. 6%), had more crashes on simulated routine and emergency driving tasks (M 2.0 vs. 1.3, p = .03), and made almost three times the number of navigational errors as the other groups (M 9.2 vs. 3.2, p = .001; see Figures 16.4 and 16.5). In contrast, the HIV-negative and HIV-positive, NP normal participants performed similarly on all evaluations, indicating that HIV seropositivity alone does not increase the risk for driving impairment. Performance on the

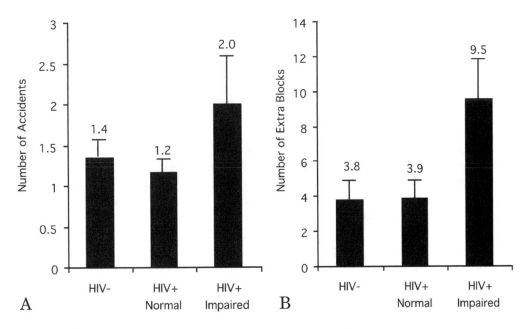

FIGURE 16.4. Comparison of group performance on number of simulator accidents (A) and number of city blocks beyond optimal performance on the Virtual City (B). From Marcotte et al. (2004). Reprinted with permission from Lippincott Williams & Wilkins.

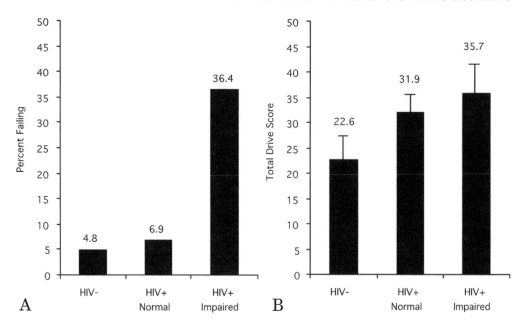

FIGURE 16.5. Group comparison of percentage of subjects failing the on-road driving evaluation (A) and total on-road drive score (B). From Marcotte et al. (2004). Reprinted with permission from Lippincott Williams & Wilkins.

neuropsychological tests, number of crashes on city driving, and route efficiency on the navigation task were all independent predictors of on-road performance, suggesting that direct assessment of driving skills (e.g., via simulator) yields data relevant to real-world performance above and beyond NP data alone. In this study impairment in executive functioning was the strongest predictor of failing the on-road evaluation. Notably, some of the individuals who failed the on-road driving test lacked awareness of their performance (these individuals had impairments that were generally greater than mild, particularly in executive functioning and learning), indicating that clinicians should be cautious in relying on a patient's self-report of driving ability.

We have also investigated whether the inclusion of visual attentional processing data could assist in identifying HIV-positive individuals who are at risk for poor driving performance (Marcotte et al., 2006). We utilized the Useful Field of View (UFOV, Visual Resources, 1998) test, which has shown particular success in identifying older at-risk drivers (e.g., Ball, Owsley, Sloane, Roenker, & Bruni, 1993; Myers, Ball, Kalina, Roth, & Goode, 2000; Owsley et al., 1998). The UFOV is a computerized measure that assesses the amount of time it takes an individual to accurately acquire both central and peripheral visual information without head or eye movements. We found that HIV-positive participants performed significantly worse on the UFOV compared to HIV-negative participants, with the greatest differences seen on a divided attention subtest. These declines in visual attention were not solely the result of advancing disease or high levels of general cognitive impairment, as individuals impaired on the UFOV covered the spectrum of disease stages and severity of cognitive impairment, suggesting a process occurring at least partially independent of disease progression, as well as a cognitive deficit not entirely captured by conventional NP tests. Importantly, the UFOV "high-risk" group had a significantly greater number of on-road crashes in the previous year compared to those who were not at high risk. Furthermore, a classification of "NP impaired" *and* "high risk" on the UFOV yielded a positive predictive value of 75% and a negative predictive value of 95% for crashes in the past year. This finding suggests that UFOV impairment may be riskiest in the presence of other cognitive impairments, as individuals may not be able to compensate for the UFOV deficit with other cognitive skills, such as deciding on an appropriate driving action (i.e., executive skills) or executing an appropriate motor response (i.e., motor skills).

Other Factors Affecting Everyday Functioning

In recent years investigations have focused on additional areas of functioning that are relevant not only to the everyday abilities of HIV-infected patients, but also to the management and prevention of the disease. Decision making and risky behaviors have been emergent areas of research, given that high-risk sexual behavior can both increase the spread of HIV and endanger already infected individuals by potentially exposing them to drug-resistant strains of the virus. In addition, risky decision making can lead to an increase in (1) drug abuse; (2) poorer everyday outcomes; and (3) likelihood of transmitting the disease through injection drug use, which currently is estimated to account for almost 20% of new HIV cases in the United States (Centers for Disease Control and Prevention, 2006).

Infection with HIV has long been associated with high-risk behaviors, such as unprotected sex, promiscuity, and intravenous drug use (e.g., Wolitski, Valdiserri, Denning, & Levine, 2001). A number of factors has been associated with increased risk behaviors in HIV-infected samples, including demographic factors such as ethnicity (e.g., Lemp et al., 1994) and age (e.g., Mansergh & Marks, 1998), drug abuse (e.g., Rhodes et al., 1999), beliefs about HIV and its treatment (e.g., Dilley, Woods, & McFarland, 1997), and mental health status (e.g., Otto-Salaj & Stevenson, 2001). However, recent studies have also investigated the cognitive and personality factors that may be associated with risky behavior in relation to HIV and drug use. Martin and colleagues (2004) used the Iowa Gambling Task (IGT) to investigate whether HIV-infected individuals with substance dependence would display poorer decision-making abilities than substance-dependent individuals without HIV infection. The IGT, created by Bechara, Damasio, Tranel, and Damasio (1997) to assess various cognitive components of decision making, involves selecting cards from four decks that have different contingencies for monetary rewards and losses, with the overall goal of making as much money as possible. Over time, prudent decision makers realize that two decks offer large payoffs but also increased losses (resulting in a net loss by the end of the task), whereas two decks offer smaller gains but fewer losses (resulting in a net gain by the end of the task). Martin and colleagues found that the HIV-positive individuals with substance dependence made significantly more disadvantageous choices on the IGT and did not learn to avoid the disadvantageous decks over time, indicating that HIV infection may be associated with an increased level of cognitive impulsivity.

The IGT was also employed by Hardy, Hinkin, Levine, Castellon, and Lam (2006), who similarly found that HIV-positive individuals evidenced worse performance on the IGT compared to HIV-negative individuals (see Figure 16.6). Notably, they also found that HIV-positive participants had an increased likelihood of selecting cards from a deck that resulted in infrequent, large penalties (as opposed to frequent, small penalties). In addition, selection of cards from this deck was associated with measures of inhibitory processing and delayed recall in exploratory analyses, suggesting that individuals who frequently chose from these decks might have difficulty inhibiting their selections and remembering the previous losses due to their infrequency.

Recent studies also indicate that personality traits may be worth considering in predicting engagement in risky behaviors; that is, longstanding traits, which may predate active substance use or HIV disease, may influence an individual's decision making. A number of studies has reported that the dispositional trait of sensation seeking, defined as the need to maintain a high level of arousal accompanied by a willingness to take risks to reach that arousal state (Zuckerman, Bone, Neary, Mangelsdorff, & Brustman, 1972), is associated with risky sexual practices among individuals with HIV (e.g., Crawford et al., 2003; Kalichman, Heckman, & Kelly, 1996). Gonzalez and colleagues (2005) investigated the contributions of executive functions, HIV serostatus, and the trait of sensation seeking on risky sexual practices in polysubstance abusers. Sensation seeking, but not executive functions, was associated with risky sexual practices in the past 6 months in both HIV-infected and HIV-seronegative groups, but this relationship was primarily driven by the association between the two within the HIV-infected group. Based on the results of these

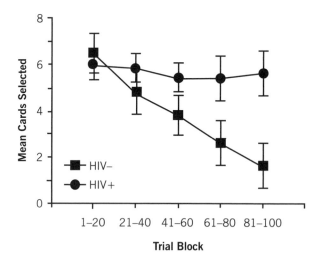

FIGURE 16.6. Average number of cards selected from a disadvantageous deck across five blocks of trials on the Iowa Gambling Task for an HIV-positive and HIV-negative group. Means are presented with *SE* bars. From Hardy et al. (2004). Reprinted by permission of the American Psychological Association.

and similar studies (e.g., Moore et al., 2005), both decision making and temperamental characteristics are important to consider in assessing risk-behavior patterns in HIV-infected individuals, especially when taking into account the actions that an individual might undertake in the real world, such as driving.

Another area of recent inquiry in HIV infection is the construct of prospective memory, which has shown promise as a predictor of everyday functioning in other neurological and medical disorders. Prospective memory denotes the ability to execute a future intention (i.e., "remembering to remember") in the absence of explicit cues, and is conceptually dissociable from retrospective memory, which refers to remembering information from the past in response to overt prompts. Examples of prospective memory in daily life include remembering to take a medication after a meal or remembering to mail a letter on the way home from work. Prospective memory is hypothesized to be a stronger contributor to the independent performance of several IADLs (e.g., medication adherence) than retrospective memory (Park & Kidder, 1996). Prospective memory therefore has particular relevance to HIV, for both its dependence on the integrity of frontostriatal circuits (Simons, Scholvinck, Gilbert, Frith, & Burgess, 2006) that are commonly affected by HIV and for the critical importance of medication adherence in the treatment of HIV/AIDS. In fact, the most commonly reported reason that HIV-positive persons give for missing medication doses is "forgetting" (Chesney et al., 2000).

Initial studies indicate that HIV infection is associated with a breakdown in the strategic (i.e., executive) encoding and retrieval aspects of prospective memory. HIV-infected individuals report more frequent prospective memory failures than seronegative individuals, in particular complaints of failures on self-cued tasks (i.e., intentions for which no salient, external cue is available, such as remembering to take a medication at a particular time) (Woods et al., 2007). On a performance-based measure of prospective memory, Carey and colleagues (2006) reported that individuals with HIV infection displayed deficient performance when the task demands involved self-initiated retrieval, but normal performance when retrieval demands were minimized with a recognition posttest. Studies have indicated that HIV-associated prospective memory impairment is correlated with worse performance on measures of strategic verbal encoding, verbal working memory, and executive functions, attesting to its construct validity in HIV (Carey et al., 2006; Martin et al., 2007).

Importantly, preliminary evidence also points to the ecological relevance of prospective memory in HIV infection. Studies have shown prospective memory impairment to be associated with high-risk behaviors in HIV-positive polysubstance users, such as medication nonadherence (Beauvais, Raskin, Dieckhaus, Miller, & Rosen, 2005) and risky sexual and injection drug use behaviors (Martin et al., 2007). Furthermore, prospective memory has been reported to be a significant, independent predictor of both subjective (Woods, Moran, et al., 2008) and objective (Woods et al., 2009) medication adherence in non-drug-abusing HIV-infected samples. In the latter study, individuals with HIV-associated prospective memory impairment at baseline were almost six times more likely to be classified as "nonadherent" (based on pill-bottle cap opening data) at 5-week follow-up than participants whose prospective memory performance fell within normal limits. Prospective memory has also been associated with increased risk of dependence in self-reported IADL functioning (e.g., financial management) in an HIV-infected sample, above and beyond that which is explained by retrospective memory impairment and affective status (Woods, Indicello, et al., 2008). Such studies suggest that prospective memory may be a unique and ecological aspect of cognitive functioning that, although ubiquitous in daily life, is not captured by traditional assessment techniques. In addition, prospective memory abilities may be important for HIV-positive individuals to maintain their health and reduce risky behavior. As Martin and colleagues (2007) hypothesized, the capacity to maintain drug abstinence, safe sexual practices, and even medication adherence may depend not only on one's ability to plan and actually retrieve, but also on one's ability to remember to retrieve appropriate risk reduction and medication management strategies.

Summary

Extensive research has suggested that HIV-associated cognitive impairments significantly influence one's ability to carry out common activities required for independent, productive daily living. These activities include such behaviors as managing and adhering to medications, driving an automobile, maintaining premorbid levels of employment and vocational skills, and avoiding risky behaviors. Although these deficits are more likely to be seen in individuals with more severe HAND (e.g., MND or HAD), it appears that even the milder impairments that are most often associated with HIV infection can influence daily functioning (e.g., Albert et al., 1995; Heaton et al., 2004) and even survival (e.g., Ellis et al., 1997). And although these impairments occur only in a subset of HIV-infected individuals, they still impart large societal costs, including increased costs of care, reducing the available workforce, and potentially spreading drug-resistant strains of the virus with inadequate antiretroviral adherence. Because of these costs, interventions to improve various aspects of everyday functioning have begun to emerge (e.g., medication reminder devices for adherence), although this important research is still in its nascent stages.

The process of isolating HIV-associated functional deficits has proven complex, as there are a number of factors that could contribute to deficits in daily functioning, including comorbid medical conditions (e.g., hepatitis C), psychiatric cofactors (e.g., depression), and substance abuse (e.g., methamphetamine dependence). Within the HIV population, there is a relatively high prevalence of psychiatric disorders, including substance use disorders. As the study by Heaton and colleagues (2004) illustrates, psychiatric factors (e.g., depression) need to be carefully considered as potential sources of functional impairment, as they may predict functioning independent of NP and/or functional performance. Often, studies do not thoroughly assess for psychiatric cofactors that may be contributing to functional difficulty, despite the high rates of disorders such as depression in HIV-infected populations. If these factors do not directly affect an individual's capacity to perform an activity, they certainly affect whether he or she *actually performs* the activity, as well as the accuracy of self-report measures that assess functional impairment. Indeed, the identification and remediation of psychiatric symptoms may prove important in preventing disability and negative functional outcomes as individuals continue to live longer with HIV infection (Rosenbloom et al., 2007; Sadek, Vigil, Grant, & Heaton, 2007).

Future Directions

An important emerging area of study involves cultural considerations in everyday functioning. HIV significantly impacts the ability to carry out common activities required for independent living. However, most research has been conducted predominantly in Western countries with mostly English-speaking populations. With the increasing rates of transmission in non-Western countries, and in ethnic minority populations within Western countries, it becomes important to characterize the complex relationships between HIV, neurocognitive impairment, affective symptoms, and everyday functioning. Although we might expect a disease to have similar effects across cultures, the fact that there are different viral subtypes around the world (e.g., clade C in India vs. clade B in the United States), the potentially differing everyday demands, the diverse nature of affective and psychiatric illness across cultures, and the general complexity of these relationships suggest that more focused and comprehensive study is needed to better answer such questions.

With translation and some minor adaptations, Mindt and colleagues (2003) employed the functional battery developed by Heaton and colleagues (2004) in a pilot study investigating the relationship between HIV infection and functional impairment in a Spanish-speaking sample. Similar to Heaton et al., they found that HIV-associated cognitive impairment was strongly associated with global functional impairment, and both, in turn, were associated with QOL and employment reports, but not to acculturation. A few studies have also investigated QOL associated with HIV in non-Western cultures, but there are surprisingly few other investigations into these questions. Therefore, further studies are needed to more thoroughly explore cultural contributions to functional status, especially to consider the interaction of cognitive impairment and affective status in predicting functional status in non-Western populations (see Cherner, Chapter 8, this volume).

Further research is also needed to better characterize HIV-associated functional deficits in aging populations. As HIV has been transformed from an almost uniformly fatal illness into a more chronic condition through more effective drug regimens, more individuals are living longer with HIV, raising important questions about the interaction of aging and HIV-related decline.

Although a number of studies has examined HAART treatment and NP performance, there is a dearth of research regarding how this treatment translates into improvements in everyday functioning. Development of new functional measures that could be completed within the constraints of a clinical trial would help advance our knowledge regarding the impacts of such treatments on real-world performance.

Lastly, to date little has been done with respect to investigating whether impairments caused by HIV, such as reduced speed of processing, are remediable via rehabilitation approaches. Given that HIV is now a stable disease for many individuals, cognitive rehabilitation may prove a fertile theme for future research.

References

Albert, S. M., Flater, S. R., Clouse, R., Todak, G., Stern, Y., & Marder, K. (2003). Medication management skill in HIV: I. Evidence for adaptation of medication management strategies in people with cognitive impairment. II. Evidence for a pervasive lay model of medication efficacy. *AIDS Behav, 7*, 329–338.

Albert, S. M., Marder, K., Dooneief, G., Bell, K., Sano, M., Todak, G., et al. (1995). Neuropsychologic impairment in early HIV infection: A risk factor for work disability. *Arch Neurol, 52*, 525–530.

Albert, S. M., Weber, C. M., Todak, G., Polanco, C., Clouse, R., McElhiney, M., et al. (1999). An observed performance test of medication management ability in HIV: Relation to neuropsychological status and medication adherence outcomes. *AIDS Behav, 3*, 121–128.

American Academy of Neurology AIDS Task Force. (1991). Nomenclature and research case definitions for neurologic manifestations of human immunodeficiency virus-type 1 (HIV-1) infection. *Neurology, 41*, 778–785.

Andrade, A. S., McGruder, H. F., Wu, A. W., Celano, S. A., Skolasky, R. L., Jr., Selnes, O. A., et al. (2005). A programmable prompting device improves adherence to highly active antiretroviral therapy in HIV-infected subjects with memory impairment. *Clin Infect Dis, 41*, 875–882.

Antinori, A., Arendt, G., Becker, J. T., Brew, B. J., Byrd, D. A., Cherner, M., et al. (2007). Updated research nosology for HIV-associated neurocognitive disorders. *Neurology, 69*, 1789–1799.

Archibald, S. L. (1998). Neuropathological correlates of in vivo and postmortem structural MRI volumes in the subjects with HIV. *Soc Neurosci Abst, 14*, 1961.

Ball, K., Owsley, C., Sloane, M. E., Roenker, D. L., & Bruni, J. R. (1993). Visual attention problems as a predictor of vehicle crashes in older drivers. *Invest Ophtha Vis Sci, 34*, 3110–3123.

Bangsberg, D. R. (2006). Less than 95% adherence to nonnucleoside reverse-transcriptase inhibitor therapy can lead to viral suppression. *Clin Infect Dis, 43*, 939–941.

Bangsberg, D. R., Perry, S., Charlebois, E. D., Clark, R. A., Roberston, M., Zolopa, A. R., et al. (2001). Non-adherence to highly active antiretroviral therapy predicts progression to AIDS. *AIDS, 15*, 1181–1183.

Beauvais, J., Raskin, S., Dieckhaus, K., Miller, L., & Rosen, M. I. (2005). Prospective memory and adherence to prescribed medication [Abstract]. *J Int Neuropsych Soc, 11*, 121.

Bechara, A., Damasio, H., Tranel, D., & Damasio, A. R. (1997). Deciding advantageously before knowing the advantageous strategy. *Science, 275*, 1293–1295.

Becker, J. T., Caldararo, R., Lopez, O. L., Dew, M. A., Dorst, S. K., & Banks, G. (1995). Qualitative features of the memory deficit associated with HIV infection and AIDS: Cross-validation of a discriminant function classification scheme. *J Clin Exp Neuropsyc, 17*, 134–142.

Bouwman, F. H., Skolasky, R. L., Hes, D., Selnes, O. A., Glass, J. D., Nance-Sproson, T. E., et al. (1998). Variable progression of HIV-associated dementia. *Neurology, 50*, 1814–1820.

Brew, B. J., Rosenblum, M., Cronin, K., & Price, R. W. (1995). AIDS dementia complex and HIV-1 brain infection: Clinical–virological correlations. *Ann Neurol, 38*, 563–570.

Brooks, R. A., Martin, D. J., Ortiz, D. J., & Veniegas, R. C. (2004). Perceived barriers to employment among persons living with HIV/AIDS. *AIDS Care, 16*, 756–766.

Burgess, A., Dayer, M., Catalan, J., Hawkins, D., & Gazzard, B. (1993). The reliability and validity of two HIV-specific health-related quality-of-life measures: A preliminary analysis. *AIDS, 7*, 1001–1008.

Carey, C. L., Woods, S. P., Rippeth, J. D., Heaton, R. K., Grant, I., & Group, T. H. (2006). Prospective memory in HIV-1 infection. *J Clin Exp Neuropsyc, 28*, 536–548.

Carrieri, P., Spire, B., Duran, S., Katlama, C., Peyramond, D., Francois, C., et al. (2003).

Health-related quality of life after 1 year of highly active antiretroviral therapy. *J Acq Immun Def Synd, 32*, 38–47.

Centers for Disease Control and Prevention. (2006). HIV/AIDS Surveillance Report, 2005, Vol. 17. Available at *www.cdc.gov/hiv/topics/surveillance/resources/reports/*. Atlanta, GA: Author.

Chang, L., & Ernst, T. (2005). Magnetic resonance spectroscopy and functional magnetic resonance imaging in the evaluation of HIV-associated brain injury. In H. E. Gendelman, I. Grant, I. P. Everall, S. Lipton, & S. A. Swindells (Eds.), *The neurology of AIDS* (2nd ed., pp. 585–600). Oxford, UK: Oxford University Press.

Chang, L., Ernst, T., Leonido-Yee, M., Witt, M., Speck, O., Walot, I., et al. (1999). Highly active antiretroviral therapy reverses brain metabolite abnormalities in mild HIV dementia. *Neurology, 53*, 782–789.

Cherner, M., Masliah, E., Ellis, R. J., Marcotte, T. D., Moore, D. J., Grant, I., et al. (2002). Neurocognitive dysfunction predicts postmortem findings of HIV encephalitis. *Neurology, 59*, 1563–1567.

Chesney, M. A., Ickovics, J. R., Chambers, D. B., Gifford, A. L., Neidig, J., Zwickl, B., et al. (2000). Self-reported adherence to antiretroviral medications among participants in HIV clinical trials: The AACTG adherence instruments. Patient Care Committee and Adherence Working Group of the Outcomes Committee of the Adult AIDS Clinical Trials Group (AACTG). *AIDS Care, 12*, 255–266.

Clifford, D. B. (2008). HIV-associated neurocognitive disease continues in the antiretroviral era. *Top HIV Med, 16*, 94–98.

Crawford, I., Hammack, P. L., McKirnan, D. J., Ostrow, D., Zamboni, B. D., Robinson, B., et al. (2003). Sexual sensation seeking, reduced concern about HIV and sexual risk behaviour among gay men in primary relationships. *AIDS Care, 15*, 513–524.

Cysique, L. A., Maruff, P., & Brew, B. J. (2004). Antiretroviral therapy in HIV infection: Are neurologically active drugs important? *Arch Neurol, 61*, 1699–1704.

Detels, R., Munoz, A., McFarlane, G., Kingsley, L. A., Margolick, J. B., Giorgi, J., et al. (1998). Effectiveness of potent antiretroviral therapy on time to AIDS and death in men with known HIV infection duration. Multicenter AIDS Cohort Study Investigators. *J Amer Med Assoc, 280*, 1497–1503.

Deutsch, R., Ellis, R. J., McCutchan, J. A., Marcotte, T. D., Letendre, S., & Grant, I. (2001). AIDS-associated mild neurocognitive impairment is delayed in the era of highly active antiretroviral therapy. *AIDS, 15*, 1898–1899.

Dilley, J. W., Woods, W. J., & McFarland, W. (1997). Are advances in treatment changing views about high-risk sex? *New Engl J Med, 337*, 501–502.

Dore, G. J., Correll, P. K., Li, Y., Kaldor, J. M., Cooper, D. A., & Brew, B. J. (1999). Changes to AIDS dementia complex in the era of highly active antiretroviral therapy. *AIDS, 13*, 1249–1253.

Dore, G. J., McDonald, A., Li, Y., Kaldor, J. M., & Brew, B. J. (2003). Marked improvement in survival following AIDS dementia complex in the era of highly active antiretroviral therapy. *AIDS, 17*, 1539–1545.

Ellis, R. J., Deutsch, R., Heaton, R. K., Marcotte, T. D., McCutchan, J. A., Nelson, J. A., et al. (1997). Neurocognitive impairment is an independent risk factor for death in HIV infection. *Arch Neurol, 54*, 416–424.

Everall, I. P., Heaton, R. K., Marcotte, T. D., Ellis, R. J., McCutchan, J. A., Atkinson, J. H., et al. (1999). Cortical synaptic density is reduced in mild to moderate human immunodeficiency virus neurocognitive disorder. HNRC Group, HIV Neurobehavioral Research Center. *Brain Pathol, 9*, 209–217.

Everall, I. P., Luthert, P. J., & Lantos, P. L. (1991). Neuronal loss in the frontal cortex in HIV infection. *Lancet, 337*, 1119–1121.

Ferrando, S. J., Rabkin, J. G., van Gorp, W., Lin, S. H., & McElhiney, M. (2003). Longitudinal improvement in psychomotor processing speed is associated with potent combination antiretroviral therapy in HIV-1 infection. *J Neuropsych Clin N, 15,* 208–214.

Ferrando, S. J., van Gorp, W., McElhiney, M., Goggin, K., Sewell, M., & Rabkin, J. (1998). Highly active antiretroviral treatment in HIV infection: Benefits for neuropsychological function. *AIDS, 12,* F65–F70.

Goldman, D. P., & Bao, Y. (2004). Effective HIV treatment and the employment of HIV(+) adults. *Health Serv Res, 39,* 1691–1712.

Golin, C. E., Earp, J., Tien, H. C., Stewart, P., Porter, C., & Howie, L. (2006). A 2-arm, randomized, controlled trial of a motivational interviewing-based intervention to improve adherence to antiretroviral therapy (ART) among patients failing or initiating ART. *J Acq Immun Def Synd, 42,* 42–51.

Gonzalez, R., Vassileva, J., Bechara, A., Grbesic, S., Sworowski, L., Novak, R. M., et al. (2005). The influence of executive functions, sensation seeking, and HIV serostatus on the risky sexual practices of substance-dependent individuals. *J Int Neuropsych Soc, 11,* 121–131.

Grant, I., & Atkinson, J. H. (1995). Psychiatric aspects of acquired immune deficiency syndrome. In H. I. Kaplan & B. J. Sadock (Eds.), *Comprehensive textbook of psychiatry* (Vol. 1, pp. 1644–1669). Baltimore: Williams & Wilkins.

Hardy, D. J., Hinkin, C. H., Levine, A. J., Castellon, S. A., & Lam, M. N. (2006). Risky decision making assessed with the gambling task in adults with HIV. *Neuropsychology, 20,* 355–360.

Haubrich, R. H., Little, S. J., Currier, J. S., Forthal, D. N., Kemper, C. A., Beall, G. N., et al. (1999). The value of patient-reported adherence to antiretroviral therapy in predicting virologic and immunologic response. California Collaborative Treatment Group. *AIDS, 13,* 1099–1107.

Heaton, R. K., Franklin, D., Clifford, D., Woods, S. P., Mindt, M. R., Vigil, O., et al. (2009, February). *HIV-associated neurocognitive impairment remains prevalent in the era of combination antiretroviral therapy: The CHARTER study.* Paper presented at the 16th Conference on Retroviruses and Opportunistic Infections, Montreal.

Heaton, R. K., Grant, I., Butters, N., White, D. A., Kirson, D., Atkinson, J. H., et al. (1995). The HNRC 500—Neuropsychology of HIV infection at different disease stages. *J Int Neuropsych Soc, 1,* 231–251.

Heaton, R. K., Marcotte, T. D., Mindt, M. R., Sadek, J., Moore, D. J., Bentley, H., et al. (2004). The impact of HIV-associated neuropsychological impairment on everyday functioning. *J Int Neuropsych Soc, 10,* 317–331.

Heaton, R. K., Marcotte, T. D., White, D. A., Ross, D., Meredith, K., Taylor, M. J., et al. (1996). Nature and vocational significance of neuropsychological impairment associated with HIV infection. *Clin Neuropsychol, 10,* 1–14.

Heaton, R. K., Velin, R. A., McCutchan, J. A., Gulevich, S. J., Atkinson, J. H., Wallace, M. R., et al. (1994). Neuropsychological impairment in human immunodeficiency virus-infection: Implications for employment. *Psychosom Med, 56,* 8–17.

Hinkin, C. H., Barclay, T. R., Castellon, S. A., Levine, A. J., Durvasula, R. S., Marion, S. D., et al. (2006). Drug use and medication adherence among HIV-1 infected individuals. *AIDS Behav, 11,* 185–194.

Hinkin, C. H., Castellon, S. A., Durvasula, R. S., Hardy, D. J., Lam, M. N., Mason, K. I., et al. (2002). Medication adherence among HIV+ adults: Effects of cognitive dysfunction and regimen complexity. *Neurology, 59,* 1944–1950.

Hinkin, C. H., Hardy, D. J., Mason, K. I., Castellon, S. A., Durvasula, R. S., Lam, M. N., et al. (2004). Medication adherence in HIV-infected adults: Effect of patient age, cognitive status, and substance abuse. *AIDS, 18*(Suppl. 1), S19–S25.

Hinkin, C. H., Hardy, D. J., Mason, K. I., Castellon, S. A., Lam, M. N., Stefaniak, M., et al. (2002). Verbal and spatial working memory performance among HIV-infected adults. *J Int Neuropsych Soc*, *8*, 532–538.

Horne, R., Buick, D., Fisher, M., Leake, H., Cooper, V., & Weinman, J. (2004). Doubts about necessity and concerns about adverse effects: Identifying the types of beliefs that are associated with non-adherence to HAART. *Int J STD AIDS*, *15*, 38–44.

Jernigan, T. L., Archibald, S., Hesselink, J. R., Atkinson, J. H., Velin, R. A., McCutchan, J. A., et al. (1993). Magnetic resonance imaging morphometric analysis of cerebral volume loss in human immunodeficiency virus infection. *Arch Neurol*, *50*, 250–255.

Joint United Nations Programme on HIV/AIDS. (2006). *2006 report on the global AIDS epidemic*. Geneva: Author.

Kalichman, S. C., Heckman, T., & Kelly, J. A. (1996). Sensation seeking as an explanation for the association between substance use and HIV-related risky sexual behavior. *Arch Sex Behav*, *25*, 141–154.

Kaplan, R. M., Anderson, J. P., Patterson, T. L., McCutchan, J. A., Weinrich, J. D., Heaton, R. K., et al. (1995). Validity of the Quality of Well-Being Scale for persons with human immunodeficiency virus infection. *Psychosom Med*, *57*, 138–147.

Kaplan, R. M., Patterson, T. L., Kerner, D. N., Atkinson, J. H., Heaton, R. K., Grant, I., et al. (1997). The Quality of Well-Being Scale in asymptomatic HIV-infected patients. *Qual Life Res*, *6*, 507–514.

Kass, N. E., Munoz, A., Chen, B., Zucconi, S. L., & Bing, E. G. (1994). Changes in employment, insurance, and income in relation to HIV status and disease progression. The Multicenter AIDS Cohort Study. *J Acq Immun Def Synd*, *7*, 86–91.

Kielhofner, G., Braveman, B., Finlayson, M., Paul-Ward, A., Goldbaum, L., & Goldstein, K. (2004). Outcomes of a vocational program for persons with AIDS. *Am J Occup Ther*, *58*, 64–72.

Kohlenberg, B., & Watts, M. W. (2003). Considering work for people living with HIV/AIDS: Evaluation of a group employment counseling program. *J Rehabil*, *69*, 22–29.

Kure, K., Llena, J. F., Lyman, W. D., Soeiro, R., Weidenheim, K. M., Hirano, A., et al. (1991). Human immunodeficiency virus-1 infection of the nervous system: An autopsy study of 268 adult, pediatric, and fetal brains. *Hum Pathol*, *22*, 700–710.

Langford, T. D., Everall, I. P., & Masliah, E. (2005). Current concepts in HIV neuropathogenesis: Neuronal injury, white matter disease, and neurotrophic factors. In H. E. Gendelman, I. Grant, I. P. Everall, S. A. Lipton, & S. Swindells (Eds.), *The neurology of AIDS* (2nd ed., pp. 405–414). Oxford, UK: Oxford University Press.

Leigh, J. P., Lubeck, D. P., Farnham, P. G., & Fries, J. F. (1995). Hours at work and employment status among HIV-infected patients. *AIDS*, *9*, 81–88.

Lem, M., Moore, D., Marion, S., Bonner, S., Chan, K., O'Connell, J., et al. (2005). Back to work: Correlates of employment among persons receiving highly active antiretroviral therapy. *AIDS Care*, *17*, 740–746.

Lemp, G. F., Hirozawa, A. M., Givertz, D., Nieri, G. N., Anderson, L., Lindegren, M. L., et al. (1994). Seroprevalence of HIV and risk behaviors among young homosexual and bisexual men. The San Francisco/Berkeley Young Men's Survey. *J Amer Med Assoc*, *272*, 449–454.

Letendre, S. L., McCutchan, J. A., Childers, M. E., Woods, S. P., Lazzaretto, D., Heaton, R. K., et al. (2004). Enhancing antiretroviral therapy for human immunodeficiency virus cognitive disorders. *Ann Neurol*, *56*, 416–423.

Levin, H. S., Williams, D. H., Borucki, M. J., Hillman, G. R., Williams, J. B., Guinto, F. C., et al. (1990). Magnetic resonance imaging and neuropsychological findings in human immunodeficiency virus infection. *J Acq Immun Def Synd*, *3*, 757–762.

Levine, A. J., Hardy, D. J., Miller, E., Castellon, S. A., Longshore, D., & Hinkin, C. H.

(2006). The effect of recent stimulant use on sustained attention in HIV-infected adults. *J Clin Exp Neuropsyc*, *28*, 29–42.

Liu, C., Johnson, L., Ostrow, D., Silvestre, A., Visscher, B., & Jacobson, L. P. (2006). Predictors for lower quality of life in the HAART era among HIV-infected men. *J Acq Immun Def Synd*, *42*, 470–477.

Liu, C., Ostrow, D., Detels, R., Hu, Z., Johnson, L., Kingsley, L., et al. (2006). Impacts of HIV infection and HAART use on quality of life. *Qual Life Res*, *15*, 941–949.

Liu, G. G., Guo, J. J., & Smith, S. R. (2004). Economic costs to business of the HIV/AIDS epidemic. *Pharmacoeconomics*, *22*, 1181–1194.

Maher, K., Klimas, N., Fletcher, M. A., Cohen, V., Maggio, C. M., Triplett, J., et al. (1999). Disease progression, adherence, and response to protease inhibitor therapy for HIV infection in an urban Veterans Affairs Medical Center. *J Acq Immun Def Synd*, *22*, 358–363.

Mansergh, G., & Marks, G. (1998). Age and risk of HIV infection in men who have sex with men. *AIDS*, *12*, 1119–1128.

Marcotte, T. D., Heaton, R. K., & Albert, S. (2005). Everyday impact of HIV-associated neurocognitive disorders. In H. E. Gendelman, I. Grant, I. P. Everall, S. A. Lipton, & S. Swindells (Eds.), *The neurology of AIDS* (2nd ed., pp. 743–752). New York: Chapman & Hall.

Marcotte, T. D., Heaton, R. K., Gonzalez, R., Reicks, C., Grant, I., & the HNRC Group. (2000). HIV-associated neurocognitive deficits impact on-road driving abilities [Abstract]. *J Neurovirol*, *6*, 268.

Marcotte, T. D., Heaton, R. K., Wolfson, T., Taylor, M. J., Alhassoon, O., Arfaa, K., et al. (1999). The impact of HIV-related neuropsychological dysfunction on driving behavior. *J Int Neuropsych Soc*, *5*, 579–592.

Marcotte, T. D., Lazzaretto, D., Scott, J. C., Roberts, E., Woods, S. P., Letendre, S., et al. (2006). Visual attention deficits are associated with driving accidents in cognitively-impaired HIV-infected individuals. *J Clin Exp Neuropsyc*, *28*, 13–28.

Marcotte, T. D., & Scott, J. C. (2004, December). The assessment of driving abilities. *Adv Transp Stud: Int J*, pp. 79–90.

Marcotte, T. D., Wolfson, T., Rosenthal, T. J., Heaton, R. K., Gonzalez, R., Ellis, R. J., et al. (2004). A multimodal assessment of driving performance in HIV infection. *Neurology*, *63*, 1417–1422.

Martin, D. J., Arns, P. G., Batterham, P. J., Afifi, A. A., & Steckart, M. J. (2006). Workforce reentry for people with HIV/AIDS: Intervention effects and predictors of success. *Work*, *27*, 221–233.

Martin, D. J., Steckart, M. J., & Arns, P. G. (2006). Returning to work with HIV/AIDS: A qualitative study. *Work*, *27*, 209–219.

Martin, E. M., Nixon, H., Pitrak, D. L., Weddington, W., Rains, N. A., Nunnally, G., et al. (2007). Characteristics of prospective memory deficits in HIV-seropositive substance-dependent individuals: Preliminary observations. *J Clin Exp Neuropsyc*, *29*, 496–504.

Martin, E. M., Pitrak, D. L., Weddington, W., Rains, N. A., Nunnally, G., Nixon, H., et al. (2004). Cognitive impulsivity and HIV serostatus in substance dependent males. *J Int Neuropsych Soc*, *10*, 931–938.

Masliah, E., Achim, C. L., Ge, N., DeTeresa, R., Terry, R. D., & Wiley, C. A. (1992). Spectrum of human immunodeficiency virus-associated neocortical damage. *Ann Neurol*, *32*, 321–329.

Masliah, E., Heaton, R. K., Marcotte, T. D., Ellis, R. J., Wiley, C. A., Mallory, M., et al. (1997). Dendritic injury is a pathologic substrate for HIV-related cognitive disorders. *Ann Neurol*, *42*, 963–972.

Mayeux, R., Stern, Y., Tang, M.-X., Todak, G., Marder, K., Sano, J., et al. (1993). Mortality risks in gay men with human immunodeficiency virus infection and cognitive impairment. *Neurology, 43*, 176–182.

McArthur, J. C. (2004). HIV dementia: An evolving disease. *J Neuroimmunol, 157*, 3–10.

McArthur, J. C., & Grant, I. (1998). HIV neurocognitive disorders. In H. E. Gendelman, S. A. Lipton, L. Epstein, & S. Swindells (Eds.), *The neurology of AIDS* (pp. 499–524). New York: Chapman & Hall.

McArthur, J. C., Hoover, D. R., Bacellar, H., Miller, E. N., Cohen, B. A., Becker, J. T., et al. (1993). Dementia in AIDS patients: Incidence and risk factors. *Neurology, 43*, 2245–2252.

McCutchan, J. A., Wu, J. W., Robertson, K., Koletar, S. L., Ellis, R. J., Cohn S., et al. (2007). HIV suppression by HAART preserves cognitive function in advanced, immune-reconstituted AIDS patients. *AIDS, 21*, 1109–1117.

McGinn, F., Gahagan, J., & Gibson, E. (2005). Back to work: Vocational issues and strategies for Canadians living with HIV/AIDS. *Work, 25*, 163–171.

Miller, R. F., Lucas, S. B., Hall-Craggs, M. A., Brink, N. S., Scaravilli, F., Chinn, R. J., et al. (1997). Comparison of magnetic resonance imaging with neuropathological findings in the diagnosis of HIV and CMV associated CNS disease in AIDS. *J Neurol Neurosur Ps, 62*, 346–351.

Mindt, M., Cherner, M., Marcotte, T., Moore, D., Bentley, H., Esquivel, M., et al. (2003). The functional impact of HIV-associated neuropsychological impairment in Spanish-speaking adults: A pilot study. *J Clin Exp Neuropsyc, 25*, 122–132.

Mocroft, A., Phillips, A. N., Soriano, V., Rockstroh, J., Blaxhult, A., Katlama, C., et al. (2005). Reasons for stopping antiretrovirals used in an initial highly active antiretroviral regimen: Increased incidence of stopping due to toxicity or patient/physician choice in patients with hepatitis C coinfection. *AIDS Res Hum Retrov, 21*, 743–752.

Moore, D. J., Atkinson, J. H., Akiskal, H., Gonzalez, R., Wolfson, T., & Grant, I. (2005). Temperament and risky behaviors: A pathway to HIV? *J Affect Disorders, 85*, 191–200.

Myers, R. S., Ball, K. K., Kalina, T. D., Roth, D. L., & Goode, K. T. (2000). Relation of Useful Field of View and other screening tests to on-road driving performance. *Percept Motor Skill, 91*, 279–290.

Nieuwkerk, P. T., Sprangers, M. A., Burger, D. M., Hoetelmans, R. M., Hugen, P. W., Danner, S. A., et al. (2001). Limited patient adherence to highly active antiretroviral therapy for HIV-1 infection in an observational cohort study. *Arch Intern Med, 161*, 1962–1968.

Otto-Salaj, L. L., & Stevenson, L. Y. (2001). Influence of psychiatric diagnoses and symptoms on HIV risk behavior in adults with serious mental illness. *AIDS Reader, 11*, 197–204, 206–198.

Owsley, C., Ball, K., McGwin, G., Jr., Sloane, M. E., Roenker, D. L., White, M., et al. (1998). Visual processing impairment and risk of motor vehicle crash among older adults. *J Amer Med Assoc, 279*, 1083–1088.

Park, D. C., & Kidder, D. P. (1996). Prospective memory and medication adherence. In M. Brandimonte, G. O. Einstein, & M. A. McDaniel (Eds.), *Prospective memory: Theory and applications* (pp. 369–390). Mahwah, NJ: Erlbaum.

Parsons, T. D., Braaten, A. J., Hall, C. D., & Robertson, K. R. (2006). Better quality of life with neuropsychological improvement on HAART. *Health Qual Life Outcomes, 4*, 11.

Peavy, G., Jacobs, D., Salmon, D. P., Butters, N., Delis, D. C., Taylor, M., et al. (1994). Verbal memory performance of patients with human immunodeficiency virus infection: Evidence of subcortical dysfunction. *J Clin Exp Neuropsyc, 16*, 508–523.

Porter, K., Babiker, A., Bhaskaran, K., Darbyshire, J., Pezzotti, P., & Walker, A. S. (2003). Determinants of survival following HIV-1 seroconversion after the introduction of HAART. *Lancet, 362*, 1267–1274.

Post, M. J. D., Berger, J. R., & Qeuncer, R. M. (1991). Asymptomatic and neurologically symptomatic HIV-seropositive individuals: Prospective evaluation with cranial MR imaging. *Radiology, 178*, 131–139.

Rabkin, J. G., & Ferrando, S. (1997). A "second life" agenda: Psychiatric research issues raised by protease inhibitor treatments for people with the human immunodeficiency virus or the acquired immunodeficiency syndrome. *Arch Gen Psychiat, 54*, 1049–1053.

Rabkin, J. G., Ferrando, S. J., Lin, S. H., Sewell, M., & McElhiney, M. (2000). Psychological effects of HAART: A 2-year study. *Psychosom Med, 62*, 413–422.

Rabkin, J. G., McElhiney, M., Ferrando, S. J., van Gorp, W., & Lin, S. H. (2004). Predictors of employment of men with HIV/AIDS: A longitudinal study. *Psychosom Med, 66*, 72–78.

Razzano, L. A., Hamilton, M. M., & Perloff, J. K. (2006). Work status, benefits, and financial resources among people with HIV/AIDS. *Work, 27*, 235–245.

Reger, M., Welsh, R., Razani, J., Martin, D. J., & Boone, K. B. (2002). A meta-analysis of the neuropsychological sequelae of HIV infection. *J Int Neuropsych Soc, 8*, 410–424.

Revicki, D. A., Wu, A. W., & Murray, M. I. (1995). Change in clinical status, health status, and health utility outcomes in HIV-infected patients. *Med Care, 33*, AS173–AS182.

Rhodes, F., Deren, S., Wood, M. M., Shedlin, M. G., Carlson, R. G., Lambert, E. Y., et al. (1999). Understanding HIV risks of chronic drug-using men who have sex with men. *AIDS Care, 11*, 629–648.

Rosenbloom, M. J., Sullivan, E. V., Sassoon, S. A., O'Reilly, A., Fama, R., Kemper, C. A., et al. (2007). Alcoholism, HIV infection, and their comorbidity: Factors affecting self-rated health-related quality of life. *J Stud Alcohol Drugs, 68*, 115–125.

Sacktor, N. C., Bacellar, H., Hoover, D. R., Nance-Sproson, T. E., Selnes, O. A., Miller, E. N., et al. (1996). Psychomotor slowing in HIV infection: A predictor of dementia, AIDS and death. *J Neurovirol, 2*, 404–410.

Sacktor, N. C., McDermott, M. P., Marder, K., Schifitto, G., Selnes, O. A., McArthur, J. C., et al. (2002). HIV-associated cognitive impairment before and after the advent of combination therapy. *J Neurovirol, 8*, 136–142.

Sacktor, N. C., Nakasujja, N., Skolasky, R., Robertson, K., Wong, M., Musisi, S., et al. (2006). Antiretroviral therapy improves cognitive impairment in HIV+ individuals in sub-Saharan Africa. *Neurology, 67*, 311–314.

Sadek, J. R., Vigil, O., Grant, I., & Heaton, R. K. (2007). The impact of neuropsychological functioning and depressed mood on functional complaints in HIV-1 infection and methamphetamine dependence. *J Clin Exp Neuropsyc, 29*, 266–276.

Sebesta, D., & LaPlante, M. (1996). *HIV/AIDS, disability, and employment: Disability statistics report 6*. Washington, DC: National Institute on Disability and Rehabilitation Research, Department of Education.

Sherbourne, C. D., Hays, R. D., Fleishman, J. A., Vitiello, B., Magruder, K. M., Bing, E. G., et al. (2000). Impact of psychiatric conditions on health-related quality of life in persons with HIV infection. *Am J Psychiat, 157*, 248–254.

Simons, J. S., Scholvinck, M. L., Gilbert, S. J., Frith, C. D., & Burgess, P. W. (2006). Differential components of prospective memory?: Evidence from fMRI. *Neuropsychologia, 44*, 1388–1397.

Singh, N., Squier, C., Sivek, C., Wagener, M., Nguyen, M. H., & Yu, V. L. (1996). Determinants of compliance with antiretroviral therapy in patients with human immunodeficiency virus: Prospective assessment with implications for enhancing compliance. *AIDS Care, 8*, 261–269.

Sonnerborg, A. B., Ehrnst, A. C., Bergdahl, S. K., Pehrson, P. O., Skoldenberg, B. R., & Strannegard, O. O. (1988). HIV isolation from cerebrospinal fluid in relation to immunological deficiency and neurological symptoms. *AIDS, 2*, 89–93.

Stankoff, B., Tourbah, A., Suarez, S., Turell, E., Stievenart, J. L., Payan, C., et al. (2001). Clinical and spectroscopic improvement in HIV-associated cognitive impairment. *Neurology, 56,* 112–115.

Starace, F., Ammassari, A., Trotta, M. P., Murri, R., De Longis, P., Izzo, C., et al. (2002). Depression is a risk factor for suboptimal adherence to highly active antiretroviral therapy. *J Acq Immun Def Synd, 31*(Suppl. 3), S136–S139.

Stevenson, M. (2003). HIV-1 pathogenesis. *Nat Med, 9,* 853–860.

Stout, J. C., Ellis, R. J., Jernigan, T. L., Archibald, S. L., Abramson, I., Wolfson, T., et al. (1998). Progressive cerebral volume loss in human immunodeficiency virus infection: A longitudinal volumetric MRI study. *Arch Neurol, 55,* 161–168.

Suarez, S., Baril, L., Stankoff, B., Khellaf, M., Dubois, B., Lubetzki, C., et al. (2001). Outcome of patients with HIV-1-related cognitive impairment on highly active antiretroviral therapy. *AIDS, 15,* 195–200.

Tozzi, V., Balestra, P., Galgani, S., Narciso, P., Ferri, F., Sebastiani, G., et al. (1999). Positive and sustained effects of highly active antiretroviral therapy on HIV-1-associated neurocognitive impairment. *AIDS, 13,* 1889–1897.

Tozzi, V., Balestra, P., Galgani, S., Narciso, P., Sampaolesi, A., Antinori, A., et al. (2001). Changes in neurocognitive performance in a cohort of patients treated with HAART for 3 years. *J Acq Immun Def Synd, 28,* 19–27.

Tozzi, V., Balestra, P., Lorenzini, P., Bellagamba, R., Galgani, S., Corpolongo, A., et al. (2005). Prevalence and risk factors for human immunodeficiency virus-associated neurocognitive impairment, 1996 to 2002: Results from an urban observational cohort. *J Neurovirol, 11,* 265–273.

Tozzi, V., Balestra, P., Murri, R., Galgani, S., Bellagamba, R., Narciso, P., et al. (2004). Neurocognitive impairment influences quality of life in HIV-infected patients receiving HAART. *Int J STD AIDS, 15,* 254–259.

Trepanier, L. L., Rourke, S. B., Bayoumi, A. M., Halman, M. H., Krzyzanowski, S., & Power, C. (2005). The impact of neuropsychological impairment and depression on health-related quality of life in HIV-infection. *J Clin Exp Neuropsyc, 27,* 1–15.

Trkola, A. (2004). HIV-host interactions: Vital to the virus and key to its inhibition. *Curr Opin Microbiol, 7,* 555–559.

U.S. Department of Labor. (1991). *Dictionary of occupational titles* (4th ed.). Washington, DC: U.S. Government Printing Office.

Valpar International Corporation. (1986). *Microcomputer Evaluation and Screening Assessment (MESA) Short Form 2.* Tucson, AZ: Author.

Valpar International Corporation. (1992). *Computerized Assessment (COMPASS).* Tucson, AZ: Author.

van Gorp, W. G., Baerwald, J. P., Ferrando, S. J., McElhiney, M. C., & Rabkin, J. G. (1999). The relationship between employment and neuropsychological impairment in HIV infection. *J Int Neuropsych Soc, 5,* 534–539.

van Gorp, W. G., Rabkin, J. G., Ferrando, S. J., Mintz, J., Ryan, E., Borkowski, T., et al. (2007). Neuropsychiatric predictors of return to work in HIV/AIDS. *J Int Neuropsych Soc, 13,* 80–89.

Visual Resources. (1998). *UFOV: Useful Field of View manual.* Chicago: Psychological Corporation.

Wagner, G. J., Kanouse, D. E., Golinelli, D., Miller, L. G., Daar, E. S., Witt, M. D., et al. (2006). Cognitive-behavioral intervention to enhance adherence to antiretroviral therapy: A randomized controlled trial (CCTG 578). *AIDS, 20,* 1295–1302.

Wensing, A. M., van de Vijver, D. A., Angarano, G., Asjo, B., Balotta, C., Boeri, E., et al. (2005). Prevalence of drug-resistant HIV-1 variants in untreated individuals in Europe: Implications for clinical management. *J Infect Dis, 192,* 958–966.

White, D. A., Heaton, R. K., & Monsch, A. U. (1995). Neuropsychological studies of asymptomatic human immunodeficiency virus-type 1-infected individuals. *J Int Neuropsych Soc, 1,* 304–315.

Wiley, C. A., Schrier, R. D., Nelson, J. A., Lampert, P. W., & Oldstone, M. B. (1986). Cellular localization of human immunodeficiency virus infection within the brains of acquired immune deficiency syndrome patients. *P Nat Acad Sci USA, 83,* 7089–7093.

Wilkie, F. L., Goodkin, K., Eisdorfer, C., Feaster, D., Morgan, R., Fletcher, M. A., et al. (1998). Mild cognitive impairment and risk of mortality in HIV-1 infection. *J Neuropsych Clin N, 10,* 125–132.

Wolitski, R. J., Valdiserri, R. O., Denning, P. H., & Levine, W. C. (2001). Are we headed for a resurgence of the HIV epidemic among men who have sex with men? *Am J Public Health, 91,* 883–888.

Woods, S. P., Carey, C. L., Moran, L. M., Dawson, M. S., Letendre, S. L., & Grant, I. (2007). Frequency and predictors of self-reported prospective memory complaints in individuals infected with HIV. *Arch Clin Neuropsych, 22,* 187–195.

Woods, S. P., Dawson, M. S., Weber, E., Gibson, S., Grant, I., & Atkinson, J. H. (2009). Timing is everything: Antiretroviral nonadherence is associated with impairment in time-based prospective memory. *J Int Neuropsych Soc, 15,* 42–52.

Woods, S. P., Iudicello, J. E., Moran, L. M., Carey, C. L., Dawson, M. S., & Grant, I. (2008). HIV-associated prospective memory impairment increases risk of dependence in everyday functioning. *Neuropsychology, 22,* 110–117.

Woods, S. P., Moran, L. M., Carey, C. L., Dawson, M. S., Iudicello, J. E., Gibson, S., et al. (2008). Prospective memory in HIV infection: Is "remembering to remember" a unique predictor of self-reported medication management? *Arch Clin Neuropsych, 23,* 257–270.

World Health Organization. (2006). *UNAIDS/WHO epidemiological fact sheets on HIV/AIDS and sexually transmitted infections.* Geneva: UNAIDS/WHO Working Group on Global HIV/AIDS and STI Surveillance.

Wu, A. W. (2000). Quality of life assessment comes of age in the era of highly active antiretroviral therapy. *AIDS, 14,* 1449–1451.

Wu, A. W., Snyder, C. F., Huang, I. C., Skolasky, R., McGruder, H. F., Celano, S. A., et al. (2006). A randomized trial of the impact of a programmable medication reminder device on quality of life in patients with AIDS. *AIDS Patient Care STDs, 20,* 773–781.

Zuckerman, M., Bone, R. N., Neary, R., Mangelsdorff, D., & Brustman, B. (1972). What is the sensation seeker?: Personality trait and experience correlates of the Sensation-Seeking Scales. *J Consult Clin Psych, 39,* 308–321.

CHAPTER 17

The Influence of Depression on Cognition and Daily Functioning

David J. Moore, Suzanne Moseley, and J. Hampton Atkinson

In this chapter we discuss how depression may negatively influence both cognitive and everyday functioning abilities. We review the prevalence of depression and some common treatment options, followed by a discussion of underlying neurobiological and genetic correlates. A large body of research has focused on depression and depressive symptomatology, but the exact relationships among depression, cognition, and everyday functioning remain unclear. A subset of depressed individuals show mild to moderate neuropsychological (NP) impairment, and there is evidence of mood-dependent NP impairment as well as difficulties that persist in some patients after acute mood symptoms clear. Thus, a large portion of the chapter focuses on how depression affects cognition and how this effect may translate into difficulties in everyday life. We clearly recognize that environmental factors can influence the likelihood of developing depression and have included these functions in our comprehensive model (Figure 17.1); however, we do not discuss environmental factors in detail.

It is important to define depression before we begin this chapter. On the following pages, we use "depression" as a general term that refers to level of depressive symptoms as determined by self-report (e.g., Beck Depression Inventory–II) or clinician rating (e.g., Hamilton Depression Rating Scale). Studies of "depression" do not necessarily encompass the multifaceted clinical syndrome of major depressive disorder (MDD). MDD or a single major depressive episode (MDE), as specifically defined in the *Diagnostic and Statistical Manual of Mental Disorders*, fourth edition, text revised (DSM-IV-TR), can include difficulties with not only mood, but due to changes in sleep, interests, energy, psychomotor performance, and cognition (American Psychiatric Association, 2000). When studies describe research participants who have met criteria for MDD or MDE, we clearly indicate this. Otherwise, the reader can assume that the studies we discuss refer to participants with significant depressive symptoms who may or may not meet the criteria for MDD or MDE.

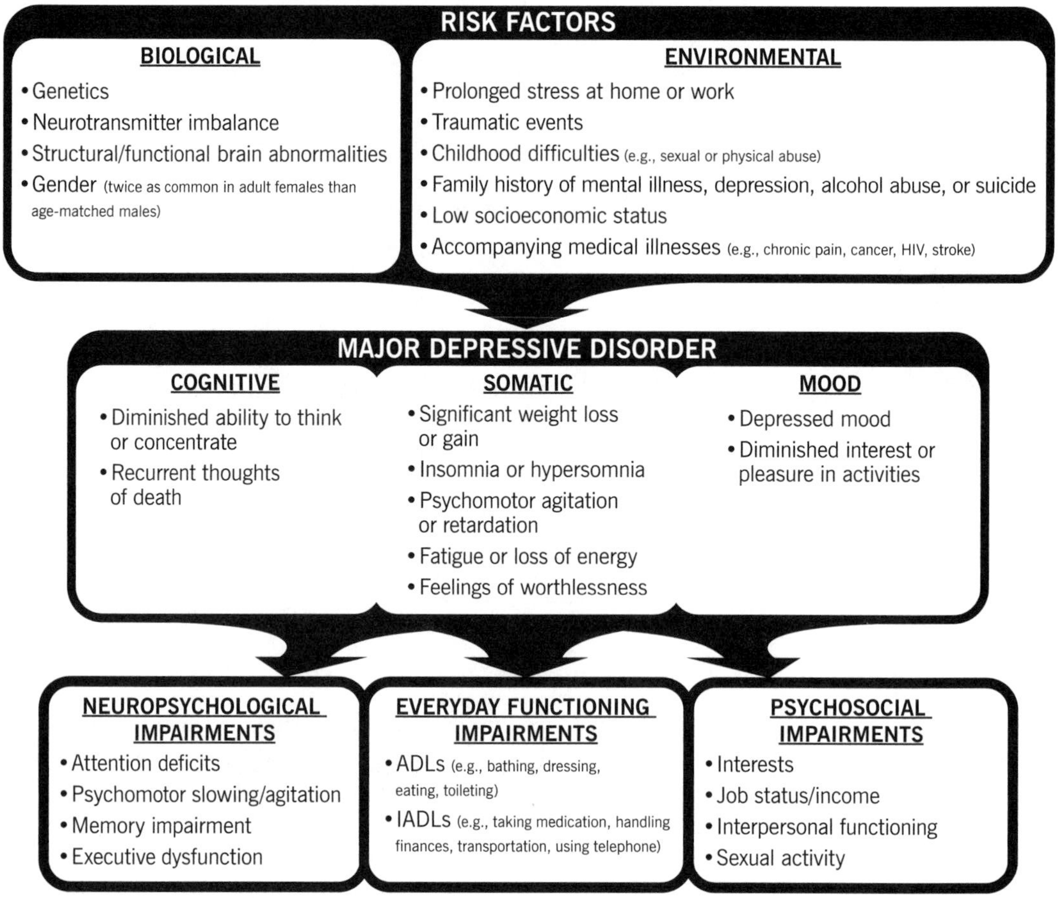

RISK FACTORS

BIOLOGICAL

- Genetics
- Neurotransmitter imbalance
- Structural/functional brain abnormalities
- Gender (twice as common in adult females than age-matched males)

ENVIRONMENTAL

- Prolonged stress at home or work
- Traumatic events
- Childhood difficulties (e.g., sexual or physical abuse)
- Family history of mental illness, depression, alcohol abuse, or suicide
- Low socioeconomic status
- Accompanying medical illnesses (e.g., chronic pain, cancer, HIV, stroke)

MAJOR DEPRESSIVE DISORDER

COGNITIVE

- Diminished ability to think or concentrate
- Recurrent thoughts of death

SOMATIC

- Significant weight loss or gain
- Insomnia or hypersomnia
- Psychomotor agitation or retardation
- Fatigue or loss of energy
- Feelings of worthlessness

MOOD

- Depressed mood
- Diminished interest or pleasure in activities

NEUROPSYCHOLOGICAL IMPAIRMENTS

- Attention deficits
- Psychomotor slowing/agitation
- Memory impairment
- Executive dysfunction

EVERYDAY FUNCTIONING IMPAIRMENTS

- ADLs (e.g., bathing, dressing, eating, toileting)
- IADLs (e.g., taking medication, handling finances, transportation, using telephone)

PSYCHOSOCIAL IMPAIRMENTS

- Interests
- Job status/income
- Interpersonal functioning
- Sexual activity

FIGURE 17.1. There are both biological and environmental contributions to the multifaceted diagnosis of major depressive disorder, which can also lead to neuropsychological, everyday, and psychosocial impairments.

It is also notable that we have not included a detailed discussion of bipolar disorder in this chapter. There is growing evidence that individuals with bipolar disorder have significant cognitive impairments and that the level of impairment may be more severe and more diffuse than that seen in persons with MDD, but less severe than the cognitive deficits observed in persons with schizophrenia (Bearden, Hoffman, & Cannon, 2001; Depp et al., 2007; Dickerson et al., 2004; Gildengers et al., 2007; Lingam & Scott, 2002; Revicki, Matza, Flood, & Lloyd, 2005; Robinson & Ferrier, 2006; Robinson et al., 2006; Sarkisian et al., 2000; Savitz, Solms, & Ramesar, 2005a, 2005b). Furthermore, there is emerging evidence that these NP impairments in persons with bipolar disorder may relate to difficulties in everyday functioning (Dickerson et al., 2004; Martinez-Aran et al., 2007). Indeed, the evidence is strong that neurocognitive deficits in persons with bipolar disorder are present outside of affective episodes, whereas the evidence for such deficits among persons with MDD is less clear.

Prevalence of Depression

Depression is extremely common; the National Comorbidity Study (NCS) estimates that 21.2% of American adults will have at least one depressive episode in their life-time (Kessler et al., 2008). Although MDD is more common among women as compared to men, the disorder affects all genders, ages, and races (Kornstein et al., 2000). Research suggests a general underdiagnosis of MDD, especially for patients who have comorbid physical illnesses such as asthma or diabetes, probably because both patients and physicians attribute depressive symptoms to medical causes (Moussavi et al., 2007). As of the year 2000, it was estimated that depression cost the United States $83 billion annually for, among other factors, health care costs and hours of work lost (Greenberg & Birnbaum, 2005). Furthermore, depression was the fourth leading source of the global burden of disease among all diseases and disorders, as measured by disability adjusted life years (DALYs), and the leading cause of disability when measured by years living with disability (YLDs) in the year 2000 (Ustun, Ayuso-Mateos, Chatterji, Mathers, & Murray, 2004). For younger persons (those ages 15–44) depression is the second leading source of disease burden. As the public becomes more informed in recognizing depressive symptoms, by the year 2020 MDD may be recognized as the second strongest contributor of lost years regardless of sex or age (Murray & Lopez, 1996).

The course of depressive illness can be quite variable. For instance, some individuals have severe depression that is treatment resistant, whereas others respond well to treatment. Even at subsyndromal levels, depression seems to have a significant effect on daily functioning and may cause particular difficulties with psychosocial functioning (Judd et al., 2002).

Individuals with depression can experience mental, role-emotional, and social dysfunction that is at least as debilitating as serious medical conditions such as coronary artery disease, hypertension, and chronic back pain (Wells & Sherbourne, 1999). To highlight the fact that disability is not just the result of a medical or biological dysfunction, the World Health Organization revised its International Classification of Functioning, Disability, and Health (ICF) in 2001, thereby strengthening the notion that disorders such as MDD should be placed on an equal footing with all health conditions (resolution World Health Assembly 54.21). Because the lifetime risk of depression is 5–10 times greater than that of many medical conditions, at a time when severe medical illness is unlikely, it may be more debilitating on a long-term and population basis. This seriousness of disability is compounded by under-recognition, consequent lack of treatment for MDD, and the fact that those in the young-to-middle age range are particularly vulnerable to this disorder. A recent study of 240,000 people in 60 countries showed that depression alone is more debilitating than chronic physical diseases, including asthma, angina, arthritis, and diabetes. Moreover, patients with the burden of such physical diseases have an increased risk of depression, and, not surprisingly, those with both MDD and a physical disease have lower health scores than those with physical health problems alone (Moussavi et al., 2007).

Despite the impact of depression on daily functioning, there has been a relative dearth of research focused on its cognitive and everyday consequences. This lack of focus on daily functioning is likely a result of several factors: (1) There are numerous efficacious treatments for depressive symptoms, and it is often assumed that cognitive and daily functioning problems will improve simultaneously with treatment of the underlying mood disturbance; (2) the severity of depressive symptomatology and functional disability can vary greatly; and (3) everyday functioning is difficult to measure, and a consensus definition for what is deemed impairment in daily functioning has not been formulated.

Treatment of Depression

Although numerous efficacious treatments for MDD exist, many individuals go undiagnosed and untreated (Gelenberg & Hopkins, 2007). Even with optimal pharmacological treatment, a significant proportion of treated persons (20–40%) continue to experience depressive symptoms (Keitner, Ryan, & Solomon, 2006). There are likely different cognitive and functional outcomes for those individuals who are treated, those who are not, and those that have failed treatment. Likewise, the treatment outcome for patients with comorbid medical issues and depression requires that both mental and physical health issues be addressed. Within this group of patients, treatment is often focused on more obvious physical diseases while depression is left unaddressed (Andrews & Titov, 2007). Taking this requirement into consideration, it is important to consider the implications of the various treatment approaches for resolution of mood, impact on cognition, and effect on everyday functioning. Below we examine both psychopharmacological and psychosocial treatments for depression.

Psychopharmacological Treatments for Depression

Psychopharmacological treatments for depression are widely used. In fact, a recent report by the Centers for Disease Control and Prevention showed that antidepressant medications are the most frequently prescribed medications in the United States (Burt, McCaig, & Rechtsteiner, 2007). More recently developed antidepressant medications (e.g., selective serotonin reuptake inhibitors [SSRIs] and related compounds) have better side effect profiles than earlier medications (e.g., tricyclic antidepressants [TCAs]), and SSRIs are commonly prescribed for the treatment of depression in the United States. A review examining 108 meta-analyses of the efficacy of antidepressant medications for the treatment of depression revealed that older antidepressants (e.g., those developed prior to the early 1980s) were equally efficacious as newer antidepressant medications. Study findings also revealed superior efficacy of serotonin and noradrenalin reuptake inhibitors (SNRIs) and a greater tolerability of SSRIs as compared to TCAs (Anderson, 2000). Finally, long-term maintenance treatment with an antidepressant medication seems important as it has been shown to provide better outcomes for individuals with depression than brief, short-term psychopharmacological intervention (Chisholm, Saxena, & van Ommeren, 2006).

The effect of pharmacological treatment on cognitive functioning has not been well established due to difficulties in disentangling the contribution of the depressive symptoms and medications. Some studies have suggested that SSRIs may negatively influence general memory abilities, resulting in forgetting, for example (Goldstein &

Goodnick, 1998; Joss, Burton, & Keller, 2003). However, the design of these studies does not allow for the disorder and treatment to be teased apart. In one study, relatively young, working individuals taking SSRI medications preformed worse on recognition and delayed recall tasks as compared to nondepressed individuals who were not taking SSRIs. However, depressive symptoms among the individuals taking the SSRIs had not yet resolved, so it is unclear if the impairments were a result of treatment or depression (Wadsworth, Moss, Simpson, & Smith, 2005).

Psychosocial Treatments for Depression

Several structured psychotherapeutic interventions have also been shown to produce substantial improvements in both mood and quality of life. Specifically, cognitive-behavioral therapy (CBT) and interpersonal therapy (IPT) have been shown to be effective in the treatment of depression. CBT is a structured therapy that can be given over a short time period. CBT focuses on the here and now and seeks to change maladaptive thoughts that may negatively affect behavior. IPT also focuses on current difficulties but in relation to interpersonal relationships, rather than maladaptive thoughts, under the premise that depressive symptoms will decrease with the resolution of interpersonal problems. The cost efficacy of psychotherapy is comparable to that for treatment with generic antidepressants, but it is less widely available (Chisholm et al., 2006).

Both psychopharmacological and psychosocial approaches to the treatment of depression appear to improve overall quality of life, including sleep, concentration, interpersonal functioning, and energy. Initial treatment with antidepressant medications and/or an indicated psychosocial intervention can lead to significant gains in terms of more years of healthy life, and long-term maintenance treatment leads to even higher gains (Chisholm et al., 2006). Furthermore, maintenance treatment with an antidepressant medication has been shown to decrease risk for relapse (Geddes et al., 2003). Antidepressants and therapy have been shown to be particularly effective in decreasing the number of days depressed (Malt, Robak, Madsbu, Bakke, & Loeb, 1999; Solomon et al., 1997).

Neurobiology/Neuroanatomy of Depression

Catecholamine Hypothesis

Conventional hypotheses regarding the neurobiological underpinnings of depression suggest that abnormal levels of monoamine neurotransmitters are associated with the illness. The so-called "catecholamine hypothesis" suggests that individuals with depression have depleted levels of several neurotransmitters, particularly serotonin and norepinephrine (Schildkraut, 1965). As a result, many antidepressant medications seek to boost the availability of these neurotransmitters either by facilitating their release into the synaptic cleft or by blocking their reuptake. Although the monoamines clearly have a large role in the development, and consequently the treatment, of depression, more recent hypotheses show that there are numerous other factors related to depression and that the underlying biology of this disorder is complex (Nemeroff & Vale, 2005; Owens, 2004).

A description of the underlying neurobiology of depression would be incomplete without mentioning the hypothalamic–pituitary–adrenal (HPA) axis, which plays a role in emotional behavior and is responsible for regulating stress. The HPA has been found to be dysregulated in persons with mood disorders and may serve to identify persons who may be at risk for development of serious depressive symptoms (Brown, Varghese, & McEwen, 2004; Goodyer, Herbert, & Tamplin, 2003; Varghese & Brown, 2001).

Neuroimaging Evidence of Brain Systems Involved in Depression

Neuroimaging studies have generally shown both structural and functional abnormalities in the frontal lobes and basal ganglia of persons with depressed mood. The specific neuroanatomical regions identified via structural neuroimaging of persons with depression reveal increased white matter abnormalities and decreased size of both the frontal lobes and the caudate nucleus as compared to persons without depression (Kanner, 2004; Krishnan et al., 1992; Sheline, 2003; Soares et al., 2001). Functional neuroimaging of people with depression shows decreased cerebral blood flow and cerebral metabolism in the inferior frontal, dorsolateral prefrontal, and anterior cingulate regions of the frontal lobe (Bench et al., 1992; Deckersbach, Dougherty, & Rauch, 2006; Fitzgerald et al., 2006; Lesser et al., 1994; Mayberg, 1994). There is evidence that the ventromedial prefrontal cortex is particularly affected in persons with unipolar depression and that damage to this region may be involved in emotional processing (Damasio, 1997). Similarly, Chamberlain and Sahakian (2006), in a review of the NP of mood disorders, have suggested that the orbital frontal and anterior cingulate regions of the frontal lobe in connection with subcortical structures may underlie the "affective" symptoms observed among individuals with depression. Positron emission tomography (PET) studies have also shown processing deficits in the frontal lobes and have related these to problems with decision making (Drevets et al., 1997). Furthermore, PET studies have revealed decreased 5-HT2 receptor density in the frontal cortex in those with remitted depression (Larisch et al., 2001). Decreased 5-HT2 receptor density may serve as an indicator of MDD susceptibility, as these receptors maintain regulation of mood, sleep, aggression, sexuality, and appetite.

Genetics of Depression

Genetic studies have sought to identify the genes that are associated with increased risk for the development MDD. Studies often focus on genes that may impact monoamine neurotransmitters. Polymorphisms in the serotonin transporter promoter region (5-HTTLPR) have received a great deal of scrutiny and have been linked to bipolar disorder, depressive traits, and suicidal behavior, but they have yet to reveal a direct association with MDD (Levinson, 2006).

Cognitive Impairment in Depression

Although there is controversy surrounding the subject, research suggests that at least a subset of persons with depression may have mild to moderate NP impairment (King

& Caine, 1996; Landro, Stiles, & Sletvold, 2001; Zakzanis, Leach, & Kaplan, 1998). Cognitive impairment appears to be more prevalent among depressed individuals who are older, have a poorer response to antidepressant medications, suffer recurrent episodes, and have a younger age of onset (Jaeger, Berns, Uzelac, & Davis-Conway, 2006).

The diagnosis of "major depressive disorder," as presented in the DSM-IV-TR, is based on a list of heterogeneous symptoms (American Psychiatric Association, 2000). Some of these symptoms are cognitive in nature. Specifically, one of the criteria, "reduced ability to think or concentrate," may be related to attentional deficits. Decreased attention and concentration can include negative thought rumination, which has been shown to impact social problem solving (Donaldson & Lam, 2004). Another of the criterion, "psychomotor agitation or retardation," is often manifested as reduced eye movements, constricted posture, shortened speaking time, slowed speech responses, poor articulation, increased restlessness at night, and continuous hand-to-head touching (Sobin & Sackeim, 1997). In NP terms these deficits may be manifested through decreased psychomotor speed and impaired speed of information processing. Such disruptions may manifest themselves differently in terms of features, severity, and permanence (King & Caine, 1996).

In the past, the term "pseudodementia" was used to describe primarily older patients with NP difficulties caused by a psychiatric illness rather than by a neurodegenerative disease. It is important to distinguish between the manifestations of cognitive difficulties in patients with these very different diagnoses. Mood-induced cognitive difficulties typically develop over a fairly short period of time and distress the patient, unlike similar changes due to a neurodegenerative disease (Arnold, 2005). Patients with dementia rarely show improvements in cognitive tests of memory, whereas many patients with depression improve their memory performance over time (Jenike, 1988). Underlying global abilities that may be lost in dementia, such as language and learning skills, are still intact in depressed individuals (Arnold, 2005). We believe that "pseudodementia" inaccurately describes the syndrome, downplaying the substantive cognitive problems experienced by individuals with depression. In other words, NP impairment should be viewed as a result of disruption in brain functioning, not just a product of depressed mood.

In terms of the severity of cognitive impairment, a well-designed study examining NP impairment in individuals with schizophrenia, nonpsychotic depression, and healthy controls showed that individuals with schizophrenia have the most significant cognitive impairment; however, individuals with nonpsychotic depression showed NP impairment in two of seven cognitive domains, as compared to zero domains among healthy comparison participants (Rund et al., 2006). Although severity of depressive symptoms did not directly correlate with NP performance, this study found that 24% of the patients with recurrent MDD had moderate cognitive impairment, and 4% of patients had severe impairment. Moderate impairment was defined as performing 1.5 standard deviations below the healthy control mean in at least two of seven NP domains, and severe impairment was defined as impairment in at least five domains. For comparison purposes, 45% of individuals with a diagnosis of schizophrenia had moderate impairment and 17% had severe impairment. For the depressed group, impairments were most apparent in the domains of working memory and reaction time.

The Impact of Severity, Clinical State, and Remission of Depression on Cognition

The evidence is somewhat mixed with regard to whether the overall extent of depressive symptoms relates to cognitive ability. The study described above reported no correlation between severity of depressive symptoms and NP performance, whereas other studies have shown that severity of depression and number of affective episodes can be associated with worse NP ability (Grant, Thase, & Sweeney, 2001; Kessing, 1998). In patients with more severe symptoms, performance on motor tasks has previously been shown to be worse, but degree of memory impairment has been shown to be negatively correlated (Jenike, 1988). However, other researchers suggests that the probability of finding memory deficits may correlate with symptomatic severity. Obviously the relationship between depression and cognitive ability is complex. There is currently no consensus as to persistence, severity, or pattern of cognitive deficits in depression (King & Caine, 1996).

The effect of an individual's current clinical state on depression is also unclear. Some studies find that level of depressive symptoms relates to cognitive functioning (Grant et al., 2001). The evidence is stronger that some persons with depression who have cognitive impairments will continue to have such problems after they have returned to a euthymic state or their symptoms have remitted (Silverstein, Harrow, & Bryson, 1994). Remitted MDD individuals in euthymic states still show significant attention and executive functioning impairments as compared to healthy controls (Clark, Sarna, & Goodwin, 2005; Paelecke-Habermann, Pohl, & Leplow, 2005). Such persistence of cognitive difficulties may suggest an underlying neural dysregulation among some persons, which influences the presentation of cognitive symptoms associated with MDD (King & Caine, 1996). The cause of NP impairment in depressed individuals does not appear to be simply a result of low mood; instead impairment may be a manifestation of many neurobiological traits.

Another important issue to clarify is whether or not subjective cognitive complaints correlate to objective findings from NP testing. Skeptics suggest that cognitive deficits in individuals with depression is a result of loss of motivation or attention, not a reproducible neural dysfunction. In one study it was found that self-reported cognitive deficits only predicted impairment in memory retention and concentration, not psychomotor speed, initial learning, or executive dysfunction (Naismith, Longley, Scott, & Hickie, 2007). The validity of self-ratings must be taken into consideration when exploring NP deficits.

The Effect of Treatment on Cognition

What remains particularly unclear is whether pharmacological treatments for depression contribute to the cognitive deficits in this disorder; however, it would be a misconception to think that cognitive problems among individuals with depression are an epiphenomenon caused by the treatment of the disorder. A recent review showed that, at least in specific executive functioning domains (e.g., set shifting), cognitive deficits do not necessarily improve with resolution of clinical symptoms. Deficits on executive functioning tasks are consistent with damage to dorsal and ventral portions of the prefrontal cortex (Austin, Mitchell, & Goodwin, 2001). These persisting cognitive deficits may have considerable implications for everyday functioning in persons treated for depression.

Cognitive Domains Commonly Impaired in Individuals with Depression

Although individuals with depression may show cognitive impairments in a range of domains, we have chosen to focus on impairments in the areas of executive functioning, learning and memory, motor skills, and psychomotor speed because they appear to be the most common (Tavares, Drevets, & Sahakian, 2003). The majority of NP deficits observed in those with depression are consistent with the frontosubcortical pathology described in the previous neurobiology/neuroanatomy section. Other cognitive abilities shown to be impaired in individuals with depression, such as an abnormal response to negative feedback and an affective processing bias, are reviewed elsewhere (Chamberlain & Sahakian, 2006; Tavares et al., 2003).

Executive functioning deficits are some of the most frequently identified and debilitating impairments among those with depression (Clark et al., 2005; Veiel, 1997). There is evidence to suggest that attention and executive functioning deficits in depression are trait-based and not a direct result of the depressive symptoms. This finding is supported by the earlier cited fact that remitted MDD individuals in euthymic states still show significant attention and executive functioning impairments, as compared to healthy controls without evidence of lifetime MDD (Clark et al., 2005; Paelecke-Habermann et al., 2005; Veiel, 1997). This does not mean that impairments in these domains are not related to clinical state. For example, in a cohort of individuals with mild to moderate levels of depression, executive functioning was the only domain of impaired functioning (attention, memory, and motor skills were normal), and certain executive functioning deficits were related to severity of depressive symptoms (Grant et al., 2001). Executive functioning impairments are more visible when the severity of the depression increases (Boone et al., 1995). Impairments in executive functioning may be particularly relevant to everyday functioning. Preliminary evidence of the effect of executive dysfunction has been shown in several areas of daily functioning, such as difficulties with planning and executing goal-directed activities. For instance, depression can lead to impairments in vocational and social abilities. Additional details regarding the effect of depression on executive functioning ability are reviewed elsewhere (DeBattista, 2005).

Learning and memory problems in some individuals with depression have been clearly identified (Goodwin, 1997). These cognitive difficulties seem to be found on both verbal and visual learning and memory tasks (Austin et al., 2001). One interesting study showed that individuals with depression (in either a current episode or with evidence of a past episode) had difficulties with delayed recall, but did not have difficulties with habit-learning tasks, suggesting dysfunction of medial temporal systems rather than striatal systems (MacQueen, Galway, Hay, Young, & Joffe, 2002). Deficits were shown to be related to number of previous episodes, but independent of current mood state. There is research, however, that has failed to find significant learning and memory problems in euthymic patients with a diagnosis of unipolar depression (Clark et al., 2005). Some have argued that learning and memory problems may largely be a state phenomenon, wherein individuals with MDD who are currently euthymic or remitted do not show these difficulties (Clark et al., 2005;

Sheline, Sanghavi, Mintun, & Gado, 1999). In short, the evidence appears to be somewhat mixed with regard to the root cause of learning and memory difficulties in persons with depression. Variation in the findings of pertinent studies may be due to methodological problems and the heterogeneity of the "syndrome" of MDD.

Psychomotor slowing is another common impairment in persons with depression, and, again, this symptom can aid in the diagnosis of a major depressive episode. This slowing can negatively influence performance on NP tests that are sensitive to generalized slowing, such as computerized reaction time measures (Elliott et al., 1996).

Cognitive Problems in Older Individuals with Depression

Some of the most consistent evidence linking depression to NP dysfunction comes from studies of older people, in whom disturbances in executive function can be prominent (Alexopoulos, Kiosses, Klimstra, Kalayam, & Bruce, 2002; Alexopoulos, Kiosses, Murphy, & Heo, 2004; Alexopoulos et al., 2000). Given that depression is prevalent in older age, and the fact that cognitive problems can increase among older adults, this is a particularly important concern (Steffens et al., 2006). Some investigators have suggested that impaired cognition may be limited to patients experiencing somatic symptoms of depression. For example, depressed patients with primarily vegetative (e.g., sleep, appetite) symptoms preformed significantly worse on NP tests of nonverbal intelligence, visual memory, and abstract problem solving, as compared to depressed patients with primarily psychological (e.g., mood) symptoms (Palmer et al., 1996). Other studies have suggested that cognitive problems are not necessarily more common with increasing age, rather that there may be "premature" aging in certain cognitive domains (e.g., nonverbal memory, word generation, and certain frontal lobe skills) (Boone et al., 1994). Given that difficulties with daily functioning can be more common among older adults, the presence of depression may exacerbate these difficulties. The particular impairments in daily functioning are further discussed in the section on depression and everyday functioning below.

Cognitive Impairment in Psychotic versus Nonpsychotic Depression

Data indicate that cognitive impairment tends to be worse in those with psychotic as compared to nonpsychotic depression, but the exact pattern of these differences remains somewhat unclear (Fleming, Blasey, & Schatzberg, 2004; Jeste et al., 1996). Some have found that individuals with psychotic depression have more diffuse cognitive impairment as compared to those with nonpsychotic depression (Basso & Bornstein, 1999). The implications of psychotic versus nonpsychotic depression for daily functioning have not been explored; however, one can hypothesize that the additional cognitive impairment in persons with psychotic depression may translate into additional functional difficulties.

Mood-Congruent Cognitive Processing

One interesting phenomenon among individuals with depression is that they tend to show preferential processing for emotional stimuli with a negative tone (Ellis & Moore, 2001). For example, depressed patients are able to more easily recall a story with negative emotional content, and they show an above-average ability to recall negative emotional events from the past (Blaney, 1986; Brittlebank, Scott, Williams, & Ferrier, 1993; Williams & Scott, 1988).

Depression and Everyday Functioning

Depression and Performance of Activities of Daily Living and Instrumental Activities of Daily Living

Individuals suffering with depression show a range of ability to independently carry out basic self-care such as personal hygiene (activities of daily living [ADLs]) and complete more complex tasks such as making and keeping appointments (instrumental activities of daily living [IADLs]). The presence of depressive symptoms is associated with a decline in performance of ADLs, particularly among older individuals. In an older population, 30–60% of individuals who have been hospitalized for a medical condition experience a drop in their ability to perform ADLs, including bathing, dressing, toileting, transferring, and eating (Hoogerduijn, Schuurmans, Duijnstee, de Rooij, & Grypdonck, 2007). Perhaps the largest study of the effect of depressive symptoms on ADLs and IADLs evaluated 572 recently hospitalized older individuals (Covinsky, Fortinsky, Palmer, Kresevic, & Landefeld, 1997). These authors found that persons with more depressive symptoms were significantly more likely to be dependent on others to help them perform ADLs as compared to individuals with no or few depressive symptoms. This finding was also true for IADLs, which include taking medicine, handling finances, managing transportation, and using the telephone. Other studies have confirmed that depressive symptoms are strongly associated with poor functional performance, and depression scores for older individuals were significantly higher for those who reported experiencing ADL decline (Covinsky et al., 1999; Lenze et al., 2005; Wakefield & Holman, 2007; Wu et al., 2000). Among community-based samples of older adults, NP impairment and depression appear to be two of the strongest predictors of daily functioning problems, even when controlling for baseline cognitive function, alcohol consumption, and chronic health conditions (Stuck et al., 1999).

Among persons with a primary major depressive episode and severe depressive symptoms (e.g., Beck Depression Inventory $M = 34.3$; $SD = 11.0$), cognitive impairment was strongly associated with impairment in IADLs, such as medication taking and finance handling, whereas level of depressive symptomatology and age were more strongly associated with impairments in basic ADLs (McCall & Dunn, 2003). Severity of depression and age were also associated with patients' satisfaction in role functioning and relationships.

Depression and Psychosocial Functioning

Like cognitive problems, psychosocial dysfunction is both a part of the diagnostic criteria for MDD as well as a consequence of the disorder. Specifically, depression is associated with declines in job status, income, and sexual activities; difficulties with marriage; and problems in familial relationships and friendships. Patients with more severe depressive symptomalogy exhibit higher levels of psychosocial dysfunction

(Coryell et al., 1993; Judd et al., 2000). Residual and pervasive depressive symptoms following treatment may lead to continued psychosocial dysfunction, suggesting that functional recovery lags considerably behind clinical recovery (Kennedy, Foy, Sherazi, McDonough, & McKeon, 2007). Additionally, problems in planning, working memory, and attention may be linked to permanent changes in the brain function of individuals with depression. These deficits in cognitive functioning may directly affect social functioning (Kennedy et al., 2007). Others may argue that low mood has less of a direct effect on neurocognitive integrity and a more consequential effect on psychosocial functioning, as difficulties in this domain may be more visibly troublesome.

Depression and Medication Adherence/Management

Although antidepressant medications are effective in reducing symptoms in many individuals with depression, this efficacy does not in itself ensure adherence to prescribed medications. In fact, randomized controlled trials of treatments for depression show that 20–40% of patients stop their treatments prior to completing a 6-month trial (Frank & Judge, 2001). In less stringent trials, the adherence rates appear to be approximately 50% (Demyttenaere, 2003). A recent review of medication adherence patterns among individuals with depression suggests that nonadherence may be largely driven by negative attitudes toward medication and depression as well as fear of medication dependence (Hansen & Kessing, 2007). Other reasons for nonadherence to medications include side effects and illness denial, although it has been suggested that beliefs about the efficacy of antidepressant medications may outweigh side effect problems (Byrne, Regan, & Livingston, 2006; Hansen & Kessing, 2007). Cognitive impairment may be another predictor of nonadherence (e.g., if a person has difficulty remembering to take his or her medication, he or she is less likely to be compliant). This is especially true of elderly patients with memory problems (Ayalon, Arean, & Alvidrez, 2005).

Several psychosocial treatments have been designed to help individuals improve their adherence abilities. Briefly, collaborative interventions that involve the patient, significant others, as well as the physician have proven to be the most helpful for improving adherence in this group (Vergouwen, Bakker, Katon, Verheij, & Koerselman, 2003). Even relatively simple adherence interventions, such as use of external reminders or construction of a positive attitude toward medication, appear to improve medication adherence (Patel & David, 2005). Cultural considerations must be taken into account when addressing the issue of adherence as some ethnic/racial groups may have different preferences with regard to the treatment of depression. For example, Hispanic individuals may have a preference toward psychotherapy or combination therapy as opposed to pharmacotherapy alone (Lewis-Fernandez, Das, Alfonso, Weissman, & Olfson, 2005).

Depression and Vocational Functioning

In addition to having a direct impact on simple daily functions, depression can negatively affect the ability to seek out and maintain employment. One study estimated the cost of time lost at work due to depression to be $31 billion (Stewart, Ricci,

Chee, Hahn, & Morganstein, 2003). Although depression may impact the likelihood of garnering employment, many individuals with depression are employed. Within the working population, depression prevalence rates have been estimated at approximately 2–4% (Dewa & Lin, 2000; Kessler & Frank, 1997; Kouzis & Eaton, 1997). It is likely that this prevalence underestimates the actual problem, given the documented pattern of individuals with depression to report physical problems (e.g., back pain) instead of emotional or psychological problems. Failure to report depression in the workplace may be driven by both associated stigma as well as compensation policies (i.e., employees may be reimbursed for physical problems but not necessarily psychological or emotional problems).

Depression has had a definitive, negative effect on short-term disability claims (i.e., loss of work for 1–30 days) among the employed. In the early 1990s the proportion of mental-health-related short-term disability claims doubled (Health Insurance of America, 1995). Furthermore, depression accounted for over half of the claims that were filed for reasons of mental health or nervous disorders.

Several studies show the widespread impact of depression on days of work lost due to short-term disability. One study showed that the likelihood of taking short-term disability among persons with depression was 37–48% as compared to 17–21% among those without depression (Dewa, Goering, Lin, & Paterson, 2002). Another study suggested that approximately 2.5% of short-term disability claims were depression-related when examining an administrative data set of approximately 63,000 Canadian employees (Dewa et al., 2002). Those who filed depression-related claims tended to be women between the ages of 36 and 55. This study also showed that among an already working population depression was more likely to cause difficulties for employees than other mental illness problems, responsible for a greater duration away from employment, and more likely to recur. Another detailed study showed that depression can be as debilitating, in terms of days lost from work, as serious medical illnesses. Specifically, in a 12-year study of employees (two-thirds of whom were women) at a major national bank, depression accounted for 65% of total short-term disability days with an average of 44 days of work lost. For comparison purposes, employees tended to take an average of 42 days for heart disease and 39 days for lower back pain. Severity and recurrence of depression were the strongest predictors of level of functional and work disability (Rytsala et al., 2005). Some effective interventions, such as the Quality Enhancement by Strategic Teaming (QuEST), which includes enhanced symptom monitoring and subsequent medication adjustments, have been applied with successful outcomes. Such enhancements in treatment appear to both increase the likelihood of returning to work and reduce the number of workplace conflicts among those returning to work following a depressive episode (Smith et al., 2002).

Depression and Driving

As has been shown in other functional domains, it is difficult to disentangle the impact of depressive symptoms and treatment for depressive symptoms on driving ability. Epidemiological studies appear to suggest that individuals who are taking sedating antidepressant medications may be at greater risk for traffic accidents (Leveille et al., 1994; Ray, Fought, & Decker, 1992). To our knowledge, only two studies have examined actual driving performance among patients with depression, and the findings have been somewhat inconsistent. One showed that patients taking an SSRI or a selective norepinephrine reuptake inhibitor (SNRI; inhibits the reuptake of both norepinephrine and serotonin) showed poorer driving performance on an on-road driving test, as compared to matched healthy controls (Wingen, Ramaekers, & Schmitt, 2006). Driving performance appeared to be related to continuing depressive symptoms, especially suboptimal arousal. An earlier study showed that driving performance was not related to improvement or decline on the Hamilton Depression Rating Scale (Ramaekers, Ansseau, Muntjewerff, Sweens, & O'Hanlon, 1997). We are unaware of any studies examining driving among individuals with depression who are not currently receiving treatment.

Depression and Quality of Life

Undoubtedly, depression can negatively impact a person's quality of life (Pyne, Smith, et al., 2003; Wells et al., 1989). The difficulty with studies of depression and quality of life is that some investigators feel that poor quality of life is simply part of the depressive illness and is not distinct from depressive symptomatology. When various predictors of quality of life are examined, severity of depressive symptoms has been shown to be most strongly associated with subjective quality of life (Corrigan & Buican, 1995). Using the self-administered and interviewer-administered Quality of Well-Being Scale (QWB), researchers have shown that level of depression is significantly correlated with QWB scores such that greater levels of depression are related to poorer quality of life (Pyne, Sieber, et al., 2003). Given the strong correlation between depressive symptoms and quality of life, one recent review called for the targeting of depressive symptoms in improving overall quality of life (Hansson, 2006).

Depression in the Context of Other Neurological/Psychiatric Conditions

Thus far we have discussed the impact of depression on cognition and everyday functioning in isolation, but it is well known that depression and/or depressive symptoms are a common consequence of many medical, neurological, and psychiatric conditions. To cover all aspects of the effects of depression on daily functioning in the context of all other medical conditions would not be feasible in this chapter; however, it is worth providing a couple of examples of how depressive symptoms can influence everyday functioning in the presence of comorbid syndromes.

Clinically significant depressive symptoms are common among individuals with HIV infection (Ciesla & Roberts, 2001). A large study of the everyday functioning abilities of individuals with HIV infection found that depressive symptoms, as measured by the Beck Depression Inventory, were a significant predictor of employment (Heaton et al., 2004). Levels of depressive symptoms and levels of functional impairment, as measured by laboratory-based IADL tests, were also correlated with patients' complaints of cognitive difficulties. Depressive symptoms uniquely contributed to participants' subjective complaints, as the symptoms did not strongly relate to levels of functional impairment. Finally, higher levels of NP impairment, functional impairment, and depressive symptoms contributed to greater dependence in the performance of daily activities such as cooking, shopping, laundry, home repair, and comprehension of reading material.

Depressive symptoms can also play a role in other psychiatric disorders. For instance, in a recent study of the functional abilities of individuals with schizophrenia, it was shown that depressive symptoms were significant predictors of real-world outcomes involving interpersonal skills and work skills independent of NP problems or other psychiatric symptoms (Bowie, Reichenberg, Patterson, Heaton, & Harvey, 2006). In conclusion, it may be important to assess for the influence of depressive symptoms on everyday functioning regardless of the clinical population.

Summary

Future Directions for Research

There is clearly a general gap in the literature with regard to everyday functioning among persons with depression. There is a sufficient body of research focusing on the impact of depression on vocational functioning and as a predictor of short-term disability. However, the interplay between cognitive functioning associated with depression and everyday skills has not yet been studied directly. Research into the interplay among depressive symptoms, cognitive abilities, functional capacity, and real-world functional outcomes would undoubtedly expand our understanding of depression and how this condition should be treated. At this point, we lack the ability to make statements about improvements in daily functioning with the resolution of clinical symptoms alone.

Conclusions

The multifaceted syndrome of depression is a common problem among individuals worldwide. The effects of this syndrome extend beyond its clinical symptoms (e.g., low mood, loss of interests in previously pleasurable activities) to problems with cognition and everyday functioning (see Figure 17.1). Cognitive problems are most prominent in the areas of executive functions, learning and memory, and psychomotor slowing. One of the major implications for everyday functioning in individuals with depression is decreased ability to function in an employment setting, and depression has been shown to be a major contributor to short-term disability claims among those who are employed. Efficacious treatments for depression are available (both pharmacological and psychosocial) and may help to resolve clinical symptoms, cognitive problems, and difficulties in everyday functioning, although it is difficult to tease apart the various contributors to cognitive impairment and everyday functioning. In sum, clinicians should be particularly sensitive to the high base rates of depression (regardless of clinical population) and the damaging effect that this illness can have on daily functioning.

References

Alexopoulos, G. S., Kiosses, D. N., Klimstra, S., Kalayam, B., & Bruce, M. L. (2002). Clinical presentation of the "depression–executive dysfunction syndrome" of late life. *Am J Geriatr Psychiat, 10*(1), 98–106.

Alexopoulos, G. S., Kiosses, D. N., Murphy, C., & Heo, M. (2004). Executive dysfunction, heart disease burden, and remission of geriatric depression. *Neuropsychopharmacology*, *29*(12), 2278–2284.

Alexopoulos, G. S., Meyers, B. S., Young, R. C., Kalayam, B., Kakuma, T., Gabrielle, M., et al. (2000). Executive dysfunction and long-term outcomes of geriatric depression. *Arch Gen Psychiat*, *57*(3), 285–290.

American Psychiatric Association. (2000). *Diagnostic and statistical manual of mental disorders*(4th ed., text rev.). Washington, DC: Author.

Anderson, I. M. (2000). Selective serotonin reuptake inhibitors versus tricyclic antidepressants: A meta-analysis of efficacy and tolerability. *J Affect Disord*, *58*(1), 19–36.

Andrews, G., & Titov, N. (2007). Depression is very disabling. *Lancet*, *370*, 808–809.

Arnold, E. (2005). Sorting out the 3 D's: Delirium, dementia, depression: Learn how to sift through overlapping signs and symptoms so you can help improve an older patient's quality of life. *Holist Nurs Pract*, *19*(3), 99–104.

Austin, M. P., Mitchell, P., & Goodwin, G. M. (2001). Cognitive deficits in depression: Possible implications for functional neuropathology. *Brit J Psychiat*, *178*, 200–206.

Ayalon, L., Arean, P. A., & Alvidrez, J. (2005). Adherence to antidepressant medications in black and Latino elderly patients. *Am J Geriatr Psychiat*, *13*(7), 572–580.

Basso, M. R., & Bornstein, R. A. (1999). Neuropsychological deficits in psychotic versus nonpsychotic unipolar depression. *Neuropsychology*, *13*(1), 69–75.

Bearden, C. E., Hoffman, K. M., & Cannon, T. D. (2001). The neuropsychology and neuro-anatomy of bipolar affective disorder: A critical review. *Bipolar Disord*, *3*(3), 106–150; discussion 151–103.

Bench, C. J., Friston, K. J., Brown, R. G., Scott, L. C., Frackowiak, R. S., & Dolan, R. J. (1992). The anatomy of melancholia: Focal abnormalities of cerebral blood flow in major depression. *Psychol Med*, *22*(3), 607–615.

Blaney, P. H. (1986). Affect and memory: A review. *Psychol Bull*, *99*(2), 229–246.

Boone, K. B., Lesser, I., Miller, B., Wohl, M., Berman, N., Lee, A., et al. (1994). Cognitive functioning in a mildly to moderately depressed geriatric sample: Relationship to chronological age. *J Neuropsych Clin N*, *6*(3), 267–272.

Boone, K. B., Lesser, I. M., Miller, B. L., Wohl, M., Berman, N., Lee, A., et al. (1995). Cognitive functioning in older depressed outpatients: Relationship of presence and severity of depression to neuropsychological test scores. *Neuropsychology*, *9*(3), 390–398.

Bowie, C. R., Reichenberg, A., Patterson, T. L., Heaton, R. K., & Harvey, P. D. (2006). Determinants of real-world functional performance in schizophrenia subjects: Correlations with cognition, functional capacity, and symptoms. *Am J Psychiat*, *163*(3), 418–425.

Brittlebank, A. D., Scott, J., Williams, J. M., & Ferrier, I. N. (1993). Autobiographical memory in depression: State or trait marker? *Brit J Psychiat*, *162*, 118–121.

Brown, E. S., Varghese, F. P., & McEwen, B. S. (2004). Association of depression with medical illness: Does cortisol play a role? *Biol Psychiat*, *55*(1), 1–9.

Burt, C. W., McCaig, L. F., & Rechtsteiner, E. A. (2007). Ambulatory medical care utilization estimates for 2005. *Advance Data from Vital and Health Statistics*, *388*, 1–15. Hyattsville, MD: National Center for Health Statistics.

Byrne, N., Regan, C., & Livingston, G. (2006). Adherence to treatment in mood disorders. *Curr Opin Psychiatr*, *19*(1), 44–49.

Chamberlain, S. R., & Sahakian, B. J. (2006). The neuropsychology of mood disorders. *Curr Psychiat Rep*, *8*(6), 458–463.

Chisholm, D., Saxena, S., & van Ommeren, M. (2006). *Dollars, DALYs and decisions: Economic aspects of the mental health system*. Geneva: World Health Organization.

Ciesla, J. A., & Roberts, J. E. (2001). Meta-analysis of the relationship between HIV infection and risk for depressive disorders. *Am J Psychiat*, *158*(5), 725–730.

Clark, L., Sarna, A., & Goodwin, G. M. (2005). Impairment of executive function but not memory in first-degree relatives of patients with bipolar I disorder and in euthymic patients with unipolar depression. *Am J Psychiat*, *162*(10), 1980–1982.

Corrigan, P. W., & Buican, B. (1995). The construct validity of subjective quality of life for the severely mentally ill. *J Nerv Ment Dis*, *183*(5), 281–285.

Coryell, W., Scheftner, W., Keller, M., Endicott, J., Maser, J., & Klerman, G. L. (1993). The enduring psychosocial consequences of mania and depression. *Am J Psychiat*, *150*(5), 720–727.

Covinsky, K. E., Fortinsky, R. H., Palmer, R. M., Kresevic, D. M., & Landefeld, C. S. (1997). Relation between symptoms of depression and health status outcomes in acutely ill hospitalized older persons. *Ann Intern Med*, *126*(6), 417–425.

Covinsky, K. E., Kahana, E., Chin, M. H., Palmer, R. M., Fortinsky, R. H., & Landefeld, C. S. (1999). Depressive symptoms and 3-year mortality in older hospitalized medical patients. *Ann Intern Med*, *130*(7), 563–569.

Damasio, A. R. (1997). Neuropsychology: Towards a neuropathology of emotion and mood. *Nature*, *386*(6627), 769–770.

DeBattista, C. (2005). Executive dysfunction in major depressive disorder. *Expert Rev Neurother*, *5*(1), 79–83.

Deckersbach, T., Dougherty, D. D., & Rauch, S. L. (2006). Functional imaging of mood and anxiety disorders. *J Neuroimaging*, *16*(1), 1–10.

Demyttenaere, K. (2003). Risk factors and predictors of compliance in depression. *Eur Neuropsychopharmacol*, *13*(Suppl. 3), S69–S75.

Depp, C. A., Moore, D. J., Sitzer, D., Palmer, B. W., Eyler, L. T., Roesch, S., et al. (2007). Neurocognitive impairment in middle-aged and older adults with bipolar disorder: Comparison to schizophrenia and normal comparison subjects. *J Affect Disord*, *101*(1–3), 201–209.

Dewa, C. S., Goering, P., Lin, E., & Paterson, M. (2002). Depression-related short-term disability in an employed population. *J Occup Environ Med*, *44*(7), 628–633.

Dewa, C. S., & Lin, E. (2000). Chronic physical illness, psychiatric disorder and disability in the workplace. *Soc Sci Med*, *51*(1), 41–50.

Dickerson, F. B., Boronow, J. J., Stallings, C. R., Origoni, A. E., Cole, S., & Yolken, R. H. (2004). Association between cognitive functioning and employment status of persons with bipolar disorder. *Psychiatr Serv*, *55*(1), 54–58.

Donaldson, C., & Lam, D. (2004). Rumination, mood and social problem-solving in major depression. *Psychol Med*, *34*(7), 1309–1318.

Drevets, W. C., Price, J. L., Simpson, J. R., Jr., Todd, R. D., Reich, T., Vannier, M., et al. (1997). Subgenual prefrontal cortex abnormalities in mood disorders. *Nature*, *386*, 824–827.

Elliott, R., Sahakian, B. J., McKay, A. P., Herrod, J. J., Robbins, T. W., & Paykel, E. S. (1996). Neuropsychological impairments in unipolar depression: The influence of perceived failure on subsequent performance. *Psychol Med*, *26*(5), 975–989.

Ellis, H. C., & Moore, B. A. (2001). Mood and memory. In T. Dalgleish & M. J. Powers (Eds.), *Handbook of cognition and emotion* (pp. 193–210). New York: Wiley.

Fitzgerald, P. B., Oxley, T. J., Laird, A. R., Kulkarni, J., Egan, G. F., & Daskalakis, Z. J. (2006). An analysis of functional neuroimaging studies of dorsolateral prefrontal cortical activity in depression. *Psychiat Res*, *148*(1), 33–45.

Fleming, S. K., Blasey, C., & Schatzberg, A. F. (2004). Neuropsychological correlates of psychotic features in major depressive disorders: A review and meta-analysis. *J Psychiat Res*, *38*(1), 27–35.

Frank, E., & Judge, R. (2001). Treatment recommendations versus treatment realities: Recognizing the rift and understanding the consequences. *J Clin Psychiat, 62*(Suppl. 22), 10–15.

Geddes, J. R., Carney, S. M., Davies, C., Furukawa, T. A., Kupfer, D. J., Frank, E., et al. (2003). Relapse prevention with antidepressant drug treatment in depressive disorders: A systematic review. *Lancet, 361,* 653–661.

Gelenberg, A. J., & Hopkins, H. S. (2007). Assessing and treating depression in primary care medicine. *Am J Med, 120*(2), 105–108.

Gildengers, A. G., Butters, M. A., Chisholm, D., Rogers, J. C., Holm, M. B., Bhalla, R. K., et al. (2007). Cognitive functioning and instrumental activities of daily living in late-life bipolar disorder. *Am J Geriatr Psychiat, 15*(2), 174–179.

Goldstein, B. J., & Goodnick, P. J. (1998). Selective serotonin reuptake inhibitors in the treatment of affective disorders: III. Tolerability, safety and pharmacoeconomics. *J Psychopharmacol, 12*(3 Suppl. B), S55–S87.

Goodwin, G. M. (1997). Neuropsychological and neuroimaging evidence for the involvement of the frontal lobes in depression. *J Psychopharmacol, 11*(2), 115–122.

Goodyer, I. M., Herbert, J., & Tamplin, A. (2003). Psychoendocrine antecedents of persistent first-episode major depression in adolescents: A community-based longitudinal enquiry. *Psychol Med, 33*(4), 601–610.

Grant, M. M., Thase, M. E., & Sweeney, J. A. (2001). Cognitive disturbance in outpatient depressed younger adults: Evidence of modest impairment. *Biol Psychiat, 50*(1), 35–43.

Greenberg, P. E., & Birnbaum, H. G. (2005). The economic burden of depression in the U.S.: Societal and patient perspectives. *Expert Opin Pharmacother, 6*(3), 369–376.

Hansen, H. V., & Kessing, L. V. (2007). Adherence to antidepressant treatment. *Expert Rev Neurother, 7*(1), 57–62.

Hansson, L. (2006). Determinants of quality of life in people with severe mental illness. *Acta Psychiat Scand, 113*(Suppl. 429), 46–50.

Health Insurance Association of America. (1995). *Disability claims for mental and nervous disorders.* Washington, DC: Author.

Heaton, R. K., Marcotte, T. D., Mindt, M. R., Sadek, J., Moore, D. J., Bentley, H., et al. (2004). The impact of HIV-associated neuropsychological impairment on everyday functioning. *J Int Neuropsychol Soc, 10*(3), 317–331.

Hoogerduijn, J. G., Schuurmans, M. J., Duijnstee, M. S., de Rooij, S. E., & Grypdonck, M. F. (2007). A systematic review of predictors and screening instruments to identify older hospitalized patients at risk for functional decline. *J Clin Nurs, 16*(1), 46–57.

Jaeger, J., Berns, S., Uzelac, S., & Davis-Conway, S. (2006). Neurocognitive deficits and disability in major depressive disorder. *Psychiat Res, 145*(1), 39–48.

Jenike, M. A. (1988). Depression and other psychiatric disorders. In M. S. Albert & M. B. Moss (Eds.), *Geriatric neuropsychology* (pp. 115–144). New York: Guilford Press.

Jeste, D. V., Heaton, S. C., Paulsen, J. S., Ercoli, L., Harris, J., & Heaton, R. K. (1996). Clinical and neuropsychological comparison of psychotic depression with nonpsychotic depression and schizophrenia. *Am J Psychiat, 153*(4), 490–496.

Joss, J. D., Burton, R. M., & Keller, C. A. (2003). Memory loss in a patient treated with fluoxetine. *Ann Pharmacother, 37*(12), 1800–1803.

Judd, L. L., Akiskal, H. S., Zeller, P. J., Paulus, M., Leon, A. C., Maser, J. D., et al. (2000). Psychosocial disability during the long-term course of unipolar major depressive disorder. *Arch Gen Psychiat, 57*(4), 375–380.

Judd, L. L., Schettler, P. J., & Akiskal, H. S. (2002). The prevalence, clinical relevance, and public health significance of subthreshold depressions. *Psychiat Clin N Am, 25*(4), 685–698.

Kanner, A. M. (2004). Structural MRI changes of the brain in depression. *Clin EEG Neurosci*, *35*(1), 46–52.

Keitner, G. I., Ryan, C. E., & Solomon, D. A. (2006). Realistic expectations and a disease management model for depressed patients with persistent symptoms. *J Clin Psychiat*, *67*(9), 1412–1421.

Kennedy, N., Foy, K., Sherazi, R., McDonough, M., & McKeon, P. (2007). Long-term social functioning after depression treated by psychiatrists: A review. *Bipolar Disord*, *9*(1–2), 25–37.

Kessing, L. V. (1998). Cognitive impairment in the euthymic phase of affective disorder. *Psychol Med*, *28*(5), 1027–1038.

Kessler, R. C., & Frank, R. G. (1997). The impact of psychiatric disorders on work loss days. *Psychol Med*, *27*(4), 861–873.

Kessler, R. C., Gruber, M., Hettema, J. M., Hwang, I., Samson, N., & Yonkers, K. A. (2008). Co-morbid major depression and generalized anxiety in the National Comorbidity Survey follow-up. *Psychol Med*, *38*(3), 365–374.

Kessler, R. C., McGonagle, K. A., Zhao, S., Nelson, C. B., Hughes, M., Eshleman, S., et al. (1994). Lifetime and 12-month prevalence of DSM-III-R psychiatric disorders in the United States: Results from the national comorbidity survey. *Arch Gen Psychiat*, *51*(1), 8–19.

King, D. A., & Caine, E. D. (1996). Cognitive impairment in major depression: Beyond the pseudodementia syndrome. In I. Grant & K. M. Adams (Eds.), *Neuropsychological assessment of neuropsychiatric syndromes* (2nd ed., pp. 200–221). New York: Oxford University Press.

Kornstein, S. G., Schatzberg, A. F., Thase, M. E., Yonkers, K. A., McCullough, J. P., Keitner, G. I., et al. (2000). Gender differences in chronic major and double depression. *J Affect Disord*, *60*(1), 1–11.

Kouzis, A. C., & Eaton, W. W. (1997). Psychopathology and the development of disability. *Soc Psych Psych Epid*, *32*(7), 379–386.

Krishnan, K. R., McDonald, W. M., Escalona, P. R., Doraiswamy, P. M., Na, C., Husain, M. M., et al. (1992). Magnetic resonance imaging of the caudate nuclei in depression: Preliminary observations. *Arch Gen Psychiat*, *49*(7), 553–557.

Landro, N. I., Stiles, T. C., & Sletvold, H. (2001). Neuropsychological function in nonpsychotic unipolar major depression. *Neuropsy Neuropsy Be*, *14*(4), 233–240.

Larisch, R., Klimke, A., Mayoral, F., Hamacher, K., Herzog, H. R., Vosberg, H., et al. (2001). Disturbance of serotonin 5HT2 receptors in remitted patients suffering from hereditary depressive disorder. *Nuklearmedizin*, *40*(4), 129–134.

Lenze, E. J., Schulz, R., Martire, L. M., Zdaniuk, B., Glass, T., Kop, W. J., et al. (2005). The course of functional decline in older people with persistently elevated depressive symptoms: Longitudinal findings from the cardiovascular health study. *J Am Geriatr Soc*, *53*(4), 569–575.

Lesser, I. M., Mena, I., Boone, K. B., Miller, B. L., Mehringer, C. M., & Wohl, M. (1994). Reduction of cerebral blood flow in older depressed patients. *Arch Gen Psychiat*, *51*(9), 677–686.

Leveille, S. G., Buchner, D. M., Koepsell, T. D., McCloskey, L. W., Wolf, M. E., & Wagner, E. H. (1994). Psychoactive medications and injurious motor vehicle collisions involving older drivers. *Epidemiology*, *5*(6), 591–598.

Levinson, D. F. (2006). The genetics of depression: A review. *Biol Psychiat*, *60*(2), 84–92.

Lewis-Fernandez, R., Das, A. K., Alfonso, C., Weissman, M. M., & Olfson, M. (2005). Depression in U.S. Hispanics: Diagnostic and management considerations in family practice. *J Am Board Fam Pract*, *18*(4), 282–296.

Lingam, R., & Scott, J. (2002). Treatment non-adherence in affective disorders. *Acta Psychiat Scand*, *105*(3), 164–172.

MacQueen, G. M., Galway, T. M., Hay, J., Young, L. T., & Joffe, R. T. (2002). Recollection memory deficits in patients with major depressive disorder predicted by past depressions but not current mood state or treatment status. *Psychol Med*, *32*(2), 251–258.

Malt, U. F., Robak, O. H., Madsbu, H. P., Bakke, O., & Loeb, M. (1999). The Norwegian naturalistic treatment study of depression in general practice (NORDEP)-I: Randomised double blind study. *Brit Med J*, *318*, 1180–1184.

Martinez-Aran, A., Vieta, E., Torrent, C., Sanchez-Moreno, J., Goikolea, J. M., Salamero, M., et al. (2007). Functional outcome in bipolar disorder: The role of clinical and cognitive factors. *Bipolar Disord*, *9*(1–2), 103–113.

Mayberg, H. S. (1994). Frontal lobe dysfunction in secondary depression. *J Neuropsych Clin N*, *6*(4), 428–442.

McCall, W. V., & Dunn, A. G. (2003). Cognitive deficits are associated with functional impairment in severely depressed patients. *Psychiat Res*, *121*(2), 179–184.

Moussavi, S., Chatterji, S., Verdes, E., Tandon, A., Patel, V., & Ustun, B. (2007). Depression, chronic diseases, and decrements in health: Results from the World Health Surveys. *Lancet*, *370*, 851–858.

Murray, C. J., & Lopez, A. D. (1996). *The global burden of disease: A comprehensive assessment of mortality and disability from diseases, injuries, and risk factors in 1990 and projected to 2020.* Cambridge, MA: Harvard University Press.

Naismith, S. L., Longley, W. A., Scott, E. M., & Hickie, I. B. (2007). Disability in major depression related to self-rated and objectively-measured cognitive deficits: A preliminary study. *BMC Psychiatry*, *7*(1), 32.

Nemeroff, C. B., & Vale, W. W. (2005). The neurobiology of depression: Inroads to treatment and new drug discovery. *J Clin Psychiat*, *66*(Suppl. 7), 5–13.

Owens, M. J. (2004). Selectivity of antidepressants: From the monoamine hypothesis of depression to the SSRI revolution and beyond. *J Clin Psychiat*, *65*(Suppl. 4), 5–10.

Paelecke-Habermann, Y., Pohl, J., & Leplow, B. (2005). Attention and executive functions in remitted major depression patients. *J Affect Disord*, *89*(1–3), 125–135.

Palmer, B. W., Boone, K. B., Lesser, I. M., Wohl, M. A., Berman, N., & Miller, B. L. (1996). Neuropsychological deficits among older depressed patients with predominantly psychological or vegetative symptoms. *J Affect Disord*, *41*(1), 17–24.

Patel, M. X., & David, S. A. (2005). Medication adherence: Predictive factors and enhancement strategies. *Psychiatry*, *3*(10), 41–44.

Pyne, J. M., Sieber, W. J., David, K., Kaplan, R. M., Hyman Rapaport, M., & Keith Williams, D. (2003). Use of the Quality of Well-Being Self-Administered version (QWB-SA) in assessing health-related quality of life in depressed patients. *J Affect Disord*, *76*(1–3), 237–247.

Pyne, J. M., Smith, J., Fortney, J., Zhang, M., Williams, D. K., & Rost, K. (2003). Cost-effectiveness of a primary care intervention for depressed females. *J Affect Disord*, *74*(1), 23–32.

Ramaekers, J. G., Ansseau, M., Muntjewerff, N. D., Sweens, J. P., & O'Hanlon, J. F. (1997). Considering the P450 cytochrome system as determining combined effects of antidepressants and benzodiazepines on actual driving performance of depressed outpatients. *Int Clin Psychopharmacol*, *12*(3), 159–169.

Ray, W. A., Fought, R. L., & Decker, M. D. (1992). Psychoactive drugs and the risk of injurious motor vehicle crashes in elderly drivers. *Am J Epidemiol*, *136*(7), 873–883.

Revicki, D. A., Matza, L. S., Flood, E., & Lloyd, A. (2005). Bipolar disorder and health-related quality of life: Review of burden of disease and clinical trials. *Pharmacoeconomics*, *23*(6), 583–594.

Robinson, L. J., & Ferrier, I. N. (2006). Evolution of cognitive impairment in bipolar disorder: A systematic review of cross-sectional evidence. *Bipolar Disord*, 8(2), 103–116.

Rund, B. R., Sundet, K., Asbjornsen, A., Egeland, J., Landro, N. I., Lund, A., et al. (2006). Neuropsychological test profiles in schizophrenia and non-psychotic depression. *Acta Psychiat Scand*, 113(4), 350–359.

Rytsala, H. J., Melartin, T. K., Leskela, U. S., Sokero, T. P., Lestela-Mielonen, P. S., & Isometsa, E. T. (2005). Functional and work disability in major depressive disorder. *J Nerv Ment Dis*, 193(3), 189–195.

Sarkisian, C. A., Liu, H., Gutierrez, P. R., Seeley, D. G., Cummings, S. R., & Mangione, C. M. (2000). Modifiable risk factors predict functional decline among older women: A prospectively validated clinical prediction tool. The Study of Osteoporotic Fractures Research Group. *J Am Geriatr Soc*, 48(2), 170–178.

Savitz, J. B., Solms, M., & Ramesar, R. S. (2005a). Neuropsychological dysfunction in bipolar affective disorder: A critical opinion. *Bipolar Disord*, 7(3), 216–235.

Savitz, J. B., Solms, M., & Ramesar, R. S. (2005b). Neurocognitive function as an endophenotype for genetic studies of bipolar affective disorder. *Neuromolecular Med*, 7(4), 275–286.

Schildkraut, J. J. (1965). The catecholamine hypothesis of affective disorders: A review of supporting evidence. *Am J Psychiat*, 122(5), 509–522.

Sheline, Y. I. (2003). Neuroimaging studies of mood disorder effects on the brain. *Biol Psychiat*, 54(3), 338–352.

Sheline, Y. I., Sanghavi, M., Mintun, M. A., & Gado, M. H. (1999). Depression duration but not age predicts hippocampal volume loss in medically healthy women with recurrent major depression. *J Neurosci*, 19(12), 5034–5043.

Silverstein, M. L., Harrow, M., & Bryson, G. J. (1994). Neuropsychological prognosis and clinical recovery. *Psychiat Res*, 52(3), 265–272.

Smith, J. L., Rost, K. M., Nutting, P. A., Libby, A. M., Elliott, C. E., & Pyne, J. M. (2002). Impact of primary care depression intervention on employment and workplace conflict outcomes: Is value added? *J Ment Health Policy*, 5(1), 43–49.

Soares, J. C., Boada, F., Spencer, S., Mallinger, A. G., Dippold, C. S., Wells, K. F., et al. (2001). Brain lithium concentrations in bipolar disorder patients: Preliminary (7)li magnetic resonance studies at 3 T. *Biol Psychiat*, 49(5), 437–443.

Sobin, C., & Sackeim, H. A. (1997). Psychomotor symptoms of depression. *Am J Psychiat*, 154(1), 4–17.

Solomon, D. A., Keller, M. B., Leon, A. C., Mueller, T. I., Shea, M. T., Warshaw, M., et al. (1997). Recovery from major depression: A 10-year prospective follow-up across multiple episodes. *Arch Gen Psychiat*, 54(11), 1001–1006.

Steffens, D. C., Otey, E., Alexopoulos, G. S., Butters, M. A., Cuthbert, B., Ganguli, M., et al. (2006). Perspectives on depression, mild cognitive impairment, and cognitive decline. *Arch Gen Psychiat*, 63(2), 130–138.

Stewart, W. F., Ricci, J. A., Chee, E., Hahn, S. R., & Morganstein, D. (2003). Cost of lost productive work time among U.S. workers with depression. *JAMA*, 289(3), 3135–3144.

Stuck, A. E., Walthert, J. M., Nikolaus, T., Bula, C. J., Hohmann, C., & Beck, J. C. (1999). Risk factors for functional status decline in community-living elderly people: A systematic literature review. *Soc Sci Med*, 48(4), 445–469.

Tavares, J. V., Drevets, W. C., & Sahakian, B. J. (2003). Cognition in mania and depression. *Psychol Med*, 33(6), 959–967.

Ustun, T. B., Ayuso-Mateos, J. L., Chatterji, S., Mathers, C., & Murray, C. J. (2004). Global burden of depressive disorders in the year 2000. *Brit J Psychiat*, 184, 386–392.

Varghese, F. P., & Brown, E. S. (2001). The hypothalamic–pituitary–adrenal axis in major depressive disorder: A brief primer for primary care physicians. *Prim Care Companion J Clin Psychiatry*, 3(4), 151–155.

Veiel, H. O. (1997). A preliminary profile of neuropsychological deficits associated with major depression. *J Clin Exp Neuropsychol*, 19(4), 587–603.

Vergouwen, A. C., Bakker, A., Katon, W. J., Verheij, T. J., & Koerselman, F. (2003). Improving adherence to antidepressants: A systematic review of interventions. *J Clin Psychiat*, 64(12), 1415–1420.

Wadsworth, E. J., Moss, S. C., Simpson, S. A., & Smith, A. P. (2005). SSRIs and cognitive performance in a working sample. *Hum Psychopharmacol*, 20(8), 561–572.

Wakefield, B. J., & Holman, J. E. (2007). Functional trajectories associated with hospitalization in older adults. *Western J Nurs Res*, 29(2), 161–177.

Wells, K. B., & Sherbourne, C. D. (1999). Functioning and utility for current health of patients with depression or chronic medical conditions in managed, primary care practices. *Arch Gen Psychiatr*, 56(10), 897–904.

Wells, K. B., Stewart, A., Hays, R. D., Burnam, M. A., Rogers, W., Daniels, M., et al. (1989). The functioning and well-being of depressed patients: Results from the medical outcomes study. *JAMA*, 262(7), 914–919.

Williams, J. M., & Scott, J. (1988). Autobiographical memory in depression. *Psychol Med*, 18(3), 689–695.

Wingen, M., Ramaekers, J. G., & Schmitt, J. A. (2006). Driving impairment in depressed patients receiving long-term antidepressant treatment. *Psychopharmacology (Berl)*, 188(1), 84–91.

Wu, A. W., Yasui, Y., Alzola, C., Galanos, A. N., Tsevat, J., Phillips, R. S., et al. (2000). Predicting functional status outcomes in hospitalized patients aged 80 years and older. *J Am Geriatr Soc*, 48(5 Suppl.), S6–S15.

Zakzanis, K. K., Leach, L., & Kaplan, E. (1998). On the nature and pattern of neurocognitive function in major depressive disorder. *Neuropsychiatry Neuropsychol Behav Neurol*, 11(3), 111–119.

CHAPTER 18

Cognition and Daily Functioning in Schizophrenia

Michael F. Green

Features of Schizophrenia

Schizophrenia is known for its dramatic clinical features, including psychotic symptoms (e.g., hallucinations and delusions), negative symptoms (e.g., flattened affect, reduced motivation, reduced speech), and disorganized symptoms (e.g., vague or tangential speech, odd behaviors) (American Psychiatric Association, 1994). Less obvious to many people is that schizophrenia is also characterized by prominent cognitive impairments (Green, 2001). Although schizophrenia has long been seen as a disorder of the brain, and one characterized by perceptual aberrations, it has not traditionally been viewed as a neurocognitive disorder. In this regard it is different from many of the other neurological conditions covered in this volume. That view of schizophrenia is changing, and the cognitive performance impairments in schizophrenia now are a recognized part of the illness. The cognitive deficits associated with schizophrenia are fairly broad and encompass a wide range of domains. This broad pattern of pattern of impairment, along with the fact that some patients perform in the normal range on certain tests, are among the reasons that it has been difficult to identify particular neural circuits that are specific to schizophrenia.

Among the many domains affected in schizophrenia, some have been selected as particularly important for clinical trials. Based on a careful literature review and consensus meetings sponsored by the National Institute of Mental Health (NIMH), the following separable cognitive domains were selected as important to assess in treatment studies of cognition in schizophrenia: speed of processing, attention/vigilance, working memory, verbal learning, visual learning, reasoning and problem solving, and social cognition (Nuechterlein et al., 2004). Although there is considerable between-subject variability in the pattern of deficits, there is also a modal neurocognitive profile that is characterized by larger deficits (in the range of 1.5 SDs or more) in verbal learning and vigilance, and lesser impairments in visual organization abilities and vocabulary (Heinrichs & Zakzanis, 1998).

Cognitive impairments are relatively common in schizophrenia. It has been estimated that 90% of patients have clinically meaningful deficits in at least one cognitive domain and that 75% have deficits in at least two (Palmer et al., 1997). Others have suggested that even these relatively high rates of impairment may be underestimates and that almost all patients with schizophrenia may perform at a level below what would be expected in the absence of illness. Such estimates are based on the cognitive performance of patients compared to their unaffected monozygotic twins (Goldberg et al., 1990) or to estimates of expected levels based on premorbid functioning (Kremen, Seidman, Faraone, Toomey, & Tsuang, 2000).

Cognitive impairments in schizophrenia have been noted and clearly described for well over a century and so cannot be considered a new discovery (Bleuler, 1950; Kraepelin, 1971). Because the impairments were appreciated so long ago, the recent surge in interest is more of a rediscovery than a discovery. At any rate, much more is known now about the nature of the deficits. The impairments are now clearly viewed as "core" features of the illness and not as secondary to the illness. The term "core" means that the impairments do not result merely from the presence of psychotic symptoms (e.g., distractibility due to hallucinations) or due to the psychopharmacological treatments (e.g., sedation due to antipsychotic medications). Evidence for the central nature of these deficits in schizophrenia comes from several lines of research. A brief listing of the lines of evidence is presented below; detailed reviews of this topic can be found elsewhere (Braff, 1993; Gold, 2004; Gold & Green, 2004; Green, 2007; Nuechterlein, Dawson, & Green, 1994).

1. Many patients demonstrate cognitive or intellectual impairments before the onset of psychotic symptoms and other clinical features of the disorder; hence the cognitive impairments predate and show a different time course than clinical features of illness.

2. Cognitive impairment (at attenuated levels) can be detected in first-degree relatives of patients with schizophrenia who are not psychiatrically ill. The presence of deficits in unaffected relatives suggests that some of the impairments reflect predisposition to schizophrenia, as opposed to the presence of the illness. For this reason, cognitive impairment is being used as an endophenotype in genetic studies of schizophrenia.

3. The magnitude of the cognitive impairment is relatively stable across clinical state, with the level of impairment on some cognitive measures being quite similar when patients are in, or out, of a psychotic episode. Hence, the impairments can occur in the absence of clinical symptoms of schizophrenia.

4. Cross-sectional correlations between cognitive performance and ratings of psychotic symptom severity are typically very small. The low correlations are especially true for psychotic symptoms. Correlations with negative and disorganized symptoms are sometimes larger, but still relatively modest.

5. The effects of antipsychotic medications are much larger on psychotic symptoms of schizophrenia than they are on cognition. There may be greater cognitive benefits for second-generation medications (i.e., atypicals) compared to first-generation medications, but even so, this discrepancy of cognitive and clinical effects is true for

both types of drugs. It suggests that the antipsychotic medications act on different neural systems from those that underlie the cognitive impairments.

Based on these converging lines of evidence, it can be concluded that cognitive impairment is a central feature of schizophrenia and that it is very prevalent. Although this conclusion seems obvious now, it reflects a recent shift in focus: away from the typical psychotic and negative symptoms that are part of the diagnostic criteria to the less dramatic, but more enduring, cognitive deficits. The focus on cognitive impairment is also consistent with the vast neuroimaging literature in schizophrenia showing a range of structural (Lawrie, Johnstone, & Weinberger, 2004; Narr et al., 2004) and functional (Glahn et al., 2005; Holmes et al., 2005) abnormalities in the disorder.

Disability and Outcome in Schizophrenia

Schizophrenia is a highly disabling illness. The illness impacts essentially every aspect of daily functioning, including social networks, closeness to family members, school and vocational success, performance of activities of daily living (ADLs), and degree of independent living. When considering all causes of disability, schizophrenia ranks among the top five causes of disability for young adults in developed countries (Murray & Lopez, 1996). This high ranking is true for both men and women, even though schizophrenia tends to have earlier onset and be somewhat more severe for men.

Functional outcome in schizophrenia is typically assessed through semistructured interviews or surveys in which the participant describes his or her participation in various daily activities (Birchwood, Smith, Cochran, Wetton, & Copestake, 1990; Weissman & Paykel, 1974). Self-report ratings of functioning can be supplemented with ratings from caregivers, but typically they are not. It is rare for outcome studies in schizophrenia to use observations of behaviors in the community, so questions are sometimes raised about the validity of self-report measures (Bellack et al., 2007). Nonetheless, self-report ratings are generally considered to be acceptable measures of functioning for patients who are clinically stable.

The relatively poor functional outcome in schizophrenia has changed little over the last century, even with the introduction of efficacious antipsychotic medications in the 1950s (Hegarty, Baldessarini, Tohen, Waternaux, & Oepen, 1994). This reality creates a confusing situation in which antipsychotic medications (both first- and second-generation medications) are highly effective in reducing psychotic symptoms, but patient outcomes have not improved. It is hard to understand why, if our drug treatments are so good, the outcomes are so bad. One way to resolve the situation is to differentiate the types of outcome in schizophrenia. There are at least three distinctly different types of outcome in schizophrenia: clinical, subjective, and functional (Brekke, Levin, Wolkon, Sobel, & Slade, 1993; Brekke & Long, 2000). The clinical outcome includes levels of persisting psychotic and negative symptoms; subjective outcome refers to how good the patients feel about themselves and how satisfied they are with their lives. Neither of these types of outcome has a strong relationship to functional outcome, which includes social functioning, vocational success, and degree of independent living.

Making the distinction among different types of outcomes helps clarify the picture. Antipsychotic drugs are clearly effective in reducing symptoms in the majority of patients, and this effect is related to clinical outcome. However, antipsychotic medications have minimal effects on other features of illness, such as cognitive impairments. As we will see in the next section, level of cognitive functioning is related to degree of daily functioning in schizophrenia. Hence, the features of illness that are related to functional outcome (e.g., cognitive impairments) are not impacted by drugs; instead the drugs improve aspects of illness such as psychotic symptoms that have comparatively less impact on daily functioning. The result of this mismatch is a major public health concern: Most patients with schizophrenia do not successfully reenter the community (defined by social or work achievements) after onset of illness (Hegarty et al., 1994; Helgason, 1990; Wiersma et al., 2000). The treatment of schizophrenia can be viewed in terms of two phases: short term and long term. When someone experiences a psychotic episode, the first challenge is to reduce symptoms and to clinically stabilize the individual. The second phase occurs after the individual and the situation are stable and he or she is seeking a return to work, school, or family. The first phase tends to be managed successfully with medications and treatment teams; the second phase tends to end in disappointing outcomes.

Cognitive Impairment and Daily Activities in Schizophrenia

There is a rather large literature on the relation between cognitive impairment and functional outcome in schizophrenia; I would estimate that around 100 data-based papers have been published on this topic. Papers started to be published in the early 1990s and have continued until the present. Many of the published studies have been included in three literature reviews from our group (Green, 1996; Green, Kern, Braff, & Mintz, 2000; Green, Kern, & Heaton, 2004). The three reviews (including one meta-analysis) concluded that cognitive deficits show reliable relationships to functional outcomes in schizophrenia. Many of the studies also included patients with schizoaffective disorder, but it is generally referred to as a literature on schizophrenia. Among the studies, functional outcomes have included types of community functioning (social outcome, vocational success, and independent living), as well as the degree of success in acquiring skills in psychosocial rehabilitation programs. Participation in psychosocial rehabilitation groups can be considered a daily activity for many patients with schizophrenia, so it is reasonable to consider success in these programs as a form of functional outcome. Across studies, the consistency of relationships is striking, and this overall conclusion is no longer a subject of debate. The strengths of the associations are typically in the medium range (e.g., $r = .3$) when separate cognitive domains are considered. The relationships can be much stronger ($r = .5$ or greater) when multiple cognitive domains are combined into composite scores (Green et al., 2000). At this point, the simple conclusion that cognitive performance is related to daily functioning in schizophrenia is clear and warranted. However, several follow-up questions deserve careful attention.

• *Do the relationships hold for prospective, as well as cross-sectional, associations?* One of the reviews was devoted to prospective studies in which baseline cognition was correlated with community functioning (defined in terms of work status, social functioning, or degree of independent living) at a minimum 6-month follow (Green, Kern, et al., 2004). This review included 18 longitudinal studies that all appeared subsequent to the earlier review that was published in 2000. Based on the survey of these studies, it appears that cognitive impairment at a baseline assessment is a reasonable predictor of later community functioning. In fact, several of the studies found good associations with outcome 2–4 years after baseline assessment (Dickerson, Boronow, Ringel, & Parente, 1999; Friedman et al., 2002; Gold, Goldberg, McNary, Dixon, & Lehman, 2002; Robinson, Woerner, McMeniman, Mendelowitz, & Bilder, 2004; Stirling et al., 2003).

Several studies in the review examined baseline prediction of *changes* in functional outcome, instead of only functional status at follow-up (Friedman et al., 2002; Smith, Hull, Huppert, & Silverstein, 2002; Woonings, Appelo, Kluiter, Slooff, & van den Bosch, 2002). Such findings of baseline cognition predicting change in functional outcome are important because they indicate that cognitive status has value for predicting how well people will benefit from interventions that are designed to improve community functioning (e.g., skills training programs). It is also possible to examine change in cognition over time, as opposed to change in functioning, and two of the studies found correlations between cognitive change and functioning (Friedman et al., 2002; Stirling et al., 2003). It should be noted that these studies examined cognitive decline, not improvement. In the absence of a potent cognitive enhancer, it has been hard to study correlates of cognitive improvement.

• *Are some cognitive domains more strongly related to outcome than others?* The findings in this regard have been mixed, with some studies suggesting that verbal learning (Green et al., 2000) or speed of processing (Gold et al., 2002) may be particularly important for functional outcome. However, looking across studies at this time, it is not obvious that one domain is particularly important to outcome compared to others. Instead, most or all of the cognitive domains appear to be related to functioning, at least when findings are averaged across subjects (Evans et al., 2003; Green et al., 2000; Velligan, Bow-Thomas, Mahurin, Miller, & Halgunseth, 2000). It is entirely possible that specific domains are more important for certain individuals. However, due to the large individual differences in which cognitive domains are most impaired, these individual patterns may wash out when the data are analyzed by groups.

• *Are specific cognitive domains related to specific aspects of functioning?* At this point it is difficult to draw connections between specific cognitive domains and particular aspects of outcome (e.g., work vs. social outcome, skill acquisition vs. independent living). Some support for specific differential relationships has come from a recent study that attempted to identify latent cognitive constructs and their relationships to outcome (Jaeger et al., 2006). Differential associations were found between cognitive domains and work outcome versus residential outcome. For example, working memory was associated with work/education outcome, but the domains of divergent thinking, cognitive flexibility, and speed were associated with residential outcome.

Some investigators have examined the cognitive correlates of specific types of outcome, such as driving ability (Palmer et al., 2002; St. Germain, Kurtz, Pearlson, & Astur, 2005). Considerations of the predictors and correlates of work performance are useful, especially because work outcome (whether someone has a job, hour many hours a week, how long he or she has maintained the job) is a rather concrete, objective, and verifiable outcome. As expected, both the likelihood of having a job and the length of job tenure are consistently related to cognitive abilities (Bell & Bryson, 2001; Bryson & Bell, 2003; Gold et al., 2002; Rosenheck et al., 2006).

One type of outcome that might be expected to be related to cognitive functioning, namely, medication adherence, is not consistently related. For example, a large-scale multisite 2-year follow-up study of patients with first-episode schizophrenia did not find level of cognitive functioning to be a predictor of medication adherence (Perkins et al., 2006). Instead, beliefs about the need for medication and the efficacy of the medications predicted adherence. Similarly, a review of the literature concluded that there is little support for cognitive status as a predictor of medication adherence (Lacro, Dunn, Dolder, Leckband, & Jeste, 2002). One might expect that lack of medication adherence would be related to memory failure, and in fact a study did find a correlation between a simulated assessment of medication adherence and the Mini-Mental State Examination (MMSE; Patterson et al., 2002). However, in schizophrenia it appears that factors related to insight, as well as belief in the need and value of treatment, may be more important than level of cognitive functioning.

Even when specific relationships to a type of outcome are uncovered, they may change over time. For example, one study reported that vigilance is more important than verbal memory in explaining work performance during a structured 26-week vocational program (12 vs. 4% variance explained)—but only for the first half of the program (Bryson & Bell, 2003). The pattern was reversed for the second half of the program, in which verbal memory was a stronger predictor than vigilance (11 vs. 6%). In this case, familiarity with the tasks appeared to change the type of cognitive demands. Given this level of complexity, it is safe to say that it will take more time and more studies with differentiated assessments to form conclusions about highly specific relationships to outcome.

- *Are the relationships present for other major psychiatric disorders?* It is clear that these patterns of relationships are not diagnostically specific to schizophrenia, but also apply to other psychiatric disorders. Chapter 17 in this volume examines cognition and functioning in depression, so here we briefly consider the data for bipolar disorder. Compared to the large number of studies on this topic in schizophrenia, the literature on bipolar disorder is paltry. However, a few findings suggest that similar relationships between cognition and functioning are present for bipolar disorder and that the strengths of these associations are comparable to those seen in schizophrenia (Dickerson et al., 2004; Martínez-Arán et al., 2004). Bipolar disorder is associated with cognitive impairment even when patients are in a euthymic state (Altshuler et al., 2004; van Gorp, Altshuler, Theberge, Wilkins, & Dixon, 1998), so many of the same concerns that apply to schizophrenia, about achieving adequate community functioning after acute treatment, also apply to bipolar disorder.

It is possible that the cognitive domains that are predictors of outcome for bipolar disorder will be different from those of schizophrenia, perhaps because of differences in the typical daily tasks for individuals with each disorder. Along these lines, it was suggested that verbal memory may be an important domain for social functioning in schizophrenia, but that executive functions are more important for community functioning in bipolar disorder (Laes & Sponheim, 2006).

Mechanisms through Which Cognition Influences Outcome in Schizophrenia

Although the connections between cognitive status and daily functioning are clearly documented at this stage, we know relatively little about the mechanisms through which the linkages exist. The identification of mechanisms is important for several reasons. One reason is that it enables investigators to test statistically the adequacy of models of outcome in schizophrenia using techniques such as path analysis and structural equation modeling (Bellack et al., 2007). Given the highly complex nature of community functioning in schizophrenia, and its reliance on a host of clinical, personal, and social factors, it is safe to assume that many of the observed effects between cognition and community activities involve mediators that act between neurocognitive processes and functional outcomes.

A second reason to identify mechanisms is that identification of key mediators can also suggest specific therapeutic targets. For example, an identified mediator of functional outcome would be a likely target for intervention in itself, especially if the mediator was thought to be more proximal to the outcome of interest. This situation could exist if a mediator, based on a well-grounded theoretical model, was thought to be closer to community outcome or vocational success than the basic cognitive process. An important goal in this area is to map out the key connections to outcome to help interpret treatment effects and to suggest new interventions.

Researchers have started to propose and test promising mediators between cognitive processes and outcome; two examples are shown in a schematic in Figure 18.1. If mediating variables are included in a model, the direct connections between cognition and functioning (shown as the single arrow with a question mark in the figure)

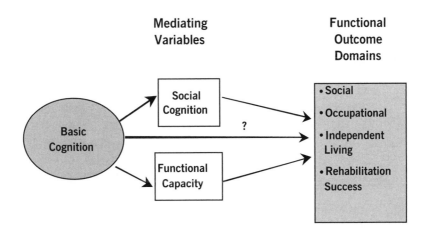

FIGURE 18.1. Cognition, mediating variables, and functional outcome.

may remain (in the case of partial mediators) or might disappear (in the case of full mediators).

One proposed mediator between cognition and functional outcome is social cognition. Studies of social cognition in schizophrenia research have examined concepts such as social perception, theory of mind, emotion processing, social knowledge and attributional bias (Green, Olivier, Crawley, Penn, & Silverstein, 2005; Penn, Corrigan, Bentall, Racenstein, & Newman, 1997). "Emotional processing" refers broadly to aspects of perceiving and using emotion. For example, an influential model of emotional processing includes four components: identifying emotions, facilitating emotions, understanding emotions, and managing emotions (Mayer, Salovey, & Caruso, 2002). "Theory of mind" typically refers to the ability to infer the intentions and beliefs of others. "Social perception" refers to the ability to judge social roles (e.g., intimacy and status) and social context; the term can also refer to one's perception of relationships between people, in addition to perception of cues that are generated by a single person. "Social knowledge" (also called "social schema") refers to the awareness of the rules and goals that characterize social situations and guide social interactions. "Attributional bias" refers to how one explains the causes for positive and negative outcomes and how the meaning of events is based on this attribution of their cause.

Numerous reports have linked measures of social cognition to basic (nonsocial) cognition, on the one hand, and functional outcome, on the other (Kee, Green, Mintz, & Brekke, 2003; Kee, Kern, & Green, 1998; Mueser et al., 1996; Penn, Spaulding, Reed, & Sullivan, 1996). More recently, studies have combined all three types of measures into single analyses and have evaluated directly whether aspects of social cognition (e.g., emotion perception and social perception) act as mediators between basic cognitive processes and functional daily outcomes (Addington, Saeedi, & Addington, 2006; Brekke, Kay, Kee, & Green, 2005; Sergi, Rassovsky, Nuechterlein, & Green, 2006; Vauth, Rusch, Wirtz, & Corrigan, 2004). Some of these studies have applied sophisticated statistical procedures, such as structural equation modeling and path analysis, to address the question of mediation. The results so far are promising and consistent: Social cognition appears to be a mediator for functional outcome. At a minimum it seems to be a partial mediator (i.e., significantly reducing the direct relationship between cognition and outcome) and, in some cases, it acts as a complete mediator (i.e., eliminating the direct relationship between cognition and outcome) (Brekke et al., 2005; Sergi et al., 2006).

Functional capacity has also been considered as a potential mediator. The term "functional capacity" refers to an individual's ability to perform key tasks of daily living (Bellack, Sayers, Mueser, & Bennett, 1994; McKibbin, Brekke, Sires, Jeste, & Patterson, 2004). Assessments of functional capacity use simulated activities (e.g., maintaining a social conversation, preparing a meal, taking public transportation, managing medications). These assessments can be conducted in the clinic and do not rely on observing the individual in the community. Good performance on a functional capacity task indicates that the person is capable of performing the tasks, but it does not necessarily mean that he or she will perform the task in the community. Performance of tasks in the community depends on other factors such as opportunity and willingness. Correlations between functional capacity measures and cognitive performance suggest good correspondence between the underlying cognitive skills and the functional capacity measure (Addington & Addington, 1999; Bellack et al., 1994; Klapow et al., 1997). A recent study using path analysis examined a measure of functional capacity, the UCSD Performance-Based Skills Assessment, that involved simulations of daily activities such as managing finances, shopping in a grocery store, and using public transportation (Patterson, Goldman, McKibbin, Hughs, & Jeste, 2001). This functional capacity measure was related to both basic cognition and community outcome, and acted as a mediator between the two for each of the functional outcome domains that were examined (Bowie, Reichenberg, Patterson, Heaton, & Harvey, 2006).

Stimulating the Development of New Cognition-Enhancing Drugs for Schizophrenia

Because of the findings that cognition is related to community functioning in schizophrenia, as well as the evidence that cognition is a core feature of schizophrenia, cognition has become a treatment target. In essence, cognition lies at the root of a major public health concern: the fact that patients with schizophrenia experience high levels of disability and have difficulty achieving acceptable goals when entering the community. A common opinion is that the antipsychotic medications may have reached the limits of their treatment potential. For these reasons, the development of new drugs to enhance cognitive functioning in schizophrenia has become both a scientific focus and a public health priority.

However, as of a couple years ago, there were notable obstacles that prevented any drug from receiving Food and Drug Administration (FDA) approval for this purpose (Marder & Fenton, 2004). First, there was no consensus on how to measure cognitive performance as an endpoint in clinical trials. The FDA had received inquiries over the years from companies that wanted to obtain approval for potential cognition-enhancing drugs. But each company used different definitions and measurements of cognition, a situation that the FDA found unacceptable. It was essential to find an endpoint for clinical trials that was based on a broad, interdisciplinary consensus process. Other significant barriers to drug development for cognitive enhancement in schizophrenia included the lack of a consensus regarding the appropriate design of clinical trials. For example, subject selection criteria, phase of illness, length of the trials, and ways to manage potential drug–drug interactions all required a consensus before the FDA was willing to moving forward. Other obstacles involved the prioritization of neuropharmacological targets (e.g., which receptor targets are the most promising) and criteria to evaluate promising compounds. Given the overriding ambiguity involving methods and measurements, and with the absence of any pathway for FDA approval, the pharmaceutical industry was understandably reluctant to make a substantial investment in the development of cognition-enhancing drugs for schizophrenia.

To resolve this situation and to stimulate the development of new drugs for cognition enhancement in schizophrenia, the National Institute of Mental Health (NIMH) launched the MATRICS (Measurement and Treatment Research to Improve Cognition in Schizophrenia) initiative. The mandate of MATRICS was to address the barriers to drug approval by holding a series of consensus meetings (with representatives of industry, academia, and government). MATRICS was charged with building a pathway for drug approval by reaching consensus on the methods and measures that would be used to evaluate promising new cognition-enhancing drugs for schizophrenia. The expectation was that once a pathway for drug approval was created, it would motivate the pharmaceutical industry to invest their resources and to develop drugs for cognitive enhancement in schizophrenia. This movement from industry, in fact, seems to be occurring.

An essential product of the NIMH-MATRICS Initiative was a consensus cognitive battery that would be the standard outcome measure for all clinical trials of cognition-enhancing drugs for schizophrenia. Selection of the consensus cognitive battery involved a thorough, multistep process consisting of several consensus meetings, evaluation, discussion, and finally a data-collection component (Green, Nuechterlein, et al., 2004). Essential criteria for the final selection of tests included (1) high test–retest reliability, (2) high utility as a repeated measure, (3) demonstrated relationship to functional outcome, and (4) demonstrated tolerability (acceptable to patients) and practicality (acceptable to testers). A relationship to functioning was selected as one of the essential criteria because part of the rationale of MATRICS was the linkage between cognitive and community functioning. It is clearly hoped that drug-related improvements in cognition will eventually lead to improvements in functioning. The components of the MATRICS Consensus Cognitive Battery (MCCB) are shown in Table 18.1. The MCCB is distributed by Harcourt Assessment (San Antonio, TX), Multi-Health Systems (Toronto), and Psychological Assessment Resources (Lutz, FL).

To evaluate the MCCB and other products of MATRICS, the NIMH recently launched another initiative to develop a clinical trials network called Treatment Units for Neurocognition and Schizophrenia (TURNS). TURNS is a network of seven aca-

TABLE 18.1. MATRICS Consensus Cognitive Battery

Domain	Test
Speed of processing	Brief Assessment of Cognition in Schizophrenia (BACS)—Symbol-Coding
	Category Fluency (Animal Naming)
	Trail Making Part A
Attention/vigilance	Continuous Performance Test-Identical Pairs
Working memory (nonverbal)	Wechsler Memory Scale (WMS)-III—Spatial Span
Working memory (verbal)	University of Maryland—Letter–Number Span
Verbal learning	Hopkins Verbal Learning Test—Revised
Visual learning	Brief Visuospatial Memory Test—Revised
Reasoning and problem solving	Neuropsychological Assessment Battery (NAB)—Mazes
Social cognition	Mayer–Salovey–Caruso Emotional Intelligence Test (MSCEIT)—Managing Emotions

demic research sites that is dedicated to identifying, obtaining, and testing the efficacy of new drugs to improve cognition in schizophrenia. This network was formed to validate the clinical trial methodology recommended by MATRICS (Buchanan et al., 2005) by conducting two or three trials that will be supported initially by NIMH. Later TURNS is expected to become self-sufficient and to obtain funds through private and federal sources. TURNS was designed as a "fast track" for evaluating promising compounds and has received numerous nominations from companies of potential compounds. The first TURNS trials started in early 2007.

Summary

This chapter has briefly summarized several topics related to cognitive performance in schizophrenia. First the evidence that cognitive performance is a core feature of schizophrenia was reviewed. It is safe to view cognitive deficits as part of the illness and not secondary to clinical symptoms or to medications. Next the literature on the relationship of cognitive performance to functioning in schizophrenia was summarized. The literature is quite large and highly consistent in showing relationships between cognitive performance and community functioning. The strengths of the relationships are medium for individual domains and large for summary scores, which indicate that much of the variance in functional outcome lies beyond cognition.

Once such relationships have been demonstrated, other questions start to emerge. One question involves the mechanisms for such relationships. It is important, for both scientific and intervention reasons, to identify key mediators that act between cognition and community functioning. So far, two promising mediators have been suggested: social cognition and functional capacity. These two constructs have been shown to be related to both cognitive performance and functioning, both reduce (or eliminate) the direct connection, and both add to the goodness of fit when added to models of outcome.

The final question is whether cognition can be a target for intervention. The NIMH launched two initiatives. The first one (MATRICS) was charged with building a pathway for drug approval through a series of consensus meetings and by development of a consensus battery. The second one (TURNS) is a clinical trial network that is currently testing the products of MATRICS. In this chapter we have focused on the efforts to develop new psychopharmacological treatments for cognitive enhancement in schizophrenia, but other efforts are occurring in cognitive remediation for schizophrenia. In all likelihood true advances in community outcome for patients with schizophrenia will occur only when cognition-enhancing drugs are combined with nonpharmacological approaches.

References

Addington, J., & Addington, D. (1999). Neurocognitive and social functioning in schizophrenia. *Schizophrenia Bull, 25,* 173–182.

Addington, J., Saeedi, H., & Addington, D. (2006). Facial affect recognition: A mediator between cognitive and social functioning in schizophrenia? *Schizophrenia Res*, *85*, 142–150.

Altshuler, L. L., Ventura, J., van Gorp, W. G., Green, M. F., Theberge, D. C., & Mintz, J. (2004). Neurocognitive function in clinically stable men with bipolar I disorder or schizophrenia and normal control subjects. *Biol Psychiat*, *56*, 560–569.

American Psychiatric Association. (1994). *Diagnostic and statistical manual of mental disorders* (4th ed.). Washington, DC: Author.

Bell, M. D., & Bryson, G. (2001). Work rehabilitation in schizophrenia: Does cognitive impairment limit improvement? *Schizophrenia Bull*, *27*(2), 269–279.

Bellack, A. S., Green, M. F., Cook, J. A., Fenton, W., Harvey, P. D., Heaton, R. K., et al. (2007). Assessment of community functioning in people with schizophrenia and other severe mental illnesses: A white paper based on an NIMH-sponsored workshop. *Schizophrenia Bull*, *33*(3), 805–822.

Bellack, A. S., Sayers, M., Mueser, K., & Bennett, M. (1994). Evaluation of social problem solving in schizophrenia. *J Abnorm Psychol*, *103*, 371–378.

Birchwood, M., Smith, J., Cochran, R., Wetton, S., & Copestake, S. (1990). The Social Functioning Scale: The development and validation of a new scale of social adjustment for use in family intervention programs with schizophrenic patients. *Brit J Psychiat*, *157*, 853–859.

Bleuler, E. (1950). *Dementia praecox or the group of schizophrenias*. New York: International Universities Press.

Bowie, C. R., Reichenberg, A., Patterson, T. L., Heaton, R. K., & Harvey, P. D. (2006). Determinants of real-world functional performance in schizophrenia subjects: Correlations with cognition, functional capacity, and symptoms. *Am J Psychiat*, *163*, 418–425.

Braff, D. (1993). Information processing and attention dysfunctions in schizophrenia. *Schizophrenia Bull*, *19*, 233–259.

Brekke, J. S., Kay, D. D., Kee, K. S., & Green, M. F. (2005). Biosocial pathways to functional outcome in schizophrenia. *Schizophrenia Res*, *80*, 213–225.

Brekke, J. S., Levin, S., Wolkon, G., Sobel, E., & Slade, E. (1993). Psychosocial functioning and subjective experience in schizophrenia. *Schizophrenia Bull*, *19*, 599–608.

Brekke, J. S., & Long, J. D. (2000). Community-based psychosocial rehabilitation and prospective change in functional, clinical, and subjective experience variables in schizophrenia. *Schizophrenia Bull*, *26*(3), 667–680.

Bryson, G., & Bell, M. D. (2003). Initial and final work performance in schizophrenia: Cognitive and symptom predictors. *J Nerv Ment Dis*, *191*, 87–92.

Buchanan, R. W., Davis, M., Goff, D., Green, M. F., Keefe, R. S. E., Leon, A. C., et al. (2005). A summary of the FDA-NIMH-MATRICS workshop on clinical trial design for neurocognitive drugs for schizophrenia. *Schizophrenia Bull*, *31*, 5–19.

Dickerson, F. B., Boronow, J. J., Ringel, N., & Parente, F. (1999). Social functioning and neurocognitive deficits in outpatients with schizophrenia: A 2-year follow-up. *Schizophrenia Res*, *37*, 13–20.

Dickerson, F. B., Boronow, J. J., Stallings, C. R., Origoni, A. E., Cole, S., & Yolken, R. H. (2004). Association between cognitive functioning and employment status of persons with bipolar disorder. *Psychiatr Serv*, *55*, 54–58.

Evans, J. D., Heaton, R. K., Paulsen, J. S., Palmer, B. W., Patterson, T. L., & Jeste, D. V. (2003). The relationship of neuropsychological abilities to specific domains of functional capacity in older schizophrenia patients. *Biol Psychiat*, *53*, 422–430.

Friedman, J. I., Harvey, P. D., McGurk, S. R., White, L., Parrella, M., Raykov, T., et al. (2002). Correlates of change in functional status of institutionalized geriatric schizophrenic patients: Focus on medical comorbidity. *Am J Psychiat*, *159*(8), 1388–1394.

Glahn, D. C., Ragland, J. D., Abramoff, A., Barrett, J., Laird, A. R., Bearden, C. E., et al. (2005). Beyond hypofrontality: A quantitative meta-analysis of functional neuroimaging studies of working memory in schizophrenia. *Hum Brain Mapp, 25,* 60–69.

Gold, J. M. (2004). Cognitive deficits as treatment targets in schizophrenia. *Schizophrenia Res, 72,* 21–28.

Gold, J. M., Goldberg, R. W., McNary, S. W., Dixon, L., & Lehman, A. F. (2002). Cognitive correlates of job tenure among patients with severe mental illness. *Am J Psychiat, 159,* 1395–1401.

Gold, J. M., & Green, M. F. (2004). Neurocognition in schizophrenia. In B. J. Sadock & V. A. Sadock (Eds.), *Comprehensive textbook of psychiatry* (8th ed., pp. 1436–1448). Baltimore: Lippincott Williams & Wilkins.

Goldberg, T. E., Ragland, J. D., Torrey, E. F., Gold, J. M., Bigelow, L. B., & Weinberger, D. R. (1990). Neuropsychological assessment of monozygotic twins discordant for schizophrenia. *Arch Gen Psychiat, 47,* 1066–1072.

Green, M. F. (1996). What are the functional consequences of neurocognitive deficits in schizophrenia? *Am J Psychiat, 153*(3), 321–330.

Green, M. F. (2001). *Schizophrenia revealed: From neurons to social interactions.* New York: Norton.

Green, M. F. (2007). Stimulating the development of drug treatments to improve cognition in schizophrenia. *Ann Rev Clin Psychol, 3,* 159–180.

Green, M. F., Kern, R. S., Braff, D. L., & Mintz, J. (2000). Neurocognitive deficits and functional outcome in schizophrenia: Are we measuring the "right stuff"? *Schizophrenia Bull, 26,* 119–136.

Green, M. F., Kern, R. S., & Heaton, R. K. (2004). Longitudinal studies of cognition and functional outcome in schizophrenia: Implications for MATRICS. *Schizophrenia Res, 72,* 41–51.

Green, M. F., Nuechterlein, K. H., Gold, J. M., Barch, D. M., Cohen, J., Essock, S., et al. (2004). Approaching a consensus cognitive battery for clinical trials in schizophrenia: The NIMH-MATRICS conference to select cognitive domains and test criteria. *Biol Psychiat, 56,* 301–307.

Green, M. F., Olivier, B., Crawley, J. N., Penn, D. L., & Silverstein, S. (2005). Social cognition in schizophrenia: Recommendations from the MATRICS New Approaches Conference. *Schizophrenia Bull, 31,* 882–887.

Hegarty, J. D., Baldessarini, R. J., Tohen, M., Waternaux, C., & Oepen, G. (1994). One hundred years of schizophrenia: A meta-analysis of the outcome literature. *Am J Psychiat, 151,* 1409–1416.

Heinrichs, R. W., & Zakzanis, K. K. (1998). Neurocognitive deficit in schizophrenia: A quantitative review of the evidence. *Neuropsychology, 12,* 426–445.

Helgason, L. (1990). Twenty years' follow-up of first psychiatric presentation for schizophrenia: What could have been prevented? *Acta Psychiat Scand, 81,* 231–235.

Holmes, A. J., MacDonald, A., Carter, C. S., Barch, D. M., Stenger, V. A., & Cohen, J. D. (2005). Prefrontal functioning during context processing in schizophrenia and major depression: An event-related fMRI study. *Schizophrenia Res, 76,* 199–206.

Jaeger, J., Tatsuoka, C., Berns, S., Varadi, F., Czobor, P., & Uzelac, S. (2006). Associating functional recovery with neurocognitive profiles identified using partially ordered classification models. *Schizophrenia Res, 85,* 40–48.

Kee, K. S., Green, M. F., Mintz, J., & Brekke, J. S. (2003). Is emotional processing a predictor of functional outcome in schizophrenia? *Schizophrenia Bull, 29,* 487–497.

Kee, K. S., Kern, R. S., & Green, M. F. (1998). Perception of emotion and neurocognitive functioning in schizophrenia: What's the link? *Psychiat Res, 81,* 57–65.

Klapow, J. C., Evans, J., Patterson, T. L., Heaton, R. K., Koch, W. L., & Jeste, D. V. (1997). Direct assessment of functional status in older patients with schizophrenia. *Am J Psychiat, 154*, 1022–1024.

Kraepelin, E. (1971). *Dementia praecox and paraphrenia*. Huntington, NY: Krieger Publishing.

Kremen, W. S., Seidman, L. J., Faraone, S. V., Toomey, R., & Tsuang, M. T. (2000). The paradox of normal neuropsychological function in schizophrenia. *J Abnorm Psychol, 109*, 743–752.

Lacro, J. P., Dunn, L. B., Dolder, C. R., Leckband, S. G., & Jeste, D. V. (2002). Prevalence of and risk factors for medication nonadherence in patients with schizophrenia: A comprehensive review of recent literature. *J Clin Psychiat, 63*, 892–909.

Laes, J. R., & Sponheim, S. R. (2006). Does cognition predict community function only in schizophrenia?: A study of schizophrenia patients, bipolar affective disorder patients, and community control subjects. *Schizophrenia Res, 84*, 121–131.

Lawrie, S., Johnstone, E., & Weinberger, D. R. (Eds.). (2004). *Schizophrenia: From neuroimaging to neuroscience*. Oxford, UK: Oxford University Press.

Marder, S. R., & Fenton, W. S. (2004). Measurement and treatment research to improve cognition in schizophrenia: NIMH MATRICS Initiative to support the development of agents for improving cognition in schizophrenia. *Schizophrenia Res, 72*, 5–10.

Martínez-Arán, A., Vieta, E., Colom, F., Torrent, C., Sánchez-Moreno, J., Reinares, M., et al. (2004). Cognitive impairment in euthymic bipolar patients: Implications for clinical and functional outcome. *Bipolar Disord, 6*, 224–232.

Mayer, J. D., Salovey, P., & Caruso, D. R. (2002). *Mayer–Salovey–Caruso Emotional Intelligence Test (MSCEIT) user's manual*. Toronto: MHS Publishers.

McKibbin, C. L., Brekke, J. S., Sires, D., Jeste, D. V., & Patterson, T. L. (2004). Direct assessment of functional abilities: Relevance to persons with schizophrenia. *Schizophrenia Res, 72*, 53–67.

Mueser, K. T., Doonan, B., Penn, D. L., Blanchard, J. J., Bellack, A. S., Nishith, P., et al. (1996). Emotion recognition and social competence in chronic schizophrenia. *J Abnorm Psychol, 105*, 271–275.

Murray, C. J. L., & Lopez, A. D. (Eds.). (1996). *The global burden of disease*. Boston: Harvard School of Public Health.

Narr, K. L., Bilder, R. M., Kim, S., Thompson, P. M., Szeszko, P., Robinson, D., et al. (2004). Abnormal gyral complexity in first-episode schizophrenia. *Biol Psychiat, 55*, 859–867.

Nuechterlein, K. H., Barch, D. M., Gold, J. M., Goldberg, T. E., Green, M. F., & Heaton, R. K. (2004). Identification of separable cognitive factors in schizophrenia. *Schizophrenia Res, 72*, 29–39.

Nuechterlein, K. H., Dawson, M. E., & Green, M. F. (1994). Information-processing abnormalities as neuropsychological vulnerability indicators for schizophrenia. *Acta Psychiat Scand, 90*(Suppl. 384), 71–79.

Palmer, B. W., Heaton, R. K., Gladsjo, J. A., Evans, J. D., Patterson, T. L., Golshan, S., et al. (2002). Heterogeneity in functional status among older outpatients with schizophrenia: Employment history, living situation, and driving. *Schizophrenia Res, 55*, 205–215.

Palmer, B. W., Heaton, R. K., Paulsen, J. S., Kuck, J., Braff, D., Harris, M. J., et al. (1997). Is it possible to be schizophrenic yet neuropsychologically normal? *Neuropsychology, 11*, 437–446.

Patterson, T. L., Goldman, S., McKibbin, C. L., Hughs, T., & Jeste, D. V. (2001). UCSD Performance-Based Skills Assessment: Development of a new measure of everyday functioning for severely mentally ill adults. *Schizophrenia Bull, 27*(2), 235–245.

Patterson, T. L., Lacro, J., McKibbin, C. L., Moscona, S., Hughs, T., & Jeste, D. V. (2002).

Medication management ability assessment: Results from a performance-based measure in older outpatients with schizophrenia. *J Clin Psychopharm, 22,* 11–19.

Penn, D. L., Corrigan, P. W., Bentall, R. P., Racenstein, J. M., & Newman, L. (1997). Social cognition in schizophrenia. *Psychol Bull, 121,* 114–132.

Penn, D. L., Spaulding, W. D., Reed, D., & Sullivan, M. (1996). The relationship of social cognition to ward behavior in chronic schizophrenia. *Schizophrenia Res, 20,* 327–335.

Perkins, D. O., Johnson, J. L., Hamer, R. M., Zipursky, R. B., Keefe, R. S., Centorrhino, F., et al. (2006). Predictors of antipsychotic medication adherence in patients recovering from a first psychotic episode. *Schizophrenia Res, 83,* 53–63.

Robinson, D. G., Woerner, M. G., McMeniman, M., Mendelowitz, A., & Bilder, R. M. (2004). Symptomatic and functional recovery from a first episode of schizophrenia or schizoaffective disorder. *Am J Psychiat, 161,* 473–479.

Rosenheck, R., Leslie, D., Keefe, R., McEvoy, J., Swartz, M., Perkins, D., et al. (2006). Barriers to employment for people with schizophrenia. *Am J Psychiat, 163,* 411–417.

Sergi, M. J., Rassovsky, Y., Nuechterlein, K. H., & Green, M. F. (2006). Social perception as a mediator of the influence of early visual processing on functional status in schizophrenia. *Am J Psychiat, 163,* 448–454.

Smith, T. E., Hull, J. W., Huppert, J. D., & Silverstein, S. M. (2002). Recovery from psychosis in schizophrenia and schizoaffective disorder: Symptoms and neurocognitive rate-limiters for the development of social skills. *Schizophrenia Res, 55,* 229–237.

St. Germain, S. A., Kurtz, M. M., Pearlson, G. D., & Astur, R. S. (2005). Driving simulator performance in schizophrenia. *Schizophrenia Res, 74,* 121–122.

Stirling, J., White, C., Lewis, S., Hopkins, R., Tantam, D., Huddy, A., et al. (2003). Neurocognitive function and outcome in first-episode schizophrenia: A 10-year follow-up of an epidemiological cohort. *Schizophrenia Res, 65,* 75–86.

van Gorp, W. G., Altshuler, L., Theberge, D. C., Wilkins, J., & Dixon, W. (1998). Cognitive impairment in euthymic bipolar patients with and without prior alcohol dependence: A preliminary study. *Arch Gen Psychiat, 55,* 41–46.

Vauth, R., Rusch, N., Wirtz, M., & Corrigan, P. W. (2004). Does social cognition influence the relation between neurocognitive deficits and vocational functioning in schizophrenia? *Psychiat Res, 128,* 155–165.

Velligan, D. I., Bow-Thomas, C., Mahurin, R., Miller, A. L., & Halgunseth, L. C. (2000). Do specific neurocognitive deficits predict specific domains of community function in schizophrenia? *J Nerv Ment Dis, 188,* 518–524.

Weissman, M., & Paykel, E. (1974). *The depressed woman: A study of social relationships.* Chicago: University of Chicago Press.

Wiersma, D., Wanderling, J., Dragomirecka, E., Ganev, K., Harrison, G., An der Heiden, W., et al. (2000). Social disability in schizophrenia: Its development and prediction over 15 years in incidence cohorts in six European centres. *Psychol Med, 30,* 1155–1167.

Woonings, F. M. J., Appelo, M. T., Kluiter, H., Slooff, C. J., & van den Bosch, R. J. (2002). Learning (potential) and social functioning in schizophrenia. *Schizophrenia Res, 59,* 287–296.

Future Directions in the Assessment of Everyday Functioning

Thomas D. Marcotte and Igor Grant

As noted throughout this volume, the neuropsychological approach to predicting everyday functioning has many advantages, including a legacy of developing standardized measures that are well characterized with respect to validity and reliability, and a rich literature addressing the relationships between brain function and real world-performance. But, as also summarized in numerous chapters, this approach still has limitations. Here, based on the material presented in this book, we briefly provide recommendations for future work linking brain function to real-world functioning.

1. *Foster development, and implementation, of new measures with greater ecological validity.* This call has gone out for decades (Heaton & Pendleton, 1981). While we can continue to refine our understanding of how tools initially developed to localize brain lesions and aid in neurological/neuropsychiatric diagnosis might predict real-world functioning, it is also worth considering new paradigms. Rather than starting with circumscribed behaviors that have been well delineated in the controlled laboratory and trying to extrapolate findings to real-world scenarios, it might prove fruitful to develop new measures whose design begins with observations of human behavior in the real world, in all of its complexity (Burgess et al., 2006; Kingstone, Smilek, & Eastwood, 2008). This may ultimately lead to new constructs regarding how we attend to, prioritize, and manage our complex lives, and also a better understanding of the component processes at work during complicated activities.

This work might be furthered by new technologies, such as virtual reality, which is increasingly sophisticated and less costly and may provide interesting opportunities for studying behaviors in a seminaturalistic manner. These methods may be particularly useful in areas such as the assessment of driving abilities, where other approaches (e.g., on-road assessments), are time-consuming, costly, and dangerous. However, "virtual" is not synonymous with "ecologically valid," and such instruments should be held to the same standards of reliability and validity as traditional paper-and-pencil and computerized tests.

It is our opinion, as well as that of others (e.g., Buchanan et al., 2005; Laughren, 2001), that functional outcomes should be a key factor in determining whether there is benefit in pharmaceutical and behavioral treatments. Unfortunately, there are limited options with respect to measures that fit within a clinical trial protocol, where time is often limited and per-site costs can significantly impact feasibility. Many trials thus rely upon brief, traditional neuropsychological tests to examine cognition and infer functional outcomes. While cognitive functioning itself is clearly an important outcome, as shown in this volume it may not always translate to everyday performance.

How can development and implementation of new measures be facilitated? Unfortunately, the current approach of relying on individual investigators/research teams to develop, refine, and apply new everyday functioning instruments to multiple populations is often inefficient. It is difficult to lay a foundation for industry standards when careers rely upon external funding and publishing, activities that almost universally require "novel" experiments and findings. As a result, although some measures have developed a wide following (e.g., Rivermead Behavioral Memory Test, Test of Everyday Attention, Six Elements Test), in many cases there is limited understanding of how measures designed to predict real-world functioning perform across different clinical groups and, importantly, few studies aim to replicate previous findings. Confidence in such measures would be greater if findings were examined repeatedly within similar patient groups and across different patient groups.

In addition to the single, "investigator-initiated" approach (which admittedly may best promote creativity), research can also be significantly advanced by the development of common methodologies that yield predictor or outcome measures that serve as standards to which other approaches can be compared. For example, if there were commonly accepted, valid instruments that predicted real-world functioning across different samples and studies, one would be able to compare the value of different interventions, as well as the relationship between brain function and everyday performance between these groups.

Such a step is likely only to occur with institutional support. It is thus our recommendation that potential stakeholders, such as the National Institutes of Health (NIH), convene expert panels to advance the development of standardized measures for assessing everyday functioning abilities. One potential high-impact focus would be developing a consensus everyday functioning battery for use in clinical trials. The NIH is undertaking a rigorous approach to developing cognitive and other assessments as part of the NIH Toolbox (*www.nihtoolbox.gov*), in which experts were formally surveyed, and investigators then selected or developed measures that would constitute a brief battery usable in clinical trials and other research. This effort does not include functional measures. In schizophrenia research, the National Institute of Mental Health supported a project that involved surveys of experts and focused conferences to define a standard cognitive battery for use in clinical trials (MATRICS; Nuechterlein et al., 2008); this effort also included the identification of "co-primary" measures that would be functionally meaningful (Green et al., 2008). While time will tell whether these efforts advance clinical research and treatment, a similar approach, perhaps on a more modest scale, might be undertaken to carefully identify, modify, or even develop everyday functioning measures that are appropriate for multiple research and clinical situations. This would likely result in more widespread use of such instruments, and facilitate comparisons across different treatments. This approach has its limitations—"consensus" does not always equate to "best"—and not all investigators would be pleased with the selected approaches and measures, but it would likely provide a needed impetus to further the cause of addressing functional outcomes in research.

2. *Improve methods for directly measuring "real-world" outcomes.* Operationalization of "real-world outcomes" is not necessarily any more advanced than the predictors being used to predict such outcomes. In order to develop useful laboratory-based measures, we need gold standards regarding what defines functioning in the real world. To establish how individuals are functioning in their daily lives, investigators/clinicians often rely on reports from patients and informants, which, while very important, have limitations, as noted in previous chapters. Developing technology may help. For example, the advent of miniaturized, unobtrusive tools (e.g., webcams) to record behavior as it occurs in the wild may significantly improve our ability to observe and measure an individual's performance under common demands/distractions. Such an approach, for example, was demonstrated in the "100-car naturalistic study" (Neale, Dingus, Klauer, Sudweeks, & Goodman, 2005), in which investigators added monitoring equipment (including videocameras) and tracked driving behavior over the course of a year. New, novel approaches to establishing the naturalistic evaluation of an individual's abilities are still needed.

3. *Develop algorithms for predicting everyday performance based on the contributions of neuropsychological and non-neuropsychological factors.* Factors such as personality/temperament, psychiatric conditions (especially depression), licit and illicit substance use, medications, disease, psychosocial factors, environmental conditions, literacy, idiosyncratic approaches to daily life, and so on, no doubt explain different amounts of variance regarding performance of everyday tasks. Predictions will have better validity (and real life meaning) if the major contributors to everyday functioning can be given appropriate weight as to their likely importance in a particular situation. For example, a prospective memory difficulty may predict everyday performance in particular areas, but in some circumstances there may be "higher-order" cognitive–dispositional–motivational complexes that determine even more of the variation in functioning, and the extent to which prospective memory problems matter. Thus, some people have trouble initiating behaviors (e.g., due to obsessional traits, or basal ganglia pathology, such as in Parkinson's disease), others may have disinhibition, some have decisional difficulties, and still others may have altered reward contingencies that affect their motivation. Attitudinal (e.g., sense of optimism) and coping (e.g., problem-solving approach, sense of mastery) variables may be powerful moderators of the path from cognitive changes to successful real-world performance. The neural bases of such complex behaviors and dispositions are only now being mapped. Disturbance in these in some instances may reflect a common pathological process that expresses itself also as a specific neuropsychological deficit; or it may reflect a long-standing disposition, or the superimposition of another problem such as mood disorder. Fatigue and pain are added features of many chronic diseases that have central nervous system injury as a component, and these can amplify everyday

difficulties. Research into how such factors separately and jointly affect everyday functioning is sorely needed in order to create clinically useful profiles and prediction estimates. Development of such multivariate models will also facilitate clinical decisions into where initial interventions might be most profitably directed.

4. *Address cultural issues when developing, and interpreting, everyday functioning measures.* Many everyday tasks are universal, and are required for successful functioning in most societies; but they can also differ substantially from culture to culture (Cherner, Chapter 8, this volume). In order to determine the effects of diseases and brain dysfunction across cultures, it would be ideal to standardize instruments as much as possible, but this may be neither easy nor appropriate. Akin to assessing whether culture-specific norms are needed for neuropsychological tests, the field may need to develop culture-specific norms for everyday functioning measures. This is true even within societies. For example, Spanish speakers in the United States may have different methods of money management and cooking than native English speakers. In some cases, particularly when individuals have very little or no education, measures of functional ability may prove to be the best way to determine whether cognitive decline has occurred.

5. *Pursue studies examining the neural basis of real-world functioning.* While the last few decades have seen dramatic progress in our ability to relate cognitive performance to brain function, this has typically been accomplished by using behavioral measures far removed from real-world tasks (Burgess et al., 2006). What are the neural underpinnings of perceiving, attending to, and making decisions in complex environments? There are a small, but growing, number of studies examining components of real-world functioning while individuals are in a scanner (e.g., Just, Keller, & Cynkar, 2008; Simons, Scholvinck, Gilbert, Frith, & Burgess, 2006), but such work is often constrained by technical limitations. A relatively new field in human factors, neuroergonomics (Parasuraman & Rizzo, 2006), focuses on using neuroimaging techniques (e.g., functional magnetic resonance imaging, electroencephalography) to capture real-time brain function during different activities; in some work-related studies, a high workload then initiates adaptive automation in which functions are distributed between human and machine. This work has been applied to military and clinical situations (Parasuraman & Wilson, 2008), and may ultimately inform future clinical studies.

6. *Translate research/clinical findings into results relevant to the individual.* Most studies involve null hypothesis significance testing in order to determine if there is a statistically significant difference between groups with and without a given brain condition. To be most clinically useful, measures of everyday functioning should help clinicians and researchers identify *individuals* at risk for impaired real-world functioning. We thus recommend that whenever possible studies report classification accuracy statistics. This includes not only the more traditional measures of *sensitivity, specificity,* and *overall accuracy (hit rate),* but even more clinically relevant measures such as *positive predictive value* (chance that someone who is impaired on a laboratory-based test also has impaired everyday functioning), *negative predictive value* (chance that if someone was unimpaired on the laboratory-based measure that he or she is also unimpaired in real-world functioning), and *risk ratios* (e.g., likelihood and odds ratios) (Woods, Weinborn, & Lovejoy, 2003). As such data expand

across many patient populations, the information will help us better understand the utility, and universality, of different approaches.

References

Buchanan, R. W., Davis, M., Goff, D., Green, M. F., Keefe, R. S., Leon, A. C., et al. (2005). A summary of the FDA–NIMH–MATRICS workshop on clinical trial design for neurocognitive drugs for schizophrenia. *Schizophrenia Bulletin, 31*(1), 5–19.

Burgess, P. W., Alderman, N., Forbes, C., Costello, A., Coates, L. M., Dawson, D. R., et al. (2006). The case for the development and use of "ecologically valid" measures of executive function in experimental and clinical neuropsychology. *Journal of the International Neuropsychological Society, 12*(2), 194–209.

Green, M. F., Nuechterlein, K. H., Kern, R. S., Baade, L. E., Fenton, W. S., Gold, J. M., et al. (2008). Functional co-primary measures for clinical trials in schizophrenia: Results from the MATRICS Psychometric and Standardization Study. *American Journal of Psychiatry, 165*(2), 221–228.

Heaton, R. K., & Pendleton, M. G. (1981). Use of neuropsychological tests to predict adult patients' everyday functioning. *Journal of Consulting and Clinical Psychology, 49*(6), 807–821.

Just, M. A., Keller, T. A., & Cynkar, J. (2008). A decrease in brain activation associated with driving when listening to someone speak. *Brain Research, 1205*, 70–80.

Kingstone, A., Smilek, D., & Eastwood, J. D. (2008). Cognitive ethology: A new approach for studying human cognition. *British Journal of Psychology, 99*(Pt. 3), 317–340.

Laughren, T. (2001). A regulatory perspective on psychiatric syndromes in Alzheimer disease. *American Journal of Geriatric Psychiatry, 9*(4), 340–345.

Neale, V. L., Dingus, T. A., Klauer, S. G., Sudweeks, J., & Goodman, M. (2005). *An overview of the 100-Car naturalistic study and findings* (No. 05-0400). Washington, DC: National Highway Traffic Safety Administration.

Nuechterlein, K. H., Green, M. F., Kern, R. S., Baade, L. E., Barch, D. M., Cohen, J. D., et al. (2008). The MATRICS Consensus Cognitive Battery, part 1: Test selection, reliability, and validity. *American Journal of Psychiatry, 165*(2), 203–213.

Parasuraman, R., & Rizzo, M. (2006). *Neuroergonomics: The brain at work*. New York: Oxford University Press.

Parasuraman, R., & Wilson, G. F. (2008). Putting the brain to work: Neuroergonomics past, present, and future. *Human Factors, 50*(3), 468–474.

Simons, J. S., Scholvinck, M. L., Gilbert, S. J., Frith, C. D., & Burgess, P. W. (2006). Differential components of prospective memory?: Evidence from fMRI. *Neuropsychologia, 44*(8), 1388–1397.

Woods, S. P., Weinborn, M., & Lovejoy, D. W. (2003). Are classification accuracy statistics underused in neuropsychological research? *Journal of Clinical and Experimental Neuropsychology, 25*(3), 431–439.

Index

Page numbers followed by *f* indicate figure, *t* indicate table